RUDOLF HESS AND GERMANY'S RELUCTANT WAR 1939–41

RUDOLF HESS AND GERMANY'S RELUCTANT WAR 1939–41

Alfred Smith

The Book Guild Ltd
Sussex, England

First published in Great Britain in 2001 by
The Book Guild Ltd
25 High Street,
Lewes, Sussex
BN7 2LU

Typesetting in Times by
Keyboard Services, Luton, Bedfordshire

Printed in Great Britain by
Bookcraft (Bath) Ltd, Avon

A catalogue record for this book is
available from the British Library

ISBN 1 85776 565 6

This book is dedicated to the memory of
Walter Packer, 2nd Battalion,
Northamptonshire Regiment who died of
wounds at Anzio, Italy, on May 23, 1944.

And if all others accepted the lie which the Party imposed, if all records told the same tale, then the lie passed into history and became the truth. Who controls the past controls the future. Who controls the present controls the past.

GEORGE ORWELL

CONTENTS

FOREWORD

Alfred Smith has written a remarkable book. It is excellently researched and highlights many new aspects relating to my father's peace mission to Britain in May 1941, including the role played by British (Air) Intelligence and the several German peace initiatives which preceded that of my father. He also opens up new perspectives on the early hostilities of 1939–41, including Hitler's order to stop further reinforcements for Goering during the Battle of Britain, the circumstances under which terror bombing was commenced and developed and perhaps most important of all, the true costs to Britain of the lend-lease arrangements with the United States of 1941. These included the handing over of the results of early research by Britain on the atomic bomb and the dismantling of the special imperial preference trading arrangements benefiting Britain and her Empire.

While I do not agree with all of the author's political views, the main conclusion which he reaches in his book is fully in accord with my own beliefs. Germany never wanted a war in the West and her preparations throughout the 1930s were solely for a preventive war against communist Russia in the East. The author describes the hostilities of 1939–41 as 'Germany's reluctant war'. I would describe them as Germany's unnecessary and unwanted war.

The graphic description in chapter ten of the events leading up to the 'miracle of Dunkirk' illustrates Adolf Hitler's true feelings towards Britain and her Empire. In May 1940, 340,000 men of the British Expeditionary Force were stranded in Flanders and could have been 'put in the bag' by the advancing German panzer forces. They were saved from that humiliation by a direct personal order from Hitler stopping the further advance of German forces. The decision was made in an effort to assist the peace initiatives emanating at that time from Lord Halifax, made through the Italian ambassador in London.

I know this to be true from conversations I had with my mother, Ilse Hess (1900–95). She told me that my father had argued strongly with Hitler that the military operations should be concluded first and only then should generous gestures be made to the British as part of the peace negotiations.

My father and others took the view that Hitler's order to stop the advance in Flanders in May 1940 was a turning point in the war. If the military option had been taken and the whole of the British Expeditionary Force captured, Britain would have been militarily naked, both as to men and material. Even with her Navy and Royal Air Force intact it is difficult to see how the British Government could then have refused peace terms which, as is now known, guaranteed the continued independence of Britain and her Empire for which Hitler had such a profound admiration.

Peace in the West would have had far-reaching effects. Germany would have been released from the threat of a war on two fronts as and when she decided to launch the preventive war against Russia. Her operations in North Africa, Greece and Crete would have been unnecessary and her total resources and military strength would have been available for use against communist Russia, which had always been the original intention. It is no idle speculation to assume that Russian communism and its threat to Europe and the world could have been destroyed in 1941.

But it was not to be. My father was right and Hitler was wrong. Hitler gave his stop order but the gesture was ignored. Nothing came of Halifax's peace initiative and the war dragged on, with unnecessary loss of life on both sides. Nevertheless, the idea of a separate peace with Britain continued to be fostered both by Hitler and my father and culminated in my father's major peace mission in May 1941, when he flew to Scotland to contact elements of the British Peace Party.

The author's conclusions as to the circumstances of my father's death in Spandau prison, Berlin, on August 17, 1987, are also correct. My father did not hang himself. He was murdered by strangulation. All the medical and other evidence to show that this was so is set down in detail in the book and the relevant appendices. It is largely through the efforts of the author that his and my conclusions on this matter are currently the subject of legal process, with a view to obtaining leave to apply for a judicial review in Britain as to the circumstances of my father's death.

Previous attempts to raise the matter by question and answer through the British House of Commons have been effectively quashed by Government intervention. If it had been accepted that my father had been murdered, the question would then have been asked as to why. The author has posed more than one answer to that question in the pages that follow. It is not surprising that discussion of the issues raised was ruled out at the highest political level.

Although the author criticises the Treaty of Versailles and rightly draws attention to the unifying effect the injustices of that treaty had on the German people, I would emphasise the deeply humiliating effect that the treaty had on a nation of 80 million who considered themselves as militarily undefeated. The German Social Democrat, Philipp Scheidemann, who proclaimed the Weimar Republic on November 8, 1918, spoke of 'the hand that must shrivel up, if it were to sign such a treaty'. It is perhaps difficult for any non-German to appreciate the extent of the deep wounds to Germany's self-esteem caused by a treaty which alienated millions of Germans from their fatherland. Some historians have said that the advent of Adolf Hitler was inevitable in such circumstances.

I am glad that the book makes it clear that my father had nothing to do with the Holocaust, a fact confirmed at the Nuremberg trials where my father was cleared of all war crimes and crimes against humanity. The author suggests that my father, because of his close friendship with Alfred Rosenberg, may have known that the Holocaust might follow in the wake of the invasion of Russia and informed his British captors of that likelihood. I am unaware if that was the case, but it may well have been. I would however mention the revisionist theories of some present-day historians as to the true nature of the Holocaust – a matter not taken up by the author.

The other point I would emphasise is the important role played by the German Resistance to Hitler at the time of the British declaration of war in September 1939. I believe this to have been a major factor in precipitating that event. The German Resistance claimed at the time that they would be unable to overthrow Hitler until war was declared. In fact, it was nearly five years into the war, on July 20, 1944, before any initiative was taken by the Resistance. If Chamberlain had known that was to be the case, I doubt very much that he would have declared war when he did.

There is of course room for many different points of view about the momentous events of the Second World War, but the facts relating to my father's peace mission and to his death 46 years later have yet to be embedded in the official records. The content of this book should do much to remedy that deficiency.

WOLF RÜDIGER HESS

Grafelfing, January 2000

PREFACE

It is very hard to remember that events now long in the past were once in the future.

F.M. MAITLAND

At 11 a.m. on Sunday, September 3, 1939, Neville Chamberlain, the British Prime Minister, addressed the nation over the radio. In sombre tones he announced a declaration of war against Germany. Only 21 years had passed since the end of the 1914–18 war which had been described as the war to end all wars.

During the six years that followed Chamberlain's broadcast the war which started as a European affair escalated into a global conflict. In the later stages it was characterised by barbarities and mass killings on a scale hitherto unknown in warfare. By August 1945, when the war ended, over 45 million men, women and children had perished.

All the participants in this bloodbath marched to war under their respective banners, parading their *causae belli* so as to give credence to what they were doing. Some invoked God on their side. All laid claims to the rightness of their cause. The Germans sought to set aside the injustices of the Treaty of Versailles, bring all Germans into one Reich and stake their claim to a place in the sun on the continent of Europe. The Japanese sought to break the stranglehold of the Western imperial powers on the raw materials in the Far East essential to Japanese industry. The Italians wished to break out from their Mediterranean prison dominated by the British and French navies and establish colonial interests. The Americans sought to frustrate Japanese ambitions in the Far East and to extend American global influence generally. Great Britain fought to preserve her historic status as a great power and to block any aggressive intent shown by those perceived as a threat to that position. Russia fought to destroy an ideology that threatened to destroy her own: hers was the Great Patriotic War.

There was of course an age-old thread that ran throughout these various aspirations. Those who wished to preserve the status quo were mortally afraid of those that did not, and those who did not were dangerously envious of those that did. Thus had wars been precipitated down through the ages. But this one was different. Twentieth-century technology and powers of destruction would see to that.

Great Britain was very much in the business of preserving the status quo. Following centuries of illustrious imperial history and world exploitation she controlled, through her Empire and Royal Navy, more than a quarter of the world's surface and resources. But by 1939 she was acutely aware of her waning industrial and financial strengths compared with the emerging star of the USA and the resurgence of old trading rivals in Europe. She also viewed with apprehension the dawn of Japanese imperial ambitions in the Far East and, nearer at home, the birth and blossoming of the rival communist and fascist/Nazi ideologies. The communists were suspected of international ambitions and the German Nazis had already manifested the threat of armed aggression. The status quo was certainly under threat from many and powerful sources. On September 3, 1939, the die was cast. The British deemed that the greatest threat to her position arose from Nazi Germany, which had already embarked upon a policy of territorial acquisition in central and eastern Europe.[1]

The British declaration of war against Germany marked the conspicuous failure of German foreign policy towards Great Britain. Ever since 1933 Hitler had sought to reassure Britain that German ambitions in central and eastern Europe would not affect the sovereignty of Britain or her Empire. The only thing Germany wanted from Britain was the hand of friendship or, failing that, a benevolent neutrality while German plans in the East unfolded. Certainly there is plenty of evidence in Hitler's personal testament, *Mein Kampf*, and in his private utterances thereafter that, in terms of major policy objectives, Germany was intent upon attacking Russia and destroying communism.

It is equally apparent from the same evidence that Hitler had no ambitions in the West. In 1934, the proposed attack on Russia was actually discussed by German army and air force chiefs with British (air) Intelligence MI6 in Berlin. The Germans even explained the new *blitzkrieg* method of attack which would be employed against the

---

[1]Although the sovereignty of Poland was the stated issue upon which war was declared it is apparent that British fears as to Nazi aggression were primarily concerned with its ultimate effect upon British interests. When Russia invaded Poland in late September 1939 there was no British declaration of war against Russia; and when the war was 'won' Poland's sovereignty was not restored.

Russians and gave details of the timing of the attack, fixed for 1941 or 1942.[2] The British therefore knew about the German plans to attack Russia some seven years before the event. They did nothing to discourage the idea. The extent to which this knowledge helped to shape Chamberlain's policies of appeasement to Hitler's demands is unclear. Certainly it is not difficult to interpret Hitler's territorial acquisitions in central and eastern Europe in the late 1930s as the acquisition of jumping-off grounds for the launch of Operation Barbarossa (the invasion of Russia) which in fact took place in 1941, as originally planned.

Chamberlain may well have made that interpretation and may well have been prepared to await the ultimate outcome of Hitler's ambitions in the East. But British public opinion did not let him. It was outraged when German troops entered Prague following on the Munich agreement of September 1938, and later when they invaded Poland, Chamberlain was obliged by British public and parliamentary opinion to declare war. He did so reluctantly, dragging his feet at every step. For Germany, the supreme irony was that on September 3, 1939, she found herself at war with Great Britain, a nation she wished to befriend, and at peace with Russia, a nation she wished to destroy.

In May 1941, in the second year of the war, an event occurred which received worldwide publicity overnight and has been hidden under a blanket of secrecy ever since. A dramatic attempt was made to stop the Anglo-German war by the Deputy Führer of Nazi Germany, Rudolf Hess. Hess flew from Augsburg on May 10, 1941, in a Messerschmitt 110 fighter aircraft and parachuted to earth in Scotland. His intention was to contact the Duke of Hamilton and talk peace. His mission was a failure. He parleyed with no one. He was identified on landing and taken into custody as a prisoner-of-war.

Hess was subsequently incarcerated for a total period of 46 years, mostly in solitary confinement, until his death in 1987. During that time he was subjected to extraordinary measures of protective security and forbidden to talk to anyone about his flight. The official German and British accounts of the flight immediately after its occurrence was that it was the lone act of a deranged individual lacking all sanction from his Government. The facts, in so far as they are now available, strongly support the remarks of the author's father in 1941, two days after the event, that 'there is more in this than meets the eye'.

Certainly the moment for a peace initiative in May 1941 could not have been more propitious as far as the Germans were concerned. The

---

[2]Details of these secret talks are given in chapter 6.

war at that stage was confined to Great Britain and Germany and her weak ally, Italy. The United States, Russia and Japan were not then participants. Military operations were almost at a standstill. France lay defeated and Great Britain had been unceremoniously ejected from a continent entirely dominated by Germany. Hitler had no more interest in the continuance of the war against Great Britain than he had in its commencement. Since June 1940, he and his generals had been engaged in the detailed planning of the great ideological war against communism and the launch of Operation Barbarossa for the invasion of Russia.

It was against this background that Hess made his dramatic flight to Scotland. If it was the lone act of a madman, its timing was singularly opportune, and after its failure the war took on a new dimension of ferocity and barbarity which led ultimately to a world conflict and those events which history will record as the nadir of mankind's endeavours in the twentieth century. In May 1941, the Holocaust, the mass terror bombings, the barbaric treatment of prisoners-of-war in the Far East and the dropping of the first atomic bomb all lay in the future.

A blanket of secrecy surrounds the Hess peace mission, 59 years after it was launched. All attempts to obtain information from Government departments have failed and the relevant papers at the Public Record Office are still embargoed. Why should this be so? What is there in terms of national security (if that be the reason for the non-disclosure) which is as sensitive today as it was in 1941?

It has been suggested that the mission had the full backing of the German Government and that its purpose was to present peace proposals to a British Peace Party[3] and to bring down the Churchill Government. It has been further suggested that this Peace Party included representatives from royalty, the landed aristocracy, business and financial interests and politicians of Cabinet rank and that disclosure of these names would cause national embarrassment. Such sensitivity must surely by now be minimal. If in the summer of 1940 the man in the street had been told what the Duke of Windsor was then up to in Portugal he might well have called for the hangman's noose. If today's man in the street was told the same story he would ask who the Duke of Windsor was. It is not difficult in hindsight (and some would claim in foresight) to present an adequate rationale for peace between Great Britain and Germany in 1941 having regard to the postwar domination of Eastern Europe by communist Russia and the prolonged cold war between East and West[4]. Present-day disclosure of the identity of

---

[3]As so described in German diplomatic papers.
[4]This view is argued strenuously by John Charmley in *Churchill, The End of Glory.*

those individuals who may have supported such a course of action (and who are for the most part now deceased) would evoke academic and historical interest rather than cries of 'traitor'. It is therefore difficult to accept that the composition of the British Peace Party, in so far as it existed at all in 1941, is the sensitive issue that compels today's secrecy.

Suggestions have also been made that British Intelligence deliberately lured Hess to this country in search of a British Peace Party that never existed. If so, why has such an outstanding coup not been the subject of public congratulation and extravagant propaganda rather than a 50-year blanket of silence? In 1941, the susceptibilities of Russia and America, soon to be Great Britain's allies, may have been factors calling for restraint. Such susceptibilities, if they ever existed, have long since disappeared. The blanket of silence has not.

Perhaps a more likely suggestion involving British Intelligence is that some of its members were themselves linked to the British Peace Party. Were they, too, actively involved in the search for peace and the bringing down of the Churchill Government? Pre-war recruitment into MI6 was largely from the British Establishment. In May 1941, there were those within that Establishment who considered communist Russia rather than Nazi Germany as the greater threat, and these views were probably as well represented within MI6 as within the Peace Party itself. This could explain present-day sensitivity, but it is unlikely that the records of the internal politics of the Intelligence Services will ever reach the public domain.

Yet another possible explanation for the extraordinary reticence of successive British Governments is linked to an issue even more sensitive today than it was in May 1941 and to events which occurred after the Hess flight: what the Germans called the Jewish problem. Racism based upon the supremacy of the Aryan was the cornerstone of Nazi beliefs. The most evil manifestation of that racism is now seen as the 'final solution' to that problem by the mass killings of innocent Jewish men, women and children. The issues raised by the Holocaust, among the most emotive of the 20th century, were very real in 1941.[5] They were or may have been relevant to the Hess flight and are therefore worthy of serious discussion.

The circumstances surrounding the death of Hess in Spandau

---

[5]Opinions differ as to the extent of the Holocaust. Total deaths have been estimated at six million but revisionist historians have questioned this figure. The release of papers from the Public Record Office in June 1997 reveal that German ciphers were being read in June 1941 and the activities of Heydrich's *Einsatzgruppen* were then known. These activities were the forerunner of the Holocaust.

Prison, Berlin, on August 17, 1987, are as controversial as those surrounding the 1941 peace mission. The death certificate issued by the British Army authorising officer stated that death was caused by asphyxia due to compression of the neck by *suspension*. The conclusion was that Hess had committed suicide. This was confirmed by a subsequent investigation conducted by the Special Investigation Branch of the British Military Police. However, over 400 pages of evidence, personal statements (including two from eminent pathologists) and other exhibits which have been submitted to the British Ministry of Defence by Hess's son, Wolf, and the author suggest that death was caused by asphyxia due to compression of the neck by *throttling*. The conclusion is that Hess did not commit suicide but was murdered. Following submission of these papers the Ministry of Defence cancelled the registration of the original death certificate, explaining that the death had been registered in the first place without proper authority. The Ministry have since refused to re-register the certificate in any terms. It appears that the only way in which these matters may be resolved satisfactorily is by applying for leave to the English courts for an application for a judicial review. At the time of writing this matter is being considered.

My thanks are due to those who have helped me on my way during my travels and researches. In particular, I found free-thinking academics and historians, both professional and amateur, unstinting in their efforts. I had not realised what a valuable contribution they make to the system of checks and balances in a working democracy. I was also fortunate to discover a team of lawyers who slotted into this same category. The suicide verdict on the death of Hess, on August 17, 1987, fitted neatly into the official version of his mental instability and the sheer madness of the solo flight; however, there is now a distinct possibility that this fiction will be effectively exposed by legal process. Thus do lawyers too march in the pursuit of truth.

By contrast, my attempts to establish a working relationship with Government departments – including the Cabinet Office, the Home Office, the Foreign and Commonwealth Office and the Ministry of Defence – have almost completely failed. To obtain meaningful information from these sources has been likened to sexual intercourse with an elephant: it is an extremely difficult and cumbersome procedure, there is very little pleasure to be derived from it, you are very likely to be squashed and there will be no result for at least two years. I encountered many such elephants on my way.

My more fruitful sources, to whom I gratefully record my thanks. include my late father, whose memorable remark on May 13, 1941, sowed the seeds of enquiry in my mind; Richard Norton-Taylor of the

Guardian newspaper; Hermann Weis of the Institüt für Zeitgeschichte, Munich, for help and encouragement in early days; L. Fowkes of Cardiff, who runs the best out-of-print book service in the business; Professor W. Van der Wile of the Department of German Studies at Birmingham University; Walter Martin of Freiburg University; Professor Richard Griffiths of Kings College, London; Dr Scott Newton of the School of History and Archaeology, University of Wales; Hugh Thomas, MD, FRCS, FRCS(C) of Brecon; the staff at the Public Record Office, Kew; the Archival Record Office at the House of Lords, the Imperial War Museum, the News International Archive Centre, the Liddell Hart Military Archives Centre at Kings College, London, the Bodleian Library, Oxford, and Churchill College, Cambridge, for their courteous help at all times; Professor Rzheshevsky Oleg Alexandrovich of the Russian Institute of Universal History, Moscow; Dr Marian Keipert of the Auswärtiges AMT Politisches Archiv, Bonn; Dr Christoph Studt and Ralph Forsbach, MA, of the Historisches Seminar, Bonn University, and Magnus Brechtken of Bayreuth University for their special help in connection with the Madagascar Plan; Patrick J. Cully, Defense Inquiries Officer at the US Embassy, London; Frau Hermann of the Bundesarchiv, Koblenz, and the Textual Records Division of the US National Archives and Records, Washington DC, for their assistance in connection with the Pfeffer file; Rhodri Morgan, MP, for his particular interest, involvement and help; Mr John T.C. Harris of Cottesbrooke, Northampton, for his valuable researches in connection with the mysterious Mary Violet Roberts; the lawyers at Turner Kenneth Brown (later Nabarro Nathanson), and in particular David O'Callaghan, Lee Newman, Michael Hales and my own son, Michael, for their patience and professional perseverance in connection with the Hess death certificate; Lesley Pitman of the School of Slavonic and East European Studies, London University; Andrew Rosthorn (for the Lynda Chalker correspondence); the London Editor of *Der Spiegel*; Adolf Galland, the Luftwaffe General; Jimmy Carter, former President of the USA; Kenneth de Courcy, freelance political consultant *extraordinaire*; Tony Mulliken of Midas Public Relations Ltd; Lord Shawcross, QC; Jack Fishman, the author; my good friend and adviser, Peter Hehir of Countrywide Communications Group; secretaries Lisa Rose, Karen Richmond and Karen Burrows, who displayed great patience and forebearance in translating my freehand scrawl into a meaningful manuscript; John Craddock, for his excellent translation services; and my son, Patrick, and his colleagues at Smith Dove, Chartered Accountants, Northampton, for their forebearance and services generally.

My special thanks and appreciation are reserved for Wolf Rüdiger Hess, Rudolf Hess's son. I was first introduced to Wolf by Hermann Weis in Munich in 1993. He, like me, was intent upon ascertaining the truth about his father's mission in 1941 and his death in 1987. We have since hunted in tandem. We do not discuss politics and I doubt that Wolf agrees with all the views put forward in this book, but that is not important. On one thing we are in complete agreement: our view as to how his father met his death in Spandau Prison. Wolf has worked constantly for more than ten years to stamp the truth as to his father's death on the historical record, and he has not given up yet. His industry, fixity of purpose and integrity have my utmost respect.

I have arranged the text of the book in four parts. Part One sets out the political situation in Germany in 1933, when Adolf Hitler assumed power. At that time Rudolf Hess was centre stage at Hitler's elbow and very much inside Hitler's mind. He had embraced with fervour all the aspirations and prejudices, if not the hates, of his friend and mentor, as expressed in *Mein Kampf*, of which he was a major contributor to the thought themes. The stage as set in 1933 shows what it was that Hess was taking on board in terms of personal commitment (this is important because of later suggestions that, blinded by his adoration for his Führer, Hess did not appreciate the portent of the policy objectives to which he was then subscribing).

Part Two plots the unfolding of Hitler's programme and the drift towards war. It also deals with the failure of German foreign policy towards Great Britain, a matter of particular importance and disappointment to both Hitler and Hess.

Part Three deals with what is called 'the reluctant war' – i.e. the period from September 1939 to May 1941. It was a war which Germany never wanted and it was riddled with attempts by both adversaries to call it off, culminating in the last great personal effort by Hess in May 1941. Emphasis is given to those instances during that period when Hitler showed his hand in prosecuting the war against Great Britain less than vigorously because of his underlying wish to end hostilities in the West before the great ideological assault on Russia. Hess's dilemma during this period is also explained. His late realisation of the excesses arising from Hitler's literalism in pursuing his policy objectives clashed with his intense personal loyalty to his Führer and friend. A major internal conflict arose as a result. It affected Hess's health and, perhaps more importantly, played a significant part in his flight to Great Britain in 1941.

Parts Four and Five deal with the two great unresolved mysteries concerning Rudolf Hess: the purpose of his peace mission and the circumstances of his death. They explore the part played in each of these events by British Intelligence, and the possibility that both may have had a Jewish dimension.

It has been said that nothing stimulates the imagination more than a mystery. Government secrecy also stimulates inquisitiveness, and the partial release of facts encourages conjecture. That is the Hess story. Let the reader decide.

ALFRED SMITH

Northampton,
January 2000

PART ONE

1933: THE STAGE IS SET

1

The Nazi accession

There is no man so dangerous as the disillusioned idealist.

GOETHE

Adolf Hitler assumed the position of German Chancellor shortly after noon on Monday, January 30, 1933. It was an appointment made in accordance with democratic process at the Reich Chancellery by President Hindenburg. Hitler was to preside over a coalition Government. It was an agreement that helped ease him into power and one which he terminated as soon as that became the case.

The appointment was a personal triumph for the 43-year-old Austrian. He came from an obscure family background, possessed little in the way of formal education and was a conspicuous non-achiever as an academic.[1] Rather did his education, development of political ideas and feeding of his personal prejudices come from his street experiences during the early years of manhood in Vienna and Munich. He had indulged an insatiable appetite for reading during those days. In Vienna, as a young man and at an impressionable age, he had experienced poverty, hunger and unemployment, relieved only by manual labour and the occasional sale of watercolour paintings. During that time, he was an acute observer of the extremes of wealth and poverty and how they lived side by side.[2] He also took in and despised the cosmopolitan nature of the Viennese populace, with its preponderance of Jews and Slavs to the exclusion of those of Aryan blood. Thus was his racism given root and nurtured.

Hitler came to Munich in the spring of 1912, at the age of 22. He described his two years' stay there prior to his army service, as 'by far

---

[1]Hitler's academic failures probably explain the contempt, even ridicule, with which he viewed those in the academic field in later life.

[2]Hitler, Adolf, *Mein Kampf*, Hurst and Blackett (1939), 22–24.

the happiest and most contented time of my life ... I came to love that city'.[3] His war service was distinguished. He volunteered to join a Bavarian regiment on August 3, 1914, and served as an infantry man, first as a private, then as a corporal. He won two Iron Crosses. The later one was First Class, an award seldom made to a non-commissioned officer. He returned to Munich after his war service. He there gave his life to political activity and the establishment of his own position at the centre of that activity. In September 1919 he became member No. 7 on the committee of the postwar German Workers Party.[4] He quickly converted it into the Nazi party and became its first leader or Führer. He then waged battle (in early days, literally) against his political opponents, chiefly the Communists and Jews. His aim was to establish the Nazi party as an electable option to the German people.

It was during this hectic time that Hitler developed those personal and political skills which were destined to carry him to the highest political office. Like any other street politician Hitler learned his political craft by hard experience. He was a master of opportunism, being well equipped with his native Austrian tactical adroitness. He soon recognised and learned the value of publicity and propaganda, of public display and its theatrical presentation, of man management, of political dealing and double dealing, of organisational techniques and the importance of planning and discipline in the holding of public meetings.

As to leadership, Hitler found, as did his colleagues, that this came to him naturally. His beliefs were held with fanatical zeal and he was able to project these beliefs so as to convince and lead others. He did this by using his powers of oratory which soon developed into his supreme skill. In both the manner of delivery and the content of his speeches he was able to reach out and touch the very heart of German postwar hopes and fears.

The 1918 betrayal by the corrupt politicians, the injustices of the Versailles *diktat*, the call of German nationalism, the purity and superiority of the Aryan race, the contamination of the Slav and other inferior races, the evils of Jewish influence, the Russian communist menace. These were all matters already lying deep within the German psyche and convenient pegs upon which to hang the frustrations and disappointments of a defeated Germany.

These were the themes that Hitler repeatedly hammered home. And he did it in an oratorical style that was soon developed into a lethal weapon capable of evoking mass hysteria and abandon among his

---

[3]*Ibid*, 80.

[4]Shirer, William L., *The Rise and Fall of the Third Reich*, Pan Books (1964), 57.

audiences. They soon flocked to hear him. In 1919 in the early days of the German Workers Party he found himself addressing audiences of six, seven or eight individuals. In the late summer of 1922 he addressed a mass demonstration of 60,000 in the Königsplatz in Munich.[5] Such were the powers of his oratory and the message he was projecting.

On November 9, 1923, the Nazi Party was dissolved and forbidden to function throughout Germany. The reason for its banishment was the part it played in the civil disorders taking place in Munich on that day. Hitler had led a failed coup. He had believed that the Bavarian Prime Minister was about to proclaim an independent Bavaria, with secession from the German Republic. The coup was designed to thwart these ambitions towards political fragmentation. It was ignominiously put down by the Army. Some demonstrators were killed,[6] others injured. Hitler himself incurred a broken collarbone. He was brought to trial on February 26, 1924, and sentenced to five years' imprisonment. He served only thirteen months and was released on December 20, 1924. His term of imprisonment was served at Landsberg on the River Lech.

Hitler's enforced stay at Landsberg was of particular political importance. During his imprisonment he wrote the first volume of his political testament, *Mein Kampf*.[7] In that task he was assisted by his friend and confidante, Rudolf Hess.[8] *Mein Kampf* is a remarkable book by any standard. It is described by the author in his preface as 'the fundamental principles of my doctrine committed to writing'. The text itself may be severely criticised. It is verbose,[9] repetitive, illogical in development and generous in hyperbole. Rhetoric runs wild in the constant emphasis of the author's prejudices, hatreds and bile, but sandwiched between these unattractive excesses there are also offered some original and penetrative thoughts. These deal, *inter alia*, with the processes of German history, the European political scene, Anglo-German relations and the factors making for successful political activity.

Most important of all, *Mein Kampf* contains a clear and reasoned statement of what Germany's future internal and external policy objec-

---

[5]Hitler, Adolf, *Mein Kampf*, Hurst and Blackett (1939), 200–302

[6]*Mein Kampf* was dedicated to their memory.

[7]The second volume was completed during the two years following the release of Hitler from Landsberg.

[8]There is some difference of opinion as to whether Hess was responsible for some of the contents of the book or merely edited it. Both are probably the case.

[9]The original suggested title by Hitler was *Four and a Half Years Struggle against Lies, Stupidity and Cowardice*.

tives ought to be and how they should be achieved. One might disagree with Hitler's political analysis and the suggested remedies but the arguments and conclusions are clearly put and suggested as a practical programme of action for the future. This is what raises the book, warts and all, to one of supreme importance when linked to the author's succession to the office of German Chancellor in 1933.The book was dismissed by so many as the ramblings of a madman. But when the madman becomes German Chancellor and starts to do exactly what he said he was going to do in *Mein Kampf*, then the ramblings become the stuff of *realpolitik. Mein Kampf* contained the authentic blueprint of Hitler's intentions as to the domestic and foreign policies of the Third Reich. It was there for all to see and study. It was one of the great tragedies and follies of the 1930s that very few did outside Germany.[10]

Lord Halifax was Foreign Secretary in Chamberlain's government and one of Great Britain's most important front men in dealing with Hitler's ambitions and objectives during the crucial period 1937–39. He apparently did not read *Mein Kampf* until after his Government's declaration of war in 1939 when Queen Elizabeth handed him a copy.[11] His Secretary of State, R.A. Butler, was an early reader. According to Butler's own rough notes, the Hitler Youth Movement and the public spirit thus engendered seems to have caught his imagination. It was hardly the book's most crucial message.

Hitler's early moves in the mid-1930s[12] demonstrated his adherence to the policies set down in *Mein Kampf* and the literalism of his thinking. He was of course a great tactical liar when dealing with his opponents on the European stage, but during the period up to 1939 he never deviated from his stated strategic policies and objectives.[13] In only one important respect did things not go according to plan. German foreign policy aimed at friendship with Great Britain failed. As a result, Hitler found himself involved in a premature and unwanted war against an adversary not of his choosing.

There is an interesting supplement to the publication of Hitler's ideas, objectives and policies in *Mein Kampf*. The book was written while he was imprisoned at Landsberg. He was not then in a position

---

[10]Where six million copies had been sold by 1940.

[11]Halifax papers, November 15, 1939.

[12]The withdrawal of Germany from the disarmament conferences and the re-occupation of the Rhineland.

[13]The annexation of Czechoslovakia after the Munich Agreement surprised and shocked Western observers. It should not have done. It was inevitable in the light of Hitler's declared policies as to *Lebensraum* in the East. Czechoslovakia and Poland were obvious springboards for the forthcoming attack on Russia. This conclusion is divined not from hindsight but from the content of *Mein Kampf*.

of political power, either within the Government or the party of opposition. He therefore had no need to bend his published views to suit the particular political climate of the day or his position in it. One can assume therefore that his views are sincerely put and nothing held back.

In 1928, some four years after his release from Landsberg, Hitler dictated a second book. This book elaborated with detailed expositions his views on foreign policy. Significantly, no new ideas were added to those already expressed in *Mein Kampf*. But his second book[14] was never published.[15] Hitler's views had not changed between 1924 and 1928, but much had changed in Germany itself. Chancellor Gustav Stresemann's policies of reconciliation had borne fruit and Germany was enjoying a brief period of prosperity. Stresemann's policies ran contrary to the ideas proposed by Hitler, who still had hopes of making the Nazi Party electable. It is probably for this reason that his second book was never published, an act of discretion in the light of electoral prospects. It was a factor which had never affected the publication of *Mein Kampf*.

What then were these policy objectives of Hitler's Nazi Party when Hitler came to power in 1933? Clearly set down in *Mein Kampf* and the 1928 book, they were almost universally ignored by Western observers. Their attempted implementation led to the World War of 1939–45 and the loss of forty-five million lives.

[14]It has no title and is referred to simply as 'Hitler's Secret Book'.

[15]The original manuscript was placed in a safe at the Nazi Party's central publishing house with strict orders that it was not to be published. In May 1945 the manuscript was found, sent to the Records Division of the US National Archives and in 1958 duly authenticated as a second book manuscript written by Adolf Hitler in 1928.

2

The German policy objectives

It is wrong to regard a nation with unalterable suspicion but what if that nation gives unalterable cause?

VANSITTART

Mein Kampf, the 1928 second book and Hitler's speeches during his twelve years in power reveal not only his policy objectives but how they were to be achieved. The policies were for the most part abhorrent to Western observers. They also sat well on the German psyche and postwar aspirations. No one knew that better than Adolf Hitler.

First and foremost, the Third Reich was to comprise only those of pure German blood. Racism was therefore to be a fundamental tenet of Nazi ideology. Other races, deemed inferior, would be excluded by segregation. This would involve the setting up of self-contained ghettoes within the Reich or deportation to areas outside the Reich, or both.[1] A second objective was that the Reich was to include all Germans within its frontiers. This would involve territorial acquisitions and frontier adjustments within Europe and a revision of the terms of the Versailles Treaty (or *diktat* as Hitler called it). A further objective was the extension of the Reich boundaries to the East. This was to provide more *Lebensraum* (living space) for the German population. The countries affected by such a policy were those of Eastern Europe and Russia, which country was specifically mentioned. Finally, Hitler's Germany sought to destroy its ideological enemy, communism. In so far as the threat of communism came from Russia armed conflict with that nation would be inevitable.

To achieve these objectives Hitler deemed three things as essential.

[1]The 'Final Solution', which was ultimately applied to the so-called Jewish problem, is not mentioned in either of Hitler's political testaments. It formed no part of German policies until after the launch of Operation Barbarossa (the invasion of Russia) in June 1941.

First, the internal political structure of the Reich was to be such that his expressed will would be executed immediately, effectively and without opposition on all matters. The constitutional tool selected was therefore to be a strong, one-party National Socialist state, based upon the *Führer prinzip*. This would encompass the denial of parliamentary and all other forms of democratic opposition. The single party would control education, press and radio news reporting, state security and all economic, culture and recreational activities. Above all, there would be a complete obedience to the iron will of the Führer.

A second requirement was that the objectives of territorial acquisitions in Europe and expansion to the East could only be negotiated, or achieved by other means, from a position of armed strength. Early rearmament was therefore essential.

Finally, a major effort would be made to reassure Great Britain that the achievement of German policy objectives would in no way affect the sovereignty of Great Britain or her Empire. Germany had no wish to enter into imperialist competition with Great Britain and repeat the mistakes of 1914–18.

All these policy objectives and the means by which they were to be achieved may be identified clearly from a reading of Hitler's two political testaments and the text of his speeches made during the 1930s. They are worthy of examination because they were originally embraced not only by Hitler but also by his friend and confidant, Rudolf Hess.

Race

The Nazi programme only made sense on the assumption of the superiority of the Aryan race. If the Germans *en masse* were a nation of supermen then all things were theoretically possible, including the rearrangement of the map of Europe. If, however, they were a nation of ordinary mortals, then their expansionist plans against other nations, strong as well as weak, could lead to disaster. In fact, of course, that is what ultimately happened. Too late, if at all, the Germans discovered that they were only ordinary people. But in 1933 they were told they were superior beings to the rest of mankind, and by 1940 they believed it. This cult of supposed racial superiority was the mainspring of all Nazi activity. Its effect, when combined with certain traits in the German (or more specifically Prussian) character, goes some way to explaining the barbarities perpetrated during the last years of the Nazi regime.

That Alfred Rosenberg, Hitler's court philosopher, could produce philosophers, both alive and dead, to elevate Hitler's racial prejudices to the status of academic thesis is a credit to his ingenuity. Darwinism as applied to mankind would establish the right of the strong to dominate, and if need be, to eliminate the weak. 'Mankind separates into races of superior and inferior quality. Divine Will subordinates the inferior and weaker to the better and stronger. Divine Will expresses the aristocrat principle'.[2] Nietzsche wrote of the coming of Superman who would rise above ordinary mortals and their ordinary morals. Houston Chamberlain, English by birth and German by adoption, preached that race was the key to all history and that the Aryan race was the only true inheritor of the world's ancient culture and civilisation. Count Joseph de Gabineau, French diplomat, man of letters and aristocrat had equated Superman with the Aryan race and identified the Germans as the pick of the Aryans (with the British earning a consolation prize).

These were the theoreticians promoted by Rosenberg to best accommodate the personal hatreds which Hitler had picked up on the streets of Vienna in early manhood. The remarkable thing is how such perversions were apparently embraced so enthusiastically by the entire German nation. They readily accepted that it was the primary duty of the State to preserve the purity of Aryan blood.[3] Every assistance was to be given to healthy Aryan women to procreate. That was their function. At the same time, if over a period all those who were physically or mentally diseased were sterilised, humanity itself would be 'fully restored and brought to a nobler era'.

Hitler also argued that if hundreds of thousands accepted celibacy by ecclesiastical precept as the basis of the priesthood then the same celibacy could be accepted by those who were diseased.[4] Sterilisation was the measure to be adopted to remove the unfit, the weaklings and the fools. Contamination of the pure Aryan blood by mixed marriages was also to be prohibited. Aryan was only to marry Aryan and Aryans were only to beget Aryans. There was to be no question of 'Germanising' other races by intermarriage, which would lead to a dilution of the pure blood content. Alien races were deemed inferior[5] and were either to be sealed off in ghettoes or deported and their land appropriated for the benefit of Germans.[6] This theme as to the preservation of pure Germanic blood from generation to generation is the

---

[2]Hitler, Adolf, *Mein Kampf*, Hurst & Blackett, London (1939), 215.
[3]*Ibid*, 220–21.
[4]*Ibid*, 227–28.
[5]Czechs, Poles, Russians and others were officially designated as such by the New Order promulgated in 1941.
[6]Hitler, Adolf, *Hitler's Secret Book*, Grove Press, New York (1961), 47–48.

constantly repeated message of *Mein Kampf* and the received wisdom of Hitler's Nazi party.

> Preservation of blood purity is in accordance with the iron law of Nature. Species keep within their own species when propagating. Every animal mates with his own species. Hybrids are sterile or the fecundity of descendants is limited. Resistance to disease is low. This urge for the maintenance of an unmixed breed prevails throughout the animal world.[7]

Such then was the Nazi thinking on the issue of race.[8] It was the cornerstone of their ideology. The thinking was both flawed and evil. It was flawed because the history of mankind provides countless examples of major contributors to world culture and civilisations who had no connection with Aryan blood, pure or otherwise. It was evil because Superman rose above all conventional morality and was answerable only to his own will. He was like a wild animal in the jungle, intent only upon survival and the domination of others. First propounded by Hegel and carried to extreme lengths by Nietzsche, there was no restriction in Superman's world of acts deemed immoral according to the cultural tenets of Judaism and Christianity. Thus was the door opened to the execution of acts of barbarity which might appal the civilised world but which would lie quite properly in the path of Superman's exercise of his iron will. These acts duly entered the record. The race that suffered worst at Hitler's hands in this manner was the Jewish race.

Race: The Jewish problem

If the supremacy of the Aryan race and the preservation of its purity were the central themes of Nazi philosophy then the treatment of the Jews as an 'inferior' race was the most devastating and evil manifestation of that philosophy. Of all the vile invective in *Mein Kampf* – and there is plenty of it – by far the worst is reserved for the Jews. Their history, their institutions, their character, their morals, their appear-

---

[7]Hitler, Adolf, *Mein Kampf*, Hurst & Blackett, London (1939), 161.

[8]It has to be said that Nazi Germany was not alone in adopting or flirting with racial policies based upon a eugenic approach to national wellbeing. Sterilisation of the unfit prevailed in Scandinavia during the period 1930–70 and its advocacy was one of the worst-kept secrets of the British intelligensia of the Left in the early part of the 20th century. The Webbs, George Bernard Shaw, Maynard Keynes, Marie Stopes, Bertrand Russell and Harold Laski all advocated the sterilisation of the unfit.

ance, their mode of living, their ambitions and their religion are all attacked. The language used illustrates more the tortured mind of the author than the subject of his remarks.

'Here was a pestilence, a moral pestilence with which the public was being infected. It was worse than the Black Death of Medieval times. And in what mighty doses this poison was being manufactured and distributed. Sometimes it went so far that one of those fellows acting like a sewage pump would shoot his filth directly in the faces of other members of the human race. One ought to realise that for one Goethe, nature may bring into existence ten thousand of such despoilers who act as the worst kind of germ carriers in poisoning human souls.'[9]

> 'The Jews are participating in shady undertakings especially in cultural life. On putting the probing knife carefully to that kind of abscess one immediately discovered like a maggot is a putrescence body, a little Jew who was often blinded by the sudden light. The charges against the Jews are grave when discovering their activities in the Press, Art, Literature and the Theatre. Nine tenths of all smutty literature, artistic tripe and theatrical banalities had to be charged to the account of people who formed scarcely one tenth of the nation.'[10]

No rational basis for this invective is included in *Mein Kampf*. In his arguments relating to the interpretation of German history, the need for revision of the Versailles provisions, the case for *Lebensraum* in the East and particularly, Germany's need for friendship with Great Britain,[11] Hitler advances a rational basis. His remarks hang together in some form of logical sequence and argument. No such rationale exists in *Mein Kampf* for his personal hatred of the Jews. There is not one word of reasoned explanation, factual evidence or specific illustration which would enable the reader to form a judgement about the reasonableness of the charges made. That some sort of pseudo-philosophical rationale for anti-semitism could be produced is unquestionable. It could have been worked out in the same way as the array of philosophers had been collected by Rosenberg to rationalise Hitler's irrational views on race generally. But it was not. It is almost as though Hitler's personal hatred for the Jews was so all-pervading that he had neither the time or patience to seek a bogus rationale.

---

[9]Hitler, Adolf, *Mein Kampf*, Hurst & Blackett, London (1939), 42.
[10]*Ibid*, 41–42.
[11]Throughout *Mein Kampf*, and throughout his life, Hitler referred to Great Britain as England.

When Hitler came to power in 1933 he let it be known that Germany had a Jewish problem. More accurately, Hitler had a Jewish problem which he was about to foist onto the German nation. It was a problem born on the streets of Vienna during Hitler's early manhood. It was there that he started to read anti-Jewish literature and 'observed the phenomena in the streets'. He refers to a great 'spiritual upheaval' at that time. 'I ceased to be a weak-knead cosmopolitan and became an anti-Semitic'.[12] When Hitler was in Vienna he was for the most part destitute. He had no home, no job and no money. In conventional terms he was a confirmed failure. He was also a man of very considerable, if undeveloped, talents. The frustrations and disappointments would therefore have been a very considerable cross to bear, especially as he observed the rich, the powerful and the successful going about their business with every advantage denied to him. It is apparent that his 'spiritual upheaval' was more in the nature of finding the convenient hook of anti-Semitism upon which to hang and get rid of his personal failures and frustrations. It was not the first time in the history of mankind that such a hook had been used. Thus are hates born and fostered.

For the remainder of Hitler's life this pathological hatred of the Jews never left him. It became his over-riding passion. It dominated his thinking on almost every subject. In ultimate terms it dictated the content of the last sentence of his last testament on the last day of his life. He even used it as a positive weapon of Nazi policy. He used it indiscriminately to explain phenomena not otherwise connected which he wished to attack. Thus were included the Jew-ridden communists of Russia, the Jewish plutocrats of the West, the parasitic Jewish capitalists of America and the Jewish infiltrators of the world trade union movement. All could be comfortably accommodated as the product of a universal scapegoat. Thus the plight of postwar Germany could be explained:

> 'If we review all the causes which contributed to bring about the downfall of the German people we shall find that the most profound and decisive course must be attributed to the lack of insight into the racial problem and especially on the failure to recognise the Jewish danger.'[13]

Although the Jewish 'problem' is set down in page after page of *Mein Kampf* there is very little to suggest what the answer to the prob-

---

[12]Hitler, Adolf, *Mein Kampf*, Hurst & Blackett, London (1939), 44–45.
[13]*Ibid*, 185.

lem might be. There is no clear policy objective, other than that dealing with racial purity generally. The search for a solution to the Jewish problem occupied many senior minds within the Nazi hierarchy during their twelve years in power. It was not easy. The treatment of Jews in Germany was not entirely a domestic matter. There were important ramifications in terms of foreign policy, particularly as affecting relations with Great Britain. The incorporation within the Reich of additional territories and peoples in the East further increased the problem. Hitler's lieutenants all knew of his abhorrence of the Jewish presence and all had their own ideas as to how they might deal with the problem. As a result, the problem was passed from department to department. There were many changes and switches in direction. Each successive measure was at one time or another described as the 'Final Solution' to the problem years before the advent of the ultimate Final Solution provided by Heydrich's SS in June 1941 and thereafter.

One inclusive Reich

One of the first demands made by Hitler on his succession to power was that the German Reich must embrace all Germans. Foreign policy relating to *Lebensraum* could not be determined until all Germans were included in the one Reich.[14] If in those circumstances there was then insufficient national territory to sustain the population, then according to Hitler, the moral right would arise for the acquisition of additional territories to the East. In 1933 the alienation of Germans from their fatherland was widespread. It arose in the main from the provisions of the Versailles Treaty signed on June 28, 1919, marking the end of the 1914–18 war. Six million Germans found themselves in Austria, two million in the new state of Czechoslovakia and a further two million in Danzig and the newly created Polish Corridor, separating East Prussia from the rest of Germany. This fragmentation was deeply humiliating.

Although an attack on the Versailles provisions was therefore an immediate target it was not necessarily enough. Hitler makes it clear in *Mein Kampf* that there was nothing sacrosanct about a return to the 1914 frontiers. Any other date would be just as relevant.[15] But Hitler was nothing if not an opportunist. He knew that the removal of the offending Versailles clauses would be a good curtain-raiser. A frontal

---

[14] *Ibid*, 13.
[15] *Ibid*, 357–58.

attack on Versailles would go to the heart of German discontent, have an immediate unifying effect upon the German populace and invoke international sympathy, especially in Great Britain where the 'fairness' card would be played. Hitler's skilful use of the 'injustices of the Versailles *diktat*' was a major policy aid in the unification of all Germans within the one Reich.

Opinions differ as to the fairness or otherwise of the Treaty of Versailles. Its primary purpose was to provide security against future German aggression against Europe in general and France in particular.[16] The granting of an even-handed peace treaty as far as Germany was concerned was low on the list of priorities. The lead players in the formulation of its provisions were 'Tiger' Clemenceau of France, Lloyd George of Great Britain, President Wilson of the United States and Orlando of Italy. Clemenceau and Lloyd George dominated the proceedings. They seemed to draft the provisions on the hoof, as their inclinations and powers of improvisation led them. Wilson was an academic rather than a politician and his Fourteen Points, upon which the armistice had been based, were pushed further and further into the background. This had an unfortunate effect, the significance of which did not become apparent until Hitler's programme began to unfold and roll across Europe.

An important part of the Versailles agreement was that the United States was to join Great Britain in her guarantee of France against future German aggression. She never did. The US Senate failed to ratify the agreement, presumably because of its remoteness from Wilson's original Fourteen Points. Thus are clever politicians too clever. The original French intention to safeguard her security was to break up Germany into small independent states, so as to avoid threats to France from a unified Germany greater in population and land area than themselves. Under pressure from Lloyd George other protective and compensatory measures were taken instead. Alsace Lorraine was restored to France and some previously held German territory was made available to Belgium. The Rhineland was demilitarised and occupied by the Allies for a period of 15 years, reverting to Germany thereafter. The Saarland was to be occupied for a period of 15 years and then a plebiscite held to determine its future.

In the East, a plebiscite was to be held in Upper Silesia,[17] Danzig became a Free City and lands previously taken by Germany when Poland was partitioned were restored to Poland. This had the effect of creating the Polish Corridor separating East Prussia from the rest of

---

[16]In respect of which it was, of course, a conspicuous failure.

[17]The plebiscite was held on March 20, 1921. 60 per cent of the population voted to remain in the German Reich. Nevertheless, the territory was partitioned, the richer part going to Poland.

Germany. Finally, territory in Schleswig appropriated by Bismarck in the previous century was restored to Denmark.

Responsibility for the war was affixed on Germany. Reparations were payable as and when the ability to pay had been assessed. This issue caused particular bitterness and provided yet another powerful boost to Nazi propaganda. The German army was fixed at a level of 100,000. There was to be no parity of arms with the Allies and no manufacture of heavy weaponry. There were to be no tanks or aircraft. The navy was to have a token force only, with no submarines or surface ships in excess of 10,000 tons.

Thus did Versailles bring to the Germans considerable losses of national territory, the occupation of further national territories by foreign troops and the alienation of millions of Germans from their fatherland. In military terms, a once proud and martial nation was stripped to the point of impotence and in economic terms she had to pick up the bill for the cost of the war. Nevertheless, the German homeland was left largely intact and although the Versailles terms were hardly generous, they compared well with those handed out by Germany to the defeated Russians on the Eastern Front at the Treaty of Brest-Litovsk on March 3, 1918.[18]

Versailles and the legends that grew up around it contributed materially to the collapse of the Weimar Republic and the accession of Hitler to power. Successive German governments had been perceived as agents of the Allied powers in the enforcement and administration of what was alleged to be 'a scandal and a disgrace and a dictate signifying an act of daylight robbery against our people.'[19] The irony was that opposition to the treaty throughout Germany was so universal that it brought a great unity to the German people – which was precisely what the Big Four and particularly Clemenceau had set out to prevent. Hitler knew that a popular and successful policy objective of Versailles Treaty revision would lead to frontier realignments, territory acquisitions and the eventual return of Germans to their fatherland. Versailles revision was therefore the important first step along the road towards one Reich for all Germans. It would also probably lead towards armed conflict with other nations,[20] and Hitler had to be ready for that.

---

[18]Russia lost territory almost as large as Austria, Hungary and Turkey combined, one third of her population, one third of her railtrack, 73 per cent of her iron ore, 89 per cent of her coal production and more than factories and industrial plants. She also picked up the reparations bill for six billion marks.

[19]Hitler, Adolf, *Mein Kampf*, Hurst & Blackett, London (1939), 260.

[20]In the event, not until September 1939 when the issue of Danzig and the Polish Corridor resulted in war. During earlier years Hitler had almost achieved his objective of incorporating all Germans within the one Reich through peaceful annexation and negotiation, albeit underpinned by the threat of military force.

The search for Lebensraum

If the implementation of Hitler's policy of Versailles revision and the incorporation of all alienated Germans within the Reich did not lead to armed conflict with other European nations then the implementation of his policy as to *Lebensraum* assuredly would. Hitler put the case for *Lebensraum* very simply. Germany could never aspire to world power status while her land resources remained so low in relation to her population. Great Britain controlled one quarter of the earth's surface. The United States, Russia and China could measure their land interests in terms of continents. Germany's land mass extended to barely 500,000 square kilometres – less than one-tenth of that occupied by any of the world powers.

The disparity is explained by the course of European history which had left Germany sidelined. She had spent most of the Middle Ages and the period leading up to the advent of Bismarck in a state of feudal isolation and/or religious controversy. Political evolution and national aspirations had been at a standstill. Unification as a single nation state under Bismarck between 1866 and 1871, after a thousand years of disunity, came very late in the day. By that time other nations, particularly Great Britain, had already staked out their claims on the world's surface by way of colonial exploitation, and they had established their world power status. Late claims by Germany were therefore bound to lead to confrontation. They did so with disastrous consequences for Germany in the 1914–18 Great War. Thus through the strategies and accidents of history was Germany deprived of what she considered to be her rightful place in the sun.

This was a powerful factor in creating the feelings of frustration, hurt and envy which prevailed on Hitler's accession to power in 1933. Germany could boast a proud cultural heritage, stemming from the 18th and 19th centuries, in music, literature and philosophy. Her people were inventive, industrious and ambitious. She was worthy of her place in the sun. But the disastrous war of 1914–18 had taught her that any threat to the existing status quo would not be tolerated by the imperial powers, in particular by Great Britain. Hitler analyses the problem in considerable detail in *Mein Kampf*. His clear conclusion was that the only effective remedy was to acquire additional territories on the land mass of Europe.

The arrogance displayed by his reasoning is breathtaking. The rights and interests of other European nations are totally ignored. He starts with the assumption that the German population was growing at the rate of 900,000 annually in a national territory static in area. He rejects two suggested remedies. Artificial birth control is ruled out as against the laws of nature. In any case, Hitler had no wish to restrict the birth of healthy Aryan stock. External colonisation would again lead Germany into competition, confrontation and eventual armed conflict with Great Britain.[21,22]

Hitler settled on the remaining alternative which called for the acquisition of further land on the continent of Europe itself. He is dismissive of existing political frontiers. He suggests that the provision of more land for the German peasantry was of a higher moral value than the preservation of the political status quo. If armed force was to be employed in upsetting the status quo and releasing land for German occupation, so be it.

> 'In considering the state of affairs today we must not allow existing political frontiers to distract attention from what ought to exist under the principles of strict justice. If this Earth has sufficient room for all then we ought to have that share of the soil which is absolutely necessary for our existence. Of course, people will not voluntarily make that accommodation available. When attempts to settle the difficulty in an amicable way are rejected, the clenched fist must take by force that which was refused to the open hand of friendship. The only possibility which Germany had of carrying a sound territorial policy into effect was that of acquiring new territory in Europe itself.'[23]

Hitler goes further. He specifies the particular area in Europe earmarked for German occupation, so as to provide the essential *Lebensraum*:

> 'We National Socialists will put an end to the perpetual Germanic march towards the south and west of Europe and turn our eyes to the lands of the East. We will finally put a stop to the colonies and trade policy of pre-war times and pass over to the territorial policy of the future. But when we speak of new territory in Europe today we must principally think of Russia and the border states subject to her. This colossal Empire of the East is ripe for dissolution... The future goal of our Foreign Policy ought to be an Eastern policy which will have to view the acquisition of such territory as is necessary for our German people.'[24]

---

[21]Hitler, Adolf, *Mein Kampf*, Hurst & Blackett, London (1939), 82–85.
[22]While Hitler did not shrink from the thought of armed conflict in pursuing his policy objectives, he expressly excludes Great Britain from that fate. The fact that a suggested remedy could bring him into conflict with Great Britain was sufficient reason for its rejection.
[23]*Ibid*, 86–87.
[24]*Ibid*, 367.

Hitler's goal was therefore Eastern Europe in general and Russia in particular. Moves to the West are expressly negatived. As Hess confirmed many years later,[25] Hitler's intention to attack Russia was consistent ever since writing *Mein Kampf*.[26]

Albert Speer, one-time Armament Minister to Hitler, provides an insight to Hitler's dreams of a German-occupied Russia when he recalled a conversation with Hitler in mid-August 1941 at Hitler's GHQ in the Ukraine. Hitler was envisaging the postwar world:

> 'The vast expanses of Russia literally cry out to be filled. The Germans who will live there in our new towns and villages will have big houses with many rooms and soon these rooms will be swarming with German children. The new Eastern territories could absorb 100 million Germans.'[27]

Hitler later described his detailed plans for the redevelopment of the occupied areas, the variety of buildings, the motorways, the wide-gauge railway tracks to accommodate spacious sleeper carriages and the villages to provide 'an ideal German landscape'.[28] Finally, he described the six-man defence bunkers complete with machine guns, anti-tank guns and flame throwers for installation 'on our final eastern boundary deep in Russia'.[29]

These were Hitler's plans for exploitation in the East, originally stated in *Mein Kampf* but still the subject of his dreams in 1942, 20 years later and well into his Russian adventure. The fact that the land of his dreams lay within the national boundaries of Russia meant that armed conflict with that nation was inevitable. That did not deter Hitler. Rather did it spur him on. The destruction of Russia, which he considered to be the Jewish-inspired manifestation of international communism, was an important policy objective in its own right.[30]

---

[25]In a conversation with Lieutenant M. Loftus at Camp 'Z', July 17, 1941. Irving David, *Hess The Missing Years 1941–1945*, Grafton Books, 1959, 253.

[26]The extent, if any, to which this clear statement of intent and major policy objective of Hitler, which underpinned his preparations for war, was taken into account by Western observers, is unknown.

[27]Speer, Albert, *Spandau: The Secret Diaries*, Macmillan Books (1976), 156–58.

[28]*Ibid*, 399–400.

[29]*Ibid*, 58.

[30]Was the apparent negligence of Western observers in not reading or taking seriously the contents of *Mein Kampf* matched by the Russians? The Russians' state of preparedness and the quality and quantity of their armaments, particularly in tanks, when attacked in 1941 suggests not. However, they appear to have been tactically surprised by the timing of the attack.

The destruction of Communist Russia

When Hitler's armies attacked Russia in June 1941 the objective was threefold. First, the vast hinterlands of Russia were to provide *Lebensraum* for the German peoples. Secondly, Aryan manhood and the Aryan sword were to demonstrate to a world audience their claim to Superman status by destroying the armies of the inferior Slavs. Thirdly, and perhaps most importantly, the national state which had embraced the Jewish-inspired communist ideology, with all its intent upon world infiltration, was to be exterminated and its influences eradicated.

Hitler's hatred of communism and communists ranked second only to his hatred of the Jews. Like that hate, it was born and nurtured in the street politics of Vienna and Munich during Hitler's early manhood. His invective against communists and all their works is sprinkled liberally through the pages of *Mein Kampf*. The language used is often indistinguishable from that used when abusing the Jews.

> 'The problem of how the future of the German nation can be secured is the problem of how Marxism can be exterminated.[31]
>
> Under the cloak of social virtue and love of one's neighbour, a veritable pestilence was spreading abroad and that if this pestilence be not stamped out of the world without delay it may eventually succeed in exterminating the human race.[32]
>
> It must not be forgotten that the present rulers of Russia are blood-stained criminals, that here we have the dregs of humanity which, favoured by the circumstances of a tragic moment, over-ran a great State, degraded and extirpated millions of educated people out of sheer blood-lust and that for nearly ten years they have ruled with such a savage tyranny as was never known before.'[33]

In one important matter, Hitler deals with his hatred of communism in *Mein Kampf* in a markedly different manner to his hatred of the Jews. Unlike the irrational invective levelled at the Jews, the dismissal of communism and all its works is aided by factual analysis and well argued criticism. It would find more than one sympathetic ear in most of the Western democracies of yesterday and today. In one short passage, for instance, Hitler shrewdly explains why armed force will always fail to eradicate an existing ideology unless a new, equally

---

[31]Hitler, Adolf, *Mein Kampf*, Hurst & Blackett, London (1939), 96.
[32]*Ibid*, 32.
[33]*Ibid*, 364.

acceptable, ideology is introduced.[34] Here is another example of how the adroit and the astute are intermingled with the mindless invective in the pages of *Mein Kampf*.

Hitler's main criticism of communism was its internationalism, its denigration of individual nationhood and its denial of patriotism. This he regarded as wholly unacceptable: it flew in the face of everything he was trying to do in his own native land. He was building a new Germany, to be founded on the superiority of the German national character and the rediscovery of Germany's heritage and self respect. Communism wished to destroy everything that he wished to reawaken (the very idea of a citizen not having a first loyalty to his fellow citizens and to his own country was anathema to him) and he therefore dismissed it as a perversion.[35] He also identified the lies, intrigues, subversions, trouble making and the sowing of seeds of mistrust that became the standard weapons of communist infiltration. Hitler was one of the first outspoken challengers of these methods and, of course, subsequent events have proved him right.

There is also little doubt that Hitler believed sincerely that the battle against communism which he was waging in the 1920s and 1930s was one of several battles that would soon be raging throughout the world. Again, subsequent events have proved him right.

> 'The Bolshevisation of Germany is only the overture to the [Communist] movement for expanding power on a wider scale and finally subjecting the world to its rule. If our state would fall victim to these oppressors of the nations lusting after blood and money, the whole Earth would become the prey of that hydra. Should Germany be freed from its grip a great menace for the nations of the world would thereby be eliminated.'[36]

As late as 1939 Hitler was suggesting that there ought to be 'a conclusive understanding between nations' as to how to deal with the communist danger as a preliminary to a general co-operation of nations.[37] The communist threat was a card he consistently played in his relations with Great Britain during the 1930s in an attempt to identify a common interest and danger. It was not successful. As well as these valid reasons for his opposition to communism Hitler had good cause to hate communists in terms of personal history and national

---

[34]A truth that eluded him when he attacked Russia in 1941, as it eluded the USA in a later adventure in Vietnam. *Ibid*, 103.
[35]*Ibid*, 43–46.
[36]*Ibid*, 342–43.
[37]*Documents concerning German–Polish relations 1938–39*, HMSO, 47.

revenge. In early postwar days in Munich they had been his main political opponents on the streets. Like his own National Socialist Party, they had a programme of mass appeal that looked for mass support; and they had a head start because of the success of the 1917 revolution in Russia.[38] The battle had been hard and long, and Hitler had been personally involved throughout.

Another matter kindled Hitler's thoughts of national revenge. In his second (unpublished) book he claims that the upper classes eliminated in Russia at the time of the 1917 revolution were largely Balts[39] – hardy German stock originating from Prussian territories bordering the Baltic Sea. According to Hitler the Slav nation of Russia had been ruled and dominated by German Balts ever since the days of Peter the Great. They had filled the upper and intellectual stratum of Russian life (in particular, the Army Officer Corps) and under their influence Russia had been able to take its place among the leading nations of the world. The Balts had been largely eliminated in the 1917 revolution. Hitler no doubt thought that old scores had to be settled.

Finally, in Hitler's mind there burned the Jewish question. This explained the phenomenon of communism and warranted the Nazi crusade against its earthly manifestation, Soviet Russia. Any link between communism and Judaism is somewhat tortuous, but it was not beyond the capabilities of Alfred Rosenberg to identify such a link. The ultimate aim of Judaism was world domination. This was to be achieved by parasitic infiltration of each nation state. There would be the gradual taking-over of the political establishments, the banks and other financial institutions, the professions and the trading and industrial concerns. The Jews would do all this under the camouflage of their religion. They had no state limited by geographical borders. Rather could they form states within states where they could live comfortably in accordance with traditional tolerances. In this manner Jews would 'undermine society, overthrow governments, plunge mankind into war and seize power throughout the world'.[40] According to Rosenberg, Tsarist Russia was the first nation to fall to these Jewish machinations as a result of the Jewish-contrived Bolshevik Revolution of 1917, but if Russia was the first nation so to fall to the communist/Jewish menace it would certainly not be the last. Nazi Germany would be the European bulwark against the spread of communism and in due course would attack and destroy the seat of its power, Soviet Russia.[41]

---

[38] Hitler, Adolf, *Mein Kampf*, Hurst & Blackett, London (1939), 202–03.

[39] Hitler, Adolf, *Hitler's Secret Book*, Grove Press Inc (1961), 135–39.

[40] Hitler, Adolf, *Mein Kampf*, Hurst & Blackett, London (1939), 174.

[41] The attack was launched in June 1941. It did not destroy Russia. It destroyed Nazi Germany.

3

Fertile soil: The German character

The Germans, a fated people, fated to make trouble for themselves and for everybody else.

MOELLER VAN DEN BRÜCK

The apparent failure of those British politicians in power during the 1930s to read and understand the significance of *Mein Kampf* must rank as one of the most inept and culpable omissions of modern British history. In its near-incredibility it is matched by the manner in which a German nation of some eighty million swallowed the contents of that infamous book without apparent question and then duly marched down the indicated road to oblivion, committing acts of depravity on the way which appalled the civilised world.[1]

The key to this German acquiescence lies within their own history and its imprint on the national character. The German nation embraced Adolf Hitler and his *Mein Kampf* because they wanted to. Hitler's plans for securing what Germans considered to be their rightful place in the sun, albeit at the expense of other peoples, was to them the natural culmination of German history that stretched back through Hindenburg, Kaiser Wilhelm II and Bismarck to Frederick the Great. It is interesting to note that the relevant historical factors seem to have produced those very facets of the national character which Hitler sought to encourage with his educational policies. As a result, Hitler

[1]It is sometimes forgotten that the camp commandants and guards who received much publicity in connection with the so-called death camps were supported by a bureaucracy of 'ordinary' Germans responsible for the logistics and administration of the operation. It may also be asked why the normal checks and balances in the life of a community (the churches, the middle classes, the judiciary, the political opposition) apparently had such little effect upon the march to oblivion. The answer must lie in the powerful effect of Hitler's message which reached to the very heart of the German character and the strength of his own leadership. Neither of these factors were matched by the policies and personalities of the more conventional forces.

produced the type of young man that the Western powers later described as a 'fanatical Nazi'. He was a character much respected, indeed feared, on the battlefields of Europe but one who was also reviled and rejected by civilised communities everywhere. Ultimately he was much pitied and subjected to psychoanalysis in the study of the abnormal.[2]

There are three factors in German history which bucked the general trend of European history and which seem to have helped mould the German character. Germany was very late to the European starting gate in staking out her claims on the Earth's surface by way of imperial adventure. The reasons why German development was so retarded up to the advent of Bismarck are not entirely clear.[3] When at last under Bismarck she became one nation and started to look outwards instead of inwards, it was too late. Worse still, when she sought to upset the status quo she received the bloodiest of noses in the disastrous Great War of 1914–18. In 1933 Germany was still looking for a place in the sun. Compared to Great Britain, America, Russia and France, measured on a land-to-population basis, she still had no such place. There was therefore real reason for the feelings of resentment, frustration, envy and jealousy which were apparent in the German national character and which had been the case for almost a century. This absence of status in international terms also spawned a deep seated feeling of inferiority which tended to manifest itself in outward show, pomp and spectacle, political bombast and the flexing of military muscle.

The second historical ingredient affecting the German character arose from a sin of omission. Prior to 1933 there is little evidence that Germany had ever made any serious attempt to embrace the principles of democratic government. The great democratic upheavals of the 17th and 18th centuries in England and France left untouched the largely feudal system prevailing in Germanic territories at that time. The scorn heaped by Hitler upon government by parliamentary democracy sat well with the totalitarian traditions coming down through a line of predecessors reaching back to Frederick the Great. This omission in terms of political evolution had much to do with an inbuilt intolerance, rigid-

---

[2]Surveys were carried out during 1942–43 by H.V. Bliss, a leading American psychologist, on German prisoners-of-war, in an attempted personality analysis of typical Nazis. Other work on the same subject was conducted by Richard M. Brickner ('Is Germany Incurable?') and H.G. Baynes ('Germany Possessed').

[3]In the Hanseatic castle of Marienberg in Prussia there is a series of painted murals. One of them depicts life as it was when the castle was built about 1280. It shows Prussian peasants clad in bearskins carrying wooden clubs. At that time the English peasantry were comparatively civilised. Winterbotham, F.W., *The Nazi Connection*, Weidenfeld and Nicholson, London (1973), 156–157.

ity of thought and absence of liberalism in the German character. To describe democracy as 'the delicate fruit of a ripe civilisation' or to quote the maxim 'I disagree with every word you say but I will defend to the death your right to say it' would bring no response or indeed, understanding from most Germans of the 1933 era. The aristocratic principle reigned supreme.

The third historical factor is perhaps the most important one influencing the German character. It was certainly the one most harnessed and manipulated by Hitler and it went to the very heart of Germanic being. It lay in the domination of the Germanic territories by the peoples of a particular part of those territories, Prussia. The core militarism, authoritarianism and disciplined codes of behaviour introduced by this Prussian domination stamped an indelible mark on the German national character. It was a characteristic that Hitler deliberately developed. If he was to negotiate, coerce or bully his European neighbours into frontier revisions and if he was to strike eastwards in the search of *Lebensraum* and the destruction of the Russian state, then he would only do so by the threat and/or use of military force. His nation therefore had to be a warrior nation. And he knew that there were too many centuries of imported Prussianism for them to be anything else, if they were properly led.

For centuries the icy waters of the Baltic Sea had washed the sandy wastes of the German coastline east of the Elbe. The environment is cold, harsh, desolate and cruel. It is hardly surprising that the natives of that inhospitable part of the world were similarly endowed. They had to be hard and cruel and hardworking to scratch a living out of that desolate wasteland. Their only hope of betterment lay in land acquisition to the east, but there lay barbarian tribes invariably on the rampage against ill defined frontiers. They therefore developed martial skills and character out of necessity. The original occupier of these lands were the Slavs from the East, but from about the 11th century these were gradually pushed back eastwards along the Baltic coast and the German state of Brandenburg was established.[4] The defeated Slavs became the landless serfs, virtual slaves to the German ruling princes, the Hohenzollerns. There was no middle class. There were the rulers and the ruled.

By the 18th century, Prussia was one of the ranking military powers of Europe. It had grown considerably in size by reason of its armed conquests. The land was still barren, there were no national resources,

---

[4]There would have been Slav blood in some of the Prussian descendants but Hitler appears to have had no difficulty in accommodating Prussians under the Aryan umbrella. Rosenberg, the racist philosopher, was a Balt, almost certainly with Slav blood in his ancestry.

no minerals and therefore no industry. The population was sparse. There were no large towns, let alone cities. There was much hard work, little leisure and less culture. There was however, one of the most efficient and ruthless military states in Europe, bearing an army that was well drilled, well equipped and well led. 'Prussia,' it was said, 'is not a state with an army but an army with a state.' The Hohenzollern reigned supreme, exercising their will through an obedient bureaucracy. No democratic nonsense here. At the height of its military powers, more than two-thirds of Prussia's state revenues were expended on the upkeep of the army. Life comprised work, obedience, honour and duty. The system was presided over by the lords and masters known as Junkers. It is no wonder, in that harsh, inhospitable land and style of living which remained unchanged over the course of centuries, that the Junkers earned a reputation as a domineering, arrogant, narrow-minded, aggressive class, with few pretensions to culture, tolerance or compassion.

The most famous Junker was Bismarck. He Prussianised the whole of Germany as part of the unification. He represented all the qualities which had made Prussia such a feared opponent to all her neighbours. It was thus that an appetite for power and domination over others was imported, based upon a stiff-necked military caste with allegiance only to the Crown. It was accompanied by a contempt for democracy and free thought and a psychological need for authority and obedience based upon prescribed rules of behaviour. By the end of the Bismarck era Germany had become an extension of Prussia and an extension of the Prussian way of life. Armed conquest continued. Successful wars were fought against Denmark (1864), Austria (1866) and France (1891). They brought unification and extension to the German state and seemed to prove the effectiveness of Prussian/German militarism. Soon Germany had aspirations to become the most dominant nation in Europe, to be rivalled only by Great Britain. It is therefore unsurprising that these ambitions should be projected forward into the 20th century as part of the German character, there to be fashioned yet again for armed conflict first by Kaiser Wilhelm II and now by Adolf Hitler. Bismarck had developed a trend towards unification and expansion. Those who came after him sought to continue that trend. The German national character was already attuned to the idea.

Perhaps the most unfortunate manifestation of the Prussian behavioural characteristics was its great capacity to hate. The total submission of self to authority, the hierarchical arrangement of society and the repression of tender and maternal instincts in the pursuit of essential manliness produced hate as a dangerous introspection. Hitler brought it to the surface. Under his tutelage, Germany became a nation of haters. They hated the Jews, they hated other inferior races, they hated communism and communists, they hated democracy and democrats and they hated their European neighbours. They took pleasure in petty tyranny and severe authority within their own homes and it was only a matter of time under Hitler's leadership before they exercised a tyranny on the grand scale throughout the continent of Europe. It was bare-knuckled Prussianism at its worst.

If then these were some of the particular facets of the German national psyche, rooted in Germanic history and now nurtured and kindled by a master psychologist for his own ends, what about the master psychologist himself? It is interesting to identify in Hitler himself the mix of personal qualities with those particular German traits of character already described. It was a chemistry that contributed so much to the devastating effect that the attempted implementation of his policies had on the world stage and to his ultimate downfall. That Hitler possessed certain exceptional skills and personal qualities is apparent from his political career and accession to power in 1933. Reference has already been made to his exceptional powers of inspirational oratory, and leadership and to his identity with and understanding of the German national character. The powers of oratory were not confined to the mass audience. Albert Speer, one-time Hitler's Armaments Minister, has confirmed that the powers were just as effective within a small group audience or even on a one-to-one basis. He refers to the mesmerising effect of a Hitler discourse. It would certainly appear that this effect was put to good use in Hitler's European diplomacy during the 1930s.

Hitler was also nothing if not a literalist, He had set down his programme of policy objectives and he never deviated from them. He was going to see them through to the bitter end and he did. That was the product of a disciplined, if twisted, mind. But in carrying out his programme he relied more upon his intuition, his opportunism and the mesmerising effect of his oratory. The demands he made against the European status quo as viewed through 1918 spectacles were for the most part outrageous. The fact that he achieved so much, at least until September 1939, without armed conflict is a tribute to his particular skills. He was a born opportunist, with a particular ability to take advantage of situations as they presented themselves. In that capacity he had far stronger nerves than his European adversaries who were eventually reduced to near impotence. He was a man of both physical and mental courage, of great fixity of purpose and an immensely strong will.

Wherein, then, lie the fatal flaws of character that brought his ultimate downfall, the total destruction of the nation he loved and the condemnation of all his works by the whole of the civilised world? Again, one must look to a particular Germanic trait of character. In the centuries prior to the advent of Bismarck, the German states were deeply introspective. They concerned themselves entirely with domestic (including religious) matters, to the total exclusion of interest in and knowledge of the outside world. Hitler inherited this attitude. His thinking was never lifted above national considerations. One of his major flaws lay in the failure of his judgement of peoples other than Germans and the likely reaction of those peoples when confronted by issues likely to involve fundamental change.

On the narrow German front his judgement was impeccable, because he was part of and thoroughly understood the German national psyche. On the international stage he inveigled and bullied foreign statesmen in much the same way as he did with his opponents in early days in Munich. He never understood or cared to understand, much less respect, the national character, resources or qualities of those people directly affected by German aspirations. All such people were inferior by definition. Apart from two visits to Italy, Hitler never travelled abroad. He had no idea why the British refused the hand of friendship during the 1930s or why they did not ask for peace terms in 1940. He had no idea why the Russian workers did not rise up against their commissars in 1941. He had no idea of the extent of American economic muscle in 1942 or her military muscle in 1944. There is an old adage, often quoted in business archives, which states 'Never assume that anyone is a bloody fool until you have proved it'. Adolf Hitler, because of his ignorant insularity, assumed that all were bloody fools except Germans. He may well have gained that impression from his dealings with Western politicians during the 1930s, but he should not have identified the politicians with the people they represented.

Another aspect of this German insularity lay in Hitler's inability to distinguish those of his objectives which were reasonable from those which were inherently evil as judged by the international community. The removal of some of the harsher terms of the Versailles Treaty would have been a natural for responsible negotiation. The lapse of a reasonable period of time and evidence of German goodwill would have seen to that. Similarly, the aspiration of one Reich to embrace all Germans was not in itself unreasonable and was an issue that could have been a subject for sensible discussion. But Hitler had coupled these issues with others that were deeply abhorrent to the civilised world. Crude racism, depicting the Aryan as some sort of superior being, was deeply insulting to Germany's European neighbours. The declared hatred of Jews and Slavs, which soon became active policies of discrimination, both legal and otherwise, bore a horrific potential which could not pass unnoticed by the international community, and the contemplated drive eastwards in pursuit of *Lebensraum* and the destruction of Russian communism was equally unlikely to gain approbation. But Hitler failed to understand or did not care about the ramifications and reactions that his radical policies would obtain within the international community. Thus were he and his regime tainted from the outset and viewed with little sympathy and active distaste by the vast majority of the civilised world. To describe Adolf Hitler as an 'evil genius' is probably a fair and valid description of the man in his early days. His evil was retained to his dying day (which he spent cursing the Jews for all the world's ills) but his genius always flawed in the manner described, became more and more impaired in the wake of character intoxication following early successes.

4

Rudolf Hess, centre stage

I have often felt a bitter sorrow at the thought of the German people which is so estimable in the individual and so wretched in the generality.

GOETHE

The facts as to the personal history of Rudolf Walther Richard Hess prior to 1933 are well established. His forbears moved into the area of Wunsiedel in the Bavarian Fichtel mountains in the early 18th century. Rudolf's grandfather, Christian Hess, who must have been a man of some enterprise, established an import business in Alexandria, Egypt, in 1865, under the name and style of Hess & Company. His two sons, Fritz and Adolf, continued the thriving business after the death of their father. Fritz was the father of Rudolf. In 1892 he had married Clara Muench, the daughter of an industrialist from Hof in Bavaria. Fritz and Clara had three children, two boys and a girl. Rudolf was the eldest child. He was born on April 26, 1894, and was christened at the German Protestant church in Alexandria on July 1, 1894. The first fourteen years of his life were spent at the family home in Alexandria with his mother and father, brother and sister. It was a comfortable, upper-middle-class environment. Its very ordinariness should have spawned a fair degree of emotional stability in the young Rudolf.

However, one feature marked it down as a household with a difference and seems to have promoted a particular trait in Rudolf's character. In accordance with German custom and tradition the family was subject to the overall authority of a father who exercised that authority with unremitting discipline. The whole household and all its routines revolved around his personal requirements, rigorously enforced. Meals, for example, were at fixed times, 'to which you could set your watch', and on those very formal occasions no one was allowed to speak except in response to conversation initiated by the father. In such a rigid atmosphere the father would seldom demonstrate any affection and love for his children. The only time when the children played together in a truly relaxed manner was when their father had left the house. The emotions thus engendered in the children towards their father were probably more akin to fear, which in later years would become resentment rather than love. If the children wanted love and affection then they looked to their mother to provide it. Prussianised Germany was alive and well in Alexandria as well as Berlin at the turn of the century. They certainly lacked for nothing in a materialist or social sense. The house was large and the gardens luxurious. The Hesses fitted well into the local well-to-do community and counted among their friends the German ambassador to Alexandria, Eberhard Stohrer.

The comparison between Hess's childhood, spent in relative material splendour, and that of Adolf Hitler, spent in abject poverty, is remarkable. There was however one important common factor which applied to both, even then. Neither had a father with whom he could establish a normal, healthy and affectionate relationship. The sort of role figure normally displayed by a father was entirely blocked out in both cases, leaving an emotional void. In the case of Rudolf Hess, the need to fill that void became a dominant psychological feature of his later life. Rudolf's first school in Alexandria, the German Protestant School, was soon found to be unsatisfactory. The services of a private tutor were then used until Rudolf reached the age of fourteen. He was then deemed fit to take up a position at a boarding school, the Evangelisches Paedogogium in Godesberg-am-Rhein in his native Germany. This he did on September 18, 1908. At that time it was assumed by his father, and perhaps tacitly accepted by Rudolf, that as the elder son he would follow his father into the family business.

Meanwhile, Rudolf was beginning to show real ability in mathematics, physics, astronomy and nature studies, subjects not usually associated with a business career. By the time Rudolf arrived in Godesberg, the family already had one foot in its native Germany. At the turn of the century, his father had built a large house in Reicholdsgrun in Bavaria, at which it was the custom of the family to spend their holidays in the summer.[1] Rudolf was at Godesberg for three years and made good academic progress. He was intelligent and anxious to learn and probably enjoyed the freedom occasioned by his separation from a dominant father. He developed a special interest in German history and continued to do well with his studies in mathematics, physics,

[1]The family were there in August 1914 and were unable to return to Alexandria until 1919.

engineering and astronomy.[2] He was popular with his peers and seems to have enjoyed this period of his adolescence.

At the end of his spell at Godesberg his tutors wished Rudolf to go on to university to study engineering. That was his own ambition too (he was now seventeen). In the event, he acceded to his father's wishes that he should embark upon a business career. He took up a one-year business course at the Ecole Supérieure de Commerce at Neuchâtel in Switzerland and then took up an apprenticeship with a shipping firm in Hamburg. He was not happy and did not excel. His work in Hamburg won him no plaudits. In his own words 'I completed the jobs given me after a fashion, poorly more often than not.' This blind alley excursion into the world of business and commerce had no interest for Rudolf. It had been instigated at the will and command of his father and it was contrary to the advice of his school tutors. It must have further widened the emotional gap between the adult young man and his father.

Most of Rudolf's intellectual powers at this time were being directed into a wide spectrum of reading, including almost everything other than business administration. He was developing a lively interest in politics and, in particular, those relating to German history. His other non-fiction reading included topics ranging from astronomy to the world's navies. In the latter case he could memorise an immense amount of detail as to the tonnage, speed, armaments and armour of all the main vessels in all the main navies in the world. He appears to have had no amorous adventures during this period. The reason for this could be his isolation from his father, which may have upset his emotional and sexual balance: that is a matter for a professional psychologist to ponder. Certainly, in terms of more mundane matters, Rudolf was an obvious misfit in Hamburg.

Relief (if that is the right word) came in August 1914 when Great Britain declared war on Germany. With his father's blessing, Rudolf immediately volunteered for service and was drafted into the Reserve of the 7th Bavarian Field Artillery Regiment being formed at Munich. He was later transferred to the 1st Reserve Battalion of the 1st Bavarian Infantry Regiment, a unit of some distinction and reputation. Hess's service career throughout the 1914–18 war was distinguished.[3] He saw early service on the front line at Ypres, the Somme, Artois and Verdun, during which time he was decorated with the Iron Cross, 2nd Class. At Verdun he was promoted to the rank of sergeant and was

---

[2]He appears to have come under the influence of a very good teacher. In later years Hess ensured for the teacher a prominent position in the Nazi Party.

[3]In this respect it runs parallel to that of Adolf Hitler.

wounded in the left hand and upper arm. On December 4, 1916, Hess was transferred to the 18th Bavarian Reserve Battalion fighting in Romania and took up the position of platoon leader.

On July 25, 1917, in the storming of the Ungureana in the battle for the western Moldavia and the mountain passes of the Carpathian border, Hess was seriously wounded. A rifle bullet passed through his left lung and exited from the back ('a clean shot through', as he described it). He was taken to hospital in Bezdivasarhely and, after surgery, convalesced over a period of months. On October 8, 1917, he was commissioned as a lieutenant and in March 1918 he was transferred to the Flying Corps for training as an officer fighter pilot. He completed his training at Flying School No. 4 in the summer of 1918 and was posted to Fighter Squadron 35 in October 1918. He served operationally at the front over Valenciennes during the first ten days of November when hostilities finished.[4]

Hess was demobilised in December 1918 and found himself on the streets of Munich without means of support. His father, whose business in Alexandria had been appropriated by the British without payment, had returned to Alexandria to pick up the pieces and rebuild the business.[5] Hess was not alone on the streets of Munich. The city was seething with unrest. It was full of ex-servicemen like Hess, young in years and old in experience of the trenches. They were bitterly disillusioned by Germany's defeat and subjected to what appeared to be a communist-inspired Bavarian government about to sever the ties with Berlin. Hess's response, as with many of his ex-colleagues, was to join the Freikorps under the command of General Franz von Epp. This body was right-wing, nationalist and anti-Semitic. Hess engaged vigorously in street politics and worked off his frustrations against the Communists and Social Democrats.

Many years later, in 1927, he described in a letter to his cousin how he felt as one of those young men tossed aside in the wake of Germany's defeat. It described how millions of other young Germans probably felt at that time and why such fertile soil awaited the advent of Adolf Hitler. 'You know how I suffer from the conditions a once so proud nation has been brought to. I fought for the honour of the flag where it is given that a man of my age must fight where the going was roughest. In the filth and the mud, in the hell of Verdun, in Artois and the other places, I have experienced the horror of death in all its

---

[4]Flying remained as Hess's active hobby until 1934. He won a civil flying competition while a Cabinet Minister but after 1934 Hitler forbade further flying as an unnecessary risk.

[5]It is perhaps indicative of the relationship between father and son that Rudolf made no attempt to follow his father and help him in that task.

variations, was shaken for days by the heaviest of barrages, slept in a dugout where half a Frenchman lay and went hungry and suffered as all frontline soldiers do. And is all that to no avail? No, had it all been for nothing then I would still regret today that I did not put a bullet through my brain the day the monstrous conditions of Versailles and their acceptance became known. At that time I did not do it, out of the one hope that one can somehow still do one's small part to alter this fate.'

These thoughts were those of a true German patriot, but Hess had a long way to go before, if at all, his patriotism was converted into the creed of National Socialism. Certainly, the faith and will to 'alter this fate' became his aspiration in 1919 and his obsession thereafter. It turned him away from an academic career for which he was eminently suited to take up politics as a full-time occupation. And ultimately that drove him into the arms of Adolf Hitler. But these decisions took time to crystallise in the mind of the 24-year-old veteran. After incurring a further wound in the leg from a street fight with the Social Democrats he decided to resume his academic career by enrolling as a student at Munich University. This he did in 1920. His subjects for study were history, economics and geopolitics. He never graduated. His continuing political activities always gained precedence over his academic studies. However, his attendances at the university exerted a particular significance on Hess's future career. He came under the influence of his professor and lecturer in the subject of geopolitics, Karl Haushofer.

Haushofer had returned from the war with the rank of major-general. In terms of academic study he had dedicated himself to geopolitical theory – the study of the relation between territorial space and the requirements of the indigenous population. In the light of Germany's position in 1918 and the impending impositions of the Versailles Treaty, this subject was very attractive to a young nationalist of Hess's stamp. Here was a rational basis for German's claims to land and her place in the sun. It was not long before the concept of land acquisition to feed population requirements was transmitted by Haushofer's young student and eventually became firmly bedded in the political testament of Adolf Hitler. Thus through Hess was the seeking of *Lebensraum* legitimised.

It is little wonder that the relationship between the young student and his professor became intimate. Hess was a frequent visitor to the Haushofer household and he does not appear to have been in any way disturbed by the fact that Haushofer's wife was Jewish, the daughter of George Mayer, a Jewish merchant from Mannheim. No doubt, the common identity of academic interest with its political relevance, heightened the degree of intimacy between the professor and his pupil.

But practical politics on the streets of Munich, which were very much a part of Hess's life, meant nothing to Haushofer, the academic.[6] And it was the street politics that eventually led Hess into the arms of another father figure where the emotional ties were to be even stronger and the personal loyalty everlasting.

On July 1, 1920, Rudolf Hess joined the newly reconstructed National Socialist German Workers Party (NSDAP), led by Adolf Hitler. Hess had first met Hitler in the previous April when he heard Hitler speak at an evening meeting of the party in a room adjoining the Steinecker-Brewery in the Munich Valley. Hess was enthralled. He saw in Hitler the fusion of all his ideals and aspirations into the realm of practical politics. He saw the converting of those ideals into reality under the leadership of a man whom he found to be truly inspiring. The resurgence of his beloved fatherland, the removal of the injustices of the Versailles Treaty, the fight against communism and opposition to the Social Democrats who had betrayed the nation was all meat and drink to young Rudolf, as it became later to millions of other young Germans. And here he was, in at the very beginning at the very side of the leader in his crusade. Hitler led and Hess followed.

As the tiny Nazi Party grew in numbers and influence and the burden of the shared responsibilities became greater so the relationship between Hitler and Hess grew into one of intimate friendship. They were constantly in each other's company and up to their necks in political activity on the streets, in the beer cellars, in the meeting rooms and at the public rallies. Hess himself was one of the earliest leaders of the Nazi stormtroopers and organised a special students' battalion. There is little doubt that he was ideally happy in this environment. He was fighting (literally, on many occasions) for the things nearest to his heart at the right hand of a man he admired and respected and who relied upon him, trusted him and confided in him. As Hess himself said 'I know of the Tribune's innermost thoughts, his attitude to all questions, his whole nature. He knows me. Our mutual trust is of the very utmost. We understand each other.'[7] Here was the father figure for whom young Rudolf Hess had been looking. Adolf Hitler had replaced Karl Haushofer as the father to be admired, respected and loved.

The days on the streets of Munich were indeed sweet to Rudolf Hess. There was of course a brief interlude from the street politics when both Hitler and Hess were imprisoned in Landsberg, following

---

[6]Haushofer never became a member of the Nazi Party.

[7]Letter from Hess to his parents, April 24, 1925, on taking up the position of private secretary to Hitler.

the abortive putsch of November 1923. It was there that Hitler, with Hess's help, wrote a large part of his political testament, the first volume of *Mein Kampf*. In these circumstances, the relationship between the two men deepened further. The two minds were very close to a single orbit. As to the emotional link, this is illustrated by a particular incident. One day during their stay in Landsberg Hitler called Hess to listen to a recently written passage of *Mein Kampf*. It related to an attack in Flanders launched by the Bavarian infantry during the Great War. 'As he read, Hitler's voice became slower, the pauses between his phrases longer until suddenly he let the page drop, lowered his head into his hands and sobbed.' As Hess took his leave, they squeezed each other's hands at length. 'I am more devoted to him than ever,' Hess wrote, '*Ich liebe ihn*' (I love him).[8]

There is little doubt that this emotional intimacy with Hitler and the ongoing relationship of total dependency which hinged upon it, were abnormal. It has been suggested that this abnormality was wholly, or in the main, explained by Hess's emotional need for a father figure. It was perhaps inevitable that less than impartial observers of a later age, including other members of the Nazi hierarchy, should add two and two together to make five. There is plenty of evidence to show that Hess was quite content, indeed happy, to subordinate his personality to that of his Führer and become his shadow. There is absolutely nothing to support allegations and innuendo as to homosexual practices. For the most part, Hitler's later lieutenants were intensely jealous of the special relationship which existed between Hitler and his Deputy. It is not therefore unexpected that gossip and innuendo should flourish from such sources.

Much more objective comment on what appears to be Hess's subnormal heterosexual activity comes from the British psychiatrist, J.R. Rees who attended upon Hess following his flight to Great Britain in 1941. Rees observes that Hess was engaged for several years before marrying Ilse Prohl and then apparently only at the suggestion of Hitler. After the marriage, Hess forbade the publication of photographs of his wife and she took no part in party activities or women's organisations. She appeared very seldom in public and then only at concerts or the theatre.[9] It was ten years into the marriage before a son was born, at a time when artificial contraception between Aryans was discouraged by the Nazi Party. While imprisoned in England Hess appeared to show very little interest in his wife, in contrast to his son.

---

[8]Letter from Hess to Ilse Prohl, June 29, 1924.

[9]Of course, it may be that Ilse valued her privacy and was less enamoured of her husband's membership of the Nazi Party than he was.

When Ilse's letters failed to arrive, he did not write to her.[10] Perhaps the powerful emotions diverted by Hess towards his Führer had drained him dry of the more normal emotions associated with heterosexual behaviour. Further conjecture would appear to be idle and irrelevant.

This unique relationship withstood the test of time. As far as Hess was concerned it was apparently in no way affected by the abominations carried out in his idol's name in later days. He seemed quite unable or unwilling to allow blame and responsibility for these to interfere with his own relationship, even though they must have appalled his own conscience. Evidence that Hess loved Hitler, and that this emotion affected his ability to think straight in associating Hitler with the crimes he commissioned, is supported by a letter written by Hess to his wife in June 1945. By that time, although Hess had not been personally involved since 1941, the full enormity of the crimes committed in Hitler's name was becoming apparent. A passage from the letter referring to Hitler reads: 'It has been granted to few to take part as we have from the outset in the development of a unique personality in joy and in sorrow, in cares and in hopes, in hates and in loves and all the marks of greatness, and also in all the little signs of human weakness which alone makes a man loveable.'[11]

After their release from Landsberg Hess put all his energies into the advancement of the Nazi Party while Hitler finished the second volume of *Mein Kampf* and in December Hess finally turned his back on an academic career, rejecting an offer by Karl Haushofer to work as his assistant at Munich university. Under the older man's auspices, and with appropriate study of which he was quite capable, Hess might have achieved a professorship. It was not to be. Hess was too badly bitten by the political bug and the excitement of his new life with Adolf Hitler. He accepted the post of secretary to his political master, at a monthly salary of RM500.

At that time the Nazi Party was not universally popular, even among adherents of the political Right. A good number of educated people like Haushofer rejected it because of the bully boy element and its appetite for street brawls with the forces of the Left. The leader of this roughneck element was Captain Ernst Roehm, a regular army officer on the staff of Army Commander General Franz von Epp. Roehm was a flamboyant, aggressive character with known homosexual tendencies. He was also a close associate of Hitler and during the very early days of the German Workers Party had exercised considerable

---

[10]As reported by Rees.

[11]Letter from Hess to his wife, June 18, 1945.

influence over him. One of the first tasks allocated to Hess was to contain this rough, but at that time essential, element and fit it into a cohesive whole, subject to an overall discipline. In that he was conspicuously successful and in so doing at least partly supplanted the affections and regard that Hitler had for his former colleague.[12]

Another very early associate of Hitler had been Dietrich Eckart, writer, poet and wit. He too was a rabid racist and anti-Semite. His place as the court philosopher was soon taken by Alfred Rosenberg, the Balt who had served up the appetising dish of the Aryan Superman to Hitler and had found himself as one of the inner circle as a result. Unlike Roehm, Rosenberg soon established a good relationship with Hess and the two remained firm friends right through until 1941.[13]

At the postwar Nuremberg trials, it was correctly held that up to the time of his flight to Great Britain in 1941 Hess held the overall responsibility for all Nazi Party matters and the authority to make all necessary decisions in relation thereto in the name of Hitler. The task allotted to him by Hitler was to shape the party according to the requirements of its leader and to ensure its electability by the German people. Hess gave that task his total dedication. He travelled the length and breadth of Germany organising meetings, planning campaigns, writing pamphlets and newspaper articles, advising on publicity, assisting with the appointment of branch officers and above all, arranging the rallies at which the Führer would speak. He would also speak himself at these public events. He always plugged the *Führer prinzip* and publicly paid homage to the main role of the Führer. He also welded together all the diverse activities and personalities within the party, with the one specific objective – its electibility to power under the undisputed leadership of Adolf Hitler.

In the early 1920s the Nazi Party was poor. It had no influential backers. Hess soon rectified this. He wrote to Henry Ford in America. The motor magnate's sentiments were known to be anti-Semitic and anti-communist. It was also known that Ford used his wealth throughout the world to subsidise those factions with similar views. The Nazi Party of Germany was one such faction to benefit as a result of Hess's efforts.[14] Because of his academic background Hess was well qualified to bridge the gap between the roughneck element of the party and the intelligensia/business community which was the potential source of funding. Fritz Thyssen, the German steel magnate, is believed to have

---

[12]A resurgence of the roughneck elements after the Nazi accession to power in 1933 led to the Roehm purges of June 1934.

[13]Rosenberg is thought to have played an important part in the Hess flight of May 10, 1941.

[14]See James and Suzanne Pool, *Who Financed Hitler*, Macdonald and Janes (1978).

contributed the sum of one million marks as a result. This helped fund the move of party headquarters on January 1, 1931 from its cramped office in the Schellingstrasse to new prestigious premises in the Briennestrasse which were named the Brown House (after the Nazi brownshirt uniform).

Bolshevism was a nightmare to Thyssen, who had suffered from postwar Bolshevik activities. Other prominent German capitalists thought similarly. Largely through Hess's efforts funding was obtained through Alfred Hugenberg, the controller of a huge media complex, Kurt von Schroder, an international banker with prominent banking connections in Great Britain and the USA and Hjalmar Schacht, formerly President of the Reichsbank, whose banking connections in Great Britain and the USA included the John Pierpoint Morgan financial empire. All these connections, and many more like them, sought to exclude communist Russia from Europe, using British and American capital and the fledgling Nazi Party as the political front.

No one appreciated more than Hitler both the essential link between the Nazi Party and business interests and the need to play the communist card to forge that link. Not only would this provide funding, it would also make available the business vote. No one worked harder than Hess to establish and strengthen this liaison which was brought to fruition in time for the elections of 1930 and the eventual succession to power in 1933. Such were Hess's many duties and responsibilities as party chief during the period leading up to 1933. Hess was Hitler's chief of staff throughout and at the administrative heart of the conspiracy for power during the struggle which culminated in Hitler's seizure of office in 1933.

Two notable events affecting Hess's personal life occurred during this hectic period between the early days in the Munich beer-cellars and the accession to power in 1933. In or around 1925 Hess became friendly with Karl Haushofer's son, Albrecht. The friendship never developed into any great intimacy because Albrecht, like his father, did not embrace the tenets of the Nazi Party or the manner of their implementation. Albrecht was a man of many parts, academic, poet, musician, political theorist. Street politician was not one of them. He was a much travelled young man and his special interest was Great Britain. In so far as Hess was an early, if not the first, advocate of German friendship towards Great Britain, Albrecht's specialist knowledge was of particular interest to him.[15] Albrecht appeared to wear many political caps and the manner in which he would exchange one

[15]It will be seen how Hess sought advice from Albrecht as part of his preparations for his mission to Great Britain in 1941.

for another during the course of his freelance intelligence work could be quite bewildering.

The other noteworthy event was Hess's marriage. On December 20, 1927, Hess married Ilse Prohl, his companion and friend of many years' standing. They had first met as students at Munich University immediately after the conclusion of the 1914–18 war. Ilse had been Hess's faithful aide and loyal supporter throughout the turbulent post-war years. When Hitler and Hess were imprisoned in Landsberg she acted as their outside courier. The wedding ceremony was a civil one and the chief guests were Hitler and Karl Haushofer.[16] A small reception was held at the home of a mutual friend, Hugo Bruckmann.

Hitler's invitation to accept the office of German Chancellor in January 1933 marked the successful conclusion of his own and his party's fifteen-year struggle for power. It also marked the end of the happiest period in the life of Rudolf Hess. In January 1933, as, the first man to shake Hitler's hand after his appointment as Chancellor, Hess stood at the side of his beloved Führer at the very pinnacle of power in the Nazi hierarchy. He above everyone had the complete confidence and trust of his leader and his authority as party leader was unchallenged. Certainly he had never given his leader cause to doubt either his loyalty to the cause or his ability to discharge his responsibilities. Fired by all the enthusiasm of a young man he had embraced both Adolf Hitler and his *credo* as the means by which his fatherland might be restored to its rightful place among the great nations of the world, to redeem its self-esteem and rediscover its national pride. He had enjoyed every minute of the struggle for power and every minute of his association with his leader in that struggle. He had given his all and success was sweet, but the world that Hitler and Hess now looked upon from the pinnacles of their success was a very different one from that which had dominated their lives over the previous years. Instead of struggling ever upwards towards the plateau of power they were now encamped on the plateau. How exactly were they to use the power they had gained?

When the German panzer armies of 1940 rolled onto the Channel coast, having knocked France out of the war and then confronted the 26 miles of water separating Great Britain from the continent, they are said to have been nonplussed as to what to do next. There were no plans to deal with their success. That was not the case for the political victors of 1933. There was a blueprint already in existence,

---

[16]The same two were sponsors at the name-giving ceremony on the occasion of the birth of Hess's son, ten years later. The son was named Wolf, which was the name Hess used when addressing Hitler.

setting out in precise detail just what the Nazi policy objectives were and how they were to be implemented once the party was in power. The blueprint was called *Mein Kampf*. It had been written in the early 1920s but nothing had changed by the early 1930s. However, to write a book is one thing. To act it out is quite another. There were some awkward passages in the blueprint and some of the logical conclusions could present difficult social and moral problems. It is one thing to write 'The wishes of the individual must be subordinated to the requirements of the *Volkisch* state', but it is quite another to offer yourself for sterilisation because your grandmother was a Jewess.

The reunification of all Germans within the one Reich would lead to frontier adjustments and land acquisitions. If that did not lead to armed conflict and killings then the policy as to *Lebensraum* in the East most certainly would. If pure Germans were to be bred, what was to happen to those of impure blood or with physical or mental disabilities? Was it to be sterilisation or euthanasia or both? If the Jews and Slavs were to be segregated as inferior beings, were they to be put into ghettoes and, if so, where were the ghettoes to be? If the 'friends with Great Britain' foreign policy failed, was not a global war on the cards, with possible American involvement?

Those were the sort of difficulties springing out of the pages of *Mein Kampf* to the ordinary reader. It is inconceivable that they did not also occur to Hitler and Hess. But Hitler was a literalist. To him, writing a book and acting it out was one and the same thing. It has been said that 'Hess was the party's conscience' but Hitler had no conscience. He used the party's conscience to further his own ends. But what about Hess? Would he, like his chief, be able to interpret the dictates of *Mein Kampf* literally and ride roughshod over the moral and social issues which were bound to arise? The motivation for young Rudolf Hess's participation in the struggle for power was a straightforward patriotism. But in 1933 Hess was going to need much more than that to carry him through the implementation of National Socialism as laid down by the blueprint. He was about to find out that winning power was one thing but using it was quite another. Was he a sufficiently tough and resilient character to do both?

The facts of Hess's personal history up to 1933 provide good evidence as to his character at that time. Less satisfactory is the evidence supplied by observers on the way, some of whom were hardly impartial. That he was a man of physical courage there can be no doubt. His war record proves that. Similarly, that he was physically tough and in good health is proven by his early interest in hill climbing and walking and the leading part he played in the early street politics and fighting. That he was responsible and conscientious is borne out by the manner in which he discharged his duties as party chief. That he was intelligent is apparent from his academic record.[17] His ability to communicate with and persuade others, including the intelligentsia and the business community, is shown by the success of his fundraising efforts and the obtaining of political support from these sources.

Perhaps more importantly, Hess had shown over a period of fifteen years that he could retain control over as well as build the party and retain the ear of his leader against all comers. He was not a weak man. That he was an idealist and to that extent something of a dreamer, is demonstrated by his intense loyalty to Hitler's cause. He was serious minded: according to his wife Ilse in the early postwar days, with the fatherland in turmoil, Hess could not understand how young people could indulge in dancing and other social pursuits. He did not smoke or drink[18] and conducted himself in a sober manner at all times. He was certainly a cultured man who enjoyed good music, especially that of Beethoven. Unlike his Führer, he was no great lover of Wagner. He was shy and difficult to approach, earning a reputation for aloofness which belied his kindly nature. His personal appearance was invariably impeccable and his shining black knee-high boots were the envy of the entire Nazi hierarchy. He had a reputation for treating both his staff and his colleagues with kindness and charm. Both his ex-secretaries paid tribute to these qualities in later years. 'He was so kind and noble that one felt obliged to be the same way as much as possible and to do for him as much as one could. None of us minded working for him until far after midnight.'[19]

Many observers have made the point that Hess was not 'pushy' in an overtly ambitious way and Hess himself dismissed the professional careerist as similar to the American moneymaker fired by the injunction 'Make money, my son, honestly if possible, but make money no matter what'.[20] Hess is also on record as to his concept of honour. He had always held this to be a cardinal virtue and one which he claimed had dictated the course of his early life. 'The honour of an individual cannot be injured or even touched by the acts or expressions on the part of another. He who attempts this does an injury to his own

---

[17]J.R. Rees, the British psychiatrist, carried out an intelligence test on Hess in 1941. He was placed in Selection Group I, the upper 10 per cent.

[18]According to Ilse there was one exception. Hess was a forceful public speaker but did not relish the occasions when required to speak. He would fortify himself before the event with one glass of pink champagne.

[19]As testified by one of Hess's secretaries at the Nuremberg trials.

[20]Letter to a well-wisher, December 1932.

honour. Honour can suffer solely as a result of dishonourable conduct on the part of the individual himself.'[21]

In view of these sentiments, can it be disputed that Hess was a man of principle? It is significant that not a single observer has described him as 'a typical Nazi'. On the contrary, almost all go out of their way to make the point that he was anything but. American historian Robert E. Canot, in *Justice at Nuremberg*, described him as 'a decent and honourable man' and 'a pacifist at heart'. Wing Commander Frederick Winterbotham, a prominent member of British Air Intelligence who met Hess on several occasions during the 1930s, reports:

> 'I remember thinking how different was this man strolling rather shyly forward towards his waiting car from the ordinary run of strutting, saluting servicemen and the SS who now seemed so thick on the ground back in Berlin. We went to see the play *Coriolanus* with him. There were lots of Nazi-type Roman salutes introduced into the play. Hess was amused and remarked, 'You know, it isn't really necessary is it?' He was more interested in opera and music, especially Beethoven. On subsequent meetings I found a depth of character and intelligence often missing in the other Nazi leaders. There was a latent sensitivity in place of the ruthless efficiency of the Goerings and the Himmlers. He had poise with diffidence. Despite an apparent lack of self-confidence he certainly did not lack for courage. The ever-faithful shadow at the right hand of Hitler, he was self-effacing, quiet mannered and a dreamer, yet he had proven to be a man of decision and action if the need arose. He was a little fanatical perhaps about his leader and his country but not basically evil like some of his comrades.'

This is an opinion given by a senior British Intelligence Officer who knew Hess well and who had many discussions with him at the highest level. It is supported by another view from an equally impeccable source. Following Hess's arrival in Great Britain in May 1941 the Foreign Research and Press Service, centred at the Royal Institute of Foreign Affairs, Balliol College, Oxford, produced a survey of Hess's life and character. An extract reads: 'Two main conclusions follow from this survey of Hess's life and searches. First, that he occupied a key position both in the party and in the State and was, under Hitler, the chief individual between the two. Secondly, that he was regarded in Germany as an upright, loyal, peaceloving man

---

[21]Hess, Wolf Rüdiger, *Who Murdered My Father?*, Reporter Press, USA (1989), 87.

inspired by high ideals and this impression is borne out in his speeches.'[22]

If then Hess was so different from the other members of the Nazi hierarchy why did he, like the rest of them, tread the path to oblivion following the accession to power in 1933? If he was an intelligent being of truly academic background, why could he not apply his God-given faculties to converting the Nazi blueprint into a less-risk reality, with due regard to the great moral and social issues involved? The answer to both these questions lies in the one fatal flaw in Hess's character – the hypnotic personal effect that Hitler seems to have had on him. This seems to have suspended Hess's critical faculties. It was as though a thick mist had descended upon the summit of success which clouded Hess's vision and intellect. But he did not seem to know or to care. In emotional terms he still had his hand tightly clasped in the hands of the Tribune; whatever path the Tribune pointed to and trod would be the correct one, and Hess would follow it. One is tempted to think that if Hitler had seen the Marxist light and led the way to Moscow and conversion, Hess would have been at his side. Certainly, the indications are that by 1933 Hess was a Hitler worshipper first and a National Socialist very much second. It is interesting to speculate on what might have happened if the mist had lifted and Hess's eyes were opened to see the full effects of the implementation of the Nazi programme. Opinion was that he was a dreamer and idealist, but when the occasion demanded he was also a man of decision and action. He was to show that in May 1941.

[22]PRO HO 199–482.

PART TWO

1933–39: THE PATH TO WAR

5

The National Socialist state and rearmament

The great questions of the day will not be settled by resolutions and majority votes but by blood and iron.

BISMARCK, 1862

When Hitler assumed power he embarked immediately upon two of the three prerequisites for the successful prosecution of his policy objectives. He had to transform the constitution of the state so as to provide himself with supreme personal power. He also had to rearm the nation to provide muscle for his forthcoming territorial demands. The third prerequisite, friendship with Great Britain in the West while he turned to the East, was more longterm.

When Hitler was appointed Chancellor on January 30, 1933, he presided over a Cabinet of eleven members of whom only three were Nazis. The Cabinet was responsible to the Reichstag which was the freely elected parliament of the Weimar Republic. The populace so represented enjoyed all those civil liberties normally associated with a working democracy. Within a period of one year Hitler had overthrown the Weimar Republic, substituted his personal dictatorship for its democracy, destroyed all political parties except his own, removed all local government organisations, unified and defederalised the Reich, outlawed all labour unions, stamped out democratic institutions of every kind, driven all Jews out of public and professional life, abolished freedom of speech and the press, stifled the independence of the Judiciary and co-ordinated under Nazi rule, the whole of the political, economic, cultural and social life of an ancient and cultivated people.[1]

Hitler thus demonstrated that his powers of action were as great as his powers of oratory. Two things are remarkable about the transfor-

[1]Shirer, William L., *The Rise and Fall of the Third Reich*, Pan Books (1964). 266

mation. The first was the speed with which it was accomplished. The second was that it was achieved with the overwhelming support of the German people. The manner of its achievement illustrates Hitler's political acumen and opportunism. Immediately on taking office he made the point that the Cabinet could not function properly without Centre Party representation and that as the latter was unwilling to join the Cabinet new elections would be necessary. These were to take place on March 5, 1933. On February 27 the Reichstag building was burnt to the ground. Hitler immediately initiated a scare campaign against the Communists. Something like panic swept the country, invoking fears of a Communist take-over. On February 28 Hitler convinced the aged President Hindenburg that emergency legislation was necessary to deal with the crisis. As a result, a presidential decree was issued. It suspended seven sections of the constitution. They were the sections which guaranteed the civil liberties of the individual. They were, of course, never restored. In the meantime, Nazi propaganda poured from the state-run radio stations warning the populace of the Communist danger and asking for an anti-Communist vote on March 5. The lone voice of former Chancellor Bruening of the Catholic Centre Party was raised in opposition. He declared that he would oppose the overthrowing of the constitution and call for an investigation into the causes of the Reichstag fire.[2]

On March 5 the German people voted in the last democratic elections to be held during the lifetime of Adolf Hitler. The Nazi Party polled over 17 million votes, an increase of 5½ million on those recorded the previous November. But it was still only 44 per cent of the total vote. It was better, but still not good enough. Hitler tried a new route. He could suspend the Weimar constitution by obtaining a 75 per cent majority vote in the Reichstag itself. Eighty-one Communists and some Social Democrats were absent from their seats in the Reichstag. They had been arrested in the earlier hiatus following the Reichstag fire. By a majority of 441 votes to 84 the Nazi-dominated Reichstag thus passed an Enabling Act which effectively voted itself out of existence under the threat or imagined threat of a Communist takeover. The Act had but five brief sections. Its effect was to transfer all legislative powers from the Reichstag to the Cabinet for a period of four years. The 84 votes recorded against its adoption came from the Social Democrats. Their leader, Otto Wells, replying to

---

[2]An entry in Goebbels's diary dated January 31, 1933, reads 'In a conference with the Führer we lay down the line for the fight against the Red terror. For the moment, we shall abstain from direct counterpressures. The Bolshevik attempt at revolution must first break into flame. At the proper time we will strike.' One month later the Reichstag fire provided the opportunity.

the debate said: 'The German Social Democrats pledge ourselves solemnly at this historic hour to the principles of humanity and justice, of freedom and socialism. No Enabling Act can give you the power to destroy ideas which are eternal and indestructible'.[3]

The Enabling Act gave Hitler and his Nazi Cabinet all the power he required as dictator of the new Third Reich. If it is accepted that the arrest of Communist and (some) Social Democratic members of the Reichstag was a necessary act to preserve a threatened government, then the transfer of power into the hands of Hitler was carried out with full regard to all the niceties of parliamentary and constitutional procedures. He was not slow to use the powers so conferred. Within one year he had closed down all avenues of individual liberties and democratic process. Every venture of national life was controlled by the Nazi Party under Hess.

The vast majority of the German people acquiesced willingly to the totalitarian nature of the regime. It sat well on their German character and they were soon to see the benefits that would flow from a well ordered and disciplined economy. Those so benefiting might well turn their heads the other way and did when they heard of or witnessed the use of concentration camps for political undesirables and the extension of legislation to take in the enforced sterilisation of the unfit and its logical outcome, the practice of euthanasia.[4] If you were a German of pure Aryan blood, fit and well, and you believed in and lived for the Führer, then what happened to Jews and other inferior people, the physically handicapped, the mentally ill and the political undesirables was not a matter of personal concern. These were matters and lives to be dealt with by the State. If there were any international concerns as to this state of affairs within Germany, then they were muted. They were matters not widely publicised and in 1933 the internal affairs of a particular state were not considered to be the preserve of all.

Even as late as 1938 there was no universal condemnation from the international community as to what was going on in Germany, although by then much of it was public knowledge. The leader in the London *Times* of January 31, 1938, accurately described the blurred vision common to most outsiders. 'Today, even if full account is taken of the suppression of the political parties and the trade unions, the deplorable conflict with the Churches and the outlawing of the Jews,

---

[3]Shirer, William L., *The Rise and Fall of the Third Reich*, Pan Books (1964), 249.

[4]In July 1933 a new law was promulgated dealing with 'The Prevention of Hereditary Diseased Progeny' under which so-called experts were to advise on sterilisation. By 1937 homicidal plans were emerging from an extension of sterilisation. Experts were then to determine who should live and who should die. The experts who were to make these life and death decisions have been described as 'moral opportunists in a marginalised profession becalmed in mediocre careers'.

it is clear enough that Herr Hitler's unchallenged position does not rest on mere force. Millions of Germans regard him with burning devotion as the saviour of his country.' Thus it was that Hitler was left free of foreign condemnation to build the strong one-party state with himself at its pinnacle as the supreme dictator. It was precisely as he had originally planned and set down in the pages of *Mein Kampf*.

Hitler's second prerequisite to ensure the success of his policy objectives was to carry through a programme of rearmament. If he was to flex his muscles on the international stage and make demands for territorial acquisitions, then he had to be seen as having muscles worth flexing. Rearmament was therefore an early priority. The original programme was to straddle a ten-year period, so as to be ready for hostilities by 1943, but it was expected there would have to be some sabre-rattling on the way. Within four months of taking office Hitler took two significant steps to launch his rearmament plans. On March 17, 1933, he appointed Dr Hjalmar Schacht as President of the Reichsbank. Schacht was instructed to reshape the German economy within two years, put it on a war footing and establish an armaments industry that would produce the required armaments over the ten-year period. Two months later, on May 17, Hitler warned the world in a speech that unless Germany was afforded parity in arms production with the Western powers, she would withdraw from the world disarmament conference then in progress. She would also withdraw from the League of Nations. On October 14, no such concession having been granted, Hitler carried out his threat.

The appointment of Schacht as his economics/armament supremo was an inspired one. Hitler himself knew little or nothing about economics but his personnel selection in this area was impeccable. Schacht was a financial genius who was to bring to bear professional skills of the highest order. His contribution to the Nazi programme of rearmament cannot be overstated. Schacht accepted and endorsed the high priority of his task with enthusiasm.[5] In one of his personal memoranda to Hitler he stated 'The accomplishment of the armaments programme with speed and in quality is *the* problem of German politics. Everything else therefore should be subordinated to this purpose.'[6] He took complete control of the national economy and used the dictatorial powers afforded him within the totalitarian state to good advantage.

---

[5]The enthusiasm did not last. Schacht became disillusioned with the Nazis and they with him. In 1936 he was replaced as Armaments Minister by Goering. Nevertheless, it was Schacht who established Nazi rearmament on the scale required by Hitler.
[6]Schacht's report of September 30, 1934, made eighteen months after his appointment.

Schacht was able to reshape the economy so as to gain all the advantages of a Keynesian demands structure without the attendant inflationary pressures. The public works used to stimulate demand were predominantly in the field of arms production. The curbing of inflation was achieved by the statutory control of prices, wages and salaries, the limitation of cash dividends and the control of foreign imports by quota schemes, foreign exchange controls and barter arrangements. Small industrial units were discouraged and eventually eliminated. Large industrial units, including cartels and especially those concerned with arms production, were encouraged by tax incentives. These took the shape of extravagant capital allowances and subsidies according to the number and value of the labour employed. Wage earners lost all their rights as to industrial and political liberties, including the right to strike, the right to collective bargaining and the right to Union representation. These rights were willingly traded in for the loss of the right to starve.[7]

Because Schacht guaranteed employment for all those able and willing to work, unemployment fell from six million in 1932 to less than one million in 1936. Businesses lived in a straitjacket of state controls, both as to prices and dividend limitation (not more than six per cent of profits). But substantial profits were made because of the consistent and increasing demand for armaments which led to an overall surge in demand. All profits other than the six per cent dividend distribution had to be ploughed back into the business,[8] but this led to self-funded ambitious capital projects and further expansion all ranking for tax concessions. As a result, national production more than doubled between 1932 and 1937.

A further achievement of the Schacht era was to make Germany almost self-sufficient. Imports were severely curtailed. Where possible *ersatz* substitutes were manufactured to cut down on the import of what were previously essential raw materials and finished goods including rubber, oil and textiles. Even *ersatz* steel was made out of low grade ore.[9] The complete picture was that of a nation gearing up to a war economy (*Wehrwirtschaft*) during a time of peace. Nevertheless, the nation enjoyed a consistent run of prosperity at odds with the rest of the European scene which featured high unemployment and depressed economies. This prosperity affected the vast

---

[7]Comfortable middle-class democrats are inclined to forget that this constituted an attractive deal to an unemployed person. You cannot eat a voting card.

[8]Profit plough-back in 1932 was DM175 million. In 1938 it was DM5 billion.

[9]This policy of self-sufficiency had considerable effect upon the achievements of the British naval blockade during the early years of the 1939–45 war. Its effectiveness never reached the levels attained in the 1914–18 war.

majority of the population. It gave them financial security, strengthened their national unity and confirmed their faith in their Führer.

Schacht was the answer to Hitler's prayer as far as the economy was concerned, but he knew that the green light to proceed with rearmament had been provided by his Führer's bold handling of the Western powers shortly after Schacht's appointment. In 1933, Germany was party to international talks on disarmament. She was also still bound by the provisions of the Versailles Treaty calling for a German Army limited to 100,000, a severely restricted Navy and no Air Force. How then was Schacht to proceed having regard to Germany's international commitments? Hitler supplied the answer. In so doing he illustrated for the first time his strong nerve and political acumen, as well as the apparent lack of resolve of his opponents. These features were to become the hallmarks of the 1930s and largely explained the remarkable success Hitler had in reaching so many of his policy objectives without spilling any German blood until September 1939.

On May 17, 1933, Hitler made a speech. It was widely acclaimed as his best speech ever. It was described as a peace speech. It was universally lauded by the international community as an indicator of the new Germany's intent upon peaceful co-existence with her European neighbours[10] and her aspirations as to resettlement within the international community. But in among the grandiose phrases and extravagant claims to international brotherhood Hitler slipped in a German requirement. As a member of that brotherhood Germany must be afforded parity of treatment in the matter of arms production. It was unreal to talk about mutual trust if it was apparent that Germany was not trusted in this matter. Hitler also slipped in a threat: if his request was denied he would be obliged to take Germany out of the disarmament talks and out of the League of Nations. The international community reacted in the same way as they were to react to similar events in the future. They plugged their ears to those parts of the speech they did not wish to hear and they loudly acclaimed those parts that they found acceptable. No one took up the claim to arms parity. No one believed that Hitler would carry out his threat. Great Britain had already stated that she required an eight-year period before Germany would be allowed parity.

On October 11, 1933, Germany carried out her threat. She withdrew from the League of Nations and the Disarmament Conference. At the same time Hitler put the matter before the German people in a national

[10]This was in direct contradiction of the policy objectives spelled out in *Mein Kampf*. No one appears to have noticed the contradiction or realised its significance.

plebiscite. In a secret memorandum to his Minister of Defence, General von Blomberg, he also ordered that the armed forces were to resist any armed attack that might be made on Germany as a result of his decision.[11] The League of Nations and the Western Democracies did what they were so often to do in similar circumstances in the future. They formed Committees, passed resolutions, wrote reports, wrung their hands and took no restraining action. In hindsight, the lack of action by Great Britain and France was extraordinary. By rearming, Germany would be in clear breach of the Versailles provisions. That breach would automatically set up the right to apply economic sanctions and armed intervention if deemed necessary.

Germany was at that time virtually defenceless. Occupation of German territory by Anglo-French forces would almost certainly have brought down Hitler. He would have been unable to withstand the political and personal humiliation. It was the first and by far the easiest opportunity that the Western democracies had of enforcing their will and confronting Hitler while they held the balance of power. What was the point of the Versailles Treaty if its provisions were not to be enforced? And why did a nation wish to arm itself alongside its protestations as to peace? No one seems to have noticed how both of these unanswered questions fitted so well into the policy objectives set down in *Mein Kampf*. And if they did, was it not possible that the turning of the first page of that testament of intent might be followed by the turning of the second? This is not a case of being wise after the event. Only one British politician seemed able to penetrate the smokescreen of Hitler's public orations at that time and realise that Hitler was intent upon preparing for war; and even he seemed to have lost his compass bearings as to where the war was to be waged.

In 1936 Hermann Goering replaced Schacht as the economic supremo. The Luftwaffe chief's knowledge of economics was about on a par with that of Hitler, but by 1936 all the factors making for the *Wehrwirtschaft* were in place and running. Goering, famous for his 'guns before butter' motto, merely tightened the screw. Immediately he was appointed, he launched a four-year plan to boost arms production even further and to improve the self-sufficiency of the nation in the event of war. In private he expressed his doubts about meeting all the targets imposed[12] and of course the plan had not run its full course when war broke out. Nevertheless, Goering had followed faithfully in the footsteps of Schacht and it was largely due to these two individuals that Germany entered the war in 1939 in a markedly superior state

[11]As testified at the Nuremberg Trials.
[12]As expressed in the Christie papers.

of military preparedness than her opponents. And Hitler knew that the measures taken to ensure a state of self-sufficiency were temporary only. The real answer to Germany's ultimate economy lay in the acquisition of land to the East and in particular the steppes of the Ukraine and the oilfields of the Caucasus.

On September 3, 1939 Germany stood possessed of 1,450 fighter aircraft, 800 bombers and 1,500 tanks. These figures are set down by Burton H. Klein, the respected German economist, in *Germany's Economic Preparations for War* (published in 1959, by when most of the dust had settled on the 1939–45 period and the strident claims and counterclaims of propaganda had died away). According to Klein at the same date the Western allies had more bombers, fewer fighters and about the same number of tanks. But the number count is misleading. In terms of quality, the German forces were vastly superior. Many of the German bombers (in particular the Dornier Do17) could fly faster than most of the Allied fighters. The German bomber crews, unlike their Western counterparts, had been battle-trained in the Spanish civil war, used by Hitler for that specific purpose. Some of the British first-line air defence included Gloster Gladiator biplanes. The new Spitfires were not held in any great squadron strength. The French air force was largely obsolete and their number count almost irrelevant. The German tanks were bigger, could move faster and hit more powerfully than anything the British or French could put against them (a superiority retained throughout the war years).[13]

The inventory and analysis of German armaments held at the outbreak of war is of particular significance. It is apparent from their design that they were being used against the wrong adversaries, at least as far as the Western Allies were concerned. Their nature was clearly intended for use in large-scale land battles, to be fought primarily with armour and with supporting aircraft working in close liaison.[14] The inference that they were to be used in seeking *Lebensraum* in the East and in Russia in particular, as described in *Mein Kampf*, is as clear as the inference that they were not designed for use in any war against Great Britain. To wage war successfully against Great Britain, Germany would look to particular strength in U-boats and long-range heavy bombers. These would be used to

[13]This superiority in arms was not restricted to aircraft or tanks. British infantry in 1939 were equipped with an anti-tank rifle for use against German light armour. A colleague of the author described how the missiles literally bounced off the German armoured cars during the Flanders campaign of 1940. On the other hand, the British 25-pounder field gun was probably superior to any German field piece and the British Bren light machine gun could certainly hold its own against the German counterpart. But it was not held in sufficient numbers.

[14]In what was described as the *blitzkrieg* method of warfare.

exercise an effective blockade by sea and air against an island largely dependent upon its overseas lifelines for essential supplies of foodstuffs and raw materials.

On September 3, 1939, Germany had neither the submarines or the heavy bombers. When Doenitz replaced Raeder as Commander in Chief of the German Navy in 1943, he castigated his predecessor over the lack of U-boats when Germany entered the war. Only 47 had been commissioned, of which only ten could be operated in the Atlantic at any one time. Doenitz argued strongly that Great Britain could have been forced to her knees as early as 1941 if Germany had started the war with the 300 U-boats deemed necessary to conduct effective operations in the Western Approaches. But by 1939 the navy command had not built even half of the 24,000 tons of submarine vessels permitted under the 1935 Naval Treaty with Great Britain.[15]

Clearly submarines had never been a strategic priority in the German arms build-up. Heavy bombers had not been either. German bombers comprised the elite force of the Luftwaffe when hostilities opened, but they were not heavy, long-range bombers. They were excellent machines for the specific purpose for which they were designed. That purpose was co-operation with army units and in particular with the panzer armoured divisions. They were fast, lightly armed, of comparatively short range and carried only medium bomb loads. All of this was the very opposite of the characteristics required for a bomber force to be directed against Great Britain. These design deficiencies became apparent in the skies over south-east England in the summer of 1940 when the Luftwaffe was obliged to give battle as an independent arm against good-quality fighter aircraft and pilots.

Even when provided with comparatively short-range facilities, consequent upon the defeat and occupation of France, the German bomber force was never able to establish any mastery of the air over Great Britain. They were also unable to reach British western ports or shipping in the Western Approaches with an effective bomb load. The much-vaunted Junkers 87 divebomber (the Stuka), so effective in close co-operation with tank units in Poland and France, was literally shot out of the skies. It had to be withdrawn from the battle, as was the Messerschmitt 110 so-called long range fighter. None of the lightly armed bombers could operate safely unless heavily escorted by Messerschmitt 109 fighters, for which long-range cover was impossible. The Battle of Britain clearly demonstrated how unsuited the German Luftwaffe was for conducting independent warfare against

[15]As reported by Hitler's Armaments Minister, Albert Speer.

Great Britain. Clearly its aircraft had never been designed for that purpose.

German military thinking saw the bomber as a mobile artillery aide to the army. On September 3, 1939, Germany had a front-line army strength of 51 divisions. Five of these were heavily armoured and a further four lightly armoured. These armoured divisions and the strike force of Luftwaffe bombers working with them in close co-operation formed the key units in the *blitzkrieg* method of offensive warfare on the vast land masses of eastern Europe and Russia. In the case of Russia, the planning of these new *blitzkrieg* can be traced back as far as 1934.[16]

Two years after his accession to power, on March 16, 1935, Hitler announced national conscription and the formation of an army of half a million men. There was again no effective international comment or action about this further breach of the Versailles provisions. Schacht's programme of rearmament was then beginning to roll and Germany was free of international entanglement by way of arms control. She was therefore in a position to start making her demands. Versailles frontier revisions and the bringing of all Germans into the one Reich, perhaps the most reasonable of Germany's demands, could now be accompanied by some sabre rattling. Skilful propaganda and a strong nerve pitted against what was perceived to be the weakness of Hitler's adversaries would probably be enough to bring the required concessions by way of negotiation without the shedding of German blood.[17] Hitler had already demonstrated his skills and superiority in the use of these techniques. As Schacht and later, Goering went through the gears with arms production, so Hitler's confidence grew, as did his demands. Ultimately he knew that armed conflict lay at the end of the road when it came to the issues of *Lebensraum* in the East and the destruction of Communist Russia. But for that he would be ready. His arms build-up had been designed to feed a new military tactic, the *blitzkrieg* that would revolutionise modern warfare and show off its paces on the vast land mass that was Russia.

However, there was one further policy prerequisite that demanded attention before Hitler's policy objectives could be brought to fruition. In both of his political treatises Hitler made it clear that his plans for territorial acquisition would not in any way affect the sovereignty of Great Britain or her Empire.[18] Rather did he see the British maintaining their world status and Empire as a necessary complement to a

---

[16]When full details were imparted to British Air Intelligence at a special luncheon at the resplendent Horshers restaurant in Berlin. See chapter six.

[17]And was the case up to September 3, 1939.

[18]On the contrary, it was hoped that the destruction of Russian communism would be seen as beneficial to British interests.

Europe dominated by Germany. Hitler considered that Great Britain's hand of friendship and benevolent neutrality was an essential ingredient for his contemplated Eastern adventure.

6

The failure of German foreign policy towards Great Britain

Is it beyond the political genius of mankind to reconcile national individuality with international collaboration?

LORD HALIFAX

That Adolf Hitler actively sought the friendship of Great Britain during the 1930s there is no doubt. The need and wish had been expressed in *Mein Kampf*. It was repeated by Hitler and his colleagues, notably Hess, on many occasions, both public and private, between 1933 and 1939. On the very eve of war Hitler was still expressing his personal wish for friendship between the two nations. His sincerity was not doubted by Sir Nevile Henderson, the British Ambassador in Berlin.[1] Even in his last will and testament, written shortly before he committed suicide in 1945, Hitler reiterated that he had never wanted war against Great Britain.[2] In strategic terms he looked for Great Britain's benevolent neutrality as and when he turned to the East. In military terms he certainly did not wish to fight a war on two fronts.

There was more to it than that, however. Hitler had a genuine admiration and respect for the British and their Empire. He saw that institution as a stabilising effect in world affairs. So much had been expressed more than once in *Mein Kampf* and it was still being said as late as 1940, at the height of the French campaign. There is every evidence to show that although Great Britain declared war on Germany Hitler prosecuted the war with less than a full vigour against a country he would rather have seen as a friend than as an enemy. Punches were deliberately pulled so as to avoid inflicting humiliating defeats on the British.[3]

---

[1]Henderson, Sir Nevile, *Failure of a Mission*, Hodder and Stoughton (1940), 259.
[2]Shirer, William L., *The Rise and Fall of the Third Reich*, Pan Books (1964), 1335.
[3]Notably, in Flanders between May 24 and 26, 1940.

Also, Operation Sealion, calling for the invasion of Great Britain in the late summer of 1940, was never a practical proposition, for political and personal, as well as military reasons.[4]

It must therefore be assumed that when Hitler launched his campaign for Great Britain's friendship, shortly after his accession to power, he did so wholeheartedly and with a personal as well as a political interest in its outcome. He invested heavily in its projected success. He was bitterly disappointed when that success eluded him. Confronted with Great Britain's declaration of war on September 3, 1939, he explained to Rudolf Hess standing at his side, 'My book has been written in vain.'[5] Hitler and his colleagues (and none more than Hess) had convinced themselves of a consistent and simple theme: 'Since we do not interfere with the affairs of Great Britain or the British Empire, do not compete with Great Britain in the world markets and do not aspire to become a maritime power comparable with Great Britain, then we ask that Great Britain should not interfere with our interests on the continent of Europe.'

This was the theme that Hitler wished the British to accept as the basis of an established friendship. But the friendship was not to be. It was certainly not for the want of trying. Hitler launched his friendship campaign as a matter of priority in 1933 but he knew that it would take time and patience to bring it to fruition. The main thrust was to dress Germany up as a nation and political phenomenon worthy of inspection and then invite Britons of importance to see for themselves. These invited ambassadors would then return to Great Britain and spread the good news. They would be able to report that Germany had recovered her pride and self-esteem, that her economy was strong and her people healthy and vigorous, happy and contented. In other words, Germany was worthy of the friendship of Great Britain. The Germans would then play the Red Menace card so as to promote a reciprocal British need for friendship with Germany.

The Germans had much to show and much to hide and on the whole they did it well.[6] Their organising abilities, flair for showmanship and lavish entertainment guaranteed that the visits made by the Britons were memorable occasions. The annual Nuremberg rallies and the 1936 Olympic Games were highlights. They were well attended by British visitors. They were able to meet the Nazi dignitaries and

---

[4]This is discussed in a later chapter.

[5]Ansel, *Hitler Confronts England*, 810–11.

[6]Where necessary there was a certain amount of stage management. Street and other notices reading 'Jews not wanted here' were removed during the 1936 Olympics, concentration camps were placed out of bounds to visitors and political prisoners were kept away from the roads.

confirm for themselves the facts of National Socialist discipline, efficiency and new found respectability. Many of the Nazi leaders tried to outdo each other in terms of hospitality on offer. During the Olympic Games Ribbentrop invited 600 guests to dinner. He was eclipsed by both Goering and Goebbels. The latter topped 1,000 guests. It was left to Hitler and Hess to entertain privately and more frugally. Hitler was assured of a good foreign press coverage for his henchmen's beanfeasts because foreign journalists were paid for that purpose. The British were left in no doubt as to the message. Germany was worthy of the respect and friendship of her Anglo-Saxon cousins, and Germany was inviting that friendship to be a bond between two nations facing the threat of European communism.

The effect, if any, these extravagant occasions had in fostering the message at governmental level is doubtful. An examination of the guest lists is revealing.[7] Representatives of the landed aristocracy, press barons and retired Service officers may well have been impressed by the military splendour and pageantry of the Nazi parades, but they were in no way representative of the bulk of the British people or, even more importantly, of the British Government. They represented in the main the minority interests of the extreme right wing of British politics whose influence on the British Government was more imagined than real.

There was also a frivolous element of empty-headed socialites. To them, skipping over the Channel and flirting with Nazi ideologies at the Nuremberg rallies was a special event on a par with a visit to Ascot or Henley. Perhaps the best example of these spoiled and pampered so-called Nazi sympathisers were the two daughters of Lord Redesdale, Unity and Diana Mitford. They were figures of eccentricity rather than serious apostles of the faith. They and their like may well have adopted German thinking as to the Red Menace and the need for Anglo-German friendship in that context, but that was only because they were probably already of that mind before they arrived in Germany. Hitler seems to have selected the wrong audience. The German propaganda probably converted few. Rather did it confirm the already converted.

Attempts made to solicit front-rank British politicians were almost wholly unsuccessful. In 1934 and again in 1936 invitations to visit

---

[7]Guests at the 1936 Olympic Games and the Nuremberg rally of that year included Lord Beaverbrook, Lord Monsell, Lord Rothmere, Lady Ravensdale, Sir Harry Brittain, Lord Mount Temple, Admiral Sir Barry Domvile, Sir Frank and Lady Newnes, Lord Apsley, Sir Frank Sanderson, Sir Thomas More, Sir Arnold Wilson and Admiral Sir Murray Sueter. Such a list was fairly typical.

Hitler were extended to Stanley Baldwin, the British Prime Minster, but Baldwin did not subscribe to man-to-man diplomacy. He was not a foreign affairs man by inclination, was ill at ease with foreigners and preferred to use official channels through his Foreign Office mandarins. In 1936, Hitler had to make do with a visit from the veteran Lloyd George instead of Baldwin. Lloyd George was not in office and his influence in governmental circles was minimal. He was very much a man of the past. He was a confirmed Germanophile and a firm believer in Anglo-German friendship before he set foot in Hitler's lair at Berchtesgaden. Hitler set out his stall. He turned on the charm, sported a large photograph of Lloyd George on his desk, who duly succumbed. He returned to Great Britain as one of Hitler's most ardent supporters. The already converted had been well and truly confirmed by his visit. Perhaps Hitler marked his card for future reference. After all, the old man had led a nation out of crisis to victory. Could he lead in similar circumstances again?

Other individual visitors from Great Britain were many and various but almost without exception, they could be fairly labelled as belonging to the minority interests existing on the extreme right of the British political spectrum. They included sincere but muddled clerics like Arthur Headley, Bishop of Gloucester, second-rank and emotionally unstable politicians like Lord Lothian, misguided press barons like Lord Rothermere and Lord Beaverbrook and bought journalists like George Ward Price of the *Mail*. They also included the well meaning but naive leaders of the British Legion who believed that German offers of friendship were motivated exclusively by feelings of honour and respect for former opponents on the battlefield.[8]

This naivety was never better expressed than by the Legion's patron and representative of royalty, the then Prince of Wales. Already a confirmed Nazi sympathiser he supplied Goebbels's propaganda machine with everything it wanted to hear. At the Legion's annual conference held on June 11, 1935, the Prince expressed his personal view: 'I feel there could be no more suitable body or organisation of men to stretch forth the hand of friendship to the Germans than we ex-Servicemen who fought and have now forgotten all about it, in the Great War'. This reciprocation of German offers of friendship from a representative of royalty gave it an almost official backing to the waiting world press. In fact, it went far beyond official Foreign Office policy. There was political and domestic uproar. The Prince was reprimanded by his

---

[8]The British Legion representatives had 'a quiet supper with Herr Himmler who gave the impression of being an unassuming man anxious only to do his best for his country'. Graham Wootton, *The Official History of the British Legion*, 185.

father, King George V, but remained obdurate. His views were clearly far ahead of his Government's.

If Hitler marked the Prince's card, then for future reference he certainly must have endorsed the marking when the Prince undertook a private visit to Germany two years later, in October 1937. In the interim, the Prince had abdicated his responsibilities as King, acquired a wife who had already seen off two husbands and fallen out with his family in general and his brother in particular. His Nazi sympathies however had remained intact. He still felt he could play a part in bringing Nazi Germany and Great Britain together and probably to his own personal advantage. The visit was arranged by Charles Bedaux, a French-American millionaire later to achieve notoriety as a German agent. The Prince had been warned by the British Foreign Office that 'prolonged visits or close contacts in Fascist countries would be unwise', but he was not renowned for taking advice. Sporting the new titles of Duke and Duchess of Windsor, the couple went ahead with the visit as planned in October 1937. They were entertained by Hess, Goering and Ribbentrop. They were indulged and flattered wherever they went. The Duchess was referred to throughout as 'Her Royal Highness', which was pleasing to both of them since that title had been denied to the Duchess by British court circles.

Hitler saw the Duke privately at Berchtesgaden. No minutes of the discussion between the two men have ever been made available.[9] In the absence of the written record one may conjecture as to their content. Hitler was seeking the friendship and the benevolent neutrality of Great Britain before embarking upon his adventures to the East. By late 1937 there were growing indications that this prerequisite was not attainable. In such circumstances Hitler might find himself at war with the Western democracies before turning East. It is known that the Duke had talked to Charles Bedaux about his possible return to the British throne in the event of a German victory in any war with Great Britain.[10] He may well have expressed those same sentiments to Hitler at their Berchtesgaden meeting. It is certain that it was actively considered both by the Duke and Hitler three years later, during the summer of 1940. But here again, any progress made with the Duke of Windsor in 1937 was made with a bit player. In real terms, as opposed to his aspirations, the Duke of Windsor was out of office and out of

---

[9]The Duchess was expressly excluded from this meeting. Minutes would have been taken but they have never been made available. The same embargo applies to subsequent correspondence passing between Hitler and the Duke. Presumably these papers are withheld on the grounds that disclosure would not be in the British national interest. One ponders if it is a matter of national interest or national embarrassment.

[10]Ziegler, Philip, *King Edward VIII*, Collins (1990), 459.

favour. It was as though the German hand of friendship was not being grasped by any of the main players on the British stage but rather by players waiting in the wings. The intriguing question is whether any of these bit players would, or did they ever, make a bid to enter the main stage and bring about the happy communion that Hitler wished?

One lead player did in fact attend upon Hitler. He did not signal communion but he did signal acquiescence to Nazi adventures in central Europe, which was the next best thing. Lord Halifax visited Germany in November 1937 and spent three hours with Hitler at Berchtesgaden on the nineteenth of that month. It is not clear if the visit arose as a result of a straight invitation from the Nazi hierarchy or was engineered by Neville Chamberlain, the British Prime Minister. Chamberlain was bent on reaching some sort of understanding with Hitler. The informal visit was arranged through the Editor of *The Field*. Halifax was to attend a sporting exhibition in Berlin and then 'shoot foxes' with Goering. An invitation to call on Hitler was inevitable. Halifax was a devoted huntsman and Master of the Middleton Hounds. Chamberlain was keen for Halifax to go. The Foreign Office was less so. Halifax held the office of Lord President in Chamberlain's government. He was not Foreign Secretary but he had Chamberlain's ear more than the Foreign Secretary, Anthony Eden, ever had. Eden reluctantly agreed the visit.

Halifax was carefully instructed but ill-prepared. He had never read *Mein Kampf* and was no student of German history, or any other European history for that matter. His street experience in terms of dealing with a man like Hitler was nil. He mistook the German leader for a footman when they met at the steps leading to the Berghof (it was the black patent shoes worn by Hitler which confused him). During the interview, Halifax did most of the talking and said everything Hitler wanted to hear.

Exactly a fortnight before meeting Halifax, Hitler had held a secret meeting at the Reich Chancellery.[11] He had addressed his military leaders and Foreign Secretary and advised them that the needs of the *Lebensraum* policy in the East would almost certainly involve Germany in armed conflict. He had specifically referred to the safeguarding of the German eastern and southern flanks by occupying Austria and Czechoslovakia. He needed the green light to go ahead, in the knowledge that there would be no military interference from the West. Halifax gave him it. Halifax, not Hitler, specifically mentioned Austria and Czechoslovakia (as well as Danzig), which was the very

[11]The so-called *Hossbach* meeting.

thing that the British Foreign Office and in particular, Vansittart, had advised against. Halifax gave Hitler the clear indication that Great Britain would not fight for the protection of either.

Following the Halifax meeting, Hitler knew that the risks with Austria and Czechoslovakia were well worth taking. He perhaps did not have Great Britain's friendship, but he would not have her military interference. He also no doubt took stock for the future of the calibre of the sort of British statesmen he was likely to encounter. Hitler had formed his impression of the British character from his experience when facing the British 'Tommy' in the trenches of the 1914–18 war. It was unlikely that the audience with Halifax had enhanced that view. As to Halifax, he reported to the Cabinet on his homecoming that 'the Germans had no policies of immediate adventure. They are too busy with domestic issues. They would press claims in central Europe, but not in a form to give others cause or probably occasion to interfere'. Halifax's comments were echoed by those of Chamberlain. 'The visit had been a great success because it had achieved its object, that of creating an atmosphere in which it was possible to discuss with Germany the practical questions involved in a European settlement.'[12] These comments were made by the two leading British statesmen only a fortnight after Hitler's meeting with his military leaders and two months before German troops marched into Austria.

There was another British visitor to Germany during the 1930s who met Hitler and Hess and others of the Nazi hierarchy on more than one occasion. He also arranged reciprocal visits to Great Britain to foster the relationships he was initiating. He was not a bit player waiting in the wings but a main player at centre stage. German attempts to foster good relations with Great Britain through his intervention appear to have made some progress with at least one important sector of the British Establishment. He was Group Captain (formerly Squadron Leader) Frederick Winterbotham, Chief of Air Intelligence with MI6 throughout the 1930s.

The precise nature of Winterbotham's relationship with Rosenberg and Hess and the true purpose of his visits to Germany, are obscure. His official brief was to pose as a friend and sympathiser to the Nazi regime, obtain information as to German aircraft production and feed that information back to the British Air Ministry. This he did, but he did much more. His own political views appear to have projected his activities beyond those envisaged by his professional brief. He subscribed to the view that Great Britain should have maintained at least

[12]As reported by Chamberlain to his sisters, November 26, 1937.

the pretence of friendly relations with Germany. She should also have acquiesced to Hitler's plans on Europe and stood off as a neutral observer while Hitler embarked upon his great crusade against Russia. So much is evident from Winterbotham's personal testimony. He described his dream world as one in which the two major forces for evil in modern times, the Nazis and the Communists, had been allowed to fight each other to a standstill of destruction. This would have left a strong Great Britain able to plan her role in the translation of the *Pax Atlantica* into the *Pax Orbi*.[13]

Holding such beliefs, Winterbotham could well have genuinely worked to promote friendly relations between Great Britain and Germany. There is plenty of evidence to show that he did just that. He had better cause than most to know that the ideological clash between Nazism and communism had been programmed and would take place. He had been told so by Hitler himself when he first met him in February 1934. Later that year he had even sat in on a meeting of high-ranking Wehrmacht and Luftwaffe officers at which full details of the forthcoming attack on Russia were discussed. It is not therefore surprising that, to assist in the work of Anglo-German co-operation, Winterbotham established an off-the-record means of intelligence and communication which led from himself at the British Air Ministry, through a particular double agent and friend, William de Ropp, and Alfred Rosenberg direct to Hess and Hitler, circumventing all the usual and official channels of communication through the Foreign Office.

Fortunately, Rosenberg's diary and German diplomatic records supply plenty of evidence as to who used Winterbotham's channel of communication and for what specific purposes in the cause of Anglo-German friendship. It is known, for example, that it was used on at least two occasions during the 1930s by members of the British royal family who appeared to subscribe to Anglo-German friendship beyond the parameters prescribed by official government policy. According to an entry in Goebbels's diary dated January 21, 1935, it was used to supply King George V with information about the Saar plebiscite. The King had complained that he had been misinformed through official sources. The King also enquired as to the general situation in Germany, including the nature of National Socialism and particulars of the leading personalities of the Nazi hierarchy. According to Rosenberg's diary entry the King had made his enquiry through the Duke of Kent who had taken it up with his personal contacts in the Air

[13]Winterbotham, F.W., *Secret and Personal*, William Kimber (1969), 185.

Ministry. Winterbotham had then been in touch with de Ropp, who had called on Rosenberg. De Ropp met the Duke of Kent subsequently at a London club and supplied the required information in a conversation which lasted until 3 a.m.[14] In the previous July, Captain Fitzroy Hubert Fyers, equerry to the Duke of Connaught, had used the same line of communication to ask Rosenberg for information about the Roehm purges.

Rosenberg considered that substantial progress was being made in fostering Anglo-German relations with members of the British Air General Staff through the good offices of Winterbotham and his immediate boss, Air Commodore Archie Boyle. This is clearly shown in a personal report made by Rosenberg to Hitler in October 1935.[15] He mentions the Royal Air Force Club as 'a centre for fostering Anglo German understanding' and suggests that the Air General Staff were in direct contact with the Germans (presumably using the Winterbotham communications link) as to how to deal with any 'anti-German activities in London'. Mention is also made as to the strong anti-Bolshevik/pro-German stance taken up by *The Aeroplane*, an important British aeronautical magazine said to be under the sponsorship of the Air General Staff. The appointment of Sam Hoare as British Foreign Secretary is then mentioned, together with his previous and continuing connection with the Air Ministry. 'At his request, a Memorandum inspired by us on the intellectual foundations of National Socialism had been passed to him as he wishes to understand our movement more fully.'

It was following Winterbotham's first visit to Germany in February 1934 that Rosenberg first reported on the susceptibility of the British Air Ministry to German initiatives. 'First of all, the Air Ministry and then the staffs of the other British Service Ministries will bring increasing pressure on British foreign policy.'[16] At the time, Rosenberg was charged with personal responsibility for the fostering of Anglo-German relations. It is hardly likely that he would minimise the success of his work. Nevertheless, even taken with a hefty pinch of salt, it is apparent that the Germans considered that progress was being made with the propagation of their cause in the direction of the British Air Ministry and aviation circles generally.

It is also a matter of record that some of the officers and committee members of the British Air League were also members of certain right-wing political organisations. C.G. Grey of *The Aeroplane* has

---

[14]See Rosenberg diary entries for January 21 and February 2, 1935.
[15]Reproduced in full in Appendix II.
[16]As reported by Rosenberg to Hitler, May 12, 1934.

been described as 'the most strident and vociferous purveyor of their views'.[17] Certainly, the Germans' target in this case was an important centre of British defence. There was nothing peripheral about Air Ministry operations, Air Ministry senior staff and an Air Minister now appointed as Foreign Secretary. It would appear that if Winterbotham and his boss, Archie Boyle were truly activists in the cause, then they were meeting with some success. It is also very interesting to note that the Air Ministry, Air Intelligence M16, Archie Boyle and Rosenberg were all probably involved in Hess's peace mission in May 1941.

There were of course reciprocal benefits that flowed from this much fostered relationship. Winterbotham was given almost *carte blanche* to see for himself the Luftwaffe developments, both as to machines and personnel. As a result, he was able to supply important intelligence information to London. During his 1934 visit he even became party to the German plans for the forthcoming attack on Russia. Full details of the programmed *blitzkrieg* assault were given to him at an extraordinary luncheon party hosted by Rosenberg and attended by leading Luftwaffe chiefs and Hitler's favourite political general, Walther von Reichenau,[18] in addition to Winterbotham and the double agent, William de Ropp. All that was asked of Winterbotham was that he should return to his colleagues at the British Air Ministry and convince the authoritative sources in London as to German intent and to give assurances that the operations so described were planned exclusively for the East.[19] Disclosure of these plans would obviously not have been made to a representative of British Intelligence if Great Britain had been considered to be a potential enemy.

In those early days of the campaign seeking friendship with Great Britain it was Rosenberg who was charged with responsibility for its success and it was the double agent, William de Ropp, friend of Winterbotham, whom he used to sound out those Britons he thought would be amenable to German blandishments. Rosenberg would then arrange for invitations to be issued for visits to Germany. Rosenberg had commenced his activities in Great Britain even before the Nazi Party came to power, having been invited to London by Winterbotham in 1931. He defined his brief at that time as 'to make contact with politicians, journalists, officers and personalities of public life and to counteract the "horror" stories about the aims and methods of the

[17]Griffiths, Richard, *Fellow Travellers of the Right*, Constable (1980), 138.

[18]Perhaps the supreme irony was that Reichenau met his end by committing suicide in the snows of Russia, his *blitzkrieg* having ground to a halt.

[19]To what extent Winterbotham acceded to this request, and was successful with the assurances if he did, is unknown. What is known is that the overall German efforts to reassure Great Britain failed and as a result *blitzkrieg* warfare was used against the Western Allies before Russia.

party, stressing Germany's position as front-line defence against Bolshevism.'

On Hitler's accession to power in 1933 Rosenberg's position was confirmed. He became the first head of the party's Aussenpolitsches AMT, responsible directly to Hess. This was the party's own foreign policy section, working alongside and sometimes independently from the Foreign Office, an organisation which Hitler considered to be bureaucratic and filled with the old guard. In their work of recruiting disciples Rosenberg and de Ropp were actively assisted by Geoffrey Dawson, Editor of *The Times*. Those who rose to the bait under Dawson's inspiration were many and varied, but they were again ready-made converts, ready for confirmation, rather than new aspirants to the Nazi cause.

The dispensing of Nazi propaganda to British MPs and journalists was handled by a so-called Anglo-German Information Service, established in Parliament Street. A big push was also made to market German propaganda books. The English edition of *Mein Kampf* was published in 1933 and further propaganda issues *Germany's Hitler*, *Hitler's Wonderland* and *Adolf Hitler* followed in the next year. Propaganda was also directed toward British children. Visits to Germany were arranged. In some cases, the teachers were more susceptible to the propaganda than the children. These early attempts to woo the British were amateurish and ineffective and Rosenberg's visit to Great Britain in 1933 was unsuccessful.[20] Apart from his important Air Ministry connection through Winterbotham (which he retained), Rothenberg had only touched on the fringe of the British Establishment.

Hitler was impatient for success. In 1935 he replaced Rosenberg by Joachim von Ribbentrop as the man to lead the Nazi propaganda initiative in Great Britain. Ribbentrop already had connections with the British. He had recently concluded the Anglo-German naval agreement with Sam Hoare which had alleviated the Versailles restrictions on German naval strength. He was also a personal friend of Ernest Tennant, a British merchant banker with views sympathetic to the Nazi cause. Through him he had been able to meet both Stanley Baldwin and Ramsay MacDonald. Ribbentrop's original brief was to approach Sam Hoare and inform him that following on the naval treaty Germany was prepared to conclude a full military alliance with Great Britain. Under the terms of such treaty Germany would give all assistance to Great Britain by land, sea and in the air as might be needed to safe-

[20]Rosenberg was not the most tactful of men. He placed a large swastika wreath on the Cenotaph in Whitehall. It was removed by a former British officer and thrown into the Thames. The culprit was fined 40 shillings. Griffiths, Richard, *Fellow Travellers of the Right*, Constable (1980), 114.

guard the British Empire in return for neutrality in the event of a conflict involving Germany.

Here was German foreign policy towards Great Britain in a nutshell. The conflict Hitler had in mind was, of course, the one involving Russia. Ribbentrop served from 1934 to 1938 as Ambassador to Great Britain (he was formally appointed as such in 1936), with specific responsibility to lead the German friendship initiatives. His campaign was a complete failure. If Hitler's appointment of Schacht as his economics supremo in the previous year was inspired then his appointment of Ribbentrop as the man to bring home British friendship was calamitous. Opinions as to Ribbentrop's character and fitness for the duties Hitler had in mind were almost unanimously hostile.[21] A composite character study records:

> Ribbentrop had polished manners, a command of foreign languages, a certain political cunning and a talent for persistence. But few politicians have been the object of greater contempt and derision from contemporaries, both at home and abroad. His pretentious *parvenu* and arrogance concealed a deep sense of insecurity. He was a bombastic bore who talked and never listened. His lack of tact was proverbial (he was known as Herr Brickendrop) and his capacity for talking nonsense was legendary. Everything about him was affected, every look and gesture artificial. He seemed more like an actor reading his lines than a thinking human – a dehumanised gramophone record spouting claptrap. Goering called him Germany's No.1 parrot. To say that he was despised as an ignorant amateur by the old German diplomatic establishment would be an understatement.

It is extraordinary that Hitler should appoint such a person to sell to Great Britain what was always going to be a very difficult package. The attributes required were intellectual integrity, an abundance of tact, diplomacy of the highest order and above all, a deep humility and humanity in reaching out and understanding the British character, Ribbentrop had none of these qualities. His mission was doomed before it started. His efforts in London never got beyond an acceptance by certain sectors of the so-called smart social set and their connections whose political ambitions outstripped their abilities.

Was Ribbentrop deluded into thinking that political initiatives might

---

[21]Goering, Goebbels, Chamberlain, Halifax and Churchill are but a few of those who voiced them.

be spawned in the salons of the socialites rather than the Palace of Westminster?

It was in these sort of circles that Ribbentrop moved, and it was in these sort of circles that he got nowhere with the purpose of his mission. He was entertained royally by the Grevilles, the Astors, the Londonderrys (his liaison with Lady Londonderry earned him the nickname 'The Londonderry Herr') the Channons, Emerald Cunard ('the twittering bird and queen of Covent Garden') and Laura Corrigan (where he acquired the further nickname of 'Ribbensnob'). He met only one Cabinet minister during the whole period of his ambassadorship – Sir Thomas Inskip, Minister for the Co-ordination of Defence, whose main interest in life seemed to be that the Church of England Common Book of Prayer should not be revised. Ribbentrop regaled Inskip as to how a better Christian Church would arise in Germany under Nazi supervision. Such is not the stuff of power politics.

On another occasion, Ribbentrop sat up well after midnight with Lord Lothian and Tom Jones, one time secretary to Baldwin, long after the other guests had gone to bed. They talked about Anglo German relations. The next morning, a lengthy memorandum setting out the result of the deliberations was sent to Anthony Eden, the Foreign Secretary. It was ignored.

In March 1937 Hess sent Albrecht Haushofer to London to try and repair some of the damage done by Ribbentrop. By early June of the next year Haushofer had produced a report for Ribbentrop setting down the Anglo-German position as he then saw it. It was a sound and realistic appreciation. While it accepted that Great Britain might still be amenable to overtures as to the plans for Eastern Europe, these plans would have to be built on the basis of plebiscites rather than armed aggression or the threat of armed aggression. Haushofer also reported that Czechoslovakia's integrity was a test case for Great Britain and that the return of former German colonies was no problem. Perhaps most importantly of all, he made the point that conflict with Great Britain might well involve conflict with America sooner or later.[22] This sober and accurate assessment ran counter to the Nazi self-deception that rapprochement with Great Britain in the West was possible while armed aggression was the case in the East. Ribbentrop never forgave either Haushofer or Hess for authorising a report which denied everything he had been preaching.[23] When he returned to Germany in 1938 to take up the post of Foreign Secretary Ribbentrop was a deeply embittered man by reason of his personal failure. He

---

[22]Report by Albrecht Haushofer to Ribbentrop on Anglo-German relations, dated June 26, 1938.
[23]Douglas-Hamilton, James, *Motive for a Mission*, Mainstream Publishing, Edinburgh (1979), 81.

conveyed that bitterness to Hitler in his distorted views as to British attitudes and motives. It was largely through his influence that Hitler's views about the British hardened somewhat during 1937–38.

On August 24, 1939, Neville Chamberlain said in the course of an address to the House of Commons: 'The German Chancellor's reply includes what amounts to a restatement of the German thesis that eastern Europe is a sphere in which Germany ought to have a free hand. If we, or any country having a less direct interest choose to interfere, the blame for the ensuing conflict will be ours... We cannot agree that national interests can only be served by the shedding of blood or the destruction of the independence of other States.' It was an accurate account of how matters then stood. Here was Great Britain's answer to the German overtures of the previous six years. There was to be no friendship. There was to be no benevolent neutrality. There was fundamental disagreement and there would be war.

Why then was the German policy such a conspicuous failure? The effect on Germany was disastrous. On September 3, 1939, Hitler found himself at war with Great Britain, a country from which he wanted only friendship, and at peace with Russia, a country which he wished to destroy. He had of course picked the wrong men to head up the friendship campaign. If Rosenberg was ineffectual, Ribbentrop was a disaster. He also seemed to have attracted the wrong audience, mostly those without power or influence. But there were other, more powerful factors at work. Perhaps the most fundamental point is that by September 1939 the vast majority of the British people no longer believed that Hitler's policy objectives would not affect the interests of Great Britain and her Empire. Germany was upsetting the status quo in Europe and sooner or later that upset would affect British interests.

Great Britain had a vested interest in preserving the status quo, not only in Europe but throughout the world. She controlled nearly one-quarter of the world's surface and resources. The emergence of a nation intent upon hegemony in Europe was thus not an event likely to promote the hand of friendship. Rather did it promote apprehension and concern for its limitation. This was the Churchillian perspective. It had been promulgated by Churchill almost as a lone prophet since the mid-1930s. It was finally endorsed by the vast majority of the British people in March 1939. It was on the fifteenth day of that month that German troops crossed the Czech border and occupied Prague. It was then apparent for the first time that Hitler's territorial demands were not limited to lands occupied only by Germans.

Hitler himself had contributed to this British distrust. As the 1930s progressed he became branded by the British government and British public as an unprincipled liar. He had stated that in private life he would never break his word but for the sake of Germany he would break it 'if need be, a thousand times'.[24] Unfortunately, the tactical lying that he deemed necessary to advance the cause of Germany eventually established him as a man lacking in all integrity.[25] When a man states on January 30, 1937, that he has no further territorial claims to make and subsequently marches into Austria fourteen months later and Czechoslovakia six months after that, he is branded as a liar. And when a liar tells the truth he is not believed. So when Hitler said that his plans did not affect the interests of Great Britain and her Empire, he was not believed.

In any case, Hitler had almost certainly under-estimated the difficulties of forging a link of friendship between two nations which were so different in historical perspective and political evolution. He may well have been an admirer of the British character but seems to have had very little conception of the inner core values which produced that character. In the first place, the British were for the most part firm believers in parliamentary democracy and all those other democratic institutions and civil liberties which produce the checks and balances which rein in the excesses of the powerful. To them democracy was 'the delicate fruit of a ripe civilisation' and they had come to that conclusion over the course of centuries of rational political evolution. They would need a lot of convincing before they extended the hand of friendship to a nation which had shut down their every democratic institution and which had prohibited every form of freedom of expression. Hitler's one-party state was anathema to them.

The British were also a tolerant people and if there was an element of racism apparent in its national life it was comparatively mild and practised by a very small minority. The cult of Superman and the persecution of the infirm and unfit and the so-called inferior races, especially the Jews, was wholly abhorrent to the ordinary Britisher. Both its philosophy and its practice would be a complete bar to any question of friendship. Again, no one could describe the British as a nation of urgent churchgoers but the closure of German churches and the imprisonment of their pastors was seriously disturbing to the British democrat. He would see it as a fundamental infringement of an individual's right to worship according to his conscience. Genuine friendly relations with such a nation would therefore be very difficult.

---

[24]Irving, David, *Churchill's War*, Veritas Publishing (1997), 483.

[25]In terms of strategy, however, he remained true throughout. He had laid down his policy objectives in *Mein Kampf* and he never deviated from them. His tactical lying on the way could have been identified as such by reference to *Mein Kampf*.

There would have to be the most powerful political motive to overcome these ideological differences.

Nevertheless, most British people were sympathetic towards Hitler's early demands. They accepted that there may have been injustices in the Versailles provisions and were amenable to any arrangements that would alleviate the position. After all, it was the French who had looked to the more harsh provisions to provide territorial security. With the passage of the years these seemed less and less necessary. Also, the requirement that all Germans should live under the one roof, or Reich, did not seem unreasonable and could be the subject of national discussion. As to German internal measures, these were matters not widely publicised in early days. There was also an attitude more prevalent than today that a nation's internal affairs were very much a matter of its own business and no one else's. But as the 1930s progressed and the excesses grew, so they became more publicised.[26] International opinion in general and British opinion in particular became seriously disturbed. Any hopes of Anglo-German friendship faded.

Hitler had also hoped that the threat of international communism would constitute the common concern which would have forged the Anglo-German link. Certainly, the Red Menace card was consistently played by German propaganda. It proved to be a damp squib. Unlike in Germany, Russian communism was not on the ordinary Britisher's doorstep and he was not ruled by a government intent upon whipping up anti-communist fervour. Very few of the population had any first hand experience of communism or communists, and internal events in Russia were not widely reported by the British media. There had been no active struggle against militant communists in Great Britain and there was no great allegiance to its cause among the British working classes. The Germans perhaps failed to realise that what was to them close at hand and immediate was seen by the British as distant and long-term. The Red Menace card therefore tended to be a joker rather than a trump card. The ordinary middle class Britisher of the mid-1930s was more concerned about the runs that might flow from Bradman's bat than the blood that might flow from the Russian sickle.[27]

Although successive British governments and the bulk of the British people therefore remained unmoved by Hitler's overtures of friendship, there were certain minority groups who took a more amenable

---

[26]The notorious pogrom of the Jews on the night of November 9–10, 1938 (*Kristallnacht*), was a case in point. British public opinion was outraged.

[27]Bradman was an Australian cricketer. He was a prolific run scorer.

view. They did not accept the Churchill perspective that war with Germany was inevitable if the German policy of territorial expansion continued. They viewed such policy as the rightful reclamation of lands belonging to Germany. Some of these groups were small, unimportant and ineffective. They represented a crank element. They included those who openly admired Hitler's National Socialist state and who saw it as an antidote to the sloppy left-wing liberalism they thought responsible for British national decline. The German system should be imported lock, stock and barrel. Other crank elements included these who secretly approved of German anti-Semitism and looked forward to the import of a higher profile opposition to Jewish influence in Great Britain, by legislation if necessary.

There were other minority groups, however, which were not crank elements. They were important and powerful. Their concern was the preservation of their positions of privilege within a continuing status quo. All viewed a war as fatal to the continuation of the status quo. If peace could be preserved while at the same time safeguarding the independence of Great Britain and her Empire then it would be singularly irresponsible not to pursue that line if there was any possibility of success. German hegemony over central and eastern Europe should be accepted. They considered that the greatest threat to the status quo came not from Nazi Germany but from communist Russia. They saw Germany as the European bulwark against which international communism would founder. The engagement of a powerful Germany as a friend and ally was therefore an event to be welcomed and a policy to be worked at.

Some doubted both the wisdom and the ability of Great Britain to engage in a major military conflict with Germany over issues which were not directly concerned with British interests. They had doubts about the extent of British economic and military muscle.

During the 1930s and even during the early war years, no less than twenty-one different organisations could be identified in Great Britain which accommodated the interests of these minority groups.[28] All were to varying degrees pro-German, anti-communist and anti-Semitic. Their views on Anglo-German friendship differed radically from the Churchillian perspective and, for varying reasons, would have accepted Germany's offer of friendship, warts and all. Elements from these groups were later to constitute what the Germans described as the British Peace Party.[29] It is unlikely that they ever formed a cohesive

[28]See Appendix I.
[29]*Documents on German Foreign Policy*, Volume Eight, September 4, 1939 to March 18, 1940, paras 363–65.

whole, as that description implies. They were more or less an association of individuals with a common desire to end a war which they considered should never have started. Although a good deal is known of the activities of these various minority groups during the 1930s very little is known after September 1939. It was these elements that Rudolf Hess intended to contact when undertaking his peace mission of May 1941.

One other minority group existed during the 1930s.[30] It held a very different perspective to any of those already described, but it too would have encouraged if not friendship with Nazi Germany, then a benign neutrality. It was the view subscribed to by Frederick Winterbotham, chief of British Air Intelligence. The National Socialism in Germany and the communism of Russia were equally abhorrent to a Western civilisation based as it was in both the New World and the Old on civil liberty and the institutions of democracy. If it were the declared policy of the one to attack the other, which it was, then there would be advantage to Great Britain in adopting a stand-off position and letting the German policy objectives work themselves through to their ultimate conclusion. The ensuing military conflict between Germany and Russia could have the effect of destroying, or at least exhausting, both regimes, thus leaving the Western democracies to institute and control world peace behind the shield of the ultimate deterrent.[31] It might therefore be politic to subscribe to non-interference while German efforts to further their policy objectives unfolded across the map of Europe, to end in disaster on the steppes and in the snows of Russia.[32] Here was another faction which thought that Great Britain should not have gone to war with Germany but, having done so, should disengage as soon as an opportunity presented itself. It was a view which was not motivated by any friendship campaign of Hitler but rather by the desire for his destruction.

---

[30]As related to the author by a former member of British Intelligence MI6.

[31]Work on the uranium constituent of the atomic bomb was in progress at Birmingham University during the late 1930s.

[32]Of course, during the late 1930s, it was not known to what extent, if at all, the Russians would be able to resist a German attack. Informed opinion at the time, both British and German, was that Russian resistance would collapse within a matter of weeks. British Intelligence sources may have known differently. If a stand-off policy had been adopted by Great Britain it would have featured the active appeasement of Hitler's demands, in the knowledge that sooner or later he was going to attack Russia. British Air Intelligence at least knew that was going to happen and Chamberlain promoted a policy of appeasement throughout 1937–39. He declared war most reluctantly, dragging his feet all the way, after his appeasement policy was swept aside by the Churchill perspective in early 1939. Perhaps there was more to Chamberlain's appeasement policy than meets the eye.

7

The 1930s – the road to Armageddon

> *Politics is the art of the possible. Beyond the discernible limits of the possible lies adventurism.*
>
> MIKHAIL GORBACHEV

During the 1930s Hitler made considerable progress towards the attainment of at least some of his policy objectives without becoming involved in armed conflict. But by September 1939 the failure of his policy towards Great Britain had caught up with him. A war resulted which eventually destroyed him. What therefore appeared to be progress during the 1930s only led him down the road which ended in confrontation and his ultimate armageddon.

Hitler's one-party state, with himself as the undisputed dictator, was up and running within two years of his taking power and had continued its uninterrupted run ever since. In the matter of rearmament he had thrown down the gauntlet to the international community in 1933 and again in 1935 by defying the Versailles provisions as to limitation of both arms and manpower. A flourishing armaments industry and a self-sufficient national economy to go with it, set up by Schacht and his successor Goering, had turned the screw further. As a result, by September 1939 Germany stood possessed of armed forces second to none in Europe both as to quantity and quality. And, precisely as planned and foreshadowed in *Mein Kampf*, it was the threatened use of this military muscle, allied to Hitler's political skills and strong nerve, which had delivered two further objectives.

By September 1939 most of the Versailles provisions deemed to be offensive to German aspirations had been set aside. In addition, all Germans, apart from those in Memel, Danzig and the Polish Corridor, had been united in the one Reich. International opinion and sympathy had helped. In retrospect it was acknowledged that there may have been injustices in the Versailles provisions. At the time of the treaty, political and strategic considerations had dominated, not moral issues. French fears for their security from a defeated but potentially dangerous enemy, had to be assuaged.[1] As a result, Versailles had failed to award the Germans the same rights as to self-determination as had been granted to the Poles, Czechs, Yugoslavs and Romanians,[2] and something like twenty million Germans in the Saarland, the Rhineland, Austria, Sudetenland, Memel, Danzig and the Polish Corridor had been separated from their fatherland.

The German case for revision of what Hitler called the Versailles *Diktat* appeared more and more reasonable as memories of the 1914–18 conflict faded.[3] Or at least that was the case with most nations, and with Great Britain in particular. But the French remained more suspicious. They were obliged to return the important coal-producing area of the Saarland to Germany following the plebiscite held on January 13, 1935, when 91 per cent of the population voted for unity with Germany. Hitler formally announced that he had no further territorial claims to make against France and renounced all claims to Alsace Lorraine. The French were to some extent reassured. Hitler's assurances in 1935 perhaps carried more weight than they did in later years. The differing views as to German recovery shown by the Western Allies became more apparent in the following year.

On March 7, 1936, German troops marched into the demilitarised zone on the left bank of the Rhine. Although German territory, the Versailles Treaty had called for its demilitarisation, so as to create an arms-free buffer zone between France and Germany. In March 1935 France signed a pact of mutual assistance with Russia. On February 27, 1936, the pact had been ratified by the French Parliament. Hitler denounced it and moved his troops across the Rhine bridges 'for the safeguarding of Germany's defence and protecting the primitive rights of its people to the security of their frontiers and the safeguarding of their defence'. Hitler claimed that the Franco-Russian pact threatened Germany's security.[4] It was of course an excuse rather than a reason. The action taken was in flagrant breach of the Versailles provisions but Hitler's Germany had long since foresaken them. France saw it as a direct threat to her security, the very thing that Versailles had sought to protect. She made representations to Great Britain for joint armed

---

[1]Henderson, Sir Nevile, *Failure of a Mission*, Hodder and Stoughton (1940), 94.

[2]The Irish also claimed the right to self-determination at the same time. It was not granted.

[3]Hitler described those responsible for Versailles as 'the jugglers, who either in their malice or their thoughtlessness, placed a hundred powder barrels around Europe all equipped with non-extinguishable lighted fuses'. Documents concerning German-Polish Relations, HMSO, 22.

[4]For perhaps the first time but certainly not the last during the 1930s, Hitler used the charge of Germany being 'surrounded'.

intervention. They were rejected. As was to become the pattern for future episodes of the German adventure, the British shut their eyes to what had happened and opened their ears to the protestations of peace which featured prominently in Hitler's speech of March 7, announcing the movement of his troops that morning.

German territorial acquisitions during the 1930s (or reclamations as Hitler's Germany would claim) were always accompanied by renewed calls for peace from Hitler. The British invariably wrung their hands at the one and listened attentively to the other – Lord Lothian's notorious remark that 'After all, the Germans are only going into their own back garden' must have been poor solace for the French. It was typical of the sort of rationale that justified a policy of doing nothing. It was another opportunity missed by the Western Allies to bring down Hitler, if that was what they wished. Hitler could only muster one division to carry out the operation, according to evidence given by General Alfred Jodl at the Nuremberg Tribunal. Of course, he learned the lesson well.

Two years later (during which time his campaign for friendship with Great Britain was at its height) Hitler turned his attention to Austria, his own home and that of over six and a half million other Germans. *Anschluss*, the union of Germany and Austria, was an issue very close to Hitler's heart. It is mentioned in the very first paragraph of *Mein Kampf*. Hitler saw it as the natural culmination of the work of Frederick the Great and Bismarck. But Austria presented a different problem to the Saarland and the Rhineland. Austria was a sovereign state and its native population included many nationalities other than Germans. Agitation for union with Germany would therefore have to come from within, so that any steps taken by Germany would be seen as a response to initiatives within Austria itself. Austria already had its own Nazi Party. It had been there since 1933. It was under direct orders from Berlin. Its function was to ferment political strife within Austria and undermine the regime of the Austrian Chancellor, Dolfuss. It did the job very well. On July 25, 1934, Austrian Nazis entered the Federal Chancellery and murdered Dolfuss. Hitler waited in the wings for the call for assistance which he knew would come in the wake of the anticipated coup. But there he had to remain. Dr Kurt von Schuschnigg, who was to succeed his murdered colleague as Austrian Chancellor, led Government forces against the Austrian Nazis and snuffed out the coup almost before it had started. Hitler backed off. Italy moved troops to the Brenner Pass and made threatening noises about the independence of Austria. Russia made even more noises about the possibility of an eastern Locarno-type treaty, which would have isolated Germany and brought about concerted East/West action in the event of German aggression.[5]

Hitler had almost acted prematurely and nearly burnt his fingers as a result. It brought home to him the truth of his own *Mein Kampf* philosophy. Foreign policy aims could only become reality with the use, or threat of the use, of force. In 1934 Hitler did not have that force. He therefore bided his time and by 1938 things were different. Hitler had acquired much military muscle and a reputation that he would use it if necessary. Italy was now in his camp. The Russians had been publicly snubbed by the Western democracies[6] and there was little possibility of any East/West concerted action.

In the meantime, the Austrian Nazis had been working overtime. Their programme of disruption, destruction and murder had brought Schuschnigg's administration to the point of crisis. On January 25, 1938, Austrian police raided the party headquarters in Vienna, making it clear that a *putsch* was to be organised in the Spring of that year. When Schuschnigg intervened, German troops were to move into Austria 'to prevent German blood from being shed by Germany'.[7] Franz von Papen, Hitler's special ambassador to Vienna (who had worked tirelessly in the cause of weakening Schuschnigg's government) suggested to Hitler that Schuschnigg should be invited to Germany to meet Hitler and discuss the position.

Hitler agreed and Schuschnigg consented. The meeting took place at Berchtesgaden on February 12, 1938. It marks one of the most infamous and degrading episodes in Hitler's career. During the initial two hour session Hitler harangued, bullied and threatened Schuschnigg in an almost non-stop monologue which amazed, shocked and finally broke the old-style, gentleman diplomat. In the afternoon, the terms of an agreement were presented to Schuschnigg by Joachim von Ribbentrop, Hitler's newly appointed Foreign Minister. The terms were such that Austria's independence would be ended. She would become a vassal of the German Reich. No room was left for negotiation. Either the agreement was signed, or within three days German troops would move into Austria. This was real military muscle being used to put backbone into Germany's foreign policy. Hitler had reduced diplomacy to the simple act of bullying. Schuschnigg signed the agreement, departed and reported to his President. All the terms of

---

[5]As a mark of good faith in that direction, Russia joined the League of Nations later that year. There was no reaction from the Western democracies.

[6]In a speech in the House of Commons on March 24, 1938, Chamberlain publicly rejected a Russian suggestion that an international conference be called, either within the League of Nations or outside it, to consider the question of German aggression.

[7]The Papen papers, 404.

the agreement were to be fulfilled by February 18. Some were. Others were not. Tensions continued to rise. At last Schuschnigg courageously called Hitler's bluff. He announced that a plebiscite would be held on Sunday, March 13. The people would decide whether the *Anschluss* was to take place or not. This was too much for Hitler. On March 12, 1938, German troops entered Austria. The *Anschluss* became a fact.

In the meantime, the Western democracies were busy dealing with their own domestic crises. France had no government. Premier Camille Chautemps and his entire Cabinet had resigned two days previously. In Great Britain, the Chamberlain government was recovering from the shock occasioned by the resignation of the Foreign Secretary, Anthony Eden. Nevertheless, Chamberlain had already given the green light to Hitler in a speech in the House of Commons, stating that what had happened at Berchtesgaden was 'merely that two statesmen had agreed upon certain measures for the improvement of relations between their two countries... It appeared hardly possible that just because two statesmen had agreed on certain domestic changes in one of the two countries ... that one country had renounced its independence in favour of the other.' It is hardly likely that Schuschnigg would have agreed Chamberlain's version of events.

Hitler failed to realise the true significance of the *Anschluss*: the alienation of world opinion from his cause. This alienation, which was to sow the seeds of Hitler's ultimate destruction, arose not so much from a knowledge of his reprehensible behaviour towards Schuschnigg, which was not widely publicised, but rather from the widely publicised treatment of the non-German population of Austria after the German occupation. In *Mein Kampf* Hitler had referred to the cosmopolitan nature of much of Austria's population. He now had the problem of dealing with large numbers of non-Aryans resident in Austria. He therefore employed the same measures as he had already employed in Germany to discriminate against the non-Aryans. But because of the higher density of non-Aryan nationals in Austria the measures taken were perceived to be much more widespread.

The worst atrocities were committed by the Austrian Nazis and the German SS troops. Street beatings and other humiliations of the Jews and others were commonplace, providing entertainment for jeering onlookers. Jewish intellectuals became street and lavatory cleaners overnight. There were 70,000 arrests in Vienna alone within weeks of the occupation. A vast concentration camp was established at Mauthausen on the Danube. Jews were encouraged to emigrate. Their passages were funded by the appropriation and sale of their personal assets. A special office and organisation was set up to handle this human traffic. It was operated under the name and style of 'The Office for Jewish Emigration' by a man who was to become notorious in later years, the infamous Karl Adolf Eichmann, assistant to Reinhard Heydrich of the SS.[8] But those who emigrated also talked. The disgraceful events in Austria immediately following the *Anschluss* were not only imprinted in the minds of those emigrating[9] but were also disseminated throughout the world by a hungry press. As a result, world and particularly British, opinion hardened considerably during 1938 and was further exacerbated by the later events of that year and the next. Hitler's triumphal progress was already carrying with it the seeds of doom.

Austria had requested no help from the Western democracies when dealing with Hitler. She presided over her own death while Great Britain and France stood and watched as uninvited bystanders. In the case of Hitler's next territorial acquisition, the Sudetenland in Czechoslovakia, things were very different. Czechoslovakia requested help from the Western Allies. They, or rather Neville Chamberlain acting for both Great Britain and France, then personally presided over the death of that country, while Czechoslovakia herself stood and watched as an uninvited bystander. In this case, Hitler raised the level of his bullying to take in the leading statesmen of the West while the Western democracies seemed to reach new levels of humiliation.

Czechoslovakia was a new state created by the Treaty of Versailles (and, for that reason alone, unpalatable to Hitler). It had evolved as a working democracy, wedding together many racial minorities, including Germans, Jews, Czechs, Slovenes, Hungarians and Russians. There were over three million Sudeten Germans who aspired to union with the Third Reich. There is little doubt however that Hitler's ambitions in this case almost certainly went further than the domestic matter of incorporating the Sudetenland within the Reich. At the meeting with his military leaders on November 5, 1937, Hitler had clearly laid down the strategic importance of occupying Czechoslovakia as well as Austria in order to protect his flanks before the drive to the East and the destruction of Communist Russia. That is why Hitler expressed disappointment with the Munich Agreement signed on September 29, 1938. It gave Hitler the Sudetenland. It did not give him Czechoslovakia.

---

[8]Eichmann handled the emigrations (mostly to Palestine) very efficiently. In due course Eichmann, his office and his organisation graduated from dealing in emigration to dealing in extermination. His efficiency remained unimpaired.

[9]The events are as described to the author by the survivors of a Jewish family who were able to leave Vienna and reached Great Britain.

The events leading up to the Munich Agreement followed a well-worn path. Hitler thought he had little to fear. Chamberlain had again given him the green light. He had informed the House of Commons, in a speech on March 24, 1938, that the British Government was not prepared to guarantee Czech independence and was under no obligation to come to the aid of France if that country found itself embroiled in hostilities by reason of its pact with Czechoslovakia. Russia also had pacts with both Czechoslovakia and France, but was only obligated to take up arms to assist Czechoslovakia provided France did so first. In the absence of British support it was certain that France would not take up arms in spite of her treaty obligations.

The chain of disaster as far as Czechoslovakia was concerned was thus completed by Chamberlain's statement. She thought she had strong protection against Hitler's ambitions. In fact, she had none. For Hitler, it was the clearest of green lights. He would need a strong nerve, but he had that. As in Austria, so in Czechoslovakia, there had always been a Sudeten Nazi Party, taking orders direct from Berlin. Its leader was Konrad Henlein. Immediately after the *Anschluss* he began his work of stoking up political unrest, based upon the real or imagined grievances of the Sudeten Germans. Henlein's work was accompanied by strident propaganda from Goebbels, designed to exacerbate the tensions already fermenting within the multiracial state. As Henlein himself put it, 'We must always demand so much that we can never be satisfied.'[10] It was a tried formula. It had worked in Austria. It would work in Czechoslovakia. Tensions increased. Hitler flexed his muscles, made threats and waited on events. His nerves held steady.[11]

He did not have to wait long. Neville Chamberlain, who took it upon himself to represent not only Great Britain but also France and Czechoslovakia, duly presented himself to Hitler to receive formal notice of German demands. He attended upon Hitler on three separate occasions within a fortnight at Berchtesgaden, Godesberg and Munich. On each occasion, Hitler increased his demands. On each occasion Chamberlain succumbed to them. Eventually the Munich Agreement was signed on September 29, 1938. Hitler reclaimed 11,000 square miles of Sudetenland for the Reich, together with nearly three million Sudeten Germans. Chamberlain came home with a useless piece of paper and was welcomed as the saviour of peace. He was delighted. Hitler was less so. Chamberlain having given in to all his demands, Hitler was left with no

---

[10]DGFP II, 197–98.

[11]Not so his generals. They feared war with the Western democracies and Russia. General Ludwig Beck, Chief of the Army General Staff, tried to organise army opposition. He failed and resigned on August 18, 1938. He continued to organise opposition to Hitler.

cause of action to occupy the whole of Czechoslovakia, which was his original intention. He soon repaired the omission.

Within weeks of the Munich Agreement separate movements were being encouraged in Slovakia and Ruthenia. The Czech central government under German pressure, reacted or perhaps over-reacted. Slovakia declared its independence on March 14, 1939. The next day, the aged President of Czechoslovakia, Dr Emil Hácha, faced with the resulting political turmoil, formally requested Hitler's help to restore the situation. German troops thereupon completed their occupation of Czechoslovakia. The nation's sovereignty was to have been guaranteed under the terms of the Munich Agreement by Great Britain, France and Germany. Germany broke her guarantee. Great Britain and France both failed to honour theirs. Chamberlain explained that because Czechoslovakia had become fragmented by the political upheavals, the composite state no longer existed and neither therefore did the guarantees. Thus were legal niceties pressed into service.

This time, Hitler's triumph carried with it more than the seeds of his own destruction. His first occupation of non-Germanic territory had a most profound effect on world and, in particular, British public opinion. In the latter case, the political fall-out was dramatic. For the first time it was seen that Hitler's ambitions were not limited to the absorption of German nationals into the Reich. The acquisition of territories belonging to other national states was a very different proposition, and potentially dangerous.[12] Readers of *Mein Kampf* would of course, have known what was going on, but these seem to have been very few outside Germany. The watching world recorded deep shock. The occupation of Prague signalled the end of Great Britain's tolerance and the end of Chamberlain's policy of appeasement. The public mood in Great Britain changed overnight and the Churchill perspective took over.

Churchill had always taken the view that Hitler had been preparing for war ever since 1933 and that war was inevitable. Whether Hitler turned to the West or East was irrelevant. He was a dangerous loose cannon and sooner or later his adventures would affect British interests. He therefore needed to be stopped in his tracks. On all counts he could not be trusted. It was a simple, direct view and it was being borne out by the facts then becoming apparent. Churchill had propounded his message for years while in political isolation. It now swept the board. Even the Government caught the mood.[13] Suddenly

---

[12]Even after the absorption of Czechoslovakia, none of Hitler's acquisitions lay beyond the boundaries of the 1914 Hungarian-German Empire.

[13]But there was no move to bring Churchill into the government. Thus did party politics override national considerations.

Great Britain was spraying out pacts of mutual assistance like handbills to potentially endangered countries in Eastern Europe. Poland, Romania and Greece were all grateful recipients. Within sixteen days of Hitler entering Prague, Chamberlain was warning Hitler off Poland in the most solemn tones. On March 31, 1939, in the House of Commons, he pledged 'all support in our power' against any action 'which clearly threatened Polish independence.'

This was a new Chamberlain. It was as if the public mood had engulfed him, that his personal disillusionment and humiliation at the hands of Hitler had led him to abandon whatever view he had originally held as to how to deal with Hitler's aspirations. As a result, German agitation for the return of Danzig and the Polish Corridor to the Reich, which was set in train in early 1939, was met not by concession and appeasement but by a brick wall. Hitler had, of course, always known that sooner or later, and in particular when he drove to the East, he would find himself involved in armed conflict. He was ready for that and he had spent years preparing for it. But he was not prepared for a war on two fronts. The failure of Hitler's foreign policy towards Great Britain had come home to roost. With the Western democracies standing firm the eastern adventure would have to be deferred until the threat from the West had been resolved.

Thus arose the diplomatic coup of the year. On August 23, 1939, Nazi Germany and communist Russia signed a non-aggression pact. It is difficult to imagine a more cynical piece of diplomacy. Overnight, the great ideological enemies became friends. Of course, both contracting parties gained short-term advantages. Germany gained time to deal with her problem in the West. Russia gained time to complete her preparations for the German onslaught she must have guessed would come. The arranged truce lasted from August 1939 to June 1941. By secret protocol to the treaty, Poland was partitioned between the contracting parties even before it was invaded.[14] It must have been comforting to them both to know that when eventually they came to grips the initial stages of conflict would be fought on neither party's national territory.

Having obtained Russian collusion on the proposed attack on Poland, German troops crossed the Polish order on September 1. Two days later, both Great Britain and France declared war. The absorption of Germans in Danzig and the Polish Corridor, following in the wake of the invasion, marked the successful conclusion of Hitler's policy

---

[14]When Russia invaded Poland there was no declaration of war on her by Great Britain.

objective of bringing all Germans into the one Reich.[15] But Hitler now found himself at war, not with Russia as planned, but with the Western democracies. His thinking on this new problem was clearly expressed in a conversation he had on August 11, 1939, with Carl J. Burckhardt, the League of Nations Commissioner for Danzig. 'Everything I undertake is directed against Russia. If the West is too stupid and too blind to understand that, I will first smash the West and then turn all my concentrated strength on the Soviet Union.'[16] And of course, that is what he did, or tried to do. He 'smashed' France but he failed to 'smash' Great Britain before turning his 'concentrated strength' against the Soviet Union in June 1941. Until then, he was tortured by the dilemma presented by Great Britain, an unwanted, unnecessary but nevertheless tenacious adversary.

Hitler had only one ambition as far as Great Britain was concerned and that was to grasp her hand in friendship. His view did not change with the declaration of war: he still hoped that Great Britain would see the error of her ways and come to terms with the fact that German ambitions lay exclusively to the East. As a result, his plans to deal with the West oscillated wildly between the extremes of launching peace overtures and the commitment to 'smashing' the West. Even when the military option was eventually sprung, in April/May 1940, Hitler's prosecution of the war against Great Britain was less than vigorous and certain punches were deliberately pulled.[17]

What then was the nature of Hitler's dilemma about Great Britain? His impressions had always been dominated by the glories and power of Great Britain's illustrious past and his personal experiences of the British 'Tommy' in the trenches of 1914. But were these impressions of the British character still valid in September 1939? Was Great Britain still strong enough to take up arms to thwart German ambitions? Were there really serious grounds for Hitler's hopes for an early peace?

---

[15]Earlier in that year 150,000 Germans in and around the Baltic port of Memel had greeted their Führer's annexation of the district and absorption into the Reich. Hitler's visit to the port on the pocket battleship *Deutschland* was his one and only sea voyage.

[16]Carl J. Burckhardt, *Meine Danziger Mission, 1937–1939*, 348.

[17]When issuing orders to his army commanders before the French campaign of 1940, Hitler made it clear that 'smashing the West' did not include destroying Great Britain. Late in that campaign Hitler himself issued a stop order to prevent German armour surrounding British forces prior to the Dunkirk evacuation. See chapter ten.

8

Great Britain and the British

We have got most of the world already, or the best part of it, and we only want to keep what we have got and prevent others taking it away from us.

FIRST SEA LORD, ADMIRAL CHATFIELD

A familiar sight in the classrooms of millions of British school children during the 1930s was a wall map of the world daubed with generous splashes of red. The daubs covered almost one quarter of the world's surface and embraced some 450 million people. It was truly said that the sun never set on the British Empire. Serviced by the British mercantile marine and Royal Navy, this remarkable disposition of power and influence had been built up over centuries of imperial enterprise by an island race of less than 50 million people. Those same British school children would also be taught how the Empire was won and they would venerate the national heroes. Sir Walter Raleigh, Sir Francis Drake, Clive of India, Cook of Australia, Nelson of the Nile and Wellington of Waterloo dominated the history books of the 10-year-olds. They were told that the early British explorers and adventurers had brought civilisation, Christian beliefs, education, medicines and hygiene to the native populations. Commercial exploitation was seldom mentioned.

It was not until the 10-year-olds had grown to adulthood that they realised that commercial exploitation had been, if not the original inspiration, then the main thrust of the subsequent colonisations. Of course, what was good and splendid and glorious and illustrious to the British was not looked on in the same light by others. In September 1939 Adolf Hitler was still expressing open admiration for the British Empire. It was no bar to his own ambitions, which lay in a different direction to imperial competition. But there were other nations with powerful commercial interests, particularly the relatively new trading nations like the

USA and Japan. They cast envious eyes on the British Empire and its control of so much of the world's resources[1] and markets.

There were also those with their own imperial ambitions, like the Italian dictator, Benito Mussolini. He deeply resented the control of the Royal Navy of the Mediterranean Sea, deemed Mussolini's *Mare Nostrum*, and the stranglehold exercised by the British over Italian aspirations in Africa. Nevertheless, liked or disliked, admired or envied, the British Empire still dominated the world wall maps on September 3, 1939. The splashes of red were the hallmark of conspicuous past endeavour and Hitler was well aware of the stinging rebuff handed out to Kaiser Wilhelm's Germany in the 1914–18 war. Germany had then thought fit to compete with and eventually confront Great Britain and her Empire on the issue of world resources and markets. She had received a bloody nose as a result. Was Hitler to suffer the fate as his predecessor?

But if the British Empire was still in being on September 3, 1939, and still adorning the wall maps throughout the world, it was far from alive and well. As with commercial enterprises, so with nations. Where the great swings of history bring the inevitable ebb and flow to the affairs of mankind, a nation can dominate for years in terms of influence on the basis of past reputation rather than present performance.[2] Such was the case with Great Britain. By September 1939 Great Britain and her Empire were, in comparative terms, in serious economic and financial decline. A deteriorating position, first apparent late in the 19th century, had continued its relentless downward trend ever since. In 1880 Great Britain was responsible for 23 per cent of the world's manufacturing output. The USA share was 15 per cent and Germany's 8 per cent. By 1900 the USA had overtaken Great Britain. By 1913 Germany had too. The percentages then were Great Britain 13 per cent, USA 32 per cent, Germany 15 per cent. In 1890 Great Britain's production of iron and steel were equal to that of the USA and twice that of Germany. By 1913 it was one quarter of US production and half that of Germany.

During the period running up to the 1914–18 war this rapid and consistent decline in industrial output was offset by earnings from 'invisibles' – insurance, banking and shipping services and the like.[3] There

---

[1]70 per cent of gold production, 100 per cent of rubber, 50 per cent of rice.

[2]In terms of commercial enterprises, F.W. Woolworth is perhaps the best example. This company traded for the best part of ten years during the 1950s and 1960s on the basis of its pre-war reputation before the public realised that the retailing expertise had been lost and the old values were not there.

[3]During the period of its earlier industrial strength London had become established as the financial centre of the world and had dispensed a wide variety of financial and commercial services to the international community.

was also considerable overseas income arising from investments made in the glory days.[4] The external budget was thus balanced and sterling was strong on the world markets. All that had changed with the advent of the 1914–18 war. Lacking the industrial strength to manufacture her own armament requirements, Great Britain had been obliged to turn to the industrial strength of the USA and import many of her requirements. By the spring of 1917 Great Britain's total gold and dollar reserves were down to $749 million and spending was at the rate of $80 million weekly. Financial disaster was averted only by the entry of the USA into the war and the victory in the next year. By that time London's position as the financial centre of the world had been badly battered. £1,365 million was owing to the USA in loans and the national debt stood at £7,435 million. Interest on the national debt took up 40 per cent of the Government's budget in 1920 and continued to cripple government finances throughout the next two decades.

Meanwhile, industrial output continued to slump[5] and earnings from invisibles, now stripped of a great deal of the overseas investment income, were insufficient to make good the shortfall. The balance of trade moved into the red and stayed there. These difficulties were compounded by the initiation of a policy of modest rearmament in the mid-1930s, albeit reluctantly and in the knowledge that it could not be afforded. The programme again emphasised the inability of British industry to manufacture its own weaponry. Thirty per cent of all special steels had to be imported from the USA. Armoured plates for warships had to be imported from Czechoslovakia. Over half of the required machine tools essential to modern engineering production, had to be imported from wherever they were available. They included, from the USA the specialist machine tools required for the manufacture of the Merlin engines for Spitfires.

The effect of these essential imports on the external financial position was dramatic. Imports increased by over 400 per cent between 1935 and 1937. In March 1938, gold and dollar reserves stood at £825 million. By March 1939 they were £600 million and by June 1939 they were £500 million. Foreign securities in the order of £200 million could be sold if necessary to augment these resources. Even so, it was apparent that unless credit could be arranged, available resources

---

[4]In 1939 overseas investments totalled £4 billion, representing 43 per cent of the world total. Ponting, Clive, *1940: Myth and Reality*, Hamish Hamilton (1990), 14.

[5]By the late 1930s Great Britain's share of the world manufacturing output was only one-third that of the USA. In terms of world trade, whereas in 1913 Great Britain's share was 14 per cent, by 1937 it was less than 10 per cent. British shipbuilding was only 7 per cent of its 1913 level, textile production only a third of its 1920 level, steel production was down 45 per cent and coal production 20 per cent on 1920 levels (*Ibid*, 20).

would soon run out if the scale of armament imports from the USA was to be maintained, let alone increased.

It was against this background of acute financial and economic impoverishment that strategic matters had to be considered. One of the basic problems was that in 1939, unlike in 1914, Great Britain and her Empire had too many potential enemies and rivals and too few allies and friends. Her one ally, France, was a broken reed. She had lost nearly three million dead and wounded in the 1914–18 conflict, representing one quarter of all her male adults under the age of 30. Her spirit had been badly buckled, if not broken. She had no heart for further warfare. She lacked both manpower and industrial power. The British were not helped either by the policy of isolation taken up by a potential ally, the USA. She divorced herself from European affairs and concentrated on a hardly concealed ambition to replace Great Britain and her Empire as the front runner in world trade. Her refusal to join the League of Nations virtually ensured the impotence of that institution.

The USA also used her creditor relationship with Great Britain to good effect at the Washington conference of naval powers in 1922. She was granted naval parity with Great Britain and a five-to-three superiority over the Japanese in major warships. Perhaps more importantly in terms of British strategy, she insisted that the Anglo-Japanese naval alliance in being since 1902, should not be renewed. During the 1914–18 war the Japanese navy had controlled Far Eastern waters and the Indian Ocean. It had lent valuable protection to Australasia and British Pacific possessions. No longer an ally, she soon became one of Great Britain's potential enemies. She cast envious eyes on British control of raw materials on her doorstep and over an area where sea routes could be controlled by her own navy in the event of conflict. Thus did American policy work against British interests.

In the late summer of 1938 the British Chiefs of Staff reported to the Committee of Imperial Defence. They made two recommendations. In the short term Great Britain was not in a position to go to war with Germany because the rearmament programme was not yet far enough advanced. In the long term, Great Britain might find herself in conflict on three fronts and she would only be in a position to wage war with the support of powerful allies. The three fronts in mind were Germany, Italy and Japan.[6]

The Service Chiefs' opinions were well founded. In 1938 Great Britain had five squadrons of Hurricanes and one squadron of

[6]This projection became a reality in December 1941, but by then Great Britain had acquired two powerful allies, Russia and the USA.

Spitfires. The Hurricanes had no heating mechanism for the guns. They could not fly higher than 15,000 feet. These meagre fighter resources would be matched against more than 1,000 German bombers and an equivalent number of fast modern fighters. The British bomber force was obsolete and could not be replaced before 1941 or 1942. There were no ground defences. None of the proposed 3.7 inch and 4.5 inch anti-aircraft guns were yet in production. Only 1,430 searchlights out of a required 4,128 had been delivered, along with 140 barrage balloons out of a required 450. Radar protection covered only the Thames Estuary. Civil defence had become bogged down in an argument between the Treasury and the local authorities as to who was to foot the bill.

Such were the deliberations at the heart of the British Empire at a time of national crisis. This chronic state of unpreparedness for war and the attendant financial impoverishment, the one apparently dependent upon the other, were not phenomena new to the late 1930s. They had prevailed throughout the two decades since the 1914–18 war. In spite of the dangers inherent in that position and the advice given by the Chiefs of Staff, no attempt was made until late 1939 to recruit any powerful allies to lend weight to Great Britain's cause and to increase her military muscle. Only when war with Germany appeared to be imminent was an attempt made to recruit Russia as an ally. The French were enthusiastic. Neville Chamberlain was less so. He had long since resisted any attempt to bring Russia (or, for that matter, the USA) into the European picture, preferring to handle the German and Italian dictators on a personal basis. The overture to Russia when made was too late, too slow, too half-hearted and too amateurish. It deserved to fail and did. Instead, the British woke up the fact that Germany had themselves recruited the targeted ally, at least on a temporary basis.

Nevertheless, in spite of all these difficulties and apparent inadequacies, at 11 a.m. on Sunday, September 3, 1939, Neville Chamberlain, the British Prime Minister, declared war on Germany. Hitler was shocked and disappointed. He was shocked because his Foreign Minister, Joachim von Ribbentrop, had assured him that the British would not fight. He was disappointed because he had absolutely no wish to be involved in a war with Great Britain.

Why then did Neville Chamberlain take the decision that he did? The immediate and simple answer is that he was obligated so to do under the terms of the Anglo-French guarantee of Poland's integrity and independence. The guarantee had been first given on March 31, 1939, and since then, embodied in a formal treaty. German troops had invaded Poland at dawn two days previously. But this merely moves the question back one step. Why had Great Britain chosen to bind herself in that manner to the possibility, indeed probability, of war? On September 27, 1938, at the height of the Czech crisis, Chamberlain had said 'How horrible, fantastic, incredible it is that we should be digging ditches and trying on gas masks because of a quarrel in a faraway country between people of whom we know nothing.' That was a very relevant comment. One year later the British people to whom Chamberlain was responsible were entitled to know why they were then committed to war because of another quarrel in another faraway country, between some more people of whom they knew nothing. Chamberlain's decision to go to war led eventually to the deaths of over 400,000 of the people of Great Britain and her Empire.[7] That is an awesome consequence. It is therefore not unreasonable to examine the reasons and adjudge the wisdom of Chamberlain's decision to intervene in what appeared to be a dispute between Germany and Poland and them alone.[8]

The stated reason for Great Britain's intervention was to safeguard the integrity and independence of Poland. If so, then Great Britain's motives were purely altruistic. Certainly, British propaganda both during and since the war has sought to promote this moral concept. But this motive is largely discounted by two subsequent events. In a matter of weeks, Russian troops also invaded Poland. According to the terms of the Anglo-French guarantee to Poland both parties should have declared war against Russia. They did not. In 1945, when the war was 'won', Poland's integrity and independence, for which the war had apparently been fought, was not restored and Great Britain made no representations to that end. There must have been another and more politically motivated reason for the Chamberlain guarantees. He may have thought that by their extension he could thwart Hitler's plans for further expansion which he considered to be a threat to British interests. This would represent Chamberlain's rather late conversion to the Churchill perspective.

That Chamberlain believed this by September 1939 there is little doubt. In a private letter to Lord Darnley[9] on February 19, 1940, Chamberlain wrote: 'In my view the history of the last few years proves beyond all doubt that Germany has set before herself a programme of aggression and expansion and just as the *Anschluss* was

---

[7]The war eventually escalated to one on a global scale. Total deaths were in the order of 45 million, two-thirds of which were civilian deaths.

[8]Although the German/Polish dispute was apparently over Danzig and the Polish Corridor, which was a problem rooted in Versailles, the real purpose of the German invasion of Poland was to provide a springboard for the attack on Russia. This was foreshadowed in *Mein Kampf*. It became a reality in June 1941.

[9]Darnley was a leading peace activist.

followed by the seizure of Czechoslovakia, and by the invasion of Poland so in due time France would have been assailed and the British Empire attacked.[10] This view, which has been ratified by popular British belief ever since, was originally propounded by Churchill while in the political wilderness and swept the board when German troops entered Prague. If true, it is a sufficient, and indeed praiseworthy, reason for British intervention.

This view, however, seems to depend for its validity on an important assumption. There is no doubt that Chamberlain's interpretation of the history of the 1930s is correct. Hitler's Germany did have a programme of aggression and expansion, and the content of *Mein Kampf* as well as the events of the 1930s fully supports that view. But the same *Mein Kampf* is quite specific as to the purpose and direction of such aggression and expansion. It was to ensure that all Germans were accommodated in the one Reich, to acquire territory in the East for more *Lebensraum* for the German people and to invade and destroy communist Russia. Nowhere in *Mein Kampf* or in any of Hitler's public pronouncements or private conversations, is there any suggestion that his intention was to attack Great Britain or her Empire.

Why then did Chamberlain make his assumption as to the ultimate effect of Hitler's programme of aggression and expansion? One might suggest that Chamberlain (and indeed millions who have subscribed to the view since) had never read *Mein Kampf*. He therefore did not know what Hitler's stated policy objectives were and, adding together the events of the 1930s, he came to a wrong conclusion. Alternatively, he might reasonably have assumed that Hitler's stated objectives were an irrelevance because the man had so often broken his word. However, Hitler had freely admitted that, whereas he would never break his word on a private issue, he would break it 'a thousand times' if necessary in the service of Germany's cause.[11] And he did. It is true that Hitler was guilty of tactical lying over and over again in his negotiations with others. But it is equally true that as to his strategic policy objectives as expressed in *Mein Kampf* he remained constant and true to the day he died (upon which occasion he reiterated yet again and for the last time that he had never wanted war with Great Britain).

But let it be assumed that Chamberlain (and others) were correct in their assumptions. Perhaps Hitler intended at some stage to reverse the plans set out in *Mein Kampf* and attack not Russia, the living embodiment of the communism he hated, but Great Britain, a nation he is said to have admired and respected and wanted as a friend. In such

---

[10]PRO PREM/143.
[11]Churchill expressed similar sentiments as far as Great Britain was concerned.

circumstances, it would be prudent for Great Britain, before making any decision to go to war to pre-empt such an attack,[12] to assess the state of the country's preparedness for war compared with that of the proposed enemy, particularly when war was being contemplated without the support of powerful allies. Surely before a war is declared there ought to be in terms of accountability to the nation's citizens some confidence that it can be waged successfully?

In 1933 the Versailles provisions had been breached by Germany in the matter of disarmament. In 1935 and 1936 they had been breached in the matter of the Rhineland and the proposed build-up of the army. By then, Hitler's aggression and expansionist plans had been well signalled. Armed intervention during those early days would have brought Germany to heel and Hitler to his downfall. Dictators cannot accommodate humiliation and defeat. The balance of power in terms of armed preparedness at that time lay heavily in favour of the Western Allies.[13] But the position at September 3, 1939, was very different. All the evidence then available suggested that the balance of power had swung very much to Germany's advantage. In fact, there was no reasonable case for suggesting that Great Britain could wage war successfully against Germany even if, in terms of logic or morality, she felt obliged to make the pre-emptive strike she did.

Germany had been preparing for war since Hitler's assumed power in 1933, and by September 1939 she stood possessed of the most powerful armed forces in Europe and probably the world. If British Intelligence did not know that, then it should have. And if Chamberlain thought that there were millions of 'good' Germans who were ready to overthrow Hitler at the drop of a hat (as apparently he did) then he was guilty of the most naive wishful thinking. On the other hand, Great Britain was almost totally unprepared for war. The one year respite provided by the Munich Agreement had been used to bring her air defences into some sort of order. But she had neither the industrial capacity or the financial strength (in terms of funding imports essential to the arms industry) to match German production. She just did not have the means to bring her armed forces to the required standard of readiness, either as to quantity or quality. There were some grounds for confidence in the matter of defence, through the Royal Navy's command of the seas and the build-up of RAF Fighter Command.[14] There were absolutely none as regards offensive operations.

---

[12]Which is what Chamberlain's declaration of war amounted to.

[13]Churchill's comments in this connection were entirely valid.

[14]In the event, although coming under severe pressure during the ensuing hostilities, they both remained undefeated.

The British Army at the time was totally inadequate in numbers. It could promise just two divisions for operations in France. They were poorly trained, ill equipped and, with one or two exceptions, led by officers whose military thinking was still anchored in the trenches of the 1914–18 war.[15] RAF Strategic Bomber Command was equipped throughout with obsolete machines.[16] The great strategic weapon of the naval blockade, so effective in the First World War, was a non-starter in 1939. Schacht and Goering had seen to that. Germany was almost self-sufficient and not dependent upon imports by sea.

The only hope that Great Britain had of conducting a successful war with Germany in 1939 was to enlist the support of powerful allies.[17] In September 1939 she had none. France was an ally, but she was a broken reed. British Intelligence was well aware of the state of the French nation and the state of the French Armed Forces. The French Navy had some good fighting ships and men to go with them. The French too had an air force that was almost entirely obsolete; and its army wanted only to sit in peace behind the Maginot Line, hoping and praying that the Germans would not attack them through the low countries – which of course they did.

On September 3, 1939, Neville Chamberlain committed Great Britain, devoid of powerful allies, to a conflict for which she was almost totally unprepared, against an adversary with the strongest armed forces in Europe if not the world, for a reason contradicted by everything which the adversary had said and done since his accession to power. The decision rested on no rational basis. Rather does it seem to have arisen as a consequence of Chamberlain's misconception as to his role in European affairs. Although his appeasement policies had failed, they were designed to bring about a general settlement of European affairs, and there is no indication that Chamberlain felt that he lacked the authority to take up such a centre stage position in European affairs. After all, there was a long-standing tradition of Britain concerning itself with these affairs, with British interests very much in mind.

Great Britain's assumption of the position as some sort of custodian trustee of European affairs conformed with her position as a Great Power, with all the strength, command and authority that the status implied. But by September 1939 her domestic economy and industrial

---

[15]These inadequacies were to become apparent during the early engagements in Norway and Flanders.

[16]The Wellington bomber was a possible exception.

[17]Churchill knew this. When he took office in May 1940 he assiduously wooed and eventually won over the USA to his cause.

base, her international financial position and her military unpreparedness were such that she no longer possessed those qualities. At the same time she retained all the trappings of power. Her ongoing reputation, her great traditions, her glorious pageantry, her innate instincts of superiority, her disdainful aristocracy, all still told the world, including Adolf Hitler, that she was still a Great Power. In that capacity she had a right, a duty and obligation still to sit in on, and if need be settle, the affairs of Europe.

This was the fatal misconception which by September 3, 1939, had led Chamberlain into a position where he had placed Great Britain's head on the block without the necessary clout to retrieve the situation. He had conducted the policies of a Great Power without economic, financial or military muscle. His policies of appeasement had sought to replace these with moral muscle. The British people were about to pay the price. In the event, the Royal Navy, RAF Fighter Command, 26 miles of water and the recruitment of powerful allies saved her from what would have been a self-inflicted disaster.

There was of course another option open to the British during the 1930s. It does not appear to have had much of an airing. Perhaps that is because it flies in the face of British accepted wisdom as to the rightness of the war against Hitler. It does however rest on a rational basis and may well have been the ultimate objective of Chamberlain's appeasement policy.[18] There is plenty of evidence to show that German aggressive intent would be directed exclusively to the East, and in particular against Russia. Why then could a view not be taken and a policy adopted based upon that statement of intent? Such a policy would be a policy of neutrality.

An analogous position had already arisen. In the 1930s Japan became involved in a war on the mainland of China. The interests of the USA in the Far East were not thereby directly threatened. But the attack signalled Japanese aggressive instincts and expansionist plans. That may well have represented a potential threat to American interests. The USA did not intervene in the Sino-Japanese dispute but retained a position of watchful neutrality. She then concentrated on

---

[18]There is no doubt that Chamberlain was propelled towards war by a powerful groundswell of British public opinion which had prevailed ever since German troops had occupied Prague. The new mood called for confrontation rather than appeasement of Hitler's further demands. This public mood was ignorant of Great Britain's economic, financial and military weaknesses. Chamberlain himself probably took the same view, following the personal disappointments and humiliation which he had suffered at the hands of Hitler. He would be less than human if not embittered by his experience. Nevertheless, prior to Prague he had worked assiduously at appeasing Hitler and avoiding war in the West. Even when pushed into the position of having to declare war (by both Parliamentary and public pressure) he hesitated to the very last moment.

building up her industrial base and arms production. When war with Japan eventually came ten years later, American industrial capacity proved to be the dominant factor in the defeat of Japan.

British European policy during the 1930s could have been similarly constructed, always assuming that the Churchillian option to strangle Hitler's Germany at birth or shortly thereafter was not taken. In all the circumstances, and most particularly those relating to Great Britain's internal and external weaknesses a policy of watchful neutrality would surely have been preferable to one of interference and commitment. Attempts could then have been made, if need be on Great Britain's initiative, to have German aspirations tabled, discussed and if need be, circumvented by truly international agreement and pressure. Great Britain would have avoided acting on her own and taking all the risk. If these measures had proved impossible to implement, and had Germany then proceeded with her eastern adventure, as she did, and fallen upon Russia, as she did, then that would have been regrettable. But Great Britain would have incurred no commitment to war.

As has already been pointed out, there were many in Great Britain, especially among the Establishment, who thought that Russian Communism was a greater threat to Great Britain's ordered existence than German Nazism. There were others who felt that a long and exhausting war between Communism and Nazism[19] would rid the world of two distasteful ideologies and bring nothing but benefit to Great Britain and the whole Western world. If a German drive eastwards had been promised, why not adopt a 'wait and see' policy to see if it would happen? If that encouraged the event, so be it. Neutrality plus awareness would have afforded the opportunity for Great Britain to restore her industrial base and quietly build up her defensive armaments. That would require firm political leadership and a British public who were given the facts and responded accordingly. If Hitler's drive to the east was in progress, that would provide the necessary incentive to take the required steps.

There is an added refinement. During the late 1930s, two refugee German scientists, Otto Frisch and Rudolf Peierls, completed experiments which suggested that an atomic bomb was a theoretical possibility. By September 1939 this possibility was being taken further in concentrated work both as to the physical and chemical aspects of the project at Birmingham University in England where Peierls was professor of physics. This further work was eventually to blossom into

[19]The received wisdom in both Germany and Great Britain was that the German campaign in Russia would be neither long or exhausting. It would all be over in six weeks. In the event, it was very long, very exhausting and brought warfare to new levels of ferocity and barbarity.

full-scale research work, leading ultimately to the production of the first atomic bomb. The Germans carried out very little similar research. The implications are apparent. By adopting a policy of watchful neutrality Great Britain could have worked quietly on the development of the ultimate deterrent.

Instead, perhaps the bitterest pill that had to be swallowed by Great Britain after the declaration of war, was that the results of her research work in connection with the atomic bomb eventually had to be shipped across the Atlantic to the USA under the lend/lease arrangements, in part payment for the armaments supplied by the USA to make good British deficiencies at a time of self-induced national peril.

PART THREE

1939–41: THE RELUCTANT WAR

9

The Phoney War and early peace moves

War is the greatest of all stimulants.

WINSTON S. CHURCHILL

Neville Chamberlain's declaration of war against Germany was made by radio broadcast. The tone of his voice was flat, dull and uninspiring. He seemed to view the event more as a personal disappointment than a national crisis. 'Everything that I have worked for, everything that I have hoped for, everything that I have believed in during my public life, has crashed into ruins.' He sounded and was a broken man. He was quite unfitted to lead the British nation into war.[1]

The declaration came after more than two days' delay, occasioned by a chronic lack of resolution on the part of both the Western Allies. The issue was clear cut. German troops had invaded Poland at dawn on Friday, September 1. The Anglo-French guarantees called for immediate declaration of war. But for two days nothing happened. France pleaded that she needed two days to complete her mobilisation before there was any threat of aerial bombardment. Chamberlain clutched at straws offered by the intervention of Mussolini who suggested an international conference,[2] but the public and parliamentary mood was against him. In the Commons on the Saturday there was a scathing denunciation of the Government's lack of resolution. To cries of 'Speak for England' addressed by Arthur Sinclair, the Deputy

---

[1]Chamberlain's lack of enthusiasm as a war leader is illustrated in a letter to his sister dated September 10, 1939. 'While war was still averted I felt I was indispensable, for no one could carry out my policy. Half a dozen people could now take my place while war is in progress and I do not see that I have any particular part to play until it comes to discussing peace terms and that may be a very long way off.'

[2]Mussolini was very good at calling for last-minute international conferences. He had done so at the time of the Czech crisis and he now repeated the process. It confirmed his position as a leading European statesman, which was a very pleasing and important matter to him.

Leader of the Labour Party (standing in for Clement Atlee who was ill), the assembly broke up in some disorder. Some members, including the young Harold Macmillan, rendered a version of 'Rule Britannia.'

Chamberlain was stunned. For so long he had dominated the compliant occupants of the Government benches and had dragged members by their ears along the path of his appeasement policies. All that was now dead. He probably realised then that he was no longer in touch with the mood of the people and that his days in office were numbered. Neither Lord Halifax or 'Rab' Butler, his understudy at the Foreign Office, drew that inference. They described the proceedings in the Commons as 'intolerable' and 'disgraceful'. In the words of Halifax, not one of the world's greatest parliamentarians, 'It showed democratic assemblies at their worst.' He thought that the Prime Minister 'had the temper of an archangel to put up with it.'[3]

After the Commons revolt there came a Cabinet revolt led by Sir John Simon, the Chancellor of the Exchequer. It was this that led eventually to the ultimatum put to the Germans at 9 a.m. on Sunday, September 3, expiring two hours later. It called for the withdrawal of all German troops from Poland. No reply was received. Chamberlain accordingly declared war shortly after the hour of 11 a.m. Similar declarations came from the Dominions. Only in South Africa was there serious debate about following Great Britain's lead. Hertzog, the Prime Minister, stepped down and Smuts took over and led the country into war on a vote of 80 to 67 in his Parliament. Eire remained neutral, as expected. France followed Great Britain into the war at 5 p.m. on the Sunday.

Thus began the 1939–45 war. Initially it was almost a parochial affair between Germany and the Western Allies, Great Britain and France. Poland was out of the picture in 25 days. On the fourteenth day Russian troops crossed the Polish border and took over those territories designated to them in the secret protocol attached to the Russo-German pact of the previous month. There was no declaration of war against this additional aggressor by either Great Britain or France. The Polish campaign provided a brilliant exposition by the Germans of the new style *blitzkrieg* method of warfare. It had little or no effect upon Anglo-French military thinking.

The Anglo-French plans to wage and win any war against Germany were drawn up in 1938. There were two strategic objectives. The

---

[3]Neville Chamberlain papers, September 10, 1939. There was no similar demonstration in favour of a declaration of war in the House of Lords, probably because a substantial number of members thought that there ought not to be one.

French army was to play a defensive role. It was to act as a deterrent to any German frontal attack which would founder against the fortifications of the Maginot Line. In the meantime, the British naval blockade would starve Germany of essential supplies of raw materials and foodstuffs. Germany would then realise she could not win the war. Internal economic and political difficulties would arise. They would lead to a coup and the end of Hitler and Hitlerism. A moderate German Government would then be granted generous peace terms. Chamberlain's advisers at the Ministry of Economic Warfare assured him that the British blockade would bring about this desirable state of affairs as soon as Germany ran out of oil. Industry and the war machine would then grind to a halt.[4]

An interesting insight into the equivocal nature of Chamberlain's ultimate aims is provided by a memorandum dated October 13, 1939, prepared by Chamberlain's private secretary, Arthur Rucker, presumably with Chamberlain's approval. It is a truly revealing document.

> Communism is a greater danger than Nazi Germany. It is a plague that does not stop at national boundaries and with the advance of the Soviet Union into Poland, the eastern European countries would find themselves exposed to that danger. What is needed is a moderate conservative reaction in Germany and the overthrow of the present regime by Army Chiefs.[5]

The defensive role allocated to the French army in the 1938 strategic decisions ruled out any possibility of its taking offensive action to assist the Poles. Such offensive action is specifically mentioned in the terms of the Franco-Polish military convention of May 19, 1939. 'As soon as the principal German effort develops against Poland, France will launch an offensive action against Germany with the bulk of her forces.' In other words, France was contracting to do something which in strategic terms she knew she would not do. Such was the integrity of the French diplomacy in the 1930s. In the event, French troops sat behind the Maginot Line and did nothing while German troops poured into Poland.

In any case, the French army was rotten to the core. It was incapable of adapting an effective role, offensive or defensive, in the event of war with Germany. This position was known to the British, or at least

---

[4]These plans were expressed in Chamberlain's letter to his sister of September 10, 1939. 'What I hope for is not a military victory. I very much doubt the feasibility of that, but a collapse of the German Home Front. For that to happen it is necessary to convince the Germans they cannot win.'
[5]The Colville diaries, 40–41.

to British Intelligence, within four months of the declaration of war. In early 1940, the French General, Charles Brecard, had presented an alarming report to his superiors suggesting that the French army was incapable of withstanding a German attack in strength. Kenneth de Courcy of British Intelligence, who was instructed by 'senior members of the British Government' to ascertain the strength of Brecard's report, interviewed many military and other personnel and concluded that Brecard's fears were well founded.[6]

Moreover, events in Poland had shown that French expectations that the Germans would be unable to break through or turn the fixed defences of the Maginot Line were based upon 1914–18 battle experiences which were now completely overtaken by the *blitzkrieg* concept of warfare. Thirty-five Polish divisions had been crushed or captured within the space of six weeks. Fixed lines of defence (such as the Maginot Line) were proved to be useless against attacks by concentrated armour operating on a narrow front supported by massed divebombers spreading noise, fire, confusion and panic. The lesson was not learnt, however. After the conclusion of the Polish campaign Sam Hoare was giving assurances that the German victory had nothing to do with the *blitzkrieg* methods and everything to do with Polish 'lack of communications'. What had happened in Poland would not happen in the West.[7]

If on September 3, 1939, the French army and its military thinking were suspect, the French nation itself was even more so. The French Prime Minister, Bonnet, was a defeatist. Early reports were that he had retained contact with Mussolini as a possible peace mediator. On October 2, 1939, the Italian Ambassador in Paris was reporting that the majority of the French Cabinet were in favour of a peace conference and that Marshal Pétain would play a large part.[8] The British Foreign Office were aware of these defeatist tendencies. They worked hard to get rid of Bonnet. Eventually they succeeded. Edouard Daladier of the French 'war party' took over. But Daladier faced opposition to the war from opposite ends of the political spectrum. He commented thus on right wing peace sympathisers: 'I have opened the abscess but it was so deep that the scalpel disappeared down it and had I gone on, my arm would have followed.'[9]

At the other end of the scale the Communist Party in France, unlike

---

[6]Brecard's opinion and de Courcy's confirmation were of course, fully validated by events.
[7]Letter to Lothian, September 25, 1939.
[8]DGFP VII, 197–98 and 414.
[9]'Better Hitler than Blum' was the cry of the French businessmen. Blum was the President of the hated Popular Front Government of the Left.

Great Britain, was strong, vociferous and anti-war. The war was a capitalist war. It had nothing to do with the ordinary French worker. The party propagated these views vigorously. Inroads were made into both the military and civil services, with consequent effect upon morale and national spirit. There was yet another factor. The British allies were distrusted and their commitment to the war questioned. The British sent only two divisions of troops to fight alongside the French. They had also failed to respond to a French call for half-a-million industrial workers to be exported to France from the British pool of unemployed so as to fill the vacancies in the undermanned French war industries.[10] The French felt isolated, let down and very vulnerable.[11]

The other major peg upon which the Anglo-French war policies were hinged was the British naval blockade. Much was expected of this in view of its success in the 1914–18 conflict. In the event it was almost totally ineffective. Again, the thinking upon which it was based was out of date. In the first place the new Germany had learned the lesson from the old. In her preparations since 1933 she had adopted policies under Schacht and later under Goering of making Germany economically self-sufficient which proved outstandingly successful. But there was another factor. Under the terms of the Russo-German pact of August 1939 Germany was assured of all her essential imports including wheat from the Ukraine and oil from the Caucasus. Russian ports in the Arctic, Black Sea and even the Pacific were also made available to service German imports.[12] Italy and Spain as fellow Fascist states also helped with German supply problems.

Chamberlain's faith in the effectiveness of a naval blockade of the Western sea approaches was thus seriously divorced from the facts, matched only by his belief in the political unrest leading to the coup that would overthrow Hitler. He seemed to think that Germany of 1939 comprised a group of gangsters (his word) presiding over a vast majority of 'good' Germans. These were kept in a state of unwilling subjection by the Gestapo. If a wedge could be driven between the 'bad' Germans and the 'good' Germans there would be a coup and the gangsters would be overthrown. Such thinking displayed a woeful ignorance of the German character and the true state of affairs.[13]

Unlike the British, to whom it would be an anathema, for a German

---

[10]Thompson, Laurence, *1940: Year of Legend, Year of History*, Collins Fontana (1968), 14.

[11]This resentment grew into bitterness as the tragic events of 1940 unfolded.

[12]The Arctic port of Teriberka, east of Murmansk, was also made available to German U-boats requiring refuelling and repair facilities.

[13]The irony is that in October 1939, in reply to an abusive speech by Ribbentrop, Chamberlain remarked: 'This tragedy of our time is that [the Germans] could not understand either the policies or character of the British people.'

life in a totalitarian state was a life of normality stemming from centuries of German history and tradition. Hitler had given the ordinary German worker a decent standard of living, full employment and a fair wage. The ordinary German businessman had been given the opportunity of earning good profits and expanding his activities. Hitler had also restored to all Germans their sense of national pride and self-esteem. He had strung together a whole list of quite outstanding diplomatic successes and brought all Germans into the one Reich. And he had now topped all that by an outstanding military success in Poland. Under the circumstances, it is hardly surprising that when the coup came, it was against Chamberlain not Hitler.

If the Franco-British war policies were shot through with holes they were better than Hitler's because he had none. His immediate war policy was therefore to bring it to an end. His eyes were fixed on the East and all his military hardware was tailored for that purpose. He had no long range bombers to attack Great Britain and no long range fighters to protect them. The production of U-boats, a major aim in this conflict with Great Britain, had never received any priority in the German rearmament programme. On September 3, 1939, Hitler could deploy just ten U-boats for active service in the Atlantic.[14] The war in the West was unwanted and unnecessary. Germany's war policies were therefore designed to get rid of it as quickly as possible.

Hitler knew that French resolution to pursue the war was less than total. Within days of the declaration of war, the German envoy in Luxembourg was reporting the receipt of French peace feelers. François Poncet and other French Ministers were known to be in touch with the German legation in Rome for the same purpose. On September 17, only fourteen days into the war, a courier from the Quai d'Orsay visited the German envoy, Radowitz. He reported that there were strong right-wing opposition forces pressing for an honourable way to peace.[15] Hitler accordingly resolved to detach France from her British ally and bring about a separate peace, without the need for armed intervention. As to Great Britain, he still clung to his long-established beliefs. Any plans he had for further territorial acquisitions did not affect either Great Britain or her Empire, and he would convince Great Britain that this was the case. But he would detach France first.

Hitler therefore launched a diplomatic peace offensive. A series of public speeches by member of the Nazi hierarchy followed. All

---

[14]Admiral Doenitz later stated that if the U-boat strength had been 300, which it should have been to wage war on Great Britain, 'the war would have been over by 1941.' (Speer, Albert, *Spandau, The Secret Diaries*, Macmillan, 1976, 120.)

[15]Martin, Bernard, *Friedensinitiativen und Machtpolitik im Zweiten Weltkrieg 1939–1942*, Droste Verlag, Dusseldorf (1974). Translation summary.

made the point that the war was unnecessary. All were directed in particular at France. In the meantime, the German armed forces were held on a very tight lead to give the peace offensive a chance of success. During the first month of the war both Hitler and Goering made important 'peace' speeches. Goering spoke to the staff of the Rheinmetall Sieg armament works in Berlin but with an international audience very much in mind. Goering had been especially selected for the job. He was popular, respected and reputedly a member of Hitler's team who had worked assiduously but without success in the pursuit of peace up to September 3. Hitler's speech followed on September 19.

The content of their speeches was almost identical. Both men congratulated the armed forces on their role in Poland. Both then drew the attention of their audience, and the whole world, to the unnecessary war in the West. Both made it clear that they held Chamberlain personally responsible. Finally, both stated that Germany was ready for a decent peace and confirmed that the French frontier was inviolate. The speeches were cleverly constructed. They were genuine gestures of peace. They also cleared Germany's position before the rest of the world and provided an alibi against what might lie ahead by way of military action. Hitler knew that the French were prepared to make concessions relating to German occupation of Polish territories. He therefore deliberately delayed the political and constitutional reconstruction of the subject Polish state. He would then accommodate French requirements in the event of peace.

The Franco-British reaction was not encouraging. The British said simply that Hitler's word could not be trusted. The French reshuffled their government and put Daladier and his war party in control in place of the defeatist Bonnet. These rebuffs caused Hitler to think for the first time, and then only tentatively, of perhaps bringing the war in the West to an end by military means rather than making peace overtures. A land offensive directed at France might knock her out of the war very quickly. The demise of France would then bring Great Britain to the peace table. He would then be able to resume his main strategy of attacking Russia. Great Britain would be a weakened but perhaps not unfriendly neutral in the war. Nevertheless, he did not hurry things. He continued to adopt a hands-off policy in terms of military operations. He was still anxious to give every opportunity for any seeds of peace to bed down and blossom. It was only during the last month or so of 1939 that the military option began to run as a serious parallel with the diplomatic peace offensive. In the new year it took over as a first priority. Even then, Hitler seemed anxious to keep open whatever channels of communication had been established, especially those with Great Britain.

The plain fact is that neither side was interested in fighting. Hitler thought that the longer he held back military operations the more chance there was that the Western Allies would realise that the Polish issue had been settled and there was no point in continuing the war. The Western Allies thought that the longer the military stalemate lasted the more chance there was that Hitler would realise the war could not be won: Hitler and Hitlerism would be deposed and peace would ensue.[16]

These aspirations had two extraordinary effects during the period between the outbreak of hostilities in September 1939 and the Norwegian campaign in April 1940. They introduced an element of farce into the proceedings: Armies of men, running into millions, who were supposed to be at war sat looking at each other across the Franco-German frontier, with hardly a shot fired in anger. Secondly, every so often, flurries of peace overtures were sent wafting around the neutral capital cities of Europe. These were spawned sometimes by the belligerents themselves, at others by heads of states, kings and queens and the Pope, and others by a crowd of enthusiastic amateurs and out-and-out cranks. It is no surprise that this period is dubbed the 'Phoney War.'

In Great Britain there was little to signal that the nation was at war. The black-out occasioned by the threat of air raids that did not happen, was a major inconvenience. The evacuation of children from the cities thought to be vulnerable to the same threat led to considerable social upheavals and frustrations. But these were comparatively minor irritations with what might have been. Apart from the appointments of Winston Churchill to the Admiralty and Anthony Eden to the Colonial Office the same Government was in control of the nation's affairs. Labour and Liberals were invited to serve in a National Government. Both refused to serve under Chamberlain, who was delighted. The appeasers of yesterday – Chamberlain, Halifax, Hoare and Simon – all remained in office, running the war in much the same way as they had run the peace. There was no state control over industry, no direction of labour and no restriction on the movement of capital out of the country.[17] Rationing of food was introduced only reluctantly. Conscription of young men for service with the armed forces was restricted, slow and cumbersome.

Churchill alone badgered the Prime Minister with ideas for prose-

---

[16]It is extraordinary that, with all the belligerents intent upon bringing the war to an end before hostilities started, this did not happen. It was of course the conditions for peace which provided the barrier. Hitler would have dealt with anyone, but Chamberlain would not deal with him.

[17]So the wealthy moved private funds to the USA and elsewhere.

cuting the war more vigorously.[18] These were invariably sidelined by referring them to the Service Minister concerned, where they received scant attention. The average age of the Cabinet was 64. It comprised a collection of fairly old has-beens, mostly of appeasement stock, who were well out of their depth in an environment of war. The population who could see no signs of actual warfare could not understand why they should have to put up with the attendant frustrations and inconveniences. They were bewildered by the lack of action. They were of course unaware that the belligerents were deploying diplomacy rather than action.

The British sent two divisions of men to France as their share of land forces opposing the Germans on the Western Front. While Great Britain fielded an army for duties throughout the world, of one and a half million, France with a smaller population fielded six and a half million. No wonder that German propaganda peddled the theme that Britain was ready to fight to the last French soldier. British military thinking was firmly rooted in the conflict of 1914–18. As a result, the British had just one, incomplete armoured division, neither fully equipped nor trained. British officers were sent into battle armed with no more than a pistol. The first British casualty arising from patrol activity occurred on December 9, more than three months after hostilities commenced.

While the armies sat looking at each other[19] British bombers flew over German cities at night. They dropped not bombs but leaflets. The leaflets told the German people that Great Britain had no quarrel with them, only with their leaders. This pathetic gesture was made in lieu of any attempt to mount any sort of military assistance to the Polish forces under intense pressure in the East. Poland duly bled to death. Only at sea was there any sign of normal wartime activity. In the South Atlantic the three British cruisers, *Exeter*, *Ajax* and *Achilles*, took on the German pocket battleship the *Graf Spee* and caused its ignominious scuttling. Her Commander, Captain Langsdorf, committed suicide.

German military activity in the West, as in the case of her adversaries, was nil. Those garrisons left in the West while their comrades demolished Poland sat gratefully watching the Franco-British forces also sitting and sometimes sunbathing on the other bank of the Rhine. Even when reinforced after the Polish campaign the German forces

---

[18]It was not until February 5, 1940, that Churchill was allowed to attend a meeting of the Supreme War Council, and then only as an observer.

[19]At the postwar Nuremberg Tribunal, General Jodl of the German Staff stated that during the Polish campaign 110 French and British divisions comprising some 1½ million men were faced by 23 German divisions comprising 350,000 men on the Western Front. The Allies' inactivity was taken as evidence of their unwillingness to fight.

continued to sit. The air fleets of the Luftwaffe which had wreaked such havoc in Poland remained grounded under strict embargo. They were not even to fly over any French or British cities, let alone drop any bombs on them. On September 7 Hitler told Admiral Raeder that his U-boats were not to attack passenger ships in the Atlantic and were not to attack French vessels at all.[20] They were also to abide strictly to the terms of the Hague Convention, which forbade attacking a ship without warning.

All these military restrictions were designed to help ease the way for German peace moves. But as 1939 drew to a close with no real peace negotiations in place, the military option for the removal of France began to grow in importance. As early as September 27 Hitler, perhaps with tongue in cheek, had fixed a provisional date of November 12 for a Western offensive. The date was confirmed on October 10 and 27 and cancelled on November 7. No less than 15 later dates were followed by postponement before Hitler's offensive was eventually launched in May 1940. Some postponements were because of bad weather, others through peace moves, either real or rumoured.

On October 17, 1939, there was a revealing note by Hitler to General Keitel of his operations staff which again confirmed Hitler's long-term plans. 'Polish territory is important to us from a military point of view as an advanced jumping-off point and for strategic concentration of troops. To that end, the railroads, roads and other communicative channels are to be kept in order.'[21] Here was the main reason for the German occupation of Poland. It had to do with Danzig. It had to do with the German-speaking population of the Corridor. It had to do with righting the wrongs of Versailles. But more than all these matters, it had to do with the search for *Lebensraum* and the launch of Operation Barbarossa.

The strange, almost unreal, atmosphere of the Phoney War prevailed throughout the first six months of the war. But under the surface and outside the knowledge of the vast majority of the British and German peoples there were plenty of diplomatic activity, particularly on the German side. Its objective was to bring the war to an end. Initiatives from the belligerents were sometimes supplemented and often obscured by others from neutral countries and private individuals. It was sometimes difficult for the belligerents to distinguish those that arose from sources of real authority from those that represented the pious hopes of well-meaning amateurs, albeit sometimes of royal blood and bearing the highest rank in business or social circles.

---

[20]Führer's conferences on naval affairs, 1939, 16–17.
[21]Nuremberg Documents 864, 5.

There were also difficulties with neutrals. Often they were acting more in the interests of their own national security rather than a genuine concern for the interests of the belligerents (consider for example initiatives arising from Belgium and The Netherlands, sandwiched between the belligerents). They were inclined to exaggerate the likelihood of their success and sometimes there were doubts as to their integrity. Some were friendly neighbours of one or more of the belligerents. There was also the suspicion that a neutral could be 'flying a kite' for a belligerent to sound out an adversary's resolve and strategic intentions rather than seeking to close a genuine deal for peace.

The most persistent and constructive attempts to bring about peace during the Phoney War came from the German side. The two early September speeches made by Goering and Hitler both called for an end to what was described as an unnecessary war. Immediately thereafter, Hitler authorised a series of peace overtures. These were made through Goering and Rosenberg. Their instructions were to peddle specific terms for peace which might be acceptable to the Allies, who were to be assured of Germany's genuine desire for peace.

Hitler had picked his peacemakers well. Unlike Ribbentrop, both Goering and Rosenberg were reasonably well respected by the British and deemed to be men of integrity with whom one could safely negotiate. That their efforts eventually involved both Chamberlain and Hitler personally is a measure of their near-success (only the Sumner Welles mission of February 1940 came nearer to the achieving of the goal of peace). In briefing them, Hitler made only one condition upon which he was inflexible. According to Walter Hewel, a member of Hitler's inner circle, 'Hitler wants peace with Great Britain and will try to make it as easy as possible for them ... but he will never give up his resolve to have a free hand in Eastern Europe, for he is convinced that if ever he made this concession to Great Britain he would not be able to undertake his big campaign against Russia.'[22]

Goering had good connections in Sweden. It was a country well known to him as a haven after his 1914–18 service. He had a particular link with Birger Dahlerus, a Swedish businessman who had been used in connection with the abortive peace efforts prior to September 3, and he resolved to use this link again. Dahlerus had the ear of the British Ambassador in Sweden, Sir Gilbert Forbes. On September 4, 1939, just one day into the war, Dahlerus telephoned Sir Frank Roberts of the British Foreign Office direct from Goering's residence, Karenhall, in Germany. Goering stood at his side. The message was

[22]Hesse, Fritz, *Hitler and the English*, Allan Wingate, London, 1954, 92–93.

clear. Goering was prepared to fly to London immediately to discuss peace terms. Roberts dismissed the offer out of hand. He did not even consult his Foreign Minister, Lord Halifax.

On the next day, Dahlerus was in touch with Forbes, advising him that Goering was wanting peace and asking for terms. Roberts again advised outright rejection. But Halifax asked that the peace terms acceptable to Germany should be set down. Goering consulted with Hitler. As a result, Dahlerus flew to London with the required terms. They were rejected.[23] The reason for rejection raised a fundamental issue that would dog all future attempts by Goering and others to place acceptable terms before the British. The issue was that no terms which originated from Hitler as the continuing head of a Nazi Government could be considered. Hitler's word could not be trusted. Hitler and his 'gang' must go first. Then and only then could peace proposals be considered.

There followed an interesting interlude which seemed to take up and deal with this very point. On September 28 Dahlerus was again in London. He presented German peace proposals first to Sir Alex Cadogan, Permanent Secretary at the British Foreign Office, and on the next day to Chamberlain and Halifax. The proposals included a suggestion that General Ironside, Chief of the Imperial General Staff[24] should meet a German general on neutral soil to negotiate an armistice as a preliminary move. An unusual provision within the peace proposals was that although Hitler would remain as the titular head of the German state, Goering would take over as the executive head (the Western analogy being that of President and Prime Minister). Goering would then carry through certain reforms, so as to reconstruct Germany on lines more acceptable to the Western democracies. These changes would include an end to the persecution of the Jews, the removal of SS and Gestapo powers and a general toning down of racial legislation. These internal measures would be accompanied by a restoration of Poland to her 1914 frontiers and the granting of some sort of autonomy to Czechoslovakia, albeit under German sovereignty. There would also be negotiation with Russia as to *Lebensraum* in lieu of the impending 'war of annihilation.'[25]

These radical proposals were put to Chamberlain and Halifax by

---

[23]See summary of Principal Peace Feelers, September 1939–March 1941, per Foreign Office Digest, April 14, 1941, PRO PREM 4–100–8 PRO and Documents on German Foreign Policy, Series D, Volume 7 140–43.

[24]It was hardly a coincidence that the suggested representative for the Western Allies should be a person known to hold extreme right-wing political views.

[25]Martin, Bernard, *Friedensinitiativen und Machtpolitik im Zweiten Weltkrieg 1939–1942*, Droste Verlag, Dusseldorf (1974). Translation summary.

Dahlerus as originating from Goering. It is not known if they had been agreed with Hitler. It is interesting to speculate as to Goering's motives. Was it a genuine attempt to end the war on terms which would as far as possible meet British requirements? Was it an excuse to indulge Goering's personal ambitions? Was it a trick to lure the British to the negotiating table without any real chance of loosening Hitler's overall authority? The British took the latter view. They rejected Goering's proposals. There were no definite proposals to rid Germany of the Nazi hierarchy in general and Hitler in particular.

Nothing daunted, Goering replaced Dahlerus with another peacemaker who had valuable British and European connections. He was Prince Max Hohenlohe, a Sudeten German landowner of independent means who operated around Europe as a freelance diplomat. He appears to have been universally respected as a man of integrity, one with whom discussions could be meaningful and constructive. Immediately following Goering's speech in early September. Hohenlohe had been in touch with a representative of the British Government in Switzerland[26] and a series of meetings took place between September 9 and 19. According to Hohenlohe, Goering's speech had created a good impression in London. Goering was a person acceptable to the British for the purpose of negotiation. An international conference should be convened and the USA asked to attend. There was one restriction. Great Britain would not accept Hitler as a part of the talks. Hohenlohe reported to Goering in Berlin. No action was taken. It is probable that the Hitler shut-out had been fatal. The report never got further than Goering's desk.

On October 7 Hitler made his 'victory speech' following on the conclusion of the Polish campaign. He appealed for 'Germany and England to come to an understanding.' He again described the war in the West as 'unnecessary'. He called also for an international conference to resolve all European issues and to agree upon disarmament proposals. The French rejected the proposals within 24 hours of the speech. There was delay with the British rejection. Chamberlain had received some 2,450 letters from private individuals, three quarters of which advocated the commencement of peace talks. Twenty Labour MPs called for a 'considered reply' to Hitler's offer.

Four days later Dahlerus was again in London and in consultation with Halifax and his Minister of State, R.A. Butler. He was not rebuffed. He was asked to supply the specifics underlying Hitler's offer. The next day, October 12, these were cabled to London. It was

---

[26]Believed to have been Group Captain Malcolm G. Christie of British Intelligence MI6.

made clear that negotiations would have to be conducted with Hitler and his Government. On the same day, Chamberlain formally recorded Great Britain's rejection in the House of Commons. 'The Government had no quarrel with the German people except that they allow themselves to be governed by a Nazi Government... No reliance can be put on the promises of the present German Government.'[27]

An interesting document among the Christie papers[28] depicts Hitler's state of mind in October 1939, suggesting that he was genuinely seeking peace at that time. A memorandum dated October 28 describes a twelve-hour discussion between Christie and Hohenlohe who claimed (correctly) to have had Goering's confidence. Hitler is described as 'depressed'. He had firmly believed that the war could have been localised to the Polish campaign and that coming to terms with Great Britain and France thereafter would not have been difficult. He now knew that was not the position. The Western Allies were apparently resolved to fight on. All the German diplomatic measures to bring about peace had failed. If Chamberlain was not prepared to negotiate with Hitler under any circumstances then Germany had a full-scale war on her hands. That was something never anticipated. In those circumstances, Hitler was prepared to hand on to Goering to 'get him out of the quagmire'.

The Christie memorandum then goes on to list those items which according to Hohenlohe would be Goering's radical suggestions for peace. They included the reconstruction of Poland by international agreement, autonomy for the Czechs, the democratisation of German political life, disarmament, revision of German foreign policies and no reparations. Most importantly Goering was to replace Hitler as Chancellor and Hitler was to retain the title of Führer in a presidential-style, non-executive capacity. Hohenlohe suggested that peace soundings on this suggested basis should be made through Sweden or the USA.[29]

There is no end result reported from these alleged suggestions. They may not have been true and may have been fed to Hohenlohe by Goering for reasons best known to Goering. But if the Holenlohe

---

[27]Diaries of Harold Nicolson, October 12, 1939.

[28]The Christie papers comprise the personal correspondence, memos etc. of Malcolm Grahame Christie, described in the archive records as 'an independent investigator of German and Central European affairs.' He was Air Attaché at the British Embassy, Berlin until 1930 when he retired from full-time employment (at the age of 49) with the rank of Group Captain. Thereafter, he used a network of agents and connections throughout Europe and compiled regular intelligence reports for Sir Robert Vansittart of the Foreign Office from 1934 onwards. He may perhaps be fairly described as a freelance MI6 officer (some of the correspondence on file is addressed to 'Colonel' Christie).

[29]Christie papers, October 28, 1939.

report is accurate and Goering's comments true, the notes do indicate just how far Hitler was prepared to go to call off a war which he thought should never have happened. It is probable that he became more optimistic after the end of October. The Goering/Dahlerus/Holenlohe attempted peace talks faltered and faded and Hitler began to consider the military option to close off the West before driving East. Goering continued to dabble in peace diplomacy, using Dahlerus, Holenlohe and another Swedish businessman contact, Baron Bonde. But his proposals always lacked the imprimatur of Hitler and they found only 'off the record', unofficial responses from Great Britain.

Reciprocation from the British seemed to come mainly from 'Rab' Butler, Halifax's Secretary of State, who seems to have taken it upon himself to play the part of a roving, freelance peacemaker, certainly without official government backing but probably with the personal backing of his master, Halifax. Butler had a particular connection with the Italian Ambassador in London, Giuseppe Bastaniani. In November, he was assuring Bastaniani that Germany could secure peace without withdrawing their troops from Poland and that Churchill's bellicose speeches were not representative of the Government's views.[30] Two weeks later he met Carl J. Burckhardt, then head of the international Red Cross but with direct links with Berlin. The occasion was the final session of the League of Nations held in Switzerland. Butler saw Burckhardt as a potential peace emissary. A report to Berlin made it clear that Butler was acting as a freelance: 'Rab operating on his own. Not sure of the relationship Halifax has with Rab.' Butler's conduct was described as 'feline'.[31]

The other avenue of covert approach to the British used by Hitler during the early period of the Phoney War was via Rosenberg, who claimed that his connection went to the very heart of the British Establishment through the good offices of the double agent Baron William de Ropp and his close colleague, Squadron Leader (later Group Captain) Frederick Winterbotham, Chief of British Air Intelligence MI6 at the Air Ministry. Mention has already been made of the part played by Winterbotham in the mid-1930s, when he had been taken into the confidence of General Reichenau and his Luftwaffe colleagues about the planned attack on Russia. It was a channel of communication which circumvented the official channels, and according to the official documents on German foreign policy files it was still alive and well on September 3, 1939. But its target was very different

[30]DGFP 427.
[31]Letter Hohenlohe to Hewel, June 20, 1940.

from the Goering/Dahlerus/Holenlohe connection which sought an accommodation with the British Government.

The Rosenberg/de Ropp connection sought contact with those of the British Establishment who for one reason or another were in favour of ending the war and ousting Chamberlain and his so-called warmongering colleagues, Churchill and Eden. On October 5 there is an unsigned (but almost certainly a Rosenberg) note on the German file.[32] It refers to a meeting between a German agent from the German *Aussenpolitisches*, AMT (controlled by Hess) with de Ropp at Montreux in Switzerland. An invitation is extended to de Ropp to visit Berlin for peace discussions. The invitation is turned down but de Ropp confirms that he is prepared to talk to the British Air Ministry 'at the appropriate time.' These views are confirmed in a further note dated October 10.[33] This refers to a cable received from 'Fred' in London.[34] Talks with the Germans are described as premature, although the Air Ministry is described as having no wish to be a party to a policy of waging a war to the finish. Representations would be made as soon as it became apparent that the Luftwaffe was the force that would dominate the war. In the meantime, it was suggested that de Ropp should remain in Switzerland as the mutual British/German contact. Daniels, the press attaché at the British legation in Berne who apparently had excellent connections at the Foreign Office agreed. De Ropp was to present himself in Berlin 'as soon as Fred wired him that the time was ripe.'

Further notes during late October and early November[35] report that the strength of the British Peace Party was increasing. As soon as it was adjudged that this party was enjoying an ascendancy over the warmongers, 'R' (presumably de Ropp) would be authorised to travel to Berlin and open up negotiations, preferably at a time of British military reverses.[36] He would be called to London first, so that he could accurately represent the views of the British Peace Party. Rosenberg is reminded of the importance of 'his direct connections with England' and mention is made of the use of codes 'health poor' (time not ripe) and 'health good' (time ripe) to indicate the timing of de Ropp's planned visit. It is noted that the anticipated peace talks would be conducted by 'Christian' (Rosenberg? Hess?) and not by his Foreign Minister, Ribbentrop.[37]

---

[32]DGFP 224–25.
[33]DGFP 261.
[34]Presumably Frederick Winterbotham.
[35]DGFP 363–66.
[36]The same requirement apparently dictated the precise timing of the Hess flight in May 1941.
[37]DGFP 363–66.

There are no further notes on file relating to the Rosenberg/deRopp/Winterbotham/Air Ministry connection or the British Peace Party. These have presumably succumbed to official weeding. There is no reason to believe other than that the connection remained in being, even though the records did not.[38] Of course, there may be more than one explanation for the rather extraordinary state of affairs[39] disclosed by those notes, left on file either purposely or in error. Each side may have been attempting to bluff the other. The Germans may have wished to stimulate British interests in peace to give themselves time to complete preparations for their Western offensive. The British may have been stimulating German interests in peace so as to prolong the military stalemate in the West. But the connection, first established in 1936, was long-standing. It was also between individuals, both British and German, who were of one mind about the dangers of Russian communism. In view of the unfortunate outbreak of hostilities ascribed to Churchill and his warmongering, it would be reasonable to suppose that the ties between those individuals of the same mind would have become stronger rather than weaker in their search for peace.

The peace moves initiated by Great Britain through government sources during the early period of the Phoney War were circumscribed by a condition affixed by Chamberlain himself. The condition was that the Chamberlain Government would only negotiate with a moderate German Government. Hitler and his Nazi colleagues would have to go first. Such a condition effectively wrecked any possibility of reaching agreement. It is quite apparent that the content of a peace settlement would itself present no particular difficulty.[40] But there was no question of negotiating with Hitler. Of course, Chamberlain could argue that his 'don't trust Hitler' policy was based upon bitter experience. But Chamberlain's personal animosity towards Hitler clearly came into the equation. Hitler had humiliated him before a world audience during the diplomatic preludes leading up to the outbreak of hostilities, and he was not a man used to defeat or accommodating it without personal rancour.

The most important peace initiative launched by Great Britain during those early days occurred in November 1939. It was an initiative

[38]And in the opinion of the author had an important bearing on the Hess peace mission of May 1941.

[39]At the relevant time de Ropp was a serving officer in the RAF, with the rank of Squadron Leader.

[40]The granting of autonomy to Czechoslovakia under the overall sovereignty of Germany and the partition of Poland into a German-speaking area incorporated into the Reich, an area for the resettlement of European Jews and a third area for the Poles under the name and style of 'Congress Poland' apparently represented arrangements acceptable to all three belligerents.

that had the full backing of Chamberlain, Halifax and the British Cabinet.[41]But it was initiated and controlled by interests outside Chamberlain's Government. They were interests prepared to sidestep Hitler's villainy and Chamberlain's injured pride and bring an end to an unnecessary war. Their efforts culminated in what has become known as the Venlo incident. The full details of the events leading up to the Venlo incident of November 9, 1939, are not known. The relevant documentation is embargoed and will not become available until 2039.

The facts so far reported are well known. Very soon after war was declared Major Richard Stevens, head of British Intelligence MI6 stationed in Holland, and Captain Sigmund Payne Best, a prominent member of Claude Dansey's highly secret 'Z' organisation in MI6, reported that one of their agents, Dr Franz Fischer, had established contact with a group of important German dissidents. They were anxious to overthrow Hitler and end the war. This was reported to Halifax alongside a MI6 picture of general anti-Hitler dissatisfaction in Germany, particularly among the generals of the Wehrmacht.

These reports fitted like a glove into Chamberlain's policy of calling upon the 'good' Germans to oust the 'Nazi gangsters.' Every official encouragement was therefore given to Best and Stevens. If possible, they were to contact the dissidents and arrange preliminary talks prior to a coup. In fact, Fischer was a double agent working for the Gestapo and led Best and Stevens into a trap. The British officers were supposed to meet a dissident German general in the village of Venlo, on the Dutch/German border. He was supposed to represent an important group of organised German opposition. In the event, they were met by the Gestapo and kidnapped. They were taken to Düsseldorf and subsequently incarcerated at Dachau. Under Gestapo pressure they gave such information to their interrogators that MI6 operations throughout Germany and Europe were compromised and the Gestapo provided with a list of names and details of the MI6 personnel.[42]

The incident is listed as one of official embarrassment[43] and a matter of gross negligence on the part of the two officers concerned.[44] But further examination of the known facts, including those supplied after the war from German sources, reveals much more than that reported in the official account. In the first place the picture painted by MI6 to

---

[41]Except for Churchill. He dissented.

[42]*The Venlo Affair*, Callum A. MacDonald, *European Studies Review*, Vol 8, No 4, 443–64.

[43]'D' notices were issued to newspaper editors at the time prohibiting publication of the details.

[44]Stevens and Best turned up at the end of the war in Austria. They were never charged with negligence but were not re-employed by MI6.

Halifax of widespread Hitler dissatisfaction among the German populace was almost wholly inaccurate and must have been known to be so by the intelligence sources. Reporting that there were dissident elements goes without saying, but there was no evidence to suggest other than that such opposition was weak and ineffective and certainly not widespread.[45] If that were the case, and known to be the case, why did MI6 report otherwise? In the second place it is now known[46] that the proposed negotiations for peace as far as the Germans were concerned were genuine. They originated not from a band of dissidents but from the German Government itself.

Having ascertained from their double agent Fischer that the Chamberlain Government was prepared to negotiate a peace, Himmler, with Hitler's full knowledge and consent, let the hare run. Walter Schellenberg, Chief of the Gestapo's counter-intelligence unit, was appointed to oversee the operation. Like Himmler, his superior, Schellenberg thought that the war with Great Britain should never have started and that both countries ought to be allies against the threat of Russian Communism.[47] According to Schellenberg's own memoirs there was a meeting with Best and Stevens on October 30, 1939, at which preliminary proposals for peace were agreed. Hitler was to remain as Reich Chancellor, Ribbentrop was to be deposed and Austria, Czechoslovakia and Poland were to be reconstructed . There was also to be agreement as to the role to be played by each belligerent in relation to the Russian Communist threat.

Schellenberg makes the interesting point that these proposals were referred not to the British Cabinet but to Halifax alone, who approved them. There was to be a further meeting in London at which the peace terms would be finalised.[48] But at some stage in early November it appears that Hitler or Himmler or both had second thoughts. It is known that Hitler's attitude towards peace hardened somewhat after the negative reaction to his peace speech of October 6 and the subsequent failure of the Goering/Dahlerus/Hohenlohe initiatives. By November he was beginning to think seriously of the military option to rid himself of the problems in the West. Anyway, for whatever

---

[45]And so it remained until military defeats much later in the war illustrated the fallibility of the Nazi regime. Prior to that, German opposition to Hitler comprised little more than a series of clandestine meetings in private houses or military establishments which never rose much above the level of local debating societies. After Venlo any German dissidents asking for details of what sort of peace could be negotiated were told to carry out the coup first and then find out. Much confusion but no action arose from this chicken-and-egg situation.

[46]Callum A. MacDonald, *The Venlo Affair*, 448.

[47]Schellenberg later appears as a lead player during the summer of 1940, when efforts were made in Spain and Portugal to enlist the Duke of Windsor to the Nazi cause.

[48]Walter Schellenberg, *The Schellenberg Memoirs*, Deutsch, 1956, 106.

reason, Schellenberg was instructed to abort the operation and take the two MI6 officers into custody. This he did on November 9 in a snatch operation at Venlo with typical Gestapo efficiency. According to Schellenberg he nevertheless continued in radio contact with MI6 sources and did not finally break off contact until November 29.[49]

If these reported circumstances are true we have a position somewhat different to that originally stated. MI6 were reporting widespread anti-Hitler dissidence which did not exist. They were also reporting that one of their agents, who was in fact a double agent, was in touch with a body of dissidents who did not exist. This false information is then fed through to Chamberlain and Halifax. The report squares precisely with Chamberlain's concept[50] as to how peace might come about. MI6 are therefore instructed to proceed. Best and Stevens then agree some preliminary peace terms with Schellenberg, including a provision that Hitler would remain in office.[51] These terms are then reported, not to Chamberlain and the British Cabinet but to Halifax alone. A further meeting is then to be held in London.

The clear inference from all this is that interests within MI6 itself initiated the peace moves, that they were content to negotiate with Hitler and Hitler's Government, that Chamberlain and his Cabinet were deliberately misled and that Halifax alone was aware as to what was really going on. In the light of subsequent events it is not difficult to cast Halifax and certain elements within MI6 in the suggested roles of peacemakers, more in touch with certain interests within the British Establishment than the Government of the day.

Secrecy and Halifax's extra-governmental activities as a peacemaker are also the ingredients in what became known as the Tavistock Peace Proposals of January 1940. These were initiated by Lord Tavistock (later to become the Duke of Bedford) and his colleague, Lord Darnley. Both were members of the landed aristocracy and both were of the opinion that the war should never have started and should be brought quickly to an end. Tavistock had apparently been in direct touch with Henning Thomson, Secretary to the German Legation in Dublin. He had obtained, or had negotiated on his own initiative, peace terms which he later claimed had been officially approved by the German Government. These terms included the restoration of Poland and Czechoslovakia, the establishment of a national home for Jews in Poland, a plebiscite in Austria, reconstruction of the League of Nations, programmed disarmament and the return of German colonies.

---

[49]Callum A. MacDonald, *The Venlo Affair*, 459.
[50]Some might say wishful thinking.
[51]Best himself is adamant on this point (S. Payne Best, *The Venlo Incident*, Hutchinson, 7).

The terms were presented to Halifax by Darnley and were later discussed with both Tavistock and Darnley.[52] Tavistock then attended again upon the German legation in Dublin to obtain confirmation and clarification of some of the terms. Presumably, this was for Halifax's benefit, he having consented to the visit, albeit informally. Considerable correspondence then arose between Tavistock and Halifax. This led eventually to considerable Government embarrassment because Tavistock published the correspondence in pamphlet form, under the title of *The Fate of a Peace Effort.*[53] He also wrote a letter to Sir Joseph Ball's scurrilous right-wing publication, *Truth*, which was published on February 9. He also leaked the full proposals to the *Daily Telegraph*, who published them on March 1. Widespread publicity arose as a result. Government embarrassment was complete. Here was another example of Halifax involving himself in peace moves quite outside Cabinet knowledge and approval. His apparent sanction of Tavistock's visits to Dublin to make direct contact with the enemy in time of war, was highly questionable behaviour on the part of a Minister of the Crown. As to Tavistock, it is difficult to assess his direct contacts with the enemy as anything other than treasonable.

Halifax had been involved earlier with the encouragement of globetrotting activities by well-meaning but amateur peacemakers. His hope was that someone would bring home a realistic proposition for peace upon which the British Government could bite. They included J. Lonsdale Bryans, great-nephew of Lord Grunthorpe, who had connections with the Hassell group of German dissidents and James D. Mooney, a vice-president of Ford Motors, based in London, who had connections with Dr Walthart, economic adviser to Goering. But all suggestions of peace talks foundered on the Chamberlain condition that such talks could only be meaningful if conducted with a moderate German Government, after Hitler and his Government had been deposed. Nevertheless, and apparently in direct contradiction to the stated condition, both Halifax and his Minister of State, Butler, continued to make it clear to all who cared to listen that Great Britain was still prepared to negotiate a peace if suitable terms were on offer.

After talks between Halifax, Butler and the Russian Ambassador in London, the German Ambassador in Moscow was reporting that the talks with Butler in particular had been 'most interesting.'[54] This readiness to negotiate by Great Britain encouraged a steady procession

[52]Diaries of Sir Alexander Cadogan, January 22, 1940.
[53]At High Wycombe in 1940 and published in the right-wing publication 'Action', January 11, 1940.
[54]DGFP 269–325.

of neutral countries to step into the ring with their own versions of acceptable peace overtures. These attempts proliferated during the Phoney War in direct proportion to the perceived imminence of a military settlement in the West. Neutrals naturally assumed that they might well be caught up in any conflagration and they rushed to stop something before it started. At least 20 attempts to initiate peace proceedings were made by neutrals between September 1939 and April 1940. They included the Vatican, Belgium, Holland, Italy, Spain, the Scandinavian countries and Romania. The initiatives came through kings and queens, heads of state, religious heads and prominent businessmen. And they all floundered on the twin rocks of Chamberlain's intransigence and Hitler's growing interest in the military option.

One exception came very close to bringing the war to an end. It came from the most powerful neutral country in the world, the USA. Anticipated American involvement as a guarantor of any European settlement that might be agreed at last caused Chamberlain to move from his previous intransigence. On February 9, 1940, the American President, Franklin D. Roosevelt, announced that he would be sending his representative, Sumner Welles, to Europe on what was described as a 'fact finding tour'. The universal interpretation was that if the facts fitted, a major peace initiative would result. Sumner Welles was the second man at the American Ministry of Foreign Affairs. He was also Chairman of the Advisory Committee for Foreign Relations. He was a close friend of the President and anti-German in his views. But he was also mindful of and in agreement with, the President's views as to non-participation in the European conflict.

The motives for the Welles tour were perhaps many and various. The most cynical view was that it was an exercise in public relations. Roosevelt was approaching the election for his next term of office. An image of 'the angel of peace' to the warring factions in Europe would sit comfortably on the laps of the American electorate. An altruistic view was that the President was genuinely concerned as to the effect hostilities could have on the peoples of Europe, their culture and the visible evidence of their civilisations in their architecture, art and ancient institutions. A more worldly and perhaps realistic motive was that Roosevelt saw an opportunity of stamping American political authority on the world conscience. The USA had already established herself in the forefront of the world economies but still played an unwanted secondary role in political terms to Great Britain and the other major states of Europe. Here was an opportunity to extend her political power.

There was also an economic factor. For four months the American President had watched Great Britain piling up a considerable and increasing external debt owing to the USA. The only manner in which Great Britain could repair her inadequacies in armaments was to draw heavily on American manufacturers. Her own industrial output was not up to it. The American President would have noted that the British were funding, or partly funding, the American debt by the sale of some of her overseas investments. Perhaps therefore the President's eyes looked beyond the European conflict to the postwar aftermath. The USA needed international markets and cheap raw materials to feed her booming manufacturing potential. The countries of the British Empire seemed particularly vulnerable in present circumstances. They were of course bound together by protective trade barriers and imperial preferences. Perhaps those barriers could be lowered by careful American exploitation.

Probably, it was a combination of all these factors which brought about Roosevelt's special springtime initiative. His announcement of February 9 was universally welcomed, even by the Germans. They promised that senior members of the Nazi hierarchy would be pleased to meet Welles. In fact Hitler had committed himself to the military option in the new year. But he also knew that any peace initiative launched by the USA with American guarantees attaching to any agreed terms would stand every chance of bringing the war to an end. Hitler therefore rode the horse, even though by the spring of 1940 it was an outsider. There was open approval of the news in Rome, a friendly reception in Paris and guarded optimism with some criticism in London. Welles started in Rome. Mussolini was flattered and suggested a joint mediation by the USA and Italy. Foreign Minister Ciano warned Welles that Hitler's attitude towards peace would have hardened after the rejection of his own proposals.

Hitler had no wish to compromise his position as a result of the Welles visit. His Ministers were therefore carefully briefed. Ribbentrop got carried away and entertained (or otherwise) Welles to a two-hour monologue that had graced, or disgraced, so many London society salons during the 1930s. Hitler himself told Welles that he was already committed to the military option because of Western intransigence.[55] Hess and Goering were courteous but uncompromising. They both made the point that Great Britain had declared war over an issue that did not concern them.

This unity of view met by Welles in Berlin was in sharp contrast to that encountered in Paris. Daladier presented himself as the only realist in the camp. He backed Chamberlain's point of view as to Hitler's

[55]On the very day that Welles arrived in Berlin, Hitler signed the order for the occupation of Norway and Denmark.

untrustworthiness. Territorial matters were not an issue. Even he was defeatist in terms of a belief that the war could not be won as opposed to not losing it. Reynaud harped back to traditional French concepts of security as originally envisaged at Versailles, but this time with US backing and guarantees.

If Welles found intransigence in Berlin, he found it also in London, at least on his first visit on March 11. Chamberlain remained rooted to the issue of Hitler's credibility. Ribbentrop's diatribe was matched by that of Churchill's. There could be no peace with the present German Government. Poland and Czechoslovakia were to be restored to full independence. Germany was to be taught a lesson. Germany should be occupied for 50 years. Berlin should be razed to the ground. German hegemony over Europe should be broken once and for all.[56] All this was hardly helpful. It must have stirred Welles's sentiments in sympathy with those of his countrymen holding isolationist views.

So far Welles had spent most of his time listening. It was when he started to talk and explain the possibilities of American involvement in the peace process, and perhaps more importantly in its aftermath (unlike Versailles), that the talkers started to listen. In particular Welles's remarks seem to have injected some realism into Chamberlain's thinking. Perhaps the full realisation of the country's predicament following his declaration of war helped. Nevertheless, he eventually signalled to Welles a complete reversal of view. Providing the suggested peace plan was underpinned by concrete American guarantees and security he was prepared to advise his Government to enter into negotiations with Hitler's Germany. The territorial and constitutional adjustments would have to encompass the reconstruction of Poland, Bohemia and Moravia, with a referendum for Austria. Welles could see no great difficulty with these provisions. The suggested presence of the American umbrella of security seems to have been the main reason for Chamberlain's change of heart, but there was perhaps another factor which would have been important to a man of Chamberlain's character. If the negotiated peace arose through and because of the intervention of the USA it could be carried through without loss of face.

It was clear that for whatever reason, Welles had achieved a major breakthrough. He needed only to sell it to the Germans. He was too late. Hitler was already travelling down the road of military ambition. Ribbentrop had warned Mussolini that this was the case. When Welles returned to Rome to enlist the support of Mussolini in approaching

---

[56]The equivalent Ribbentrop phrase was 'eliminate British influence over Europe for ever'.

Hitler, he was met with a very different reception from that on his first visit. Mussolini refused to help.[57] Welles thereupon offered Mussolini territorial inducements in the Mediterranean area to help him change his mind.[58] Welles telephoned his President to obtain sanction for this move but Roosevelt instructed him to venture no further and close down the negotiations. Roosevelt himself finally nailed down the coffin of possible peace by making a speech to the US nation, but with a worldwide audience. He made it clear that the USA was 'not looking for an appeasement peace'.

It is difficult to interpret the President's actions in shutting down the Welles negotiations at the very point when his emissary had achieved a major breakthrough. His action appears to give added weight to the less attractive of his motives for instructing Welles in the first place. Welles must have brought back to his President most valuable intelligence as to European affairs. It would have included a valuable assessment of how future military operations were likely to go, how the British and more particularly, the French might react, how Great Britain might become increasingly dependent upon America and how that might beneficially affect America's postwar position.[59]

It is clear that American motives for the Welles mission were mixed and ultimately concerned with American interests above anything else. It is also clear that German readiness to see Welles was more of a pose than a genuine desire to join in a peace process. Any restriction or control arising out of agreed peace terms involving American guarantees and American military muscle would have been intolerable to Hitler. It would have cut right across his ideological plans which comprised the mainspring for all that he wished to do. He certainly wanted to be free of entanglements and commitments in the West, but not at the cost of cramping his style in the East. He had decided upon the military option as the means of resolving his problems in the West before Welles set foot in Berlin. He no doubt saw the Welles mission as a means of escaping the charge of irresponsible warmongering.

The real lessons of the Welles mission were twofold. It illustrated how Hitler had turned away from considerations of peace in the West, following the failure of his own initiatives in October/November; he

---

[57]Following Ribbentrop's advice, Mussolini had promised to take up arms at the side of Germany – a promise that he subsequently retracted on the grounds that he had neither the men or the munitions to indulge in such an extravagance.

[58]It is extraordinary that Welles should contact his President to sanction the bartering of Mediterranean territories which could only have come from the Anglo-French treasure chest – unless of course the issue had already been discussed in London/Paris.

[59]The most important factor missing from the Welles file, and the one which was to have the most telling effect on American postwar aspirations, was of course the Russian factor.

had made a conscious decision to 'smash the West' by feat of arms and his military planning was far advanced. It also illustrated Great Britain's essential weakness. While sitting at a negotiating table with Hitler was publicised as unthinkable on a one-to-one basis, it immediately became a proposition when the same negotiating table sat underneath the American umbrella of guarantee and security. For the first time, Great Britain was realising that she was no longer capable of extracting herself from major commitment without American help.

The summer months that followed those of the Phoney War illustrated clearly the inability of both Great Britain and France to measure up to the commitments that they had freely undertaken. In the case of France, that inadequacy proved fatal. In the case of Great Britain, it was not so. Great Britain was saved from oblivion by 26 miles of water and the advent of a national leader equal to the task that confronted him. His name was Winston Spencer Churchill.

10

April–June 1940 – the military option is sprung

At last I had the authority to give directions over the whole scene. I felt as if I were walking with destiny and that all my past life had been but a preparation for this hour and for this trial.

WINSTON S. CHURCHILL, MAY 10, 1940

The Norwegian fiasco and Churchill's accession to power

The Norwegian campaign of April–May 1940 brought about the downfall of Chamberlain and his Government and the accession to power of Winston Churchill. The campaign was a disaster for the Western Allies. It also clearly indicated that the Chamberlain Government was unfitted to wage war against what was now seen to be a strong, efficient and resolute enemy. Belatedly, reluctantly and far from unanimously, the House of Commons at last caught the mood of the British people and brought Chamberlain down in a memorable debate of May 7 and 8, 1940. The political aftermath was Churchill's accession to power. The Norwegian campaign, although a military disaster, therefore marks a political event of far-reaching importance in Great Britain's prosecution of the war. Churchill was not Chamberlain and he did not inherit any of the former Premier's views as to how the war might be ended. In particular, he was not a peacemaker. He was a warmaker.

The clash of arms in Norway arose because each of the belligerents considered that country and its coastal waters to be important to their strategic requirements. The Germans saw the occupation of its western seaboard as a means of nullifying the Royal Navy's stranglehold on the North Sea and the wide stretches of the North Atlantic. Deep-water ports would be available for U-boats and surface raiders of the pocket-battleship class. Air bases could be established hundreds of miles nearer to the homeland of the main rival, Great Britain. Plans for the invasion of Norway and neighbouring Denmark had lain on file at the headquarters of Hitler's Navy Chief, Grand Admiral Raeder, for some time.[1]

The strategic importance of Norway to the Allies was more complex. There were two issues which soon fused into one. The first was clear cut, the second obscure. Ever since the declaration of war, Churchill, in his capacity as First Sea Lord, had advocated the mining of what were known as the Norwegian 'leads'. This was the name applied to the narrow strip of water lying between the western coast of Norway and the outlying islands which ran from the northern port of Narvik down to Stavanger. Ships with valuable cargos of iron ore for German steel production sailed down the leads to the Baltic. The iron ore was produced at the Gällivare mines in Sweden. In summer, the iron ore was shipped direct to Germany from the Gulf of Bosnia and across the Baltic. In winter, this was not possible because of thick ice. The iron ore had to come overland from Gällivare to Narvik and then by sea down the leads to Stavanger and then to Germany. It was this shipping which Churchill wanted to attack with mines.

Although illegal,[2] the intent made strategic sense. Certainly, it stood well in comparison with the second issue affecting Allied plans. On November 30, 1939, Russia attacked Finland. There was immediate international condemnation. The British Cabinet, in consultation with the French, decided in their wisdom to put together an expeditionary force of some 100,000 men to go to the aid of Finland. They would land at Narvik and travel overland through Norway and Sweden to Finland. In January 1940 both the Norwegian and Swedish Governments refused permission for these movements of foreign troops through their countries. No doubt they feared possible German and Russian reaction.

During the next two months, the British Cabinet debated the issues on no less than 60 different occasions[3] before they finally decided to go ahead in any case. No doubt Churchill saw the opportunity of closing down the leads for good and possibly destroying the Gällivare iron ore mines into the bargain. But they were too late. On March 12 the Russians and Finns came to terms and hostilities ceased. The Allies

---

[1]The plans had been prepared by Admiral Rolf Carls, third ranking officer in the German Navy. They carried the full support of Raeder.

[2]The mining of the leads in Norwegian territorial waters constituted the first infringement of international law in the 1939–45 conflict.

[3]A.J.P. Taylor, *English History, 1914–1945*, Oxford University Press (1965), 469.

were humiliated. Once again they had promised help to a small nation subjected to the aggression of a powerful neighbour and had failed to deliver. The French Government fell. Reynaud replaced Daladier as Premier.

The fall of the French Government provides a clue to the underlying motives for the proposed Anglo-French expedition to Finland. In military terms it was a madness. Having embroiled themselves in a war with Germany for which they were totally unfitted, the Western Allies now sought conflict with Russia as well. Admittedly, in certain quarters there was frustration at the lack of action during the Phoney War and Finland was an area of operations which would carry international approbation.[4] There was also French interest in any military action that took the spotlight off the Western Front, which could then stagnate to their advantage and comfort. But these factors alone would not explain a decision which added up to military madness. There must have been important political reasons.

There were of course strong and vociferous right-wing elements in France who thought that the Franco-German war was unnecessary and that both nations and Great Britain should be leading an anti-Communist crusade against Russia instead of squabbling amongst themselves. There were similar right-wing interests in Great Britain who thought the same way. They were not so vociferous as their French counterparts but appeared to have influence up to and including Cabinet level. How else would the British fall into line with a French suggestion that at first sight appeared to have been one of strategic lunacy?

If the Anglo-French Expeditionary Force had reached Finland and carried on the fight with Finland against Russia, within little more than one year the enemies on the Western Front would have found themselves as allies on the Eastern Front. In such circumstances, the 'war' in the West, which might never have got beyond the phoney stage, would have collapsed. Was this a strategic objective? There may well have been covert political thought behind the apparent military madness.[5] The full record of events leading up to the Norwegian campaign are not yet available for public scrutiny; they may make for interesting reading when they are.

The collapse of these grandiose Allied ambitions did not deter

---

[4]It was suggested that the expeditionary force should conduct its operations under a League of Nations banner.

[5]One might ask whether, while the expeditionary force was making its laborious way through the northern snows of Norway and Sweden, the Norwegians, Swedes, Germans and Russians were expected to be passive observers.

Churchill. He continued to agitate for the mining of the leads[6] and eventually a decision to proceed was taken on April 9, 1940. As a precautionary measure, the original expeditionary force was to be sent to Narvik, in case there was any German reaction. The Germans were aware of these plans.[7] Rosenberg had a strong connection with Vidkun Quisling, the former Norwegian Defence Minister and fellow spirit with Rosenberg in the proposed formation of the Nordic Nazi Empire. Both had important connections with the British Establishment.[8] Quisling had been in constant personal attendance on Hitler to update his knowledge of the Norwegian situation.

On March 15 there occurred an event which appears to have had a marked effect upon Hitler's decision to move against Norway and deploy Raeder's plan, known as Operation Wesser. On that day, a British destroyer, HMS *Cossack* intercepted the German supply ship *Altmark* in Jösing Fjord lying well within Norwegian territorial waters. The *Altmark*, which was carrying merchant seamen prisoners, was boarded by crew members from the *Cossack*. Two hundred and ninety-nine prisoners were released and taken on board the British destroyer. Apart from demonstrating the Royal Navy's offensive spirit (for which Hitler is said to have expressed his admiration) the incident demonstrated the Royal Navy's apparent contempt for the finer points of international law.

Hitler had himself said that history judged by success or failure and that alone. Here was the Royal Navy thinking along the same lines. The British had serious intent and, coupling this with the Quisling/Rosenberg intelligence already to hand, Hitler decided to launch Operation Wesser as a pre-emptive strike. The Commander-in-Chief for the operation was named as General Nikolaus van Falkenhorst. Falkenhorst knew all about conducting war in Arctic conditions. He had fought in Finland at the conclusion of the 1914–18 war. Goering was outraged. He was not informed of the appointment until after it had been made. He then found that his beloved Luftwaffe had been placed under the command of Falkenhorst. The German navy was to play the lead role but with inter-services support, in particular from the Air Arm.

---

[6]Churchill had advocated this course of action since the outbreak of hostilities. One of his fiercest opponents was Rab Butler.

[7]In contrast, the British were taken completely by surprise when German troops landed in Norway. British Intelligence had reported increased naval activity in German Baltic ports as a prelude to a break-out of naval units into the North Sea. Apparently they could not distinguish troop transports from battleships. Chamberlain ordered an enquiry into MI6 failures. No action resulted.

[8]Rosenberg's connections have already been mentioned. Quisling had received the British CBE decoration for his services in protecting British interests in Russia following the 1917 communist revolution.

To the British nation the Norwegian campaign was a blessing in disguise.[9] The humiliations were great. The much vaunted Royal Navy which had ruled the oceans of the world since Trafalgar failed to prevent the enemy landing in strength on a coastline only a few hundred miles from Great Britain's own naval bases.[10] The Anglo-French expeditionary force was hurriedly evacuated within days of landing in Norway. But at least the scale of the disaster and the humiliations suffered opened the eyes of the British nation as to the reality of the deep crisis that engulfed them. The evidence was laid before the nation by the events in Norway – events which were preceded by some of the silliest recorded comments of the whole 1939–45 war.

On April 4, Chamberlain addressed a conference of the Conservative and Unionist Association. He referred to German military preparations and the expectation of an early military assault, commenting that in its absence 'Hitler had missed the bus'. On the same day, under a *Daily Express* headline of '"Come on Hitler" dares Ironside', the Chief of the Imperial General Staff said in interview that 'we would welcome a go at him. Frankly, we would welcome an attack. We are sure of ourselves. We have no fears.'[11]

In the event, eight battalions of British troops, including five battalions of half trained, half equipped territorials and some French Alpine troops, landed in Norway to do battle with 51 battalions of German troops. The Germans had been landed in Norway on April 7–8 without any serious interference from the Royal Navy.[12] The British troops went in without reconnaissance or Intelligence reports. They held out-of-date terrain maps. They were under-trained and badly led. They had no artillery, no armour, no transport and no anti-aircraft guns. Most important of all, they had no air cover. They did have a full complement of office equipment, quartermasters' ledgers and accounting forms.[13] Some of the troops were issued with so much Arctic clothing and accessories they could hardly move. Others had no Arctic clothing. None had the one essential cold-climate requirement, snow skis.

Norwegian civilians dreaded the arrival of British troops because of the incessant heavy bombing that always followed them. Norwegian houses were made largely of wood. They were razed to the ground by incendiary bombs. Orders, counter-orders and muddle pervaded Allied command structures from top to bottom. There was disagreement at

---

[9]Except for those unfortunate young men who were sent into battle under-equipped, half trained and badly led.
[10]Churchill's boast that 'every German ship using the Kattegat will be sunk' was wholly unfulfilled.
[11]*Daily Express*, April 5, 1940.
[12]Denmark was occupied at the same time. There were few casualties.
[13]Thompson, Laurence, *1940: Year of Legend, Year of History*, Collins Fontana (1968), 50.

the highest level as to which should be the main target of attack. Was it to be Narvik in the north or Trondheim with its deepwater harbour? In the event, both were attacked. An already weak force was further weakened by the dissipation.

There was supposed to be a pincer movement to take Trondheim. Troops were landed north and south of the town at the small fishing ports of Aandalsnes and Namsos. The pincers never met. The British were heavily bombed and completely outfought by a well armed, well trained and well led ruthless enemy. The British casualties at Aandalsnes were due to the pitiful state of their fighting capacity. Four officers and 17 other ranks were killed, 21 officers and 128 other ranks were wounded; no less than 76 officers and 1,156 other ranks were taken prisoner.[14] The remaining British force were obliged to conduct a humiliating evacuation from their original post of disembarkation. They were in Norway for less than one month. Much the same happened at Namsos. Narvik was eventually captured on May 28 but evacuated on June 8 in the light of developments on the mainland of Europe. All other British troops were out of Norway by May 2.

The Royal Air Force was almost totally absent from the operations. Complete supremacy over the skies over Norway was exercised by the Luftwaffe. It was the single most important factor which led to the defeat of the Anglo-French forces. The occupation of Norwegian airfields had been a first priority for the invading German forces. Incredibly, RAF bombers were instructed not to attack these air bases in either Norway or Denmark until April 11 because of the possible danger to civilians. Appeasement tacticians were alive and well, in war as in peace. They had every prospect of losing the war as they had lost the peace.[15] The RAF had no long-range fighters capable of operating over Norway. With all the airfields occupied by the Germans, there were no bases from which their short-range fighters could operate either. The Luftwaffe reigned supreme.

The cardinal lesson that should have been learned from the whole sorry business, but was not, was that without domination of the air, land and naval forces were impotent. When operations commenced, Churchill remarked 'our hands are now free and we can apply our overwhelming sea power on the Norwegian coast.' He could not have been more wrong. The overwhelming power exercised during the Norwegian campaign was exercised not by the Royal Navy but by the German Luftwaffe. There were a few material gains to the Anglo-French arising out of the Norwegian campaign. The German navy lost

---

[14]Thompson, Laurence, *1940: Year of Legend, Year of History*, Collins Fontana (1968), 63.
[15]Rouse, A.L., *All Souls and Appeasement*, Macmillan (1961), 106.

three cruisers and ten destroyers. A further two heavy cruisers and a pocket battleship were damaged and put out of action for a while.[16] The Allies also gained over a million tons of Norwegian merchant shipping. But these material items in no way compensated for the humiliating defeat incurred in the first direct military confrontation of the war.

International opinion drew their own conclusions. Joseph Kennedy, American Ambassador in London, described Great Britain as inefficient and degenerate. In his opinion, she would lose the war.[17] The political repercussions in London were even more important. They were immediate and far-reaching. The poor performance of the nation's armed forces in and around Norway was such that Chamberlain's Government was now deemed incapable of prosecuting the war successfully.[18] It also clearly demonstrated the extent of Great Britain's unpreparedness for war and the neglect of the pre-war Chamberlain and Baldwin Governments. They had failed to match Great Britain's assumed world power status with equivalent world power muscle.

For these reasons, Chamberlain's Government had to fall, and it did. First-hand knowledge of the amateurish bungling in Norway reached the House of Commons through some of their own members who had served with the expeditionary force. One of them, Captain Martin Lindsay, sought an interview on his return to Great Britain on May 5 not with his Conservative colleagues but with the Leader of the Labour Opposition. To him he imparted the full details of the incompetence and inadequacies that had prevailed. It was part of a deliberate attempt to bring Chamberlain down.[19]

That eventually occurred in the wake of a memorable Commons debate on May 7 and 8. There were of course small dissident groups in the Commons who had opposed Chamberlain and his policies even before the Norwegian campaign. There was Churchill's group of supporters, there was the so-called Eden group, and there were those who had collected around Duff Cooper following the Munich Agreement and Cooper's subsequent resignation. These dissidents, originally few in number, now coalesced and were joined by others who became active following the Norwegian campaign. The Marquess of Salisbury

---

[16]These losses became a factor in connection with the German Operation Sealion, the proposed invasion of Great Britain.

[17]According to Kennedy a meeting of US attachés had agreed that England was going to lose the war. Thompson, Laurence, *1940: Year of Legend, Year of History*, Collins Fontana (1968), 68.

[18]A Gallup poll taken in March measured confidence in Chamberlain's Government at 67 per cent. In May it was 32 per cent.

[19]Thompson, Laurence, *1940: Year of Legend, Year of History*, Collins Fontana (1968), 59.

was chairman of the small but powerful Watch Committee. Following Salisbury's talks among Conservative MPs, he advised Halifax at the Foreign Office that the position warranted the formation of a truly National Government with Liberal and Labour representation. On May 6 the same point was taken up by the *Evening Standard*. For the first time, suggestions were being made that Chamberlain should stand down.

Opinions differed as to his replacement. The *Evening Standard* favoured Halifax. Others favoured Churchill. Similar articles appeared in the *Times*, the *Daily Telegraph* and the *Manchester Guardian*. On May 7, an open letter by Stafford Cripps appeared on the front page of the *Daily Mail*. Cripps was a lawyer of some distinction and a prominent former member of the Labour Party. He had been travelling abroad extensively. He had been listening to international comment on the Norwegian defeat. In his letter he advocated a truly National Government, a small War Cabinet holding no departmental responsibility comprising Churchill, Lloyd George, Eden, Morrison and Attlee (from the Labour Party) and the replacement of Chamberlain by Halifax as Prime Minister. Significantly, Cripps the lawyer, saw no difficulty in accommodating Halifax from the House of Lords as Prime Minister.[20]

The real issue was that there could not be a National Government with Chamberlain as its head. Representatives from the Labour opposition refused to serve under him. This is what ultimately sealed Chamberlain's fate. He was unwilling and unable to form the National Government which all now saw as a necessary first step in the right direction.

It is remarkable that during the period which followed the conclusion of the Norwegian campaign and the crucial debate on May 7 and 8, neither Chamberlain or Halifax seemed aware of the possible outcome. The *Daily Express* under Beaverbrook and the Kemsley Press continued to support Chamberlain to the very end. Chamberlain wrote to thank Beaverbrook: 'When so many are sounding the defeatist note over a minor setback it is a relief to read such a courageous and inspiring summons to a saner view.' Meanwhile, Lord Kemsley was reassuring Chamberlain that 'the overwhelming mass of the people regard the hysteria of your critics with contempt.'[21] Thus

---

[20]This was an issue raised later, as an excuse by Halifax and as a reason by Churchill, as to why Halifax could not take up the Premiership. It could have been dealt with by a simple change to the Standing Orders of the Commons by means of a Commons resolution or by Act of Parliament, if deemed necessary. It was a convenient red herring used by a different people for different purposes.
[21]Chamberlain papers, 7/11/33/117. Kemsley to Chamberlain, May 9, 1940.

do press barons pretend what public opinion is that they are supposed to reflect. On May 6, the day before the Commons debate, Halifax recorded in his diary: 'Considerable political, clamour but I doubt whether this, at present at all events, will amount to much.' Nevertheless, according to the same diary, Halifax saw Morrison on that day about the possibility of Labour joining the Government.[22] It may be that Halifax had a shrewder idea of where things were going then he had publicly declared.

The debate in the Commons started calmly enough on May 7. It ended in near turmoil on the following day. At first it was not the intention of the Labour Party to force a division. But they had second thoughts after the first day. The vote on the division brought down the Chamberlain Government. Two hundred and eighty-one members voted for the Government, 200 voted against. Sixty-five members who would normally have voted in support of the Government abstained. Thirty-three Conservative members actually voted against the Government.[23] The Government majority of 81 compared with the equivalent figure at the time of Munich of 222. Under the circumstances, the Government was unsustainable in its existing form. The Commons had at last caught the mood of the British people.

In retrospect, the only surprising feature about the vote was that 281 MPs still voted for the continuance of a Government already damned by its own performance. The debate which preceded the vote produced good speeches, some including a theatrical touch. All in their different ways contributed to the inevitable end-result. Sir Roger Keyes, resplendent in the uniform of an Admiral of the Fleet and one of the worst speakers in the House, was bitterly critical of the Government's performance. His very incoherence and inaudibility seemed to carry an even greater weight of sincere conviction. Leo Amery, normally a rather boring speaker, excelled. He criticised not only the conduct of the Norwegian campaign but of the war generally. It was he who quoted the famous words of Cromwell and directed them at the Chamberlain Government. 'You have sat too long here for any good you have been doing. Depart, I say, and let us have done with you. In the name of God, go!' Amery was a personal friend of Chamberlain. He was MP for a neighbouring constituency in Chamberlain's home city of Birmingham. It was probably his speech which at last brought home to Chamberlain the extent of the threat to his personal position.

---

[22]Joining which Government? Chamberlain's or his?

[23]They included Leo Amery, Duff Cooper, Richard Law, Robert Boothby, Edward Spears, Harold Macmillan, Emrys Evans, Ronald Tree, Lord Woolmar and serving officers like Quintin Hogg, John Profumo and William Anstruther-Grey.

The following day, Morrison opened for the Opposition and announced the intention of forcing a division. His attack was factual and irrefutable. Chamberlain's reply was a disaster. He seemed ill-prepared and he lacked his usual arrogance of delivery. He attempted to drag the debate down to a personal level. He called upon his friends to support him in the voting lobbies that night. It is sad that at a time of grave national crisis he should have deemed entitlement to votes on the strength of personal relationships. It is even sadder that he should say as much in the debate. Sam Hoare followed Chamberlain and applied his usual balm to try and smooth things down. It was the calm before the storm.

As Hoare sat down, Lloyd George got up. He delivered a bitter personal attack on the Prime Minister. There was a mutual antipathy between these two parliamentary veterans going back 20 years to the 1914–18 war. Lloyd George was unlikely to pass up the opportunity of humiliating his old rival in front of the packed assembly of the Commons. He was of course one of the best speakers in the House and was well prepared. His indictment was detailed and it was complete. He also supplied the remedy:

> It is a not a question of who are the Prime Minister's friends. It is a far bigger issue than that. The Prime Minister must remember that he has met this formidable foe of ours in peace and war and he has always been worsted. He is not in a position to appeal on the grounds of friendship. He has appealed for sacrifice. The nation is prepared for any sacrifice so long as it has leadership. I say solemnly that the Prime Minister should give an example of sacrifice because there is nothing which can contribute more to victory in this war than that he should sacrifice the seals of office.

One great orator of the House was followed by another as Churchill rose at 10 p.m. on May 8 to wind up for the Government. Churchill's job was immense. He had to reconcile the irreconcilable. He had to convey his loyalty to Chamberlain. At the same time he, more than most, knew that there was something drastically wrong with the conduct of the war at the highest level. He had to shoulder the burden of blame for at least part of the operations in Norway without being seen to be disloyal to the armed forces. He also had to avoid seriously damaging his own personal position. Like Halifax he probably had a good idea as the ultimate outcome. He had to play his cards very carefully. He knew that the majority of the Conservative members of the Commons were still Chamberlain men. They were not yet Churchill men.

The manner in which he took all these factors into account was remarkable. Lloyd George commented: 'Mr Churchill must not allow himself to be converted into an air raid shelter to keep the splinters from hitting his colleagues.' There was near tumult at the conclusion of proceedings and after the voting had been announced. Some members rendered a raucous version of 'Rule Britannia', others shouted 'Who missed the bus?' and 'In the name of God, go'. Not all viewed the scenes of jubilation in the same light. Rab Butler commented: 'The final scene in the House was very distasteful. It reminded me of certain episodes in the history of Peel. The singing of "Rule Britannia" by Harold Macmillan was much resented by Neville who rose looking old and white haired as he has become and marching out, realising as he did, that he could not go on.'[24]

Halifax was amazed at the hostility displayed towards Chamberlain. A friend of Halifax reported a conversation he had with him at the time: 'We discussed the chances of his having to take over that ghastly and thankless job. He thought it would never work, this difficulty of the Lords and Commons being impossible and having someone to deputise for you would always be unsuccessful. He dreaded the thought.'[25] This was hardly the view of a man anxious and eager to embrace the top responsibility. It appeared also that he was already arranging the peg upon which he could hang his hat of refusal.[26]

Outside the Commons there was a groundswell of public opinion that Churchill, not Halifax, should replace Chamberlain. The ordinary Britisher viewed Churchill as the only action man in the Government, an inspirational and larger-than-life figure, spoiling for a fight and in their view the only man capable of giving the leadership required.[27] But all this was lost on the Conservative Party machine at Westminster. The Conservative whips were concerned only as to the ways and means of propping up the Chamberlain Government. On the day following the debate they made frantic efforts to come to terms with the dissident Conservative groups by agreeing concessions. Their hope was a reconstructed Government under Chamberlain and without Labour representation. Thus did party politics take precedence over public accountability at a time of national crisis.[28]

---

[24]Butler papers, G13. Diary note, May 8, 1940.

[25]Roberts, Andrew, *The Holy Fox*, Weidenfeld and Nicolson (1991), 197.

[26]As the possibilities of appointment became more and more imminent, Halifax also developed a persistent stomach ache.

[27]The relevant quote by the author's father at the time was 'If it's a scrap you're after then Winston is your man.'

[28]Even later, after Churchill had assumed the position of Prime Minister, he was not accepted by the majority of the Conservative Party in the Commons, although he was clearly the people's choice. A national crisis was not allowed to disturb the serious business of party politics.

The efforts of the party Whips were unrewarded. The dissident groups required a truly National Government. Labour refused to serve under Chamberlain. They were adamant. Chamberlain therefore had to go. The only issue was as to who was to replace him. In the event, it was Churchill. At first sight, that would appear to be extraordinary. Chamberlain had already told Halifax that in the event of his enforced resignation he would look to Halifax to succeed him.[29] Chamberlain also knew that the parliamentary Conservative Party did not consider Churchill as an acceptable candidate. How then did Churchill assume power? It has been reported and accepted that Halifax was offered the Premiership by Chamberlain and declined it. The offer was made at a meeting at 10 Downing Street during the late afternoon of May 9. In addition to Chamberlain and Halifax, Churchill and the Conservative Chief Whip, Captain David Margesson, were in attendance. Halifax declined the offer because of the difficulties envisaged in a situation where a peer was Prime Minister but responsible to the Commons. Churchill then took by default.

In fact, far more was involved than the constitutional issue. It is clear that Chamberlain and Churchill conspired together to bring about the result that they both desired. Chamberlain does not win many accolades for the part he played in one of Great Britain's more unfortunate periods of history, but here was one properly due but never publicised. Having regard to the shooting war that had now started, Churchill's appointment as a war leader turned out to be truly inspired. It awakened the people of Great Britain to the dangers that confronted them and it led them to wage war with total commitment. The one man responsible for that appointment was Neville Chamberlain.

Chamberlain and Churchill did not conspire together by direct contact. They did it through Kingsley Wood, a close friend of Chamberlain. Churchill was invited to lunch with Eden on May 9. He was surprised to find Kingsley Wood there as a fellow guest. Although a close friend of Chamberlain, he was not particularly close to either Eden or Churchill. He seemed to know about the meeting fixed for later that afternoon. He carefully primed Churchill as to how to play his hand. In particular, he advised Churchill that Halifax would raise the constitutional issue and when he did, Churchill was to say absolutely nothing.[30] Churchill duly attended the meeting with Chamberlain, Halifax and Margesson at 4.30 p.m. that same afternoon. Everything

---

[29]In accordance with the procedures then applicable (later changed) the outgoing Conservative Prime Minister had the right and obligation to nominate his successor to the Sovereign for approval.
[30]The fact of the conspiracy was confirmed to Beaverbrook by Kingsley Wood shortly before the latter's death in 1943 and is the subject of a memorandum in the Beaverbrook papers.

went exactly as anticipated. Chamberlain said that he was prepared to serve under either Halifax or Churchill. Margesson stressed the need for unity. That was not now possible under Chamberlain. Chamberlain offered the Premiership to Halifax. Halifax raised the constitutional issue. Neither Chamberlain or Churchill said anything. Neither sought to reassure Halifax that the difficulty could be overcome (which it could). Halifax responded by suggesting that Churchill was more fitted to act in time of war. Both Chamberlain and Churchill accepted Halifax's verdict. With (according to Halifax) suitable expressions of regret and humility, Churchill said that 'he could not but feel the force of Halifax's arguments'. The matter was thus resolved.

The meeting was a sham. Chamberlain and Churchill had together conspired to bring about one of the most vital decisions taken during the entire course of the 1939–45 war, at least as far as Great Britain was concerned. It is interesting to consider the thoughts of the three main players as they sat there that afternoon. Those of Halifax and Churchill are not difficult to analyse but Chamberlain's are intriguing. It is quite apparent that Halifax was more than apprehensive about the responsibilities that were going to be heaped upon his shoulders. He knew nothing about war, which he abhorred.[31] The thought of re-entering the hurly-burly of the Commons probably appalled him too. He had always found life in the Commons distasteful in his early days. The constitutional issue was a godsend to him, as was Churchill's acceptance of the post. Halifax's stomach ache, which had persisted up to 4.30 p.m. on May 9, no doubt immediately eased thereafter.

Churchill got what he wanted. He knew the constitutional issue was a red herring; but it served a purpose, so he left it there. He felt perfectly at ease with himself: 'At last I had the authority to give directions over the whole scene. I felt as if I was walking with destiny and that all my past life had been but a preparation for this hour and for this trial'.[32] Chamberlain's thoughts were no doubt more complex. By May 1940 he was consumed by a deep personal hatred of Adolf Hitler. There were many people in Great Britain who hated Hitler and everything he stood for. But theirs, in the main, was a hearsay hatred. Chamberlain's hatred was personal, born out of bitter experience. As Lloyd George had pointed out in the recent debate, Chamberlain had been worsted by Hitler in both peace and war. Chamberlain did not take kindly to being worsted. He was not that sort of man. He must have dearly wished to bring Hitler to his knees, either one way or

---

[31]The German invasion of the Low Countries was thought to be imminent. No doubt this was a further cause for apprehension as far as Halifax was concerned.
[32]Winston Churchill, *The Second World War*, Vol I, 601.

another. He also knew, in the wake of the Norwegian disaster, that Hitler had taken up the military option, was now intent upon a shooting war and was capable of waging it with ruthless efficiency. He must have known that the die had been cast and the only hope Great Britain had of surviving was to wage war with equally ruthless efficiency. It followed that his successor would have to be a person with a similar view and the ability to convert the concept into reality.

What were Chamberlain's personal thoughts about the two candidates? To what extent had each of them demonstrated their loyalty to Great Britain's name and their commitment to the war effort? Certainly, Churchill had demonstrated his personal loyalty to Chamberlain ever since his appointment to the Cabinet as First Sea Lord at the outbreak of hostilities. Chamberlain himself had said 'To me personally, Winston is absolutely loyal'.[33] It may be, of course, that the reasons for Churchill's loyalty were two-faced. His own position in the Conservative parliamentary party was fragile. He was considered to be, and was, a rebellious, free-thinking, volatile maverick by nature. He knew that if he put a foot wrong with Chamberlain, his Cabinet position would be in jeopardy. But there was more to it than that. Churchill retained in his character a certain amount of old-style chivalry. He was grateful to Chamberlain for his restoration to office. He also had an instinctive sympathy for Chamberlain for his treatment at the hands of Hitler.

For all these reasons Churchill had never wavered in his personal loyalty towards Chamberlain. Nowhere better had he demonstrated this than in the recent Norwegian debates. If there was no doubt in Chamberlain's mind as to Churchill's loyalty and commitment to war, there must have been serious doubts as to Halifax, on both counts. On more than one occasion Halifax and his acolyte, Rab Butler, had far exceeded their Cabinet authority to indulge their freelance peacemaking activities. Halifax had encouraged Tavistock, and Tavistock had been in direct contact with the enemy through their Dublin legation. Halifax also appeared to know more about the Venlo incident than had been passed onto the Cabinet. Butler had talked peace with Hohenlohe in Switzerland. Halifax had set in motion more than one amateur peacemaker to travel the neutral capitals of Europe.

Of course, disloyalties of this kind will not affect relations with the injured party if they pass unnoticed. But that would not be the case with the Halifax/Butler freelance activities. Chamberlain had his own personal intelligence service. It had been operated for several years

---

[33]Thompson, Laurence, *1940: Year of Legend, Year of History*, Collins Fontana (1968), 69.

through his personal friend and confidant, Sir Joseph Ball. It was very efficient. The Halifax/Butler indiscretions would have been well researched by Ball, noted and passed on to his chief. Chamberlain therefore knew that Halifax was a pacifist, concerned primarily with peacemaking activities. He was not concerned with the vigorous prosecution of the war. He was therefore not the person to take the helm in the particular circumstances prevailing in May 1940.[34]

Chamberlain's attendance upon the King on the evening of May 9 proved difficult. The King was a solid Halifax man. He was no great lover of Churchill, the man who had supported his brother in the abdication crisis. Halifax was a personal friend of the King and his confidant. He was a frequent visitor to the Palace for dinner and often walked through the Palace gardens when on his way to Downing Street from his suite at the Dorchester. Lady Halifax was a lady-in-waiting to the Queen. The King had expected Chamberlain's recommendation to be Halifax. Chamberlain explained the constitutional difficulty. The King suggested that Halifax's peerage could be placed in abeyance. When Chamberlain declined to consider this obvious solution, the King became bitterly opposed to Chamberlain's recommendation of Churchill. He considered it to be a royal snub.[35]

Queen Mary and Queen Elizabeth both subsequently wrote personal letters of sympathy to Chamberlain on the occasion of his resignation. No similar letter was ever received from the King. According to Mrs Chamberlain this omission caused her husband deep hurt.[36] Queen Mary also wrote to the mother of Jack Colville, assistant private secretary to Chamberlain, advising her to encourage her son not to serve under Churchill. Churchill may have been the people's choice. He certainly was not the choice of the British royal family.[37]

Others were equally unenthusiastic. Late that evening, in the under-secretaries' room at the Foreign Office, Colville and his colleagues Rab Butler, Alexander Dunglass (Chamberlain's principal private secretary, later Lord Douglas-Home) and Chips Channon, Butler's private secretary, drank champagne. They raised their glasses to Chamberlain with the Jacobite toast 'to the King over the water'. Butler had much to say, possibly prompted by the champagne. Referring to the Churchill succession, he opined that 'the good clean tradition of British politics had been sold to the greatest adventurer of modern

---

[34]Had Halifax succeeded Chamberlain in May 1940, he might well have negotiated peace terms after the fall of France. That this did not happen is due to Chamberlain as well as Churchill.

[35]Why did Chamberlain not tell the King the truth, that Halifax was a pacifist and therefore, in Chamberlain's view, unsuited for the job in hand?

[36]Letter from Mrs Neville Chamberlain to Alan Lascelles, January 12, 1954.

[37]Halifax diary, May 10, 1940.

political history'. Butler claimed that he had tried 'earnestly and long to persuade Halifax to accept the Premiership, but the sudden coup of Winston and his rabble was a serious disaster'. He blamed Chamberlain, who had 'weakly surrendered to a half-bred American whose main support was that of inefficient but talkative people of similar type'.[38]

Hitler's reaction to Churchill's appointment was surprising: 'Perhaps it is just as well that the man responsible for England's war against us will now be fully and officially responsible. I hope all the more that some day I shall have the chance of coming to an understanding with the man. If I succeed in doing so, we shall find him a really good and reliable friend.'[39] Even this contribution to wishful thinking from Hitler mentions yet again the two points he had always made as his view on Great Britain: he had never wanted war and he hoped to come to an arrangement which would bring it to an end. With Churchill in the saddle, that was a near impossibility.

The German view of peace therefore soon took on the same perspective as had been Chamberlain's. It was essential to distance the British people from 'Churchill and his gangsters'. Unfortunately for the Germans, this belief had the opposite effect. The propaganda affixing Churchill with the label of Public Enemy Number One helped enormously to ease him into the position of Public Hero Number One with the British. This was much helped by Churchill's own flamboyance and flair for personal publicity. Unlike Chamberlain, he did not categorise the German nation into good Germans and bad Germans and seek to detach the one from the other. In Churchill's eyes there was only one problem, and that was the German nation itself. It had to be brought to its knees in mortal combat. Thus, with Hitler already taking up the military option in the West, the prospects for peace faded.

There was irony in the situation. Chamberlain had rejected early peace proposals because he could not trust Hitler. Hitler had gradually lost patience and had turned to the military option: he would knock France out of the war and isolate Great Britain. Great Britain would then have to accept reasonable peace terms. The way would then be clear to seek *Lebensraum* and destroy Russia. When Sumner Welles brought the promise of American guarantees to underpin a negotiated peace, Chamberlain had second thoughts. But this was too late. Hitler was no longer interested in parleying. He had committed himself to the military option. His exercise of that option had brought down Chamberlain. In his place, there was now a man of war. Thus the

---

[38]Colville diaries, 122.
[39]Hesse, Fritz, *Hitler and the English*, Alan Wingate (1954), 98–99.

possibilities of peace in the early summer of 1940 had receded more by the accident of events than by design, to reappear as soon as it became apparent that France was falling apart and Great Britain was indeed isolated. The Phoney War had ended. The Shooting War had started.

Flanders, Dunkirk and a political intervention

The lifting of almost all the British Expeditionary Force from the beaches around Dunkirk in May/June 1940 and their evacuation to England has been described and widely publicised as the 'miracle of Dunkirk'. It is an apt description, at least from the British point of view.[40] Apart from the God-given benign weather which prevailed throughout and provided calm seas, the miracle was man-made. The German generals were confident that no one would escape their advancing armies. The British Government reckoned on a lift of no more than 45,000 over a maximum period of two days. In fact, 338,226 men were lifted in an operation that extended over a seven-day period from May 27 to June 3.

The embarkations were conducted by 860 ships of all shapes and sizes, including pleasure steamboats, ferries, river cruisers, fishing smacks and outboard motorboats as well as the ships of the Royal Navy.[41] Every sort of amateur sailor and volunteer was involved. The German Luftwaffe, which had played such a dominant role in the events leading up to the evacuation, had no strategic effect on the operation. They were met for the first time by British Spitfire fighter aircraft operating from bases across the English Channel. They were more than a match for the Messerschmidt 109 and had lethal effect against the German bombers.[42]

Three hundred and ninety-four German aircraft were destroyed in combat, against RAF losses of 114. On the ground, British beach discipline and improvisation were in the main part exemplary.[43] Losses

---

[40]The French considered it an act of desertion. On May 24, General Weygand, the French Commander-in-Chief, ordered Blanchard, one of his generals, to organise an extensive defensive perimeter around Dunkirk. It was to be used as a supply port for a northern bridgehead. At the same time, the British Government were instructing Gort, Commander in Chief of the British forces to evacuate through the port. (Thompson, Laurence, *1940 Year of Legend, Year of History*, Collins Fontana (1968), 131).

[41]A.J.P. Taylor, *English History, 1914–1945*, Oxford University Press (1965), 486.

[42]These circumstances were of particular significance in view of what was to follow after the fall of France.

[43]An unfortunate exception was the killing of Major General Bernard Montgomery's operations officer by lawless French soldiers alleging betrayal (Brooke papers 5/2/1, Kings College, London).

of military equipment were substantial.[44] Two hundred and forty-three ships were sunk, including six Royal Navy destroyers, and a further nineteen destroyers were damaged. But these losses did not distract from the fact that almost the entire British Expeditionary Force had been brought back to its homeland to fight another day. Not a victory by any means, but certainly a miracle of human endeavour.

Extraordinarily, the Dunkirk miracle was preceded by an earlier, man-made miracle which has not enjoyed the same publicity, although without it the Dunkirk miracle would never have occurred. General Gerd von Rundstedt, German Commander of Army Group A at the time, described it in retrospect as 'one of the great turning-points of the war'. The circumstances were indeed remarkable. On the morning of Friday, May 24, 1940, Allied forces comprising nine divisions of the Belgian Army, ten divisions of the British Expeditionary Force and remnants of the French First Army, comprising in total 375,000 men, were trapped on the French/Belgian coast. Their backs were to the sea and they were surrounded on three sides by strong German forces.

Their predicament had arisen following the launch of the long-awaited German invasion of the Low Countries on May 10, 1940. This had been followed by the breakthrough of concentrated armour with air support through the Ardennes at Sédan, the race to the Channel coast at Abbeville and the turn northwards to roll up, isolate and finally trap the Allied forces north of the Somme.[45] By May 24 these Allied forces had been compressed into a small triangle. Its base ran along the Channel coast from Gravelines to Ostend. The apex was just short of Valenciennes, some 70 miles inland. The north-eastern side of the triangle was defended in part by the Belgian Army. They were to capitulate some four days later. British and French units were also involved in that area. The south-western side of the triangle was defended in the main by the British.

Their defences were strung out along the north side of the so-called canal line which comprised the Aa and other inter-connected canals and canalised rivers stretching some 20 miles from the coast down to St Omer and then a further 40 miles from Aire to Béthune and La Bassée, where they joined up with the Deurle canal, turning eastwards just short of Valenciennes. This canal line was the only natural defence line available to the British. It was manned by a scratch force hastily

---

[44]They comprised 475 tanks, 7,000 tons of ammunition, 9,000 rifles, 400 artillery pieces.

[45]The campaign was a brilliant exposition of the *blitzkrieg* method of warfare. Conceived by the British military strategist, Captain Basil Liddell Hart, embraced by forward-looking German generals and first introduced in the Polish campaign, it swept all before it in the Low Countries and France during May/June 1940.

improvised from line-of-communication troops and half-trained divisional troops who had been employed as pioneers. The main British fighting force had been involved further east, in what was known as the Arras salient. A single battalion defended the 20-mile stretch of the Aa canal between the coast and St Omer. The defending forces were equally weak down the lower reaches of the canals.

There were bridges across the canals, not all of them wired for demolition. In the case of four of the bridges elements of General Guderian's 19 Panzer Corps were already across to the western side of the canal. They were within 15 miles of Dunkirk. Guderian's forces formed part the Kleist and Holt Armoured Groups which were then poised to make the final assault across the canals to Dunkirk, break through the weak southern defences and crush the remaining Allied forces against General Bock's 6th and 8th Armies advancing from the north. Three hundred and seventy-five thousand men would be 'put in the bag'. As the diary entry of General Sir Alan Brooke records on May 24, 'Nothing but a miracle can save the BEF now'.[46]

At 11 a.m. on that same day the miracle duly arrived. For two whole days, until the afternoon of Sunday, May 26, the German tanks sat on the southern banks of the canal line, idle and impotent. They did not advance one inch from the positions they had taken up on the previous Friday morning when they had seized the four bridgeheads. In fact, some units who had reached Hazebrouck, north of the canals, fell back to the canal line. The British were thus provided with two days' freedom from attacks. They were able to spend this invaluable waiting time in strengthening their defences on the northern banks and making appropriate redispositions of their forces.[47] They were also given the time to organise the pending evacuation of troops from Dunkirk, which commenced a few days later.[48]

The effect of the delay was critical in strategic terms. The war diary of 39 Corps of the Holt Armoured Group records that 'as foreseen, the two-day halt on the southern bank of the canal line produced two results. The troops suffered considerable casualties when they eventually attacked across the canals and there was no interception of the

---

[46]The Alan Brooke papers, King's College, London.

[47]In particular, the British 5th and 50th Divisions, earmarked for an attack southwards on May 26, were switched to the northern front to strengthen the defence against Bock's Army Group B, a move which proved inspired in view of the capitulation of the Belgian army on May 28. Thompson, Laurence, *1940: Year of Legend, Year of History*, Collins Fontana (1968), 127. It was this switch, without notice to the French, which later led to charges of deserting the French.

[48]A colleague of the author graphically described the two-day pause thus: 'We had two days in which to eat, sleep, wash, shave and shit.' As well as these domestic priorities the military tasks described above, also received attention.

British/French forces escaping westwards from the hills area towards the Channel'. Three hundred and seventy-five thousand Allied troops were not put in the bag. General Brooke's miracle had arrived and General von Rundstedt's turning point of the war had occurred. The two-day standstill had lost the German generals a quick, easy and total victory which would have involved the complete destruction of the British Expeditionary Force and all its equipment. It also made possible the miracle of Dunkirk.

How and why, then, did the enforced halt to the German advance occur? The first is easily answered, the second more open to debate. The advance halted because Adolf Hitler ordered it to halt. The order was unequivocal. It was issued by Hitler from the headquarters of General von Rundstedt's Army Group A at Charleville, near Sédan at 11.32 a.m. on Friday, May 24, following a conference between Hitler and Rundstedt during the morning. It was phrased clearly: 'By order of the Führer. Attack north-west of Arras is to be limited to general line Lens, Béthune, St Omer, Gravelines. The canal line will not repeat not be crossed until further notice.'[49] The further notice to resume the offensive operations followed on the following Sunday afternoon, May 26.

No reason has ever been given for Hitler's intervention in the battle or his attendance at Rundstedt's headquarters. Things were going extraordinarily well for the Germans. They were about to apply the *coup de grâce*. Although Hitler was not above 'advising' his generals, at this early stage in the war he rarely intervened to give a direct order himself on strictly military matters. Why did he intervene on this occasion? Why did he give an order which he must have known, or would have been advised, might allow the British forces to escape?

It is a difficult question to answer. Much controversy has raged over the years between those generals personally affected by the decision, politicians wishing to make political capital out of the consequences and researchers seeking the truth. One explanation is that the decision was a military necessity. If so, none of Hitler's staff officers or his operational generals subscribed to that view. Their professional opinions, given both at the time and retrospectively in postwar interrogations, varied from the contemptuous to the sarcastic. The diary entry of Hitler's Chief of Staff, Halder, for May 24 reads: 'The entire left wing which has no enemy before it will thus be stopped dead in its tracks by the direct order of the Führer.'[50] Guderian, Operations

[49]Hans Jacobsen and Jürgen Rohwer, *Dokumente zum Westfeldzug*, Frankfurt (1970), 120.
[50]Ellis, Major L.F., *The War in France and Flanders 1939–1940*, HMSO (1953), 350 and Appendix II, 398.

Commander of the 19 Panzer Corps, states that he and his chief, General von Kleist, were 'utterly speechless'.[51] General von Bock, Commander of Army Group B pressing in from the north, commented that 'unfortunately, the armour was held back for two days. To this I say I regard the seizure of Dunkirk now as absolutely necessary, otherwise the English might transport out of Dunkirk what they please, right under our nose.'[52,53] Major von Treskow, one of Rundstedt's staff officers, describes the decision as 'pure madness'.[54] Halder commented further: 'The troops are frozen to the spot when the enemy's rear could be cut at any time you wanted to attack.'[55]

Hitler himself mentioned the unfavourable terrain for tanks. He was referring to the low-lying flatlands of northern Flanders. No doubt his own experience of 1914–18 mud would have been brought to mind. But General Guenther Blumentritt, Rundstedt's Chief of Operations has since pointed out: 'The Panzer divisions had coped with even more difficult ground in the swamps and mud at the River San, Lemberg and Grodek in Poland and Hitler knew that.'[56] In any case, Hitler cleared the tanks two days later and the terrain had not changed. RAF reconnaissance, reporting the halt of armour on May 24, suggested that the need for fuel replenishment and maintenance work were possible reasons for the halt; but the Panzer columns had long since learnt the art of feeding off the country for fuel (no 'scorched earth' policies were adopted in France). Blumentritt, Rundstedt's Chief of Operations, has also confirmed that ongoing maintenance had received every priority during operations and 'before Dunkirk the number of our tanks was growing again'.[57] In any case, Dunkirk was 15 miles away, not 150.

In the overall battle plan for the final phase of operations, the major share of the fighting had been allocated to Bock's northern Army Group because it contained a heavier weight of infantry. This was no reason why the Panzers in the south should halt in their tracks. A rapid advance along the coastal stretch through Dunkirk to Ostend presented the best opportunity for completing the encirclement of the BEF. The same point arises in connection with the suggestion that there was a need to preserve the armour for the operations then pending south of the Somme. It is true that Rundstedt's thoughts were already turning

---

[51] *Mit den Panzer in Ost und West*, 46.
[52] Von Bock's diary entry, as quoted in *Hitler Confronts England*, 86.
[53] Which is of course precisely what happened.
[54] Kurt Assman, *Deutsche Schicksalsjähre*, 167.
[55] Von Bock's diary, as above.
[56] Liddell Hart papers, 9/24/218 KUL. Blumentritt to Liddell Hart, May 17, 1950.
[57] Liddell Hart papers 9/24/218 KUL. Halder diary, May 23, 1940.

in that direction; his Group War Diary records on May 25 that 'The task of Army Group A can be considered to have been completed in the main.' In the light of the priority to be given to Bock in the final stage of the operation, that was certainly true; but it did not imply that Army Group A were to opt out of the obvious military advantage now presented. Rundstedt was not that kind of general. A further advance of a mere 15 miles against weak opposition would ensure the encirclement of 375,000 Allied troops.

Hitler's generals are of one mind in condemning Hitler's decision as inexplicable in military terms. In their opinion, there was no military reason why 375,000 Allied troops should not have been put in the bag and Great Britain deprived of almost the whole of her army. If, then, there was no good military reason for Hitler's decision, is it possible that it was guided by political considerations of which the Army generally were unaware?[58]

One internal German political factor has been raised as a reason for the decision, but on examination fails to warrant serious consideration. On May 23, Hermann Goering, Commander-in-Chief of the Luftwaffe, intervened in the battle. He telephoned Hitler and demanded, rather than suggested, that the National Socialist Luftwaffe should be given the honour of destroying the British Army. Exactly how it was to destroy an army was not explained. During the afternoon of May 24 Hitler certainly agreed that the Luftwaffe could 'seal off' the Dunkirk area; but according to Goering's own Intelligence Officer this agreement was not signalled to Goering until several hours after Hitler's meeting with Runsdtedt and the issue of Hitler's stop order. Goering's fanciful thinking was therefore unlikely to have been the factor underlying Hitler's decision.[59]

Hitler's decision on the morning of May 24, 1940, takes on the nature of true significance and meaning only in the light of external political matters. Hitler himself referred to the matter much later in the war, when he dictated his so-called political testament on February 26, 1945, when, even to him, defeat must have seemed inevitable. The time for pretence had gone. In the testament he expressed his deep regret that Churchill 'had been quite unable to appreciate the sporting spirit with which he had hesitated to destroy the British Army five years earlier'.[60] This is confirmed by his true friend and personal con-

---

[58]Hitler never blamed his generals, which suggests that the decision was not based upon military considerations. Churchill blamed Rundstedt and the generals. This is a pointer in the same direction. Churchill would wish to avoid any suggestion of a political dimension.

[59]Notes by General Adolf Heusinger, staff officer at Oberkommando des Heeres (Supreme Command of the German Army), cited by Pierre Galante in *Hitler Lives*, 91.

[60]H.R. Trevor Roper, *Hitler's War Directives, 1939/1945*, 26–29.

fidant, Rudolf Hess. According to an entry dated June 27, 1940, in the diary of the doctor then treating Hess, Dr Kersten, Hess had told him:

> We'll make peace with England the same way as France. The Führer has spoken of the great value of the British Empire. Germany, France and England against the enemy of Europe, Bolshevism. This was the reason why the Führer allowed the English Army to escape to Dunkirk. He did not wish to upset the possibility of understanding. He can't imagine England running her neck into the Soviet noose instead of saving it by coming to an arrangement with us.

The Hess comments come from a man with the reputation of 'being in Hitler's mind'. They echo views that Hitler had consistently expounded ever since he had written *Mein Kampf* with Hess at his side, and they confirm that Hitler's decision of May 24, 1940, was linked with his hopes at that time of some sort of settlement with Great Britain.[61] Blumentritt, who was present at the conference between Hitler and Rundstedt on the morning of May 24, recalls:

> Hitler was in good humour and gave his opinion that the war would be finished in six weeks. After that, he wished to conclude a reasonable peace with France. Then the way would be free for an agreement with Britain. He then astonished us by speaking with admiration of the British Empire, of the necessity for its existence and the civilisation that Britain had brought the world. He said that all he wanted from Britain was that she should acknowledge Germany's position on the continent. He concluded by saying that his aim was to make peace with Britain on the basis that she would regard as compatible with her honour to accept.

Blumentritt might well feel astonishment: Hitler was expressing these thoughts about his enemy in the heat of battle. But of course, he was only repeating a message taken almost verbatim from the pages of *Mein Kampf* and propagated by Hitler ever since the book was written. He was to further propagate these views over the weeks which followed to his generals, Mussolini, Ciano and finally in public. Ciano, the Italian Foreign Minister, was astonished to find, a month later with France prostrate and Hitler master of all Europe, that the Führer was

---

[61]In all Hitler's remarks about his relationship with Great Britain about this time, he constantly refers to an 'arrangement' or 'settlement'. He never uses the words 'victory' or 'defeat'.

still obsessed with the importance of maintaining the British Empire as a factor in world equilibrium.[62]

What then was in Hitler's mind if in fact his halt order was motivated primarily by political considerations? It was unlikely that he intended or anticipated that the British would escape through Dunkirk. Until quite late in the day that was deemed impossible by the German High Command, although Bock had signalled the danger. Goering had wanted to use the Luftwaffe to 'seal off' the sector and boasted that he would prevent any evacuation from Dunkirk. Rather would Hitler have looked at the trapped British forces as they appeared to be on the morning of May 24. They could be used as a huge hostage holding factor, pending the development of peace moves which were already in process.

On the very day of the halt order Halifax, the British Foreign Minister, was beginning his attempts to obtain Cabinet approval for an approach to Mussolini. The suggested approach was ostensibly to buy him off from joining the war at Hitler's side by bribing him with real estate from the Mediterranean treasure chest. In reality, it was Halifax's intention to talk to Bastaniani, the Italian Minister in London, with a view to obtaining Italian intervention in a general European settlement.[63] Hitler knew that with Halifax still prominent in the British Cabinet, there was always a good chance of peace moves blossoming. His judgement was not misplaced. He must have felt that the trapping of the British Expeditionary Force was going to be a powerful bargaining counter to help him on the way. Unfortunately for him the trap started leaking badly through Dunkirk, and after two days the halt order had to be rescinded. It was too late. The miracle of Dunkirk was now possible.

Events in France moved quickly to a climax following the Dunkirk evacuation. The evacuation itself prompted serious debate in the French Cabinet and led to the seeking of armistice terms. The French considered that they had been badly let down by the British. On May 26, Reynaud was in London reporting that the war was lost. The French had lost 120,000 killed, 250,000 wounded and one and a half million prisoners. The British had lost 3,500 killed in six weeks' fighting, almost the same as the Dutch in only a few days.[64] Military events south of the Somme were a formality. The so-called Weygand Line was breached on June 5–6. German troops entered Paris on June 14. Three days later Reynaud resigned and was replaced by Marshal

---

[62]Ciano diaries, 265–66.
[63]See Appendix III.
[64]Ponting, Clive, *1940: Myth and Reality*, Hamish Hamilton (1990), 95.

Pétain who, promptly asked for peace terms. Hostilities ended on the same day and an armistice was concluded at 6.50 p.m. on June 22. After a personal intervention by Hess, Hitler agreed that the armistice terms should be honourable throughout.[65]

The terms were in fact, generous. The French army was to be demobilised and all armaments surrendered. Germany was to occupy most of France from Dunkirk to the Pyrenees, including Paris and the whole of the northern and western seaboards. The Pétain/Laval French Government was to retain possession of that part of France running south from the Loire to the Mediterranean. The French fleet was to return to home ports and there to be demobilised and disarmed under German/Italian supervision.[66]

An interesting footnote to the French armistice conditions again illustrates Hitler's political input. Goebbels had issued a draft order relating to the French/British prisoners. They were to be treated in such a manner that their general vitality would be lowered. In the case of the French they were to be told they would never see France again. All French manpower between the ages of 18 and 35 were to work for their German masters in Germany. The brutal intent was to destroy France for good by destroying its manpower. Hitler cancelled the order. He replaced it by instructions 'for political reasons' that all prisoners taken in the West were to be afforded proper treatment. Under no circumstances were any of them to be interned in German concentration camps. Meanwhile, Hitler urged the military authorities to behave 'with great clemency' in France, because 'nothing deepens hatred between nations as much as excesses on the part of the occupying power'.[67] It is difficult to resist the conclusion that the French armistice terms and the measures taken thereafter were drafted with more than France in mind. Hitler was seeking to impress upon the world in general and Great Britain in particular, that he was a reasonable man when it came to negotiating peace terms.

So ended the military campaign in the Low Countries and France. Within the space of six weeks. France had been destroyed and Great Britain driven from Europe. Everything that the Germans had displayed in Norway in terms of military prowess had been repeated on an even greater scale and with even greater success. The equipment, training, discipline, generalship, tank/aircraft co-operation, morale, physical fitness and sheer fighting ability of the German troops were far superior to anything that the Western Allies could put up against

---

[65]Hess, Wolf Rüdiger, *My Father, Rudolf Hess*, W.H. Allen (1986), 51.
[66]Italy had entered the war at the side of Germany on June 10.
[67]Hesse, Fritz, *Hitler and the English*, Allan Wingate (1954), 101.

them. German mastery of the new techniques of *blitzkrieg* warfare had established the Wehrmacht as the most formidable army in the world. It was in these circumstances that Great Britain and her new Prime Minister found themselves alone in June 1940. It remained only for Hitler to come to his 'arrangement' with Great Britain and then turn his attention to his unresolved long-term policy objectives. He would be able to establish German *Lebensraum* in the East and destroy the seat of communism by falling upon Russia. It is no wonder that Hitler was in jubilant spirits in the high summer of 1940.

11

Summer crisis – a man for the hour

Let us therefore brace ourselves to our duties and so bear ourselves that if the British Empire and Commonwealth lasts for a thousand years, men will say 'This was their finest hour'.

WINSTON S CHURCHILL, June 18, 1940

After attending the preliminary proceedings of the French armistice at Compiègne on June 21 1940, Hitler went off with Hess and others to tour the old 1914–18 battlefields. He had, after all, spent most of his formative years there. No doubt he dwelt upon the turnaround of events in the previous 25 years since. He visited occupied Paris. He did not return to his headquarters at Tannenberg in the Black Forest until June 29. He held no military conferences between June 23 and July 11. He did not need to. The war was over. The threat from the West had been removed by force of arms. He could now turn his eyes towards the East. In Berne, the German Minister had hosted a ball 'to celebrate the end of the war.'[1] Halder's diary refers to demobilisation and plans for Germany's peacetime army in the West.

On June 15 Hitler had actually issued an order for the partial demobilisation of the army, reducing the number of operational divisions from 160 to 120. As a precautionary measure there was to be no demobilisation of navy or Luftwaffe personnel, pending the agreement of peace terms with Great Britain. That Great Britain would ask for such terms Hitler had no doubt. It is now known that he was ready, willing, even anxious to respond to any such request. Hitler even had in mind his appointee, Ernst Bohle, for the post of German Ambassador to London. He probably knew that there was little realistic prospect of coming to an arrangement with a Churchill Government.

There were other possibilities, however. A steady stream of British

[1]Sir David Kelly, The Ruling Few, Hollis & Carter (1952), 268.

right-wing and other sympathisers had visited him before the war. Advice had been received through the various intelligence sources as to early peace initiatives undertaken by the British during the Phoney War. It was believed that there was a small but potentially powerful faction in Great Britain that had representation right up to and including senior Foreign office and Cabinet levels. They had always had an abiding interest in making peace. Hess and Rosenberg had connections which went to the very heart of the British Establishment. It was only a matter of opening up channels of communication with these people so that they may be encouraged to speak out.

As for the vast majority of the ordinary people of Great Britain, surely they were sensible enough to realise that Germany's strength and Great Britain's predicament were such that the war that should never have started should now be brought to an end. Given a proper lead, Hitler felt, they would eject Churchill for an alternative Government led by people like Lloyd George and Halifax who would accept the generous peace terms that would be on offer. Germany would then become her ally, not her enemy. Germany would then take on Russia and remove the threat of communism from Europe for good. It was all so inescapably rational. All that Hitler had to do was to open up the channels of communication and sit and wait.[2]

One month later Hitler was still sitting and waiting, although with markedly less patience. Of course, if Great Britain would not come to the peace table voluntarily then she would have to be brought there by force of arms. Perhaps one further display of German armed strength was called for, although that cut across Hitler's strategic plans. He had little stomach for such a course of action. On July 13 at a conference General Halder noted Hitler's comments: 'If we smash England militarily, the British Empire will disintegrate. Germany however would not profit from this. With German blood we would achieve something from which only Japan, America and others will profit.'[3]

Nevertheless, with Churchill's defiant rhetoric in full flow across the English Channel it became necessary to go through the motions of planning an actual invasion of Great Britain. Alternatively, consideration could be given to forcing her to her knees by naval and air warfare. No one seems to have had much enthusiasm for these tasks. There had been no military thinking on such subjects before the war and the German

---

[2]It may be argued that if Hitler wanted peace so badly, why did he not initiate the peace moves himself? He probably found that incompatible with his status as the victor, with a string of diplomatic and military successes behind him. When the several unofficial and semi-official initiatives from the British side were effectively snuffed out by Churchill, then Hitler did initiate moves himself. The supreme initiative came from Hess in May 1941. These matters are dealt with in later chapters.
[3]Thompson, Laurence, *1940: Year of Legend, Year of History*, Fontana (1968), 165.

armed forces had never been assigned or organised with these objectives in mind. In the case of an invasion, the thought of amphibious operations across 26 miles of hostile water, in perhaps hostile weather seemed to have sapped the professional zeal of Hitler's generals.

Also, no one knew better than the Germans that air superiority was the vital ingredient to the success of any naval or military operations. Could that be guaranteed over the Channel and southern England against home-based Hurricanes and Spitfires supported by a highly sophisticated system of radar defences? The performance of the Luftwaffe in combat with the RAF at Dunkirk had been anything but encouraging. It was doubtful if it could dominate British air space to the extent required for an amphibious landing operation. Hitler dragged his feet. On May 21 Admiral Raeder sounded him out on the invasion prospects. He got no response.[4] On June 10, the Italians came into the war. They suggested that the peace terms for France were too generous and proposed an early invasion of Great Britain. There was no response.

On June 20 General Jodl, Hitler's chief planner of military operations, was explaining to naval staff officers that the Führer did not want the High Command to undertake studies and preparation for an invasion of England because of 'the possibility of making peace with Great Britain after the defeat of France.'[5] On July 22 Halder's diary records: 'Crossing the Channel appears very hazardous to the Führer. On that account, invasion is to be undertaken only if no other means is left to come to terms with Britain.'[6] Finally, on July 16 and with reluctance, Hitler issued Directive 16 to his planners 'to prepare for a landing operation against England and if necessary, to carry it out'. The last few words are significant. The fundamental truth was that the invasion of Great Britain conflicted with Hitler's personal feelings as well as his strategic objectives. As he confided to one of his inner circle, 'I shall in any case offer England an honourable peace. I do not want to conquer her. I want to come to terms with her. I want to force her to accept my friendship.'[7,8]

---

[4]Hitler believed that given the option, the British would ask for and get peace with honour.

[5]Costello, John, *Ten Days that saved the West*, Bantam Press (1991), 321.

[6]Meeting between Hitler and General Walter von Brauchitsch, Thompson, Laurence, *1940: Year of Legend, Year of History*, Fontana (1968), 173.

[7]Hesse, Fritz, *Hitler and the English*, Allan Wingate (1954), 114.

[8]There is more in these words than military strategy. They seem to express most clearly Hitler's feelings towards Great Britain. They echo his words in *Mein Kampf*. One wonders as to what terms of 'friendship' he had in mind in June 1940. Great Britain had suffered a string of humiliating defeats on both the diplomatic and, now, the military fronts. The British people had not yet shown their mettle or fighting spirit and Hitler must have been intoxicated by his success. Had he in mind a very junior partnership, which would have been unacceptable to Great Britain? This point is argued strenuously by Professor Bernard Martin in his excellent *Friedensinitiativen und Mach-politik im Zweiten Weltkrieg – 1939–42*, Droste Verlag, Dusseldorf (1974).

Even by the end of June Hitler was changing direction. He began to suggest that a naval blockade by U-boats and air warfare would 'if necessary' convince the British of the hopelessness of their cause. On July 31 he was confirming that view to his Army Chiefs. 'A U-boat war and an air war can decide the war. It will last one to two years.' As late as September 8, when his naval chief called on Hitler to discuss some of the details of Operation Sealion (the invasion project) he found Hitler regarding the operation as unnecessary. 'He is finally convinced that Britain's defeat will be achieved without a landing.'

In fact, Hitler's real interest during the summer of 1940 lay in plans not for the invasion of Great Britain but for the invasion of Russia. Even though Great Britain had not yet come to the peace table he was quite prepared to go ahead with these plans. His generals warned him of the dangers of a two-front war. He countered their fears by suggesting that his attack on Russia and resulting victory would be the event which would finally convince Great Britain and bring her to terms. He argued was that the involvement of the USA was Great Britain's only hope of salvation. That would not happen if American interests in the Far East were threatened by a Japan released from any danger from Russia. It was of course a fatal mistake. Hitler's enthusiasm for his eastern adventure was outweighing consideration of basic strategy. The two front war would in due course destroy him.

Nevertheless, Hitler made the position very clear to Ribbentrop shortly before making his speech on July 19 marking the end of the land operations in Europe.

> I have decided to march against Russia. I am resolved to put an end once and for all to the Bolshevik menace and to secure in Europe those colonies[9] which alone can guarantee our future. This is my life's whole making, for that I have fought, for that alone have I made such sacrifices and that is my task. I must defeat Russia while England is prostrate. Only when I have defeated Russia will the English be ready to make peace and recognise my conquests.'[10]

It is apparent that Hitler had little interest in what lay on the other side of the English Channel, other than removing the British as an unnecessary and unwanted adversary and coveting their friendship. On July 21 Hitler issued instructions to commence the detailed planning for the invasion of Russia under the code name *Aufbau Ost*

---

[9]The reference to 'colonies' in Europe relates to the claim for *Lebensraum*.
[10]Hesse, Fritz, *Hitler and the English*, Allan Wingate (1954), 107.

(Reconstruction East). One of the few persons aware of these plans and intentions was Rudolf Hess.[11] Ten days later a formal conference decision was made to dispose of Russia in the spring of 1941 with a total build up of the army to 180 divisions. In Hitler's notes of the conference is included 'Camouflage: North Africa, England, Spain.' Operations against Great Britain were therefore to be a side-show to mask Hitler's real intent. On November 12, the very day when the Russian Foreign Secretary was in Berlin to consider participation in a proposed agreement with Germany, Italy and Japan, instructions were being issued from Hitler's headquarters: 'All preparations for the East are to be continued. Directives on this will follow as soon as the outline of the Army's plan of operations is submitted to and approved by me.'[12] On December 18 formal instructions were issued for the implementation of Operation Barbarossa. Preparations were to be completed by May 15, 1941. There was some opposition from the army chiefs. They again warned that Great Britain should be brought to the peace table before Barbarossa was launched. They were overruled by Hitler.

It is apparent that in June 1940 Hitler considered Great Britain more of an irritant than a serious adversary and one that ought, and would, come to terms as soon as she realised the hopelessness of her cause. In the event, this assessment was grievously in error. Although Hitler consistently expressed his admiration and respect for the British, he never seems to have understood the facets of character that had produced the features he so admired. This failure to read the British character was never better illustrated than in his big peace speech delivered at the Reichstag on July 19, 1940, to celebrate the end of hostilities in Europe. The occasion itself was a glittering success in terms of public relations and a great tribute to Hitler both as a showman and an actor. But his particular references to Great Britain and Winston Churchill had precisely the opposite effect to that intended. Personal abuse and invective were heaped upon Churchill and 'the Jewish warmongers who were responsible for the war.'

In July 1940 Churchill embodied the spirit of the British people. He articulated their hopes and fears. He drew heavily upon their illustrious history. He *was* the British people. When Hitler personally abused and ridiculed him, Hitler was personally abusing and ridiculing every Britisher. Nothing was better designed to increase their existing bloody-mindedness in the matter of peace and keep them away from any parleying. As to the 'Jewish warmongerer' who had caused the war,

---

[11]Walter Warliment of Hitler's operational staff at OKW was instructed to keep Hess fully informed as to developments. Walter Warliment, *Inside Hitler's HQ*, 33–34.
[12]Hitler Directive, November 12, 1940.

the average Britisher dismissed the view as a reflection of the psychotic disorder that was part of Hitler's mental make-up (and which was true).

Hitler referred in his July 19 speech to an 'appeal to reason'. The average Britisher considered it as anything but. Here was one reason why Hitler's wait and see policy could never come to fruition in the manner Hitler expected. The other factor was Winston Churchill himself. Unlike Hitler, he *could* read the British character and he knew of their latent talents and endeavour which had left such an indelible mark on the world in the past. He believed that, given proper leadership, they were capable of rising to the present predicament. Churchill's task in providing that leadership in the circumstances of that summer was enormous. He had no knowledge of Hitler's innermost thoughts or of his obsession with Russia and *Lebensraum* in the East.[13] All he knew was that Hitler and his apparently invincible war machine were 26 miles away and that Great Britain was hopelessly equipped to deal with what the whole world now considered to be the inevitable invasion.

Hitler's wait and see policy had at least handed the initiative to Churchill during May and June. He had used the time to good advantage. He had strengthened his hold on public affection by his rhetoric. He had mended his fragile relations with the Conservative Party. Most importantly, he had demonstrated to the world in general, and the USA in particular, Great Britain's resolve to continue the struggle. Nevertheless, he knew that Great Britain was faced with a predicament worse than any it had ever faced in its long history. The balance sheet at June 1940 reflected a crushing preponderance of liabilities over assets. Churchill was faced by the world's most formidable fighting forces who had demonstrated their skills and superiority in such an outstanding fashion in both Norway and Flanders. They now had naval and air bases which dominated the British Isles.

Against the 150 battle-hardened divisions of the Wehrmacht, Churchill had just two divisions fully trained and 14 in training. They were armed only with rifles.[14] The men saved at Dunkirk were available but they were disorganised, largely unarmed and bereft of all equipment. There were fewer than 1,000 tanks, most of them obsolete, unserviceable or both. No division had a full complement of anti-tank guns or artillery pieces. There were fewer than 40 Thompson submachine guns in the whole island. The Local Defence Volunteers,

---

[13]It is not known if Churchill had ever read *Mein Kampf.* He had his own personal assessment of Germans and all things Germanic.

[14]Minutes of the 13th Supreme War Council Meeting, May 31, 1940, PRO/CAB/99/3.

forerunners of the Home Guard, were armed with wooden mock rifles, pitch forks and a few shotguns.

On May 27 the Chiefs of Staff had reported the obvious. 'The land forces are not strong enough to repel the Germans once they are ashore.'[15] To stop the Germans getting ashore would be the responsibility of the Royal Navy. They certainly enjoyed a clear superiority in numbers of naval craft against anything the Germans could put to sea. Again, the Chiefs of Staff had stated the obvious. The Royal Navy could not hold up the invasion without adequate air support.[16] At least the lessons of Norway were at last being learnt by the die-hards at the Admiralty. Air superiority was therefore the crux of the matter.

No one knew that better than Hugh Dowding, the air officer commanding RAF Fighter Command. On June 1 he reported to the War Cabinet that he had 244 Hurricanes and 280 Spitfires available for the defence of the United Kingdom. He considered these numbers to be an irreducible minimum. He warned the Cabinet against sending any further squadrons of fighter aircraft to France. He also warned against a possible shortage of pilots.[17] How was the RAF to withstand the Luftwaffe assault which would surely involve aircraft numbered in thousands? And if the island resources were so slender, how much more so were the resources available to defend the Empire. This great sprawling mass of countries and peoples stretching across the world was virtually defenceless against any enemy who chose to attack it.

Potential enemies far outweighed potential allies – another adverse entry on Churchill's balance sheet. Italy, Spain, Japan were all totalitarian states with similar ideologies to those of Germany. They were all potential enemies with a view to pickings from the Empire. Japan in particular represented a real threat in the Far East. As to the powerful neutrals, the USA was generally sympathetic to Great Britain's cause but sympathy was the extent of her involvement, apart from the commercial business of supplying arms. Russia was antagonistic and distrustful towards the British. Perhaps that was with good cause, having regard to the rebuffs handed out by Chamberlain during the appeasement years. Nearer at home there were more fundamental weaknesses. In terms of running a war, the British had demonstrated a woeful amateurism with almost everything that they had touched since September 1939. There was incompetence and muddle from top to bottom in the command and operational structures both political and military. Heads needed to roll and to roll quickly.

---

[15]Taylor, A.J.P., *English History 1914–1945*, Oxford University Press (1965), 490.
[16]*Ibid.*
[17]This issue became the crucial factor in the subsequent Battle of Britain.

There was also a severe problem with the general populace. Churchill would have to work hard on this particular issue. There is no doubt that before his advent the British people as a whole had their heads firmly planted in the sands of complacency. Even after the military defeats suffered in Norway and France, this extraordinary complacency as to the perils that beset them was slow to dissolve. Unlike their European counterparts, the British people had experienced very little of the real deprivations of modern war during the nine months to June 1940.[18] In the summer of 1940 hotels, cinemas, theatres and other places of amusement were still crowded with pleasure seekers while France and the Low Countries went up in flames. As to feelings about the war, for three centuries Britishers had been free from any foreign encroachment of their native soil. They seemed to think that this state of affairs would continue indefinitely as a fact of nature. Although the facts said otherwise, they still considered themselves as a Great Power, if not the Greatest Power in the world.

Tradition had it that the British always lost every battle in a war except the last one. The Britishers still believed that in June 1940. Their complacency was breathtaking. Just 3 per cent of the populace thought in May 1940 that Great Britain might lose the war.[19] Denied any real leadership, they had been fed on fairy tales and wishful thinking for so long by successive Governments afraid to dispense the truth, apparently because it would have lost votes. The ordinary Britisher was completely out of touch with reality. Churchill had to pierce this great protective shell of complacency. Somehow he had to release the ingrained qualities he knew to be there if Great Britain was to come to grips with the very real peril that was about to engulf her.

Churchill also had to deal with another segment of British society which concerned him to a far greater extent than he or anyone else has ever recorded. Its members were not complacent. They were ready to contemplate the ejection of Churchill from power and coming to the peace table. They comprised what the Germans termed the British Peace Party. Churchill knew that these dissenting interests existed and he knew that he had to deal with them before they established any meaningful contact with the enemy.

The last liability on Churchill's balance sheet was as simple as it was devastating. In June 1940 Great Britain was financially bankrupt. On August 22, Kingsley Wood, the Chancellor of the Exchequer,

---

[18]They had experienced minor inconveniences like the blackout and rationing, but no aerial bombardment or land fighting.
[19]According to a Gallup Poll taken in that month.

presented a most secret financial report to the Cabinet. So grave were the contents that all copies of the report were gathered in at the conclusion of the meeting and retained by the Chancellor. The report advised that total gold and dollar reserves of £775 million at the beginning of 1940 were down to £156 million at June 30. They would be completely exhausted by the end of the year. Unless open-ended assistance was forthcoming from the USA, Great Britain would not be able to continue the war because she would not be able to pay for the supplies and armaments she had to have.[20] This parlous position had already been brought to the attention of the US Secretary to the Treasury, Henry Morgenthau, early in the summer by Sir Frederick Phillips, a senior British Treasury official. No comment by way of reply had been received by August 22 when Kingsley Wood presented his report.

This litany of problems gives some idea of the immense burden of responsibility undertaken by Churchill in the summer of 1940. It has become somewhat fashionable among latter-day historians to debunk Churchill. They have exposed some of his weaknesses and the errors of judgement he made during the course of his wartime administration. There is assuredly value to such studies, in that perspective and balance may be added to the overall picture of the man. Absolutely nothing, however, can detract from the truly inspired leadership and personal courage that Churchill displayed during the summer crisis of 1940.[21] During that time, and for a year thereafter, Great Britain under Churchill's leadership continued to resist and refused to parley. As a result, for a full year she was obliged to withstand alone the full force of German U-boat warfare and aerial bombardment from the Luftwaffe in an attempt to break her morale and bring her to the peace table before the onset of Operation Barbarossa.

It may truly be said of this period 'come the hour, come the man', and it is on this count that Churchill takes his rightful place in history. Only a man with depth of character could have embraced with apparent enthusiasm and little rancour all those grave problems inherited from and created by others of lesser stature. Only a man of tenacious courage and immense personal resource could have worked so assiduously at each one of these problems and in due course of time, overcame them all. On the way, he may have made some mistakes. Having regard to the immensity of the task, they were inevitable. The man who never made a mistake never made anything. Churchill made

---

[20]As disclosed in Kingsley Wood's most secret paper, 'Gold and Exchange Resources', August 21, 1940.

[21]Britain's 'finest hour' was no myth. The author has been there.

many things, including some mistakes. But perhaps most importantly of all, only a man of outstanding vision and faith could have inspired both himself and the British nation to believe that at the end of the 'blood, sweat and tears' there was a way ahead and that Great Britain would find that way ahead to victory.

Churchill was a man of simple beliefs. He was an unashamed imperialist. Ironically, like Hitler, he believed that the British Empire still had an important role to play in terms of world equilibrium and the advance of civilisation. He saw it as his duty and that of Great Britain to resist the ambitions of Adolf Hitler whom he considered to be an evil man propagating an evil doctrine. His vision and faith were of course fully vindicated when the scales of justice tilted in his favour a year later.

With the launch of Operation Barbarossa, Russia became an ally, to be followed six months later by the entry of the USA at the side of Great Britain. By that time, Great Britain could no longer be described as a minor and ineffective irritant to Germany's cause. Rather had she become an experienced and skilful war combatant and major adversary. She possessed realistic war policies that aimed towards survival in the short term and offensive action in the longer term.

The skills Churchill used to bring about this remarkable turnaround were many and various. He made haste slowly in ridding himself of the high-ranking appeasers. Churchill knew that his own political position was so fragile, and so much in the hands of the Conservative Party (of which he was still not the leader), that any other policy would have been inappropriate. He acted with swift and brutal resolve against the French navy at Oran. This was to preserve British control of the seas and demonstrate to the world in general, and the USA in particular, British resolve to continue the war. That same swift and brutal resolve was in evidence in removing and replacing the dead wood associated with the earlier conduct of the war.

Churchill also included blackmail among his skills when enlisting the support of the USA in the matter of arms supplies. The threat of the surrender of the British fleet in the event of peace (which would have seriously imperilled the American eastern seaboard) was sufficient to provide the necessary accommodation. Short term policies bent on survival depended upon the shoring up of the inland defences, gearing up war production to feed the defences and revitalising the populace so as to bring out their latent powers of resilience and endeavour. At the same time, the USA had to be coaxed to supply the answer to the financial predicament.

As to longer term strategy directed towards possible offensive operations, Churchill already had an eye on Germany's weak partner,

Italy.[22] The prospect of naval action in the Mediterranean and military action in North Africa was attractive. Churchill also had in mind the building up of a long range strategic bomber force powered with new four-engined aircraft which would eventually carry the war into the heart of Germany. Most important of all, superimposed on these plans was Churchill's strategic centrepiece. This involved the full economic and financial support of the USA and eventually, her involvement in the war as an active partner. Churchill knew that this was the only real hope of establishing a victory. He was prepared to gamble with very high stakes to ensure its outcome. He did so and won. The USA entered the war against Germany in December 1941 and she accommodated all Great Britain's economic and financial requirements for the interim period prior to that. The cost to Great Britain was very high. Some say it was too high. But immediately after his accession to power his eyes had turned instinctively across the Atlantic to the United States of America.

---

[22]In retrospect, it is apparent that Italy would have been more use to Germany as a friendly neutral, with an implied threat to the British position in the Mediterranean. As a participant, Italy allowed Great Britain to pick up some easy victories which boosted her battered morale. Germany spent an inordinate amount of her time and resources in constantly pulling Italian chestnuts out of the fire.

12

The American factor

The Japanese are our unrelenting enemies and the Americans are our unrelenting creditors.

BEAVERBROOK, January 1941

Churchill's rhetoric, for all its value of lifting the morale of the British people and inspiring the will to resist, could not buy military hardware. And Churchill knew that unless Great Britain obtained supplies of arms in the quantities she required, she would not survive. Great Britain's own industrial capacity was such that it was incapable of reaching and sustaining the levels of production required. The penalty was now being paid for the years of neglect in funding investment in plant, machine tools, heavy equipment and the modern production techniques that went with them.

Churchill looked to the USA to remedy the deficiency. He knew that America had an enormous industrial potential and that Americans were in general sympathy towards Great Britain and her cause. Who better to make friends with, and who better to ask for help in a time of need? Churchill tended to romanticise on the subject. He foresaw a grand coalition of the English speaking peoples of the world, united by a bond of kinship that was expressed in the democratic principle and the freedom of the individual. The coalition would unite the vast American industrial strength with Great Britain's dominance of world markets through her existing Empire. No doubt he saw such a union as a positive step forward in the advance of civilisation. He looked to the USA in the short term for the supply of urgently needed arms and other materials, in the medium term to its involvement as an active partner in the war against the dictators, and in the long term to a lasting and dominate partnership in a postwar world.

Such were Churchill's plans and ambitions. He had even expressed these sentiments in the conclusion of his speech in the House of Commons on June 4.[1] This visionary aspect of Churchill's thinking formed an important part of his main strategic policies during 1940 and 1941. However, they sat uncomfortably with those important practical difficulties which almost aborted the strategy. The first and most immediate difficulty was that Great Britain could not pay for the supplies already on order, let alone the further supplies needed. The second difficulty was that Roosevelt did not share Churchill's vision of global partnership. Churchill saw America as a helpmate at a time of crisis. Roosevelt saw Great Britain as a country to be helped but on a strictly commercial basis and only if that help was tied to American interests. The third difficulty was that during May and June Roosevelt could not make up his mind about Great Britain's chances of survival. He seemed more intent upon what he could get out of the liquidation than on lending support to avoid the liquidation.

In the event, Churchill got his supplies of arms and other necessaries and means were found for payment in kind rather than in cash. The USA entered the war as Great Britain's ally and it succeeded Great Britain as the dominant postwar political world power. So Churchill got what he wanted in the short and medium term and Roosevelt got what he wanted in the long term. Maybe that was a fair outcome of the Anglo-American liaison. Criticism in Great Britain as to the long-term consequences has come mainly from these armchair critics who were not around in 1940 to appreciate the crisis-level pressures then prevailing. Churchill did. When the USA entered the war in December 1941 Churchill expressed his deep sense of relief. 'I went to bed that night saturated and satiated with emotion and sensation and slept the sleep of the saved and thankful.'

It is perhaps indicative of the style of Churchill's new-look Cabinet that when Kingsley Wood presented his devastating financial report on August 22, advising them that all gold and dollar reserves would have disappeared by the end of the year, the agreed solution was to immediately increase the size of orders to the USA. One thousand Stuart light tanks were ordered straightway.[2] The question of payment was ignored. There was of course method in the madness. Beaverbrook made the suggestion. Churchill backed it. Both knew that the American

---

[1]These rather optimistic and expansive views as to the unity of purpose with the USA were perhaps influenced by the fact that Churchill's mother was an American and that he had been personally funded by the American benefactors, Charles Schwartz, the steel magnate, and Bernard M. Baruch, the financier, during those years when he was out of office, out of favour and out of friends. He was also in personal and friendly contact with President Roosevelt, having established ongoing correspondence with him since 1939 when at the Admiralty.

[2]Costello, John, *Ten Days that Saved the West*, Bantam Press (1991), 387.

industrialists were hungry for business. If they became over committed in terms of unpaid production the US Government would have to intervene and provide the credits to fund the purchases.

That the industrialists were hungry for business, there was no doubt. On that they had presidential backing. As early as September 1938 Roosevelt himself said 'Europe's gold is now flooding into the USA to purchase munitions. They might even have to use navy ships to ferry the gold across. British and French citizens owned US securities of enormous value and would be forced to sell if war broke out. The USA would only profit from a war.'[3] No doubt Roosevelt could see how America's vast pool of unemployed might be drained dry by a heavy and consistent demand for American production.

The Beaverbrook/Churchill policy of unrestrained ordering continued throughout the summer of 1940. Great Britain also took over all the outstanding French orders after their collapse.[4] Total orders for USA for the one year 1940–41 were worth $10 billion. Great Britain had gold and dollar reserves at December 31, 1940, of £3 million. Eventually, special arrangements for financial help were made through the Lend/Lease agreement which received Congress approval on March 11, 1941. But long before that Bill arrived on the statute book the US administration was insisting that Great Britain 'scrape the barrel'.

The maximum possible was to be realised from Great Britain's own resources before any special legislation was wheeled into place. All British-held securities in the western hemisphere were sold. Gold by the shipload was also transferred to America throughout 1940 from wherever it could be found or raised. That included contributions from governments in exile[5] and Vichy French gold was appropriated in London.[6] British cruisers and even battleships were sometimes detached from operational duties to carry gold to America. Roosevelt even suggested at one stage that an American battleship call on South Africa and load up gold direct from the mines.[7]

Roosevelt himself referred to the end of the 'scraping of the barrel' operation: 'We have been milking the British financial cow which had plenty of milk at one time but which has now run dry.'[8] Beaverbrook aired his own thoughts on the same subject: 'They (the Americans) have conceded nothing. They have extracted payment to the uppermost

---

[3]Harold Ickes diary, September 18, 1938.
[4]Ponting, Clive, *1940: Myth and Reality*, Hamish Hamilton (1990), 205.
[5]Only the Dutch and Norwegian Governments refused.
[6]Ponting, Clive, *1940: Myth and Reality*, Hamish Hamilton (1990), 9–10
[7]Churchill referred to 'the Sheriff collecting the last assets of a helpless debtor'.
[8]Harold Ickes diary, January 19, 1941.

for all that they have done for us. They have taken our bases without valuable consideration. They have taken our gold. They have been given our secrets and offered us a thoroughly inadequate service in return.'[9] Beaverbrook mentions two particular payments in kind as well as the gold shipments. The leasing of British naval bases in the West Indies to the USA in 'payment' for 50 old American navy destroyers received much postwar publicity and adverse comment. The reference to the Americans being 'given our secrets' as payment received little postwar publicity, but which included items of much more fundamental importance. Even Beaverbrook was probably unaware of the precise nature of the secrets so conveyed and their effect upon the future conduct of the war.

The lease of Britain's West Indian bases was the subject of protracted and at times, ill-natured negotiations. Churchill originally raised the issue of destroyers on May 15, only days after his accession to power. He reactivated his request on June 10, following a Roosevelt speech pledging support to Great Britain. Roosevelt replied by tying in a request for the lease of the West Indian bases.[10] His original request, then indignantly refused by the British Cabinet, had been made on May 27. Eventually, the two requirements were tied together by negotiation (although in terms of publicity and for the sake of British prestige they were put up as matters independent of each other). The USA took possession of the bases.[11] Great Britain took possession of the 50 destroyers. They were of 1914–18 vintage. They had four funnels and a great propensity to roll when at sea. They all required a four month refit before they were deemed fit for service with the Royal Navy. They were described variously as 'worthless heaps' and 'wallowing rust buckets'. They were not popular with Royal Navy personnel.[12]

The destroyers-for-West-Indian bases exchange can scarcely be described as one of Churchill's better deals during that summer of crisis, but it is necessary to appreciate the needs of the hour. America was in the driving seat while Great Britain, under extreme pressure, was running alongside with begging bowl in hand. Immediate needs were the pressing priority. Fifty extra destroyers in the Western Approaches were probably deemed of greater importance than the Stars and Stripes flying over bases on the other side of the Atlantic.

---

[9] Irving, David, *Churchill's War*, Veritas, Australia (1987), 487.

[10] The requirement was for a 99-year lease on bases situated in Newfoundland, Bermuda, The Bahamas, Jamaica, St Lucia, Trinidad and British Guyana.

[11] Since described as 'the start of the disintegration of the British Empire' (Charnley).

[12] A colleague of the author who served on one of the destroyers described them thus: 'They didn't sail. They rolled along and you had to roll with them. But at times they were bloody handy.'

The other payment in kind mentioned by Beaverbrook refers to the export of British 'secrets' to America. That was a much more serious matter. On August 14, Sir Henry Tizard, the Air Ministry's principal scientist, took to the USA the blueprints of the latest developments with British radar and other items.[13] American radar techniques at the time were described as 'belonging to the Stone Age'. Thus began the enforced and continuing leak of British scientific and technological data taken in payment for the supply of arms.[14]

A secret of even greater importance was conveyed to the Americans in that same month of August 1940. During the late 1930s two refugee German scientists, Otto Frisch and Rudolf Peierls, had carried out experiments that led them to the conclusion that an atomic bomb was a theoretical possibility. Both had fled from Hitler's Germany and became naturalised Englishmen, continuing their experiments in this field at Birmingham University in England.[15] The prevailing view by 1939 was that the bomb was not a practical proposition because the uranium that had to be used in its manufacture was far too heavy for the bomb ever to become airborne. Frisch and Peierls experimented further. By the summer of 1940 they had developed the means to produce a refined type of uranium known as U-235. Using U-235, the critical weight of the bomb could be measured in pounds rather than tons. The bomb had become a practical proposition.

The Frisch/Peierls memorandum setting out their findings and constituting the first practical blueprint for the manufacture of the atomic bomb was then conveyed to the USA, where it provided the basis and vital stimulus to the American Manhattan project. Both Frisch and Peierls continued to advise on the complex technology associated with the separating out of U-235 from natural uranium, and Peierls later worked under Robert Oppenheimer at the Los Alamos laboratories in the New Mexico mountains on the actual design and manufacture of the first atomic bombs.[16] It is difficult to value the real worth, or indeed the wisdom, of exporting to America this scientific data which converted the atomic bomb from a theoretical concept into the practical proposition.

Wise or otherwise, blueprints for the future were willingly exchanged

---

[13]They included microwave radar, new air-to-surface vessel radar (ASV), a specimen of the cavity magnetron capable of increasing radar power a thousandfold. Other items included chemical warfare formulae, details of the new RDX explosive, data on rocket defence for ships, Bofors pom-pom predictors and the proximity fuse being used in Frank Whittle's jet engine and in German magnetic mines.

[14]Irving, David, *Churchill's War*, Veritas, Australia (1987), 397–98.

[15]Under the code names 'Maud' and later 'Tube Alloys'.

[16]U-235 was used in the Hiroshima bomb. Plutonium was used in the Nagasaki bomb.

for present-day armaments of war in the unseemly scramble for survival in the high summer of 1940. The ultimate arrangement which formalised and made legal what really had amounted to horse-trading was expressed in a Lend-Lease Bill which received the consent of the American Congress on March 11, 1941. Much propaganda on both sides of the Atlantic surrounded the circumstances leading up to the presentation of the Bill. It was desired that the moral principles supporting the Bill should be emphasised. We are told that while on a Caribbean cruise, President Roosevelt considered at his leisure a lengthy memorandum sent by Churchill on December 9, 1940, which once again set down the British shopping requirements and entreated American support. On his return, Roosevelt called a press conference and publicly promised such support. Shortly afterwards, there followed the well-publicised 'fireside chat' broadcast to the American people, who were told about the neighbour with the fire, borrowing a hosepipe to deal with the emergency and then returning the hosepipe or something else in lieu when the danger had passed. The analogy, even if inaccurate, was highly effective in creating the illusion of altruistic motivation.

Churchill, for obvious reasons, described the Bill as 'the most unsordid act in the history of any nation.' He would have been hard put to find a seconder and certainly not one among the unborn generations of British still paying for the garden hose 50 years after the event. Under the terms of the Bill, the President of the United States was provided with the authority to 'sell, transfer to, exchange, lease or otherwise dispose of defence articles to the government of any country.' The consideration would be by 'payment or repayment in kind or in property or in any other direct or indirect benefit which the President deemed satisfactory.' There was no longer any need to pay in gold or dollars. The door was opened to barter and payments in kind. But who assessed the value of the benefits in kind being exported by Great Britain?

The benefits acquired by the USA were enormous. The whole of Great Britain's system of Imperial Trade Preference based upon the Ottowa Agreement of 1932 was dismantled. All trade barriers around Great Britain and her Empire came down. This single provision virtually ensured American domination of the postwar world markets. Many other restrictions were placed upon the British by the same provisions which were given statutory authority in the Master Agreement of February 23, 1942. No lend-lease supplies to Great Britain were to be exported by her. Imports other then lend-lease supplies from America were to be restricted, British exports to new markets were prohibited where they would be in competition with American exports.

All unused war material supplied under the arrangements was to be returned to the USA after the war. All sterling area exchange controls were to be dismantled. Maximum and minimum gold and dollar reserves to be held by Great Britain were to be fixed by the USA. Finally, Great Britain's dependency upon the USA could be easily increased by switching a category of goods out of lend-lease terms so that payments had to be made out of gold and dollar reserves.[17] To all intents and purposes the lend-lease provisions as they were in fact used and abused effectively stripped Great Britain of all her trade advantages, placing her in a financial straitjacket subject to the control of the USA.

Before notification of the Bill the USA Senate hearings included public statements by the British Government as to the assets they still owned but which were deemed unrealisable. The procedure was in the style of a bankrupt's public examination. After the Bill had been placed on the statute book it was then used or misused for political purposes quite divorced from its original purpose but in furtherance of American foreign policy. In November 1944 it was used to bring pressure to bear on Churchill to persuade British delegates at the international civil aviation conference to drop their opposition to free competition on the world air routes. It was also used to 'persuade' Great Britain to restrict her imports of Argentinian beef to help American attempts to pressurise the Peronist regime there.

A postscript to the arrangements occurred one week after the Japanese surrender, when the provisios ended and Great Britain was called upon to pay for all supplies then in the pipeline in gold or dollars. The bill was $60 million. There is little doubt that when Churchill was first informed of what Roosevelt had in mind by way of payments or the transfer of benefits he had no idea as to the extent to which Roosevelt would then turn the screw. There is even less doubt that Roosevelt knew only too well just how well he would turn it.[18]

These different understandings arose out of the different concepts that each leader had of the Anglo-American relationship, which was the second great difficulty with which Churchill had to contend in his dealings with Roosevelt. Churchill did not consider that Great Britain's inability to pay for war materials was fundamental. He took the view that the responsibilities of the USA went much further than that of a commercial transaction. He saw the USA as a partner with Great Britain in the struggle against the dictators. Great Britain was in

---

[17]Tobacco was a case in point.

[18]There is also little doubt that Roosevelt had very much in mind the postwar implications of what was happening.

the frontline and the USA was the 'arsenal of democracy'. Arms should be made available to the frontline, if need be outside the normal commercial conventions. Roosevelt's approach was very different. He treated everything on a strictly commercial basis. American interests, and these alone, were uppermost in his mind. He may have had some measure of personal sympathy with the predicament of the British people, as did probably the majority of Americans, but that is as far as his and their feelings went.

There were aspects of the British way of life and their history which were repugnant to the average American. He did not look kindly upon the British class system based upon privilege, or on the somewhat patronising and disdainful air of the British aristocracy towards the ex-colonials (some would say more imagined than real), or on British attitudes to Ireland or her performance in the Boer War. Perhaps most of all, the average American resented Great Britain's privileged political position in the world, based upon the glories of the past rather than its 20th-century achievements.

On January 9, 1941, in a world-wide broadcast, Churchill uttered the memorable words 'Give us the tools and we will finish the job.' But there was never any question of the Americans giving anything. Every scrap of material or morsel of foodstuffs that crossed the Atlantic would have to be paid for one way or another. And if that meant stripping Great Britain and her Empire of all her wealth and international trading advantages, so be it. The British Empire meant everything to Churchill.[19] It meant very little to Roosevelt, other than as a potential market for American production. Nowhere was this approach better illustrated than in the early days of the summer crisis. France was in her death throes and there was every prospect of the entire British Expeditionary Force going 'into the bag' in Flanders. On the basis of not throwing good money after bad, all pleadings from France for more supplies of arms were turned down. Roosevelt's thoughts were concentrated rather on the destiny of the ships of the Royal Navy in the likely event of a British defeat.

This was Churchill's third difficulty in his relationship with Roosevelt. He had to convince the American President that Great Britain was not only willing but was able to continue the struggle with real chances of survival. Roosevelt was unlikely to back Churchill's request for more supplies unless he was assured on this point. In fact and for that reason and in spite of the most strenuous representations from Churchill, no arms at all were dispatched from the USA during

[19]And even something of value to Hitler.

May, June and July 1940. During that time Great Britain was virtually defenceless. On the last day of July the S.S. *Britannic* arrived from New York with a full cargo of arms. By then, Churchill had apparently convinced Roosevelt that expectations of the early demise of Great Britain and her Empire were premature and that Great Britain was in the fight to stay.

Roosevelt's earlier preoccupation (some would say obsession) with the destiny of the British fleet and his need for confirmation of Great Britain's will and capacity to fight on were perhaps understandable. At the time, the friendly British fleet constituted, in fact if not in law, America's Atlantic defence. It enabled her to concentrate very substantial naval forces in the Pacific area as a deterrent to Japanese ambitions. If the British fleet was surrendered or otherwise compromised as part of any armistice terms agreed between Germany and Great Britain, that defence would have gone. Worse still, Roosevelt could see a nightmare scenario of the American navy being confronted at some stage by the combined navies of Germany, Italy, Japan and Great Britain.

This nightmare was perhaps the factor that impelled Roosevelt to act in a manner which, in retrospect, it is difficult to describe as other than thoroughly reprehensible. On May 25, immediately prior to Dunkirk, the British Expeditionary Force faced almost certain encirclement and destruction. On that day, Roosevelt secretly approached Mackenzie King, Prime Minister of Canada, and asked him if he would advise Churchill to keep the British fleet intact until all was lost and then ship it across the Atlantic to American ports. The analogy has been drawn of a mother trapped by fire, throwing down her jewel box from the bedroom window before succumbing.[20] Mackenzie King's interpretation was that if that happened Germans were unlikely to be generous with any peace terms with Great Britain. In other words, Roosevelt was suggesting that Great Britain should invite harsh terms for peace so that the Americans could hive off the British fleet for their own protection. Mackenzie King told Roosevelt 'that he would rather die' than do as Roosevelt suggested. He saw no reason why the USA should protect herself at the expense of Great Britain.[21]

The significance of Roosevelt's request was not lost on Churchill. Not for the first time[22] he realised that the destiny of the British fleet

---

[20]Memorandum from Mackenzie King to Prime Minister, May 26, 1940.

[21]Thompson, Laurence, *1940: Year of Legend, Year of History*, Fontana (1968), 183.

[22]As early as October 1939 Churchill had told Joseph Kennedy, the American Ambassador, 'If the Germans bomb us into subjection one of their terms will certainly be that we hand over our Fleet. And then your troubles will begin.'

was the one and only trump card he had in his hand that would help him in his dealings with the President. He worked hard with his trump card. On May 19 he informed Roosevelt that 'If members of the present (British) administration were finished and others came into parley amid the ruins, you must not be blind to the fact that the sole remaining bargaining counter with Germany would be the Fleet and if this country was left to fate no one would have the right to blame those then responsible if they made the best terms they could.' This was said in the same breath as 'whatever happens, we intend to fight to the end on this island.' In other words, make available the arms to make sure we do not fight in vain or see the British fleet in the hands of the enemy.

This was blackmail. And it was given a boost by what appeared to be a strange decision by Churchill. In the middle of his negotiations with Roosevelt, Churchill suddenly invited David Lloyd George to join his Cabinet. Many opinions have been advanced as to the true motives behind Churchill's invitation.[23] One of them may have been to increase Roosevelt's apprehensions about an alternative to Churchill's Government. Lloyd George was a pacifist. Mackenzie King added his own spice for Roosevelt's benefit. He emphasised to Roosevelt the tremendous strain that Churchill was under, the possibilities of a stroke and the spectre of an alternative Government.[24] He also sent Canada's only three destroyers across the Atlantic to join the British fleet. This demonstrated to Roosevelt how Canada felt about bringing Royal Navy vessels across the Atlantic in the opposite direction. Churchill's trump card therefore eventually won the day and supplies were begun on July 31.

The reason for the three months' delay from May were many and various. The American Neutrality Act authorised the trans-shipment of only those arms considered to be surplus to America's own requirements; there were bureaucratic procedures to be followed and in May 1940 the so-called arsenal of democracy was more potential than actual. Priority also had to be given to the expansion and re-equipping of America's own armed forces.[25] There was also American public opinion to accommodate. Not all were in favour of the shipment of arms to Great Britain. Great Britain's military performance in Norway and Flanders had been anything but illustrious and her population had yet to show the resolve that was necessary to

---

[23]One of which is discussed in chapter 15.
[24]Thompson, Laurence, *1940: Year of Legend, Year of History*, Fontana (1968), 185.
[25]In June 1940 the American Army comprised only 200,000 men and its Army Air Force totalled no more than 1,800 aircraft.

survive.[26] But these factors did not fully explain the stand-off position adopted by the USA during this crucial period, when Great Britain most needed help and received none.

During that time, and for a good deal longer in some cases, Roosevelt was being fed with almost unanimous reports and opinions from his advisers that Great Britain was finished and would have to ask for terms. In that, they agreed with Hitler's assessment. All efforts should therefore be directed towards rescuing whatever was possible from the wreck and in particular, if possible, the British fleet. All this seemed inescapable logic to the American administration. It certainly explains American attitudes at the time given that their only interest was American interest. Requests for urgent help during that period therefore fell on deaf ears. Churchill himself described the American attitude graphically as 'a rather distant and sympathetic manner that one adopts towards an old friend dying of cancer'.[27]

Roosevelt's senior advisers were General Marshall and Secretary of State, Cordell Hull. The judgement of these advisers was based principally on the reports both were receiving from the respective American ambassadors in Paris and London. They, after all, were the Americans closest to the action. Unfortunately, both individuals were less than kindly disposed towards Great Britain, even before they took up their ambassadorial duties. William C. Bullitt in Paris had soaked up a good deal of the French version as to the campaign in Flanders and in particular the British 'desertion' at Dunkirk. According to Bullitt the British had no stomach to fight. Bullitt was a straight defeatist, much influenced by the French experience.

Joseph Kennedy, the American Ambassador in London, was something much worse. A hardened Irish-American businessman from Boston, there was much in his family and national history that provided him with an inborn dislike, if not hatred, of the British and prevented him from forming any sort of judgement which might have pretensions as to objectivity. His prophecies of gloom, despondency and defeatism commenced in September 1939 and continued through to October 1940, when he was recalled to Washington and sacked.

The catalogue was unrelenting. In September 1939 he sent a report to Roosevelt on the subject of British decadence. Two months later he was warning Roosevelt to keep out of the war. In April, during the

---

[26]There was a noticeable change of view later in the year as the effect of Churchill's leadership became apparent, the Battle of Britain was fought and won, the Battle of the Atlantic was joined with total commitment and, perhaps most importantly, resistance to the aerial bombardment of the 'blitz' demonstrated the resilience and courage of the British people.
[27]Cecil King diary, February 19, 1941.

Norwegian campaign, his cables to Washington were emphasising British irredeemable muddle and inefficiency. In May, when Churchill was first pressing Roosevelt for urgent help, Kennedy was advising Cordell Hull to send none. On June 12 Kennedy was again advising Roosevelt to keep clear of the war and Churchill. Two days later he was reporting what he believed, or perhaps what he wanted to believe, were the feelings of the British people: 'They are beginning to say we have everything to lose and nothing to gain and what is the use of fighting. If the English people thought there was a chance of peace on any decent terms, an upheaval against the Government would come.'[28] On July 31 Kennedy was reporting that German air power would put the RAF out of commission. 'After that, Britain's surrender would be inevitable because without American support they have not got a Chinaman's chance of survival.'[29]

Perhaps most revealing of all of Kennedy's prejudices against Great Britain is the cable sent to Roosevelt on September 26. By that time, there was plenty of evidence available both as to Churchill's leadership qualities and the British will to fight on. In particular, the Battle of Britain had been fought and won and the Luftwaffe had conspicuously failed to win supremacy of the air space over Great Britain. Nevertheless, Kennedy reported to Roosevelt: 'I cannot impress upon you strongly enough my complete lack of confidence in the entire conduct of the war. If by any chance we should ever come to the point of getting in to this war we can make up our minds that it will be the USA against Germany, Italy and Japan aided by a badly shot-to-pieces country which in their last analysis can give little, if any, assistance to the cause.' But by this time, Kennedy was on his way out. He left London for the USA on October 22, boasting that he was going to wreck Roosevelt's ambitions to be re-elected to an unprecedented third term as President. Arriving in Washington, Kennedy was transported direct to the White House. There was a long discussion. Kennedy emerged as a Roosevelt supporter and endorsed Roosevelt's candidacy in a nationwide radio broadcast.[30]

In July Roosevelt had sent William J. Donovan, a prominent

---

[28]This calumny is more indicative of Kennedy's inborn prejudices than the mood of the British people.

[29]Kennedy to State Department, July 31, 1940, and August 2, 1940. 740. 0011 4923/29.

[30]The reason for Kennedy's volte face and the content of his discussion with Roosevelt have never been disclosed. Roosevelt may have had knowledge of Kennedy's more clandestine activities while in London. There had been security leaks through the American Embassy and these had been picked up by British Intelligence MI5. Opinions differ as to whether the leaks were inspired by Kennedy himself. If they were, it raises the question as to Kennedy's true function and status when in London.

Republican lawyer, on an independent fact finding mission to London. His report differed materially from those of Kennedy. The Donovan report backed up by the reports of respected journalists and commentators like Ed Murrow and Quentin Reynolds and other independent sources, all brought about a vital change of opinion not only by the President but also by the American people. This change of heart, together with his re-election as President which followed on November 2, enabled Roosevelt to give serious thought not only as to Great Britain's immediate survival but also as to how that survival could be strengthened and prolonged. It was this thinking that eventually led to the lend-lease provisions. Roosevelt's motives throughout remained that of American self interest. The maintenance of Great Britain and her fleet constituted America's front line of defence against the dictators. In the meantime, Great Britain would have to pay in cash or in kind for every item of material sent across the Atlantic.

Kennedy disappeared from the political scene following his dismissal from London. When Roosevelt was re-elected President he allocated no office, high or low, to Kennedy. That did not stop Kennedy from making speeches up and down the country airing his personal political views. It is interesting to consider these views in the context of his position as ambassador in London during 1939 and 1940 and the reported security leakages from the American Embassy. In California, at the Hollywood Film Studios he spoke off the record for three hours. He laboured the need for America to isolate itself from the European war. He thought Hollywood should stop making anti-Nazi films. He thought that the Jews had caused the war. He said that anti-Semitism was growing in Great Britain. On May 31, 1941, speaking to graduates at Notre Dame, Indiana, he described Adolf Hitler as the 'greatest genius of the century'. He also described Hitler's diplomatic and military ability as 'superior to anything that the British could muster. Britain is hopelessly licked and there will be a negotiated peace within sixty days.'[31] Churchill neither liked or trusted Kennedy.[32] He was not alone. A favourite British quote in the early summer of 1940 was 'I thought my daffodils were yellow until I met Kennedy.'

---

[31]This prediction appears to be wildly irresponsible unless Kennedy had information he was not disclosing. This is not impossible. The Hess peace mission had been launched on May 10.
[32]The antipathy was mutual. Kennedy described Churchill as 'a fine two-handed drinker'.

13

The Battle of Britain – Goering brought down

Never in the field of human conflict was so much owed by so many to so few.

WINSTON S. CHURCHILL, August 20, 1940

The Battle of Britain was the first occasion in the 1939–45 war when the German armed forces met with defeat. The defeat was inflicted on the Luftwaffe by Fighter Command of the RAF. The Luftwaffe brief was 'to sweep the RAF out of the skies' and establish German air superiority over British air space. The purpose was to provide the essential prerequisite to an invasion of the British Isles. Alternatively, such air supremacy might bring the British to the point of surrender in which case the invasion would be unnecessary. In the event, air supremacy was not gained, there was no invasion and Great Britain was not brought to the point of surrender.

The RAF victory demonstrated to the world, and particularly the USA, that the German armed forces were vulnerable in circumstances not of their choosing. It also demonstrated that in favourable circumstances, the British could fight with skill and resolution and win. Hitler showed little interest and less involvement in the Battle of Britain.[1] He wanted an arrangement with Great Britain, not a battle. The planning and operation of the Luftwaffe offensive was therefore left largely to its chief, Hermann Goering and his staff. Goering was a flamboyant character. He would not have failed to see the prospects of much personal glory if the efforts of his air force could lead to victory without the need of an invasion. The RAF victory was a close run thing. It hinged upon a major strategic error by Goering and his high command and a late in the day fundamental disagreement between Hitler and Goering.

[1]In marked contrast to the campaign in the Low Countries and France, where he was actively and enthusiastically involved in both the planning and execution of the operations.

There were other factors, too, which accounted for the RAF success. At first sight, it would appear that the Germans had every advantage. Goering was able to arraign against the RAF three air fleets totalling over 2,000 aircraft and comprising 963 fighters, 998 bombers and 315 divebombers. The RAF could put up between 700 and 800 fighters. The standard German fighter aircraft was the Messerschmitt 109. It was fast, well armed with cannon. It had proved its worth in the Polish, Norwegian and Flanders campaigns. In this case however, it was well matched by the standard British fighters, the Spitfire and Hurricane. The Spitfire was as fast as the Messerschmitt. The Hurricane, while slower, was more manoeuvrable. The concentrated fire of the British fighter from its eight machine guns matched the cannon of the Messerschmitt. It was soon found that the German bombers, unless escorted by the German fighter force, were sitting ducks for the British fighters. The German bombers were comparatively slow and poorly armed. This was particularly the case with the Stuka Junkers 87 divebombers which had wreaked such havoc in Poland and France.[2]

The crucial factor therefore was not straight numerical superiority but the fighter strength ratios, and in that the two combatants were almost evenly matched. There was also an even balance in fighter pilot skills. The Messerschmitt pilots were well trained and battlehardened. Most of the RAF pilots engaged in the early stages of the battle were pre-war fliers because that was their enthusiasm. They learned quickly. Both sets of men fought with bravery, skill and chivalry.

However, there were other factors heavily weighted in favour of the RAF. The German aircrews, both bomber and fighter, fought over ground (and water) that was not of their choosing and in a style of combat for which they had not been trained and had no experience. The bombers of the Luftwaffe were not designed for use as a long-range heavy bomber force[3] but as an air arm to be used in close support of advancing land forces, almost as short-range artillery support. But their effectiveness depended upon the skies being swept clear of enemy fighter opposition. This had been the case in Poland, Norway and France. It was never the case over southern England during the summer of 1940. In general terms, the Spitfires took on the Messerschmitts while the Hurricanes got in among the bombers. Only on rare occasions did the bomber enjoy an unmolested run up to its target.

Another important factor was that the British fighters were sup-

---

[2]The Stukas were withdrawn for the battle in August because of heavy losses.
[3]As Churchill had in mind with the RAF.

ported by a highly sophisticated aircraft warning and defence system, based upon the use of radar together with centralised and decentralised control through strategically placed sector air stations and their satellite airfields. As a result, RAF fighter command knew before the event the direction and approximate strength of each German attack before the aircraft became visible to the naked eye. This developed technique enabled the RAF fighters to take off and position themselves without wasting time and fuel in speculative patrolling. The fuel and time therefore available for actual combat was thus maximised. The opposite was the case for the German fighters. They had to fly a round trip of anything up to 200 miles from and to their bases in France and the Low Countries. Their time for actual combat was thus strictly limited. Also, because combat took place for the most part over south-east England, any German pilot, or complete aircrew in the case of a bomber, baling out from a damaged aircraft was taken prisoner. His British counterpart in similar circumstances would, with luck, rejoin his squadron and fight again.

There was a final factor. RAF Fighter Command was commanded by a strong-minded, independent, professional airman. Air Chief Marshal Dowding was afraid of and bowed to no one, and that included Churchill if need be. He controlled the battle not only skilfully but also with a nerve that remained steadfast throughout. He knew what he was doing and would brook no interference from well-meaning amateurs (like Churchill). He was served by an equally strong subordinate commander, Air Vice-Marshal Mungo Park, who commanded 11 Group, covering most of the area of battle.

Very different circumstances prevailed in the German camp. The German operational commanders were incapable of standing up to Goering and acquainting him with unpalatable facts as to the state of the battle. In similar fashion Goering as with the rest of the Nazi hierarchy other than Hess, fed naive and uninformed optimisms to his master Hitler. In particular, Goering was incapable of standing up to his chief when Hitler made what must have seemed to Goering, two strategic blunders which affected the course of the battle.

The British version of events notes the commencement of the battle as July 10. The German version logs August 13. Between these two dates the Luftwaffe was attacking shipping in and around the south and east coasts of England. The raids were not heavy. They were more a flexing of the muscles and an invitation for the RAF to come up and fight. The RAF declined the invitation and conserved their resources. On August 1 the German offensive operations were notched up several gears. Directive 17 from Hitler stated: 'In order to establish the conditions necessary for the final conquest[4] of England,[5] I have decided to continue the air and naval war against the English homeland more intensively than heretofore.' Goering immediately committed himself to a self-imposed and ridiculous timetable. He would gain air superiority within four days and the complete destruction of RAF Fighter Command within one month.[6]

Neither target was achieved. The German assault under the new directive began on August 13, designated Eagle Day by Goering. The primary target was the airfields of Mungo Park's 11 Group and in particular, its sector stations. The next day saw the first of Goering's optimistic reports to Halder. He claimed that eight major British air bases had been knocked out and 15 per cent of the RAF and bomber and fighter forces destroyed. German loses were reported at 3 per cent. The report was nothing but wishful thinking. No bases had been knocked out. British losses were significantly less than the German. On the next day, August 15, the massed attacks continued. In addition to continued attacks on airfields in the south of England, an attack was launched across the North Sea by aircraft based in Norway and Denmark. It was hoped that with the heavy attacks in the south RAF reserves would have been sucked in, leaving the north coast vulnerable.

The German hopes were groundless. The Luftwaffe lost 23 aircraft out of an attacking force of 157. Very little damage was done by the bombers. These Scandinavian based aircraft never reappeared in the battle. Meanwhile the heavy attacks in the south continued. On that day over 1,000 German planes were over Great Britain at one time or another. After a further three days of massed attacks there was a lull in the fighting between August 19 and 23, caused by bad weather. Massed attacks were resumed on the 24th. The main targets remained unchanged, the airfields of Mungo Park's 11 Group. German estimates of remaining RAF fighter strength were 300 aircraft. In fact, it was still 700. Factory production was keeping pace with combat losses.

The developing problem to the RAF was not machines but pilots.[7] These losses represented almost one third of the total fighter pilot strength. The losses were experienced pilots. Their replacements were comparatively raw. Many died early in combat. Those experienced pilots still in action in late August were tired and battleweary. These

---

[4]Note 'conquest' rather than 'invasion'. It was hoped that if Goering's onslaught was successful there would be no need for the latter.

[5]This new 'get tough' directive followed on immediately after the collapse of the Windsor negotiations (chapter 15 and appendix V). Hitler was perhaps losing patience again.

[6]Thompson, Laurence, *1940: Year of Legend, Year of History*, Fontana (1968), 199.

[7]*Ibid*, 205.

factors were reflected in the loss ratios. They had dropped from over three to one in the early days of the battle down to almost evens in the early days of September.

The cumulative damage to the airfields was also building up. By early September it was apparent that a critical period had been reached. The official RAF history designates the period August 28 to September 5 as 'a critical period when the damage to sector stations and our ground organisation was having such a serious effect on the fighting efficiency of the squadrons who could not be given the same good technical and administrative service as previously'. During that period, a daily average of over 600 German aircraft were pressing home their attacks with great resolution in spite of heavy losses. Six out of the seven RAF sector stations had been seriously damaged and RAF casualty rates of 200 monthly were exceeding the output of trained, but raw, pilots.[8]

It was at this moment of crisis, on September 1, that a decision was made at a Luftwaffe conference of senior staff officers that virtually decided the battle in favour of the RAF. It was a major strategic error. The decision was made to switch the attack from the much-damaged airfields to the city of London. The first such attack was launched on Saturday, September 7. Most grievous though that was to the citizens of London's East End, the relieving effect on the RAF defence system was immediate. The freedom from attack enjoyed by the sector stations and their satellite airfields enabled the work of repair and rehabilitation to proceed quickly and without interruption. In a matter of days the defence organisation was again fully back in business. New machines were rolling off the production lines in greater numbers than the losses. RAF fighter command, although weakened and hard put to fill their ranks of combat pilots, were once more capable of effective resistance to the German attacks.

The reason for the extraordinary decision by the Luftwaffe High Command, fully backed by Hitler, is obscure. An early explanation was that due to a navigational error on the night of August 24, a German bomber or bombers had inadvertently dropped bombs on London, having overshot the oil tanks at Rochester and Thameshaven which were the targets for that night. This brought a retaliation attack on Berlin ordered by Churchill, which in its turn caused Hitler to vent his spleen on London. The Luftwaffe attacks were switched accordingly. This explanation is too facile. Far more important motives were in play than the venting of personal spleens either one way or the other.

---

[8]*Ibid*, 205.

The first massed attack on London began during the afternoon of Saturday, September 7 and continued through the night of September 7–8. When the bombers arrived at about 5 p.m. the city was bathed in warm sunlight. It offered the perfect target. RAF fighter defence was for once caught off balance by the unexpected switch in attack and a considerable number of the total attacking force of 625 bombers and 648 fighters arrived over the capital unmolested. Three hundred tons of high explosive bombs were dropped together with 13,000 incendiary bombs.[9] Woolwich Arsenal, gas works, power stations and the whole of London's docklands to the east of the city were set ablaze. At that time, it was the most devastating air raid ever undertaken. Over 1,500 civilians were killed or injured. The previous bombing of Warsaw and Rotterdam, much exaggerated for propaganda purposes, were mere pinpricks by comparison.

These human and material losses were of course grievous. But in terms of strategic objective they achieved nothing for the German High Command. The breathing space afforded to the RAF defence system by the switch in attack was crucial. The effectiveness of the restored defences was soon in evidence the succeeding days, when German planes continued to be shot out of the skies. They were still being met by undiminished numbers of Hurricanes and Spitfires. In Hitler's own words to his military chiefs a week later on September 14, 'The enemy fighter forces are not yet completely eliminated. The enemy recovers again and again. Our own reports of success do not give a completely reliable picture.'[10]

On the next day, Sunday, September 15, the battle reached its climax. Massed attacks by over a thousand aircraft were made on London, Portland and the Spitfire works at Southampton. This time the RAF fighters were ready and well directed by a rejuvenated defence system. Fifty-six German aircraft were shot down, for the loss of only 26 British fighters. The loss ratio of two to one was as in the early days of battle. The British air defences held firm. RAF Fighter Command were clearly undefeated.[11] It was the end of the battle.

The defeat of the Luftwaffe was decisive. On October 2 it suspended all daylight bombing of London and acknowledged defeat. They had lost a total of 1,733 aircraft, together with most of the crews. RAF losses were 915.[12] During the course of the battle the date for the

---

[9]Shirer, William L., *The Rise and Fall of the Third Reich*, Pan Books (1964), 921.
[10]Thompson, Laurence, *1940: Year of Legend, Year of History*, Fontana (1968), 209.
[11]On July 10 RAF first-line strength in fighters was 656. On September 25 it was 665. Taylor, A.J.P., *English History 1914–1945*, Oxford University Press (1965), 500.
[12]*Ibid.*

proposed invasion of Great Britain, if in fact it was ever to occur, was shunted backwards and backwards. On September 17 the proposed date was postponed indefinitely. It was never resurrected.

There is an interesting political postscript to the Battle of Britain, as there was to the Dunkirk evacuation. It again reveals Hitler's innermost thoughts and his intentions as to both Russia and Great Britain during the summer of 1940. On or about September 15, at the climax of the battle, there was, according to Doctor Fritz Hesse, personal assistant and adviser on English affairs to Hitler and one of his inner circle, a violent disagreement between Hitler and Goering. It was already clear that the strength of the air forces directed against RAF Fighter Command was almost used up but Goering and his High Command were not willing to admit defeat. They requested, even demanded, of Hitler that German squadrons stationed in Poland in preparation for Operation Barbarossa should be transferred to the West. The 'final blow' could then be delivered against the RAF.

The orders for the transfer had been made out when Hitler intervened. He 'raged like a madman' on the telephone and expressly forbade the transfer and any interference of his military dispositions. Air squadrons which had been kept in readiness for the Russian campaign were not to be wasted on 'a senseless enterprise', which Goering countered by saying that the measure was necessary to win the victory over the British. Hitler replied that he 'knew these things much better than Goering' and would not tolerate any interference with his *political* decisions. He asserted that 'Goering did not even now understand that he (Hitler) wanted to keep the British down but not to lay them flat.'[13]

The transfer of additional squadrons from the East might well have been the prelude to the 'final blow' that Goering was suggesting, although Goering's forecasts were nothing if not optimistic. But if Hitler believed Goering's opinion to have been correct, or even that it might be correct, his intervention echoed that which prevailed in Flanders on May 24. Hitler was again intervening to save Great Britain from complete military defeat. Another punch was being pulled. Just as there is a possible unsung miracle underpinning the miracle of Dunkirk, is it possible that there was another unsung miracle underpinning the miracle of the Battle of Britain?

---

[13]Hesse, Fritz, *Hitler and the English*, Allan Wingate (1954), 118.

14

Aerial bombardment – the road to Nemesis

The British initiative as to indiscriminate bombing is clear ... The 'Blitz' began only after the British had been bombing German towns for five months between May and September 1940.

A.J.P. TAYLOR

The decision by the Luftwaffe High Command, early in September 1940, to switch attacks from the RAF airfields and defence establishments to the city of London constituted a major strategic blunder, marking the turning-point in the Battle of Britain. Why was this decision made and who was responsible?

There have been many candidates for the position of Germany's post-war scapegoat. Albert Kesselring, Commander of Air Fleet 2 which was the one most heavily involved in the battle, is one. At the high level conference held on September 1 he had advocated the switch. He reported that RAF Fighter Command defence had been destroyed and that the way was clear for the final blow, aimed at the heart of London. He was wrong in fact and premature in expectation. But his opinion was backed by Hans Jeschonnek, the Luftwaffe Chief of Staff. Not for the first time, he openly advocated the mass bombing of the industrial areas of London so as to stimulate civilian panic. No doubt Goering took note of this advice from his two lieutenants, but it was he who made the decision and it was he who was guilty of misreading the military position. But Hitler also came into the picture. He brought pressure to bear because of his need to retaliate to persistent, if ineffective, attacks on Berlin by RAF bombers. These RAF attacks had commenced on the night of August 25. Lastly, and most importantly, Winston Churchill comes into the picture.

The timetable of events leading up to September 7, when the first mass retaliatory raid on London took place, indicates clearly that the bombing of London on that date arose out of a deliberate policy by

Churchill to entice, even invite, the bombing of British cities and towns and that the German High Command rose to Churchill's bait. Churchill anticipated that American public opinion would be outraged by the bombing. It would then swing behind Great Britain to such an extent that America would enter the war at her side. Churchill also believed that violent enemy action directed against the civilian population would harden their resolve and would quell any suggestion of peace moves by those minority interests whose commitment to war was less than total.

The involvement of the USA in the war at the side of Great Britain was essential to Churchill's strategy for survival and eventual victory. There is little doubt that he was quite prepared to take any necessary steps to bring about that desirable state of affairs. If the aerial bombardment of British cities would bring the USA in then he would not shrink from enticing the Luftwaffe. Joseph Kennedy reported to his President on June 12, following a meeting with Churchill: 'Desperate people will do desperate things if that is all that is needed.'[1] It was one of Kennedy's more penetrating views. Churchill was certainly desperate in June 1940. His views about the bombing of British cities and the hoped for reaction by the USA are a matter of record, as are his views about stiffening of British resolve. On June 7, after Churchill had called on Kennedy, the latter reported to his President: 'By his conversation, I should judge that he believes that with the bombing of well known places in England, the USA will come in.'[2]

Ten days later, when lunching with the Hungarian Ambassador, Gyorgy Barcza, Churchill is reported as saying, 'You are on good terms with Hitler. You could do a little favour. The British are still not aware of the danger that they are in or the seriousness of their situation. We'll have to do something to wake them up. Would you tell Hitler to start a little bombing of London? That would wake up the most indolent Englishman.' Barcza replied that he felt sure the raids would soon start. Churchill replied 'Well, the sooner the better. London is full of ugly buildings. At least we can build some new ones.'[3]

During that same month Churchill had told his Cabinet that he expected the German bombing of England to have a powerful effect upon the Americans.[4] On August 4, when with Charles de Gaulle, the

---

[1]Kennedy to State Department, No 1603, June 12, 1940.
[2]*Ibid*, No 1579, June 10, 1940.
[3]Unpublished memoirs of Gyorgy Barcza, Hoover Library, 206.
[4]Charmley, John, *Churchill: The End of Glory*, Hodder and Stoughton (1993), 421.

leader of the Free French Forces, Churchill raised a clenched fist in the garden at Chequers and exclaimed: 'Why won't they come?' When de Gaulle asked why Churchill was in so much of a hurry to see British cities and towns smashed to bits Churchill replied, 'The bombing of Oxford, Coventry and Canterbury will cause such a wave of indignation in the USA that they'll come into the war.'[5]

As early as May 16, in the early days of the Flanders campaign, Churchill had advocated the strategic bombing of the Ruhr industrial complexes. He had then expressed the view that faced with bombing attacks on his Reich, Hitler would be bound to retaliate with bombing raids against Great Britain. This would draw off the Luftwaffe from their activities in the Low Countries and thus relieve the French. Churchill confirmed the proposal to Reynaud and the bombing of towns and cities in the Ruhr was commenced. In spite of optimistic reports which described the Ruhr as 'a mass of ruins' and from the British Foreign Office which 'proved the terrible effects of British bombing operations in the Ruhr,' there were no reprisal raids on Great Britain. The Luftwaffe continued to fulfill its proper function as an air arm in support of the German ground forces.[6]

Shortly after the collapse of France, Anthony Eden and Halifax were both of the opinion that Churchill had become obsessional over the need to bomb Berlin. Eden suggested that if Wellington bombers were available they should be sent to the Middle East theatre of operations where they could best be used. Churchill was adamant that they should be used to mount an attack on Berlin.[7] On July 8 he was asking Max Beaverbrook, his Minister of Aircraft Production, when sufficient bombers would be delivered so that he would be able to launch 'an absolutely devastating exterminating attack by very heavy bombers.'[8] He probably had in mind the new four-engined Stirling bomber which had been promised for early squadron service.

On July 20, Churchill summoned Sir Charles Portal, Air Officer Commanding the RAF Bomber Force, to his private residence and instructed him to arrange for the night bombing of Berlin as soon as Churchill gave the word. A tentative target date was fixed for September 1.[9] The date of that meeting and the subject matter of the discussions is perhaps significant. Hitler had delivered his 'peace' speech on the previous day, July 19. There were rumours

[5]Thompson, Laurence, *1940: Year of Legend, Year of History*, Fontana (1968), 196.
[6]PRO PREM 3/193/6A.
[7]PRO FO/800/321/142.
[8]Beaverbrook papers D414, Churchill to Beaverbrook, July 8, 1940.
[9]PRO AIR 14/1930.

of peace moves initiated by Lord Lothian, the British Ambassador in Washington, on the very day that Churchill saw Portal in the evening. Also on that day, Churchill was asking Archibald Sinclair, his Secretary of State for Air, what bombers were available for an attack on Berlin and how soon they could be made available. Full details were supplied to him. They included the numbers and type of aircraft, their availability, bomb loads and speed of approach to the target.[10] On August 4 Portal was again dining at Chequers. Professor Lindemann (later Lord Cherwell), Churchill's scientific advisor, was also in attendance. He was an advocate of area bombing. Portal next attended Chequers on August 17, and on that date a decision was taken to bomb Berlin.

It is impossible to justify the decision on military grounds. At that time, Germany possessed ten times the bombers available to the RAF.[11] With their new bases in Norway, Denmark and the Low Countries, their bombers had only very short distances to travel to targets in Great Britain.[12] If there was to be a retaliation, it was going to be a very one-sided affair. Once again, it is apparent that political issues outweighed the military. On the night of August 23–24, due to a navigational error, German bombs from a single errant bomber intended for targets at Rochester and Thameshaven were inadvertently dropped on London. They were the first bombs dropped on London since the Zeppelin raids of 1918.[13] They provided the pretext that Churchill needed to raid Berlin.[14]

The very next day, August 25, Churchill telephoned Bomber Command Headquarters, circumventing both his Minister of State for Air and his Chief of Air Staff, and personally ordered a raid on Berlin that night. Cyril Newall, Chief of the Air Staff, intervened and indicated Leipzig as the target for that night. Arthur Harris, standing in for Portal, Chief of Bomber Command, then had Berlin reinstated. The attack went ahead. Eighty bombers were mustered. Less than fifty found Berlin. Casualties and damage was negligible.[15] There was no retaliation. A further British raid took place on the night of August 28–29. Ten civilians were killed. There was no retaliation. On August

---

[10]PRO PREM 3/14/2.

[11]Production of bombers had taken second place to the production of Spitfires and Hurricanes during the Battle of Britain.

[12]Irving, David, *Churchill's War*, Veritas, Australia (1987), 403.

[13]Shirer, William L., *The Rise and Fall of the Third Reich*, Pan Books (1964), 931.

[14]The decision to bomb Berlin was taken by Churchill on August 17. The errant bomber provided a convenient pretext, not the reason, for the raid on Berlin on August 25–26. It could be described as the flight of the red herring.

[15]Costello, John, *Ten Days that saved the West*, Bantam Press (1991), 388.

30, retaliation by the Luftwaffe was considered but ruled out by Hitler because of continuing peace feelers.

On September 6 Berlin was bombed again. This time, Churchill succeeded in obtaining a full reciprocation on the following night. The lifting of the embargo on the bombing of London which had been in place and honoured since September 3, 1939, had been threatened by Hitler in his speech two days earlier at the *Sportspalast* in Berlin: 'Since they attack our cities, we will extirpate theirs.' He went on: 'When people are very curious in Great Britain and ask "Yes, but why doesn't he come?" We reply: "Calm yourselves! Calm yourselves! He is coming! He is coming".'[16]

And so he came. On the afternoon of September 7 and through the following night he delivered what was up to that time, the heaviest air raid ever made in the history of aerial warfare. It was always claimed by the Germans that only military targets were attacked, but inevitably there were civilian casualties. Hitler was reportedly furious when told that the fires had encroached into central London. According to his aide, Fritz Hesse, the original Luftwaffe plan was to reduce Great Britain to economic impotence by destroying all the main centres of transport, communications, food dumps, harbours and road and rail links. There was never any intention of mass bombing as a terror weapon.

This objective was confirmed at a Führer conference held a week later on September 14. Hitler then again ruled out of order a suggestion by Jeschonnek to bomb London residential areas. 'Bombing calculated to produce mass panic will be left to last.'[18] On September 17, the Air Ministry instructed RAF Bomber Command to attack Berlin at night. 'at the first opportunity during the present moon phase with the maximum number of heavy bombers possible'.[19] Retaliation was following upon retaliation. It was only a matter of time before both the Germans and the British, whatever good intentions they might have had as to bombing military targets, soon descended into the realms of indiscriminate or so called area bombing of civilian populations. The Germans were first into the chase and the heavy and consistent bombing of London soon broadened out into night attacks on most of the cities of Great Britain. To that extent, Churchill was provided with the first part of his American equation.

Churchill's expectations that American revulsion would be such that public opinion would push the USA into the war were premature.

---

[16]Thompson, Laurence, *1940: Year of Legend, Year of History*, Fontana (1968), 209.
[18]*Ibid*, 208.
[19]PRO PREM 3/14/2.

Roosevelt had needed the best part of three months earlier that summer to convince himself that Great Britain could survive and he would need a further 16 months before the USA entered the war,[20] even though during that period Great Britain suffered most grievously from heavy and sustained bombing. Nevertheless, it is true that the sustained bombing and the British reaction to it influenced American public opinion greatly. No longer was there any doubt about British resolution and their powers of resistance and this eased the passage of the lend-lease agreements for the supply of arms. It was a half victory for Churchill in the short term.

Churchill's enticement policy was to have one other consequence. One of the saddest features of a war is that the longer it goes on, the more escalatory it becomes in terms of brutality and excesses. Every action leads to reaction and every reaction to counter-reaction. Eventually, all morality disappears. In no war was this truth better illustrated than the war of 1939–45. And nowhere within that war is there a clearer example than the road trodden in the pursuit of the supposed prizes of aerial bombardment. The bombing of London on September 7, 1940, marks a milestone along the road to Nemesis. In August 1939 Goering, with the full support of Hitler, used his peace envoy, Dahlerus, to obtain assurances from the British that, in the event of war, they would confine any bombing to military targets only. In America at the same time, Roosevelt made it clear that no military or other aid would be made available to any nation which bombed civilians.[21] Hitler confirmed the German position in a Reichstag speech September 1, 1939. 'I have already made known to the Reichstag itself and to the rest of the world, that is to say, I will not wage war against women and children. I have ordered my Air Force to confine itself to attacks on military objectives.'[22] This outright condemnation of unrestricted bombing did not receive any direct reciprocation from across the water.

It is only fair to point out that the German concept of aerial warfare at that time was as a close support weapon for army co-operation. The aircraft had been designed and the aircrews trained for that purpose. They did not envisage a heavy bomber strategic force to be used as a weapon in its own right, as did Churchill. It was therefore easier for them to give an undertaking as to the avoidance of civilian targets. Nevertheless, British intentions as to bombing seemed as peaceful as those of the Germans in the early days of the war. Under the

---

[20]And even then only as a result of a declaration of war on her by Germany.
[21]Commercial considerations eventually took precedence over Roosevelt's moral stipulation.
[22]DGPR 161.

Chamberlain administration bombing of land targets of almost any nature was ruled out of order. In the first month of the war Halifax was advising against any bombing of Germany because of the danger of retaliatory raids, which would harden public opinion and make the ground less fertile for the receipt of peace proposals. This was Churchill's argument in reverse. Halifax was nothing if not tireless in his efforts to smooth the way for peace.[23] At the same time, Kingsley Wood was advising the Cabinet that the Black Forest in Germany could not be bombed because so much of it was private property.

For a full eight months before May 1940 the aerial truce held. It was an important component of the Phoney War. On May 16 the truce was broken. British bombers attacked targets in the industrial area of the Ruhr and continued to do so. Four months later, on September 7, following attacks on Berlin by the RAF, there occurred the first mass raid on London by way of retaliation. 1,500 civilians were killed. During the eight-month 'blitz' that followed, 40,000 civilians were killed and 900,000 houses destroyed. Three years later, as a result of an RAF Bomber Command attack on Hamburg over three consecutive nights, 43,000 civilians were killed and 60 per cent of the city's houses destroyed. In February 1945, three months before the war with Germany ended, an undisclosed number of civilians died as a result of a single attack by RAF bombers on the city of Dresden. The German historian, Friedrich Reichert, has estimated the dead at 25,000. Others have estimated the figure at 35,000. The German Government reported 250,000 at the time.

With the exception of the dropping of the first atomic bombs on Hiroshima and Nagasaki three months later, the raid on Dresden was the most horrific of the war. In the space of 25 minutes, 1,477 tons of high explosive bombs were dropped, to be followed three hours later by thousands of incendiaries. The fires became a conflagration consuming great quantities of oxygen. Outside, air rushed in with the force of a hurricane. Victims were suffocated and burned to ash within a moment. An eyewitness reported:

> Several people, although dead, were cowering by the entrance (to the basement). Others were on the steps. You could recognise that the corpses had human shapes but they were without clothes, hair or eyes, just charred remains. If you touched one, it fell apart into ash. There was no skeleton, not even individual bones. It was the most ghastly sight of my life.

---

[23] Liddell Hart papers 3/109, August 27, 1939.

By 1945, aerial warfare had come a long way since the pious hopes expressed in 1939. At Dresden, the only military targets in the shape of the large army barracks to the north of the town and the railway junction were untouched.[24] The total number of German civilians killed by aerial bombardment during the entire course of the war was 590,000. A further 800,000 were seriously injured. Over seven million were made homeless.[25] Churchill's enticement policy set in motion an escalation which culminated with Dresden and the atomic bombs. The indiscriminate area bombings of German cities and their civilian populations by RAF Bomber Command reached their full fruition in the years 1944 and 1945. Whatever the military advantages, real or imagined, that arose from such a policy, its implementation ranks high on the list of the barbaric practices to which mankind descended during the 1939–45 war.[26] There is little point in totting up points for the evils perpetrated by the belligerents in their search for victory in a climate of total war. But aerial bombardment and the horrific climax it had reached by 1945 is a clear example of its evil dynamics.

[24]*Guardian* newspaper report, February 9, 1995, on the occasion of the 50th anniversary of the raid.
[25]Ponting, Clive, *1940: Myth and Reality*, Hamish Hamilton (1990), 162–63.
[26]Confirmation of the British initiatives in strategic aerial bombardment is provided by A.J.P. Taylor in his *English History, 1919–1945* (534) and by J.M. Speight, Principal Assistant Secretary to the Air Ministry, *Bombing Vindicated* (73–74).

15

Fight on or make peace?

> *Future generations may deem it noteworthy that the supreme question of whether we should fight on alone never found a place in the War Cabinet agenda. Never was the possibility of a compromise peace ever mentioned.*
>
> WINSTON S. CHURCHILL

Divided Cabinet, errant diplomats and free-ranging agents

Churchill's unequivocal statement, contained in his Nobel Prize-winning five-volume history, *The Second World War*, is untrue. Publication of Cabinet and other records[1] discloses that there was a series of discussions at Cabinet level during May 1940 at which the matter of a negotiated peace was considered, that the War Cabinet was deeply divided on the issue, and that these divisions were not confined to the Cabinet. There were many instances during the latter part of 1940 when senior British diplomats, both at home and abroad and with or without the sanction of their masters at the Foreign Office, were initiating peace moves. Finally, if German diplomatic records are to be believed, 'hundreds' of British MI6 agents were instructed to sound out their German counterparts as to what sort of peace conditions were available for use as a basis for negotiation.

Given the widespread nature of these peace initiatives and the manner and skill with which Churchill eventually carried the day at Cabinet and all other levels to fight on, it is difficult to understand why his historical account of this period should be so incomplete. One

[1]These disclosures are still not complete. Some items in the relevant minutes are omitted completely. Others are partially blacked out.

would have thought that an account of his victory over the faint-hearted would have been an important and interesting feature in the history of those times. It must therefore be assumed that Churchill considered the preservation of the national myth of complete unity at a time of national crisis to be more important than the truth of the matter. The minutes relating to the Cabinet meeting held on Sunday, May 26, further suggest that Churchill's own personal view as to fighting on was expressed with rather less resolution than in the later meetings. Perhaps he did not wish that what might be considered a slight blemish on his own performance should enter the public domain.

The case for a negotiated peace was strongly presented at Cabinet level by the Foreign Secretary, Lord Halifax. The issue was argued during a series of Cabinet meetings which extended from May 26 to May 28. At that time, France was fighting for her survival, with every prospect of losing the battle. The British Expeditionary Force was virtually surrounded in Flanders, with every prospect of 'going into the bag' in its entirety. Halifax believed that with France beaten and the BEF lost, Great Britain could not fight on alone with any prospect of victory. If a peace could be negotiated which preserved the integrity and independence of Great Britain and her Empire, then that opportunity ought not to be lost.

On the basis of the known facts, Halifax's view was not unreasonable. He received varying support within the Cabinet for his views. Chamberlain usually but not always supported him. Eventually, Halifax found himself in a minority of one. Churchill opposed him throughout, with a resolution that grew with each succeeding meeting. He believed that the sort of generous terms that Halifax had in mind were not obtainable from Hitler and that, even if they were, Hitler could not be trusted to abide by the agreed terms. He was wrong on the first count but he may have been correct on the second, at least in the long term. We now know that in the summer of 1940 Hitler was prepared to negotiate a peace on precisely the terms Halifax had in mind. Hitler's aspirations lay in the East not the West. Generous terms were therefore available to end an unwanted and unnecessary war.

It is of course a matter of conjecture as to whether a peace guaranteeing the independence of Great Britain and her Empire would have held in the long run. Hitler had demonstrated in the past an alarming tendency to change direction according to changing circumstances, irrespective of past and present agreements and guarantees. With eyes fixed on Russia, peace in the West was essential. He could afford to be generous with the terms. But with Russia out of the way,[2] what then? Churchill's fears may have been well-founded. After Russia, Hitler might well have turned to the West as a next objective in a programme of world domination. There is no documentary or other evidence to suggest that this was Hitler's ultimate ambition, but the intoxication of continuing success on the battlefield might well have led him in that direction.

Churchill also had good reason, in the circumstances prevailing in the summer of 1940, to doubt that Hitler's conditions for peace would be generous. Great Britain had suffered a string of diplomatic defeats during the 1930s at the hands of Hitler, followed by an even more ignominious series of military defeats in Norway and Flanders. At no time during the decade leading up to the summer of 1940 had Great Britain displayed anything like the resolution, leadership and adventurous spirit one might have expected from a people with such an illustrious history. Was it not therefore entirely reasonable to expect nothing but the most humiliating terms from the man responsible for all the past humiliations?[3]

Personal factors, too, helped to promote the different views of the two adversaries in Cabinet. Churchill loved war and he loved to wage war. He no doubt found it instinctively distasteful to even talk in terms of peace so soon after he had donned the mantle and paraphernalia of the supreme War Lord. He was not bowed down by the responsibilities he had assumed on May 10. On the contrary, he had embraced them with enthusiasm. Halifax on the other hand, was a pacifist. He abhorred war and everything to do with it. He would soon demonstrate, both in Cabinet and out of it, and with Churchill's consent or without it, that he was prepared to go to almost any lengths to bring the war to an end. He was nothing if not a supremely rational being[4] and his reason told him that in the circumstances of May/June 1940, and in particular, the imminent demise of France, there was no rational basis for the continuance of the struggle. The war could not be won and countless British lives would be lost in the losing. Churchill, on the other hand, saw his mission as a crusade. It was to be fought

---

[2]Informed opinion at the time, both German and British, was that Russian resistance to a German invasion would last for a few weeks only. In the event, it lasted for four years, by which time Germany herself lay defeated.

[3]In 1950 Churchill confessed that his greatest fear in 1940 was that Hitler would publicly offer peace terms so generous that thay would have been impossible to ignore (*The Second World War*, Vol II, 199).

[4]In the circumstances of European turmoil prevailing in the 1930s and early 1940 this was not necessarily an all-pervading virtue. Halifax could never grasp the fact that mankind aspires as well as thinks and that issues are often settled by passions far removed from the cloistered calm of All Souls, Oxford. Halifax's restricted vision was a severe handicap. He never understood Churchill, any more than he ever understood Hitler.

against the evil forces of totalitarian barbarism and it was to be fought to the death. Halifax saw it as a useless exercise in the wastage of human life. If it could be ended with British sovereignty intact, then it should be.

There was yet another element which heightened the drama played out in the Cabinet exchanges of May 1940. Its ramifications went far beyond the obvious. When the first crucial Cabinet meeting took place on May 26, Churchill's tenure of office as Prime Minister was but a fortnight old. Chamberlain, not Churchill, was still the elected leader of the Conservative Party. The Conservative Party still dominated the Commons. Most of its members would have seen Halifax succeed Chamberlain rather than Churchill. Churchill also knew that the same view was held by the Monarch and court circles generally. He knew that his own political position was therefore not strong. He also knew that there were members of the Conservative Party in the Commons, and more particularly in the Lords, who represented those who had the most to lose in terms of privilege and material wellbeing by a continuation of the war. For that reason he knew that there were others behind Halifax. Halifax was not alone in the pacifist camp. Was he in fact, the tip of an iceberg? And if he was, how big was the iceberg?

Probably because of these factors, a reading of the record of the early Cabinet exchanges suggests that Halifax rather than Churchill dominated the proceedings and ensured that the possibilities of peace found a place on the agenda. It was only later when Churchill's leadership qualities had been demonstrated and his confidence boosted by public backing, that he gained the ascendancy and began to dominate the proceedings. A chronological account of the entire Cabinet discussions of May 1940, together with notes as to the attendant circumstances and comments, is set down in Appendix III. They reveal the deep divide in opinion prevailing at the topmost level.

Churchill's views as to fighting on eventually prevailed. One would have thought that thereafter, in accordance with the doctrine of collective responsibility and as a matter of personal loyalty to their Prime Minister, the Cabinet would then have closed ranks and displayed that same unity which was already emerging among the general populace[5] and which would eventually become the case in the Commons. But this was not so. Halifax and his Minister of State, Rab Butler, not only continued to hold open the door to possible German peace overtures but also to initiate them, both personally and through their Foreign Office representatives abroad. The British Ministers in Geneva (H.B.

---

[5]Albeit largely based on Churchill's rhetoric, a disdainful national arrogance born of successive centuries of political ascendancy and an ignorance of the true facts.

Livingston), Berne (Sir David Kelly), Washington (Lord Lothian), Stockholm (Sir Victor Mallet) and Madrid (Sir Samuel Hoare) all became heavily involved in peace traffic during the latter part of 1940, in spite of the Cabinet decision to fight on.

This peace traffic is a matter or record, both German and British. Those details presently (January 2000) available are reproduced in Appendix IV, together with relevant comments, but there is no certainty that the record is complete. According to Dr Fritz Hesse, the German Foreign Office adviser on English affairs,[6] 'hundreds of British (MI6) agents had been instructed to establish contacts with their German counterparts to sound them out.'[7] It is therefore apparent that in addition to the professional diplomats known to have been involved, British Intelligence agents were also receiving instructions to sound out the peace possibilities. These details are for the most part undisclosed; but MI6 involvement appears to be confirmed by the strange connection of Sir William Stephenson, the Head of British Security Co-ordination in the USA, with the extraordinary Wiseman/Princess Stephanie meetings of October/November 1940.[8]

What is not clear, and poses one of the most intriguing questions of this period, is who instructed those now known to have acted in direct contravention of a Cabinet decision of major policy, and why. The chain of command controlling the professional diplomats leads back to the Foreign Office and Foreign Minister Halifax and his Minister of State, Butler, and thence to the Cabinet. The chain of command controlling the intelligence agents leads to the MI6 Chief, Stewart Menzies, and thence to the Prime Minister. The instructions may have originated from Churchill himself. Technically, there is a difference between holding the door open so as to listen and find out what peace terms were available and actually initiating peace moves as a positive step in that direction.[9] In fact, the two activities merge. It may be that Churchill acknowledged, albeit privately, that defeat was a possibility and that he ought to know what terms for peace were on offer. In those circumstances, authorisation would have been issued to leave the door open and listen.

That Churchill did, in his private moments, have thoughts as to defeat and his own position in that eventuality is perhaps supported by a decision he took at the very height of the crisis. On May 18, just as

[6]Hesse had been head of the official German News Agency in London before the war and he was well respected. There is no reason to doubt the truth of his report.
[7]Thompson, Laurence, *1940: Year of Legend, Year of History*, Fontana (1968). As reported by Hesse to Ribbentrop.
[8]See Appendix IV (iv).
[9]The Hesse report refers to the British agents 'sounding out' their German counterparts.

the crisis was deepening in Flanders and only one week after his own accession to power, he sounded out Chamberlain about inviting David Lloyd George to join the Cabinet. At that time, Lloyd George shared with Halifax the distinction or otherwise of being the country's leading pacifist, not to mention defeatist. What was the reason for Churchill's extraordinary decision? Was it that he knew full well that the king across the water, Lloyd George, was lurking in the wings, waiting to take over as soon as peace terms were on the Cabinet table, and that Churchill would rather have him on the opposite side of the table, where he could perhaps handle him better?

There is another explanation. Churchill had demonstrated his firm grasp of arithmetic when he brought in Archibald Sinclair, so as to give him a clear majority at the crucial Cabinet meeting on May 27 (see Appendix III). The pretext for Sinclair's inclusion was that he was the Leader of the Liberal Party. The real reason was that he was Churchill's friend and would vote accordingly. The advent of Lloyd George to the Cabinet would have the opposite effect. Lloyd George, Halifax and Chamberlain could have produced a deadlock, in which case Churchill could have honourably resigned and thus avoided any personal responsibility for a subsequent acceptance of German peace terms. This is perhaps an extreme, even cynical hypothesis; but Churchill was nothing if not a professional and astute politician. It would not be beyond his wit to cover his tracks for every possibility.[10] He may well have ordered a 'leave the door open and listen' policy.

A more likely suggestion is that Churchill authorised the instructions to both the diplomats and the agents so as to mislead the Germans. Rumours of peace moves would, and did, delay the military assault on Great Britain. That is a very plausible explanation and one which has been advanced subsequently by diplomats explaining their actions.[11] Another reason, also advanced by diplomats, is that, by reason of their own centuries-old traditions, Foreign Office personnel believed that every problem had a diplomatic answer and it was their job to find one. That was their training. Senior diplomats like Kelly, Mallet and Livingston were skilled in the art of opening up channels of communication in every conceivable (diplomatic) situation. If peace traffic was in the air, their every instinct would be to follow it up and if necessary put flesh on the bones. There was no possibility of military victory. Why not encourage diplomatic activity? Senior diplomats sited in ideal locations for handling peace traffic would hardly need instructing. Nevertheless, this reasoning appears to be wrongly based in view of the

---

[10]Lloyd George refused the invitation to join the Cabinet (see chapter 20).

[11]The Kelly negotiations, for example. See Appendix IV(iii).

decisions made at Cabinet level, inclusive of the Foreign Secretary, to fight on. There remains the most straightforward, if no less extraordinary, explanation of the instructions given to the diplomats and agents: that they were given not by Churchill but by Halifax and Menzies, without Churchill's knowledge, or more precisely, without his consent.

Halifax was, of course, intent upon peace and it will be suggested in a later chapter that his enthusiasm was matched by that of Menzies. But even if that were the case, it is still extraordinary that such instructions could be issued in open defiance of Churchill's wishes and the Cabinet decision to fight on. It is as though those in charge at the Foreign Office and in the MI6 Intelligence Services did not seriously care if Churchill was aware of what was going on. If that was the case, it suggests that the divided Cabinet reflected much wider divides within the nation.

That hypothesis is supported by the nature of Halifax's actions and the man himself. In the events immediately prior to Churchill's accession to power, Halifax had demonstrated his lack of will when faced with the opportunity and responsibility of accepting the premiership. The thought of accession to supreme power had elated Churchill. It had given Halifax the belly-ache. If Halifax wanted peace so badly, which he did, how better to wrap up the whole wretched business than by succeeding Chamberlain when he had the opportunity, excluding Churchill from his inner Cabinet, and then asking for terms? But Halifax had not done that. Instead, he had accepted a position under Churchill. There he sought to undermine Churchill's position by initiating through Butler and his team of senior diplomats a succession of peace moves apparently designed to put peace terms on the Cabinet table as a *fait accompli*.

In those circumstances, a major political crisis would have been precipitated with the possible demise of Churchill. Who would have succeeded Churchill? Who would have picked up the peace terms and had the courage to face the British people, tell them that the Government was going to negotiate terms to end the war and face up to negotiations with Adolf Hitler? It would not have been Halifax. He had turned down that option on May 9.

Was it possible then that someone else was waiting in the wings, ready to replace Churchill once acceptable peace terms were available? Such a hypothesis poses both the existence of the so-called British Peace Party and the possibility that Halifax was not a principal but an agent. Halifax had always shaped up well as Chief of Staff but never looked big enough to fill the shoes of the Commander-in-Chief. This would also explain Churchill's quite extraordinary action, or lack of it, when confronted with the facts as to the dissemination of peace talks through the Foreign Office and Intelligence Service. He did not dismiss Halifax or Butler immediately, as he had every right to do. His own political position was too fragile for that. Rather did he bide his time until his own position was strengthened.

In December 1940 Churchill rid himself of Halifax by sending him off to Washington as British Ambassador.[12] In similar fashion, the clandestine activities of Butler in June 1940 received only the mildest reproach at the time[13] but a posting out of the Foreign Office and into the Ministry of Education a year later.[14] Certainly, Churchill's less than vigorous approach to the problem of these two senior renegades during the summer of 1940 indicates the frailty of his own position and the knowledge that he was perhaps dealing with a problem larger than the two individuals concerned.

Another factor points in the same direction. Many of the senior diplomats posted to neutral countries, where they would be ideally placed to handle peace traffic, were either pacifists or sympathetic to Germany's cause, or both. All had been appointed by Halifax, with Chamberlain's approval. It is as though the stage had been set by Chamberlain and Halifax in September 1939 to end the war almost before it had started – presumably as part of the wishful-thinking policy to wait for the 'good' Germans to overthrow the Nazi regime, whereupon generous peace terms would be on offer. It was unfortunate for Churchill that he inherited this position. It was fortunate for Halifax that he had a ready-made peace force at his disposal.

One of the most extraordinary postings Halifax ever made (or one of the cleverest, if the foregoing suggestion is correct) was the appointment of Sam Hoare as British Ambassador to Spain on June 1, 1940.[15] Churchill had jettisoned Hoare from the Cabinet as soon as he had taken over. 'Slippery Sam' was a notorious defeatist and appeaser of the old school, and he had been in the pay of Beaverbrook, the press baron. He could count among his friends all the leading pacifists, appeasers and defeatists of the day, including Halifax, Butler, Lothian and the Duke of Windsor. During the pre-war decade, dominated by political dwarfs, he had been over-promoted to hold most of the senior

---

[12]It might be thought that Washington was an inappropriate posting for a man of Halifax's pacifist tendencies; but Churchill himself was handling most of the important diplomatic traffic with Washington through his personal correspondence with President Roosevelt.

[13]See Appendix IV(i).

[14]Churchill's hand of retribution did not end at the Ministry of Education. It extended to 1956. Butler has been described as 'the best Prime Minister Britain never had'. In fact, Butler had no chance of succeeding Eden as Prime Minister, or for that matter Macmillan, while Churchill was alive. On both occasions, Churchill attended upon the Monarch and advised upon the succession.

[15]PRO FO 366/1096/7.

offices of state. In that capacity he had contributed much to the misfortune which beset the nation in September 1939. He was a man of little vision and less courage. He possessed all the social skills[16] and had an undoubted talent for administration. When Hoare and his wife were preparing to leave Great Britain for Spain, at the height of the summer crisis, Alexander Cadogan at the Foreign Office commented: 'The rats leaving the sinking ship. The quicker we get them out of the country, the better. I'd sooner send them to a penal settlement. The Quisling[17] of England when Germany conquers us and I am dead.'

On arriving in Madrid, Hoare took up residence next door to the German Ambassador in Spain, Eberhard von Stohrer.[18] He propounded defeatist views from day one. Such was the man. Madrid, the capital city of Fascist Spain, was friendly with both Germany and Italy. The French armistice proposals were spawned there. Marshall Pétain, the leading French defeatist, had been the French Ambassador to Spain.[19] Halifax in his wisdom united the man and the Spanish environment. Can there be any doubt as to the inspiration of the appointment? Where else, or who else, could better spawn another armistice?[20]

Other Halifax appointments were in the same mould. He appointed Philip Kerr (Lord Lothian) to be Ambassador to Washington on September 1, 1939. Lothian, heir to the Scottish title and some 28,000 acres of land was an accomplished young man. He had charm, wit a persuasive tongue, a fluent pen and all the social graces. He was the Prince Charming of the Liberal persuasion. He had a quick brain, fertile imagination and intellectual aspirations. He was in frequent attendance at All Souls, Oxford, where he met and became friendly with Halifax, Simon, Dawson and other appeasers. He was deeply religious and sought to bring morality into politics, a notoriously dangerous cocktail.[21] Unfortunately, in spite of his brilliance Lothian was also confirmed as thoroughly unstable and volatile in his opinions.[22] He

---

[16]Lord Birkenhead said of him 'he looked like he had come from a long line of maiden aunts', such was his fastidiousness.

[17]Vidkun Quisling was a prominent Norwegian traitor.

[18]Hoare, Rt Hon Sir Samuel, *Ambassador on Special Mission*, Collins (1946), 22.

[19]DGFP 523/524 and DGFP 200.

[20]Hoare was involved in the Duke of Windsor affair (see Appendix V). He tipped off the Spanish Foreign Minister, Beigbeder, as to the arrival of his friend in Spain on June 23 and probably suggested to Beigbeder that the Germans contact him, which they did. Rudolf Hess also instructed his friend, Albrecht Haushofer, to open up a channel of communication with Hoare and this was done in late 1940 and early 1941.

[21]He was not alone in this aberration. Religious faith and a professed morality underpinned the behaviour of most of the main appeasers of the 1930s, including Halifax, Hoare and Dawson.

[22]Even his religious faith successively encompassed Roman Catholicism, liberal agnosticism and finally Christian Science, which saw him to a premature death in the British Embassy in December 1940 with no doctor in attendance.

went to Russia and was imbued with communism. He went to America and was imbued with capitalism. Unfortunately, he also went to Germany and was imbued with Hitler. He was always apt to be the victim of his most recent experience. For that reason Lothian was considered to be a rather naive political lightweight and little more than a gifted amateur.[23]

Lothian never attained high political office. His one abiding political view in the late 1930s was his love for Germany, its leader and his aspirations. He became a prolific writer of letters to and articles for the *Times*, advocating Hitler's cause. He gave a pre-war view of European affairs: 'Mussolini and the Pope are the worst kind of dictators, closely followed by Litvinov. Hitler, who is a visionary rather than a gangster, was the least eerie of the lot and the Germans in themselves are much better people than the Italians and Russians. Hitler was one of the creative figures of the generation.'[24] This was the man appointed by Halifax to fill one of the most prestigious positions in the diplomatic service on the outbreak of war with Germany. President Roosevelt objected to the appointment, referring to Lothian's 'attitude of complete despair'. Similar doubts were expressed by Lothian's predecessor, Sir Ronald Lindsay.[25] Lothian was not removed.

Perhaps the most revealing of the Halifax appointments was that of Sir David Kelly as the Foreign Office representative to Switzerland in December 1939. He had been considered for Stockholm but Halifax eventually sent him to Berne. (Both Stockholm and Berne, situated in prominent and near-at-hand neutral countries, were perhaps likely to become busy post-offices for the passage of peace traffic if the belligerents so decided.) Kelly later wrote his autobiography, *The Ruling Few*, in which he also expounds in some detail upon his political philosophy of government. His father was the son of a landowner with estates in County Londonderry, Northern Ireland. His mother, née Sophie Armstrong d'Arenberg, was part-German and her family took the German side in the 1914–18 war. Kelly's public school was St Paul's. He then went to Magdalen College, Oxford. During his school and university holidays he spent a good deal of time in Germany. He learnt the language and became enamoured with the manner of their government, which he described as 'paternal benevolent despotism'.

Kelly saw European evolution in terms of strong historical Toryism. He criticises modern democracy, claiming that the vast mass of

[23]J.R.M. Butler, *Lord Lothian*, 237.
[24]Lothian letters of May 1 and 7, 1936, as quoted by Butler (p254) and by Martin Gilbert in *Britain and Germany Between the Wars*, 99.
[25]PRO FO 1794/18.

mankind busy themselves with their day-to-day affairs and leave an elitist minority to rule them. In Great Britain the elitist minority are the products of the public schools and Oxbridge. 'The man in the street has no more direct say in a modern democracy than he had under the Habsburgs or Hohenzollerns.' Kelly extols the virtues of the dictators Cromwell, Atatürk and Salazar, and he deals at some length with the threat of communism.

These political thoughts might provide good raw material for intellectual debate. But they also happen to represent the political views of a person placed in a sensitive diplomatic post at a time of national crisis. It is apparent that Kelly was not only of German ancestry but also of German inclination, that he was no democrat, that his right-wing political views were more aligned to Nazi thinking than that of a British democrat, and that he considered communism a greater threat to British social structures than fascism. It is hardly surprising that Kelly figures prominently in the British peace initiatives set down in Appendix IV.[26] His appointment and the others described give cause to ponder upon the wisdom of such appointments and, indeed, their true purpose. Churchill's inheritance was truly burdensome.

In the circumstances prevailing in midsummer 1940 the initiating of the peace moves described in Appendix IV is unremarkable. What is remarkable is that the initiatives never convinced the Germans of British intent to carry the negotiations through to a conclusion at the highest level. As a result, anyone who may have been waiting in the wings, pending Churchill's demise, never had an opportunity to make an appearance and Churchill never relinquished the spotlight. He first dealt with Halifax and his pacifism at Cabinet level, albeit by the narrowest of margins. and was then able to snuff out the widespread peace nibbling in Halifax's domain overseas by constantly making bellicose 'fighting on' speeches in the Commons and repeating them over the radio to a worldwide audience.

Churchill's defiant speeches inspired the British people and carried them with him. Perhaps more importantly, they also made it clear to the Germans that peace was just not on the agenda. The Germans were put in constant disarray by the discrepancy between Churchill's defiance and the apparent willingness to talk peace as peddled by Halifax's diplomats and Menzies's agents. Perhaps the crowning inconsistency, and the crowning confusion for the Germans, was when Churchill coerced (there can be no other word for it) Halifax into making the broadcast reply on the evening of July 22 to Hitler's much-

[26]In 1949, Kelly was appointed British Ambassador to Moscow. The Russians took more than two months to approve the appointment. Approval is normally given within a week or so.

publicised 'peace speech' in Berlin three days earlier. Hitler's peace invitation was rejected outright. Coming from the lips of Halifax, the rejection must have dulled German enthusiasm for any further peace dabbling by British overseas diplomats and agents.

German initiatives

The odd situation that prevailed during the summer of 1940 was that Germany, which had swept all before it in terms of military prowess, wanted a compromise peace and Great Britain, with a string of military disasters behind her, wanted war. At least, that was the declared intention of Churchill's Government irrespective of the activities of some of his more wayward Ministers. Hitler thought that the vanquished should be asking for terms from the victor and that is how he expected matters to evolve. He therefore sat on his hands during June 1940, waiting for the inevitable to happen. But the inevitable did not happen. Any peace nibbling that resulted from British initiatives lacked the final *imprimatur* of Churchill.

By early July, Hitler's patience was beginning to wear thin. He felt himself pushed into having to prepare a final military strike to enforce a peace. He was singularly unenthusiastic about that option, for both military and personal reasons. He therefore resolved to try another option. He was due to speak in early July at a session of the Reichstag to formally announce the successful conclusion of military operations in the West. He could also use the speech to make it clear to Great Britain and the world that Germany was ready to consider any realistic proposals for peace that Great Britain might care to make. On July 8 he postponed the date of the Reichstag speech because reports were reaching him that there was about to be a reshuffle of the British Cabinet.[27] When these reports proved to be unfounded, the Germans, tired of sitting on their hands, decided to do something themselves.

An invitation was extended to Dr Carl Burckhardt, President of the Red Cross, to visit Berlin. There he was instructed to sound out the British and make it clear that generous peace terms would be on offer.[28] Burckhardt said that he would talk to a friend in Switzerland. The friend was David Kelly.[29] On July 8 Burckhardt met Kelly and

---

[27]General Franz Halder (Hitler's Chief of Staff) diary entry.
[28]The only concessions Great Britain would have to make from the status quo would be minor ones to satisfy Italian territorial ambitions.
[29]Kelly to Foreign Secretary, July 14, 1940 (PRO FO 371/24401).

Paravincini, the Swiss Minister to London, in Berne. He made it clear that the assault on Great Britain was being withheld in anticipation of British peace proposals and would continue to be so withheld, providing something concrete was forthcoming. Kelly raised the difficulty occasioned by Hitler's apparent lack of trustworthiness. These sentiments were echoed in London and for that reason the approach never gained strength.

At the same time as instructing Burckhardt, the Germans made similar overtures through the Papal Nuncio in Berne, Dr Salazar in Lisbon and the Prime Minister of Finland. These various approaches eventually reached the desk of Roger Makins, a senior official at the British Foreign Office. He appears to have taken up the position of Churchill's watchdog at that establishment. The approaches were ignored.

In spite of these rebuffs, or perhaps because of them, Hitler now put considerable effort into his big speech, now scheduled for Friday, July 19. The speech, subsequently known as the *Friedensredf* (peace speech), was a showpiece performance. Some say[30] it was one of Hitler's best. From a flower-bedecked podium, he spoke for over two hours. In a touch of pure stagecraft, he broke off half-way through to make awards and laudatory remarks about his generals, ministry officials and others who had contributed to the victory in the West. Twelve generals were promoted on the spot to the rank of Field Marshal during the interlude. Goering went the one step further. He took up the rank of Reichsmarschall, a rank created especially for the purpose. All the grandeur and celebration of success produced an atmosphere of unity between Hitler, the Nazi Party under Hess and the military chiefs. It was also conducive to acceptance by the audience of almost anything Hitler had to say. He did not waste the opportunity.

Hitler was well aware of the world-wide audience for whom his speech was being broadcast in addition to his adoring disciples packed into the Reichstag.[31] Apart from some personal invective directed at Churchill, which was ill-judged and unnecessary, Hitler successfully promoted the image of a magnanimous victor being both fair and reasonable in his suggestions to a vanquished foe. His speech constituted what appeared to be a sincere public avowal of a wish for peace and it was delivered in a respectable and reasonable manner. There was no screaming and shouting.

---

[30]William L. Shirer, the distinguished American commentator and author, was one of them.
[31]Shirer, William L., *The Rise and Fall of the Third Reich*, Pan Books (1964), 903.

> In this hour I feel it to be my duty before my own conscience to appeal once more to reason and common sense[32] in Great Britain as much as elsewhere. I consider myself in a position to make this appeal since I am not a vanquished foe begging favours but the victor speaking in the name of reason. I see no reason why this war need go on. I am grieved to think of the sacrifices it must claim. A great Empire will be destroyed, an Empire which it was never my intention to destroy or even harm.[33]

Hitler had not stated any specific terms for peace, but he had certainly left the door wide open to British overtures. According to William Shirer, who was present on the occasion, there was never any doubt that Great Britain would grasp the friendly hand and come to terms.[34] Yet within one hour of the speech ending the BBC broadcast a firm rejection. They had not even waited for official Government sanction. There was no formal debate on the speech or its implications in the British Commons. Formal rejection of Hitler's invitation was included (significantly) by Halifax in a routine ministerial broadcast on July 22. The door opened by Hitler had been firmly shut in his face.

Certainly, there were rumours of peace moves immediately thereafter, but no active negotiations emerged. It was reported that Lothian, Lloyd George and the Duke of Windsor were all urging a positive response to the speech. Lloyd George and the Duke of Windsor were both said to have written to King George VI advocating the dismissal of the present Government and its leader and its replacement by a new peace cabinet of Lloyd George, Halifax and Chamberlain. The *Gazzetta di Popolo* of Turin even quoted the fact of the Duke of Windsor's cable to the King and the issue was taken up by *The New York Times.*[35,36]

Hitler's expectation of a domestic upheaval within the ranks of the British Establishment and the ejection of the Churchill Government appears to be confirmed by reports to Vansittart filed by MI6 agent Christie and included in the Christie papers retained at Churchill College, Cambridge.[37] A Christie report of July 23 states that Hitler was concerned at having to conduct war on two fronts, and wished to

---

[32]It is no coincidence that these are the precise words used by Halifax in connection with the Prytz affair (see Appendix IV).
[33]Shirer, William L., *The Rise and Fall of the Third Reich*, Pan Books (1964), 904.
[34]*Ibid.*, 905.
[35]The content of the cable is unknown. Presumably the cable rests with the royal archives.
[36]*The New York Times*, July 23, 1940, page 3.
[37]Christie had a network of intelligence connections throughout Europe, including those he had developed through the Catholic Church.

deal with Russia free of the impediment to his rear. Hitler planned to defeat Great Britain from within and the peace invitation was made with this end in view. Christie referred to what he called the 'fifth column'[38] correspondence in the *Times* just before the outbreak of war. Hitler believed that, as with France, there were Nazi sympathisers in Great Britain.[39]

On August 3 Churchill himself made a belated response to Hitler. He called for 'effective guarantees by deeds, not words' and the evacuation of all the German-occupied countries before negotiations for peace could start.[40] Hitler's reaction to Churchill's response is unknown, but German peace nibbling continued. Albert Plessman, the founder of the Dutch KLM airline, was pressed into service by Goering. Plessman came up with a plan based on the principle that the industrial nations of the world should be co-operating not warring. At the same time, the German Ambassador to Turkey, Franz von Papen, made proposals through the Netherlands Minister in Ankara to the British Ambassador to Turkey. This approach arose as a result of conversations between Hitler and von Papen.[41] On August 31, Dr Ludwig Weissauer, a Berlin lawyer, was sent to Stockholm to contact the British Minister there, Sir Victor Mallet, using the President of the Swedish High Court of Appeal, Dr Eckberg, as a go-between. None of these well meaning attempts to start negotiations were fruitful. Frank Roberts, a senior official at the Foreign Office and another of Churchill's watchdogs, saw to that: 'I see no reason to depart from the uncompromising attitude laid down.'[42]

These rejections appear to have closed down all thought of peace overtures from the German side. Hitler had certainly opened the door, but Churchill's position was one of intransigence. Germany had to evacuate all the occupied countries in Europe before negotiations could commence. That was Churchill's view and that was the British Government's view while Churchill continued to hold the reins. However much Halifax and his followers may have thought, like Hitler, that there was plenty of room for manoeuvre and negotiations, the problem of Churchill *in situ* had to be dealt with. It never was. It was Churchill's will, not Halifax's or Hitler's, that prevailed.

---

[38]The term originated during the Spanish civil war. It designated traitorous assistance within the ranks of the enemy.
[39]Christie papers, 1/16.
[40]Churchill, *The Second World War*, Vol II, 231.
[41]PRO FO 371/24408, August 21, 1940.
[42]*Ibid*, September 7, 1940.

Neutral interventions

Various attempts to promote peace initiatives were also made by neutral countries during the summer crisis of 1940 and thereafter. They were made for a variety of reasons but were totally ineffective. Most of them came from European neutrals fearful of further German expansionist plans which would affect their own sovereignty. Such countries were small and carried little diplomatic weight. Their efforts were usually treated with suspicion by the warring parties who accused each other of using neutrals to cloak their own peace moves which might have been construed as a sign of weakness if undertaken direct.

Neither of the two powerful neutrals, Russia and the USA, was inclined to launch initiatives, for reasons which were not dissimilar. The conflict suited Russia. Germany was less likely to attack Russia while she was committed in the West by an undefeated enemy. The conflict also suited the USA. With Great Britain kept in the fight but reduced to a position of total dependence upon American supplies, the USA could see her way clear to taking on the postwar mantle of economic and political leader of the world democracies.[43] This inclination to stand off rather than take any initiative towards peace is illustrated by the peace efforts made by Dino Alfieri, the new Italian Ambassador in Berlin. In late June, with the direct authority of Hitler, Alfieri called on the American chargé d'affaires in Berlin. He explained that Hitler's wish for peace was genuine and that generous terms were available. Alfieri asked that the USA should mediate. His request was conveyed to Cordell Hull in Washington, who replied that the USA would require Churchill's authority as well as Hitler's if the USA were to mediate. The initiative thereupon collapsed.

Other soundings came from Sweden, Turkey, Switzerland, Spain, Japan and the Vatican. Even the Pope's motives were not of the purest. No doubt he was concerned about the moral issues involved in major warfare. But he was perhaps also concerned that the Catholic Church in Europe, its institutions, fabric and community life should not be impaired by a continuance of the conflict. He was also an Italian. He was therefore no doubt concerned as to the future of his native land. Certainly, the Vatican launched several initiatives during the summer. On June 22 and 26 approaches made personally by the Papal Nuncio who visited Sir David Kelly in Berne were rejected in London. Subsequent interventions by the Pope himself were similarly rejected.

[43]Russia's expectations were not realised. America's were.

At the end of July an offer of mediation was received by King George VI from King Gustav of Sweden. Both the King and Churchill guessed correctly that Gustav was merely a mouthpiece for a German approach. Churchill was dismissive of Gustav and of his own Foreign Office who handled the original approach: 'The ideas set forth in the Foreign Office memo appear to me to err in trying to be too clever and to enter into refinements of policy unsuited to the strategic simplicity and grandeur of the times and issues at stake.'[44] Churchillian rhetoric was not confined to parliamentary occasions.

Another Scandinavian approach followed, this time from Finland and was rejected out of hand by both the British and the Germans. Perhaps the most bizarre initiative of the year came from the Japanese Foreign Secretary, Josuke Matsuoka. Matsuoka's ambitions outstripped his abilities. He had mediated successfully in comparatively minor border disputes between China and Thailand and later on between Thailand and Vichy France, following the defeat of France. Matsuoka planned to step onto the larger stage and bring the Anglo-German conflict to an end. He travelled to Europe, displayed an ignorance of the issues involved and was dismissed both by Anthony Eden, the new British Foreign Minister and Ribbentrop. Matsuoka's visit seems to have been singularly ill-prepared and motivated more by personal ambition than true intent to bring the conflict to an end. Other attempts at reconciliation by the neutrals and by well-meaning amateurs were all ineffective. British disbelief of Hitler's stated intentions proved to be an insurmountable obstacle to any meaningful progress towards peace.

The Duke of Windsor

No account of the peace moves during the summer of 1940 would be complete without referring to the extraordinary lengths to which the Germans were prepared to go to use both the Duke and Duchess of Windsor in their overall plan for peace. A detailed account of these activities in Spain and Portugal during June and July 1940 is therefore included in Appendix V. If the behaviour of Halifax and Butler in 1940 can fairly be described as disloyal and near-treasonable, that of the Duke of Windsor falls fairly and squarely into the latter category. On two separate occasions in that year, either the Duke or Duchess or both were knowingly in direct touch with the King's enemies; on the

---

[44] Thompson, Laurence, *1940: Year of Legend, Year of History*, Fontana (1968), 173.

second occasion, they offered help to those enemies. The Duke was never brought to trial, presumably because as the brother of King George VI he was a prominent, albeit disgraced, member of the royal family and thus, enjoyed a privileged immunity.

The Duke's whole life had been one of privilege, occasioned by his birth as Edward, Prince of Wales. Groomed to assume the responsibilities of the King of England he had been a constant source of embarrassment during his apprenticeship; and soon after the assumption of those responsibilities he abdicated them in favour of a twice-married American lady totally unfitted to become his Queen. Throughout his life Edward had relied upon privilege rather than ability to make his way. Apart from a certain boyish charm and inquisitiveness, he gave little in return. In his entrance examinations for the Royal Navy he secured 291 marks out of 600, in spite of receiving private tuition by way of preparation. The marks constituted a 'fail' but he was admitted. In the navy examinations of March 1910 he was placed 48th in geometry and 45th in trigonometry out of a class of 59.[45] He then went up to Oxford, although he had no academic qualification so to do.[46] He left after the second year and took no degree.

During the 1914–18 war the Prince was commissioned into the 1st Battalion Grenadier Guards, although not of the required height. When that battalion left for action in France he was transferred to the 3rd Battalion, which stayed at home. In 1916 he was awarded the Military Cross, having never been in action.[47] At the end of 1916 his two equerries, Claud Hamilton and Joey Legh, introduced the Prince to the delights of an experienced French prostitute, Paulette. 'From that moment, sex became one of the Prince's most urgent preoccupations.'[48]

This depressing litany of non-achievement and the generous rewards flowing from a position of privilege would have been acceptable had the monarch-to-be recognised a commensurate responsibility in terms of public duty. But Edward never did so, either as Prince or as King. He never accepted that he had two lives to lead, one private the other public. Edward lived only one life, his own. It was a constant embarrassment to his family and his Ministers of State.

A good and strong wife might have presented at least part of the

---

[45]Ziegler, Philip, *King Edward VIII*, Collins (1990), 24.

[46]Examples of his spelling while at Oxford include 'chaplin', 'chapple', 'colision', 'dammaged' and 'explaned' (*ibid*, 40).

[47]*Ibid*, 67.

[48]*Ibid*, 89.

answer to the problem. But there was no wife in early days, just two mistresses, Freda Dudley Ward and Thelma Furness, and a host of philandering in-betweens. When he finally proposed taking a wife she was a twice-divorced American lady, Wallis Simpson, whose main interests appeared to be the accumulation of wealth and the scaling of the social heights rather than affairs of state. An American press comment caught the picture well, following Edward's visit to the USA in 1924 as Prince of Wales. The impression conveyed 'was that of a desperately unhappy, wilful, dissipated boy without much brain who could be very charming when he chose but who was always seeking to avoid the duties of his position.' His aide, Alan Lascelles, went further: 'The Prince never grew up. There was an inability to establish and maintain a mature relationship with another adult. There were fits of depression. He expressed interest in unemployment and housing but had neither the stamina, education or temperament to do anything about it.' Such were the opinions of those close to him of the boy born to be King.

The road ahead would have been hard enough with these shortcomings, but there was more. Edward's early and growing allegiance to the politics of the Right and an admiration for Nazi Germany and its leader became a source of acute embarrassment and concern to Baldwin's Government of the mid-thirties. He had, of course, inherited German connections. In terms of ancestry he was more German than British.[49] Most of his twelve godparents were German.[50] He spent a good deal of his holidays in Germany ('I felt more at home than in France because I stayed mostly among relatives'). He had all the trappings of a Nazi follower. He was a racist,[51] had an obsessive fear of communism and its consequences[52] and saw Nazi Germany as the bastion against the spread of communism. He went one step further. 'Of course it is the only thing to do. We will have to come to it, as we are in great danger from the Communists too.'[53] Apparently, he was suggesting that Great Britain should embrace National Socialism.[54]

---

[49]He was five-eighths of German blood, if the author's arithmetic is correct. He conversed regularly in German with his mother, Queen Mary (previously Princess Mary of Teck).

[50]Ziegler, Philip, *King Edward VIII*, Collins (1990), 5.

[51]When entertaining distinguished guests during a tour of Sierra Leone which included some coloured dignitaries he exclaimed: 'I've flatly refused to dance with black women! That's too much!' (*ibid*, 158).

[52]This was a family inherited characteristic. In 1929, he acted for his father, King George V, in receiving the Russian Ambassador at Court. His father had refused to see the Ambassador (*ibid*, 196).

[53]*Ibid*, 206.

[54]There is little doubt that Ribbentrop's appointment as special Ambassador to Great Britain in 1936 was influenced by the possibility of establishing a special relationship with the new King. Unfortunately for Ribbentrop, the King's main, if not only, interest at the time was Wallis Simpson.

Such a candidate for the British throne must have been a mouth-watering prospect for the Nazi hierarchy.

By 1936, Baldwin and his colleagues thought that matters with the young Prince should be brought to a head. His behaviour was considered unfit to serve as the next King of England and his character deficiencies and indiscretions were becoming public knowledge. Baldwin, MacDonald and Simon resolved to attend upon the Prince, but on January 20, King George V died and Edward succeeded to the throne. By that time Wallis Simpson was dominating his life. Freda Dudley Ward had curbed his self-indulgence, at least to some extent. Thelma Furness had encouraged it. Wallis Simpson depended upon it. It therefore ran wild. Wallis Simpson and King Edward VIII were as one. No one else existed. Nothing else existed. It was therefore no surprise, and with a great deal of relief as far as his Ministers were concerned, when the new King abdicated his throne on December 10, 1936. It had been made clear to him that Wallis Simpson would never be Queen of England.

The Germans always maintained that the abdication was engineered in a political plot to rid the country of a monarch with professed Nazi views and that the unsuitability of Wallis Simpson to be Queen was an excuse, never the reason. This has always been denied by the British. Only an understanding of the peculiarly British moral rigidity which applied to matters of state and sovereignty at that time could explain that denial. Nevertheless, Edward's Ministers were glad to see the back of him and his place taken by a much more sober individual who took his responsibilities seriously.[55]

Edward's exit from office did not end the embarrassments. The visit to Germany by the Duke and Duchess in October 1937 was a case in point. Described as a private visit, it was used as a public snub to the British Government and King George VI. The Duke and Duchess were feted wherever they went. They met all the top Nazi leaders including Hitler and Hess and they received world-wide publicity. Goebbels made a point of addressing the Duchess as 'Your Royal Highness', which was the title denied to her by King George VI and his advisers in Great Britain. This further exacerbated the already existing rift between the two brothers. They were already in serious disagreement as to the financial terms of the abdication. But the main cause of the estrangement was the failure of King George VI and his wife to accept Wallis Simpson into the royal circle. As quite childish rebuffs and countersnubs occurred between the two brothers, so the estrangement

---

[55]George VI blossomed into a much respected and well-liked monarch, supported by a Queen of strength and total personal commitment to her King.

hardened into something approaching hatred, not only between the King and his brother but also the two women linked by destiny as well as marriage.

These matters were of course domestic, but they contained an underlying political importance. They may, in all their perversity, have driven the Duke even faster along the road towards assimilation of the tenets and practices of National Socialism and a drawing closer to the King's potential enemies. Certainly, the Duke's intense anger with his brother and sister-in-law affected his judgement on the issues before him in Spain and Portugal in June and July 1940. Thus do personal matters crowd in on political issues.

The Duke's long standing love affair with Germany and its Nazi leaders remained with him throughout the war years and even thereafter. For that reason, he and his wife were under constant surveillance by both British and American intelligence. His friends were invariably well disposed towards the Nazi regime, if not active agents in their cause. When the Duke and Duchess were married on June 3, 1937, the ceremony took place at the *Château de Candé,* a villa owned by Charles Bedaux, a personal friend and Nazi sympathiser. Bedaux was eventually arrested by the American FBI and charged with treason. Another friend, also a Nazi sympathiser, was the Swedish businessman, Axel Wenner-Gren; both became involved in illegal currency deals after the Duke had taken up a post in the Bahamas. Churchill had advised the Duke against associating with Wenner-Gren, who was 'suspected of being in communication with the enemy'. Sumner Welles considered Wenner-Gren to be a German agent and Harry Hopkins, personal aide to President Roosevelt, described him as 'violently pro-Nazi'. Such was the company that the Duke kept.

In February 1940 military intelligence was leaked to the Germans relating to Allied defensive plans in the event of a German offensive through Holland and Belgium. The German Ambassador at The Hague was able to relay to Berlin precise details of the French defensive positions. The information came from Charles Bedaux, a constant companion of the Duke in Paris where, as a liaison officer with the British Military Mission, he was party to the joint discussions with the French as to important military strategy.

In December 1940, the Duke gave an interview to Fulton Oursler, for the American magazine *Liberty*. In Oursler's own words, 'I did not believe my ears.' The Duke enthused about his personal regard for Hitler, saying that 'it would be a tragic thing for the world if Hitler was overthrown. He was the right and loyal leader of the German people.' He then apparently asked Oursler if Roosevelt would consider intervening to stop the war. The next morning, the Duke's aide-de-camp, Captain Vyvian Drury, went further: 'Tell Mr Roosevelt that if he were to make an offer of intervention for peace, then before anyone in England would oppose it, the Duke will instantly issue a statement supporting it and that will start a revolution in England and force peace.' Oursler subsequently sought advice from Roosevelt as to whether he should publish the interview. Roosevelt advised not, commenting: 'I am amazed to find that some of the greatest people in the British Empire, men of the so-called upper classes, men of the highest rank, secretly want to appease Hitler and stop the war.'[56]

After the war, the British Government never considered the Duke for employment in any diplomatic post. There were too many skeletons in the cupboard, not all of which have yet seen the light of day. Some fell out and became public property when the official German diplomatic documents became available. In spite of great efforts by both Churchill and Ernest Bevin, the postwar British Foreign Secretary, to keep the records under wraps they, or at least some of them, were eventually published in 1957.

The final twist to the bizarre saga of the Duke's wartime activities is provided by Anthony Blunt, one-time royal art historian, wartime intelligence officer and latter-day traitor. Blunt was dispatched to Germany with Owen Morshead, the librarian at Windsor, to recover certain documents contained in a trunk. According to one version, the trunk contained letters by Queen Victoria written to her daughter, the Empress Frederick. They were retrieved by Blunt and Morshead and taken to Windsor Castle for safekeeping, pending a return to normality in Germany. There is another version: that the document-hunting expedition had nothing to do with Queen Victoria's correspondence with her daughter and everything to do with the Duke of Windsor's correspondence with Adolf Hitler and other Nazi leaders. This second version also suggests that Blunt's secret mission for the royal cause earned him immunity from prosecution for his traitorous activities as a Russian spy until such time as he eventually confessed his misdemeanours. The reader may draw his own conclusions.

This was the Duke of Windsor's story or at least that part of it that has surfaced through the official documents. It is a sad story. By all accounts the Duke was not happy as a young man and was not particularly bright, falling heavily at every intellectual hurdle. He lived on privilege divorced from ability and was never able to appreciate the relationship between privilege and public service. He was groomed for

---

[56]As reported on a Channel 4 television programme, *Edward VIII, The Traitor King*, November 16 and 23, 1995.

a job which he failed to do and was besotted by a woman whose vision never rose higher than what she could buy.

By any standard, Edward was a thoroughly bad egg, a traitor to his country and his King. When the German diplomatic documents were published in 1957 with revelations as to his exploits in Spain and Portugal in the summer of 1940, an official Foreign Office statement was issued stating that 'His Royal Highness never wavered in his loyalty to the British cause.' It is one of the saddest features of the British Establishment that bad eggs must always be projected as good eggs when it is felt that the truth would be damaging to the Establishment itself. Why should such organised hypocrisy constitute an integral part of present-day British democracy?

PART FOUR

MAY 1941: THE HESS MISSION

16

Rudolf Hess: The mould is broken

It is one thing to write a book. It is quite another to act out its pages.

ANEURIN BEVAN

In chapter four an account has been given of the early life of Rudolf Hess, his career, his alignment to the Nazi cause and the part he played in bringing the Nazi Party to power in 1933. It was there suggested that the period of his political struggle with the Nazi Party had been the happiest period of Rudolf Hess's young life. In Adolf Hitler, Hess had found the father figure for whom he had been searching. He had also found a man who seemed to have the vision and grasp of practical politics that would bring to reality all the aspirations of this young veteran of the 1914–18 conflict.

The restoration of German self-esteem, the righting of the wrongs of the Versailles *diktat*, the unification of all Germans into the one Reich, the elimination of communist and Jewish influences from German affairs and the replacement of a weak and vacillating bureaucratic democracy by a strong nationalist Government, based upon the old Germanic virtues of obedience and service – these were the issues, real or imagined, that loomed large in the mind of young Hess as they did in millions more young Germans at that time.

No one understood these needs of the German psyche better than Adolf Hitler and he had nailed his political programme to their realisation. His accession to power in 1933, after years of struggle, was the first great step in that direction. When Hitler took up the seals of office on the morning of Monday, 30 January 1933 it was for Rudolf Hess as much as it was for Adolf Hitler, a moment of intense triumph. Hess knew at that moment that he was the man nearest to Hitler, not only in terms of political idealism and concept but also in terms of emotional bond. They had fought side by side for over a decade and they remained as one in mind and intent. Rudolf Hess had indeed been a happy man on that January morning in 1933.

Seven years later, by the summer of 1940 Hitler stood possessed of a long catalogue of diplomatic and military triumphs which had brought in their wake the accomplishment of many of the policy objectives marked out in *Mein Kampf*, by Hess as well as Hitler. But by then, Rudolf Hess had become a very different man. The enthusiasm and idealism of his youth had gone. He was a deeply disillusioned, unhappy and sick man, living very much on his nerves. Still tied by a deep and lasting emotional bond to his Führer, he had become increasingly disturbed as to the manner in which the implementation of the policy objectives had been carried through during the 1930s. He was also deeply apprehensive about what lay ahead and his treading of the path into the future at the side of his mentor.

There were also unresolved and major strategic problems in the summer of 1940 which Hess viewed in more pessimistic terms than did Hitler. Hess's own wife, Ilse, described his physical and mental condition as well as anyone: 'He was moody and never talked about himself or his plans. At home, he was complaining of stomach trouble, liver trouble and gall bladder trouble but the doctors could not find anything wrong. I think it was mainly his nerves.'[1] There was no doubt that Hess's illness was genuine. It would cause absences from his office of up to 14 days at a time.[2] But there was no basis for the symptoms in terms of physical cause or defect. The illness was psychosomatic in origin, caused by nervous stress. It also accounted for Hess's general demeanour, far removed from the heady days of 1933.

There is no evidence to suggest that Hess's nerve trouble was caused by any self-doubt as to his own competence or his ability to hold down his job. Appointed Deputy Führer on April 21, 1933, his responsibility was that of party boss, in which capacity he was to continue shaping the Nazi Party in accordance with Hitler's requirements. He had been well groomed for that responsibility. He had spent an arduous ten years in building up a party organisation and public image that had convinced the electorate as to the rightness of its policies and its promised performance. He set to with enthusiasm to accommodate his Führer's ambition to build the German Reich in accordance with the much-vaunted *Weltanschauung* described in *Mein Kampf*.

As Deputy Führer, Hess's authority in party matters was absolute. After his appointment as Minister of State without portfolio on December 1, 1933, he also became involved in matters of state,

---

[1]PRO FO 371/46780.

[2]Testimony of Alfred Leitgen, Hess's personal adjutant: Alfred Leitgen papers, Institüt für Zeitgeschichte, Munich, ZS262 F18. December 3, 1965.

particularly after Hitler had dispensed with the democratic nicety of the Reichstag and started to rule by decree.[3] Hitler decreed and Hess interpreted and drafted the required legislation. The internal transformation of Germany into a totalitarian one-party state, devoid of all democratic institutions, was rapid. Rudolf Hess was largely responsible. There is no reason to believe that he was anything other than completely happy about the part that he played. The reconstruction was fully in accord with his own as well as his leader's concept of a proud and strong Germany, unencumbered with effete manifestations of liberal thought and variant philosophies.

Some of the measures taken in furtherance of the reconstruction – measures with which Hess was heavily involved[4] – are of course distasteful to the Western democrat. But they were not untypical of the measures taken by other European, one-party totalitarian states claiming similar allegiance to nationalist considerations and the elevation of a particular ideology to the status of a morality transcending all other moralities. Communist Russia, fascist Italy and (later) fascist Spain all trod the same path in the 1930s. There is therefore no reason to believe at least in those early days, that Rudolf Hess had any qualms about treading the same paths at the side of his Führer or that he lacked the administrative and organisational skills to give effect to Hitler's requirements.

Hess's responsibilities in early days were all embracing. Based at the Brown House in Munich and with the industrious Martin Bormann as his deputy, he executed control over no less than 19 different departments of the party organisation.[5] They included those dealing with the press, education, universities and high schools, employment, fiscal and taxation policies, the Todt organisation (responsible for public works including construction of the autobahns), race policies, kinship investigations (the tracing of Jewish blood) and cultural activities.[6] There were no less than four separate departments within the party dealing with foreign affairs. These were in addition to, and often in direct competition with, the Reich Foreign Office which, until the advent of Ribbentrop, was under the control of the old-style professional diplomats.

This multiplicity of similar functions in different departments, apparently in direct competition, was a feature of the Nazi Party

[3]Hess was Hitler's confidential secretary as well as party boss.

[4]In September 1935, Hess signed the infamous Nuremberg Laws 'for the protection of German blood and German honour' under the terms of which Jews were forbidden to marry or to have extra-marital relations with a German or someone of kindred blood.

[5]Douglas-Hamilton, James, *Motive for a Mission*, Mainstream Publishing, Edinburgh (1979), 132.

[6]Padfield, Peter, *Hess: Flight for the Führer*, Weidenfeld and Nicolson (1991), 71–73.

organisation, or otherwise.[7] But ultimately, all the threads of responsibility and authority led back to the one man whom Hitler trusted above all, Rudolf Hess. This was also the case in early days with the various departments handling state and party intelligence. There was a State Intelligence Department which was the Department of Military Intelligence under Admiral Canaris. But alongside this state department there were no less than eight other intelligence agencies operating at both state and party levels, all concerned with different aspects of intelligence-gathering but all responsible ultimately to Hess. Hess was therefore in a unique position to gather intelligence information under conditions of great secrecy.

Two of these intelligence networks call for special mention in the light of the events of May 1941. Hess had the exclusive use of a diplomatic intelligence network operated through Captain Franz Pfeffer von Salomon. Salomon was an original member of the old SA under Roehm but had been deposed at the time of the Roehm putsch in 1934. Hess had employed him thereafter to develop and extend a special secret intelligence operation which had been in existence since the 1914–18 war and had originally been army-based. One of its chief intelligence officers was Colonel (later General) von Reichenau, a regular and later Freikorps officer who had joined the ranks of the Nazi Party. It was he who had provided both the opportunity and means, out of secret army funds, to use the old network. It was he also who had taken British air intelligence into his confidence in 1935, when he had explained the new *blitzkrieg* methods which were to be used in the attack on Russia.

According to Salomon, his intelligence contacts, gathered over many years, extended deep into the respective embassies of Great Britain, France and Russia and provided insights into all matters of economic and political importance.[8] If Saloman's claims were valid then Hess held an exclusive and deeply penetrative source of intelligence which could have led to those personal connections in Great Britain which were perhaps sympathetic to Germany's cause.[9] The second intelligence leak available to Hess and worthy of note in view of the events of May 1941 is the one linking Rosenberg to the British

[7]There was method in the madness. The 'divide and rule' maxim applied and worked to Hitler's personal advantage. The four separate party departments dealing with foreign affairs are of particular interest because it was through one or more of these departments, with their intelligence offshoots, that Hess gathered the information and means of help that prompted his flight to Great Britain in 1941.

[8]Pfeffer to Dr Bennecke, April 21, 1963.

[9]According to Ilse Hess, a copy of Hess's peace plan which he brought to Great Britain on May 10, 1941, was contained in 'the Pfeffer file' which was placed in a Munich bank for safekeeping after his departure. The file has not been located (see chapter 22) but the name of the file suggests that the Pfeffer von Salomon intelligence link may have been used in connection with the Hess mission.

Air Ministry, used during the 1930s to circumvent normal diplomatic channels.[10]

A review of the position in 1940 would have revealed fundamental changes. The changes were not in the organisational structures, which remained largely undisturbed, but in the command structures. Various departments had been floated off under their respective heads who were now accounting, if at all, direct to Hitler. This applied to Himmler (Gestapo), Heydrich (Secret Intelligence Services) and Bormann (generally). Ribbentrop had been appointed Foreign Secretary, with responsibilities outside the party, and Goering had undertaken military duties as Commander-in-Chief of the Luftwaffe. Hess's influence with Hitler could have been downgraded in these circumstances and partially replaced by new allegiances, but there is no evidence that this was the case.

The decentralisation of the party's affairs and the independent floating-off of department heads was an inevitable consequence of the expansion of activities during the 1930s. The Reich of 1940, together with its occupied territories, was a very much bigger and more complex entity than it was in 1933. The departmental heads under Hess in 1933 were men of ambition. It was natural that in an expanding entity they would take their places in the Nazi hierarchy at the same level and not below that of Hess. That was providing they could show that their performance matched their ambition. There was an inevitability about the situation which had little to do with the personalities involved[11] and there is no evidence to indicate that Hess did not accept the process with good grace, although he may have had some qualms as to the character of some of the lieutenants so appointed.

It is true that on the outbreak of war in September 1939 Hitler named Goering rather than Hess as his successor, but that was almost certainly because Hitler felt that Hess's authority with the armed forces (with which he had little contact) was not sufficient to hold the balance between the armed forces and the party.[12] Hitler was by then engaged more with foreign affairs and the preparations for war than with the party matters which had been his whole life up to 1933 and he thus necessarily had more to do with the officers of the armed forces and Ribbentrop and less with Hess. The latter would not be human if he did not witness with some reservations the dynamic rise

---

[10]Rosenberg flew from Berlin to be with Hess on the morning of his departure on May 10, 1941. British air defences took no action as Hess flew into British airspace on that day.

[11]The same circumstances are met in an expanding business. There arises a need to float off separate departments or groups of activities under their own departmental heads.

[12]Henderson, Sir Nevile, *Failure of a Mission*, Hodder and Stoughton (1940), 72.

to power of some of his old departmental heads; but there is no reason to suggest that this evolutionary process was responsible for the extreme nervous tension, stress and inward turmoil which he was showing by the summer of 1940.

The contention that Hess's personal relationship and influence with Hitler in 1940 was anything other than it had always been is equally unproven. The bond between the two was partly emotional: Hess was Hitler's trusted and loyal friend, and that friendship had been forged in the very earliest days of Hitler's struggle for power. One of Hitler's redeeming features was the strong personal loyalty which he retained for at least some of those who had helped him in early days and in particular circumstances.[13] It is unlikely that the Hitler/Hess bond would have been broken by the rise to stardom of people like Ribbentrop and Himmler. Hitler could trust Hess as he could trust no other member of the Nazi hierarchy. That trust was fully reflected in the particular offices which Hess held at the outbreak of war as Hitler's deputy. These were a measure of Hitler's personal confidence and trust in him. When Hess's son was born on November 18, 1937, Hitler was pleased to accept the invitation to act as the boy's sponsor, together with another of Hess's old friends, Karl Haushofer. In Christian terms, they would be described as the boy's godparents. The boy was named Wolf, which was the name Hess used to call Hitler in early days.[14] It is difficult to interpret this event other than as an expression of continuing mutual regard and affection between the two men.

Finally, it may be noted that only a matter of days before Hess's flight to Great Britain, Hitler and Hess emerged from a room in the Chancellery in Berlin (where they had almost certainly been discussing the proposed flight). Hitler's arm was around Hess's shoulder and they were talking in an animated and friendly fashion. If the relationship had withered and Hess's influence with Hitler gone there is no evidence to support any contention of an estrangement, and it is unrealistic to advance such a contention as the cause of Hess's discomfiture in 1940.

One must look much deeper to identify the cancer of concern. One does not have to look far. Hess was no fool and unlike some of his colleagues, he was not obsessed or blinded by the pursuit of power for its own sake. He had a well-developed intellect and was well able to stand apart from the crowd and take a rational view reaching beyond the

---

[13]The best example was his conspicuous and unrelenting loyalty to the Italian dictator, Mussolini. He had held back Italian troops along the Austrian border at the time of the Anschluss. Mussolini became an intolerable burden to Hitler during the war years but Hitler remained loyal throughout.
[14]PRO FO371/26566.

horizons prescribed by personal ambition. He could foresee the results of the continued and increasing use of Hitler's proven powers when his policy objectives came to be realised. These results had been demonstrated with frightening impact during the 1930s, both within and outside the Reich frontiers, and Hess did not like what he saw. In fact, he was terrified by what he saw. Worse still, he knew that Hitler could see the same picture and was content.

Here was Hess's dilemma. As Hitler's literal interpretation of his policy objectives unfolded during the 1930s, and as the vision of the future became clearer and clearer, Hess had become deeply disenchanted and disturbed. How could he continue to serve his beloved Führer with all the loyalty and devotion that the relationship demanded? He was tied to Hitler by emotional bonds that were deemed unbreakable and he must have tried a thousand times to convince himself that his fears were groundless. But the fears were founded on Hess's own character and fed by his personal experiences. They would not go away. Rudolf Hess's world was falling apart.

What then were Hess's fears during that crisis summer of 1940? The first item that must have caused him considerable disquiet, as it did to Hitler, was a strategic matter. Hess saw the consequences in an entirely different light to Hitler. There is little doubt that both Hitler and Hess were completely baffled by the continued resistance of Great Britain. If it had been said once it had been said a thousand times that Germany wanted nothing from Great Britain other than a free hand in Europe. Hess believed passionately that Germany and Great Britain should be friends, not enemies, and that Great Britain should regard a strong, German dominated Europe as the shield against the encroachment of Russian communism into Europe and ultimately, into Great Britain. He had expressed the view over and over again through the years. He just could not understand why the British were not convinced of what he considered to be self-evident.

In the early days of 1933 Hess had addressed Geoffrey Shakespeare, a British MP and a friend with whom he had spent holidays in the Bavarian Alps, thus 'There was no reason why Germany could not exercise supreme powers in Europe without lessening the powers of the British Empire in the world.'[15] Four years later, in 1937, he repeated the same thoughts when entertaining the Duke and Duchess of Windsor during their visit to Germany. According to Ernst Bohle, who acted as interpreter during a luncheon engagement: 'We all talked about Germany and England. During the whole talk there was nothing

[15]Irving, David, *Hess. The Missing Years 1941–1945*, Grafton Books, Collins (1989), 44.

but an understanding between Germany and England and not in the diplomatic or political way but rather coming from the depth of his (Hess's) heart. That was his opinion. There was no doubt of that.'[16]

In April 1941, only a few weeks before his flight to Great Britain, Hess was taking tea with a friend, Schwerin von Krosigk, and told him of his 'despair' that two Germanic nations should be tearing each other apart. 'There had to be the possibility of bringing the madness to an end. The British had shown no interest in the Führer's peace proposals unfortunately, yet if one could speak to influential Englishmen oneself, show them the danger threatening Western culture and could make them believe that Germany, and above all Adolf Hitler, wished nothing from England, then an agreement would be possible.'[17] He dismissed his friend's well-founded objection that British statesmen would find it difficult to negotiate with Hitler after all his broken promises. 'The point was to bring Hitler's entire conception and the dangers of Bolshevism to the attention of the British.'[18]

It is possible that Hess's respect for the British and his admiration for her Empire went back to his own childhood spent in Alexandria, Egypt, which was a British protectorate at the time. Certainly, that regard was expressed in the (intercepted) mail to his family in Alexandria sent while he was in Germany.[19] But irrespective of any emotional tie, there was of course a strong political motive for the required friendship of Great Britain. It was important that when Operation Barbarossa was launched it would be launched with a friendly rather than a hostile Great Britain to the rear. A war on two fronts was a frightening prospect and Hess 'had argued that the Führer would court military disaster by launching Barbarossa before coming to terms with England.'[20]

On this important strategic point Hess was in fundamental disagreement with Hitler, who believed that the destruction of Russia would in itself bring Great Britain to the negotiating table.[21] Hess was bitterly anti-communist. 'To be sure, Hess was stamped with an almost pathological aversion to the Asiatic Bolshevik *Weltanschauung*.'[22] He considered Ribbentrop's German/Soviet pact of August 1939 'a

---

[16]Postwar interrogation of Ernst Bohle, September 26, 1945. Imperial War Museum papers.
[17]This is the clearest statement of Hess's views and intent, made only weeks before his flight. That it was sincerely given there is no doubt. As to its truth, that is another matter.
[18]Padfield, Peter, *Hess: Flight for the Future*, Weidenfeld and Nicolson (1991), 172.
[19]Irving, David, *Hess. The Missing Years 1941–1945*, Grafton Books, Collins (1989), 49.
[20]PRO WO 208/4170.
[21]Hess was right. Hitler was wrong. Operation Barbarossa with a hostile Great Britain to the rear ended in disaster.
[22]Testimony of Alfred Leitgen, April 1, 1952.

betrayal of Nazi principles.'[23] It is clear that this strategic loose end filled Hess's mind with much misgiving. But by the summer of 1940 he had already made up his mind what he personally was going to do about that particular problem.

There was another strategic shortfall in the summer of 1940. It had even more serious ramifications for the future, and Hess knew that. The so-called Jewish problem, so central to Nazi philosophy, was still largely unresolved. As new territories had been acquired, so as to bring all Germans into the one Reich (Austria and Sudetenland), jumping-off grounds acquired for Operation Barbarossa (Czechoslovakia and Poland) and further lands acquired as a result of victory in the West (Norway, the Low Countries and France), so also had been acquired new and extensive colonies of Jews. How were these people to be accommodated within the boundaries of the Greater Reich and the occupied territories, and upon what terms?

Hess was a racist, like his Führer, and he believed that Germany's ills, and indeed those of the world in general, were due to Jewish influences. He was a willing signatory to the infamous Nuremberg Laws which had marked an important step towards the exclusion of Jewish blood and Jewish influence from German society[24] and to encourage their emigration. But that is a far cry from the ultimate 'Final Solution' which began to take effect after the commencement of Barbarossa in June 1941. By that time responsibility for dealing with the Jewish problem had been passed from the German Foreign Office to Heydrich's SS.

The full development of Nazi policies to deal with the Jews, which is crucial to an understanding of Hess's mind when he flew to Great Britain in May 1941, is traced in chapter twenty-one. Hess himself always maintained his complete innocence in the matter of the reported extermination of six million Jews arising as a result of the Final Solution. This was confirmed by the postwar Nuremberg military tribunal, which found Hess not guilty of any crimes against humanity. In a 1974 biography of Hess written by Wolf Schwarzwaller, a respected author from Vienna, Hess is quoted as saying: 'I never wanted an extermination of the Jews nor have I ever planned one. I am completely convinced that the Führer never intended any such thing either and he cannot have ordered it.'[25]

---

[23]PRO WO 208/4170.

[24]In the interests of semantics it could be argued that the Nuremberg Laws protected the purity of Jewish blood by denying the opportunity of admixture by German blood.

[25]There is no evidence that Hitler ever directly 'ordered' the extermination of the Jews. He let his underlings (Himmler, Heydrich, Eichmann, etc) know that he wanted to be rid of the Jews and they did the rest. Hitler knew what was going on but did not stop it. He perhaps did not 'order' it but was content to see it happen.

What Hess had in mind to accommodate the Jews was something like the South African policy of Apartheid in geographical terms: that is to say, a closed, ethnically delineated settlement of the Jews on German territory, the sort of settlement for which the Eastern Territories in conquered Poland was being considered in 1940.[26] When in Spandau prison, following the Nuremberg trials, Hess spoke to a French pastor, Charles Gabel, with whom he had established a friendly relationship. He described to Gabel how moved he was by the plight of the Jews. At the same time he made it clear to Gabel that he held no personal responsibility for their plight.[27]

In November 1938, Hess's office had issued emphatic instructions forbidding anti-Jewish outrages.[28] According to the diary of Ulrich von Hassell, one of the leaders of the German resistance to Hitler, Hess was 'in despair' over the later nationwide pogrom known as the *Kristallnacht* occurring on the night of November 9/10 when mobs were invited to rampage Jewish shops, businesses and homes. According to Hassell, Hess had been depressed 'as never before' and had left his friends in no doubt that 'he thoroughly disapproved' what had happened. He had besought Hitler to refrain but without success. Goebbels, he said, had been the instigator of the action.[29]

At the Nuremberg trials, Hess sought to introduce Ingeborg Sperr, one of his secretaries, to give evidence 'that he most strongly condemned the actions' following on the events of *Kristallnacht* as part of his defence against the charge of persecuting the Jews.[30] Hess certainly appeared to have little personal animosity towards individual Jews. The wife of his early mentor, Karl Haushofer, was half-Jewish. Her father was George Mayer, a Jewish merchant from Mannheim.[31] This did not prevent Hess eating at her table when he was a young student. In fact, Hess protected both her sons who, strictly speaking, came within the terms of the Nuremberg Laws. He also protected Alfred Pringsheim, a friend of Karl Haushofer and of Jewish descent, until he emigrated in September 1939.[32]

According to the tenets of the Nazi faith, Hess was anti-communist and anti-Jewish. There is not much doubt from the evidence which was the more abiding passion.[33] He had watched with alarm the

---

[26]As formulated (and subsequently abandoned) in the Lublin Plan.
[27]Gabel, Charles, *Conversations interdites avec Rudolf Hess*, pp59–60 and pp254–55.
[28]As testified at Nuremberg.
[29]Ulrich von Hassell, *Vom Anderen Deutschland*, 43.
[30]PRO FO 1019/32.
[31]Douglas-Hamilton, James, *Motive for a Mission*, Mainstream Publishing, Edinburgh (1979), 22.
[32]Hess, Wolf Rüdiger, *Who Murdered my Father, Rudolf Hess*, Reporter Press, USA (1989), 159.
[33]Unlike his Führer, who held both in equal contempt.

Kristallnacht excesses against the Jews, he was well aware of the developments and trend of official policy to deal with the Jewish problem,[34] and he had already witnessed the frightening literalism with which Hitler and some of his lieutenants had implemented some of the other Nazi policy objectives. If that same literalism was applied to 'solving' the Jewish problem, what was the solution likely to be? If Rudolf Hess was astute enough to ask the question, which he was, then he was astute enough to supply the answer, which he almost certainly did. Here was an issue of potentially terrifying consequence which must have exercised Hess's mind in midsummer 1940. He had witnessed Hitler's literalism at first hand. He knew it existed and he knew the philosophy behind it. The morality of superman was intrinsic in the action taken. No other morality existed.

The events of the *Kristallnacht* were a good example. On November 7 a young German Jew had shot and killed the Third Secretary of the German Embassy in Paris. Goebbels ordered and Heydrich organised and carried out a 'spontaneous' demonstration against Jews throughout Germany. It was a night of horror. Synagogues and Jewish homes, shops and factories went up in flames and Jewish men, women and children were shot or otherwise killed trying to escape from their burning homes. No one was charged with murder.[35] No insurance monies were receivable by the Jews for the damage caused to their property. On the contrary, the Jews were fined collectively a sum of one billion marks as punishment 'for their abominable crimes.'[36] Here was Hitler's racism running rampant.

The events of *Kristallnacht* and their aftermath were an outrage to all conventional morality, but superman was not subject to such restraints. The end justified the means. The effect upon Hess has been noted. It was not the first time that Hess had been introduced to the sheer brutality of Hitler's literalism. In early 1934, just one year into power, Hitler had been obliged to choose between his own party's Brownshirt SA troops, organised under one of his closest colleagues and friends, Ernst Roehm, and the Reichswehr regular troops. Roehm, believing himself to be in a strong position and becoming increasingly independent, was advocating a second revolution to submerge the middle classes and have his own troops take over from the regular army. Hitler made his choice. Rather than destroy the forces of the German

---

[34]See chapter 21.
[35]Although, by a strange twist of Nazi law, those guilty of rape were so charged. The Nuremberg Laws had been infringed.
[36]As decreed by a meeting of German Cabinet Ministers presided over by Goering on November 12, 1938 (Shirer, William L., *The Rise and Fall of the Third Reich*, Pan Books (1964), 527).

Establishment he wished to harness them. Roehm was becoming too dangerous and would have to go. And so he went, on the night of June 30, 1934, which later became known as the Night of the Long Knives.

Roehm was murdered in cold blood, with hundreds of his supporters. But that was not all. The opportunity was taken to rid the Nazi regime of other political undesirables at the same time. Erzberger, the Catholic leader and signatory to the Versailles Treaty, Walter Rathenau, unionist and saviour of Germany in 1917, and Gregor Strasser, an early colleague of Hitler were among those who perished in the Roehm purges for no other reason than that their political views were at variance with the prescribed Nazi model. Roehm had been a personal friend of Hitler and one of the chosen few in early days. But he had strayed from the prescribed path and therefore had to be eliminated. As one commentator put it, 'If this is what they could do with their comrades, think that they would do with their enemies.[37]

The Roehm purge was carried out on a nationwide basis by the SS under Heydrich and controlled by Goering and Himmler, who had planned the operation with General Reichenau. Hess sat with Hitler in the Brown House at Munich arguing about the names on the death list. According to Hess's adjutant, Alfred Leitgen, there was 'protracted and heated' argument. 'Hess fought passionately with Hitler over individual names, not allowing himself to be intimidated even by Hitler's strongest outbursts. There were many, it will never be known how many, he saved.'[38]

Hess was much affected by the Roehm experience. In 1952 his former adjutant stated: 'This example of Hitler's personal brutality on June 30, 1934, was one of the hardest blows Hess suffered which deeply wounded his marked, almost feminine sensitivities and aged him by years. Hess had envisaged that the victims of the purge would be consigned to the concentration camps, like the communists and socialists in the past. Their murder was a great shock to him.'[39]

Perhaps the worst example of Hitler's terrifying literalism and its progressive nature lay in the field of racial purity, the very cornerstone of Nazi philosophy. If those who were degenerate or had physical or mental disabilities were prevented from procreating issue, then in due course the degeneracy would disappear. Compulsory sterilisation was therefore introduced as a formal Nazi programme in the interests of racial purity. Those affected were those who were deemed 'hereditarily ill.' That included the congenitally feeble-minded, schizophrenics,

---

[37]Rouse, A.L., *All Souls and Appeasement*, Macmillan (1961), 30.
[38]Testimony of Alfred Leitgen at Nuremberg, April 1, 1952.
[39]Ditto.

manic depressives, the insane, epileptics, the hereditary blind or deaf, those suffering from grave physical deformities, homosexuals and hereditary alcoholics. Sterilisation of the inadequate was therefore necessary and moral as far as superman was concerned.[40] But sterilisation was a delayed-action remedy. Why wait a generation for sterilisation to take effect? There was no effective answer to this rhetorical question. So, after the Polish campaign plans were drawn up and experiments carried out using carbon monoxide and properly designed gas chambers for the purpose of organising the systematic murder of the unfit.[41] Superman regarded the decision as one determined by efficiency. Conventional morality did not come into the equation.

Hess's reaction to these developments is not recorded. He must have known what was taking place. The impact of contemplated murder of the most vulnerable on a national scale in the interests of racial purity upon his 'marked, almost feminine sensitivities' leaves little to the imagination. And if state-inspired killing was in the frame for degenerates, it required no great intellectual jump to work out what the final solution to the Jewish problem was likely to be, particularly with Operation Barbarossa in prospect.

It was this harsh reality that Hess now had to confront. To assist his Führer in the writing of *Mein Kampf* was one thing. To act out its pages was something quite different. It was this which was producing the inner conflict for which there was no remedy. Hess was by nature an idealist, a philosopher and a dreamer. He had fought with Hitler in early days for certain ideals and had been gloriously happy in fighting to put those ideals before a nation. But he now had to test out their worth in terms of their implementation. In 1934, when addressing a mass rally, Hess had referred to National Socialism as 'nothing but applied biology'. But what is compulsory sterilisation if not applied biology?

In January 1937 in a speech to the officers of the German Wehrmacht in Berlin, Hess referred to those Germans then outside the boundaries of the Reich. 'They are being instructed in National Socialist ideology. They are being re-educated to a proud sense of being German, to cohere amongst themselves, to respect one another so as to make them realise that they stand higher than any other national group.'[42] That

---

[40]These measures had been legitimised by legislation introduced immediately after Hitler's accession to power in 1933. The declared objective was the 'prevention of hereditary diseased offspring'.
[41]Lifton, Robert Jay, *The Nazi Doctors*, 63.
[42]Hess, Rudolf, *Essence and Endeavour of the National Socialist German Workers (Nazi) Party*, January 16, 1937.

was all good sound stuff for the master-race audience but what is to be done with those inferior or impaired members of other national groups in our midst? Do we deny them the rights of intercourse with Germans? Do we compulsorily sterilise them? Do we poison them with carbon monoxide in gas chambers? Hitler was quite able to accommodate the reasoning. Hess could not.

There was yet another factor which exacerbated Hess's discomfiture. However flawed Hitler's actions were in terms of conventional morality, he always condoned or explained his deplorable actions in terms of a principle. Hess had accepted Hitler's principles, even enthused over them, but he could not stomach the action taken in their implementation. There was now a further breed of men, those who had risen to take their places as Hitler's lieutenants. They gloried in the actions taken and sought no principle other than the satisfaction of their own ambitions. These new lieutenants embraced the philosophy but that issue was not the mainspring of their activities. The philosophy became an academic matter. The prospect of power leading by reason of success to megalomania became the reality.[43]

Those who were engaged in the detailed planning and execution of the *Kristallnacht* pogrom, the Night of the Long Knives purge, the enforced sterilisation and the first experimental gas chambers were not Hess or even Hitler but Goebbels, Goering, Himmler, Heydrich and Eichmann. All these sadists were the action men in positions of power and influence in the summer of 1940 and these were the men who were to be Hess's companions as he drove down the road into the future.

It is not difficult to identify the factors which were the cause of Hess's deep disquiet and personal turmoil in the summer of 1940. The continuance of an unwanted and unnecessary war with Great Britain was to Hess a matter of great personal regret as well as contributing an important and worrying strategic loose end. He considered that there was great risk in undertaking Operation Barbarossa with an undefeated enemy in the rear, but he knew that Hitler was intent upon such action. He also knew that the Jewish problem was still outstanding and he feared greatly as to what the final solution to that problem might be. Finally, he had watched a gangster element enter the court of his Führer which embraced not the original purity of the Hitler/Hess philosophy but the brutal excesses apparently demanded by its literal implementation. They were men of unbridled ambition and very little else.

All this was very foreign and deeply disquieting to a basically

---

[43]Winterbotham, F.W., *The Nazi Connection*, Weidenfeld and Nicolson (1978), 61.

decent man. Hess had been propelled into the Nazi cause in the first place by nothing more than a burning patriotism and the hero-worship of a man who appeared to him to be a demi-god and the father figure for which he had always thirsted. Such motives were in no way dishonourable. But underneath his patriotic aspirations there lay a kindly and soft nature which was totally unfitted to embrace the evil and immoral manifestations of a philosophy which, in his own mind, had never really got beyond the academic. It was no wonder that Hess was a deeply unhappy man in that crisis summer of 1940. But he had shown in the past that, when the circumstances warranted it, Rudolf Hess, the dreamer and philosopher, could also be a man of action. During June 1940 he toured the old 1914–18 battlefields in France with Hitler. They talked at length about England. It was then that Hess started thinking about a way to resolve the problems that beset him.

17

Dreamer turned action man – the preliminaries

When two friends fight, the third rejoices. Russia rejoices today.

ADOLF HITLER, June 1940

At 5.45 p.m. on Saturday, May 10, 1941, Rudolf Hess, Deputy Führer of Nazi Germany, took off from Augsburg, some 40 miles north-west of Munich at the controls of a Messerschmitt 110 twin-engined fighter plane. At 11.09 p.m. the plane crashed near the village of Eaglesham in Renfrewshire, some 8 miles south of Glasgow, the pilot having parachuted to safety nearby. When picked up, Hess asked to be taken to the Duke of Hamilton, who lived at Dungavel House, nearby. He later stated that he had come on a peace mission and that it was for that reason that he wanted to see the Duke.

The official version of the Hess flight is that it was the personal act of a deranged individual which lacked all backing from his Government and was prompted by an irrational desire to contact a British Peace Party which did not exist, so as to bring the Anglo-German war to an end.[1] The fact that this lie, as lie it is, has not yet passed into history as a truth is a tribute to those historians, both professional and amateur, who have pointed out in a number of well-researched and erudite publications that the official version just does not measure up to the known facts. In May 1941, the author's father remarked 'There is more in this than meets the eye', a comment which is as relevant today as it was 59 years ago.

The full facts relating to the Hess flight are not known and probably never will be. The embargo on the relevant papers at the Public Record Office and elsewhere is complete and relentless. Hess's incarceration in prison, for the most part in solitary confinement, for over 40 years

[1]It is odd that a person wishing to bring to an end a war which ultimately claimed the lives of 45 million people should be deemed deranged and irrational.

and his eventual death in 1987 effectively removed any possibility of anything emerging, as it were, from the horse's mouth.[2] This lack of information has, of course, stimulated both the curiosity and the imagination of those attempting to put together a credible account of the flight, the reasons for Hess's prolonged incarceration and the manner of his death. For this reason, those facts that are available may be assembled to present more than one version as to the complete story.

It is the author's belief that Hess's flight, far from being a solo exhibition of derangement, bore the *imprimatur* and backing of Adolf Hitler in a last-ditch attempt, before the onset of Operation Barbarossa, to make the British realise that peace really was on offer, on terms which ought to be acceptable. Further, that Hess's mission was supported and part organised by both German and British Intelligence (MI6) and was directed towards a British Peace Party that not only existed but which included elements of British royalty and was backed by industrial, commercial and financial interests with representation up to and including Cabinet level. Like Hitler and Hess, they too wanted the war to end.

Hess also knew that Operation Barbarossa was imminent and that responsibility for seeking a solution to the 'Jewish problem' was about to pass from the German Foreign Office to Heydrich's SS. He knew what the final solution to that problem was likely to be, and he may well have communicated his fears to his British interrogators, to no effect. If all these circumstances had become common knowledge they would have seriously detracted from the official British histories of that time and could have been greatly damaging to Great Britain's international reputation. This would explain why Hess was subjected after his capture to a protracted incarceration extending to 46 years, for the most part in solitary confinement, under the most stringent security precautions and finally met a violent end on August 17, 1987, when his release from prison had become imminent. Let the reader determine the validity of this hypothesis, based upon the background of circumstances already described and those now to unfold.

There is evidence to show that Hess's concept of a flight for peace was conceived as early as June 1940. It was during that month that he toured the old 1914–18 Flanders battlefields with Hitler following the defeat of France. Hitler had then talked at length, as he had written in *Mein Kampf*, about his admiration for the British, the need for their friendship and the value of the British Empire in terms of world equilibrium. The need to come to terms with Great Britain before turning

---

[2]This possibility may have been a factor related to his death.

eastwards was paramount. The postwar interrogation of Ribbentrop confirmed an entry in the diary of Felix Kersten, dated June 24, 1940. Kersten was treating Hess for stomach pains. The entry recorded that Hess had resolved then to embark upon a personal peace mission.[3]

The timing of Hess's decision is also confirmed by an application he made at the Nuremberg Trials. He requested the attendance of one of his secretaries, Hildegard Fath, to give evidence on his behalf that she had known that 'the plan and preparations for the flight to England went back as far as the month of June 1940.' She had been charged with the responsibility of obtaining weather reports of conditions prevailing over the British Isles, the Channel and the North Sea.[4]

Further confirmation comes from Helmet Kaden, the airfield manager at Augsburg, who has stated[5] that in August 1940 Hess had requested for his own personal use a Messerschmitt 109 single-seater fighter. The request had been declined. All the aircraft in question were being transferred to Regensburg, and in any case an Me109 was not an easy machine to handle without appropriate training. In September, Hess had requested a Messerschmitt 110 twin-engined two-seater aircraft for his own private use. He 'liked' aircraft No. 3869 VJ OQ and this aircraft was allocated to him. It was placed under special guard and Hess asked that two extra exterior fuel tanks be fitted. Each of these tanks had a capacity of 900 litres which, together with the normal fuel load of 1,200 litres, would provide for approximately ten hours flying, or a range of something like 4,000 kilometres. This does not indicate that Hess intended to fly to Great Britain but it does indicate, together with his reported statements that he had in mind some sort of personal peace mission to Great Britain, that he had in mind flying somewhere for that purpose.

On August 15, with the Battle of Britain at its height, Hess summoned Albrecht Haushofer to his residence to discuss the possibility of putting out peace feelers to Great Britain.[6] His choice of adviser is unsurprising. Albrecht Haushofer, who became a leading player in the Hess initiative, was the elder son of Karl Haushofer, Hess's mentor and father-figure of early years. Although no longer under the influence of the old man, Hess had remained good friends with him and

---

[3]The decision had probably been made following Hess's discussions with Hitler during and after the campaign in Flanders.

[4]PRO FO 1019/32.

[5]In a lecture to the Rudolf Hess Society in Munich on November 23, 1989.

[6]Most of the facts relating to the events of August/September 1940 are taken from letters between Hess and the Haushofers as reproduced in the official German diplomatic documents for the period (Volume II).

his family. He had known Albrecht since the early 1930s. Like his father, Albrecht was a brilliant academic specialising in political geography and geopolitics. He was an acknowledged expert on foreign affairs. He had travelled extensively and his connections were worldwide. Of all the countries he had visited, Great Britain was his favourite. He had a good number of English friends and acquaintances at all levels of political and diplomatic activity. In particular, he knew those committed to the cause of Anglo-German friendship.

Hess had been seeking Albrecht's advice on foreign affairs generally, and on Great Britain in particular, for a number of years. They were not close friends but there was a particular link which bound them together. Albrecht was part-Jewish and Hess had extended protection to Albrecht and his brother in early days because of Hess's relationship with their father. Albrecht was therefore indebted to Hess. Because of this protection, allied to his ability, Albrecht, part Jew, had made considerable progress in a Nazi environment. He had expressed his appreciation to Hess on more than one occasion. Here then in August 1940 was an opportunity for Albrecht to repay some of the debt.

There was another factor which must have increased Albrecht's sense of obligation to Hess. Albrecht was not a member of the Nazi Party and was very much a free spirit as far as his personal politics were concerned. Hess knew that but still helped him with his career. Like Hitler and Hess, Albrecht had all the post-1918 conventional German views as to the iniquities of Versailles, the need for the Anschluss, opposition to French designs for the fragmentation of Germany and German ambitions as to the domination of central and eastern Europe.[7] Like Hitler and Hess, he was very much opposed to war with Britain. In the knowledge that the USA was likely to stand behind Great Britain in the long term, and in the knowledge of Hitler's ambitions to the East, Albrecht made a prophetic judgement to an academic friend on October 8, 1939: 'There are only two ways for the future of Europe now, the Russian way or the American way.'[8]

Albrecht was not an admirer of Hitler and trod a dangerous path in establishing links with the German Resistance. This latter grouping, although it never aspired during the early years of the war to be much more than a fragmented debating society, nevertheless laid claim to the fundamental truth that appeared to have escaped Hess, that peace with Great Britain was not possible while Adolf Hitler and the Nazi Party

---

[7]Douglas-Hamilton, James, *Motive for a Mission*, Mainstream Publishing, Edinburgh (1979), 33.
[8]*Ibid*, 112.

ruled Germany. Albrecht had said as much to Fritz Hesse in September 1939: 'There will be no deal with Hitler by Great Britain. Germany's chance of an understanding with her opponents would only present themselves after Hitler's downfall.'[9]

No doubt the German Resistance considered Albrecht a good catch, but it was a dangerous game to play by a man under contract and obligation to Hess in a private capacity and to the Nazi Party for his employment. Perhaps Albrecht's vanity sustained him in the belief that by working in all three guises he could help achieve his objective of peace and the bringing down of Hitler. His end was perhaps inevitable. In 1945 he was murdered by the Gestapo.[10] Such was the man whose advice was sought by Hess in the late summer of 1940.

Hess knew that Albrecht was part-Jewish, that he was not a member of the Nazi Party and was less than enamoured with Adolf Hitler and the Nazi Party's activities. But he also knew that Albrecht had British connections, knew the British mind and like Hess, looked for an early peace with Great Britain. These were the important matters as far as Hess was concerned. On August 31, a fortnight after meeting Albrecht to discuss the possibility of peace feelers to Great Britain, Hess met Albrecht's father at Hess's home at Hartschimmelhof in Bavaria. It was intended that the meeting was to be with Albrecht but he was away and the old man took his place. Perhaps Hess was in a hurry. The meeting lasted some nine hours. It included a three-hour walk through the beautiful Grünwalder forest.[11] It may be imagined that Hess would have been in an expansive mood as he explained his plans to bring peace.[12] Nevertheless, it is clear from a letter that Karl wrote to Albrecht on September 3 that Hess had not disclosed just how personal the initiative was likely to be.

On September 8, Hess met Albrecht at Bad Godesberg. The meeting lasted two hours. According to Albrecht, Hess almost pleaded with him: 'I was asked about the possibility of making known to persons of importance in England, Hitler's serious desire for peace. It was quite clear that the continuation of the war was suicidal for the white race. Even with complete success in Europe, Germany was not in a position to take over the inheritance of the British Empire and did not want it even today. Was there not someone in England who was ready for peace?' Albrecht's reply was adamant and unequivocal. 'Practically

---

[9]*Ibid*, 121.
[10]His father committed suicide the next year.
[11]Irving, David, *Hess. The Missing Years 1941–1945*, Grafton Books, (1989), 84. It was 2 a.m. before the two men parted.
[12]It appears that Hess took on a new lease of health during the latter part of 1940 and the early part of 1941, as his plans matured towards the actual flight.

all Englishmen who mattered regarded a treaty signed by Hitler as a worthless scrap of paper.'[13]

It was an accurate assessment and Albrecht gave Hess examples of how Hitler had broken his word, including the ten-year treaty with Poland, the non-aggression pact with Denmark and the guarantee of the Czech border after Munich. Albrecht went further: 'For the British of all classes Hitlerism was the reincarnation of all that they hated, all that they had defended themselves against for centuries. In the worst case, the English would rather give away their Empire piece by piece to the Americans than subscribe to a peace which handed mastery in Europe to National Socialist Germany.'[14]

Albrecht could not have put the issue more clearly. And the advice was totally ignored. Apart from enquiring why the British would rather do a deal with the Americans than the Germans, Hess pressed on with his next item of enquiry, the names of some of the important people in England who would listen. This rejection of good advice is extraordinary. It suggests that Hess had already made up his mind as to what he was going to do before he talked to Albrecht and was not going to be deterred. Had he already been in touch with a channel of communication which was already giving him the green light?

Pressed on the point as to who might listen to Hess's proposals for peace, Albrecht suggested that 'the British who have property that they stand to lose. The more calculating elements of the plutocracy are those likely to be ready to talk about peace.'[15] He explained the use of the word 'plutocracy' as meaning the land-owning aristocracy. Again, his advice was impeccable. Albrecht then mentioned specific names. They included Sir Owen O'Malley, the British Minister to Hungary, Sam Hoare in Madrid (described as 'half sidelined, half lying in wait') and most especially, Lord Lothian in Washington. Albrecht made it clear that Lothian was his first choice. He then added, 'As the final possibility, I then mentioned that of a personal meeting on neutral soil with the closest of my English friends, the young Duke of Hamilton, who had access at all times to all important persons in London, even to Winston Churchill and the King.'

Albrecht mentioned the obvious difficulties of making contact with Hamilton, who was a serving officer with the RAF. There is no note of any reaction by Hess to the Hamilton suggestion. The conversation was then closed by Hess, who said that 'he would consider the whole

---

[13]Thompson, Laurence, *1940: Year of Legend, Year of History*, Collins Fontana (1968), 210.
[14]Foreign Colonial Office library, C109 002190.
[15]Irving, David, *Hess. The Missing Years 1941–1945*, Grafton Books, (1989), 88.

matter thoroughly once more.' Two days later, on September 10, Hess wrote to Karl Haushofer. He had decided to go ahead in spite of everything Albrecht had said. Hamilton was to be his contact. The earmarking of the Messerschmitt 110 aircraft for his personal use indicates how the contact was to be made, although not where.

Hess's letter to Karl Haushofer also contained some rather complicated instructions as to how the initial contact with Hamilton was to be made. It was to be done by letter and for that purpose an accommodation address was to be used in Portugal. The address was Post Box 506, Lisbon, Portugal, and the addressee to be used was a Mrs Mary Violet Roberts. Mrs Roberts was an old family friend of the Haushofers. In Karl's letter to his son of September 3 he had mentioned 'as a sign of fate' that he had recently received a card from Mrs Roberts giving the Lisbon address for a reply. The address and addressee could therefore be used for the Hamilton letter.

Two decisions made by Hess in connection with these arrangements are difficult to understand – the selection of Hamilton as his contact and the use of the Lisbon accommodation address. Albrecht had recommended Lothian as a first-choice contact. Hess had chosen Hamilton. Lothian was a known appeaser, with an existing track record of attempted peace moves through his own volition. Both the German *chargé d'affaires* in Washington, Hans Thomsen, and Minister of State Weizsacker at the German Foreign Office knew that. Lothian was a Halifax man through and through. Hamilton was a serving RAF officer, with no such recorded history. Why then did Hess choose Hamilton? As for the advent of Mrs Violet Roberts and the 'sign of fate', how and why did these fortuitous events coincide precisely with the needs of the hour? Was there the possibility of a contrivance and, if so, who was contriving what and why? Hess had a number of his own foreign and intelligence contacts in Portugal. Why then entrust such a vital matter to a complete stranger?

Consider first of all, Hess's choice of Hamilton as his contact against the advice of Albrecht. Douglas Douglas-Hamilton, aged 37 in September 1940, was a true, blue-blooded member of the Scottish aristocracy. Previously the Marquis of Clydesdale, he had succeeded to the dukedom of Hamilton and Brandon on the death of his father earlier that year. As the 14th Duke of Hamilton he was the premier Scottish duke, Keeper of the Royal Palace of Holyrood House and Lord Steward of His Majesty's Household, in which capacity he was the King's representative in Scotland. That office gave him the right of personal attendance upon the King, if need be over the head of the

Prime Minister and the Government of the day.[16,17] Educated at Eton and Balliol College, Oxford, Douglas-Hamilton acquired early skills and form as an amateur boxer. He was also a daring and skilful aviator. In 1933 he had won international fame as the first aviator to fly over Everest. He had been a flying instructor for the RAF and in September 1940 he was a serving officer as CO of No 602 City of Glasgow Fighter Squadron. He also commanded a Wing and was charged with the responsibility of defending Scotland and Northern England from air attack.

Hamilton was also an MP, the Conservative member for the constituency of Renfrewshire, East, and had been the second youngest member in the Commons before succeeding to the dukedom. His politics had always been well right of centre. In the early days of the war he had subscribed to Chamberlain's view that there were 'good' Germans and 'bad' Germans, and that if the two could be separated peace would be possible with a 'good' German Government. He wrote a letter to the *Times* on October 6, 1939, expressing these views. While condemning Hitler and all his works, he also referred to 'a healing peace negotiated between honourable men.'[18] Hamilton's letter clearly indicated his respect and regard for Germany and things Germanic.

This apparent Germany kinship and an examination of Hamilton's pre-war record tend to distract somewhat from first impressions of him as a simple, no-nonsense, uncomplicated young Scottish peer, putting his aviation skills to good use for his country as an operational commander in the RAF. Before the war, as Marquis of Clydesdale, he had been a prominent member of the Anglo-German Fellowship, an organisation devoted to the cause of Anglo-German friendship but also noted for its anti-communist and anti-Semitic stance. In 1936, he was among a small band of British right-wing MPs invited to the Olympic Games as guests of the German Government. Hess said that he had met Hamilton on that occasion. Hamilton denied that, but all the evidence suggests that such a meeting did take place. A diary note by 'Chips' Channon confirms a luncheon appointment.[19] On May 14, 1941, a German official radio announcement confirmed it.[20] On August 23, 1943, the British Minister of Information, Brendan

[16]The previous incumbent, Lord Buccleuch, had been removed from the post because of his pacifist activities. He was under house arrest at his castle in Scotland.
[17]It will be seen that Hamilton exercised this right shortly after Hess's arrival in Scotland.
[18]These views coincided precisely with these of Albrecht Haushofer and the German Resistance.
[19]Rhodes James, Robert, *Chips: The Diaries of Sir Henry Channon*, Weidenfeld and Nicolson (1967), 304.
[20]PRO PREM 3 219/4.

Bracken, confirmed it to a New York press conference.[21] One has to remark that it would have been extraordinary if Hamilton had not met Hess. The small band of MPs invited to the Games were wined and dined at every opportunity. They were all hand-picked ardent right-wingers with known German sympathies, and the vigorous wooing of their inclinations constituted an important part of German efforts to promote Anglo-German friendship.

When the Marquis married in 1937 he received a handsome personal wedding gift of silver-gilt porringers from Ribbentrop. According to newspaper reports at the time, Clydesdale's name appeared on the guest list of a banquet held at the Berlin Chancellery hosted by Hitler and the Nazi leadership on the evening of August 12, 1936. As favoured guests the British MPs would certainly have been formally introduced. It is also a reasonable assumption that Clydesdale's introduction to Hess would have gone beyond a few words. Clydesdale was a skilled and enthusiastic aviator. So was Hess: had he not won the prestigious 'Round the Zugspitz' air race in 1934? He was fascinated by flying and everything to do with it. It is known that Clydesdale's *A Pilot's Guide to Everest* was included among Hess's reading material.[22] It is inconceivable that the two fliers did not find time and space to talk about their mutual interest. Nevertheless, for reasons known only to the Duke and those advising him, he denied to his dying day (in 1973) that he had ever met Hess prior to their meeting in 1941.

It has been suggested that before the war, Hamilton had been involved in intelligence work for Stewart Menzies of British Intelligence MI6.[23] 'Certainly, it is known that he was engaged in pre-war undercover operations. On January 16, 1983, Hess's wife, Ilse, sent a letter to Alfred Seidl, Hess's lawyer, stating that immediately before the outbreak of war in September 1939, Hamilton had arrived by private plane at Brunswick to attend upon Alfred Rosenberg, to see if there was any possibility of averting war.[24] For whom and on whose authority was such a flight made? Also, according to his son, Hamilton had spent a lot of time in the Tyrolean Alps in the 1930s. The suggestion has been made that he was working for British Intelligence MI6, in the attempted fermentation of trouble to encourage German/Italian friction over the proposed Anschluss. If the verdict that 'There is more in this than meets the eye' can be applied to the whole

---

[21]PRO INF 1/912.
[22]It was being read by Ilse Hess on the day that her husband flew to Great Britain.
[23]Padfield, Peter, *Hess: Flight for the Führer*, Weidenfeld and Nicolson (1991), 138.
[24]Hess, Wolf Rüdiger, *My Father, Rudolf Hess*, Lengen Müller Verlag GmbH (1984), 146.

Hess episode, it may also be fairly ascribed to Hamilton and the part he played in it.

Hamilton's personal relationship with Albrecht Haushofer further complicates the issue. Apparently, a 'professional friendship' existed between the two men. It is difficult to understand why. Hamilton was the typical good-looking, clean-cut, modest, outgoing, sporting and action-loving Englishman. Albrecht was a fat, weak, brilliant dreamer-philosopher. They appeared to be opposites in every way. And yet they had been in regular attendance upon each, other either personally at their respective residences or in correspondence, throughout the 1930s. What was the common interest that drew them together? There are two possibilities. In accordance with the modern vogue there has to be considered the possibility of a homosexual relationship between the two men. Both were unmarried when the relationship commenced at the time of the Berlin Olympic Games in 1936. The Gestapo investigated Albrecht for alleged homosexual activities in 1941,[25] but then that was a favoured subject for Gestapo investigation to supply grounds to put away an undesirable of whatever sexual orientation. After the war Beaverbrook alleged that Hamilton and Albrecht had both been members of a homosexual network patronised by the British ruling classes[26] but he brought no evidence to support his allegation.

Hamilton's family has never released the pre-war Hamilton/Albrecht correspondence, which may or may not be significant. But none of these circumstances constitute any real evidence to suggest that the Hamilton/Albrecht relationship was homosexual in nature. A much more likely bond between the two men was the strong mutual wish for an Anglo-German rapprochement and the exploring of the ways and means to bring that about. They certainly had the necessary connections. Albrecht had the ear of Hess and in early days, that of Ribbentrop. He was on first-name terms with most of the Nazi hierarchy, was in touch with the German Resistance, had plenty of international political and diplomatic connections at senior level and had his own means of intelligence. Most importantly, he had English friends as committed as he was to the cause of Anglo-German friendship.

As to Hamilton, he had been an active MP in the Commons and by 1940, a respected member of the House of Lords. That brought him into contact with those elements of the British Establishment that wanted peace. If those factions included royalty then Hamilton could

---

[25]As reported by Heinz Haushofer (Albrecht's brother) to the historian, David Irving. Irving, David, *Hess. The Missing Years 1941–1945*, Grafton Books, (1989), 122.
[26]Costello, John, *Ten Days that saved the West*, Bantam Press (1991), 409.

count on direct access to the King himself if necessary. Winston Churchill may have dispelled the Chamberlainite views as to 'good' Germans and 'bad' Germans from official thinking, but that did not necessarily include Hamilton who had strongly aligned himself to the Chamberlain view. Hamilton also had connections with British Intelligence MI6. Both he and Albrecht had been enthusiastic members of the Anglo-German Fellowship, an organisation infested with intelligence agents for obvious reasons which provided plenty of interplay and freedom for those interested in rapprochement between the two countries.

Two other factors would have appealed to Hess in selecting Hamilton as his contact. In the first place, unlike Lothian and other overseas diplomats, Hamilton could be contacted and confronted on a one-to-one, face-to-face basis, without the need for middlemen, nominees and all the other diplomatic protocol which had bedevilled other attempts to talk peace. Secondly, Hess had said that he wanted to talk to important people in Great Britain who would be prepared to listen. Well, Hamilton was important and his background and history indicated that he was likely to listen. Moreover, Albrecht had described Hamilton as a man 'who had access at all times to important persons in London, even to Winston Churchill and the King.'

It is apparent from Hess's subsequent and persistent references to the King that this was a matter of importance to him, and that he believed the British royal family would be a fertile field to explore in the cause of Anglo-German rapprochement. He was of course aware of the political proclivities of the Duke of Windsor and his then current behaviour in Spain and Portugal. He was also probably aware of the deep friendship that existed between the pacifist Lord Halifax and his wife with King George VI and Queen Elizabeth and how much they would have preferred to see Halifax rather than Churchill succeed Chamberlain in the previous May. Hess would also have known that the royal family had inherited from King George V and Queen Mary (formerly Princess Mary of Teck) a rigid anti-Russian stance, following the murder of their cousins by the Bolsheviks in 1917, and that they were natural sympathisers towards Germany by reason of their blood and other ties of friendship.[27]

Hess's good friend, Alfred Rosenberg, also had a good reason to

---

[27]King George V and Queen Mary were personal friends of Baron Konstantin von Neurath, one-time German Foreign Minister, and Queen Mary was a childhood friend of Baroness von Neurath. Neurath was sentenced to a 15-year prison sentence at Nuremberg but served only nine years. His early release was apparently due to his frail health, but there is some evidence from the PRO papers that royal pressure was brought to bear to secure his release.

believe that such ties existed. He would have confided to Hess the details of the strange story relating to the German sympathies of King George V, the then sovereign's father. In 1934, George V had apparently used an unofficial channel of communication through British Air Intelligence and double-agent Baron William (Bill) de Ropp to Rosenberg to ascertain the true position about the Saarland plebiscite and about National Socialism 'down to the last detail.'[28] Rosenberg would also have confided to Hess the part played in that subterfuge by the present King's younger brother, the Duke of Kent. For all these reasons, Hess apparently fixed upon King George VI as one of his principal targets. Hamilton's personal connection with the King was therefore important to him.

According to the Sunday *Empire News* of October 13, 1953, Hess said in conversation with a Spandau prison officer that 'I knew that I must fly to the Duke of Hamilton who could take me to see King George with an offer of peace from Germany. I felt sure that the King would get rid of the warmongers in the British Government and replace them with a Party for Peace.' It is clear from these reported remarks that Hess did not understand the constitutional elements of British democracy. Whereas the Sovereign was party to all state papers and had the benefit of weekly consultations with the Prime Minister and others, he held no executive powers or responsibilities in Government. He certainly could not of his volition 'get rid of the warmongers'.

Whatever the personal sentiments of King George VI and Queen Elizabeth in 1940 as to the continuance of the war with Winston Churchill at the helm, they were unlikely to be converted into overt action by exercise of any constitutional powers. Their acquiescence in acting as figureheads to a different Government, with different views to those of Churchill and his colleagues, was of course, a different matter. This fundamental misconception of the nature of the British monarchy in the 20th century does not appear to have been appreciated by Hess when making his plans. Thus, Hamilton's connection with the King appears to have been a considerable plus factor in Hess's choice.

---

[28]This strange episode is recounted in full in the Rosenberg report to Hitler in October 1935, as shown in Appendix II. The odd thing is that Frederick Winterbotham of British Air Intelligence and the author of *Secret and Personal*, published in 1969, provides the reader with a full statement of the Rosenberg report. But in his later book, *The Nazi Connection*, published in 1978 and covering much the same ground, he refers to the matter only in passing and identifies the King in question as King Edward VIII (later the Duke of Windsor). That could not, of course, have been the case because the Rosenberg report is dated October 1935 and refers to the King's request 'at the end of last year'. King Edward VIII did not succeed to the throne until January 20, 1936. It would appear that some necessary but injudicious editing had taken place between the two publications.

If there was more than met the eye about Hess's selection of Hamilton as his contact then there was even more than met the eye about his choice as to the suggested manner of contact through Mrs Violet Roberts. As finally decided, Albrecht was to draft a seemingly innocuous letter to Hamilton.[29] A suggested meeting was to take place in Portugal the purpose of which was to be understood by Hamilton but no one else who might intercept and read the letter. The letter was to be addressed to Mrs Roberts in the first place at her PO Box 506, Lisbon, and she would then clear the letter to London for onward transmission to Hamilton. The first point to note is that the involvement of Mrs Roberts was unnecessary. Hess himself had scores of accommodation addresses he could have used in Portugal, all known personally to him or his overseas organisation. Why then use the services of a complete stranger?

In any case, no accommodation address was necessary. During the war, correspondence was possible between Germany and Great Britain and *vice versa.* The service was provided by and through the international travel agents, Thomas Cook. All mail destined for Great Britain was cleared through a single Thomas Cook accommodation address. It could then go to Cook's London office in Berkeley Street for formal censorship and onward transmission to the addressee. Cook's accommodation address for this purpose was PO Box 506, Lisbon.[30] That address was therefore not particular to Mrs Roberts. Why had she apparently suggested otherwise to the Haushofers? And why did not Hess and the Haushofers with all their intelligence and other connections know about what was in fact, a common procedure for the clearing of mail to Great Britain? And why did they apparently not know that all mail cleared through PO Box 506 would end up on the censor's desk in London and that, however 'innocuous' the letter from Albrecht was to be, it would in fact be seen as a missive of importance?

The questions can be extended to include the mysterious Mrs Violet Roberts. She was to be entrusted with initiating what could possibly lead on to events of truly historic significance. According to the Haushofers, she was an elderly English lady of 76 years, retired and resident in Bath, England. What then was she doing in Portugal in the middle of a war, exchanging pleasantries with enemy nationals? Who in fact was she and how and why did she fit into the overall picture?[31]

---

[29]The text of this letter is reproduced in Appendix VI.
[30]This information is given in *Undercover Addresses of World War II*, published by Chavril Press.
[31]The author is indebted to his fellow accountant, John Harris, for his admirable researches relating to much that follows in connection with the mysterious Mrs Roberts.

It is easy to say who she was not. She was not, as reported by Heinz Haushofer, Albrecht's brother, and repeated in several publications since, the daughter-in-law of the former Viceroy of India, Lord Roberts of Kandahar. She was in fact the daughter of Patrick and Louise Maxwell and she acquired her married name when she married Ainslie Roberts, a distinguished Cambridge mathematician, in 1894. The Haushofers and the Roberts became friends in the 1920s and regularly visited each other. Ainslie Roberts died in 1932. There was one son, Patrick Maxwell Roberts, a diplomat with extensive international experience and a friend of David Kelly and of Victor Mallet, who was killed in a road accident in Greece in 1937. Mrs Roberts had a nephew, Walter Stewart Roberts. He too was a diplomat, serving in the British Foreign Office from 1940 to 1948, when he was awarded the CBE.

Roberts spent the entire war period at Woburn, part of the Bletchley Centre, which was originally a codebreaking centre but early in the war became the head of signals intelligence world-wide and a base for all political intelligence. By 1946 Roberts was its deputy head. If his professional career is interesting in the context of the Hess mission then his school and social contacts are more so. Roberts attended Eton between the years of 1902 and 1908 and was a member of the Eton Society, 'Pop', the prestigious prefectorial body of senior boys. Also at Eton at the same time, and president of 'Pop', was one of his close friends and colleagues, Stewart Graham Menzies (later knighted), who became head of British Intelligence MI6, known as 'C'.

It does not require much imagination to infer from these facts that Karl Haushofer's little old lady friend, who appeared as 'a matter of fate' at just the right moment, was in fact a cover for British Intelligence MI6. The intriguing question is not who she was and what she represented but who knew who she was and what she represented. A clear indication that the Haushofers at least knew of the involvement of British Intelligence in the guise of Mrs Roberts is provided in *The Crown and the Swastika* by Peter Allen, published in 1953. Allen refers to the role of the 'old lady' in the Duke of Windsor affair (see Appendix V), and records that a cable purporting to have been sent by Walter Schellenberg, Ribbentrop's agent, to Albrecht in July 1940 read 'Our friend Tomo met with C and Willi this morning. Urgent you contact the old lady as soon as possible S.' 'Tomo' was the known code for Hess. 'Willi' was the known code word for the Duke of Windsor. 'S' stoods for Schellenberg. The reference to 'C' is uncertain, the only known designation being the Head of British Intelligence MI6.

It is apparent from this cable that Hess was in Spain and Portugal during July 1940, that he had met the Duke of Windsor and that

Albrecht was to keep British Intelligence informed. It is also apparent that Albrecht was the link with British Intelligence and that 'the old lady' was a code name for MI6. Having regard to all these circumstances, it is unlikely that Mary Violet Roberts had ever left her retirement home in Bath, let alone set herself up in Portugal to exchange postcard greetings with enemy nationals.

The 'innocuous' letter which was to initiate the Albrecht/Hamilton meeting is also open to suspicion. Albrecht suggested to Hess on September 19 that such a letter be written and that he should draft it in English.[32] On September 22 Hess instructed him to go ahead. The letter was sent the next day and, for some reason not made clear, backdated to September 3. The letter is reproduced in full in Appendix VI. It is anything but 'innocuous'. If British and German nationals of important status with 'friends in high places' are to meet on neutral ground in the middle of the war it is fairly obvious that matters of importance were on the agenda for discussion. It is impossible to believe that Hess and Albrecht could be so naive as to think such a letter would survive interception and censorship and arrive in the hands of Hamilton with its security intact. So why did Albrecht draft such a 'giveaway' letter, and why did Hess authorise its dispatch? It is almost as though Albrecht had no interest in a venture which he believed to be forlorn in any case and that Hess had no interest either because he had already made his plans outside the scope of Albrecht's letter.

These reported events, which are for the most part extracted from British and German official records, prompt as many questions as answers. It is known that Hess had been planning a peace mission since June 1940 and had reserved the use of an aircraft for his personal use for that purpose. It is also known that at least one of Hess's advisers to the project was Albrecht Haushofer, a man of many parts and many connections. But when Albrecht advises against the project, Hess rejects the advice. When Albrecht is pressed to name a British contact, he suggests Lothian. Hess selects Hamilton. His selection of Hamilton is, on investigation, less surprising than first impressions might indicate. Hamilton's politics were well to the right, he had German sympathies and known connections with British royalty, the British aristocracy and MI6. He had met Hess in 1936 and had maintained a pre-war personal relationship with the anglophile Albrecht of such intimacy that it was unlikely that they had any secrets from one another in the field of Anglo-German rapprochement or the intel-

[32] Irving, David, *Hess. The Missing Years 1941–1945*, Grafton Books, (1989), 91.

ligence and diplomatic connections that went with these activities. These factors made much sense of Hess's selection.

Finally, it is clear that the introduction of Violet Mary Roberts as the initial contact by the Haushofers was nothing more than a cover for British Intelligence MI6 involvement. In dealing with these matters, or rather not dealing with them, the official records are both incomplete and misleading. The available Haushofer/Hess correspondence is detailed, but what cutting and editing have they undergone before insertion (by the Allies) in the official German records? It is known that the Haushofers kept personal diaries but these have never surfaced for public scrutiny. They were removed from the Haushofers' mountain lodge on the Partnach Alm by British Intelligence immediately after the end of the war. They have never been seen since.[33]

[33] *Ibid*, 95.

18

September 1940 to May 1941 – a tortuous eight months and some false starts

Nothing stimulates the imagination more than mystery.

ANON

The same incompleteness of available records applies to the period between the dispatch of Albrecht's letter to Hamilton in September 1940 and the day when Hess took off from Augsburg on May 10, 1941. There is, for example, a three-month gap in the Air Ministry records relating to the personal file of Hamilton. All the documentation relating to Air Ministry instructions to the Duke between February and April 1941 have been removed.[1] The Air Ministry records relating to the Albrecht letter surfacing in the hands of the British authorities are incomplete and confusing. Some of the deficiencies are made good by reference to the Duke's own records but it is apparent that much happened for which no records are available.

The official version of the receipt of Albrecht's letter is told simply, but again makes for more questions than answers. On November 2, 1940, some six weeks after it had been posted, the Albrecht letter landed on the desk of the British Postal Censor, Examiner 1021, Table II of Department PR4 of Terminal Mails (Private Branch) of British Censorship HQ, situated immediately adjacent to British Intelligence MI5 HQ, then at Wormwood Scrubs. The examiner had noted 'writer possibly a German possibly writing from Berlin. Requested addressee to forward to Duke of Hamilton.' No information is available as to the cause of the six weeks' delay in the letter reaching the desk of the censor. This raises the possibility of prior interception and processing by another agency before it reached the official censor. The original letter

---

[1]Irving, David, *Hess. The Missing Years 1941–1945*, Grafton Books, (1989), 95.

was then passed on to Department M112 (counter-espionage) of MI5 and a copy sent to the Foreign Office.[2] The 'innocuous' letter had ended up precisely as anyone could have reasonably predicted, not in the hands of Hamilton but in the hands of the British Censor and MI5.

No information is available as to what decisions or actions were taken within MI5 thereafter, and it was not until four months later, on February 26, 1941, that Hamilton received a letter from Group Captain F.G. (Freddie) Stammers, OBE, of Air Intelligence MI5. Stammers requested Hamilton to call and see him when next in London. Hamilton did so on March 15, taking ten days leave from March 8.[3]

It is difficult to know what was in the mind of Stammers. There were at least two possibilities. The Albrecht/Hamilton relationship apparent from the letter may have alerted MI5 to the dangers inherent among the 'people in high places' and the possible existence of a British Peace Party among Hamilton's connections. It is reported that the MI5 file on the Duke of Hamilton had become 'inches thick'[4] and may be that since the official receipt of the letter in November 1940, a protective research exercise had been undertaken into these connections. But there was a second possibility. Should Albrecht's invitation be taken up by engaging first in preliminary correspondence to ascertain what the ultimate result might be in terms of British advantage? It might be possible to bait the hook by using Hamilton's name to hijack or snatch a Nazi personage of some importance, lured into a trap by the possibility of meaningful peace talks. This would represent a spectacular replication of the infamous Venlo incident, this time to British advantage.

MI5 operated a special Double X Section under Major 'Tar' Robertson. It specialised in deception plans built around turned agents. Robertson's appearance at a meeting with Hamilton in April lends weight to this option. At the earlier Stammers/Hamilton meeting, on March 15, Stammers produced a copy of Albrecht's letter and asked Hamilton what he had done with the original. Hamilton replied that he had never received any original. That was certainly correct, because the original had disappeared into the MI5 system, immediately following its receipt on November 2. It is extraordinary, indeed unbelievable, that Stammers, having been supplied with a copy of the letter had not been informed as to the circumstances of its original receipt.[5]

---

[2]*Ibid*, 114.
[3]*Ibid*, 116.
[4]*Ibid*.
[5]Padfield, Peter, *Hess: Flight for the Führer*, Weidenfeld and Nicolson (1991), 158.

A further meeting was held at the Air Ministry on April 25. Hamilton this time saw Group Captain D.L. Blackford, Chief of Air Ministry Security, and Major Tar Robertson. It was on this occasion that Hamilton was formally asked if he would go to Portugal and see Albrecht. According to Hamilton, he was not keen but would go if ordered. He was told that it would be preferred if he volunteered for the job and there the matter was left.[6] Hamilton then took advice and on April 28 wrote to Blackford saying that he was prepared to go ahead, subject to certain conditions. He was to have Foreign Office consent, the British Ambassador in Portugal was to be informed and Albrecht was to be provided with an adequate reason as to why there had been a seven month delay in dealing with the letter.

On May 3 Blackford acknowledged receipt of Hamilton's letter, calling the whole thing off 'having discussed Hamilton's letter with Air Commodore Archibald Boyle, Chief of Air Intelligence.' It is suggested that there was particular significance attaching to this stop order and the official authorising it. 'Archie' Boyle had been an essential link in the pre-war intelligence channel of communication that had led from the British Air Ministry through Boyle and Wing-Commander 'Freddie' Winterbotham to the double agent, Baron 'Bill' de Ropp, and from him to Alfred Rosenberg, personal friend of Rudolf Hess. Boyle may have stopped Tar Robertson's plans for a deception exercise (a copy of Blackford's letter to Hamilton calling the whole thing off was sent to Robertson) because he was aware of other plans about to reach fruition. Hamilton acknowledged Blackford's letter on May 10. That evening Hess landed in Scotland.

Two other points arise from Blackford's letter to Hamilton of May 3 which illustrate the lack of reliable records dealing with these events. Blackford apologises for not being present 'when you came to London', which was not the case unless he was referring to a meeting other than that held on April 25 when Blackford *was* present. If there was such a meeting then there is no record of it. Blackford also suggested in the same letter to Hamilton that the seven months' delay in dealing with Albrecht's letter could be put down to 'another department having mislaid the papers'. Such false representations were hardly likely to convince Hamilton, Albrecht or anyone else as to the true reason for such a delay.

This lack of information relating to the true motive and movement of the Albrecht letter of September 23, is matched by the lack of information relating to the movement and motives of the Duke of Hamilton

---

[6]Irving, David, *Hess. The Missing Years 1941–1945*, Grafton Books, (1989), 117.

during the same period. It has already been noted that Air Ministry instructions to Hamilton during the three months period February to April 1941 are missing from Hamilton's file. Why should such *official* instructions through the Air Ministry still be embargoed, 59 years after the event? It is also extraordinary that Hamilton should take so much leave during the period in question. After all, it was a time of grave national emergency and Hamilton was the operations commander of a Fighter Command Station and charged with the responsibility of the air defence of Scotland. Why then did he take such a lot of leave from his operational duties – unless, of course, he was engaged on equally important duties in a sphere somewhat divorced from those associated with a Fighter Command Station?

On Tuesday, November 12, 1940, six days after Albrecht's letter landed on the desk of the British censor, Hamilton handed over to his second-in-command, Wing Commander Pinkerton, and took ten days' leave. It is not known how or where he spent it.[7] It may be thought that Tuesday was a rather odd day to commence a leave unless there was some sort of urgent necessity so to do. On Sunday, January 26, 1941, Hamilton took a further ten days' leave. Again, it is not known how or where he spent it. It may nevertheless be significant that the period coincided precisely with Albrecht's visit to Sweden, ending on February 5. It also coincided with Jacob Burckhardt's approach to von Hassell in Switzerland on behalf of 'the British circles who still believed in a reasonable peace.'[8] Immediately following February 5, 1941, there are two Foreign Office files closed to public scrutiny[9] and later in the same month, another three files are closed.[10] On March 8, 1941, Hamilton took yet another ten days' leave which straddled the meeting with Stammers on March 15. This was the third of such leaves, totalling a whole month in four months – a quite extraordinary state of affairs in the absence of explanation.

Another extraordinary feature in Hamilton's behaviour occurred immediately prior to the arrival of Hess. During the afternoon of Saturday, May 10, 1941, the very day of the Hess flight, Hamilton piloted a Hurricane fighter aircraft based at his Fighter Command station at Turnhouse and took it to Drew aerodrome, near North Berwick at the entrance to the Firth of Forth. From there he engaged in a mock dogfight over the Firth with his second-in-command. Operations records at Turnhouse make no note of this spectacular and

---

[7]PRO AIR 28/863.
[8]Padfield, Peter, *Hess: Flight for the Führer*, Weidenfeld and Nicolson (1991), 181.
[9]They are PRO FO371/26945/C1052 and C1104/306–41.
[10]They are PRO FO371/26542/C1303 and C1687 and C1954/324/18.

highly unusual activity by its commander but does record that 'A' flight from 602 Squadron was moved to Drew from Turnhouse and 'B' flight from Drew to Turnhouse.[11] Was Hamilton really practising his dog-fighting techniques over the Firth of Forth or was he patrolling the area for a very different purpose? Certainly, his absence from operational duties, the removal of Air Ministry instructions from his personal file and his activities on that afternoon suggest that he was involved in extra-curricula activities during the 1940–1941 period leading up to the Hess flight quite apart from the Stammers/Blackford discussions.

If consideration is also given to the recorded events in Germany leading up to Hess's flight, the result again falls short of a full explanation. The history relating to the maintenance and preparation of Hess's aircraft and his practice and other flights are clear enough if the account given by the airfield manager, Helmut Kaden,[12] is to be believed. As noted previously, Hess's original request had been for an Me109 aircraft but he had been allocated an Me110. The reasons given were that all the Me109s were being transferred to Regensburg, and in any case the Me109 machine was not easy to fly. There may have been another reason for the change. The Me110 was a two-seater, twin-engined machine with a much longer range than the Me109. There may, at some stage, have been a change of venue for any meeting Hess had in mind – perhaps a switch from Switzerland to Scotland.[13] Soon after Hess acquired the Me110 the aircraft's radio was switched from the rear seat to the front clearly indicating that the flight would be solo.

At the beginning of November Hess wrote a brief farewell note to his wife and son referring to a flight he was going to undertake 'in the next few days' which would be 'crowned with success'. Probably, having completed his practice flights which he started in the September, he was ready to embark upon his mission. This again indicates that his arrangements lay outside the Albrecht/Hamilton correspondence, since the Albrecht's letter to Hamilton had not landed on the censor's desk until November. Hess's completion of arrangements for the flight by November also links up with the completion of the translation of a long letter from Hess to Hamilton by Hess's friend, Ernst Bohle. The letter in English was to be taken by Hess on his flight.

The first recorded flight by Hess after writing his farewell note in early November was not until December 21, 1940, when full fuel loads

---

[11]PRO AIR 25/233.

[12]At a meeting of the Rudolf Hess Society held at Munich on November 23, 1989.

[13]As testified by Ernst Bohle at Nuremberg. Hess, Wolf Rüdiger, *My Father, Rudolf Hess*, W.H. Allen (1986), 58.

totalling 3,000 litres were taken on board. Hess had spoken by telephone to the sea weather station at Hamburg. He boarded the aircraft with two document files and took off at 1330 hours. He returned three hours later with a blocked rudder.[14] On January 10, Hess made a further attempt. He had received weather reports for two secret locations, 'X' and 'Y'. On take-off he handed two sealed envelopes to his adjutant, Captain Karl Heinz Pintsch. One was addressed to Pintsch, the other to Hitler. Pintsch was instructed that the letters be actioned if Hess did not return within four hours of take-off. Hess returned very shortly afterwards, no reason being given. In the meantime, Pintsch had opened 'his' envelope and had therefore become aware of Hess's plan.[15] On January 18, Hess made a further attempt. He took off at 1330 hours but returned at about 1700 hours, having failed to pick up the Kalundborg transmitter signal which he needed for navigational purposes. Kalundborg is in Denmark. It was used regularly by German bombers based in northern Germany en route to Great Britain.

During February and March and much of April no flights were possible out of Augsburg because of heavy snow. On April 30 Hess was about to make a further attempt, but at the very last moment before take-off he was obliged to take an urgent telephone call from Hitler. Hitler was due to make his scheduled May Day speech to the workers at the Messerschmitt works but wished Hess to stand in for him.[16] The intervention may have been significant. Hitler knew where Hess was and, presumably, what he was doing, and he may have had second thoughts. It was on that very day that Hitler had instructed his generals that Operation Barbarossa was to be launched on June 22. Hess does not appear to have been put off by Hitler's intervention. After delivering the speech to the workers on May 1, Hess spent time with Willi Messerschmitt agreeing the latest modifications required to the Me110 which was to be ready for May 5.[17] Nine days later Hess flew to Scotland.

The record clearly indicates that Hess had been ready to make his flight to Great Britain as early as November or December 1940, and that he had written a lengthy letter to Hamilton in October. It was translated into English by his aide and confidant, Gauleiter Ernst Bohle, the head of Hess's overseas organisation and a man almost as fanatically pro-British as he was.[18] Bohle was never fully taken into

---

[14]As reported by Helmut Kaden, the airfield manager. Hess himself made no mention of the December flight. Hess, Wolf Rüdiger, *My Father, Rudolf Hess*, W.H. Allen (1986), 59.

[15]Irving, David, *Hess. The Missing Years 1941–1945*, Grafton Books, (1989), 97–98.

[16]Given under oath by Kaden in a report for the Hess family, May 4, 1941.

[17]Padfield, Peter, *Hess: Flight for the Führer*, Weidenfeld and Nicolson (1991), 184–185.

[18]The letter has never surfaced. It is known that it was written and translated. It may have been sent to Hamilton or more probably, brought by Hess on his flight for personal delivery to Hamilton.

Hess's confidence as to Hess's destination, and in early days he believed that his chief would be flying to Switzerland.[19] On October 9 he was summoned to Hess's residence in Berlin for an evening meeting; he was handed a draft letter to Hamilton and asked to translate it into English (he spoke and wrote fluent English). Hess asked him to make an immediate start.[20] Bohle, who believed that Hitler knew of the existence of the letter but that no one else did,[21] attended upon Hess at regular intervals thereafter[22] and continued to work on the translation until January 7, 1941, when his work was completed. Significantly, at the Nuremberg Trials there was no probing as to the content of this letter or as to its whereabouts.[23]

Why did it take Bohle over three months to translate the content of a single letter, albeit one that may have been of considerable length? It may be that there was never just one letter to translate but rather an exchange of letters between Hess and Hamilton, or even of those purporting to be from Hamilton. As well as the all-important letter, other relevant documents and details are missing. The flight details would have had to be discussed and agreed before the flight. The precise route and destination, time of arrival, manner of approach and landing and reception details would all need careful attention and appropriate documentation. None of these items are available.

Although it is apparent that the flight was scheduled to take place as early as January, there were additional factors in May which made the reasons for the flight even more pressing. In particular, Operation Barbarossa was imminent; Great Britain had suffered further military defeats in Greece and Crete, and not least, other peace moves by other people were in the air which could have been ruinous to Hess's personal plans. Nevertheless, nothing gave any impression of panic or emergency to Hess's demeanour during his last few days on German soil. However, he attended two meetings which could have had special significance in terms of the purpose of his flight and the manner in which it had been organised. The first, on Monday, May 5, was with Adolf Hitler. The second, the very morning of his departure, was with Alfred Rosenberg.

On May 4 Hitler had addressed the members of the Reichstag at the

---

[19]Irving, David, *Hess. The Missing Years 1941–1945*, Grafton Books, (1989), 93. This ties in with Hess's original request for a Messerschmitt 109.

[20]Hess, Wolf Rüdiger, *My Father, Rudolf Hess*, W.H. Allen (1986), 58–59.

[21]Postwar interrogation of Ernst Bohle, September 26, 1945.

[22]In November Bohle asked Hess if he could accompany him on the flight and act as interpreter. It is a matter which Hess may well have considered. Irving, David, *Hess. The Missing Years 1941–1945*, Grafton Books, (1989), 94.

[23]This is inexplicable except as a deliberate omission for a good but unstated cause.

Kroll Opera House in Berlin, on the occasion of the recent German occupation of Crete. Hess was in attendance. His arms were folded and he was composed throughout the proceedings. Afterwards, and in reply to his query, Hitler confirmed that the tenets of Nazi faith as set down in *Mein Kampf* still staked out the guidelines of Nazi policies.[24] It can be presumed that Hess had in mind the need for friendship with Great Britain 'at any cost'. On May 5, Hess obtained maps from Hans Bauer, Hitler's personal pilot, indicating those areas of Germany over which flying was prohibited. Later that day, he had a four-hour meeting with Hitler in the Führer's study at the Reich Chancellery. No one else was in attendance and the proceedings were not minuted.

Detective Josef Portner was in an outer office throughout the meeting and he reported to Ilse, Hess's wife. He was unable to pick up the words used but said that the voices 'sometimes rose considerably'. When the door to the inner office finally opened and the two men finally emerged Hitler had 'put an arm around Hess's shoulders' and 'took his leave of Hess almost cheerfully', saying 'Hess, you always were pig-headed'. There is little doubt that the two men had been discussing Hess's contemplated flight. It may be assumed from the manner of their leaving that Hess had obtained his Führer's final, if somewhat reluctant, blessing. Presumably, they would have discussed the courses of action to be adopted in the event of both the success and failure of the venture and the role to be played by each of them in either eventuality.[25] It appears that Hess was confident of success, Hitler less so.

Hitler may have thought that Hess was the only person capable of pulling off such a coup. He was deemed to be the conscience of the party, a decent and honourable man and one with whom the British might well parley. But Hitler would not have wished to be officially connected with the mission until and unless it was successful. The seeking of peace by a victorious Germany would be seen as a weakness.[26] A private affair that could develop into a public matter, if successful, was a different matter.

On May 9 Hess wrote to Walter Darré, the Minister for Agriculture, and told him that he would be unable to keep an appointment for mid-May, saying 'I am going on a long trip and don't know when I shall be back.'[27] More importantly, on that day he attended a meeting of the

[24]Irving, David, *Hess. The Missing Years 1941–1945*, Grafton Books, (1989), 104.
[25]It is probable that Hess's role as a 'deranged' individual in the event of failure was agreed at this meeting.
[26]Padfield, Peter, *Hess: Flight for the Führer*, Weidenfeld and Nicolson (1991), 192.
[27]Hess, Wolf Rüdiger, *My Father, Rudolf Hess*, W.H. Allen (1986), 83.

Nazi hierarchy in Berlin. In attendance were Hitler, Goering, Ribbentrop, Himmler and Rosenberg. There is no record of the proceedings at this meeting, but it is reasonable to assume that the Hess mission fixed for the next day was disclosed to those of his colleagues who were not already party to the plan.

The presence of Rosenberg is the key. Rosenberg was a personal friend of both Hitler and Hess, going back to the early party struggles on the streets of Munich. But in later years he had been bypassed in terms of status as a front line member of the Nazi hierarchy. Why then was he at the meeting? His presence suggests that he was an essential part of the plot and one does not have to look far to find out what his connection was likely to have been. As already noted, Rosenberg had a very special line of communication which led direct from the Nazi hierarchy straight to the British Air Ministry. It circumvented all official channels of diplomacy. It may well have been used to plan, organise and carry out the Hess mission.

After the meeting, Rosenberg remained in Berlin, Hess returned to Munich. Later that day, Hess contacted Rosenberg again by telephone. He requested Rosenberg's immediate presence in Munich. Rosenberg said that was not possible, but Hess was adamant. He laid on a special aircraft to bring Rosenberg to Munich that same evening. The two men met the next morning, May 10, for an early lunch at Hess's residence at Harlaching. There was a long discussion in private in the dining room. The servants were requested to leave. There is no record of the discussions and again, significantly no questions were asked of either men at the Nuremberg trials or elsewhere as to the nature of their discussions.[28]

Presumably, the flight itself would be discussed and perhaps Hess needed to check the details as to the manner of his reception at the British end of his flight. But there is another point which Hess may have wished to clarify before setting off which would have been of sufficient importance to warrant Hess's urgent summons of the previous evening. Just three weeks previously, on April 20, Hitler had appointed Rosenberg as his own personal delegate to the Central Planning for Questions of the East European Area, a post which was to be upgraded to Reichsminsister for the occupied Eastern Territories, following the launch of Operation Barbarossa.[29] In that capacity, Rosenberg would be brought into intimate contact with the Jewish question, since the territories to be occupied contained a large indigenous population of Jews and Slavs.

---

[28]Interrogation of Rosenberg, November 16, 1945. Papers at Imperial War Museum. FO 645 Box 160.
[29]Padfield, Peter, *Hess: Flight for the Führer*, Weidenfeld and Nicolson (1991), 190–91.

Responsibility for the 'Jewish problem', prior to the invasion of Russia, had been in the hands of the German Foreign Office. With the launch of Barbarossa this responsibility was to pass to Heydrich's SS.[30] The consequences of that transfer may well have formed the main topic of discussion at the lunch on May 10. Certainly, any threatened excesses inherent in the SS take-over would be of concern to Hess. What might happen would happen under the nose of and, indeed, under the ultimate authority of his good friend Rosenberg; it was to him that Hess would speak about matters causing him unease.

Rosenberg left Hess at 1300 hours. He did not return to Berlin. He motored direct to Hitler at the Berghof, a distance of some 150 kilometres. He almost certainly arrived there before Hess took off from Augsburg at 1745 hours. After Rosenberg left, Hess seemed both calm and cheerful. It was a fine, sunny day and he spent time walking alongside the river with his son and his three dogs. He had written a 16-page letter to Hitler to be carried to the Berghof by his adjutant, Karl Heinz Pintsch, after his departure. He wrote other letters to his wife, Ilse, his parents, brother Alfred, Albrecht Haushofer and Himmler.[31] Ilse was ill in bed, apparently reading Hamilton's book, *A Pilot's Guide to Everest*. That she was unaware of her husband's plan, as she always maintained, strains credulity. Hess himself then took a rest and, after taking tea to Ilse at about 1430 hours and donning his uniform of a Luftwaffe captain, completed his goodbyes and set off for Augsburg in his Mercedes. His driver, Lippert, was at the wheel and Hess's personal detective accompanied them. Hess carried with him a small suitcase containing his homeopathic medicines, Ilse's camera, the letter to Hamilton, charts of his route and a wallet containing family photographs and the visiting cards of Albrecht and Karl Haushofer.[32]

Shortly before reaching Augsburg, realising that he was ahead of schedule (he planned to make landfall in Scotland after sunset), Hess stopped the car and spent half an hour walking through the woods with his driver. At Augsburg, being Saturday, the Messerschmitt works were deserted, apart from the guards. On the airfield were his Messerschmitt 110 and a small departure group. Hess donned a flying suit and boots, climbed into the aircraft, transferring the contents of

---

[30]This was the case. The invasion of Russia on June 22 and the resulting ideological war marked a period of warfare of unparalleled ferocity and barbarity. From the earliest days, Heydrich's *Einsatzgruppen* (snatch squads) systematically murdered Jews and Russian commissars. These activities were later developed and legitimised. Eventually they resulted in what became known as the Holocaust.

[31]None of these letters have ever been traced.

[32]Although more than one inventory was taken of Hess's personal possessions on landing in Scotland, the inventories are missing from the files at the Public Record Office.

his suitcase to his pockets and hanging the camera around his neck. After going through the normal start procedures, he took off. It was 1745 hours as he flew off into the sunlit evening sky.[33] This time he did not return. It would be four years before he saw his native Germany again. By then it would have been reduced to a devastated wasteland.

[33]Padfield, Peter, *Hess: Flight for the Führer*, Weidenfeld and Nicolson (1991), 195.

19

Albrecht's hares keep running

I cannot think that espionage can be recommended as a technique for building an impressive civilisation. It's a lout's game.

REBECCA WEST

Albrecht Haushofer had little confidence in Hess's plans for peace, or what he supposed were Hess's plans for peace. He was of the opinion, like his friends in the German opposition, that peace was only possible with Great Britain if Germany first ridded herself of Hitler and the Nazi Party. That was unlikely to be high up Hess's agenda. That did not stop Albrecht setting his own hares running in the pursuit of peace, sometimes with and sometimes without Hess's blessing. The period from September 1940 to May 1941 sees Albrecht very busily engaged in the pursuit of peace, wearing all sorts of hats (for Hess, for Hitler, for the German opposition and even for Himmler in one case).

The extent to which Hess was involved personally in these initiatives is uncertain. One of Albrecht's most fruitful contacts was Sam Hoare, the British Minister in Madrid. Albrecht was able to approach Hoare through one of his own former pupils, Heinrich Georg Stahmer, then serving as a secretary at the German Embassy there. Another of his valuable contacts was the Swiss, Jacob Burckhardt, late League of Nations High Commissioner in Danzig, now of the International Red Cross. He was a veteran of peace moves in the past.

Albrecht first contacted Hoare through Stahmer in September, he suggesting an early meeting in either Spain or Portugal.[1] It took place sometime during the winter of 1940–41 through the good offices of the Swedish Legation in Madrid. The two of them agreed that the

[1]Hess, Wolf Rüdiger, *My Father, Rudolf Hess*, W.H. Allen (1986), 80–81.

essential prerequisite of peace was the exclusion of both Hitler and Churchill.[2] It is unlikely that Hess was aware of these discussions.[3]

In the meantime, Albrecht's other contact had been active. Burckhardt was in touch with Sir David Kelly, British Minister at Berne who was requesting that his earlier talks with Max Hohenlohe be resumed, so that information could be obtained as to what peace terms were on offer from Germany.[4] During January, Burckhardt was claiming that he had unofficial confirmation from London that the views previously and consistently put forward by Hitler were acceptable, but not if negotiations were to be conducted with Hitler. Albrecht saw Burckhardt. He wanted assurances from Great Britain as to the terms of peace that would be on offer in the event of a German revolution against Hitler.[5] In the circumstances prevailing in early 1941, with Germany basking in the sunlight of military success, Albrecht was pursuing a point of pure theory.

Between February 21 and 24 Albrecht consulted with Hess. The subject of their discussion is unknown. In the meantime, Stahmer in Madrid was proposing that there should be a meeting in Spain or Portugal in February or March. Great Britain should be represented by Halifax and Hoare and Germany by Hess and Albrecht. In that event, Hess would have to be told of the pre-condition excluding Hitler from any follow-up peace talks. That presented a fundamental problem. Again, the suggestions were unrealistic.

In March, the Kelly request for a resumption of talks with Hohenlohe, started the previous December, bore fruit. The terms of peace requested by Kelly had been conveyed to Sam Hoare in Madrid and on March 5 Hohenlohe met Hoare there. Hohenlohe's account of the meeting has been preserved in the present-day Italian archives. The account is totally different from the one supplied by Hoare to his superior in London. According to Hohenlohe, Hoare said that Churchill's position was insecure and he could no longer rely upon a political majority. Hoare said that sooner of later he (Hoare) would be 'called to London to take over the Government, with the precise task of concluding a compromise peace. Eden as Foreign Secretary would be replaced by Butler.'[6]

According to Hoare's version, Hohenlohe was told that there was no

---

[2]This was fairly typical of the so-called peace moves of Albrecht and the German opposition. The getting rid of Hitler and Churchill was a nice point of principle but in the absence of realistic plans for implementation, was purely academic and led nowhere. Hess had other ideas.
[3]Hess, Wolf Rüdiger, *My Father, Rudolf Hess*, W.H. Allen (1986), 80.
[4]Costello, John, *Ten Days that saved the West*, Bantam Press (1991), 456.
[5]Hess, Wolf Rüdiger, *My Father, Rudolf Hess*, W.H. Allen (1986), 82.
[6]Documenti Diplomatici Italiani, 1939–43, 9th Series March, 14, 1941.

possibility of peace because Hitler's word could not be trusted, and in any case Great Britain would not tolerate Europe under German domination.[7] These reported comments were of course strictly in accordance with the official Churchillian line. If the Hohenlohe version is correct then there must have been more than one meeting because the original arrangements were that the meeting should take place at the flat of Brigadier Torr, the British military attaché in Spain. Hoare would not have said the things attributed to him by Hohenlohe if he was speaking in front of Torr. If Hohenlohe's version was correct then Hoare's remarks as to the insecurity of Churchill's position may have acted as a further spur to Hess's plans, if indeed he was in need of one.

Burckhardt, still hopeful that something solid could come out of the peace rumours abounding in the early months of 1941, asked Albrecht to come to Geneva for further discussions, while at the same time passing on to Albrecht cordial greetings 'from old friends in England.'[8] This was in early April and it is known that Hess and Albrecht met between April 12 and 15.[9] Presumably, they were discussing Burckhardt's initiative and deciding if Albrecht should accept the invitation. As well as this Swiss strand of peace they probably also discussed the Spanish lead through Hoare, as rumours were rife in Madrid at that time as to the existence of a Scottish Peace Party opposed to the Churchill administration.[10] The rumours included a report, subsequently officially denied, that Hess had flown to Madrid.[11]

Another feature of this rather frantic period of peace gossip was Hoare's absence from his post as ambassador in Madrid. Protocol demands that ambassadors stay put in their embassies. People who wish to see them come to the embassy. During April Hoare took unauthorised leave, travelled to Seville and Gibraltar and explained the purpose of his travels to no one, least of all to his superiors in London.

On April 26 Hess gave permission to Albrecht to take up Burckhardt's invitation and meet him in Geneva. Significantly, Albrecht asked that the visit be cleared in terms of authority by Hitler himself. Albrecht knew that if he were to be engaged in any peace process he would be reporting to more than one principal, according to the hat or hats he was wearing. In the present case he would be acting for Hitler/Hess, but he would be reporting also to members of the

---

[7]PRO FO371/26542/C2505/324/18.

[8]Irving, David, *Hess. The Missing Years 1941–1945*, Grafton Books, (1989), 100.

[9]Hess, Wolf Rüdiger, *My Father, Rudolf Hess*, W.H. Allen (1986), 70.

[10]Costello, John, *Ten Days that saved the West*, Bantam Press (1991), 456.

[11]But confirmed by Hitler's secretary, Rolf Inliger, when convening the Hitler/Goering/Hess meeting of May 4, 1941. PRO FO371/46780 and PRO FO371/26945.

German opposition and exceptionally to Himmler.[12] Himmler had apparently suggested that any peace offensive should be launched in the name of Hess but that Hitler should be replaced by Himmler at any subsequent negotiating table.[13] The ultimate cover of Hitler was very necessary to Albrecht in these circumstances.

Albrecht and Burckhardt met on April 28. There is no record of the proceedings but Albrecht delivered a report to Hitler. It reported that 'Burckhardt said that he had a visit in Geneva from a person well respected and well known in London Conservative and City circles. The person spoke of the desire of important Englishmen to review peace prospects and he mentioned Albrecht as a contact.' Albrecht had then suggested to Burckhardt that a meeting be arranged with the person in question in Geneva.[14] It was after his meeting with Albrecht that Burckhardt was visited by an agent acting for Himmler. Himmler had suggested that he should replace Hitler as the German representative at any peace talks.[15] The agent was probably Dr Carl Longbehn who had introduced Albrecht to the Wednesday Club, a group of the Hitler opposition.

On April 30 Albrecht returned from Geneva. He was pleased with the progress made.[16] He planned to return to Geneva, see Burckhardt again and then fly on to Madrid to see Sam Hoare.[17] He was working hard to pull together the Swiss and Spanish peace threads. But the permanency of Hitler and Churchill remained as the fundamental problem. Apart from the Himmler suggestion, no new step had been put forward.

It seems that all the Hohenlohe/Burckhardt/Albrecht /Hoare talks dwelt lengthily and lovingly with the position that they all wished to achieve without any realistic thought as to how it was to be achieved. Albrecht was an academic by nature, training and experience. He tended to achieve academic results. It is not difficult to appreciate that men like Hitler and Hess may have long since taken the view that Albrecht was very busy running around in circles getting nowhere. It was as though a group of theoreticians was gathered around a swimming pool engaged in academic discussion as to the temperature of the water. Hess was about to jump in and find out.

According to Karl Haushofer, Hess – who had authorised Albrecht's

---

[12]In later years it was Himmler who sounded out the Americans as to a possible peace.
[13]Irving, David, *Hess. The Missing Years 1941–1945*, Grafton Books, (1989), 101.
[14]Padfield, Peter, *Hess: Flight for the Führer*, Weidenfeld and Nicolson (1991), 178.
[15]Ulrich Hassal Diaries, May 18, 1941.
[16]Martha Haushofer diary entries May 3, 1941, and May 5, 1941.
[17]Confirmed by Karl Haushofer in a postwar interrogation, October 5, 1945. Imperial War Museum FO645 Box 155.

meetings with Burckhardt and Hoare – was prepared to meet Hoare himself in Madrid sometime late in May 'but decided to fly to Great Britain instead.'[18] In fact, Albrecht saw Hoare on May 6 but the meeting was abortive.[19] As Hess's son points out,[20] Hess could see that these various initiatives and others, prompted by well meaning neutrals, globetrotting amateurs and wishful thinkers[21] and all leading nowhere, could get in the way of his own plans. Decisive action was necessary without further delay.[22]

Hess's mission and motives were partly personal. He knew exactly what he wanted to do and thought he knew how to do it. He certainly did not wish to get involved in a whole mish-mash of conflicting interests and motives inspired by a man wearing three or four peace hats at the same time. Although he had authorised at least some of Albrecht's many-tracked initiatives, he had quietly and secretly gone about the business of organising his own mission quite independently.

A clue to the intelligence aid used by Hess points again to the Rosenberg/de Ropp/Winterbotham/Boyle/Air Ministry channel of communication, which was seen to have been in full working order only two months prior to Hess's flight. On March 7, 1941, 'Bomber' Harris and Sholto Douglas, respectively commanders of British Bomber and Fighter Commands, were caught up in a bizarre incident which was never reported. They awaited the arrival at Lympne airfield in Kent of a German four-engined Condor aircraft piloted by Hitler's personal pilot, Hans Bauer. The passengers aboard would include Hitler and some of his entourage, the aircraft having been hijacked by Bauer, disillusioned by the war and anxious to end it. The information had been taken seriously by the Air Ministry. Signals had been agreed for Bauer's approach to the British coast, a reception arranged at Lympne and a Ford V8 box-body touring car with escorting motor cycles was on stand by.

Nothing in fact happened on the night of March 7. But the important point is that the Air Ministry had maintained an ongoing communication for a matter of months direct with Bauer. It is possible that the Air Ministry/Winterbotham/de Ropp/Hess connection had been used.[23] This channel had been used in the 1930s. Was it still being used

---

[18]As reported by E. Mann, *Glasgow Evening Citizen*. 1945.

[19]Reported by Albrecht shortly before his death to Walter Wehrenberg, one of his pupils.

[20]Hess, Wolf Rüdiger, *My Father, Rudolf Hess*, W.H. Allen (1986), 83–84.

[21]See PRO FO 371/26542 for examples.

[22]Ironically, on the very day of Hess's departure a cable arrived from Stahmer in Madrid urging an Albrecht/Hoare meeting for May 12. Irving, David, *Hess. The Missing Years 1941–1945*, Grafton Books, (1989), 105.

[23]Padfield, Peter, *Hess: Flight for the Führer*, Weidenfeld and Nicolson (1991), 159–60.

in March 1941? Was it used in May 1941? Bauer flew with Hess in early practice flights. Hess was a particular friend of Rosenberg. Just as Bauer had used the channel to agree arrangements as to route, navigational signals, landing arrangements and reception, did Hess use it for the same purposes? As with so much that happened between October 1940 and May 1941 these details must remain matters of conjecture. That is because of the embargo still in place on these documents at the Public Record Office[24] and elsewhere which would illuminate this period of covert action by the different factions.

[24]They include FO 371/26542/C1303, C1687 and C1954/324/98 and FO 371/26945/C4456, C4487/306/41 and C4038

An early volunteer. Hess as a young soldier in the 1914/1918 War

Rudolf Hess the academic who preferred politics

The family man. Hess with his son before his flight to Britain

Rudolf Hess: Nazi Party Leader

Hess with Hitler and Göring at Nazi Party rally

Hess with Hitler, Himmler, Goebbels and General Blomberg. The best polished boots in the business

Early days as brownshirts. Hess with Hitler, Göring and other party leaders

Hess. An able speaker but a glass of pink champagne was usually called for before the event

Early days. Hitler marching with his aides. Hess on his left in 1931

Hitler and his faithful deputy at a torchlight procession, 1938

The Messerschmitt 110 aircraft used by Hess for his flight to Britain

Memorial stone marking the spot where Hess landed on the night of 10 May 1941. The stone was subsequently vandalised and destroyed

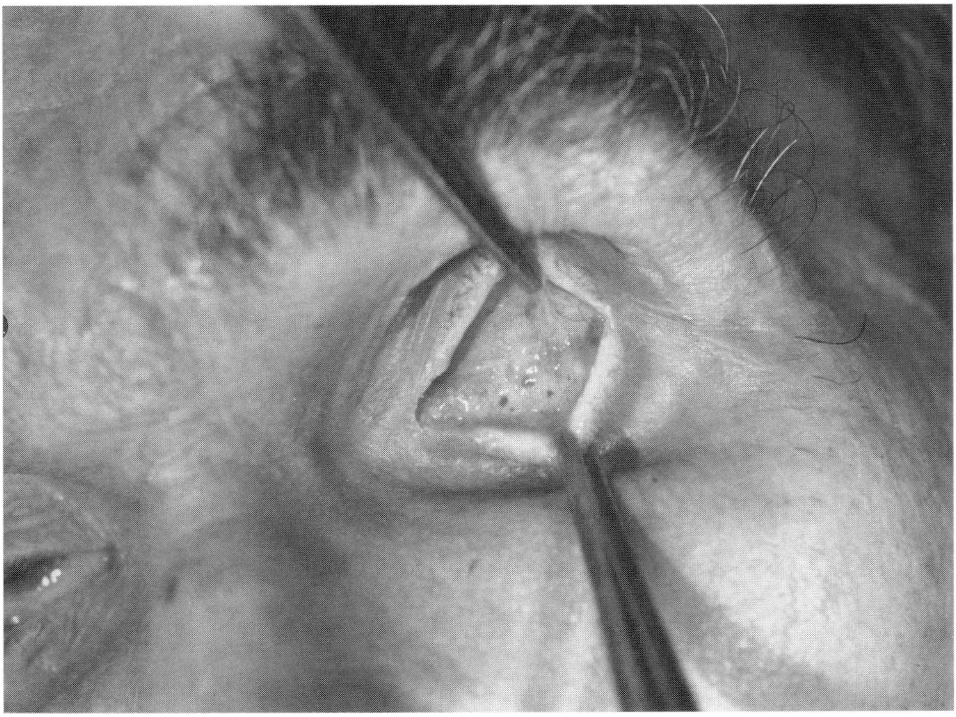

Post-mortem view of Hess's eyes and the haemorrhaging, an indication of death by strangulation

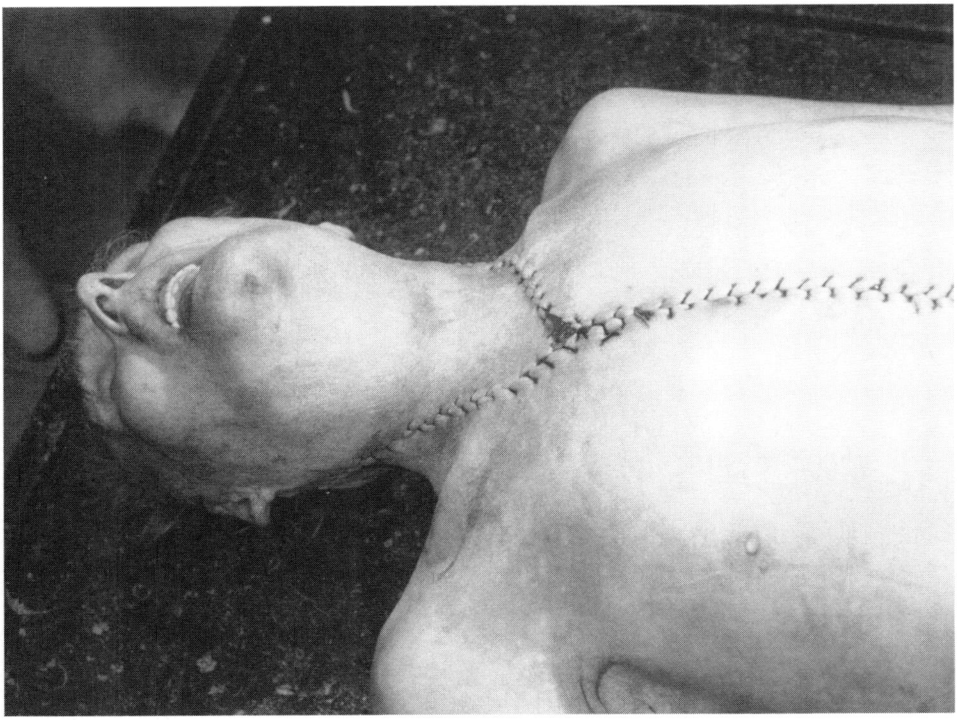

Post-mortem view of the front of Hess's neck showing the horizontal strangulation marks

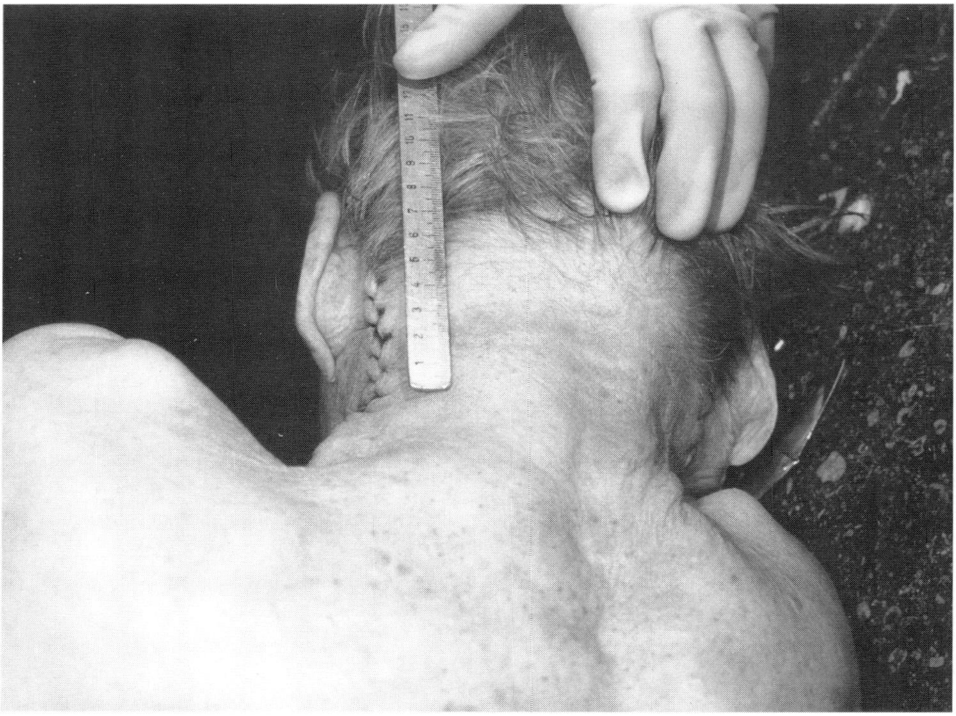
Post-mortem view of the back of Hess's neck showing the horizontal strangulation marks

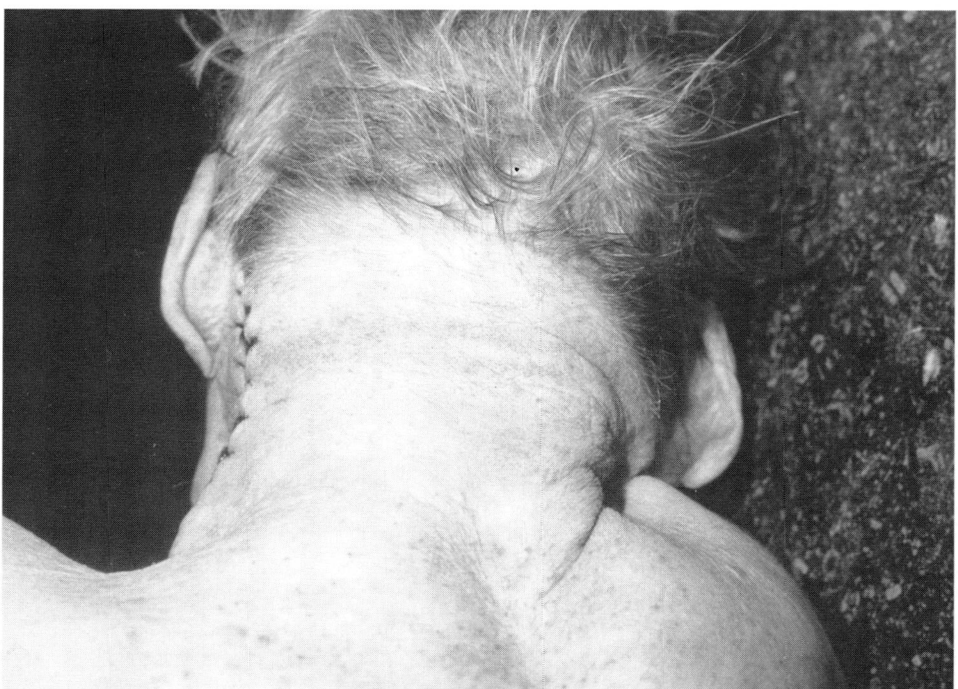
Another post-mortem view showing the horizontal strangulation marks

20

The British Peace Party

Is it beyond the political genius of mankind to reconcile national individuality with international collaboration?

LORD HALIFAX, June 25, 1939

When Rudolf Hess took off from Augsburg on the afternoon of May 10, 1941, his objective was to land in Great Britain and make contact with representatives of a British Peace Party. The term 'British Peace Party' is used in the official German diplomatic records.[1] It is not recognised or used in any official British record. As a formal political party it never existed. As a loose association of individuals and institutions having a common desire, albeit for different reasons, to come to terms with Germany and make peace, it almost certainly did. In the main, it comprised elements from the so-called British Establishment. In that context, in May 1941, it included representatives from British royalty, the land-owning aristocracy, industrial, commercial and financial interests, senior politicians, diplomats and members of the Intelligence Services.

The British Establishment has been likened to a club[2] of not more than five or six thousand people who are said to run Great Britain[3] and who are superimposed on the general population of some 57 million people. These chosen few are said to occupy the real positions of power and privilege in government, the public offices, the armed forces, the financial institutions and land property. Their positions of power are then said to be preserved in near perpetuity by inheritance provisions and a specialised system of private education. That system

[1]Documents on German Foreign Policy, Volume 8, December 4, 1939, to March 1940, paras 363–65.
[2]By the distinguished American journalist, Richard Critchford. See *Guardian* article of August 13, 1990.
[3]Or more precisely, the people who *control* the people who run Great Britain.

is based upon the English public schools and the ancient Oxbridge universities which feed successive generations into the system as required.

The Establishment's one over-riding fear is the fear of change. Its members' positions of privilege are rooted in the status quo. Anything that is likely to attack the status quo is to be regarded with suspicion and if need be, resisted. The continuance of the war with Germany was likely to affect the status quo. It was costing money, causing high taxation and losing export markets. More importantly, it was likely to bring political and economic changes in its wake, and most dangerous of all, the threat of social change.[4] To some within the Establishment ranks, a German-dominated Europe was the best protection possible against the encroachment of communism into Europe and eventually into the domain of the British Establishment. For this reason of naked self interest and protection some within the Establishment thought that Mr Churchill's war should be brought to an end.

In May 1941 the strategic position was such that there was a discernible, rational basis why the war should be brought to an end. An increasing number of freethinkers were no longer toeing the Churchill line. They were not motivated by self-interest alone. They were intelligent, responsible people who honestly thought that the continuance of the war was pointless and should be brought to an end. This rationalist wing of the Peace Party gave it further strength and added somewhat to its dignity of purpose. The rationalists would argue that the absence of a discernible path to victory for Great Britain was very real in 1941. That fact should be recognised. If the sovereignty of Great Britain and her Empire could be guaranteed, then the sensible thing was to negotiate a peace.

Churchill knew from the day he assumed power that victory over Germany by way of armed conflict could only come about through the involvement of America in the conflict. This had been his constant policy theme thereafter. No sacrifice had been too great and no subterfuge too devious to bring that desired state of affairs into being. He had invited, indeed initiated, the Luftwaffe bombing offensive against British cities, in the mistaken belief that American public opinion would be so outraged that it would bring pressure upon their Government to join in the anti-Nazi crusade. He had bombarded President Roosevelt with personal missives advocating American intervention. He had blackmailed Roosevelt into the lend/lease arrangements for the supply of arms by threatening the loss of the British Atlantic fleet in the event of a British defeat. But in May 1941, America

---

[4]Which was the case in 1945.

was still an onlooker, the battle of the Atlantic lifeline was reaching crisis proportions and the nightly bombing of British cities and towns was seemingly unrelenting. Perhaps most disturbing of all, the British army had again demonstrated its clear inferiority in combat with its German counterpart in the recent campaigns in North Africa, Greece and Crete. This continuing failure to take on and defeat the German land forces in almost any and every circumstance seemed to mark a permanent state of affairs that denied any possibility of ultimate victory.

There was another factor which compounded the rationalist approach. Churchill's political position had been fragile ever since he had assumed the position of Prime Minister and by May 1941 he was in great personal difficulty. He was having to face severe criticism for the military defeats in the Middle East and that criticism was merging into a general criticism of his overall war direction and style of government. If the German successes in North Africa continued and Rommel reached the Suez Canal it was difficult to see how Churchill could survive. The door would then be open for positive peace moves by those representing the British Peace Party.

At the beginning of May, Hugh Dalton, Chief of Special Operations in Europe, noted in his diary: 'A titanic struggle was about to break out between those who wanted a premature peace and those who intended to fight to the finish.' On May 7, formal opposition to Churchill's direction of the war was expressed in the House of Commons by Lloyd George, supported by Hore Belisha, the former Secretary of State for War.[5,6] Criticism of Churchill's 'dictatorial methods' were also being voiced by Robert Menzies, the Australian Prime Minister, then in London, and Cecil King in the *Daily Mirror* was advocating immediate Cabinet changes.

Churchill's position was insecure, the Germans and some of the most powerful elements within the British Establishment wanted peace, and there appeared to be a rational basis for its realisation. Who then among the ranks of the Peace Party had the courage, will and political ability and status to put himself forward as a prospective leader and take on Churchill? Who would have jumped on the bandwagon and taken office in the new peace Government?[7]

---

[5]See Hansard records.

[6]But when the issue was put to the test in a vote of confidence, Churchill emerged with a majority of 447 to 3. Churchill described Lloyd George's speech as one which could have been made by Marshal Pétain in the dying days of Reynaud's French Government. Pétain of course, led France's surrender. Lloyd George never forgave Churchill for this indirect accusation of treason.

[7]It is interesting to note in hindsight that no one from the Peace Party was prepared to take on Churchill and go public on a pacifist platform. Rather like the German opposition, and for the same reasons, the British Peace Party never rose much above the status of drawing-room theorists.

It has been suggested that the man waiting in the wings to take over on the demise of Churchill was David Lloyd George. He said as much to his private secretary: 'Victory is not possible. I shall do nothing until called upon. I shall wait until Winston is bust.'[8] There is no suggestion there of taking on Churchill in direct confrontation. Rather is there a willingness to take over as and when Churchill was forced aside by events. This ties in with the efforts of Halifax and Butler and their senior colleagues to put a peace deal on the Cabinet table as a *fait accompli* and thereby promote a political crisis and a Churchill resignation.

Lloyd George was a confirmed defeatist from the first day of war. Flattered by Hitler's *Mein Kampf*,[9] he appears to have been impressed by at least some of the Nazi ideals and even more so by its leader. After visiting Hitler in 1936 he became his vociferous and public advocate and devotee. He expanded his views consistently through the British press, preaching the need for Germany's friendship and the threat of communist encroachment into Europe. Perhaps the thing that impressed Lloyd George most of all about Nazism and blinded him to a good deal else was the Nazi solution to the problem of unemployment and the stability achieved between prices and workers' wages.

When war came in 1939 Lloyd George was dismayed. Within a month he was urging the Government not to reject out of hand the peace offer made by Hitler immediately following the Polish campaign. His political reputation thereafter was that of a defeatist. He fully lived up to that reputation. For this reason and others[10] he was never invited by Chamberlain to join the Government. Nevertheless, he was or had been, a man of immense political stature. He had revolutionised Asquith's administration in the 1914–18 conflict and never more so than when he had taken over the Premiership himself in 1916.[11]

Whether at the age of 78 in 1941, Lloyd George was the political giant of yesteryear is a matter of conjecture. But as a former distinguished statesman with an enviable past reputation he would certainly have fitted the bill as a temporary Premier to inaugurate the initial peace talks, rather in the same way that Marshal Pétain had done in the case of France. Certainly by May 1941 he had committed so many indiscretions in pursuing his near obsession for peace that nobody

---

[8] Diary of A.J. Sylvester, Lloyd George's private secretary, October 3, 1940.

[9] Hitler paid tribute to Lloyd George's oratorical skills and his powers of communication with his people. He rather spoiled the flattery by referring to Lloyd George as 'that great Englishman'.

[10] He and Chamberlain had been political enemies since the 1914–18 war.

[11] His succession to Asquith was likened to the 'substitution of dynamite for a damp squib' (Memoirs of Sir Almeric Fitzroy, 191).

could mistake where his loyalties lay. He was in open collusion with Richard Stokes the Catholic pacifist MP for Ipswich, who led a group of some 40 MPs of similar mind in the Commons. He corresponded regularly with Beaverbrook, who could never quite make up his mind where his loyalties lay and was at various times quite prepared to talk about peace.

Lloyd George's constant adviser in connection with his peace policies was the military historian, Basil Liddell Hart. On August 28 Liddell Hart had attended upon Lloyd George at the latter's residence in Wales. Between the two of them, they drafted a detailed memorandum setting out the terms for a just and lasting peace. A copy was sent to Beaverbrook. In November, further copies were provided for Lord Lothian, British Ambassador in Washington, and Roosevelt. Early in 1941 a copy found its way into the hands of A.V. Alexander, the First Lord of the Admiralty who passed it on to Churchill. Churchill described the document as 'defeatist and treasonable', but no action was taken.[12]

Churchill, of course, knew Lloyd George of old. He certainly did not trust him in the circumstances prevailing in 1941. Shortly after his own succession to power he had invited Lloyd George to join his Cabinet, where he could keep an eye on him. Lloyd George refused the invitation, preferring to retain his own freedom of action. He was unwilling to associate himself with an adventure under Churchill which he believed could have no successful outcome. It is significant that on the death of Lothian on December 12, 1940, Churchill's first choice as a replacement in Washington was not Halifax but Lloyd George. Churchill no doubt considered Washington as a convenient repository for the faint-hearted or worse. Both Lloyd George and Halifax threatened Churchill's position, but Lloyd George was apparently considered to be a greater threat. Lloyd George again turned down Churchill's invitation. Churchill settled for Halifax.

On the very day of Hess's flight, the Duke of Bedford[13] wrote to Richard Stokes proposing that Lloyd George, who was 'so obviously the one man who could save the country', should make a public statement indicating the peace terms to which Germany could respond.[14,15]

---

[12]Costello, John, *Ten Days that saved the West*, Bantam Press (1991), 398.

[13]The Duke was a member of the land-owning aristocracy, typical of those wishing to bring the war to an end.

[14]Day, David, *Menzies and Churchill at War*, Angus and robertson (1986), 184.

[15]Hindsight tells us that Lloyd George never did commit himself to a public statement. Whether he never considered the time and circumstances opportune or whether in the end he chose to remain loyal to his old colleague Churchill is not known. Churchill perhaps thought that the latter was the case. On December 18, 1944, Churchill offered Lloyd George an earldom. Lloyd George this time accepted Churchill's invitation and he became the Earl Lloyd George of Dwyfor. He died three months later.

If the post of Premier in the new theoretical Peace Government was to be taken up by Lloyd George, then senior Cabinet posts would certainly be found for the two peace protagonists who had beavered away so assiduously to bring about the demise of Churchill and open the door to peace by laying terms on the Cabinet table as a *fait accompli.* The Foreign Secretary Lord Halifax and his Minister of State, Rab Butler, deserved no less.

Halifax was a true-blooded member of the Establishment. His mother was the daughter of the Earl of Devon who could count three Emperors of Constantinople among her Courtenay ancestors. His father came from good Yorkshire Tory stock and the Northumbrian Whigs of Lord Grey. Just prior to the start of the industrial revolution, Halifax's father had bought land near Doncaster. He found that he was sitting on hundreds of acres of some of the richest and deepest coal seams in Great Britain.[16] Young Edward never had cause to earn a living and drifted through Eton and Oxford with all the ease and air of the born aristocrat. He was very good at taking and passing examinations and finished up as a Fellow of All Souls, Oxford, where in accordance with the traditions of the day he entered into public service. He chose politics. He was a very religious, high-minded young man who tended to mix his morals with his politics. He had little practical experience of anything outside academia and estate management.

As Viceroy of India between 1927 and 1932 Halifax had administered British rule in accordance with well-established and proven imperial custom. On the whole he had handled competently the aspirations of Gandhi, a rational, educated, non-violent nationalist with whom he could converse on equal terms. By contrast, he was completely out of his depth in dealing with the aspirations of Adolf Hitler, the irrational, street-educated, violent nationalist with whom he had nothing in common.

Remarkably, though, Halifax's views on peace identified very closely with those of Adolf Hitler. Halifax was of the view that, providing the integrity and independence of Great Britain and her Empire could be guaranteed, Great Britain should not lose the opportunity of ending the war. And if that meant German domination of Central and Eastern Europe, so be it. That view coincided precisely with that of Hitler. Halifax was and always had been a committed pacifist. He abhorred violence and he abhorred war. If negotiations could bring the present conflict to an end then the investment in negotiations should be made. This had been his firm view during the summer crisis of

[16]In some places the seams were 70 yards in depth, yielding best-quality coal.

1940. It had not changed a year later. Certainly his inclinations in that direction outstripped in terms of priority any personal loyalty he may have had towards Churchill, a man he understood about as well as he understood Hitler. Nevertheless, Halifax was right and Churchill wrong about the sort of peace terms that could be obtained from Hitler in 1940, and the position had not changed a year later. Halifax would have taken his place in any Cabinet pledged to peace with enthusiasm.

Rab Butler was not of the Establishment but married into it.[17] Like a convert to a new religion, Butler became more enamoured by the Establishment and all its glitter than any true aristocrat. As a result of his marriage, he entered the world of the important and influential and he liked it.[18] He was provided with a safe Conservative seat at Saffron Walden and was relieved of all financial need. Previous to his marriage his academic career had been somewhat flawed compared with his illustrious forebears in that field, most of whom had entered the Colonial Service. Butler failed an Eton scholarship. He went to Marlborough instead, where he was anything but happy. His subsequent career at Cambridge was somewhat marred by illness. He suffered more than one nervous breakdown. He had expressed a wish to enter the Diplomatic Service but did not take the examinations. He married a Courtauld instead.

Butler therefore had better cause than most to wish the status quo to continue unharmed and unthreatened.[19] Churchill's war should be brought to an end. Germany was far more use as the bulwark against Russian communism, the real threat to everyone's status quo. Butler had fallen easily and naturally into the ranks of those seeking to appease Hitler, and he had certainly demonstrated since the onset of hostilities that he was still of the same mind. With or without Halifax's knowledge and consent and certainly without Churchill's he had talked peace to anyone who was prepared to listen. The Prytz affair (see Appendix IV) demonstrated that, like Halifax, Butler was quite prepared to put his loyalty to Churchill on the back burner and talk peace, in direct contravention to the Cabinet decision to fight on. Again like Halifax, he was quite happy to jump onto the peace wagon as soon as it was seen to move.

If Halifax and Butler were steadfast in their quest for peace and less than lukewarm in their loyalty to Churchill, Beaverbrook was volatile

---

[17]He had married Sydney Elizabeth Courtauld, the only daughter of Samuel Courtauld, the textile magnate.

[18]Howard, Anthony, *The Life of R.A. Butler*, 29–30.

[19]When Sam Courtauld died in 1947 the vast bulk of his personal fortune went to his only daughter, Butler's wife. Butler personally inherited the Gatcombe Park estate in Gloucestershire (now owned by the Princess Royal).

on all counts. A self-made millionaire, this Scots-Canadian son of a presbyterian minister, born William Maxwell Aitken, was the world's greatest pragmatist. He owed no allegiance or loyalty to anything or anyone other than himself He had learned in the hard school of the business world that practical options serving his own ambitions were the only things that really mattered. He was as practical as Halifax was theoretical and he would switch sides and allegiances as often as it pleased him. In the early days of the war he was a strong supporter of Richard Stokes, the pacifist MP. He no doubt saw the war as a direct threat to his newspaper empire.[20] Like Lloyd George, he was a disciple of the defeatist military strategist, Basil Liddell Hart. He published his views regularly in all his newspapers. In those early days, Beaverbrook belonged to that group who advocated a stand off position as far as Europe was concerned. Let the warring factions and ideologies tear each other to bits while Great Britain stood off and watched. For that reason, his newspapers vigorously supported Chamberlain's pre-war policy of appeasing Hitler.

Churchill recognised Beaverbrook as a threat. He therefore invited him into his Cabinet and gave him one of the most important tasks of the day, Minister of Aircraft Production. Beaverbrook was flattered, his ego assuaged and his ambitions fired. He accepted Churchill's invitation. He then produced precious fighter aircraft, just as he had produced newspapers. Churchill ran out of fighter pilots before he ran out of fighter aircraft. The crisis over, Beaverbrook reverted to type. By May 1941 he was playing both the Churchill and the Lloyd George cards. He pleaded with Churchill to release him from high office pleading excessive strain. Churchill accordingly moved him away from the front-line ministries. At this stage, Beaverbrook belonged to the group who believed that while Great Britain could probably survive there was no way in which she could win the war. The stalemate should therefore be brought to an end by a sensible peace agreement.

Beaverbrook had always maintained a close but odd relationship with ('Slippery') Sam Hoare, one of the arch-appeasers of pre-war days. Hoare had been relegated from the Cabinet on Churchill's accession to power and then sent by Halifax to take up the post of Ambassador in Madrid. Halifax may well have felt the posting to be of some importance. Hoare had been kept financially alive by Beaverbrook before the war. He had been paid well to provide Beaverbrook with Government information and to play the part of Beaverbrook's puppet, to be jerked this way and that by his master's strings. The position had

---

[20]He owned the *Daily Express*, *Sunday Express* and the *Evening Standard*. He was the greatest newspaper proprietor since Northcliffe.

not changed since the onset of war.[21] A prominent member of Chamberlain's Big Four team of pre-war appeasers, by 1941 Sam Hoare was up to his neck in peace diplomacy[22] and there is little doubt that he would have been in close touch with his paymaster. Hoare, like his master, was ready to jump on the peace wagon in May 1941 providing there was a driver securely in place.

Perhaps the most powerful behind-the-scenes operator for the British Peace Party, and the one nearest to the real centre of power within the British Establishment, was the head of the Secret Intelligence Service MI6, Stuart Menzies. Menzies had succeeded the previous head of MI6, Admiral Sinclair, on November 29, 1939, and there may be some significance in the timing of the appointment. Reference has already been made to the extraordinary appointments to senior positions in the Diplomatic Service during the late 1930s, all connected by the common thread of appeasement. Lothian in Washington, Kelly in Berne, Livingston in Geneva and Mallet in Stockholm were all Chamberlain/Halifax appointees. They were all confirmed appeasers and pacifists. The appointment of Menzies was in the same mould and Churchill was very much against it for that reason. But in the early Chamberlain Government, Churchill was in a minority of one. The appointment therefore stood. Menzies had then become involved in the infamous Venlo affair, when MI6 contacts with 'good' Germans to commence peace talks turned out to be contacts with the SS. The whole of the British intelligence system in Europe was compromised as a result.

There were other reasons why Churchill was unhappy about the Menzies appointment. He knew that the only trump card that he might eventually be able to play was American involvement in the war. He knew that Menzies, like most of the Establishment grandees, was deeply suspicious of the Americans and their ambitions[23] and wanted nothing to do with them. Churchill also knew that Menzies's contacts ran deep into Establishment territory to its very roots. Not only was Churchill not a part of that territory, he was also a cause of much displeasure to it, and on his accession to power in May 1940 it was confidently expected that Menzies would be replaced. Instead, he sacked Sir Vernon Kell, head of MI5.[24] He also inserted Major

---

[21]In May 1940, when Hoare was posted to Madrid, Beaverbrook paid Hoare's debt owing to Lloyds Underwriters. About £6,000 was involved. (Beaverbrook papers, May 29, 1940).

[22]Reference has already been made to his meeting of March 5, 1941, with Hohenlohe when, according to the latter's report, Hoare had told him that he was expecting a call to return to London to take over.

[23]A suspicion well founded, as events were to show.

[24]Kell was obsessed with the communist threat and had organised the British counter-intelligence forces accordingly.

Desmond Morton as his personal intelligence officer to deal with Menzies on his behalf: in effect, a personal spy to keep an eye on the head of MI6.[25]

It was rumoured that Menzies was the illegitimate son of the Prince of Wales, later King Edward VII. His mother was Lady Holford, a court favourite and a great beauty. She married Sir George Holford, a grandee of King Edward's court. Whatever his true antecedents, Menzies was intimately connected with the court, high Tory interests in the City and the service chiefs. He was literally at the hub of the Establishment. As a private person his interests did not appear to extend much further than his old regiment, the Life Guards, the Beaufort Hunt and White's Club.[26] He had served with distinction in the 1914–18 war, winning the DSO and MC. He had migrated into the intelligence services while still serving in the army. He was no intelligence giant but, having seen at first hand the carnage on the Western Front, he was an ardent pacifist. In that capacity, he would view peace negotiations as an act of patriotism. In all the circumstances, he was unlikely to be the soul-mate of Winston Churchill.

Lloyd George, Halifax, Butler, Beaverbrook, Hoare and Menzies were therefore likely candidates to take their places among the hierarchy of a possible alternative Government bent on peace rather than war. And the Duke of Windsor would certainly have been willing, indeed anxious, to provide a royal ingredient by replacing his brother as the ruling monarch. A full account of the Duke's Nazi proclivities and his treasonable activities in Spain and Portugal during the summer crisis of 1940 are set down in Appendix V. On the Sunday morning of August 1, 1940, before departing from Lisbon for the Bahamas, he had made it clear to his host and German agent, Espírito Santo, that he was prepared to return to help Germany in its efforts to open up peace negotiations with Great Britain, as and when the time was considered opportune. He had even left a code word which was to be used in that eventuality. The motives for the Duke's pro-German stance were numerous and have been noted in chapter 15. There was a strong personal element directed against his brother, King George VI. The Duke had been incensed by the rejection by the royal family of his wife the Duchess, dissatisfied with the financial arrangements made at the time of the abdication and, more latterly, probably jealous of his brother's competent performance as Sovereign during a period of national crisis. But his motives went deeper than that. He was and always had been an open admirer of Adolf Hitler and all his works and would

---

[25]Padfield, Peter, *Hess: Flight for the Führer*, Weidenfeld and Nicolson (1991), 118.
[26]*Ibid*, 113.

have liked to have seen National Socialism preached and practised in Great Britain. He had said as much.[27] It has to be said that only a monarch or near-monarch living in splendid isolation, could be so out of touch with the ordinary Britisher as to think that he could or would embrace the tenets of National Socialism.

Windsor was not alone with his thoughts of adopting National Socialism as a cure for Great Britain's ills. There were others who believed that all the sloppiness and licence introduced by a liberal democracy had sent the nation into steep decline and that the nation needed the discipline inherent in National Socialism. Among them were Admiral Sir Barry Domvile, founder of The Link, Sir Oswald Mosley of the British Union of Fascists and Lord Tavistock, author of the Tavistock proposals. There were many more. Most of the landed aristocracy held rather less extreme views but actively supported those who worked to negotiate a peace. In early 1940 there had been so many peacemongers in the House of Lords that Lord Ponsonby had been obliged to request that the House go into secret session before discussing possible peace terms. The position had not altered by May 1941. In fact, many thought there was an even more urgent need for peace negotiations.

The individuals and groups in Great Britain who would be interested in the commencement of a peace process[28] may have had different motives, but there was a common objective. The various sectional interests were represented by politicians of calibre. They were also backed by substantial material resources. But where was their leader who would take on Churchill and go public when Rudolf Hess arrived with his peace initiative? And how would the Churchill Government deal with that situation, as and when and if it arose? These were the questions that were shortly to be asked and answered.

---

[27]Ziegler, Philip, *King Edward VIII*, Collins (1990), 206.

[28]Appendix VII sets down some of the prominent members of the Anglo-German Fellowship, the Link and the Right Club in the summer of 1940. These were three of the more important organisations established in Great Britain and engaged in pro-German/anti-communist/anti-Semitic activities. It is likely that a good number of the members listed would be attuned to the views ascribed to the British Peace Party in the main text

21

The Jewish factor

The English, the French and the Italians are strong enough and old enough to ignore or absorb the Jews but in Germany they remain a constant intellectual provocation to a people always sensitive to the newness of their nationhood.

W.E.D. ALLEN

It is sometimes difficult to realise that the past was once in the future. In May 1941, the Holocaust did not exist. It lay in the future. In May 1941 the 'final solution' to the German so-called Jewish problem was not the Holocaust. It was a deportation scheme called the Madagascar Plan which has long since departed both the memory and the history books.[1] Its implementation was dependent upon Germany coming to terms with Great Britain, and that did not happen. When Rudolf Hess took off from Augsburg on May 10, 1941, he knew what the alternative to the Madagascar Plan might be if the invasion of Russia went ahead with Great Britain undefeated. Thus was added a further imperative to his mission for peace. The failure of his mission and the ramifications of the Jewish issue are perhaps the biggest single factor explaining the continuing official British secrecy concerning Hess's mission and the manner of his death in August 1987.

The nature, extent and importance attached to the Jewish problem as seen through German eyes in the 1930s has been described in earlier chapters. The Germans were not alone with the problem. The assimilation of the Jewish people into the various nation states in which they had settled after the 1914–18 war was a matter of concern to many. The Jews were of a distinctive race, religion and culture but had no national home. Their integration into the mainstream living of

[1]But which remains on file at Bonn.

their host nations tested the patience and tolerance of both Jew and Gentile. Nations genuinely subscribing to the democratic ideal, such as America, Great Britain and France, made a rather better fist of it than did those which adopted more authoritarian principles, such as Poland, Romania and (pre-Hitler) Germany. Even in the Western democracies which accommodated a high proportion of the Jewish intelligentsia and well-to-do, the integration was sometimes more apparent than real. There was a good deal of drawing-room anti-Semitism in England, for example, especially among the ranks of the Establishment. This found expression in many ways, in the protective exclusivity of certain clubs and right-wing political organisations, restrictions within the higher echelons of the learned professions and prohibition of entry into the more venerable public schools.

In literature, a Jewish flavour was often attached to the anti-hero. T.S. Eliot's poetry, Shakespeare's Shylock, Sapper's Bulldog Drummond, the novels of Dornford Yates and John Buchan all provide examples.[2] Jews were tolerated rather than welcomed in Great Britain during the period when Hitler held sway in Germany. Nor was it exclusively the Establishment ranks which raised the defensive front. Jewish emigrés from Europe competed for jobs and housing against the native working population. Considerable friction arose particularly in the East End of London, giving much comfort and courage to Oswald Mosley and his Blackshirt agitators. Nevertheless, in spite of private prejudices manifested in various and often petty-minded vendettas and exclusions, the overall public attitude in Great Britain towards Jews was one of tolerance and forbearance in accordance with the tenets of an established democracy. Only the lunatic fringe of the extreme Right would have adopted a different stance and they had no democratic mandate with which to back their extremist views.[3]

---

[2]Sapper (H.C. McNeile) introduces his villain thus: 'The newcomer wore a heavy fur coat though the evening was warm. A silk scarf was wrapped round his neck, an opera hat was on his head. His face was swarthy, his dark eyes gleamed with vitality. And his hooked nose proclaimed his race.' (*Bulldog Drummond at Bay*).

[3]It is interesting to speculate on what new attitudes might have been adopted towards Jews if the checks and balances provided by a healthy democratic regime had been removed. Later experience is not encouraging. In 1940, after her defeat, France voted into power the ultra-conservative Marshal Pétain. Under his regime, 74,500 French Jews passed through Drancy concentration camp, six kilometres from the centre of Paris, en route to Auschwitz. 2,500 survived. French bus-drivers brought the Jews to Drancy and French train-drivers took them to Auschwitz. Frenchmen responded willingly to a policy of Jewish deportations promulgated by a properly constituted French Government. French Jews were rounded up for deportation in Vichy (unoccupied) France as well as in German-occupied territories.

In June 1940 the British Channel Islands were occupied by German armed forces. There was no resistance. On the contrary, there was active co-operation with the occupying forces. 16,000

Continued next page

Imperfect as attitudes may have been in Great Britain, they were totally unlike those running parallel at the same time in Nazi Germany. Racial purity was the keystone of Nazi philosophy and the ostracising of the Jews was the clearest manifestation of that philosophy. In Great Britain there was no fundamental Jewish problem. In Germany, the Jewish problem had caused all the other problems, or so the teaching went. Jewish politicians were responsible for Versailles, Jewish revolutionaries were responsible for communist Russia, Jewish plutocrats in the West had frustrated Germany's legitimate aspirations and Jewish insurgents had infiltrated the German trade union movement. Everything that had ever gone wrong, every problem that had arisen, every frustrated ambition could be comfortably accommodated as the product of the universal scapegoat, the Jew. The resolving of the so-called Jewish problem was therefore a major policy objective of Hitler's Reich.

How were Jewish influences to be eradicated from German national life? What was to be done with the Jews themselves who were living within the Reich boundaries? What was to be done with those Jews acquired as a result of frontier adjustments and land acquisitions in the East? The nature of the problem is stated in pages and pages of invective in *Mein Kampf*. But to state the problem is not to solve it, and *Mein Kampf* does not supply a great deal by way of a solution.

Two suggestions are apparent from the text. Those persons of inferior status (the Jews) were to be collected and sealed off in ghettoes on Reich or Reich-occupied territory, or they were to be lifted and transported elsewhere to establish their national home outside Reich territory. Both suggestions were to be adopted in later years.[4] There is certainly no mention in *Mein Kampf* of the 'final solution', as was ultimately the case, and there is no evidence of any long-term conspiracy with that object in mind; yet such a solution was inherent in and consistent with the literalism of Nazi philosophy.

The keystone belief in Aryan racial superiority and the Superman

---

Continued from previous page

foreign workers, including many Jews were imported and used as virtual slave labour in the construction of defensive fortifications. The workers were treated abominably. They were beaten, starved and over 3,000 were literally worked to death, with no medical care. Victor Carey, Bailiff of Guernsey, supplied the Germans with the names of all Jews resident on the island and co-operated throughout. The German Alderney Commandant, Major Carl Hofmann, was never brought to justice for his ill-treatment of Jews and others, for fear that the scale of British collaboration would become public knowledge. A secret report on this collaboration by Captain Theodore Pantcheff of British Intelligence MI9, commissioned immediately after the liberation in 1944, has never seen the light of day. Victor Carey was awarded a knighthood (see *The Model Occupation* by Madeleine Bunting).

[4]Heydrich's Lublin Plan was an example of the former, the Madagascar Plan of the latter.

ideal which carried that belief beyond conventional morality had an obvious relevance to the Jewish question. This sort of logical progression in Nazi thinking had already been demonstrated in dealing with the problem of the unfit, the mentally deranged, the incapacitated, the psychiatric inadequates. Those embarrassments to the ideal of Aryan supremacy had to be eradicated. Morality did not come into it. The end would justify the means. The logical thread was discriminatory legislation, voluntary sterilisation, compulsory sterilisation, euthanasia. By June 1940 euthanasia centres had been established to bring to an end the lives of those deemed incurably unfit. It was therefore a logical projection to believe that there would arise a parallel with the Jewish problem.

The search for a solution to the Jewish problem and the development of relevant policy objectives occupied many senior minds within the Nazi hierarchy during the 1930s. But the matter was still unresolved in terms of execution in May 1941. Rather had the problem been much accentuated by the acquisition of territories, both before and since the commencement of war. The Jewish populations of Austria, Czechoslovakia, Poland, Norway, France and the Low Countries added to the problem. At first sight, it is not apparent why the problem had not been attacked immediately on Hitler's accession to power in 1933. Ernst Roehm and his Brownshirt followers thought that it should have been and were punished for their beliefs in the Night of the Long Knives on June 30, 1934. But Hitler was a cleverer political animal than Roehm and knew that he had to play the Jewish card carefully. German rearmament and friendship with Great Britain were early policy objectives. Both were affected by the Jewish issue.

Economics Minister Hjalmar Schacht looked to the private owners of industry to produce the required economic miracle. Some were Jews and others included Jews among their senior and middle-order management. Neither Hitler or Schacht were going to disturb those arrangements in early days by any sort of discriminatory legislation. The goose that was to lay the golden eggs was to be undisturbed. In the same way, Hitler knew that any radical design and implementation of policy as to the Jews might well affect the susceptibilities of the British. The British were to be befriended as a prelude to adventures in foreign policy. They were not to be antagonised by anti-Semitic legislation and behaviour. Hitler alone decided priorities.

In the early days of power, the Jewish problem was for the best of reasons, left on the back-burner. Relegated in terms of political expediency it may have been. Fundamental tenet of faith, it remained. The internal organisation of both the State and the Nazi Party were also a factor. There was no single department or departmental head charged with the specific task of supplying an answer to the problem. As a result, many hares were set running by departmental heads in charge of other activities. It was known that the Führer wanted rid of 'the Jewish nightmare' and he did not need to issue specific instructions to specific members of his hierarchy to get the ideas flowing. But the growth and eventual size of the problem went far beyond the scope of suggestions made; which in any case were usually squeezed out of consideration for implementation by the sort of priorities already mentioned. That did not prevent every and any suggestion made being labelled 'the final solution', an expression of hope rather than accomplishment.

The earliest attempts to attack the problem took the form of discriminatory legislation emanating largely from Rudolf Hess. The legislation was designed to eradicate Jewish influences from German national life by planting obstacles in the way of Jewish advancement in public and private life. This would demean the Jew and, it was hoped, would lead to his voluntary emigration. Voluntary emigration to Palestine was encouraged by the Haavara Agreement under the terms of which Jews could emigrate to Palestine and take at least some of their financial resources with them, providing the arrangements were tied in with reciprocal arrangements for German exports to the Zionists.[5,6] The Hess legislation was on the statute book in 1933, the first year of his administration as party boss. It restricted the participation of non-Aryans in the Civil Service, the legal and medical profession and certain educational establishments.

This legislation was popular in Germany. It evoked no particular comment abroad. The general view was that the internal matters of a particular state were not the concern of other states. The German national saw the legislation as a natural continuance of an anti-Semitism already in evidence before the advent of Hitler. As to outsiders, their own drawing-room anti-Semitism no doubt sedated any feelings of moral outrage. In any case, most outsiders, and certainly Great Britain, had far more on their political plates by way of unemployment and economic depression to concern themselves about the rights of foreign nationals and wandering Jews in far-away countries.

Pressure for more extreme legislation soon followed. After the

---

[5]Yisraeli, David, *The Third Reich and the Transfer Agreement: Journal of Contemporary History*, VI/2 (1971), 129–31.

[6]In 1937 Rosenberg told Winterbotham of British Air Intelligence that it was hoped to encourage Jewish voluntary emigration to Brazil (Winterbotham, F.W., *The Nazi Connection*, Weidenfeld and Nicolson (1978), 140). As late as 1940 Himmler was fostering a plan for the emigration of Jews to America in exchange for hard currency (Padfield, Peter, *Hess: Flight for the Führer*, Weidenfeld and Nicolson (1991), 131).

demise of Roehm and his disciples agitation for further action against the Jews was taken up by Julius Streicher, the Gauleiter of Nuremberg and noted Jew-baiter. This pressure culminated in the infamous Nuremberg Laws promulgated by Hess in September 1935. These laws attacked a fundamental civil right, the right to marry whoever one should choose. Both marriage and extramarital relations between Jews and Aryans were specifically forbidden by the legislation (as was the hiring of young Aryan maids by Jewish households). Although fundamental human rights were now being trampled underfoot, foreign reaction was again muted.

In the following year, the soft pedal was applied. It was the year of the Berlin Olympic Games. There would be many distinguished British visitors. They were not to be affronted by overt displays of anti-Semitism. The pedal was not easy to apply. Public opinion in Germany was running ahead of Hess's legislation. Jew-baiting was a popular pastime. Street notices were appearing in towns and villages throughout the Reich which read 'Jews strictly forbidden in this town', 'Jews enter this place at own risk', 'Drive carefully. Sharp bend. Jews at unrestricted speeds'.[7] Apart from such insulting notices, all of which had to be taken down before the (mainly) British visitors arrived, there were other restrictions. Some shops refused to serve Jews, some hotels would not provide accommodation, chemists would not supply medicines and dairies would not supply milk for Jewish children.[8]

In 1938 the German Jewish issue began to receive attention from the international press for the first time. There had been significant developments in the size and nature of the problem and the measures taken to alleviate it. In March 1938, German troops occupied Austria. Hitler's long-awaited dream of the Anschluss had become a reality. There were two important consequences in terms of the Jewish question. An immediate consequence was the appalling physical ill-treatment handed out to Austrian Jews by Austrian Nazis while German troops of the occupying army stood aside. This ill-treatment certainly equalled, if not exceeded, anything that had already been the case in Germany. Jews of all classes, but particularly the intelligentsia and academics were dragged out into the streets and publicly humiliated in front of jeering crowds. University professors were ordered to sweep the streets and act as lavatory attendants. Those in public

---

[7]Shirer, William L., *The Rise and Fall of the Third Reich*, Pan Books (1964), 290–91.

[8]In view of the privations and indignities suffered by the Jews in Germany as early as 1936 and the trend towards more extreme measures, it is remarkable that more Jews did not take the opportunity of leaving Germany and starting a new life elsewhere. In 1938 there were still 400,000 Jews left in Germany, half of whom were unemployed.

service were stripped of their offices and their places taken by those of Aryan blood, irrespective of their academic or other qualifications.[9] There were 70,000 arrests in Vienna alone in the first weeks of the occupation and a vast concentration camp was constructed at Mauthausen on the Danube.

The further consequence of the German occupation was the first attempt to use mass emigration (deportation would be a more accurate word) as a means of ridding the Greater Reich of Jews. Reinhart Heydrich of the German Secret Police sent his Jewish expert, Adolf Eichmann, to Vienna to organise the mass emigration of Jews to Palestine. In legal terms the emigration was voluntary, but the terror tactics and threats which later became commonplace were used by way of persuasion. In some cases, this persuasion included the payment of the costs of emigration of the poorer Jews by others more generously endowed. In the short term and from a German point of view the Eichmann plan was successful.[10] It also established Eichmann and the SS as acknowledged specialists in dealing with the Jewish question and guaranteed SS involvement in any future schemes;[11] and it proved that the movement of the Jews *en masse* could be organised, by terror tactics if necessary, provided that a base for their resettlement had been established first. The suggestions contained within *Mein Kampf* were becoming practical possibilities.

Nevertheless, the brutal treatment of the Austrian Jews and the manner of their emigration to Palestine were widely reported, and for the first time the world at large – Great Britain and America in particular – became aware that the abuses being perpetrated went far beyond what might be expected of a modern European state with any pretensions to civilised standards of behaviour. In addition to a generally hostile world press, those Jews who emigrated to Palestine talked when they arrived and corresponded with their friends and relatives in Great Britain and America. German persecution of the Jews thus became an international topic for discussion.

Later in the same year, on the night of November 10–11, a further demonstration of Nazi violence against the Jews rejuvenated the international press campaign against the Nazi Government. The circumstances relating to the *Kristallnacht* have already been explained. On that night, Reinhard Heydrich executed a plan suggested by Goebbels

[9]As recounted to the author by a personal acquaintance, an Austrian Jewess who fled the country after the Anschluss.

[10]In the long term it had the opposite effect. The flood of immigrants to Palestine caused the British to install a system of quotas. This shut the door to the further mass movement of Jews from Germany/Austria to Palestine.

[11]This involvement became an important factor in connection with the Madagascar Plan.

and approved by Hitler for a 'spontaneous' demonstration of violence and fire-raising, directed against Jews throughout Germany and Austria in their homes, their synagogues, their shops and other business establishments. There was widespread death, destruction and damage, all for the first time Government-inspired and encouraged, and these facts were reported. World opinion, shocked and revolted, expressed itself accordingly. The mood had much changed. In October of the previous year, the leader on *The Times* was still stating 'German internal policies, however awful, are no one else's concern except in matters of religious persecution.'[12] One year later, after *Kristallnacht*, a letter to the *Times* was stating 'I cannot believe that [Adolf Hitler] can have given his sanction to this deplorable action, especially at this crucial moment in the international situation.'[13]

Those last few words were so true. If Hitler was still looking for Great Britain's hand in friendship the recent activities in both Austria and Germany had done much to make such an event an impossibility. A British opinion poll conducted immediately following the receipt of reports concerning the *Kristallnacht* pogrom asked the question 'Do you think that the persecution of the Jews in Germany is an obstacle to good understanding between Great Britain and Germany?' Seventy-three per cent responded with a 'Yes', 15 per cent said 'No', 12 per cent were undecided. In spite of (or perhaps even because of) these serious repercussions abroad, Hitler, or rather his lieutenants, appeared to have taken the bit between the teeth in making a positive attempt to deal with the Jewish question.

The screw was turned further. Hermann Goering was appointed to co-ordinate all the work being done in connection with Jewish affairs. One of his first acts was to 'Aryanise' German industry by dismissing those Jewish personnel whom Schacht had previously retained in positions of responsibility. They were replaced by those of Aryan blood. At the same time, Heydrich was advocating the large-scale emigration of Jews. The Eichmann initiative in Austria was quoted as the type of operation which could be reproduced.

There were difficulties, however. Palestine was subject to British immigration quotas. Other countries were not anxious to receive what they saw as impoverished refugees without resources and without skills – there was a good deal of anti-Semitic feeling, especially in Eastern Europe – and there were logistical problems. Not least, every emigrant Jew carried with him virulent anti-Nazi propaganda that

---

[12]It was not explained to *Times* readers why religious persecution was not acceptable but the persecution of Jews was.
[13]*The Times*, November 16, 1938.

served no good cause as far as German foreign policy was concerned. By 1938, Germany was virtually free of Jewish interests and influences. She was not free of Jews. There were still 400,000 Jews living in Germany and Austria. In January 1939, Goering gave support to Heydrich's concept of mass emigration. He authorised Heydrich to establish a Reich control office for the purpose of organising Jewish emigration, along the lines already demonstrated by Eichmann in Austria. Meanwhile, the problems became exacerbated. The onset of war in September 1939 closed down emigration as an option. At the same time, a series of military successes led to the acquisition of additional territory and additional Jews. Clearly, new thinking was necessary.[14]

The new thinking came not from Goering or Heydrich but from the German Foreign Office. In terms of history the German Foreign Office had always looked to a moderated approach to the problem. Most of its personnel were mildly anti-Semitic and like most Germans viewed with little satisfaction the heavy emigration of Jews into Germany from the East immediately after the 1914–18 war. It supported Hess's discriminatory legislation and looked to encourage voluntary emigration. It was also more aware than most of the susceptibilities of foreigners to any perceived ill-treatment of Jews and the effect that might have on Anglo-German relations. In early days it had supported the orderly emigration of Jews to Palestine, under the terms of the Haavara Agreement and Schacht's retention of Jews in some of the key industrial posts.

In 1938 Baron von Neurath was replaced by Joachim von Ribbentrop as Foreign Minister. Neurath was an old-style diplomat. Ribbentrop was a new-style Nazi. He did not take kindly to being left on the side lines while Goering and Heydrich were let loose to promote policies in connection with the Jews which could be so damaging to German foreign policy. Ribbentrop soon gained representation on the committee of the Reich Central Office dealing with all Jewish emigration. The advent of war in September opened the door wider for Foreign Office involvement in Jewish affairs. There were two reasons. The war had brought the Goering/Heydrich emigration policies to a standstill. Palestine was no longer an option and the British Navy controlled the seas. In the second place, any peace treaty drawn by Germany with any defeated enemy (which would of course be the responsibility of the German Foreign Office) would have to include terms to cover the

[14]There is no evidence to suggest that this new thinking included considerations of systematic extermination. Both the alternative suggestions made were along the lines suggested by Hitler himself in *Mein Kampf*, and both therefore had his support.

proposed treatment of the Jewish population.[15] This was to be the case particularly as far as Great Britain was concerned.[16]

The German diplomatic documents contain a memorandum of a conversation between Dahlerus, the Swedish peace mediator, and Hitler in the presence of Goering on September 26, 1939. A German peace overture is about to be made to Great Britain. Dahlerus makes the point that the British would have to be satisfied as to the fate of the Polish and other Jews and appropriate terms would have to be included in any peace treaty. Hitler's reply is significant. It repeats his original comments in *Mein Kampf* and also foreshadows the arrangements that were then actually in hand. His reply was 'The organisation of Poland would provide any asylum there for the Jews.'

That position is further confirmed in the same official German diplomatic documents covering October/November 1939. Correspondence from William de Ropp, the double agent, to Rosenberg asks what was to become of Poland under the terms of any peace treaty. Rosenberg's reply confirms that of Hitler. Part of Poland would go to Germany for exclusive use by German residents, the second part to be known as Congress Poland would be for the exclusive use of Polish residents. The third part would be reserved for occupation by the Jews.

These official pronouncements made as it were, from the horse's mouth tally with what was actually happening. Blocked from any solution provided by emigration, Heydrich had turned his attention to the possibilities of mass deportation and the setting up of a massive Jewish ghetto around the Polish town of Lublin. By his decree of September 21, with backing from Hitler, all Jews throughout Germany and the occupied territories were to be relocated in cities adjoining the west/east railway which would ultimately carry them eastwards to Lublin, which would become an area designated exclusively for Jewish resettlement.

The deportations commenced in December 1939 and in the first two months 200,000 Jews were transferred to the Lublin area. It was perhaps inevitable that logistic problems with the mass movement of so many would intervene, and this was soon the case at the resettlement area. In March 1940 Goering was obliged to call a halt. The operation was not resumed. The Lublin Plan, brainchild of Heydrich and Eichmann was dead. Up to then, the contribution from the German Foreign Office towards Jewish affairs had been minimal. Others had dominated the field. Hess had brought in his discriminatory legisla-

[15]It will be seen how the details of the Madagascar Plan were to be included in any peace terms offered to Great Britain.
[16]Documents of German Foreign Policy, Volume 8, September 4, 1939, to March 18, 1940.

tion, Goering had Aryanised German industry, Heydrich and Eichmann had pursued a vigorous but, in the long term, a failed policy of voluntary then enforced deportation and resettlement. All had failed.

In May 1940 the German Foreign Office under Ribbentrop reorganised its department dealing with Jewish affairs and reconstituted it under the name and style of Jüdenreferat DIII. New blood was introduced into the department. It was headed by Franz Rademacher aged only 34 at the time of his appointment. Within a matter of three months the new incumbent had produced a comprehensive plan to deal with the Jewish question in all its aspects. The plan was well thought out, carefully researched and well presented. It was known as the Madagascar Plan. Rademacher's immediate boss was Martin Franz Julius Luther, second man at the Foreign Office to Ribbentrop. Luther's background was dubious (he was a bankrupt and had faced embezzlement charges), he was an emotional and physical cripple and almost universally disliked by his superiors. He was also ambitious, very good at his job and an excellent manager of staff, who repaid him with a fierce and lasting loyalty. He was anxious that the new Jüdenreferat DIII under Rademacher should make its mark and push the Foreign Office representation in Jewish affairs to centre stage, and he was fortunate in the selection of Rademacher as section leader. Rademacher was young and anxious to win his spurs at senior level. His origins were ordinary (he was the son of a train driver) but his rise to professional prominence had been rapid. He was a self made man. His education had led him into the legal profession, his Nazi indoctrination into Roehm's Brownshirts. He had found the two spheres of activity incompatible, had resigned his position with the SA and migrated into the Foreign Office, where he had become well versed and well read on the Jewish question. Luther's ambitions sat comfortably on the shoulders of young Rademacher.

The concept of Madagascar as a national home for European Jewry cannot be ascribed to Rademacher. Some 20 years previously the Dutch anti-Semite, H.H. Beamish, had suggested Madagascar as the island to which all Jews should be transported.[17] Thereafter, the idea had been resurrected from time to time by various members of the Nazi hierarchy in their sometimes frantic hunt for a quick solution to an extreme problem. Certainly, the concept fitted to what we know of Hitler's own thoughts. In *Mein Kampf* he had suggested that those of 'inferior' race should either be collected together in ghettoes in Reich or Reich-occupied territories or that they be removed entirely from

[17]Rademacher affidavit, July 20, 1940.

Reich territories and resettled elsewhere.[18–19] But Rademacher developed the Madagascar concept into a detailed plan and obtained the approval not only of his superiors at the Foreign Office but also of Hitler himself. The manner in which he developed the concept and obtained his approvals is related in various memoranda and copy correspondence held in the German Foreign Office archives at Bonn which are still open for public inspection.

Rademacher produced his first draft memorandum on the Madagascar project for internal circulation around his department within less than one month of his appointment. This suggested that all European Jews should be deported and that the only three realistic alternatives in terms of destination were Lublin, Madagascar or Palestine.[20] On June 24 there is copy correspondence from Heydrich to Ribbentrop acknowledging that although 200,000 Jews had emigrated voluntarily since January 1939 voluntary emigration could no longer cope with the size of the problem. There had to be a territorial solution, with a particular territory earmarked for the deportation.[21] It is apparent from this correspondence that Heydrich knew that the Foreign Office was working on some plan and Heydrich did not wish to miss out in its participation. Rademacher acknowledges this in a further memorandum on July 2, headed *Plan zur Lösung der Jüdenfrage*, which refers to the requirement that France was to cede Madagascar to Germany under mandate. Subject to the reservation of strategic points as military bases, the remainder of the island was to accommodate the Jewish immigration. Madagascar would then become a self contained and self operated Jewish community subject to overall German control through the SS.[22]

On July 3 a further Rademacher memorandum makes it clear that the Madagascar Plan was to be included in the peace treaties to deal with the Jewish question.[23] Twenty-five thousand French residents on the island were to be repatriated to France.[24] On July 17 there is a memorandum showing Rademacher's researches into the number of

---

[18]An Oswald Mosley pamphlet of January 21, 1939, suggested that 'the final solution to the Jewish problem was a national home in some waste but potentially fertile area'.

[19]Winston Churchill was apparently aware of German thinking. In February 1941, only a matter of weeks before Hess's flight, he had taunted the Australian Prime Minister, Robert Menzies, saying 'Adolf Hitler thinks that sixteen million Jews ought to go and live in Australia. What do you say to that?' (Menzies Diary, March 2, 1941).

[20]PA Inland IIg 177 T120/1512/372108.

[21]*Ibid*, 372047.

[22]*Ibid*, 372104.

[23]By then a peace treaty with Great Britain was confidently expected in addition to that with France, already defeated.

[24]PA Inland IIg 177 T120/1512/372109/11.

European Jews involved and how they could be accommodated within the confines of the island. Dr Burgdorfer, a well-known demographer and president of the Bavarian State Office of Statistics, had calculated an ultimate Jewish population of 10.3 million. The population density was calculated at 16 per sq km, which was stated to be about the average for the world's surface and only about one tenth of that then prevailing in Germany.[25] On August 2 Luther informed Rademacher that Ribbentrop had formally approved the plan in principle.[26] On August 15 Luther reported to Rademacher in a letter that 'the Führer has said at the beginning of August in a speech about France that he wants to evacuate all Jews from Europe after the war.'[27]

Thus encouraged, Rademacher completed his researches into the climatic conditions and mineral resources of the island and then dealt with the economic aspects of the proposed deportations. Monies received from the confiscated property and assets of the Jews in Europe were to be used to fund the costs of the deportation, provide initial capital for a Central Bank in Madagascar for development purposes and to finance individual Jewish enterprises on the island. His detailed proposals are set down in his memorandum of August 12, *Gedanken über die Gründung einer intereuropäischen Bank für die Verwertung des Jüden Vermögens in Europa.*

On August 30, in response to Ribbentrop's request. Rademacher set down the full details of the Madagascar Plan for inclusion in the peace treaties. The document is lengthy and detailed. The plan was Rademacher's dreamchild and he had spent much time in its preparation. It covered every aspect of the proposed deportations, the inclusion of the plan in the peace treaties, SS involvement, transport arrangements, the administration of the island, a four-year plan for development, economic and financial arrangements, publicity and propaganda, the participating agencies and a proposed commission, with Rademacher as the project co-ordinator. In September, Hitler informed Mussolini and Ciano that the Madagascar Plan was the answer to the Jewish question. All was to take place 'after the war', that is as and when terms for peace had been agreed with Great Britain.[28]

The Madagascar Plan was of course stillborn. Hess's peace mission failed. Great Britain continued to control the seas and the plan could not be implemented even though it had been approved at the highest

---

[25]PA Inland IIg A/B 35/2 T120/3071/D612577-80.
[26]PA Inland IIg 177 T120/1512/372108.
[27]*Ibid*, 372049.
[28]*Ibid*, 372050-2.

level. Perhaps the most significant document on file in Bonn is a copy of a memorandum from Goering to Heydrich, dated July 31, 1941. By that time, the failure of Hess's mission had become apparent. The memorandum simply states 'Find a solution to the Jewish problem and include all organisational and economic details.'[29] Heydrich did just that. The Holocaust followed. On January 20, 1942, Heydrich's new 'arrangements' which he had operated since the commencement of Operation Barbarossa were formalised at the infamous Wannsee Conference. Four days later Rademacher acknowledged that the Madagascar Plan was dead in a memorandum to his boss, Luther.[30]

There is a further significant document on file. A memorandum dated August 21, 1942, sets down in summary and chronological order the various steps which had been taken to find a solution to the Jewish problem. The document records the 1940 solution as the Madagascar Plan, which is specifically stated to be 'Führer Approved'. It then follows up with the crucial date of July 31, 1941, as mentioned above, when Goering gave authority to Heydrich to find an alternative solution. The third date included is the date of the Wannsee Conference which formally approved Heydrich's 'Final solution in the East'.[31]

The documents on file at the German Foreign Office archives at Bonn have been quoted extensively for two reasons. When from June 1941 onwards the Jews were being transported to the East to take their place in Heydrich's extermination camps, they were sometimes told that they were en route for Madagascar. At that time the Madagascar project was used as a cover name for the extermination camps. For this reason, it has been suggested that the Madagascar Plan was never anything other than a cover for the Holocaust, which was always the original intention. There is no evidence for this. The documents at Bonn are genuine and prove otherwise. They show that the plan was a genuine attempt to solve the Jewish problem, approved for implementation at the highest level. The plan looked to deal with the problem by the resettlement of Jews in an island territory which would have become their native home.

The other important point turns on the significance of the dates. On May 10, 1941, at the time Hess flew to Great Britain in search of peace, the Madagascar Plan was the official German plan to deal with the Jewish problem and would have been a suggested term for inclu-

---

[29] *Ibid*, page 190.
[30] *Ibid*, page 185.
[31] *Ibid*, 371976/94.

sion in any peace treaty negotiated with Great Britain.[32] Rudolf Hess knew that. He almost certainly knew also what Heydrich's solution to the problem would be if his peace mission failed and Operation Barbarossa launched.

[32]Having regard to the continuous strife and bloodshed caused by the eventual Jewish settlements in Palestine, the proposed allocation of island exclusivity in Madagascar for the setting up of a Jewish national home may, in retrospect, have had advantages not fully appreciated at the time. Of course, voluntary emigration was one thing. Compulsory deportation was quite another. The Holocaust was yet another.

22

Saturday, May 10, 1941

Raid 42. Bandits on the Filter Board at 2200 hours. Normal action to intercept and shoot down.

RAF TURNHOUSE, May 11, 1941

According to the official version of events, after Hess took off from Augsburg in his Messerschmitt 110 fighter aircraft during the early evening of Saturday, May 10, 1941, he first flew across heavily defended German airspace in the Rhineland and north-west Europe without permission but without attracting any attention or alerting air defences. He then navigated himself across the North Sea alone, unaided and unescorted. His unarmed aircraft then crossed the British coast in broad daylight, avoiding all British air defences. He then intended to land his Me110 aircraft on the hillside landing strip at Dungavel House in Renfrewshire, the residence of the Duke of Hamilton, and there conduct peace talks with the Duke who he hoped would be in residence together with other representatives of a British Peace Party that, in fact, did not exist. If that were all true, then Hess certainly was deranged, as the official version describes him. Fortunately, in the interests of his sanity and ours, the facts tell a very different story.

In the first place, Hess could not have flown his aircraft unmolested across some of Germany's most heavily defended airspace without authority being given at the highest level and the defences alerted to take no action. Radar was being used extensively by Germany in 1941 and a *Himmelbett* (Heavenbed) radar zone covered the whole section of north Germany and Holland over which Hess flew, including the coastal areas and at least 40 miles beyond that out to sea. Hess's aircraft must therefore have been plotted and, in so far as it was unmolested, the flight must have had official blessing. Much has been made about a telephone call made by Goering to Adolf Galland, the

German fighter ace, then commanding a German Fighter Group on the Channel coast. Galland was instructed by Goering to intercept Hess's aircraft and shoot it down. Goering had apparently been tipped off by Pintsch that Hess was flying out of Germany on a peace mission and had to be stopped. Galland confirms these circumstances in his own memoirs.[1] He stated that he scrambled some fighter aircraft but in view of the fading light (described as 'ten minutes to darkness') no contact was made and the fighter aircraft returned to base.

The significant factor in Galland's account is the reference to the fading light. That puts the time at approximately 2200 hours mid-European time, by which time Hess was in fact approaching the Northumberland coast. There was therefore never any possibility of an interception. It is apparent that Goering's telephone call which led to Galland's subsequent belated action was part of a charade to sustain the story of Hess's individual escapade. It also confirms that both Goering and Hitler were playing their respective parts. If then, the Hess flight had official backing is it at all likely that Hess would have been unescorted on his long and arduous flight over the North Sea and on the approach to British airspace? It is an unreasonable assumption.

Hess had been a competent flyer in the later stages of the 1914–18 conflict and in the years thereafter, but by 1941 he was no longer a young man or an experienced flyer. Also, the Messerschmitt 110 aircraft was not an easy machine to fly. It was an aircraft vulnerable to attack. Its record in the Battle of Britain had been anything but distinguished. It lacked manoeuvrability and had been a sitting duck for British Spitfires and Hurricanes. And Hess's aircraft was unarmed.

In these circumstances, and having regard to the importance of the mission, prudence demanded that Hess be escorted. There are three clear indications that he was. In the first place, the time actually taken on the flight does not equate with the distance travelled. There must have been some sort of diversion which took up air travelling time. A meeting up with others could provide an explanation. According to Helmut Kaden,[2] the airfield manager at Augsburg and a man closely associated with Hess in all his previous training flights, Hess's route would have taken him northwards from Augsburg. He would have passed over Würzburg, Hanover and Hamburg and then continuing northwards he would have flown up to the Frisian Islands to Jutland before turning west across the North Sea. He would then use as his navigational aide the radio beam emanating from the Danish station of

---

[1]And in correspondence with the author. Galland confirmed that Goering's call was 'at about 10 o'clock just as the light was fading.'
[2]In an address given in Munich on November 23, 1989.

Kalundborg. This would set him on course for the Northumberland coast.[3] This northerly route suggested by Kaden is supported by Hess's own booking of his training flight on the morning of May 10, when he entered his destination as Norway. The Kaden route to the Northumberland extended in total to some 1,600 kilometres, well within the range of the Me110 with its extra fuel tanks.

On the basis of a cruising speed of approximately 400km an hour, Kaden estimated that Hess would have made landfall on the Northumberland coast at about 2200 hours mid-European time, or 2100 hours Greenwich time. In fact, Hess crossed the coast at about 2208 hours Greenwich time. He was over an hour late. Where had he been and what had he been doing? We do not have far to look. When Hess first approached the coast, the radar defence screens at Ottercops Moss, midway between Newcastle and Farne Islands, reported not one blip on their screens but 'three plus aircraft'. As Hess neared the coast he brought his aircraft down to 50 feet. This took his aircraft off the radar screens. Radar then reported that the echoes on Raid X42 were fading and moving back out to sea in a north-easterly direction. The operational record books of the RAF coastal defence fighter squadrons show clearly that there were no RAF fighters in that area at that time. It is therefore apparent that the fading 'blips' were German fighter-escort aircraft returning to base. It is also apparent that whatever arrangements had been made for the rendezvous over the North Sea so that Hess could meet up with his fighter escort would account for the extra hour of Hess's flight time.

It is even possible to identify at least one of Hess's escorts. By doing so, it draws attention to the importance placed on the mission by Hitler. The escort in question was Reinhardt Heydrich, Chief of the SS Security Service. Heydrich was the sort of man who involved himself personally in any major secret mission undertaken by his department. He played a major part in the Venlo incident of November 1939. He had personally organised the Polish frontier incidents which had provided the pretext for the invasion of Poland in September 1939. In a postwar interview, Heydrich's widow confirmed that on May 10 her husband had been flying a Messerschmitt 109 aircraft from a base on the Channel coast. Confirmation of these activities is also provided by Heydrich's Chief of Police, Arthur Nebe. Nebe had told his contacts

[3]Kaden rejects the flight plan reportedly drawn by Hess while in British custody and which has received considerable publicity ever since its first (and incongruous) inclusion in the 1947 book by J.R. Rees, dealing with Hess's psychiatry. Kaden was adamant that Hess would not have reproduced his actual flight plan because it would have revealed its dependence upon the then highly secret use of radio beams as navigational aids.

with the German resistance that Heydrich was flying over the North Sea on May 10, 1941.[4] Heydrich was a busy man and an important man in the Nazi hierarchy. The fact that he was detached from his other responsibilities to ensure Hess's safe delivery to Great Britain in complete secrecy indicates the degree of importance attached to the project.

Perhaps the most extraordinary part of the Hess flight was yet to come, after he entered British airspace and crossed the Northumberland coast. His progress was plotted meticulously as reports from the Royal Observer Corps (ROC) posts and radar defences were fed into the nerve centres of the RAF defence system. But no defences swung into action. No fighter aircraft of the RAF or anti-aircraft fire from the Army disturbed the single German aircraft as it flew across the whole breadth of Scotland from east to west and back again in broad daylight. Either the British defences were extraordinarily incompetent or Hess's unimpeded flight was in accordance with previously agreed arrangements.[5]

There is plenty of evidence to show that the latter was the case. As Hess crossed the coast near the Farne Islands he skimmed over the village of Belford at rooftop level.[6] At 2223 hours the (ROC) post A2 at Embleton on the coast, ten miles south of the Farne Islands, was reporting a second bearing on Hess's aircraft. At 2225 hours ROC post A3 at Chalton, ten miles south-west of Belford, was reporting an Me110 at 50ft. Further sightings of the Me110 were subsequently reported at 2230 hours from ROC post F2 across the Scottish border at Jedburgh and at 2231 hours from ROC post G1 at Ashkirk. The RAF controller at Ouston, south of Newcastle, initially dismissed the reports of an Me110. Having regard to the aircraft's supposed return journey the controller concluded that an Me110 was way beyond its range of operation. He therefore substituted a Dornier Do210 instead of an Me110. The Controller of Fighter Command followed suit[7] Their reasoning was correct. Their conclusions were wrong.

Meanwhile, ROC centre No 34 in Glasgow was continuing to plot the Me110 flying westwards at 300 mph. ROC post G3 at Kilbride on the Firth of Clyde, 25 miles south-west of Glasgow, saw the Me110 flying below the level of the observer post and then swing round over the Firth to head back across Scotland in an easterly direction. Finally,

---

[4]*Reinhard Heydrich: Schlüsselfigur des Dritten Reiches*, Edward Calic.

[5]It is perhaps significant that after capture, Hess never enquired how it was that he had avoided all contact with British defences while over British airspace.

[6]The Royal Observer Corps sightings which follow are a matter of record.

[7]Padfield, Peter, *Hess: Flight for the Führer*, Weidenfeld and Nicolson (1991), 200.

ROC post H2, situated on the edge of Eaglesham Moor some 12 miles north-west of Dungavel House, saw Hess bale out of his aircraft, having run out of fuel.[8] It was 2309 Greenwich time. All these sightings had been fed into the ROC and RAF nerve centres, providing the data for appropriate defensive action.

Examination of the records now available show that no defensive action was taken. Fighter Command Instruction 17 issued in March 1941 to 13 Group, which included the air space in question, makes it clear that standing patrols by single-engined fighter aircraft were to be maintained constantly to intercept any enemy attacks made between Glasgow and Newcastle-upon-Tyne.[9] According to the RAF Operational Record Books (ORB) for May 10, 1941, no such patrols were in the air at 2200 hours. The coast patrols landed at 2110 hours. These were Spitfire patrols completed well before Hess crossed the coast. They were not replaced. There is an official report from RAF Turnhouse west of Edinburgh, dated May 11 as to the action taken to deal with the Hess aircraft, designated as Raid 42. There is no reason why the report should have been made by RAF Turnhouse. The Hess aircraft crossed the coast in a defence sector south of that controlled from RAF Turnhouse, which therefore should have had no operational responsibility for the defensive measures taken or not to be taken.

The Commanding Officer of RAF Turnhouse was Wing Commander the Duke of Hamilton, who was on duty that night. His report referred to 'bandits on the Filter Board at 2200 hours. Normal action to intercept and shoot down.' Hamilton issued a later statement. According to his recollection 'Spitfires at Drem [in East Lothian] were brought to readiness and a section of Hurricanes from Acklington or Bulmer [in Northumberland] were dispatched but went very wide of the mark.'[10] Hamilton's report and subsequent recollections are not supported by the ORB records. No Hurricanes were dispatched from either Acklington or Bulmer. A single Spitfire was scrambled from 72 Squadron at Acklington, but that was not until 2220 hours, a full 12 minutes after Hess had crossed the coast and 15 minutes after the first radar plot had been received. The Spitfire was not airborne until 2223 hours, by which time the Me110 had long since departed travelling west. The Spitfire pilot, Flight Sergeant Pocock, has since confirmed that he was scrambled far too late to make an interception.[11]

Why then was there the delay? It appears that the scramble was

---

[8]As confirmed by Hess in a letter to Ilse.
[9]PRO AIR 25/242.
[10]Air Vice-Marshal Sandy Johnstone, CB DFC, *Where no Angels Dwell*, London (1969), 90.
[11]Costello, John, *Ten Days that Saved the West*, Bantam Press (1991), 6–7.

more of a gesture than any real attempt to do battle with the Me110. The only other aircraft actually scrambled according to the record was a Boulton Paul Defiant Fighter from 141 Squadron at Ayr on the west coast. The Defiant neither saw or attacked the Me110. That is no surprise. The Defiant was a conspicuous failure as a front-line fighter aircraft. It was cumbersome and slow, with a rear gun turret necessitating a second crew member. It had no hope of catching an Me110 in full flight. In a later official report from RAF Turnhouse it was reported that 'a Defiant was scrambled from Prestwick and was soon hot on the tail.'[12] In fact, the Defiant was scrambled from Ayr, not Prestwick, and sat on no one's tail.

The really significant point about the Defiant's entry into the story is that as it lumbered into the air, Spitfires and Hurricanes sat on the Ayr tarmac watching it. As in the case of Galland's ineffective scrambling of the German coastal fighters and the late scrambling of the Acklington Spitfire, so the lone Defiant appears to have been invited to take his place in the charade. Hard evidence that defensive intent was never there is provided by Cecil Bryant, then aged 20, who was a radio telephone operator employed in the 'R' Sector control room at Usworth, near Sunderland. This was the sector directly responsible for operations against the Hess aircraft and which in particular controlled the Spitfires at Ouston in Northumberland and Acklington. As a radio telephone operator, Bryant was the direct link between the sector controller and the fighter aircraft under command. Bryant reported two facts. First of all, when Raid 42 was first plotted following the radar and ROC reports there was a delay of 15 minutes during which no action was taken. During the delay the bandit aircraft was moved across the plotting board and was almost out of the sector at the end of the 15 minutes. This action, or lack of it, was quite outside all normal procedures.

The second fact was even more significant. Bryant reported that he clearly overheard over the telephone the instruction 'This aircraft is not to be attacked.' At the side of Bryant there sat an army major who was in charge of the sector's anti-aircraft defences. Bryant stated that the major was instructed in exactly the same terms.[13] It is hardly surprising that the RAF records relating to the Usworth sector control room are not now available. It is however clear that the RAF response to the Hess intruder aircraft designated Raid 42 comprised the scrambling of a single Spitfire from 72 Squadron at Acklington on the east

---

[12]PRO INF 1/192.

[13]Interview and correspondence with John Costello, November 1989. Costello, John, *Ten Days that Saved the West*, Bantam Press (1991), 6.

coast a full 15 minutes after the Hess aircraft had passed over the coast at 300 mph, to be followed by one obsolete Defiant taking to the air at Ayr on the west coast while any number of available Spitfires and Hurricanes stood idle on the tarmacs at Acklington, Bulmer, Drem and Ayr, all apparently following the general instruction 'This aircraft is not to be attacked'.

On May 22, the Secretary of State for Air reported 'All the usual action was taken to intercept this aircraft and in fact had he not baled out, Hess was in imminent danger of being shot down.'[14] This statement is as untrue as the earlier report from RAF Turnhouse stating that 'normal action had been taken to intercept and shoot down the enemy aircraft.' A comparison of the ORB entries before and after the Raid 42 entries clearly demonstrates the difference between normal defence activities and those applied, or not applied, in the case of Raid 42.[15] It is apparent that the air defences were inoperative for the very good reason that Hess and his aircraft were expected. They were to be protected, not shot down.

It is of course no coincidence that the commanding officer at RAF Turnhouse and the man responsible for the misleading reports as to the defensive action taken was Wing Commander the Duke of Hamilton and Brandon. It was he who on the evening of Saturday, May 10, 1941, when Hess flew in from the North Sea, was on duty as controller in the operations room at RAF Turnhouse when Raid 42 was first picked up by radar. But Hess's aircraft did not cross the coast in the sector controlled by Hamilton. He came in on the sector to the south of Hamilton's. Was it not the case then that had Hess crossed the coast in the 'right' sector he would have been escorted in under Hamilton's control and put down safely to a friendly reception party, rather than having to bale out over Eaglesham Moor? After all, the purpose of the Hess mission was to meet up with Hamilton. Hess said as much when landing by parachute. How better to do that than by approaching the British coast in a sector where the air defences were controlled by Hamilton?

In the event, Hess 'took the wrong turning', missed his escort and finished up having to bale out of an aircraft running out of fuel, a manoeuvre for which he had received no training. The suggestion that Hess was looking for Dungavel House and intended landing the Me110 on the adjoining airstrip is an absurdity. The airstrip was situated on the side of a hill and was suitable for use by only the lightest of aircraft landing at low speeds. It would have been impossible for

[14]PRO AIR 19/564.
[15]PRO AIR 28/624 Ouston ORB.

Hess, a comparatively inexperienced Me110 pilot, to put down a twin-engined Messerschmitt 110 with a high landing speed on a sloping airstrip in the semi-dark. It was never a possibility. It may be that the Dungavel story was inserted as an explanation for Hess's circuitous route flown over Scotland. It is more likely that Hess was looking for promised landing facilities that he had missed by crossing the coast in the wrong sector.

There was of course a most significant point arising from the navigational error arising at the end of Hess's flight. Although he entered the 'wrong' airspace not personally controlled by Hamilton, the defences encountered were still neutered. Hamilton may well have been the personal contact Hess was seeking, but the reception and the arrangements made to silence the air defences must have gone much deeper than any private arrangements between Hess and Hamilton. The British Air Ministry, or at least some of its personnel at senior level, appears to have been overseeing the operation, a role that follows easily and naturally in the light of Hess's known intelligence contacts with MI6 and in particular, British Air Intelligence.

There are two interesting postscripts to the events of May 10, 1941. One again seems to confirm that the Hess mission was backed by Hitler. The other comprises a mysterious confirmation that, at least in Scotland, Hess's arrival was expected. On the night of May 10–11, a matter of a few hours only after Hess had taken off from Augsburg, over 500 bombers took off from their bases in north Germany and the Low Countries to deliver the heaviest aerial bombardment yet against the city of London. Using mostly incendiary bombs, the city was attacked by successive waves of bombers. Over 2,000 fires were started, some of which blazed for days before they were brought under control. Casualties were severe. Over 1,400 Londoners were killed and over 1,600 injured. One of the severely damaged buildings was the House of Commons. Thereafter, the bombing of London and other British cities and towns ended. The airpower of the Luftwaffe was then turned eastwards in preparation of Operation Barbarossa. It is as though this heaviest-ever raid was intended as a curtain-raiser to the Hess peace initiative and to create the right sort of climate for its sympathetic consideration. Hitler was master of the velvet glove/mailed fist technique and here was perhaps yet another example.

The second postscript is one of mystery. In a little village just south of Glasgow, Walter Ramsey was out walking with his young son of the same name. It was late during the evening of Saturday, May 10, 1941. When they heard the sound of aircraft engines approaching, Mr Ramsey said to his son, 'That's probably Rudolf Hess'. Almost immediately thereafter, Mr Ramsey told his son 'Forget what I have just said and talk to no one about it.' From that day until his death, Mr Ramsey never again mentioned the incident. Neither did his son until he met Rudolf Hess's son in February 1976 at Sanaa in the North Yemen, when he recounted the story of the incident. Walter Ramsey was a well-known and well-respected engineer, as indeed was his son in later life. There is no reason to disbelieve the incident.[16] It has been said in hindsight that Scotland was awash with rumours as to a Hess/Hamilton meeting of minds, particularly with Hamilton's pre-war pro-German views in the background. That matter was fairly common knowledge among Scots. But the actual arrival of Hess on the night of May 10–11, 1941, was quite another thing.

If, as appears to be the case, the Hess flight was planned and enabled by those German and British factions interested in bringing an unwanted and unnecessary war to an end, what were the terms for peace that Hess brought with him? It is known that they were set down in a personal letter from Hess to Hamilton which had been translated into English by Hess's confidant, Ernst Bohle. Hess had the letter with him when he flew from Augsburg, but it was taken from him when he was captured. It is one of the many documents presently embargoed by the British Government, but it is not difficult to guess as to at least some of its main contents. Hitler had been as consistent about the conditions under which Anglo-German war could be ended as he had been in the pursuit of his political objectives. In essence they amounted to the simple proposal 'Give me a free hand in central and eastern Europe and I will guarantee the independence of Great Britain and her Empire.' *Mein Kampf* tells us that Hitler's ambitions in central and eastern Europe comprised the acquisition of *Lebensraum* and the destruction of Russian communism. In view of Hitler's consistency of outlook in terms of Anglo-German relations it is hardly likely that the peace terms brought by Hess differed materially from the previous main theme.

In comparative terms these conditions for peace in 1941 were more advantageous to Great Britain than they had ever been before because by May 1941 Hitler already enjoyed a complete hegemony over Europe by reason of his conquests. Any peace proposals were simply to bring to an end the ongoing hostilities. If these terms on offer were in essence the same as those which had been public knowledge since 1939,[17] why has the Hess/Hamilton letter never seen the light of day? Of course, Hess would have brought with him more than the bare

---

[16]Hess, Wolf Rüdiger, *My Father, Rudolf Hess*, W.H. Allen (1986), 21.

[17]They were broadcast to the world in the Hitler peace speeches of October 6, 1939, and July 19, 1940.

bones of the main theme. It is known that Bohle was working on the English translation over many months. Pintsch delivered a 14-page version of the letter to Hitler on May 11.[18] While in captivity Hess prepared a 45-page supplement for Hamilton.[19] None of these documents is available. It is therefore apparent that the need for secrecy relates not so much to the main theme content of the proposals as to the supplementary proposals and comments.

Even Churchill noted at the time, in his own handwriting on one of his memoranda, 'Hess also made other declarations whose revelations could not be in the public interest.'[20] Of course, Hess may have made representations both in the letter to Hamilton and subsequently as to particular British personages who were members of the British Peace Party. He would certainly have mentioned the forthcoming Operation Barbarossa and he may have made suggestions as to Great Britain's active or passive role in that adventure. He may have included suggestions as to American encroachment on the preserves of the British Empire and the sort of protection that would be afforded by an Anglo-German understanding. He would almost certainly have dealt exhaustively with the threat to Europe of Russian communism, a favourite theme of his, and he may have called British relations with Russia into question.

These were of course, sensitive issues at the time. They are of academic or historic interest only in 2000. And yet the secrecy remains. Such issues cannot be the reason for the secrecy. There must be something else that Hess brought with him that is as sensitive today as it was 59 years ago. According to the papers at the Public Record Office inventories of Hess's personal possessions after his parachute landing were taken on at least three separate occasions. His personal possessions would have included the Hamilton letter. Details of the inventories are not to be found among the PRO documents. They have been removed. Bohle was interviewed in 1945 by Robert Kempner, who subsequently served in the American prosecution team at Nuremberg. The notes of that interview are not available. Bohle appeared subsequently at Nuremberg. He was not questioned as to the content of the Hamilton letter.

One piece of guesswork as to the letter's content became prevalent following the launch of Operation Barbarossa and has some evidence to support it. The suggestion was made that if Hess's mission had been successful Barbarossa would not have been necessary. German claims

---

[18]PRO WO 208/4170.
[19]The Commandant's Diary, August 7, 1941. The manuscript was never delivered.
[20]PRO PREM 3/217/4.

against Russia by way of *Lebensraum* and supplies of Caucasian oil and Ukrainian wheat would have been settled by negotiation. Certainly there are pointers that indicate that the launch of Barbarossa was linked in some way with the Hess mission. On February 17, 1941, nearly three months prior to the Hess flight, Sir Robert Corbett, the British Ambassador to Stockholm, reported that his contacts had indicated that Hitler would soon declare that German territorial demands were at an end. There was no point in the continuance of the war as far as Germany was concerned. Germany would submit detailed proposals to end the war and they would be placed before an international conference for negotiation. The onus for the continuance of the war would then be placed on Great Britain. By inference, any claims that Germany had against Russia would be included in the peace proposals and settled by negotiation.[21]

It is perhaps significant that when in captivity Hess referred consistently to an agreement with Russia and never a war against, when talking about German claims against Russia. Also of course, Hitler did not fix the date for the launch of Barbarossa until May 29, 1941, three weeks after the Hess mission and in the knowledge that it had failed.[22] But most importantly of all, Hess himself confirmed that if his mission had been successful there would have been an international conference at which German claims against Russia would have been dealt with as part of an overall settlement. This confirmation was given by Hess to his son in a written reply to specific questions drafted by Hess's son and smuggled into Spandau prison through the good offices of Pastor Gabel, the Frenchman who had befriended Hess during his pastoral visits to the prison.[23] Hess makes it quite clear in his reply that Operation Barbarossa would not have taken place.

Of course, the debate as to the content of the Hamilton letter will not be settled until the document becomes available for public inspection. This should be the case in 2017, under the 75-year rule. There was of course a copy or copies of the Hamilton letter, but exhaustive research suggests that the final resting place of one particular copy is at the side of the original in the same British archive. Before Hess flew to Great Britain on May 10, 1941, a copy of the Hamilton letter was placed in a 'Pfeffer' file which was then deposited with a Munich bank for safekeeping.[24] Pfeffer von Saloman was chief of Hess's own per-

---

[21]PRO FO/371/26/542C 1532.

[22]Hess, Wolf Rüdiger, *My Father, Rudolf Hess*, W.H. Allen (1986), 176.

[23]The original questions and Hess's reply have been seen by the author.

[24]The facts relating to the missing Pfeffer file arise from comments made by Ilse Hess and research work carried out by Hess's son and the author.

sonal intelligence unit responsible only to Hess. Presumably, the Pfeffer file would have contained other documents of equivalent importance and secrecy.

In 1945 when American troops were approaching Munich, a General Gottlieb Berger of the SS took the Pfeffer file and a security box also in the bank's custody, to the village of St Josefstal, Neuhaus near Schliersee in the Bavarian Alps, with a view to their continued preservation under Berger's personal control. According to a Captain (later identified as a First Lieutenant) Joseph Stein attached to the Enemy Document Section of the US 3rd Army Intelligence Centre, who had been instructed to recover the box and papers, American troops had looted the house in St Josefstal where the box and papers had been held. Frau Berger and her daughter had apparently burnt most of the papers in the box beforehand. Stein claimed to have found a file cover entitled *Meine Besprechungen mit dem Führer*, but the papers inside the file cover had been destroyed. Stein also reported that he had found one or two pieces of table silver and a baby spoon presumed to be Hess's baptismal presents. According to Stein there was no trace of a Pfeffer file.

It is of course possible that Stein did in fact recover more than he says. The fact that he was specifically ordered to search for and recover the box and papers taken to St Josefstal by General Berger indicates the importance attaching to the recovery of the box and papers. Exhaustive enquiries have been made at the American Army Archive Center in Maryland in an attempt to locate the missing Pfeffer file, but to no avail. The American response was that any British-related captured documents would have been returned to the British Foreign Office. It is therefore likely that the copy Hamilton letter lies alongside the original in the Foreign Office files. On May 27, 1941, David Lloyd George remarked to Richard Stokes, the pacifist Labour MP, 'As to Hess, I think the British public should be informed of the substance of Hess's documents to the Government. We are treated too much like children who cannot be trusted with too much of the truth.'[25] Fifty seven years later things have not changed.

It is pertinent when considering the continuing secrecy surrounding the Hess flight to assess the degree to which he communicated his knowledge of 'the Jewish factor' to his captors, together with his misgivings on that score. He was certainly privy to the Madagascar Plan, as described in the previous chapter. He knew that if his mission failed, that plan would be stillborn because Great Britain controlled the seas

[25]The Stokes papers.

and the emigration of Jews to Madagascar would be impossible. He also knew that Operation Barbarossa would then go ahead and that the responsibility for finding a solution to the Jewish problem was likely to pass to Heydrich and his *Einsatzgruppen* (snatch squads). It was not difficult to foresee what means would be employed to justify the ends. So much had almost certainly been confirmed to Hess on the morning of his departure by his friend, Rosenberg, who had flown from Berlin overnight so as to see Hess before he left. No one knew better than Rosenberg what the consequences were likely to be for the Jews if Barbarossa went ahead. As Reichsminister for the Occupied Eastern Territories following the launch of Barbarossa, he would be in theoretical control of Heydrich and responsible for his operational activities.[25]

Were these fears included in the original letter to Hamilton? Were they expressed in Hess's subsequent letter to King George VI? Were they brought out in Hess's discussions with his British interrogators? To what extent were the Duke of Hamilton, King George VI, Winston Churchill and the British Government made aware of the position of European Jewry if Hess's peace initiative failed, there was no international conference and Barbarossa went ahead? Were they in fact warned by Hess about an impending Holocaust? Was this, and is this, the reason why the full details of Hess's peace plan will never become public knowledge? All other issues which may or may not have been sensitive in 1941 are now of academic or historical interest only.[27] The Jewish factor, on the other hand, is even more sensitive today than it was in 1941 because the full consequences of the Holocaust are now known. There is reason to believe that there will be continued secrecy into eternity.[28]

---

[25]An accusation that Rosenberg had to face at Nuremberg and which helped bring him the death penalty.

[27]The existence of a British Peace Party, the identity of its members, the pacifist/defeatist activities of leading politicians of the day, and the involvement of royalty and MI6 in the 1940–41 peace processes are unlikely to stimulate the passions (other than those of historians) in 2000. In themselves, they do not warrant the present degree of continued secrecy.

[28]It will be appreciated that these factors may also be relevant to the death of Hess in Spandau Prison, Berlin on August 17, 1987

23

The Involvement of British Intelligence

Intelligence agents in my experience are even bigger liars than journalists and the historians who try to reconstruct the past out of their records are for the most part dealing in fantasy.

MALCOLM MUGGERIDGE

That British Intelligence was involved with the Hess mission there is no doubt. The intriguing question is in what capacity it was involved. The fact that it was involved at all is, of course, evidence which rebuts the official version that the flight was the independent act of a deranged individual. It also supports the view that 'there is more in this than meets the eye.'[1]

Reports that British Intelligence was involved are many and various. Some were made at the highest level. In October 1944, at a supper in the Kremlin attended by Churchill, Stalin proposed a toast to British Intelligence 'which inveigled Hess into coming to England.'[2] Stalin's information came from a Soviet agent who had infiltrated the Vichy French Military Intelligence Service and had stolen a Hess file from the French archives. Contained within that file is Report No. 398/B, dated September 5, 1941, which referred specifically to the role played by British Intelligence MI6 in the Hess mission. The source of the French information was 'a long-standing friend of the British Trade Minister who was in touch with the Duchess of Hamilton' and who was also 'very well connected with the high-ranking members of the British Secret Services in New York'.[3]

[1]As expressed by the author's father on the morning of Tuesday, May 13, 1941.
[2]PRO PREM 3/434/7.
[3]Costello, John, *Ten Days that Saved the West*, Bantam Press (1991), 452. The reference to 'high ranking members of the British Secret Services in New York' is interesting in view of the remarks contained later in Appendix IV relating to Sir William Stephenson, Head of British Security Co-Ordination in the USA and based in New York.

The KGB files contain corroborative evidence. In October 1942 Colonel Moravec, Chief of Czech Military Intelligence (code name 'Moravetz),[4] informed the resident NKVD agent in London that British Intelligence had been involved in the Hess flight. The agent claimed that he had actually seen the MI6 file dealing with the operation. In his cryptogram N450 he had reported that 'the dissemenated story that Hess arrived in England unexpectedly is not correct. Long before his flight Hess had corresponded about his mission with the Duke of Hamilton. In the correspondence there was discussed in detail all the questions to do with the organisation of the flight. But Hamilton was not a participant personally. None of Hess's letters to Hamilton had reached him but were intercepted by the Intelligence Services where the answers to Hess in the name of Hamilton were manufactured.' So important did the NKVD top brass consider this intelligence information that they arranged a top secret briefing for both Stalin and Foreign Secretary, Molotov.[5]

There is further corroborative evidence. According to diary entries made between May 12 and June 1, 1941 by Edvard Taborsky, Secretary to President Benẽs of the Czech Government. Benes had been told by MI6 officers that they were expecting 'somebody' to arrive. Benẽs's MI6 informant was probably Robert Bruce-Lockhart. He was the MI6 liaison officer attached to the Czechs. He attended upon Benẽs constantly in the days immediately following Hess's arrival.[6] Further confirmation is provided by a member of the German Resistance, Dr Otto John, former president of the Federal Constitutional Protection Authority. John, a close friend of Albrecht Haushofer, knew all about the proposed flight and was in touch with his MI6 contact, Tony Minegod.[7]

As well as these reports of MI6 involvement it is also known that MI5 were involved. At Hamilton's meeting on April 25 with Air Ministry officials he had been introduced to Major 'Tar' Robertson of Military Intelligence, Double X Department, whose speciality was the dissemination of false intelligence data to Germany by the use of turned German Abwehr agents. Whatever Robertson had in mind about using Hamilton as some sort of double agent appears to have been brought to an end rather abruptly by the intervention of Air Commodore 'Archie' Boyle, Chief of Air Intelligence. Boyle's inter-

---

[4]Moravec passed information to Russia throughout the war in return for Russian help for the Czech Resistance.
[5]Report by Beria, Head of Russian Intelligence.
[6]Padfield, Peter, *Hess: Flight for the Führer*, Weidenfeld and Nicolson (1991), 181 and 292.
[7]Hess, Wolf Rüdiger, *My Father, Rudolf Hess*, W.H. Allen (1986), 152.

vention suggests that Air Intelligence was itself also involved. Mention has already made of such an intelligence link initiated in the mid-1930s and used by Hess and Rosenberg on previous occasions. It was Rosenberg who had been summoned to Munich for last minute discussions with Hess and it was Boyle of British Air Intelligence who was intervening at the same time on the other side of the water.

Finally, there is known MI6 involvement in the shape of the mysterious old lady, Mary Violet Roberts, acting as a cover for her nephew, Walter Stewart Roberts, who was based at the Bletchley Park Signals Centre and was a personal friend of Stewart Menzies, Chief of MI6. In 1946 Roberts was appointed head of British Political Intelligence. The little old lady friend of the Haushofers certainly had friends or relatives or both in very high places within British Intelligence.

The view that British Intelligence was heavily involved in the Hess mission is therefore beyond doubt. But in what capacity? The view most commonly promulgated is that Hess was duped by a trick into flying to Great Britain. False correspondence purporting to come from Hamilton was manufactured. This created the impression that there was a powerful British Peace Party waiting in the wings for the arrival of Hess as a prelude to the overthrow of the Churchill Government and ending the war. Hess himself firmly held that belief, otherwise he would never have embarked on his mission. Protagonists of this theory are obliged to assume that either Hess was a fool to be so taken in or that the baiting of the hook was so sophisticated and skilled that he was bound to be taken in. Careful examination of the facts suggests that neither of these circumstances applied.

In the first place, Hess was no fool. His personal background, history, education and above all, his early experience on the streets of Munich indicated otherwise. But in addition, Hess had available a personal intelligence service which was second to none and would have guaranteed his immunity from playing the part of a hooked fish. Reference has already been made to the personal services rendered to Hess by Pfeffer von Saloman who had acted as his personal intelligence chief ever since the Roehm purges of 1934. The Pfeffer service had a well-earned reputation. Hitler's ability to read the diplomatic situation in Europe so successfully during the 1930s was to a large extent due to the depth and widespread nature of Soloman's intelligence contacts in every European capital and especially in London. The feedbacks came to Hess's office.[8] These Soloman contacts were long-established and deep-rooted. They had been inherited through

---

[8]Padfield, Peter, *Hess: Flight for the Führer*, Weidenfeld and Nicolson (1991), 100.

General von Reichenau, Hitler's favourite political general and they reached back into Germany's imperial past.

It is inconceivable that Pfeffer von Soloman would not have been aware of any British Intelligence plot if it had existed. What is entirely conceivable is that Soloman was in active co-operation with British Intelligence in arranging Hess's mission. At the relevant time, British Intelligence MI5 was informing the Americans that high-level intelligence from unidentified sources in Great Britain were being passed to Pfeffer von Saloman of Hess's private office.[9] It is known also that a Pfeffer file which, according to Ilse Hess contained full details of the mission went missing after its transfer from a Munich bank to the Bavarian village of St Josefstal in 1945.[10]

The suggestion that the hook was so skilfully baited that Hitler, Hess, the Haushofers and Saloman were all bound to be taken in does not hold water either. Such skills would compare oddly with the amateurish measures taken to mask the involvement of the Intelligence Services. The use of the mysterious old lady, Violet Mary Roberts, was perhaps the best example. Hess could have used any number of addresses in Portugal as a clearing house for the initial Albrecht/Hamilton correspondence, all known to him or to his brother. Why pick a complete stranger to handle such top-secret documentation? In fact, Mrs Roberts was deliberately used as a *nom de plume* for British Intelligence MI6 acting through her nephew based at Bletchley Park who was a personal friend of Menzies, Chief of MI6. The addition of a plot or trick to this superstructure is unnecessary and there is no evidence for its existence.

Protagonists of the duping theory also contend that there was a continuing concocted correspondence covering the period September 1940 to April 1941 between British Intelligence (under the guise of Hamilton) and Albrecht Haushofer, and that this included full details of the proposed flight, the landing arrangements and reception details. Apparently, all these details would have been manufactured and forged in Hamilton's handwriting. Albrecht and Hamilton had of course corresponded for years before the war in the most affectionate terms. Their relationship was one of intimacy, and recognition of each other's handwriting would have been taken for granted. Hamilton claimed that he had no contact with any intelligence services until March 15, 1941, when he was invited to the Air Ministry to meet Group Captain F.G. (Freddie) Stammers, OBE, of Air Security. It is inconceivable that in his replies to such faked correspondence Albrecht would not have

---

[9]Thomas, Hugh, *A Tale of Two Murders*, Hodder and Stoughton (1979), 80.
[10]See chapter 22.

raised matters of personal and mutual interest quite apart from those dealing with the operational matter. How then did the fake correspondents at the British end conceal their ignorance as well as fake the handwriting? Albrecht was an articulate, intelligent, erudite academic of quality. It is inconceivable that he should be taken in by such amateurish measures.

The duping theory has a further extension. The scheme is said to have been conceived as a direct retaliation by MI6 for the humiliation heaped upon it after the Venlo incident in November 1939, as a result of which British Intelligence throughout Europe had been almost completely compromised by the capture of two senior MI6 officers, Sigmund Payne and Richard Best. Old scores had to be settled. It was almost a private matter between the British and German Intelligence Services and had resulted in landing a very big Nazi fish. If that be so, and if the duping of Hess was a special intelligence exercise which resulted in an outstanding success, why was such a coup not given the publicity it so richly deserved? The duping of the Nazi hierarchy and the capture of the Deputy Führer of Nazi Germany in the middle of the war would, if true, have represented the most important single achievement in the history of MI6.

Why then was such an achievement masked by a deafening silence which has lasted nearly 60 years? Such a silence demands an explanation. The propaganda issues that could have been brought into play are mind-boggling. Not one was in fact employed. Churchill, apparently showing uncharacteristic hesitancy and indecisiveness, made no detailed statement to Parliament or to the press or the public – hardly like Churchill at a moment of triumph. Hess disappeared into solitary confinement from which he did not emerge, except for a brief attendance before the Nuremberg Military Tribunal, until his death in 1987, 46 years after his flight.

There is yet another flaw in the duping theory. Kim Philby, the noted double agent, had supplied British secrets to the Russians over many years. In 1941 he held a fairly senior rank with the Special Operations Executive (SOE) under Hugh Dalton. The first report that the Russians received announcing the arrival of Hess in Great Britain came from Philby (code name 'Vadin'). A second report followed four days later. Significantly, neither of these two special Hess reports from Philby, an experienced and skilled agent, include anything about a British Intelligence plot.[11] Philby had the full run of all the secret files, but the

---

[11]As included in the memoirs of Robert Caice, assistant private secretary to Alexander Cadogan at the time of the Hess flight.

dog did not bark. Perhaps it did not bark because there was nothing to bark about.

Finally, it has to be said that the author has been assured in the most categorical terms by an informant who was an MI6 officer at the time of the flight that although MI6 were 'in the Hess thing up to their necks' there was never any conspiracy to lure Hess to Great Britain. That was 'only the gloss added for public consumption after the official story about the exploits of a madman became discredited.' The same informant added that in any case the brain power within the ranks of MI6 was never up to planning and working a deception plan of such importance and apparent success.

If the suggestions of duping are rejected, it is necessary to substitute some other purpose for the known MI6 involvement. The simplest inference is logical and obvious. MI6 were 'in the Hess thing up to their necks' for the very good reason that its officers, or some of them, applauded Hess's mission and the purpose for which it was made. They were prepared to welcome Hess and listen to his message. They were also prepared to join with Hess's own intelligence agencies and help plan and execute the arrangements. The suggestion is that certain of the officers within MI6 were also active members of the British Peace Party.

There were early indications that Peace Party views existed within the ranks of MI6. In October 1939, having moved his base of operations during wartime to Switzerland, Baron 'Bill' de Ropp, double agent and essential link in the Winterbotham/Rosenberg chain of communication, reported that the British Air Ministry was still of the same view as his own and 'by no means wished to be a party to the present policy of England waging war to the finish.' It is known from the record of their pre-war association that Winterbotham of British Air Intelligence, de Ropp, Rosenberg and Hess[12] shared identical views about the communist threat to Europe, but here was a sounding actually taken after the commencement of Anglo-German hostilities. The clear indication is that even though hostilities had broken out, pacifist views remained unimpaired within the British Air Ministry. The thought there was that the Anglo-German conflict was unnecessary and should be brought to an end.[13]

It is also known that Lord Lothian, a prominent pacifist although Churchill's ambassador in Washington, had used Sir William Wiseman,

---

[12]Winterbotham, F.W., *Secret and Personal*, William Kimber (1969), 24. The relationships did not survive the war years. Rosenberg begged both de Ropp and Winterbotham to give evidence on his behalf at the Nuremberg Military Tribunal. Both refused.
[13]DGFP, Vol III, October 10, 1939.

Head of British Intelligence MI6 in the USA during World War I, as a go-between for some of his peace initiatives. Wiseman had met the German consul-general in San Francisco and also the mysterious (and notorious) German Princess Stephanie who was related to Max Hohenlohe, a freelance peace negotiator known to be a German agent. Wiseman had been badly compromised by the FBI. In the course of their surveillance of the Princess, the FBI had bugged a conversation between her and Wiseman in an hotel bedroom. Wiseman had told the Princess that Halifax was heading a group seeking a lasting peace with Germany and claimed that the group had considerable backing.[14]

These glimpses of the peace activities and views within the ranks of British Intelligence warrant a look at the background and history of the intelligence services. Their method and sources of recruitment and the entrenched views of some of their senior personnel are interesting. It will be seen that most of the MI6 officers would fall naturally and easily, and perhaps with enthusiasm, into the ranks of a British Peace Party. Their roots lay within a common soil, the British Establishment. During the period up to 1941, MI6 recruited its officers almost exclusively from the ranks of the Establishment and they brought with them, at least in the main, the political views of the Establishment. It has already been noted that the greatest fear of the Establishment was change. Change could affect their positions of privilege. The war brought change. In any case, the great danger to the established order of things was communism. The Anglo-German war was unnecessary. It should be ended. Thus was the thinking of the British Peace Party that arose out of the Establishment. Thus also was the thinking of many of the recruits of MI6 who came from the Establishment. The British Peace Party, the British Establishment and MI6 were to a considerable extent made up of the same individuals. They were hardly likely to wear different hats as they moved from one world to the next.

Perhaps the most prominent member of the British Peace Party, the British Establishment and the British intelligence services was the Chief of MI6, Major General Sir Stewart Graham Menzies, KCMG, KCB, DSO, MC. He was at the very core of the Establishment. Everything about him was Establishment. Court circles and rumour said of him that he was the illegitimate son of the Prince of Wales, later King Edward VII. His mother was Lady Holford, a prominent member of court circles. By all accounts she was a 'great beauty'. She duly married George Holford after Menzies's birth and convention

---

[14]Costello, John, *Ten Days that Saved the West*, Bantam Press (1991), 399–402.

slotted in Holford as the father. Holford was also prominent in Edward's court. Menzies was educated at Eton where he was captain of the Eton XI and president of the prestigious prefectorial society, Pop. He entered the army in the Grenadier Guards but later transferred to the Life Guards where he could indulge his love of horses and riding. He married the daughter of the eighth Earl de la Warr but subsequently divorced her for granting bedroom favours to another.

During the first two years of the 1914–18 war Menzies served with great distinction on the Western Front, winning the MC and DSO. He witnessed at first hand the wholesale slaughter caused by the ascendancy of the machine gun and the absence of effective protection against it. He saw the disappearance of so many young men of his age including his own comrades and old school friends. After promotion to the staff of the British Commander-in-Chief in France, he became involved in matters of intelligence and security. This interest remained after completion of his war service. He joined a special intelligence section which had been set up to counter communist subversion and propaganda and subsequently moved into the Secret Intelligence Service, MI6. By September 1939 he was deputy head of MI6 to Admiral Sinclair.

Sinclair died on November 29 and Menzies was appointed as his successor. It was very much a Chamberlain/Halifax/Palace appointment. Churchill was very much against the appointment but he could not block it. He was in a minority of one in November 1939. He knew that Menzies was spawned from those sections of the Establishment who were looking for a compromise peace even before the actual fighting started and that he would fit naturally and easily into the make-peace lobby, alongside Halifax, Butler, Sam Hoare and John Simon.[15] Menzies had already been heavily involved in the Venlo affair and the wishful thinking policy of Chamberlain which sought to separate the good Germans from the bad.

There was another factor. Churchill knew that the only realistic way of beating Germany in armed combat was to involve America. Menzies did not agree. In conformity with Establishment thinking, he viewed the possibility of American intervention with alarm. He did not trust American long-term aims for the commercial opportunities that would become available, as and when and if the British Empire frag-

---

[15]This does not imply that Menzies was anything other than a true patriot. He believed, as did others, that the ending of the Anglo-German war was an essential preliminary to building up a coherent European defence against the threatened communist encroachment. But there was little doubt that by 1941 Menzies was also a pacifist. His experiences during the First World War had seen to that.

mented. In spite of these Churchillian fears, Menzies's appointment was confirmed. He was then 49 years of age.

Of course, Churchill could have removed Menzies when he assumed office as Prime Minister in May 1940. He chose not to. Churchill's own political position was insecure and he had already dismissed a stunned Sir Vernon Kell, MI5 Chief and Establishment elder. Churchill adopted a policy of wait and see. In fact, Menzies saw the war out. On that count he must be considered as one of life's great survivors. He knew he had to make it his business to get on with Churchill and did so. To that end he was an affable drinker, a good companion and an ardent listener.

Menzies also had one priceless weapon in his armoury. The government code and cipher services establishment at Bletchley Park was an outstanding success in reading German ciphers and the assimilation and transmission of top-secret enemy intelligence to Churchill. Churchill himself described the operation as 'the goose that laid the golden eggs and never cackled'. The delivery of top-secret decrypts to Churchill was undertaken by Menzies personally. It was the conspicuous and continuing success in the breaking of German ciphers, combined with Churchill's romantic image of intelligence work generally, that seems to have masked Menzies's shortcomings in other directions. Menzies's mind was that of a 1914–18 cavalry officer and remained so throughout the 1939–45 war. His policy of leaving operational details in the hands of subordinates without supervision led to the wholesale infiltration of MI6 by communist agents, the employment of incompetent officers and a lamentable record of non-performance in the field.

By May 1941 there was widespread dissatisfaction among the service departments as to the standard of intelligence work. There had been a long litany of failures ever since the declaration of war. Prior to that, MI6 was more like a club than a professional service department. There was muddle and incompetence everywhere and a low standard of recruitment which caused most of the departmental problems. And there was only one enemy, the Soviet Union. All the limited resources had been pitted against the Red Menace.[16] There was scant interest and few resources devoted to the plotting and combating of German expansionist plans. As with the armed forces at that

---

[16]It is sobering to reflect that if MI6 had operated a competent field operation in Germany during the 1930s, instead of obsessing itself with the Red Menace, they would have been able to report that while Germany was certainly preparing for war, that war was to be directed against Russia, not the Western democracies. Anglo-French policies might have been more enlightened as a result and they might not have blundered into war as they did. This is perhaps the most fundamental indictment of MI6 pre-war incompetence.

time, it was a completely amateur show when stripped of whatever romantic associations were attached to it.[17]

The pre-war French attitude to war and French morale generally, which was to become such a vital factor in the 1940 campaigns, was never picked up and reported to the Government. The reports of the eccentric but knowledgeable Kenneth de Courcy which highlighted French corruption, internal division and lack of will to fight, were ignored. Pre-war warship construction in Kiel in direct contravention to the Versailles Treaty passed unnoticed. The British Government received no advance warning of the reoccupation of the Rhineland in 1936 or of the Anschluss in 1938. At the time of the Czech crisis MI6 warned the Czechs that 11 German divisions were approaching the Czech border. The report was completely untrue. Hitler was enraged and the crisis worsened.[18]

In 1939, the Russo-German summer negotiations which led to the signing of the non-aggression pact in August were unknown to MI6. At that time, MI6 intelligence had been described as 'normally 80 per cent inaccurate' and the War Office were complaining that MI6 could provide no reliable information as to Germany's military capabilities, its arms build-up or its troop movements.[19] Chamberlain was using propaganda data as to the strength of the German Luftwaffe derived from the reports of Charles Lindbergh, a known German sympathiser in the USA. He had failed to obtain the information from his own intelligence services.

The pre-war catalogue of intelligence disasters continued into the war years under the stewardship of Menzies. On April 7, 1940, MI6 reported that the German navy was about to break out from their Baltic ports and enter the North Sea, making for the open Atlantic. They were not. They were preparing for the invasion of Denmark and Norway; this came as a complete surprise to the Anglo-French Chiefs of Staff who were busy planning their own invasion of Norway. Apparently MI6 could not distinguish troop transports full of soldiers from naval vessels full of sailors. On May 10, 1940, the launch of the German offensive in the West achieved complete tactical surprise. There was no intelligence from MI6 as to the planned movement of German armour through the 'impossible' terrain of the Ardennes and the concentration of armour on the Meuse before Sedan. A fortnight later, German armour reached the Channel coast. An MI6 intelligence report attached to the Chief of Staff's report of May 25, 1940,

---

[17]Knightley, Philip, *The Second Oldest Profession*, Pan Books (1997), 95.
[18]General Alfred Jodl, diary entry, May 30, 1938.
[19]Hinsley, H.F., *British Intelligence in the Second World War*, Vol I, 56.

announced that 'Germany would not wait for the final collapse of France before mounting an immediate assault on Great Britain.' The report was a complete nonsense. Not only did Hitler never attempt an invasion of Great Britain but in political terms he never had any intention of doing so, either before or after the defeat of France.

Perhaps the best example of wishful-thinking intelligence work provided by MI6 is displayed in their reports during the summer of 1940. These show so clearly how MI6 still clung to the Chamberlainite idea of 'good' Germans and 'bad' Germans, even though the new realism of Churchill's thinking was beginning to dominate government policies. During that summer Hitler was at the very zenith of his powers and popularity with the German people. Pre-war diplomatic success had been followed by wartime military success. German pride and self-esteem had been fully restored and the German people were rock solid in their support for the one man responsible for their nation's rebirth. This phenomenon, so apparent to neutral journalism, was widely reported in the international press. It apparently escaped the notice of MI6 officers. They were busy reporting that in their view there was a good deal of popular opposition in Germany to Hitler and Nazi rule.[20] It is apparent that MI6 were reporting what they thought the Government would like to hear rather than the facts.

In the spring of 1941 Germany was preparing to launch Operation Barbarossa, destined to be the greatest military confrontation in the history of land warfare, involving millions of combatants. MI6 reported the build-up of German troops in the East as 'quite normal'.[21] On March 31 of that year General Rommel launched a full-scale offensive in the Western Desert. The attack came as a complete tactical surprise. No warning intelligence was received and no information was made available as to Rommel's military strength, his troop dispositions or his intentions.[22] Two months later, after the German attack on Yugoslavia, MI6 were adamant that Hitler had no intention of invading Russia and that his main target remained Great Britain.[23] Operation Barbarossa was duly launched on June 22.[24]

Apart from the looseness of control exercised by Menzies at the top of the command structure of MI6, there were two main reasons why MI5 built up such a catalogue of operational disasters. In the first place the quality of their officers in terms of native intelligence and the train-

---

[20]Roberts, Andrew, *The Holy Fox*, Weidenfeld and Nicolson (1991), 226–27.
[21]PRO WO 190/893.
[22]Irving, David, *Churshill's War*, Veritas Publishing (1987), 535.
[23]PRO FO371/29479. CAB 79/11 and WO 190/893.
[24]A casual glance at *Mein Kampf* would have told MI6 that they had got it the wrong way round.

ing they received was very low. In the second place, the whole organisation continued to be obsessed with the Red Menace. They had little time and even less inclination to develop any sort of sophisticated techniques for use against Hitler's Germany, still considered to be a secondary target. Both these factors guaranteed that MI6 operations against Germany, even after the war had started, would be feeble and incompetent.

The same two factors counted much towards the alignment of its members in the direction of the British Peace Party. The chief recruiting officer for MI6 was Colonel Claude Dansey, head of the espionage section. He has been described as 'an incurable snob' and is said to have recruited 'his honourable correspondents' from the bars of the more fashionable London clubs, particularly White's and Boodle's. The recruits were wealthy, privileged, public-school educated, of 'good' family and considered to be 'sound'.[25] These were the Menzies/Dansey hoops through which applicants had to pass before appointment.

During the 1930s there was a general drift towards the left in political thought in Great Britain, at the expense of the traditional Conservative/Liberal viewpoints. MI6 recruitment during that period was concerned with the involvement of young men who bucked this trend. Menzies and Dansey were looking for and found young men born into the Establishment who looked rather towards a fervent belief in King, country and Empire, the preservation of the great institutions of state, the maintenance of public order and stability but, above all, to the preservation of the essential status quo and the inviolability of inherited wealth.[26] The universities of the day reflected the leftward swing and it is therefore unfortunate that Menzies and Dansey recruited very few young men with a university background. They were thus left with the educated dross who had never made it to university. It is not difficult to appreciate that standards of competence suffered as a result, at least up to the outbreak of war in 1939.

After that the so-called professionals were joined by wartime amateurs, mostly academics and professionally qualified men who had attained high status by native ability and application. This new intake,[27] having found their feet and rubbed shoulders with the incumbents, were appalled at what they found and scathing in their comments about the Establishment figures holding senior posts in the

---

[25]For some time, Roman Catholics were excluded from the latter category.

[26]Knightley, Philip, *The Second Oldest Profession*, Pan Books (1987), 86.

[27]They included Graham Greene, Hugh Trevor-Roper and Malcolm Muggeridge and men of similar calibre.

organisation. 'There were these metropolitan gentlemen whose education had been expensive rather than profound.' 'They had been educated beyond their intelligence.' 'They included a number of army middle-ranking officers who were never likely to reach senior rank and had therefore resigned to join the intelligence services.'[28] 'Most recruits to both MI5 and MI6 were right-wingers. They were in general terms as thick as planks.'[29] 'It seemed to me that the professionals were by and large, pretty stupid and some of them very stupid.' These were typical of the many remarks made by the new intake in their assessment of the old guard.

It is of course fashionable to sneer at the 'old school tie' approach; but in the case of the intelligence services there could be a case for some sort of system which relied for its security upon the fact that the unit was run on the lines of a club. Everyone had known each other over a number of years and all had the same sort of background, history and education, subscribed to the same values and pursued the same political ends. That said, and that certainly being the case with MI6 until the arrival of the new wartime intake, one is left with the strong impression that here was a collection of young and middle-aged men with no great fund of native intelligence or academic ability but with a firm hand on the tiller of inherited privilege. It is also apparent that they were welded together in the belief that the life of privilege which had spawned them and their forebears was under serious threat from the Russian Bear, now updated to the Red Menace. Such a collection of individuals made up the rump of the MI6 organisation. It is not difficult to also identify them as part of a solid core within the British Peace Party.

The obsession with the Red Menace was endemic within the ranks of MI6. The general attitude towards Russia and her evil intent as embroiled in MI6 dogma bordered on the hysterical. There is a close parallel between pronouncements on the subject by MI6 personnel and the pronouncements of Adolf Hitler himself. The following diatribe, delivered by one of MI6's more flamboyant characters, might have been taken straight out of the pages of *Mein Kampf*:

> Gracious heavens. Will the people of England never understand? The Germans are human beings. We can afford to be even beaten by them. Here in Moscow, there is growing to maturity the arch enemy of the human race. Here, the foulest and most monstrous and most obscene passions which have been suppressed and bridled

[28]Simpson, A.W. Brian, *In the Highest Degree Odious*, Clarendon Press (1992), 37.
[29]As reported personally to the author by a former member of MI6.

> by the common decency of people at large and by the strong hand of the most beneficent authority since civilisation first began, gibber and swagger in the seats of government. What is happening here is more important than any war that has ever been fought. At any price, this foul obscenity which has been born in Russia must be crushed out of existence. Peace with Germany? Yes, peace with Germany. Peace with anybody. There is only one enemy. Mankind must unite in a Holy Alliance against this midnight terror.[30]

This tirade was delivered by Sidney Reilly, an MI6 agent employed in Russia during and after the 1917 Communist Revolution. It faithfully set the tone for the future attitudes of MI6. It was also probably the first exponent of the 'you're in the wrong war' theme which became so prevalent in MI6 circles later and which became particularly resonant following the onset of the 1939 war. In 1917, the Russian revolution had produced a major impact on the Western world, particularly as to the international consequences of a declared policy of world revolution. Russia replaced Germany as the big bogey. As far as MI6 were concerned it remained so throughout the two decades leading up to September 1939. As a result, between 1917 and 1939 the bulk of the (very limited) resources of MI6 were used in attempting the penetration of the Soviet Union and the ascertainment of its true policy objectives. Operations against Germany were restricted by budget and resources, and they were unpopular and unwelcome in terms of professional interest.

The original (and wrong) thinking of MI6 was that the first encroachment of communism that would affect British interests would occur in the sub-continent of India where a few thousand British administrators ruled millions of Indians. MI6 agents were sent to India where they thought about little else. When they returned home to European or home postings, they brought their own views with them and impregnated them on their colleagues in London and elsewhere. Because of this introverted and obsessive view as to the dangers of communism and the concentration of resources and activity in that direction, MI6 were unable to supply successive British Governments in the 1930s with much in the shape of useful intelligence on other European matters. As a result, governments gleaned whatever information they could from whatever sources were available and tried to bring good sense and sound judgement into play when the required technical data were not available. It was a poor substitute.

---

[30]Reilly, Sidney, *The Adventures of Sidney Reilly*, Elkin Matthews & Marrst (1931).

There was an important and dangerous consequence of these inadequacies as MI6 became an increasingly isolated adjunct to Foreign Office activity between the wars. In March 1934 the Defence Requirements sub-committee for Imperial Defence decided in its wisdom that the principal potential enemy against which long-term defence would have to be prepared was Germany, not Russia. This decision did not accord with MI6 design. The intelligence service therefore continued to function on the basis that they knew better. The bulk of their resources remained where they were, watching Russia. In 1936 a Foreign Policy Committee was set up to advise the Government as to its foreign policy decisions, with particular reference to the expansionist activities of Nazi Germany. During the following two-and-a-half-years the committee received from MI6 relevant data on just two occasions.[31] Never was a Government served so badly by its intelligence services. MI6 remained interested in its own obsession and continued to act independently.[32] It is said that the first casualty of war is truth and Malcolm Muggeridge, himself a wartime MI6 officer, suggested that there were no bigger liars than the Intelligence Service. Certainly the lie lived by MI6 in the years preceding the 1939–45 war, in open defiance of its own government requirements, gives a clear indication of a loose cannon, armed with the most dangerous conviction that Great Britain was fighting the wrong war from day one.

It was not of course the first occasion that the intelligence services had thought of crossing swords with the Government of the day. In 1924, Sidney Reilly, the same flamboyant MI6 agent responsible for the hysterical reports received from Moscow in the early days after the Communist Revolution, perpetrated a fraud on the British public, with the full backing of his MI6 masters, which cost the British Labour Party the election during that year. The so-called Zinoviev letter was a fraud. It was purported to have been written on September 15, 1924, by Grigori Zinoviev, President of the Communist International, to the British Communist Party. It instructed members of the party to prepare for the forthcoming armed uprising by intensifying their acts of sabotage and disruption within the armed forces and by using whatever sympathies they had with the British Labour Party.

The letter was originated by Reilly, who then brought it to the atten-

---

[31]Hinsley, F.H. Thomas, *British Intelligence*, Vol I, HMSO (1979–84), 49 and 80.

[32]Such misdirected arrogance is not peculiar to British Intelligence. In 1949, a small group of American CIA officers researched the intentions of the Soviet Union. Their findings were that there was no Soviet masterplan for world domination. Such a conclusion contradicted the tenets of CIA self-belief. The report was therefore suppressed and an 'official' version published, confirming the official view. (Barnes, Trevor, *The Secret Cold War, The CIA and American Foreign Policy in Europe 1946–1956*, Part 2, Volume 25, No 3, Historical Journal (1982), 651.)

tion of his MI6 masters. They gave it their blessing and referred it to the Foreign Office. The letter was subsequently released to the press and published on October 20, 1924. The general election was to be held on October 24. Publication of the letter had a devastating effect upon Labour Party prospects. The result of the election was a foregone conclusion. Labour was voted out of a second term of office and the Conservatives regained power. A proposed Anglo-Soviet trade agreement negotiated by the outgoing Labour Government was set aside and Anglo-Russian relations soured as a result. To what extent, if at all, the Foreign Office and Conservative Central Office were party to the fraud is a matter of conjecture. What is obvious is that Reilly, an anti-communist fanatic, and his chiefs at MI6 produced the forged document and put it into circulation. They were fully committed to the use of the forged document for the purpose subsequently achieved and so prevented a leftward looking government of the day winning a second term of office. To the then MI6 hierarchy, democratic socialism was next-door to international communism and one term of government was sufficient for such an extravagance.

There was another factor. Apart from its ever-present inbuilt obsession with the communist threat, the MI6 hierarchy also knew that an incoming Labour government intended that the MI6 files be opened up and that it was even considering the suspension of MI6 pending its reorganisation.[33] These forages by the Intelligence Services in terms of independence of action from the government of the day raise the question of the accountability of the Intelligence Services to the State. It is a matter which has exercised the minds of politicians from time to time but has never been finally resolved.[34]

The author was surprised to learn direct from an MI6 source that MI6 considered that its allegiance was to the Sovereign rather than the Government of the day, 'although for administrative purposes the service came within the ambit of the Foreign Office'. It is apparently the privilege of the Chief of MI6 to call on the Monarch at any time for a private audience and without the leave of the Prime Minister or any other Minister of State. One of the badges of office held by the Chief of MI6 is the key to the side door to Buckingham Palace which is presented to him by the Monarch on his appointment – a custom which apparently commenced during the reign of Charles II.[35] Interesting as

[33]For a fuller account of the Zinoviev letter incident see Knightley, Philip, *The Second Oldest Profession*, Pan Books (1987), 62–64. Within one year Reilly, the instigator, was sent to Russia on MI6 intelligence work and was never seen again.
[34]It came to a head yet again in postwar Great Britain when there was an apparent attempt by MI6 to destabilise the Labour Government of Harold Wilson.
[35]Winterbotham, F.W., *The Nazi Connection*, Weidenfeld and Nicolson (1978), 128.

these quirks of constitutional history may be, they seem to give some credence to the MI6 view that they could steer a different course to that of the government of the day if circumstances warranted it. That is a provocative and dangerous state of affairs. This was the position that prevailed in May 1941.

Churchill at that time would have had to have complete confidence in his Chief of MI6 if he was to have his Intelligence Service conforming with his policies and working loyally with him to ensure their implementation. He knew that was not the case. Menzies embodied to the last detail a Conservative Establishment which was not committed to 'his' war and was bitterly opposed to his policy of American involvement. Churchill therefore appointed a personal spy to spy on the spies. His name was Desmond Morton. It is perhaps noteworthy and certainly disappointing that Major Desmond Morton gave instructions that on his death, all his papers were to be destroyed. And so they were. It is interesting to guess what information may have been included.

Morton's brief was to act as Churchill's personal intelligence chief,[36] so that all information, misinformation and disinformation coming through MI6 channels was first filtered and assessed by Morton before it landed on Churchill's desk. Some of Morton's reports about the exploits, authorised and unauthorised, of MI6 officers would have made interesting reading. Churchill had known Morton for a great number of years. He trusted him implicitly. In the political climate of the day, with the solid ranks of the Conservative Establishment standing against him, Churchill necessarily placed personal loyalty as the highest priority among his appointees. That is why Morton, of proven loyalty over many years, was appointed to the position of supreme intelligence authority, responsible to Churchill alone. Menzies, along with the Chief of MI5, was thus rendered subject to the authority of Morton, an arrangement hardly likely to encourage good relationships and one which may have encouraged Menzies to play a deeper and more obscure game than had hitherto been the case.

Even Menzies's sole authority with the Bletchley decrypts was attacked by Morton's appointment. A Churchill memorandum of August 5, 1940, stated 'All intercepts to Morton. He will inspect them for me. He is to be shown everything.'[37] Morton had served on the staff of General Douglas Haig during the 1914–18 war and was first posted to the Intelligence Services by Churchill when the latter was Secretary of State for War in 1919. Churchill had therefore known him for more than 20 years when he came to power in 1940. A 'bluff, pink-gin

[36]Rather in the same way that Hess had appointed Pfeffer von Saloman in the same capacity.
[37]Irving, David, *Churchill's War*, Veritas Publishing (1987), 389.

swilling' ex-army major, no particular respecter of persons and possessor of an outgoing Irish charm, Morton was an easy, comfortable companion for Churchill. During the 1920s he was for a time the Number Three at MI6. He had built up a useful information-gathering services through the good offices of foreign correspondent newspapermen.[38] But it was during the 1930s, when Churchill was in the political wilderness and snapping at the heels of successive indolent governments in the matter of war preparations, that the Churchill/Morton relationship became particularly thick and rewarding. It was this which established Morton as one of Churchill's trusted few.

Morton lived near Churchill's residence at Chartwell and was a frequent visitor and guest for Sunday lunch. While Churchill was in the political wilderness, Morton was very much part of the MI6 information-gathering service related to German war preparations. In particular he was aware of the information gathered by Air Intelligence through 'Freddie' Winterbotham who was taking advantage of his special relationship with de Ropp, Alfred Rosenberg and the Luftwaffe Air Staff. Winterbotham has stated[39] that it was Morton's custom to attend upon him on Friday evenings to discuss the latest information available as to Luftwaffe plans for expansion and German aircraft production figures. Morton would then carry this information to Churchill, together with the relevant secret MI6 files if necessary, on his weekend visits to Chartwell. Churchill in exile would therefore have the information before the Prime Minister. He would then use the figures to fire awkward questions at Baldwin and others as to the comparisons between German and British aircraft production.

There were ironic features to this exercise. The German figures of production supplied to Winterbotham were almost certainly inflated in the first place. Winterbotham's figures then became so alarming to the Secretary of State for Air, Lord Londonderry, and his department that they were either doctored or suppressed at the Air Ministry. Some of the figures never found their way onto Londonderry's desk and hardly any at all onto Baldwin's desk. Baldwin therefore quite correctly and honestly replied to Churchill's figures (originating from Baldwin's own Secretary of State's department) by saying that he had no information to offer as to German aircraft production.[40]

This service for Churchill rendered by Morton over the crucial years

---

[38]Knightley, Philip, *The Second Oldest Profession*, Pan Books (1987), 91.

[39]Winterbotham, F.W., *The Nazi Connection*, Weidenfeld and Nicolson (1978), 106–07.

[40]Eventually there was a ministerial enquiry into this extraordinary failure of the Air Ministry to supply the figures and other data being obtained by Winterbotham. Londonderry, who had already excelled himself by refusing to back Frank Whittle's jet engine project, was dismissed from office.

in the 1930s cemented the relationship. When Churchill took over in 1940 he appointed Morton as a director of what was then called the Industrial Intelligence Committee or Agency (IIA), which later became the Ministry of Economic Warfare. These were nothing more in their early days than covers for Morton's activities as Churchill's personal intelligence agent. Churchill himself referred to the MEW as the 'Ministry of Ungentlemanly Warfare.' One of the chief purposes of these organisations was the monitoring of MI6 agents who might be overzealous in the search for peace. Churchill always had a profound distrust of what he described as 'the collective wisdom of the services' intelligence organisations'.[41]

It is apparent from the foregoing that British Intelligence MI6 was deeply involved in the Hess mission. There is more than one source of information that confirms this. The plot theory was only advanced after the involvement of British Intelligence had become common knowledge and the official view that the mission was the act of a deranged madman had been discredited. The plot theory goes one step too far. It jumps over the obvious and logical explanation. British Intelligence MI6 or parts of it were involved in the Hess mission because they believed in it. Like Hess, they thought the Anglo-German war was unnecessary and ought to be ended. A united front could then be formed to face the common enemy, communist Russia. Such an explanation rests naturally and easily with the sentiments and political views of those individuals of MI6 and Air Intelligence who operated in the field. Pre-war British Intelligence had been recruited almost exclusively from the ranks of the British Establishment. Those recruits carried with them the political views of the British Establishment. Great Britain was in the wrong war. Russian communism was the real threat to the essential status quo that guaranteed their positions of privilege. They wanted no part of Churchill's war, and he knew that. That is why he had to appoint his own spy to spy on the spies.

Churchill also knew that in spite of their own record of relentless mediocrity in terms of performance, the intelligence services could have illusions of grandeur and act independently of the Government of the day. Its own history proved that. The peculiar allegiance of the Intelligence Services to the Sovereign rather than the Government constituted a serious flaw in the issue of accountability. Churchill knew he had a loose cannon on board. In hindsight, he would have realised that if Hess had not 'taken the wrong turning' when making

---

[41]Costello, John, *Ten Days that saved the West*, Bantam Press (1991), 445.

landfall on the evening of Saturday, May 10, 1941, the loose cannon might, with others, have trained its fire on Churchill and everything that Churchill stood for.

PART FIVE

MAY 1941 – AUGUST 1987
INCARCERATION

24

Post-flight trauma

The greatest secrecy is to be observed as the Prime Minister is deadly afraid that Hess's peace plan will get known and split the country. There have been peace demos in Liverpool.

W.B. MALONE, SECOND LIEUTENANT, SCOTS GUARDS

June 7, 1941

When Rudolf Hess took off from Augsburg he had high hopes of bringing to an end a war that Germany had never wanted. His confidence matched his hopes. Germany had reached the zenith of her military power. The whole of Europe lay under her control. France had been defeated and Great Britain lay prostrate and impotent. And yet the peace terms on offer to Great Britain were to be generous. There was to be no loss of sovereignty and a full preservation of her Empire. Hess had good reason to be confident. In fact, he flew into oblivion. When he landed he was treated not as a peace envoy but as a prisoner of war. He was imprisoned after capture and remained imprisoned for the rest of his life, a total period of 46 years. Twenty-three of those years were spent in solitary confinement. It was an incarceration with no equal in British legal history. Its purpose was purely political. Its occurrence constituted an indelible black mark on the libertarian ideals of a great democracy.

The days following the arrival of Hess in Scotland were marked by such confusions, omissions and contradictions on the part of those involved that the events almost degenerated into farce. They certainly gave no indication of the tragic course of events that were to overtake the potential peacebroker. The whole trouble with the reactions to his arrival was that he arrived at the wrong time, in the wrong place and among the wrong people. His navigational error in crossing the coast in the wrong sector had landed him in a wet, soggy field with a chipped ankle bone under the belligerent and some say, bleary eye of the local Home Guard. He should have been welcomed at an airfield under the control of his friends at the British Air Ministry and elements of the British Peace Party. Never has 'taking the wrong turn' had such far-reaching consequences. Most of those in the Peace Party expecting him, never set eyes on him. Others in the same party who had second thoughts about loyalties and allegiances had to deal with him. Those who did not expect him had to explain why he had arrived. Those who were warned of his coming at the last moment had to improvise policies off the hoof to deal with the situation. The official history of the events is thereby much disfigured.

The facts as to Hess's landing on British territory and the immediate aftermath are well established and amply recorded. They are not in dispute. Hess made a parachute landing (for which he was neither practised or trained) because his Me110 aircraft ran out of fuel. He landed at 11.09 p.m. in a pasture field just north of Eaglesham village, behind Floors Farm, and chipped his ankle bone in doing so. He was assisted for some 200 yards to the nearby cottage of his captor, rustic ploughman, David McLean armed with a pitchfork. Hess introduced himself as Hauptmann (Captain) Alfred Horn[1] and said that he had an important message for the Duke of Hamilton. Lieutenant Clarke, the officer commanding the local unit of the Renfrewshire Home Guard was called. Hess repeated his introduction and his request to see Hamilton. Hess was then taken under escort to Giffnock Scout Hall in the village of Busby which served as the headquarters of 'C' Company, 3rd Battalion, Renfrewshire Home Guard. Hess arrived there at 12.29 a.m. on Sunday, May 11. A telephone call was then made to the Paisley headquarters of the 14th Battalion of the Argyll and Sutherland Highlanders, a regular army unit. A request was made for a military escort to take the prisoner into custody. A sleepy pyjama-clad night duty officer seemed disinclined to take up the invitation and suggested that the prisoner be locked up in a police cell overnight. He later relented and dispatched an escort which arrived at the scout hall about one and a half hours later.

In the meantime, there had arrived at the scout hall, the first person who began to realise the true significance of what was going on. Major Graham Donald was an assistant group officer in the Royal Observer Corps. Donald had already visited the site of the crashed aircraft at Eaglesham. He had noted that the aircraft was unarmed and carried no bomb racks, not the usual garb of a German operational aircraft. Donald had spent some time in pre-war Munich. He could speak some

[1]Alfred Horn was the name of Hess's brother-in-law. Hess had used the name on previous occasions in the 1930s when travelling on holiday, incognito.

German and so when he arrived at the scout hall he could to some extent converse with Hess. Donald soon identified Hess as such and listened again to Hess's repeated plea that he had 'a secret message for the Duke of Hamilton.' The army escort arrived at 2 a.m. and Hess was driven off to Maryhill Barracks on the north-west outskirts of Glasgow where medical facilities were made available for the treatment of his ankle.

At about 1.30 a.m. on May 11 Major Donald had telephoned RAF Turnhouse where the Duke of Hamilton was the station commander. Donald's concern, in view of the prisoner's identity and stated request, was that he be interrogated in accordance with the normal procedures applicable in the case of captured enemy aircrew. Donald was told that the Duke was not available and so he left a message. The message was simple and its importance emphasised. It was that Hess had landed and that he had a special and urgent message for the Duke whom he claimed he knew personally. Donald insisted that Hamilton be given the message immediately. Hamilton was accordingly called from his bed but decided that the interrogation of Hess could wait until 10 a.m. later that morning.

This recital of facts concerning the first few hours of Hess's arrival already poses questions. In the first place, it is the normal procedure that when an enemy flyer is taken into custody, he is searched and an inventory prepared as to his personal possessions. In the case of Hess three separate inventories were prepared as he was passed from one military unit to another. The evidence of this is contained in the documents filed at the Public Record Office. But the actual inventories are not there.[2] The most important item missing is the letter which Hess brought with him for Hamilton. It is the one Ernst Bohle had translated into English for him. It would certainly have included full details of Hess's peace proposals. It may also have included Hess's views on the further prosecution of the war, including the launch of Operation Barbarossa and British attitudes thereto, Anglo-American relations and the effect of Barbarossa on the Jewish question.

The other question posed turns on Hamilton's extraordinary behaviour in ignoring Donald's urgent message and returning to bed (if indeed that is what he did) instead of making arrangements to interrogate Hess. It is standard practice in accordance with RAF procedures for captured enemy aircrew to be interrogated as soon as possible after the event. The practice is well founded. While still in a state of shock, the individual concerned may be more disposed to talk more freely

---

[2]See PRO WO 199/3288A and 3288B, the latter file being closed until 2017.

about operational details than he would several hours later after composing himself so as to exercise caution and restraint. Hamilton's omission was the subject of a formal complaint made subsequently by Colonel Firebrace, the Glasgow Area Military Commander. 'It can only be assumed that the decision to do nothing until the next morning was taken by the Duke of Hamilton. If it is true that the RAF authorities were informed before 0100 hours on May 11 that an important prisoner was anxious to make a statement then their laxity was most unfortunate.'

Hamilton's curious behaviour cannot be explained as a straight dereliction of duty. Hamilton was and always had been an efficient and enthusiastic officer and one very much on terms with the rules and regulations making for good RAF discipline. There was an obvious intent on his part that neither he or his intelligence officer Flight Lieutenant Benson, who could have been sent in his place, should enter any sort of immediate dialogue with Hess. First of all, the full consequences of Hess's arrival had to be considered and appropriate advice taken as to how to handle the situation. Presumably, those are the matters which received Hamilton's (perhaps frantic) attention during the night of May 10–11. But if he was receiving advice or instructions, from whom was he receiving them? From his friends at the Air Ministry? From Air Intelligence? Or MI6? From the Government? From elements of the British Peace Party? Hamilton may well have had a lot of hard thinking to do overnight but he seems to have resolved his position by 10 a.m. that morning. It was then that he and Benson arrived at Maryhill Barracks to interview Hess. Even then his behaviour was far from normal and remained so during that day, again raising questions as to his true role in the events now being enacted.

When Hamilton entered the small room where Hess had spent a comfortable night, Hess immediately requested that Benson and the accompanying guard withdraw. Hess wanted to speak to Hamilton alone. Hamilton acquiesced and the two men withdrew, leaving Hess and Hamilton alone. Again, the matter of correct procedure is raised and is again seen as being set aside by Hamilton in the special circumstances known only to him. Any person free of personal involvement, when interviewing such an important personage as the Deputy Führer of Nazi Germany in the middle of a war with that country, would have insisted on the presence of a guard and more importantly, a second person as a witness to what was said. That was not the case with these first Hess/Hamilton discussions.

The only version of events is that provided by Hamilton. It reveals very little and the suspicion is that the record is of questionable worth. Hamilton apparently disagreed with Hess that they had lunched together sometime during the 1936 Olympic Games in Berlin.[3] Hess made the point that he was unwilling to conduct any peace negotiations with the Churchill Government. Hamilton claims that he made it clear to Hess that there was now only one party in Great Britain. That was a war party, not a peace party. There must have been much more to the conversation than these recorded items. Presumably, they would have discussed their mutual friend, Albrecht Haushofer, and his letter to Hamilton of September 23, 1940. Hess may have enlarged upon the motives that lay behind the letter. Certainly, Hess seemed to have considered that his initial discussions with Hamilton were more fruitful than Hamilton reports because he continually requested further opportunities to meet Hamilton again in the months that followed.[4] There must have been something else in these initial discussions.

Immediately afterwards, Hamilton and Benson went to view the wrecked aircraft. According to Hamilton, Benson 'removed certain parts that he thought might be of use'. There is no mention as to what parts or for what use. Did Hess tell Benson to recover some specific item or items of importance? There is even a loose end with the RAF records relating to the removal of the wrecked aircraft itself from Eaglesham. The operational record book of 63 Maintenance Unit of the RAF shows the collection of the aircraft on May 11 and its removal to 63 Maintenance Unit. The same record then shows that Flight Lieutenant F.E. Cowlrick arrived from 43 Group five days later to take charge of the aircraft.[5] There is no corresponding entry in the operational record book of 43 Group.[6]

While Hess was being removed under strong guard to Buchanan Castle on the shores of Loch Lomond, Hamilton's curious behaviour continued throughout that Sunday. At 5 p.m. he telephoned the Foreign Office and tried to speak to Sir Alexander Cadogan, Permanent Secretary to the Foreign Secretary, to whom he was presumably going to report the events. He was unsuccessful but while engaged in animated conversation with the secretary on duty, found that his call was interrupted. A second voice, said to be that of one of the Prime Minister's secretaries, startled Hamilton by saying 'This is the P.M.'s secretary speaking. The P.M. sent me over to the Foreign Office as he is informed that you have some interesting information.' How the Prime Minister knew that Hamilton would be telephoning at 5 p.m. is not stated but as a result of this strange telephone call and its inter-

---

[3]They had. 'Chips' Channon's diary entry records the event.
[4]A request that was denied. Hess was never again allowed to see Hamilton alone.
[5]PRO AIR 29/1019.
[6]PRO AIR 25/623.

ruption arrangements were made for Hamilton to fly down to London that evening to see Churchill.[7]

There are many different accounts, all of which are contradictory, as to the events related to Hamilton's telephone call to London. It is apparent that more than one contrivance has been wheeled into place to mask the reality of what occurred. Again, a number of points arise in connection with the events of the Sunday. In the first place Hamilton, having interviewed the Deputy Führer of Nazi Germany at 10 a.m., apparently decides to report the fact to his Government at 5 p.m., some seven hours after the event. The normal expectation would be that such an important matter would have been reported immediately after the event. What was Hamilton doing during the intervening seven hours? It is known that he went to see Hess's wrecked aircraft with Benson. According to his own notes he then spent the rest of the morning and the afternoon trying to find a letter he had received from Albrecht Haushofer in July 1939 and writing a two-page report of events. There is no explanation as to why he was searching for an old letter or why he should spend several hours putting a two page report together. All that is known is that these two activities received his attention before he thought fit to telephone and report the fact of Hess's arrival to his political masters.[8] One ponders as to what other activities, unrecorded and unreported, occupied Hamilton's time during that Sunday.

Hamilton was not alone with his curious behaviour on that day. His version of the extraordinary telephone conversation with the Foreign Office is confirmed by Cadogan's diary entry for that day. It is also contradicted by Sir John Colville, Churchill's secretary, and both versions are contradicted by Churchill himself. Cadogan's diary records that he was home during the afternoon of Sunday, May 11. At about 5.30 p.m. he received a telephone call from his private secretary, John Addis, who was on duty at the Foreign Office on that day. Cadogan's diary records that 'Addis reported that a German pilot had landed near Glasgow and had asked to see the Duke of Hamilton The latter was so impressed that he was flying to London and wants to see me at Number 10 tonight. Half an hour later, heard that the PM was sending to meet His Grace at the airfield and would bring him to Chequers.'

Colville, the Prime Minister's secretary, gives a totally different version in his published diaries of the same incident. He says the call from Hamilton came on Sunday morning, not in the afternoon. He reports that after attending morning service he had walked over to the Foreign

---

[7]Irving, David, *Hess. The Missing Years 1941–1945*, Grafton Books, (1989), 130.
[8]PRO PREM 3/219–7. The Hamilton Report.

Office where he had found Nicholas Lawford, a Foreign Office secretary, in a heated telephone conversation with the Duke of Hamilton. Colville records Lawford as saying 'Hold on a minute. I think this is your man.' According to Colville's version he then took the telephone and said to Hamilton 'Has someone arrived?' After a long pause, Hamilton replied and said 'Yes, please be at Northolt to meet me.'

It is unacceptable that experienced senior civil servants of the status of Cadogan, Addis and Colville should in innocence record such differing accounts of the same event. It is apparent that one or more versions are contrived. It is likely that the Hamilton/Cadogan version is nearer the mark. Lawford's own (unpublished) diary shows that on the date in question he was not on duty at the Foreign Office. He was with his parents on their Hertfordshire estate. Lawford has also confirmed that his colleague, John Addis, was on duty at the Foreign Office on that day. All the versions make it clear that Churchill was already aware of the arrival, if not of Hess, then of someone of political importance. Churchill himself denies this. He says that news of Hess's arrival 'came late in the evening after dinner.' The dinner to which he refers was the one he attended at Dytchley Park, near Oxford.

In fact, it is now known from more than one source that Churchill was aware of Hess's impending arrival before the event. He had been informed on the Saturday evening that Hess was on his way. His informant was his Minister of Labour, Ernest Bevin who had telephoned the news from the Queens Hotel, Leeds. Bevin had received the information from Albert James Head, an area representative of the Transport and General Workers Union who had an industrial contact inside the Messerschmitt works at Augsburg.[9] Corroborative evidence is provided by Lady Nancy Tree, Churchill's hostess at the Dytchley Park dinner. She recalls how she was puzzled 'by the strange request by the Prime Minister on the Sunday morning that the Duke of Hamilton would be joining the guests at Dytchley Park that evening'. Churchill then added the words 'Truth is sometimes stranger than fiction' and told her not to breathe a word to the other guests.[10]

When Hamilton duly arrived at Dytchley with his news as to Hess's arrival, Churchill was able to indulge his play-acting abilities before the assembled guests who included, perhaps significantly, Archibald Sinclair, his Secretary of State for Air. Churchill's words when Hamilton arrived have been well reported: 'Come and tell us this

---

[9]This remarkable intelligence is related in detail by Albert Head in the *Yorkshire Post* issue of November 4, 1969.

[10]Tree, Ronald, *When the Moon was High. Memoirs of Peace and War 1897–1942*, London (1962), 130.

funny story of yours' But even the funny story had to wait until Churchill and the other guests had sat through a full-length Marx Brothers film. It is not difficult to imagine the frustration and anxieties of the tired Hamilton as he was obliged to watch the antics of Churchill's favourite film funny men. Churchill's prolonged play-acting to stir up the elements of surprise at the announcement of Hess's arrival may have impressed the home guests but had no significance beyond that. Much more important was the three-hour discussion between Churchill, Hamilton and Sinclair that took place after midnight when the film show had been packed away and the other guests banished to bed. There is no record of these discussions but they appear to have precipitated a day of near crisis on the following day, Monday, May 12.

Churchill arrived at No. 10 Downing Street first thing in the morning, after a headlong high speed dash by car from Dytchley, dropping Hamilton off at the Foreign Office. There then followed a series of high-level discussions with his senior ministers, service chiefs, Menzies and not least, Desmond Morton. Churchill confided to Eden, his most senior colleague, 'I don't believe the story.' It is interesting to conjecture just what Churchill *did* believe at this point and ponder as to the part then being played by Hamilton. Hamilton had delayed interrogating Hess when he had first arrived and had delayed in reporting the matter to Churchill and representatives of Churchill's Government. Were these delays due to Hamilton's indecision as to the role he wished to play personally in response to Hess's arrival? He may have spent the best part of the Sunday in communication with others who may have represented the British Peace Party. As a result, he seems to have come to the final conclusion that he was a Churchill man. He was therefore acting accordingly.

There is an interesting supplement to Hamilton's behaviour following Hess's arrival. After his headlong dash to London with Churchill on the Monday, Hamilton spent time with Cadogan at the Foreign Office. According to the latter's diary for May 15 Hamilton expressed a wish to see King George VI. Cadogan advised Hamilton to see Churchill first, but Hamilton made his own arrangements and lunched with the King on May 16. Churchill was only informed subsequently.[11] As the holder of the senior Scottish dukedom, Hamilton had the right to approach the Sovereign direct. Nevertheless, it is interesting to note that he apparently did not consider that Churchill should be informed of, or be a party to, his visit or be informed as to its purpose. As for

---

[11]PRO INF I/912

Churchill, the three hour discussion with Hamilton on the Sunday evening may well have enlightened him as to the true nature and extent of the Hess peace initiative and the cannons it intended to turn loose.

Meanwhile, on the other side of the water in Germany, Churchill's play-acting was being well matched by Hitler. Forewarned by Rosenberg on the Saturday evening (probably before Hess took off from Augsburg) that Hess was on his way, he had to play the part of a dumbfounded onlooker as agreed with Hess at their meeting at the Berlin Chancellery five days previously. He played the part well when Pintsch, Hess's adjutant, arrived at the Berghof with news of Hess's initiative at noon on the Sunday. He immediately summoned Goering and Ribbentrop to the Berghof. Significantly, Himmler and Goebbels who were not party to the plot did not join them until later. By then, Hitler was giving an appropriate display of play-acting to all and sundry and expressing his shock and amazement at Hess's exploit. As General Karl Bodenschatz, Goering's adjutant, commented, 'The Führer's shock and surprise on hearing of Hess's flight was an example of his superb acting.'[12] Hitler knew that, as agreed with Hess, he had to play the insanity card but not until he knew that Hess's mission had failed. In the early hours after Hess's departure that was not the case. He therefore rejected the opinion of the Luftwaffe general, Ernst Udet that because of the prevailing westerly winds, Hess would never have made landfall in Great Britain. He had almost certainly flown into oblivion somewhere in the North Sea. By Sunday evening, Hitler had received no coded message announcing the success of Hess's mission. He was therefore obliged to come to terms with Udet's assessment and assume that Hess and his aircraft were at the bottom of the North Sea. Thereupon, Hitler succumbed to genuine grief at the supposed loss of his most trusted and loyal friend, a fact confirmed by both Goebbels and Mussolini, to whom he telephoned the news of Hess's loss.[13]

Goebbels was not brought into the picture until Monday, May 12, by which time the preliminary broadcast announcement had been drafted by Hitler's press secretary, Otto Dietrich. In accordance with Hitler's agreement with Hess, it referred to Hess having gone missing 'apparently in a fit of madness' and having left a letter which revealed 'a mental breakdown'. The broadcast went out on German radio at 8 p.m. on that Monday evening. Goebbels was not pleased. He had not been consulted about either the plot or the broadcast. He was of the opinion that the reference to madness and mental breakdown was

---

[12]See statement by General Milch, May 20, 1945, PRO WO 20/4170.
[13]The Ciano diaries, 1939–43, 352.

damaging to the Nazi image. He did not know of course that the insanity card was to be played in the event of failure of the mission.

There was a further extension to Hitler's play-acting. He had to go through the motions of uncovering the preparations for Hess's flight. Others may have been involved and they had to be punished. Albrecht Haushofer was summoned to the Berghof, put in a small room with a guard and told to prepare a written report for Hitler setting down all Albrecht's connections and in particular, those that might have been used by Hess in terms of peace initiatives. Albrecht's report was detailed. It was also specific as to names.[14] Halifax and Butler received special mention.[15] Albrecht was subsequently arrested and interrogated by the Gestapo but released after eight weeks.[16] Hitler's play-acting finally finished when he appointed Martin Bormann as Hess's successor as party leader. It was an unfortunate appointment that traded crude barbarity and craven ambition for integrity and loyalty.

Meanwhile in Great Britain it had been agreed that Ivone Kirkpatrick, a senior officer at the Foreign Office, should fly to Scotland with Hamilton to see Hess. Kirkpatrick possessed considerable pre-war experience in Berlin at the British Embassy, where he had been in contact with most of the Nazi hierarchy, including Hess. He would be able to formally identify Hess and invite him to explain the purpose of his visit. The two emissaries flew off that same day, May 12, and arrived at Buchanan Castle at midnight. Hess was roused from his sleep. He did not recognise Kirkpatrick, although the latter was convinced of Hess's identity. According to Kirkpatrick's report, Hess delivered a three-hour homily, referring constantly to some of his handwritten notes which he produced from a brown envelope. He dealt at length with a number of items. These included a German version of Anglo-German relations since the 19th century, the hopelessness of Great Britain's current military position, the pointless nature and waste of human life occasioned by a continuance of the war, the German wish for friendship with Great Britain and the peace proposals on offer – including the assurance as to the continuance of British sovereignty and independence, and that of her Empire. These items held nothing that was new, but there may have been other matters that may have been edited out.

---

[14]Those mentioned included Alec Douglas (later Lord) Home, Astor, Balfour, Lindsay, Winterbotham, Derby, Stanley, Lothian, Strang, Mallet, Hoare, Halifax and Butler.

[15]Three weeks later Churchill moved Butler out of the Foreign Office and into the Ministry of Education. Presumably Churchill thought he could do less damage there.

[16]He was re-arrested some three years later, when his knowledge of British affairs was of no further use to the Nazi administration. He was shot by the SS on April 23, 1945. His father Karl lived peacefully through the war but committed suicide in 1946.

From this point, all the records relating to conversations with Hess, his imprisonment, his actions, behaviour and in particular his health, both physical and mental, are Churchill-government inspired. By the time Kirkpatrick and Hamilton had flown up to Scotland, Churchill, after the uncharacteristic hesitancy and indecision apparent on the Monday morning, had decided how to play the Hess event. It is therefore probable that at least some of the official records now on file were edited to accommodate the course of action on which he had determined.[17] The report by Kirkpatrick and later ones by Sir John Simon and Lord Beaverbrook may be cases in point.[18]

Early the next morning, May 13, Kirkpatrick and Hamilton returned to RAF Turnhouse and at 10.30 a.m. Kirkpatrick telephoned his first brief to Cadogan. The fact that Kirkpatrick was sent back to Buchanan Castle on two further occasions to question Hess would indicate that there was some item or items of particular interest to London; but Kirkpatrick's second and third reports, as filed, are even briefer than the first and contain nothing new.

There is however one further detail contained in Kirkpatrick's report of May 13. It refers to Hess being in the best of health and states that the doctors had confirmed that there was no trace of drugs.[19] This clean bill of health on arrival in Great Britain was paralleled by an equally clean bill of health shortly after Hess arrived in Nuremberg some four years later. It is suggested that particular regard should therefore be paid to the several reports of his ill health, physical and mental, during the interim period when he was imprisoned in Great Britain, and to the possible cause of such debility.

On the evening of Monday, May 12, the German radio announced that Hess was missing and that he had taken an aircraft and flown off from Augsburg, 'apparently in a fit of madness.'[20] It occurred to Beaverbrook that if the German version of Hess's madness and mental breakdown was being broadcast to the world then it would be no bad thing if the British broadcast nothing that would dispel that notion. It would certainly counter the rumours that were already surfacing that

[17]According to Philby's reports to the Russian NKVD, Eden and Beaverbrook both visited Hess during the first week of his captivity. Neither visit is the subject of any official British record. (Costello, John, *Ten Days that Saved the West*, Bantam Press (1991), 442.)

[18]Kirkpatrick's official report of the three-hour discussions comprised just 2½ pages of manuscript. By the time the report was presented to the Nuremberg Military Tribunal it had shrunk to 1½ pages. Such vigorous pruning is hardly likely to have left the fundamentals intact, even if they were there in the first place (Nuremberg Documents, M117/118/119).

[19]PRO PREM 3/219/7.

[20]The delay in the German announcement arose because Hitler waited a full two days for news of Hess's success. When the previously agreed code message failed to arrive, Hitler released the story of Hess's madness, also as previously agreed.

peace feelers were in the air and that this was the true purpose of the Hess flight (which was, of course, the case). Beaverbrook claims that he mentioned the idea to Churchill while walking through St James's Park. It seems that the plan had already been adopted and was being implemented by the time Hess arrived at his first permanent place of imprisonment at Mytchett Place, near Aldershot, on May 20, having spent an uncomfortable four days in the Tower of London, after being moved south by train on May 17.

Sinister overtones became apparent as soon as Hess moved into Mytchett Place. He found himself being attended by several psychiatrists who quickly produced a myriad of symptoms, diagnoses and treatments, accompanied by the administering of unspecified drugs. It is difficult to resist the suggestion that if Hess was not a psychiatric case when he arrived in Scotland, he would soon become one as a result of the treatment he was about to receive in England.

With Hess safely locked away, Churchill turned his attention to the public relations aspect of Hess's arrival. His wish was to lend credence to the Germans' own version by default. He dare not openly confirm Hess's 'insanity', for the good reason that he was not insane. Also, he did not wish to openly suggest anything of that nature because it could lead to a claim for repatriation. He therefore determined on a policy of complete silence. At 11 p.m. on Monday, May 12, and in response to the German announcement made three hours earlier, a press conference was held at the Ministry of Information. The Minister, Duff Cooper, read out a short statement confirming Hess's arrival. There was no mention as to his mental state or the purpose of his mission. In particular, there was no mention as to any peace proposals. It fitted in well with the German announcement. Immediately thereafter, at 11.20 p.m., the BBC broadcast the same statement. Churchill then drafted a fairly full statement and this time included a reference to peace proposals, albeit dressed up as the product of a deranged mind, which he intended to present to the House of Commons. His senior advisers were adamant that he should not do so. They included Eden, Cadogan, Duff Cooper and Beaverbrook, who all seemed more aware than Churchill as to the inherent danger of mentioning peace proposals in any context. After some angry words, in particular with Eden over the telephone, the statement was eventually scrapped altogether.[21]

MPs had to live on the scraps of information offered to them through the BBC. They were not pleased. Churchill, besieged in the Commons, stonewalled throughout. 'I have nothing to add at present

---

[21]Cadogan diary, May 14, 1941.

to the statement on the wireless. I think this is one of those cases where the imagination is somewhat baffled by the facts as they present themselves.'[22] This sort of statement hardly helped. It told very little and stimulated the demand for more. Rumour and speculation abounded. The press in particular were up in arms at the lack of news about an event which truly deserved the epithet 'sensational'. Many angry letters were received from members of the public.

It is interesting to consider the furore that would have been caused by the publication of Churchill's original statement, as drafted, mentioning the fact of a peace overture. On the margin of that typewritten draft Churchill had pencilled, in his own handwriting, 'He (Hess) has also made other statements which it would not be in the public interest to disclose.'[23] These 'other' statements by Hess were not available in the public interest then and they are still not available in the public interest now, almost 60 years after the event.

The furore would have been increased if it had been known that, whereas Churchill apparently could not trust the details to his own Parliament and people, he could do so to his confidant across the Atlantic. Roosevelt was sent a shortened version of Churchill's draft (minus the pencilled note) as originally intended for the Commons. Churchill added the comment, 'If Hess expected to contact members of a peace movement in England whom he could help oust the present Government then this is an encouraging sign of the ineptitude of the German Intelligence Service.'[24] Roosevelt was having none of it. In discussions with his advisers, Harry Hopkins, Sumner Welles and Robert Sherwood, he posed a question: 'I wonder what is really behind this story?' Sherwood supplied the answer, hitting the nail on the head: 'A small but powerful minority in Great Britain were not averse to peace talks.'[25]

It was of course only a matter of time before rumours started to accumulate around the name and reputation of the Duke of Hamilton. On May 19, the Air Ministry was having to assure the House of Commons that 'the Duke had never met and had never been in correspondence with Hess'. This succeeded in combining an untruth with a half truth to effect a denial of the Hess/Hamilton connection.[26] Harry Pollitt and his British Communist Party were undeterred. Pollitt made a personal attack on Hamilton in one of the party's pamphlets. He published details of Hamilton's pre-war membership of the Anglo-

---

[22]Hansard, May 13, 1941.
[23]PRO PREM 3/219/4.
[24]PRO PREM 3/468/409.
[25]Sherwood, Robert, *Roosevelt and Hopkins*, New York (1948), 374.
[26]PRO INF 1/912.

German Fellowship. Hamilton was obliged to sue for libel and Pollitt took up the challenge, at one stage threatening to call Hess as a witness of Hamilton's Germanic sympathies. After Government intervention the libel action was dropped, but not before a good many Churchillian feathers were ruffled.[27]

Soon afterwards, the transatlantic confidence also leaked. This gave rise to further embarrassment for Churchill in the Commons at the hands of Sidney Silverman and 'Manny' Shinwell. Silverman asked the question which was on everyone's lips: 'There are many people in this country who believe rightly or wrongly that Hess has arrived here with a definite plan for peace. Is that the case or not? Why should the Government be afraid to say this was so and let us know what the proposal was? Why the USA but not us? The people are entitled to know.'[28] But Churchill was adamant. He continued to stonewall, with the words 'I have nothing to add'.

If Churchill had not initially been aware of the danger to his own personal position from the advent of Hess, he adjusted to that idea within a matter of days. It is probable, through Morton, that he had himself investigated the strength of the British Peace Party and obtained a realistic assessment of the threats it posed. His initial hesitancy as to how to deal with Hess was replaced by a Beaverbrook-inspired policy which he believed would stifle the threat, and did so. The Hess flight was to be made a non-event. It was to be set down as a lunatic act by a deranged individual, precisely as the Germans had already announced.

Thus it was that a fairy-story dreamed up initially by Hitler and Hess became the stuff of official record. Hess could be shut away in isolation out of sight and, hopefully, soon out of mind. There would be no bulletins, no news, complete secrecy as to his whereabouts and activities and the tightest security arrangements at all times. Last but not least, Hess could be handed over into the care of psychiatrists who would be free to prescribe such drugs as were thought appropriate.[29] The policy may fairly be described as one of 'isolate and forget'. The policy was an unqualified success. Gradually, the clamour for information died away. No elaborating statement was ever made to the House of Commons and the British Peace Party were left to dwell upon what might have been.

---

[27]PRO AIR 19/864.

[28]PRO PREM 3/219/7.

[29]The J.R. Rees book, *The Case of Rudolf Hess*, deals at some length with Hess as a psychiatric subject; but, remarkably, no mention is made of the drugs prescribed for him during his imprisonment.

Much has been made of the glaring omission to use the presence of Hess on British soil for propaganda purposes. But of course the added publicity that would have been generated would have cut right across the 'isolate and forget' policy. There were strong advocates in favour of propaganda use but Churchill ruled all the suggestions made as being out of order. Hess was never used for propaganda purposes. Across the water, Hitler, Goebbels and the whole German people were astounded by the omission. Goebbels's comments were colourful: 'We are dealing with dumb amateurs. What we would do if the positions were reversed?'[30] Goebbels was not party to Churchill's deeper game.

There is an important postscript to the trauma experienced by all the interested parties immediately following the arrival of Hess. Reference has already been made to the handwritten note appended by Churchill to his initial draft of a statement he was preparing for submission to the Commons. Churchill had written the words 'He (Hess) has also made other statements which it would not be in the public interest to disclose.' Hess had apparently said something of importance in discussion which Churchill felt should not become public knowledge. On May 13, only three days after Hess landed, Churchill sent a memo to his colleague, Anthony Eden, which perhaps suggests what the other statements by Hess were about. It concludes with the words 'Like other Nazi leaders this man is potentially a war criminal and he and his confederates may well be declared outlaws at the close of the war. In this his repentance would stand him in good stead.'[31] Why did Churchill describe Hess as a *potential* war criminal? At the Nuremberg Military Tribunal, held after the war, Hess was acquitted on all charges of being a war criminal. The 'crimes against humanity', and in particular the Holocaust, did not take place until after the launch of Operation Barbarossa in June 1941, a month after Hess's flight. Hess was not therefore involved. When Churchill used the words 'potentially a war criminal', no war crimes had been committed.

The only construction that makes sense of Churchill's remarks is that he was aware of the war crimes *that were going to be committed in the future*.[32] Hess knew what might happen if Operation Barbarossa was launched and full rein given to the Heydrich/Eichmann Final Solution to the Jewish problem. Had he told Churchill or his interrogators? Was this included among the 'other statements' that Churchill felt were not for public consumption? It would explain not only Churchill's reference to Hess as a potential war criminal (i.e. as

---

[30]Goebbels diary, May 19, 1941.
[31]Churchill, Winston, *History of the Second World War*, Vol III.
[32]And were.

someone in some way responsible for what was going to happen) but also his reference to Hess's 'repentance', which might well relate to Hess's declared attitudes in 1941 to Nazi excesses in the past and those that lay in the future.

25

Isolate and forget

No visitors, no contact with the outside world, special guards, no newspapers, no wireless.

WINSTON CHURCHILL, May 1941

On May 20, 1941, Hess was transferred under heavy guard and in complete secrecy from the Tower of London to Mytchett Place near Aldershot. If Mytchett Place was to fit into a scheme to reduce Hess's considerable qualities of resilience and help produce the psychiatric case required by Churchill's policy in conditions of complete secrecy, then it was an ideal choice. A red-brick, run down Victorian mansion, it was dark, gloomy and foreboding. It was heavily policed by Grenadier and Scots Guards. Around the structure itself were perimeter defences, including slit trenches, barbed wire entanglements and road blocks. The external approaches could be floodlit if required. Within the building there was a 24-hour guard. Hess was the sole resident, apart from staff, and his personal quarters were encased in a wire-mesh cage which was under lock and key. His only companions were to be 'Lieutenant Colonel Wallace' (probably Lieutenant Colonel Thomas Kendrick), Major Frank E. Foley and 'Captain Barnes'. They were all intelligence officers and Hess knew that. His personal quarters were bugged for the benefit of his companions and Hess knew that too.[1] It goes without saying that the bugged tapes have never been made available for public scrutiny.

The implementation of the 'isolate and forget' policy was prosecuted assiduously. Hand in hand with the complete shutdown of all news items and comments as to Hess's whereabouts and activities, an incarceration was conducted at Mytchett Place which in its total effect bordered on torture. It seems that conditions were specifically

[1]PRO PREM 3/219/7.

designed to break Hess's spirit and reduce him to a psychiatric case, incapable of mounting a threat as a political personage. Churchill's original instructions for Hess's imprisonment included the injunction 'No visitors, no contact with the outside world, special guards, no newspapers, no wireless.'[2] And thus it was. Hess complained incessantly about his isolation, the lack of amenities and the constant noise which he claimed was deliberate and which prevented him from sleeping. He knew that he was surrounded by intelligence officers, that his quarters were bugged and that he was under constant surveillance, even in his most intimate moments. But his main complaint and fear concerned the activities of several psychiatrists who attended upon him.

In 1941, it was fair comment to suggest that anyone placed in the care of a psychiatrist was deemed 'mad'. That suited Churchill's book and that is presumably why the psychiatrists descended upon Hess. There certainly was no medical reason. Hess was given a clean bill of health, both physical and mental, soon after he had arrived in Great Britain. Psychiatry in 1941 was even less of an exact science than it is today and here was a specimen patient available as a human guinea pig. It is therefore unsurprising that a series of psychiatrists who examined Hess during the four years of his solitary imprisonment in Great Britain, prior to his attendance at Nuremberg, spawned a myriad of symptoms, diagnoses and remedies all of which were generously underpinned with the application of unspecified drugs. The varying conclusions were such that it is difficult to determine which of the minds were the most confused, the patient's or the doctors'.

Hess seems to have entered into the spirit of things by inventing his own 'hysterical amnesia', feigning loss of memory and then recovering it again as and when the mood took him. Apart from the hysterical amnesia, Hess was variously diagnosed as suffering from delusions of persecution, delusions of grandeur, hallucinatory tendencies, paranoia and paranoid schizophrenia.[3] The psychiatrists could not agree among themselves. Colonel John Rawlings Rees was in overall charge, but he did not accept the diagnosis of his hands-on delegates, Colonel Gibson Graham and Major Henry Victor Dicks.[4] Dicks was of Jewish ancestry and was openly hostile towards Hess. Rees produced a book in 1947 entitled *The Case of Rudolf Hess*. It included many things quite divorced from psychiatry, including an account of Hess's reputed

---

[2]Irving, David, *Hess. The Missing Years 1941–1945*, Grafton Books, (1989), 148.
[3]Editorial comment, *The Lancet*, December 8, 1945.
[4]It goes without saying that none of them diagnosed Hess as normal.

flight plan which is highly suspect.[5] More significantly and surprising in a textbook on psychiatry, it gives no prescription list of the drugs prescribed for Hess in response to the several diagnoses made. It is an unexpected and unexplained omission and it is difficult to resist a sinister interpretation.

Hess himself was under the impression that he was being systematically drugged while at Mytchett Place. He was suspicious as to the content of his intake of both food and drink. Distressing side-effects were produced, including stomach pains, diarrhoea and constipation and the involuntary retention of urine necessitating the use of a catheter. If there was in fact the relentless application of unspecified drugs added to the other privations described, do we not have a picture of a peculiarly British brand of gentle torture and the manufacturing of a required psychiatric case?[6] Whether or not the inference is correct, the result was certainly a consequence of Churchill's policy of isolate and forget.

When Hess was moved away from Mytchett Place and its attendant psychiatrists in June 1942 he was subjected to further medical examinations at Maindiff Court Hospital at Abergavenny. The medical opinion given then was that 'his condition was such that the account given of his medical state at Mytchett was almost incredible'.[7] The account given was of course entirely credible if Hess had been under the influence of drugs. In any case, it was perhaps inevitable that the deprivations at Mytchett Place and the effect of the drugs then administered would produce, at some time, a state of clinical depression. This likelihood grew with the realisation, as every day passed, that his mission had failed.

On June 15 an incident occurred which has been described as a suicide attempt. In fact, it seems to have been more an act of desperate frustration. Unable to sleep during the night, Hess dressed himself in the full regalia of a Luftwaffe officer and, when the cage door to his quarters was opened to admit Major Dicks, dashed out, made a hurdle-type jump over the banisters and fell down the well of the stairs. He was not badly injured and soon recovered. It may be that there was a special significance to the date of this incident and the effect that it may have had on Hess's behaviour that day. On March 27, Hitler had put back the date for the launch of Operation Barbarossa,

---

[5]It is rejected out of hand by Helmut Kaden, the airfield manager at Augsburg from where Hess flew on May 10.

[6]The evidence of gentle British torture is not unknown to the author. He was involved in the questioning of some ex-SS prisoners of war at Mestre in Northern Italy in 1946. They were stripped naked 'for the purpose of interrogation'.

[7]Rees, J.R., *The Case of Rudolf Hess*, William Heinemann (1947), 68.

from May 15 to June 15. The delay was caused by the anti-German insurrection in Yugoslavia and the German need to take the necessary military action to secure the southern flank before attacking Russia. In fact, Hitler made a further postponement on April 30 fixing the date at June 22, but Hess may not have been aware of this postponement before he flew to Scotland. To him, June 15 would have marked the beginning of Operation Barbarossa, with all its probable consequences. If Hess had already advised his British interrogators of these dangers, with particular reference to the Jewish problem, and had received nothing by way of a response, then he had good cause to be both depressed and frustrated on June 15.[8]

Nevertheless, Hess's sense of failure was not entirely complete while at Mytchett Place. He still made efforts to bring his representations before those he thought could help him. During the final week of June he prepared a paper for submission to the British Cabinet which has been described as 'a model of clarity, exposition and logical argument.'[9] On August 7 he prepared a 45-page document for the Duke of Hamilton, and on November 13 he wrote a personal letter to King George VI, to be delivered through the Swiss Ambassador – a letter which was chased by another with instructions that if it were not possible to deliver the letter to the King, it was to be redirected to Hamilton. The receipt of these missives was never acknowledged and no replies were ever received. They have never been made available for public inspection.

On June 9 Hess was visited by Viscount Simon, the Lord Chancellor, a liberal academic and a noted appeaser of the pre-war years. During that time he had been Foreign Secretary and, in that capacity, had met Hess in Berlin. The visit was apparently suggested to Churchill by Ivone Kirkpatrick. It was felt that Hess might be disposed to open up about German war plans if the conversations were held with a known appeaser of the Chamberlain school and the sort of person who Hess might think had connections with the British Peace Party.[10] Simon was to be accompanied by Kirkpatrick, an interpreter, a stenographer and, at Hess's request, a German witness, by name Kurt Maass. The conversations were to be conducted in great secrecy. News of the forthcoming meeting appears to have had a considerable effect upon Hess. He became excited, nervous and extremely agitated.[11] Of course, he

[8]Hess's comment on being told of the actual launch of Operation Barbarossa on June 22 was 'so they have started after all.' The last two words are perhaps significant. They tend to indicate that Hess knew all about Barbarossa but had the incorrect earlier date in mind.
[9]Rees, J.R., *The Case of Rudolf Hess*, William Heinemann (1947), 35–36.
[10]Cadogan/Kirkpatrick conversation, May 13, 1941. PRO PREM 3/219/7.
[11]Rees, J.R., *The Case of Rudolf Hess*, William Heinemann (1947), 37.

had no way of knowing that the discussions were to be anything other than genuine peace talks. His apprehension is therefore understandable. He probably thought that this would be his one and only chance to press his case. He was never in with a chance. War secrets, not peace secrets, was what Churchill was after and he made that clear in his original instructions to Simon.

Simon and his colleagues duly arrived on the morning of June 9. Simon, Kirkpatrick and Hess were supplied with aliases. Simon and Kirkpatrick became Dr Guthrie and Dr MacKenzie respectively and Hess became 'Jonothan'. The reason for the aliases is unknown. Perhaps the oddest name within the group belonged to Kurt Maass, the German witness to the proceedings brought in at the request of Hess, who was described as an interned junior German consular official.[12] The same name also featured as the signatory on the 'Wanted' notices which appeared in South Africa when Churchill was on the run as a young man. It is an odd coincidence. Did it have an equally odd significance?

According to Simon's report of the proceedings at the meeting, Hess launched into his now familiar (at least to Kirkpatrick) German version of Anglo-German relations and reiterated the German wish for peace and the hand of Great Britain in friendship. Again after two hours, as reported by Simon, Hess stated the peace terms in simple terms. They were the same as those put to Kirkpatrick and Hamilton at their earlier talk with Hess at Buchanan Castle. Great Britain and her Empire were to retain their independence and Germany was to enjoy hegemony over Central and Eastern Europe. In addition, the previously owned German colonies were to be returned, indemnity given for all war losses and peace terms agreed with Italy as part of the overall settlement. In answer to a Simon query, Hess confirmed that German hegemony in Europe would include continental Russia. That would arise as a result of negotiations with that country, not armed conflict. In spite of judicial probing by Simon as to German war policies and intentions, no significant data were forthcoming from Hess.

All that Hess is reported to have said had already been reported as said previously. Certainly, Simon's conclusions fitted tidily into what was then the official line. Perhaps that was the real purpose of the visit. Simon concluded that Hess came of his own initiative without the consent or knowledge of Hitler, that Hess imagined the existence of a British Peace Party and that he had continually requested that he be put in touch with the 'opposition' Party. Churchill's own comments sit

[12]Diary of Commandant of Mytchett Place, Lieutenant Colonal A. Malcolm Scott, June 9, 1941.

equally well with the official file. 'I have read the Guthrie and Jonothan transcripts which seem to consist of the outpourings of a disordered mind. They are like a conversation with a mentally defective child who has been guilty of murder or arson.'[13] Churchill was perhaps unaware that a day or so before Hess met the Simon delegation he had been asked to do the standard British army intelligence test.[14] His rating was in the top 10 per cent of intelligence distribution.[15]

There is a second recorded visit to Hess by an important political personage. On September 1, Lord Beaverbrook, then Churchill's Minister of Supply, had been appointed by Churchill to head up a Cabinet mission to Russia to consider ways and means of increasing the supply of military aid to Russia. Operation Barbarossa had been launched on June 22 and deep inroads made into Russian territory by German forces. Beaverbrook's mission to Moscow was to take place on September 19. Beaverbrook knew he would run into questions about Hess and no doubt he wished first to get the story from the man himself. Having obtained the necessary permission from Churchill and Eden, he duly attended upon Hess at Mytchett Place on September 9. No record is available as to the content of their talks. They were certainly taped and the (edited?) tape handed over to Stalin by Beaverbrook when they met. It has never been made available to the British public. The unedited version may well have been interesting.

There was a certain meeting of minds in Beaverbrook and Hess on more than one topic. Beaverbrook was a maverick. He blew hot and cold in his support for Churchill and his loyalty was always in serious doubt. He was a noted anti-Semite, had met Adolf Hitler on three occasions pre-war and had expressed his open admiration for the man. No records are available of the Beaverbrook/Hitler pre-war talks. Perhaps they have been destroyed to avoid embarrassment. Beaverbrook was also a staunch supporter of the British Empire and its independent status. He was himself a Canadian. He clashed, sometimes violently, with Churchill over Churchill's pro-American stance.[16]

Both Beaverbrook and Hess gave some indication of the subject matter of their discussions in later circumstances. When Stalin bluntly asked Beaverbrook why Hess had flown to Great Britain he received an equally blunt: 'To persuade Great Britain to join Germany in making an attack on Russia.'[17] Also, when Hess was due to appear before

[13]PRO PREM 3/219/5.
[14]The Raven Progressive Matrices Test.
[15]Irving, David, *Hess. The Missing Years 1941–1945*, Grafton Books, (1989), 192.
[16]*Ibid*, 275.
[17]Beaverbrook papers.

the Nuremberg Military Tribunal after the war, he prepared one of his long dissertations setting down all the facts and circumstances to be used in his defence. He listed his complaints relating to his imprisonment in Great Britain, in particular his claim that he had been drugged, and he referred to his conversation with Beaverbrook on September 9, 1941, stating that he had told Beaverbrook 'some things in connection with the German/Russian war which had just broken out.'[18] What were the 'some things' to which he was referring? Did they concern Heidrich, Eichmann and the Jewish problem?

On June 26, 1942, Hess was moved from Mytchett Place to Maindiff Court at Abergavenny in Wales. Maindiff Court had been used as an admissions hospital for entry into Monmouthshire Mental Hospital some 1½ miles away.[19] It was a good move for Hess. The atmosphere was more relaxed and most of the irksome practices and privations suffered at Mytchett were abandoned. An entire wing of the hospital was made available to Hess and the guards were reduced in number. There were no hidden microphones. Hess was even taken out of his new prison for some hill climbing in the nearby Welsh hills. The walks were comparatively short and under guard, but they did go to make a much greater measure of freedom than had previously been the case.[20] This relaxation of security went hand in glove with the relaxation in the political significance previously attached to the Hess flight. Churchill's policy had succeeded and the political turmoil had died away.

In August 1942, Brendan Bracken, then Minister of Information and in America, was guilty of a major indiscretion when he said that Hess had flown to Great Britain 'expecting to find Quislings who would help him to overthrow Churchill and make peace.' Bracken also confirmed that Hamilton had met Hess before the war. This of course, contradicted Sinclair's earlier statement to the House of Commons.[21] Eden was obliged to make a statement to the Commons to protect Hamilton's position, and this he did on September 23: 'The Wing Commander has no recollection of the prisoner and is not aware that he has ever seen or met Rudolf Hess.'[22] Stalin, among others, was not impressed.

In the meantime, Hess continued in the more relaxed climate of Maindiff Court. He was still under the enforced care of professional

---

[18]James Lessor, *The Uninvited Envoy*, 117–18.
[19]Irving, David, *Hess. The Missing Years 1941–1945*, Grafton Books, (1989), 332–33.
[20]Thomas, Hugh, *Hess: A Tale of Two Murders*, Hodder and Stoughton (1988), 113.
[21]Padfield, Peter, *Hess: Flight for the Führer*, Weidenfeld and Nicolson (1991), 296.
[22]*The Times*, September 23, 1943.

psychiatrists, however, and the prescribing of unspecified drugs continued. On August 15, 1943, on the occasion of a visit from the Swiss envoy, he elaborated upon the hysterical amnesia game that he had played at Mytchett and which he continued to play at Maindiff Court: 'I again, deceived them as to loss of memory. I persisted in pretending that I had lost my memory. I learned from my mistakes. Soon, I didn't make any more mistakes. I came through tests like the sudden appearance of persons whom I had known before and I pretended not to recognise them any more. Finally, I was ready to answer questions falsely even in my dreams by keeping up the pretence of loss of memory.'[23]

While it is surprising that Hess was able to fool professional psychiatrists in this manner, it is interesting to consider his motives for so doing. He revealed these a year or so later, when talking to his then consultant, Dr Ellis Jones. He confessed that as his induced hysterical amnesia had not led to his repatriation, further continuation of the pretence appeared futile.[24] Nevertheless, Hess used the ploy again when he reached the International Military Tribunal at Nuremberg, where it served him well. On October 8, 1945, Hess's stay in Great Britain came to an end. He was driven by car to Madley in Herefordshire. From there he was flown to Brussels for onward flight to Nuremberg where he was to stand trial with some of his ex-colleagues as a war criminal. The chief American prosecutor, Justice Robert Jackson, had commented that 'the list should not be overloaded by the inclusion of Rudolf Hess.'[25] But it was, and Hess stood trial with the others. Hess's words on coming in to land at Nuremberg were prophetic. 'Within ten years, Great Britain will agree with everything I've ever said against Communism. It will then be the world's biggest enemy.' By 1955, it was.

---

[23]Rees, J.R., *The Case of Rudolf Hess*, William Heinemann (1947), 122.
[24]*Ibid*, 124.
[25]Irving, David, *Hess. The Missing Years 1941–1945*, Grafton Books, (1989), 423.

26

Nuremberg

International law is a combination of legal niceties originating in the mind and will of the strongest powers.

IVAN MAISKY

Hess arrived at Nuremberg on October 6, 1945. He was then 51 years old. He was placed in prison with some of his former Nazi colleagues to await trial by the International Military Tribunal which had been established in that city. The tribunal was constituted in accordance with the London Agreement of August 8, 1945, and its attached charter which set down its composition, powers and procedures. Its purpose was 'the trial of war criminals whose offences have no particular geographical location whether they be accused individually or in their capacity as members of organisations or groups or in both capacities.'[1] The defendants were to face charges under four counts: conspiracy to commit the crimes referred to in the other counts, crimes against peace, war crimes (those against the law and conventions of war), and crimes against humanity (inhuman acts against civilians and persecution for political, racial or religious reasons).

Twenty-four persons deemed to be major war criminals, including Hess, were indicted. Proceedings commenced on November 20, 1945. The verdicts were announced some ten months later, on October 1, 1946. The court conducted its business at the Palace of Justice. It was protected by the most stringent security arrangements throughout. Eight judges presided, two each from the USA, Russia, Great Britain and France, and the court sat for a total of 217 days. Of the 24 defendants, 12 were condemned to death (including Martin Bormann in his absence), one (Ley) committed suicide before the proceedings began, seven (including Hess) received varying prison

[1]Ann and John Tusa, *The Nuremberg Trial*.

sentences, three were acquitted and in one case (Krupp) proceedings were postponed.

These varying sentences seemed to discount Goering's remarks that 'it's just a cut and dried political affair' or the harsher judgement that it was 'a tribunal of revenge'. Nevertheless, even the most preliminary of examinations would cause serious criticisms to be made as to the true validity and value of the proceedings. What is apparent to latter-day observers did not seem to be the case to the politicised lawyers who were actually involved. Ivan Maisky, one-time Soviet Ambassador in London, has described international law as 'a combination of legal initiatives originating in the mind and will of the strongest powers.'[2] He may well be right. Certainly, such a view would explain, for example, why Article Six of the IMT charter only applied to the vanquished and not to the victors at Nuremberg.

Article Six refers to 'the wanton destruction of towns and villages.' To anyone other than a Nuremberg-trained lawyer the wanton destruction wreaked by the RAF carpet bombing on German cities and towns during the latter years of the European war and the total erasure of Hiroshima and Nagasaki by atom bombs at the conclusion of the Far Eastern war must qualify under Article Six as prime war crimes. No International Military Tribunal has yet sat to deal with these matters. Similarly, it is noteworthy that when Goering was sentenced to death for his war crimes, no mention was made of his Luftwaffe terror bombing of Warsaw, Rotterdam, London and Coventry which had excited so much passion in earlier years. These crimes were conveniently omitted because, of course, they would be trumped a thousand times over by the Allied bomber offensive that followed.

The same sort of argument applied to the legal framework that determined the proceedings at Nuremberg. The 'mind and will of the strongest powers' thought fit to change international law as had been previously practised. Past misdeeds were brought into charge by new legislation which was to be applied retrospectively. Also, heads of state and other political leaders who were in charge of a country's affairs were to be held personally liable for that country's misdemeanours. Neither of these concepts had any place in international law as it existed prior to the outbreak of war in September 1939. International law was changed in 1945 so that the individuals in the dock could be faced with charges arising from the misdemeanours of Germany since 1939. This use of retrospective legislation and the indictment of individuals for a nation state's misdeeds cast a particu-

---

[2]Roberts, Andrew, *The Holy Fox*, Weidenfeld and Nicolson (1991), 304.

lar slur upon the use of politicised law in international relations. These concepts, erroneous in principle and potentially corrupt in their application, were also thoroughly bad in law. They prevailed at Nuremberg because it was politically desirable that they should.

Perhaps the crowning inconsistency to the proceedings, and the one that removes all true justice from its deliberations, was blatantly political in nature. Two of the judges represented the Soviet Union, a country equally responsible with Germany in a particular act of aggression specifically mentioned in the indictment. The act of aggression in question was the invasion of Poland in September 1939. By a secret protocol attached to the Soviet/German Non-Aggression Pact of August 23, 1939, it was agreed that particular spheres of interest were marked out for Russia as well at Germany in both Poland and the Baltic states. In furtherance of these agreements, Russia invaded Poland on September 17 and occupied some 200,000 sq km of Polish territory, an area greater than that occupied by Germany. There was no provocation for Russia's action and her act of aggression against Poland was no less than that of Germany.

At Nuremberg, while Germany stood in the dock, Soviet Russia occupied the seats of their accuser and judge. This patent absurdity was raised by Alfred Seidl, Hess's lawyer, during the course of his defence of Hess. The actual words are worthy of record. 'The position is that at least one of the signatory powers of the London Agreement of August 8, 1945, appears in the present proceedings not only as an author of the law, but as prosecutor and judge ... but also as a participant in a plan and a contracting party to, an agreement which under Article Four, paragraph 20 of the IMT Charter renders those responsible liable to punishment.'

Seidl, a young but brave lawyer, was suggesting that Russia should be a defendant, not a judge. He was ordered to remove his remarks from the pleadings. But the point was picked up by *The Economist*, which published the following editorial comment:

> Baron von Weizsacker, State Secretary of the (German) Foreign Office from 1938 to 1943, testified about a secret agreement that was added to the (German/Soviet) Non-Aggression Pact and provided for the territorial division of six European nations and their apportionment between Germany and the Soviet Union. The counsel for the prosecution made no attempt to refute this testimony. Still, the court ignores it totally. Such silence, unfortunately, proves that the Nuremberg court was an independent court only within certain restrictions. In a proper criminal trial, it would be most remarkable if a judge in a proceeding against a murderer

> were to leave out of consideration testimony about an accomplice's part in the murder because that testimony revealed that the judge himself had been that accomplice. That no one in the Nuremberg trial considers such a concealment to be out of the ordinary shows just how far removed we are from anything that could be called 'the rule of law' in international matters. In 1939, Moscow boasted openly of military collaboration with Germany for the destruction of Poland.[3]

Having regard to what appeared to be the most serious flaws in the validity of the proceedings at Nuremberg it is perhaps not surprising that Hess's attitude was one of marked disinterest throughout. He spent most of the time sitting in the dock reading a book. He also continued to play the hysterical amnesia game prior to his appearance in court, much to the bewilderment of all concerned. It is interesting to note that when Hess was medically examined on arrival at Nuremberg and passed as fit to plead, of the triumvirate of British doctors involved, only Lord Moran, Churchill's doctor, voted against the general view.[4] This fitness to plead was the subject of a special court hearing on November 30, 1945. It started with weighty words from the professional psychiatrists and was adjourned in uproar at 6.30 p.m. when Hess made a formal statement to the court stating that he had been faking his amnesia throughout.

Seven psychiatrists, two neurologists and two internists had all been taken in by Hess's performance.[5] The dramatic admission by Rudolf Hess that he had been fooling the court at Nuremberg was bound to raise questions of psychiatric diagnosis. It certainly did and does. Hess himself thought that his play-acting with the amnesia had a bearing on the absence of a death penalty in his case and said so: 'If it had not been for my acting ability, I would have been sentenced to death.'[6] He was of course well practised in his act. On arrival in Nuremberg he successfully failed to recognise any of his old Nazi colleagues or even his two personal secretaries, Ingeborg Sperr and Hildegard Fath. Albert Speer's memoirs confirm Hess's charade and how he felt about misleading Ingeborg Sperr. He records that on November 20, 1946, when showering, Hess disclosed that his loss of memory was faked. 'The psychiatrists all tried to rattle me. I came close to giving up when my secretary was brought in. I had to pretend I didn't recognise her

[3]See issue of October 5, 1946.
[4]Was Churchill concerned about Hess taking the stand? In the event, Hess refused to do so.
[5]Rees, J.R., *The Case of Rudolf Hess*, William Heinemann (1947), 164.
[6]Fishman, Jack, *The Seven Men of Spandau*, 26–27.

and she burst into tears. It was a great effort by me to remain expressionless. No doubt she thinks I am heartless.'[7]

At the commencement of the trial Hess had first refused to appoint a lawyer to represent him. He then appointed one and then sacked him. Eventually, Alfred Seidl, an abrasive but brilliant young lawyer from Munich, took his case and served him well.[8] Seidl advanced other arguments in Hess's defence. He emphasised the inconsistency of accusing Hess of crimes against the peace when the sole object of his 1941 mission was to end the war. 'By his flight to Great Britain, he committed his entire person in an attempt which sprang from the desire to avoid further bloodshed at all costs.'[9] Seidl also claimed that when Hess flew to Great Britain he did so as Hitler's authorised representative, as a peace plenipotentiary. Hess himself had claimed that status in a personal letter written to King George VI on December 12, 1941. As a peace envoy he should have been protected under the provisions of the Hague Convention of 1907 from bodily harm, imprisonment or any other form of detention and also from conviction for any crimes committed prior to the commencement of his peace mission. No charges should therefore be brought against him at Nuremberg.[10]

Seidl also made the point that any plotting of war by Germany arose directly out of the iniquities imposed upon Germany at Versailles. Hitler was an inevitable consequence of Versailles. If it had not been Hitler, it would have been someone else in his place. This argument was brought as a defence or explanation of Germany's preparations for war, in which Hess was admittedly involved.[11] To what extent Seidl's arguments were taken into account may be gauged by the court's verdict on Hess. He was found guilty on counts one and two of conspiring with others in carrying out crimes against the peace. He was acquitted on counts three and four of committing war crimes and crimes against humanity.

Hess was therefore cleared of all involvement in the excesses and barbarism that followed the launch of Operation Barbarossa and in particular, the Holocaust. He was found guilty of the one charge of taking an active part together with others in the preparations for war. No account was taken of any justification occasioned by Versailles,

---

[7]Speer, Albert, *Spandau: The Secret Diaries*, Macmillan (1976), 20.
[8]And continued to do so until Hess's death in 1987.
[9]Thomas, Hugh, *Hess: A Tale of Two Murders*, Hodder and Stoughton (1988), 136.
[10]Hess, Wolf Rüdiger, *Who Murdered my Father, Rudolf Hess?*, Reporter Press (1989), 4–5.
[11]Reference was made to the importance of Hess in the Nazi Party, his close contact with Hitler and all his policies and his personal involvement in the Nuremberg race laws, the Anschluss, the Sudetenland and Poland (Hess, Wolf Rüdiger, *My Father, Rudolf Hess*, W.H. Allen (1986), 218).

which was dismissed on the grounds of remoteness.[12] And irrespective of whatever participation Hess may have had in the preparations for war, no account was apparently taken of his mission in 1941, the purpose of which was to bring the war to an end. It is a remarkable omission.

Ironically, it was Hess's 1941 mission that nearly brought him the death penalty. Certainly, that was the wish of the chief Russian prosecutor, Major-General I.T. Nikitchenko. He made the point, and it was not easy to challenge it, that if Hess's mission to Great Britain in 1941 had been successful and peace terms agreed between Great Britain and Germany, then either with or without British involvement, the German onslaught on Russia would have been that much more difficult to resist. As a result, even more Russian lives would have been lost than the 25 million already claimed. Of course, Nikitchenko's argument depended for its validity upon the assumption that in the event of an Anglo-German peace, Germany would still have attacked Russia. Hess would have denied this, but Nikitchenko's assumption was firmly affixed to the pages of *Mein Kampf.*

As it was, Hess was sentenced to life imprisonment, which in Western European terms meant release after 15 to 20 years, subject to satisfactory behaviour during the imprisonment. It was by no means a satisfactory verdict for a man who had sought to end the war, but at least he could reasonably expect to rejoin his wife and family at some time and live out his last years with them. Alas, it was not to be. There were political motives which would make that impossible.

[12]Versailles 'remoteness' may have held up in a court of law. It was anything but remote in political or historical terms to the ordinary German of the 1930s.

27

Spandau

Cruelty, persecution and inhumanity cannot be more or less tolerated according to which end of the political spectrum it comes. Neither should it be believed that oppression is a thousand times worse if it is imposed on a thousand people rather than one. If through lack of charity and human feeling we demean Rudolf Hess, we demean ourselves and all mankind.

LORD CHALFONT

It was decided that those defendants sentenced to terms of imprisonment by the International Military Tribunal should serve their sentences in Spandau Prison, Berlin. On July 18, 1947, Hess, together with six fellow prisoners was transferred from Nuremberg to his new place of imprisonment, a giant, forbidding, fortress-like prison situated in the angle between Wilhelmstrasse and Schmidt-Knobelsdorfstrasse in the British-occupied zone of Berlin. His companions on the journey to Spandau were Baron von Neurath (sentenced to 15 years' imprisonment), Eric Raeder (life), Walter Funk (life), Karl Doenitz (10 years), Albert Speer (20 years) and Baldur von Schirach (20 years).

Spandau Prison had been built in 1876 for use as a military establishment. It was a virtual fortress, with thick external walls of considerable height topped by electric fencing and with six watchtowers dominating the interior garden area as well as the external walls. The whole of these external areas could be floodlit if required. Originally, there was accommodation for 600 prisoners in single-cell units. Each cell was sparsely lit and was 1.30 metres wide, 2.80 metres long and 2.40 metres high, with a single barred window less than one metre square and some 2.40 metres high at the end of the cell. During the Nazi era the prison had been used as an interrogation clearing centre for political prisoners before dispatching them to concentration camps.

The administration and security arrangements for 1947 with its high status occupants were to be handled in monthly turn by each of the Four Powers, the USA, Russia, Great Britain and France. Each assumed responsibility in consecutive calendar months. Some 32 external and 18 internal guards were to be provided to ensure the safe custody of the seven prisoners. In addition, there were 28 other members of staff, including doctors, nurses, cooks, interpreters, secretaries and cleaners. In total, there were something like ten members of staff to look after each prisoner.[1]

Hess soon found a sharp contrast apparent in the stringent conditions applied at Spandau compared with the relaxed atmosphere which had prevailed at Maindiff Court. In the early days of their imprisonment, the inmates were not allowed to speak to one another, were not allowed to use knives and forks and were subjected to endless inspections of their cells and persons. These latter procedures were sometimes carried out throughout the night, making sleep impossible. Of course, during the early postwar period, each day was bringing news of some new barbarity committed during the war years and it was inevitable that those perpetrated by the vanquished should receive maximum publicity. The attitude of the Spandau guards drawn from regular military units of the victorious powers towards the high-ranking Nazis in their charge, could not be unaffected.

Hess did not help himself in this respect. His attitude throughout the Nuremberg trials was that the proceedings had no legal validity. He therefore ignored them. The same attitude continued at Spandau and his behaviour was that of non-co-operation. As a result, he was not the most popular prisoner at Spandau and any good behaviour image that he might have acquired to claim early release was not enhanced. He also contributed to his own isolation in a manner which is difficult for a non-German of the old school to understand. In their early days at Spandau each prisoner was allowed one visit each month from a relative. The visit was not to last more than 15 minutes and was to be made with the tightest security arrangements, guards being present throughout. Hess never took advantage of his particular concession until the Christmas of 1969. For the first 22 years of his imprisonment at Spandau Hess did not see either his wife Ilse or his son, Wolf (who had been only 3½ years old when his father had flown to Scotland).

This extraordinary state of affairs was the subject of an explanatory comment by Ilse. ‘Rudolf has built a mental wall about himself as a protection against the strain he is under but I know and he knows it is only a thin wall. That is why he is afraid of my visiting him in

---

[1]Hess, Wolf Rüdiger, *My Father, Rudolf Hess*, W.H. Allen (1986), 259–61.

Spandau. I might cry. The strain and the emotion would be too much for both of us. We have not seen each other for a long time and Rudolf is afraid that my presence would smash his defences. Once breached, a wall so thin might be beyond repair and then God knows what would happen. His mind might go completely. And so he will not see me or our son. He cannot bear the thought of our boy seeing his father as a felon.'[2]

The sting is in the tail. The honour of the father figure in the German family unit is a powerful factor in the German psyche. It has been centuries in the making. The only visits that Hess therefore had in the 22-year period from 1947 to 1969 were those from his lawyer, Alfred Seidl, who first came to see Hess on November 18, 1964, and thereafter on a regular but infrequent basis. During that period the prison regulations gradually began to relax, prisoners were allowed to converse during their period of recreation, which they usually spent in the prison garden under the watchful eye of the guards. They were also allowed books to read. Hess immediately indented for over a hundred titles. They were also allowed to write one (censored) letter home each month.

When visits from Hess's wife and son commenced after Christmas 1969 the most stringent regulations were applied. Application for each visit was to be made two weeks in advance and the visit was to be entirely at the option of the prison directorate. All conversations were to be in German and there was to be no mention of the Third Reich or its leader, National Socialism, the war, the flight of May 1941 or the Nuremberg trials. There was to be no physical contact during the visit and witnesses at prison directorate level were to be present to ensure that these requirements were met.[3] These conditions were of course extraordinary. They applied to no other prisoner and demonstrated the special precautions taken in the case of Hess to ensure that his remarks were kept clear of all sensitive issues.

Baron von Neurath, sentenced to 15 years' imprisonment, was released in 1954, having served only half of his sentence. The grounds for early release were his ill health. There was perhaps a little more to it than that. Before the war, von Neurath and his wife had been great personal friends of King George V and his wife, Queen Mary. Queen Mary's German mother, Princess Elizabeth of Teck, and Queen Mary herself had spent a great deal of her childhood years at the von Neurath estate in Würtemberg. She had formed a close friendship with Baroness Neurath, and in later years, Baron and Baroness von Neurath

---

[2]Fishman, Jack, *The Seven Men of Spandau*, 29.
[3]Hess, Wolf Rüdiger, *My Father, Rudolf Hess*, W.H. Allen (1986), 331–33.

were frequent visitors to Buckingham Palace.[4] That does not detract from the fact that von Neurath, 81 at the time of his release, was a sick man and was rightly released on humanitarian grounds. It may have been that a little pressure from English court circles oiled the wheels.

In the following year Eric Raeder, serving a life sentence, was also released on the grounds of ill health. He had served only nine years of his life sentence. He was followed the next year, 1956, by Karl Doenitz, who was released after serving his full sentence of ten years. In the next year Walter Funk was released on the grounds of ill health, having served only eleven years of his life sentence. Nine years later, in 1966, Albert Speer and Baldur von Schirach were both released, having served their full term sentences of 20 years. Examination of the circumstances of these releases discloses a regular pattern. Either the prisoner had served his full-term sentence or he had been released prematurely because of ill health. There was also an added circumstance, based upon well established practice in Western Europe that life imprisonment was usually commuted to a lesser sentence of something in the order of 15 to 20 years.

In 1966, after the release of Speer and Schirach, Hess was left alone in Spandau. Although at that time his health was good for a man then aged 72, he had by then served 20 years of his life sentence. It was therefore reasonable for him and his family and friends to expect his early release, like the other prisoners and in accordance with the standard practice. In fact, he was never released. He died as a prisoner in Spandau, 21 years later, aged 93, a tired, frail old man crippled with arthritis and heart disease. By then he had served a total of 41 years' imprisonment in Spandau, the last 21 of which were in solitary confinement. Obviously there was something very special about Rudolf Hess and the reasons for his incarceration until death.

Many powerful and distinguished voices were raised in protest at the inhuman and unusual treatment meted out to Hess. They included those of Sir Hartley (later Lord) Shawcross, the eminent lawyer and the chief British prosecutor at Nuremberg, Bernard Levin, the respected Jewish columnist and A.J.P. Taylor the distinguished historian. Shawcross expressed his opinion strongly within a year of Speer and Schirach being released.[5] It represented the view of civilised people throughout the world.

---

[4]Queen Mary retained the characteristics of her German upbringing throughout her life. She regularly conversed in German with her son, David, when Prince of Wales and used to help her granddaughter, Elizabeth, later Queen Elizabeth II, with her German lessons.
[5]Hess, Wolf Rüdiger, *My Father, Rudolf Hess*, W.H. Allen (1986), 286–397.

> Most civilised people with a concern for humanity even nowadays inflict punishment for retaliation or revenge. From the human aspect therefore it now appears to be necessary to release Hess. Continuation of his imprisonment is a pure act of revenge and retaliation, a disgrace to great and powerful nations. A judgement that banishes a human being behind bars for his whole life threatens to destroy his soul. Only a few who suffer such a punishment are anything more than a wreck at the end. Imprisonment for life is more cruel than a verdict of death since it robs the prisoner of all hope... Many states pronounce sentence of life imprisonment but I know of no country claiming to be civilised which does not remit the rest of the sentence after a certain period of time. In Britain 'life' imprisonment with good conduct means twelve to fifteen years. Never has a 'life' prisoner served more than twenty years. I assume that at least the British and American judges at Nuremberg anticipated when pronouncing a life sentence that the procedure would be similar in the case of Hess.

Similar statements were made as the years passed and Hess's incarceration continued. All expressed concern and moral outrage. All assumed that it was Russian intransigence which was causing the problem but there was an answer to that problem. The Western Allies could give notice to the Russians that Hess would be released, with or without Russian consent, the next time a Western Power assumed its monthly responsibility at Spandau. It would only be repaying the Russians in kind. The Russians had erected the infamous Berlin Wall in direct violation of the four-power agreement of June 5, 1945, and without the consent of the Western Allies. If the Western Allies had proceeded unilaterally in that manner, there is little doubt that they would have carried with them the overwhelming support of the vast majority of ordinary people in Western Europe and the USA.

It was not as though the published views of Shawcross, Taylor and others were isolated examples from an intellectual minority. Hess's son, Wolf, only four years of age when his father had flown to Scotland, had grown to maturity during his father's imprisonment. Motivated by a deep sense of the injustice meted out to his father, he was determined to secure his father's release, so that he could spend the remaining years of his life with his family. Together with others, he formed a 'Freedom for Rudolf Hess Association', a registered society, whose main purpose was the dissemination of information as widely as possible as to his father's plight and the bringing of pressure to bear through the media for his release. An 'October Declaration' was sworn in 1966, following the release of Speer and Schirach calling attention to the lone prisoner at Spandau and requesting his release in the name of humanity. It was intended as a world-wide citizens' initiative and the declaration was given generous press coverage both in Germany and abroad, particularly in Western Europe and Great Britain. Copies were sent to the heads of state of the Four Powers primarily concerned and to the Pope, the World Council of Churches and the United Nations Commission for Human Rights in an attempt to arouse international feeling.

Wolf Hess himself travelled extensively in Great Britain and America, obtaining plenty of press coverage. In Great Britain he also obtained the signatures of more than 200 MPs petitioning for Hess's release. But nothing happened. There was no move by the governments of the West to approach Russia to secure Hess's release or any move to act unilaterally. Russian intransigence was still deemed to be the problem. The Russian attitude at Nuremberg was being projected forward to explain why Hess's incarceration for life was to be for life.

The Russians had said at Nuremberg that if Hess's mission in 1941 had been successful then many more Russian lives would have been lost. Russia would have lost an ally. Germany would have gained one. Russia would have been even more hard pressed than she was. There was of course logic to the Russian argument. But it depended upon the assumption that Germany would still have attacked Russia in the event of peace with Great Britain. Certainly, that assumption is enshrined in *Mein Kampf* but is disputed by Hess. There is written evidence to that effect by way of a memorandum smuggled out of Spandau by Wolf, signed by his father. According to Hess, if his mission had been successful it would have been followed up by an international conference at which all outstanding matters would have been discussed. But even if the Russian case could boast a rough logic it still made no concession to humanitarian considerations, having regard to Hess's advancing age and the term of imprisonment already served. One has to assume that these issues counted for little in the Russian mind against the grievous losses occasioned by the war recently ended.

It is also impossible to understand why the Western Powers did not take unilateral action anyhow. Humanitarian considerations demanded it, the means were there to do it, by building the Berlin Wall the Russians had supplied the pretext to do it and the ordinary people of Western Europe and America would have applauded it. But it did not happen. In spite of all Wolf's efforts, his father remained alone and apparently forgotten in Spandau. Churchill's policy of 'isolate and forget', adopted in 1941, was still alive and well in 1966 (and in fact, survived until Hess's death in 1987).

After these failures to obtain Hess's release in 1966, humanitarian considerations came more and more to the forefront as Hess aged and his health deteriorated. Considering his age, Hess's health at 72 in 1966 was good, but the solitary confinement that followed soon had its effect. On November 19, 1969, Hess suffered a perforated stomach ulcer and was rushed to the British Military Hospital. Arthritis was also beginning to take its toll. On December 29, 1978, at the age of 84 he suffered a stroke which left him seriously incapacitated. His vision was impaired, he was left with a permanent weakness in his left arm and hand and his left knee tended to buckle. His walking became laboured. He was obliged to move with a pronounced shuffling gait and a loss of balance. His spine became curved from the arthritis and he had developed a limp. He had great difficulty in turning his head. At Christmas 1979, A.J.P. Taylor, in the knowledge of Hess's impaired physical condition, wrote an impassioned article for *The Sunday Express* which appeared on December 23.

> Rudolf Hess is now sick and aged and he will enjoy no Christmas with his family. A man who is still condemned to the loneliness he has had to suffer for thirty-seven years, he wishes to be reunited with his wife and son. What human tyrant has refused him the fulfilment of this wish, particularly at Christmas, the time of goodwill? This refusal is an act of brutality. But this inhuman act is the work of civilised people who boast of charity and of overflowing Christmas sentiment. It is the governments of the Great Powers, Great Britain, France, Russia and the USA, who keep Hess prisoner. This crime is being committed in our name. We are told we must respect the law. In 1946, the International Military Tribunal at Nuremberg sentenced Hess to life imprisonment. He cannot therefore be released until all Four Powers give their consent. What kind of hypocrisy is this? It is of course desirable to respect the law. But there are higher considerations than the law. Do we have to applaud the massacre of the Innocents because the decree to do so was issued by Herod? And who would accept the Crucifixion because Pontius Pilate authorised it? If Hess is not allowed to go and see his family for Christmas our creed of charity and Christmas principles become a farce. We are guilty, everyone of us.

Four years later, Hess was again admitted to the British Military Hospital with 'wet' pleurisy. He had also developed heart and circulatory problems, bringing palpitations and breathing difficulties. This latest stay in hospital coincided with a further application for his release. A new formula was tried. As part of the application, Hess gave his word of honour that if released, he would give no opinions on political or historical matters or partake in any form of political activity. Such activity would have been impossible in any case, by reason of his age and infirmity. His wish was only to spend the rest of his days with his family. He was then 88. The application, as with all others, failed. There were further applications but they too failed, in spite of the most strenuous efforts by Hess's son aided by Dr Seidl. In January 1984 a special lift was installed in the prison to enable Hess at first-floor level to reach the garden at ground-floor level. The old man was incapable of negotiating the narrow spiral stairs. The cost of the lift installation was DM13,000. It appeared to be a clear indication that there was no question of Hess leaving Spandau.

In July 1986, Pastor Charles Gabel who served the prison was transferred away. This was a great disappointment to Hess. Gabel had befriended Hess during his solitary confinement and his visits had been a great source of comfort to Hess. The two men would talk about their mutual love of the Viennese school of composers, particularly Beethoven, Mozart and Schubert. They would also discuss science, exploration, philosophy and history, all subjects of particular interest to Hess since his student days. The occasion of Gabel's dismissal was the discovery of a document drafted by Gabel for Hess's signature. It was a written expression of regret by Hess for his past actions. It was intended that the declaration should support a further application for release – Gabel had suggested a statement of regret would be more supportive to an application for release than yet another attack on the invalidity of the Nuremberg decisions.

With the New Year of 1987 there came about a radical upturn in Rudolf Hess's fortunes and, for the first time ever, his release began to shape up as a realistic proposition. In January, Wolf Hess sent a letter to the Soviet Embassy in Bonn as part of his continuing efforts on behalf of his father. For the first time in 20 years he received a reply. It referred his enquiry to the Soviet Embassy in East Berlin. Wolf wrote to the Embassy and arrangements were made for a meeting there on March 31. Wolf was much encouraged by the new attitude of the Soviets, which appeared to be a direct outcome of Mikhail Gorbachev's new policies of rapprochement and *détente* towards the West. Wolf was attended by Vladimir M. Grinin, ambassadorial adviser. The conversation was lengthy and courteous throughout. Grinin explained that public opinion in Russia presented a problem but this would ease with the passage of time. He praised Wolf's efforts on behalf of his father and Wolf promised that as and when his father was released there would be no question of a 'political sideshow'. Wolf came away much encouraged. At least the Soviets were at last talking in terms of his father's release.[6]

Prior to his meeting, Wolf had visited his father at Spandau to tell him of the good news. He had found his father mentally alert but physically very frail. He could walk only with the assistance of a stick and the arm of a guard. He was suffering from cardiac arrhythmia, with a variable heartbeat and breathing difficulties. At the same time as Wolf's visit to the Soviet Embassy in East Berlin, Margaret Thatcher, the British Prime Minister was attending a summit meeting with Gorbachev in Moscow. The German President, Weizsäcker, would also be visiting Gorbachev later that year. The release of Hess was on Weizsäcker's agenda. It is thought that it may have been on Thatcher's too, but for a very different purpose.[7] On April 12, less than a fortnight after Wolf's visit, *Der Spiegel*, the influential and internationally read German journal, ran a headline 'Will Gorbachev release Hess?' The article that followed, which appears to be well-informed, referred to Weizsäcker's forthcoming visit and the fact that Hess's release would be on the agenda. The cat was out of the bag. The news item was picked up by more than a hundred newspapers throughout the world. There was little chance of a secret release, which is what Wolf had in mind.

On June 21, correspondence with the German-speaking Russian Division of Radio Moscow originating from 'a loyal citizen of West Germany' (in reality a member of the Rudolf Hess Support Group) elicited a reply which read: 'Recent statements by our head of Government, Mikhail Gorbachev, give rise to hope that your many years of effort towards the release of war criminal, Hess, will soon be crowned with success.' Wolf believed that a statement of that importance would not have been made by the Russian state-controlled radio unless it had been approved at the highest level.[8] Wolf's confidence grew. He had kept his father fully appraised as to the developments and had noted the joy and relief that the old man had felt at the thought of his going home after 46 years in exile.

The Soviets were expected to make their announcement of agreement to release during their monthly on-duty period of administration at Spandau. Weizsacker would be the guest of Gorbachev in July and the next Soviet on-duty month thereafter would be November, when the announcement would be made. But it was not to be. On August 17, 1987, Hess died in Spandau Prison. The official verdict on his death

[6]Hess, Wolf Rüdiger, *Who Murdered my Father, Rudolf Hess?*, Reporter Press (1989), 152–53.
[7]See later text relating to the correspondence with Rhodri Morgan, MP.
[8]Hess, Wolf Rüdiger, *Who Murdered my Father, Rudolf Hess?*, Reporter Press (1989), 167.

was that he committed suicide by hanging himself. In the circumstances described the stated cause of death is incomprehensible. In the summer of 1987, for the first time in 46 years, Rudolf Hess had reasonable hopes of an early release to spend the remaining years of his life with his wife, his son and his grandchildren. Why then would he commit suicide? Or did he?

There is of course another line of thought that seems to fit the fact of his death, but not its nature, more rationally than the reported suicide. The Russian intransigence card had been well played down through the years. On December 21, 1979, for example, a spokesman for Margaret Thatcher had told Wolf: 'As you will be aware, the British Government together with the United States and France have for the past twelve years expressed themselves in favour of the unconditional release of Rudolf Hess on humanitarian grounds. The Prime Minister has asked me to assure you that the British Government, for its part, is continuing to press for agreement among the Four Powers for his release.'[9] But if the Russian intransigence card was now to be removed and Hess released, what would become of Churchill's original 'isolate and forget' policy. That card too had been well played down the years. If Hess was released he would no longer be isolated. And if he chose to talk about his 1941 mission he would no longer be forgotten. There were matters which Hess had mentioned in 1941 that Churchill considered would not be in the public interest to know about. These matters may have been the details of a peace plan, the identity of members of the British Peace Party or notice of a forthcoming Holocaust. Perhaps disclosure of these matters by Hess in 1987 would be as lethal to British national interests then as it would have been in 1941. There may have remained a strong motive for Hess's continued incarceration as far as the British Government was concerned.

The removal of the Soviet intransigence card may have removed the skirt behind which the British Government had been hiding for years. Under these circumstances, one would expect to see British pressure to ensure Hess's continued imprisonment. There is evidence to support this contention. On March 24, 1994, the author wrote to Mr Rhodri Morgan, MP for Cardiff West in the following terms: 'My present information is that during the early summer of 1987 the British Ambassador to Moscow personally intervened in the matter of Hess's detention at Spandau and specifically requested Mr Gorbachev not to give his consent to the release of Hess. I would respectfully enquire if

[9] Hess, Wolf Rüdiger. *My Father, Rudolf Hess*, W.H. Allen (1986), 298–99.

you have any information or means of information in your possession which would support my information.' Mr Morgan replied on April 29, 1994. His reply is illuminating.

> As regards the point about the British Ambassador to Moscow personally intervening in relation to Hess's detention at Spandau, it fits in with my general understanding of what occurred. I have never been able to get confirmation of this in writing from any German source, although I have had three separate and almost identical versions of events in relation to what happened when the German President, Richard von Weizsäcker, visited Moscow in 1987. My information was that von Weizsäcker had put in a plea to Gorbachev to release Hess to spend the remaining years of his life at home with Wolf Rüdiger Hess, his son. The German President was not suggesting releasing him for forgiveness but simply on humanitarian grounds. Mr Gorbachev said that this would be OK but he would have to give him a few months[10] to square it with the other Allied Powers and with Russian public opinion. The British then vetoed it while always hiding behind the Russian refusal to release Hess.

It was not long before expert medical evidence became available that contradicted the nature of Hess's death as officially reported, adding weight to the alternative line of thought indicated above and which reached its logical conclusion at 4.10 p.m. on Monday, August 17, 1987.

---

[10]This reference is important. It indicates that the release would probably have taken place in November, when the Russians would again be on duty at Spandau.

PART SIX

AUGUST 1987
THE CURTAIN COMES DOWN

28

A most convenient death

There are only two things certain in life. One is death and the other is rent day.

ANNIE SMITH, CIRCA 1935

The morning of Monday, August 17, 1987, dawned bright, clear and warm. It was a beautiful late summer day. It was Rudolf Hess's 16,898th day of imprisonment but this one was to be special. It was his last. He would be dead by ten minutes past four that afternoon.

The early part of the day passed uneventfully, just like all the other days at Spandau since Hess had been left as the sole occupant after the release of Speer and Schirach. Hess's orderly, nurse and friend, Abdullah Melhaouhi, reported for duty as usual at 6.45 a.m. Melhaouhi, a Tunisian on the civilian staff at Spandau, had looked after the old man for over five years and knew him well. There was a mutual affection between the two men. Hess was already up when Melhaouhi arrived. After giving him a massage, trimming his hair and shaving him, Melhaouhi helped Hess shower and dress. He then helped Hess into the small dispensary where he checked and recorded his weight, blood pressure, temperature, pulse and respiration, all of which were matters of established routine. After breakfast which he hardly touched, Hess asked Melhaouhi to go into Spandau to make some purchases for him. The pot which Hess used to boil his water for tea needed replacing and he also needed tissues, toilet paper, stationery, and a ruler.[1]

According to the Spandau prison diary, Melhaouhi left the prison at 11.05 a.m. in the company of one of his colleagues, Boulanger, the head guard. In the meantime, Hess had been helped down into the

[1]Unless they were a 'blind', these purchases appear to indicate Hess's intention to live on, not die.

prison garden where he could make the best of the good weather. Although he could only stand and walk with assistance he still enjoyed being outdoors in the fresh air. At 11.30 a.m. he was subjected to the usual routine body search and at 12.15 p.m. he was served with his lunch. It was fifteen minutes late. The old man ate only the crab cocktail. Perhaps it was the heat that turned him off his food. He then returned to his cell for his usual after-lunch rest until 2.30 p.m. when he was awakened, dressed and again accompanied to the garden. His escort on this occasion had changed from that of the morning. His new guard was the American, Jordan. Jordan was black. There was no love lost between the prisoner and this particular escort. Hess had previously complained about Jordan's antagonistic manner and had asked that Jordan be moved to other duties. The request had been ignored.

At 3.15 p.m. a guard in one of the watchtowers reported seeing Hess sitting in the garden on one of the seats, with Jordan in close attendance. At 3.30 p.m. the same guard reported that Hess and Jordan had both entered the small summerhouse situated in the garden. At this point, the guard's vision was obscured by one of the trees.[2] It was unusual that Hess should enter the summerhouse with his guard. The summerhouse was very small. It was only 3.7 metres long and 2.2 metres wide. There was hardly room for more than one occupant. It was the custom for Hess to sit in there alone for a while. He might read, or meditate or doze. He could take the sun as he sat there because the whole of the rear side of the structure was made up of a sliding glass door. The entrance door and a window were on the opposite wall facing the prison. The Russians used to call the summerhouse, Hess's little *datscha* (home or den). It was simply furnished with a bench, a small table, a chair and an easy chair. The only fixture was an electric lamp with a flex attached. While Hess took his ease in the *datscha* it was also the custom of the guard to sit outside on a garden seat or under a tree, taking his ease too but at the same time keeping an eye on his prisoner.

On this occasion Jordan left Hess alone in the summerhouse, having apparently been called to the main prison building to answer a telephone call. This again was unusual. The prison regulations called for the personal surveillance of Hess at all times. There is no account available as to what happened next or what Jordan found when he returned to the summerhouse. His evidence has never been made public. Melaouhi reports[3] that having completed Hess's shopping in Spandau and had his lunch, he returned to the prison 'in the early after-

[2]Hess, Wolf Rüdiger, *Who Murdered my Father, Rudolf Hess?*, Reporter Press (1989), 93.
[3]And has submitted a signed statement under oath in support.

noon.' He was confronted at the prison gates by a guard with the news that 'something had happened' in the summerhouse. This is confirmed by the prison diary record which records that Jordan reported an 'incident' in the summerhouse at 2.30 p.m.[4]

Melaouhi describes vividly the scene which confronted him 'When I arrived in the summerhouse I found the scene looking as though a wrestling match had taken place there. The ground was churned up and the chair in which Hess usually sat, lay on the ground a considerable distance from its usual spot. Hess himself lay on the ground, lifeless. He reacted to nothing. His respiration, pulse and heartbeat were no longer measurable. Jordan stood nearby, near Hess's feet and obviously quite beyond himself.' Melaouhi was surprised to see two strangers present, in addition to Jordan. They were both dressed in American army overalls. This was most unusual. No one had access to that part of the garden in which the summerhouse was situated. Above all, all personal contact with Hess was strictly forbidden. According to Melaouhi the two strangers were quite calm, in sharp contrast to Jordan who was much more agitated. Melaouhi attempted resuscitation and asked the two strangers to assist. One began to massage Hess's chest but did so with such force that nine of Hess's ribs and his sternum were broken.[5] When all attempts at resuscitation had failed, Hess was removed by ambulance to the British Military Hospital. He was pronounced dead at 4.10 p.m.[6]

At 6.45 p.m. Donald W. Keane, the American prison director on duty that month telephoned Hess's son, Wolf, at his home near Munich, and told him that his father had died at 4.10 p.m. that day. He said that he was not authorised to give any details at that stage. According to Wolf, Keane was nervous and ill at ease. Wolf, accompanied by his father's lawyer, Dr Alfred Seidl, flew to Berlin and arrived at Spandau the next day. They were not allowed into the prison and had to await publication of the first press release to ascertain the cause of death. The official press release reported that Hess had attempted to take his own life. He had been discovered in the summerhouse with an electric cord around his neck. Attempts at resuscitation had failed and he had been declared dead at 4.10 p.m. A formal

---

[4]Although according to the *Figaro* magazine p115, the figure '3', as included in the reported time ('14.30 hours'), appears to have been entered over a previous figure which has been erased. (Hess, Wolf Rüdiger, *Who Murdered my Father, Rudolf Hess?*, Reporter Press (1989), 259.)

[5]This performance, or lack of it, would indicate that the two strangers were not medics, as was later claimed.

[6]There is an apparent discrepancy in the reported timings. The 'incident' in the summerhouse was reported at 2.30 p.m. and yet Hess was not removed to hospital until nearly 4 p.m. The attempts at resuscitation would not have continued for one and a half hours.

investigation into the circumstances and a thorough post-mortem were described as 'ongoing.'

Both Wolf and Dr Seidl were incredulous that the cause of death should be thought to be suicide. They both knew that in August 1987 Rudolf Hess had more reason to live than at any time during his long incarceration because it was probable that his incarceration was about to end. They were anxious to know the facts and circumstances surrounding the death. All they had to go on initially was the content of the press release.

In the meantime, arrangements were proceeding for the formal investigation into the circumstances of the death and the post-mortem. The investigation was to be undertaken by the Special Investigations Branch of the British Military Police, acting under orders from Major J.P. Gallagher of BAOR headquarters staff. Its findings were that Hess had throttled himself by passing the two ends of the electric flex from the lamp through the roof structure of the summerhouse, putting his head through the loop and then pulling down hard. This would cut off his breathing which would induce a blackout leading to death.[7] The post-mortem examination was to be carried out during the morning of Wednesday, August 19, by Professor James M. Cameron, Professor of Medicine at London University since 1973 and Chief Pathologist to the British Army. He had been flown into Berlin specially to do the job. All four Allied prison directors and representatives of the Special Investigation Branch team were in attendance.

Professor Cameron's finding was that death was due to asphyxia, caused by compression of the neck arising from suspension. No mention was made as to suicide but clearly that was the inference. The medical evidence supported the findings of the Special Branch investigatory team. No photographs or video record of the post-mortem proceedings were taken. That was unusual. On August 19, the death certificate was issued by Cameron and signed by Anthony le Tissier, the British prison director, as witness. The cause of death as stated on the certificate was 'asphyxiation resulting from compression of the neck due to suspension.' On the same day, and almost by way of tidy conclusion, a suicide note was produced. This had been discovered in Hess's coat pocket as the body had been undressed in preparation for the post-mortem. Lieutenant N. Lurcock, one of the Special Investigations Branch team had produced it and its discovery had been witnessed by all those in attendance at the post-mortem.

The completion of the investigation and the post-mortem followed

---

[7]Thomas, Hugh, *Hess: A Tale of Two Murders*, Hodder & Stoughton (1988), 181.

by the issue of the death certificate would normally have completed the formal proceedings relating to the death. But in this case these formalities set in train a series of enquiries and doubts into what appeared to be unsatisfactory features. Some of these were precipitated by the authorities themselves. Immediate confusion and query arose because of the differing versions, all originating from the Four Powers themselves, as to what had happened in the summerhouse. The official investigation had referred to Hess looping the flex around the summerhouse roof structure. A second version issued by the French Military Government referred to Hess hanging himself with an electric flex extension cord attached to a window bolt.[8] On August 24, a third version was released to the press by the Allies, acting apparently in unison. It stated that Hess 'had wrapped around his neck part of an extension cord that was already attached to the ceiling or wall of the summerhouse. He then apparently let himself drop off the bench on which he had sat.'[9] As if to clinch the matter this last official version was supported by the publication of a photograph of the interior of the summerhouse showing the offending electric flex extension cord hanging from the window frame.

Unfortunately, an earlier photograph of the interior of the summerhouse is available which was taken within two hours of Hess's death by a warrant officer in the Royal Engineers. The photograph clearly shows that there was no extension cord flex attached to any window catch or frame.[10] Furthermore, both Melaouhi, Hess's constant nurse and attendant, and Pastor Gabel who had sat for hours in the summerhouse with Hess, have both confirmed that an extension cord had never existed. They both make the same simple point. The summerhouse was so small that there was never any need for an extension cord for the lamp. The cord attached to the lamp measured 70 cm and the summerhouse itself was only 3.75 metres.[11] It is difficult to resist the thought that an electric flex extension cord was affixed to the window frame after the event for the purposes of an official photograph. This would then support at least one of the three authorised versions as to what happened.

Perhaps even more importantly, since it attacks the suggestion of suicide head on, is that Hess was quite incapable of carrying out the physical manoeuvres necessarily entailed in hanging himself in the various ways described. Hess was 93 years of age, generally infirm

---

[8]This report was made available to Wolf Hess on July 12, 1988.
[9]As reported by the Berlin office of the American News Bureau Associated Press.
[10]See *Guardian* article, August 17, 1989.
[11]Hess, Wolf Rüdiger, *Who Murdered my Father, Rudolf Hess?*, Reporter Press (1989), 86.

and suffering from advancing arthritis, heart disease and circulatory problems. He was quite incapable of tying a simple knot and he could not stand or walk without assistance. To suggest that he could be looping flex around the roof structure or tying the flex around his neck or throwing himself off the bench is bizarre. This was a view shared by Melaouhi, Hess's personal nurse, who was better acquainted with Hess than anyone; by Hugh Thomas who was the surgical consultant at the British Military Hospital in Berlin and had treated Hess; and by the Matron at the same hospital who had attended Hess there with a perforated stomach ulcer in 1969.[12]

Melaouhi made the further point that if Hess was intent upon committing suicide by hanging he could have done this in the privacy of his own cell. There was an electric cord in his bathroom which was twice the length of the one alleged to have been attached to the fixture in the summerhouse. There were other features that even to the most impartial observer invited enquiry and the view that the truth was at some variance with the authorised version. The death occurred during August. That was a month when the Americans were on duty, and yet all the arrangements to do with the death were taken over by the British. A British pathologist was specially flown in to carry out the post-mortem and issue the death certificate. A British team carried out the investigation into the circumstances surrounding the death. The British director at Spandau, Anthony le Tissier, was the sole witness to sign the death certificate. No reason was ever given for the British dominance of affairs, which continued to be the case.

Within one week of Hess's death, British troops of the King's Own Scottish Borderers moved in to supervise the complete destruction of the entire Spandau prison premises. The summerhouse and its contents, including the offending flex or flexes if in fact they ever existed, were totally destroyed. Hess's son and Hess's lawyer, who had been refused permission to view the scene of death and inspect the garden and the inside of the summerhouse, took the view that there was a deliberate destruction of evidence as to the circumstances of the death. The official explanation was that Spandau Prison was erased in accordance with the Four-Power Agreement, so that the site could not become a shrine or monument that would encourage neo-Nazi activities. Be that as it may, the immediate effect was to destroy items which could perhaps have supplied evidence for an alternative view of the death. This did not escape the notice of those who were already forming these views.

---

[12]See *Guardian* article, June 12, 1992.

As well as the refusal to visit the site of the death, other permissions and information were being withheld from an increasingly angered and frustrated son, feeding his doubts as to the true nature of his father's death. The only information he had was that conveyed in the official press releases and nine months after his death that was still the position. On May 30, 1988, Wolf wrote to each of the four Allied directors and formally requested as a member of the Hess family 'an official communication regarding the circumstances and the cause of death of my father.' Each of the three Western Allies replied in the same terms. Each sent him the official press release of September 17, 1987. This referred to death by hanging by the use of an extension cord. As Wolf knew from Melaouhi, Gabel and the post-death photograph of the interior of the summerhouse, that no such extension cord had ever existed, this was less than satisfactory. The Russian reply merely referred Wolf to the Americans who were on duty during August 1987. As the Russians must have known that it was the British who had taken over all the arrangements, this reply too was unsatisfactory.

A request was then made for a copy of the report of the Special Investigations Branch of the British Military Police who had carried out the official investigation into the circumstances surrounding the death. In particular, Wolf called for a copy of the testimony of the guard, Jordan, who appeared to have been the last person to see Hess alive. The request was formally refused by each of the three Western Allies and no reply was ever received from the Russians.[13] It was subsequently learned that Jordan had been flown back to the USA shortly after Hess's death.

If there was to be any serious attempt to question the validity of the death certificate and the reported circumstances leading up to the death, attention would needs turn to the medical evidence provided by Professor Cameron's post-mortem findings and the suicide note. So the release of Rudolf Hess's body to his family, which took place on August 20, constituted a major aberration on the part of the prison director. The original Spandau regulations had called for cremation in the case of any death occurring at Spandau; but in 1982 it had been agreed that in the case of the last survivor the body would be released to the Hess family for private burial. And so it was that Hess's body was handed over to Hess's son at the USAAF base at Grafenwöhr. There was no private burial. The body was taken to Munich University Institute for Forensic Medicine for the purposes of a second post-

[13]Subsequent requests by the author for the same documents have also been refused.

mortem examination, which would confirm or otherwise the validity of Professor Cameron's findings. This was carried out at 9 a.m. on Friday, August 21, 1987 – i.e. within 48 hours of that carried out by Cameron.

The officiating pathologist was Professor Dr Wolfgang Spann, assisted by Professor Dr Wolfgang Eisenmenger, Dr Tutsch-Bauer, Dr Packratz and M. Lohr, all from the Munich University Institute for Forensic Medicine. The leader of the team, Professor Spann, was a skilled, experienced and respected pathologist. His findings agreed with those of Professor Cameron that death was not due to natural causes but to asphyxia caused by 'violence to the neck' by means of a ligature. But his findings differed fundamentally from those of Professor Cameron as to the manner in which the violence to the neck had been applied. He was of the opinion that the marks around Hess's neck and other forensic indications were more typical of death from throttling or strangulation than from suspension by hanging. He also called attention in his report to a large circular bruise on the corpse's head which had been described by Cameron as a minor abrasion.

The forensic details leading to the different conclusion were necessarily technical. Wolf Hess therefore asked Professor Spann to prepare a supplement to his report stating his opinion as to the manner of Hess's death and whether the explanations as to the death already given by the Allied Governments were consistent with the findings of his own post-mortem examination. Spann delivered the required supplement to Wolf Hess on December 21, 1988. An extract containing his expert comments is shown in Appendix VIII. Their fundamental point is understandable even to the lay person. Spann states that 'in forensic science the course which the ligature mark makes on the neck is considered to be a classic indicator for the differentiation between the forms of strangulation, of hanging and of throttling.'[14]

In the case of hanging, the ligature mark will ascend in the direction of the attachment point of the device being used. In the case of throttling, horizontal marks around the throat are characteristic. The marks around Hess's neck were horizontal. They are clearly shown as such in coloured photographs taken by Professor Spann. They are visible even on the back of the neck, where one would expect little if any marks in the case of a hanging. Cameron does not deal with the direction of the ligature marks on the neck in his post-mortem report. He

---

[14]Hanging is defined as the compression of the neck by the core of a ligature used passively through the weight of the victim's body. Throttling is the compression of the neck by means of the encirclement of the neck and the active constriction by another person or, very rarely, by the victim himself.

does not therefore appear to have considered the possibility of death by throttling.

In answer to Wolf Hess's original question Professor Spann clearly indicates that the account of Rudolf Hess's death given by the Allied Governments was not consistent with the findings of his own post-mortem examination. His findings were that the death was more likely to have been caused by throttling than hanging. It is a view that was shared subsequently by Professor David Bowen of Charing Cross Hospital, who read both the Spann and the Cameron reports.[15]

Professor Cameron's failure to take note of the direction of the ligature marks on the neck and to then consider the possibility of throttling is extraordinary, in terms of both forensic procedure and common sense. So also is the omission to highlight the extent and nature of the significant bruise to the head. What Cameron described as 'a circular bruised abrasion' was in fact a central bruising about two inches in diameter and raised half an inch from the level of the scalp.[16] It was a major injury, which could have been caused by a blow to the head as well as from a fall. Professor Cameron's professional reputation had not been enhanced by the widely publicised Australian Lindy Chamberlain 'dingo' case of 1980, in which his expert opinion had been seriously challenged. But it has to be said in the Hess case that there may well have been non-forensic considerations which dictated the final form of Cameron's post-mortem report and its apparent omissions.

This suggestion is supported by another extraordinary feature. Hugh Thomas was a consultant in general surgery at the British Military Hospital in Berlin. He had attended Hess in that capacity. According to him, Professor Cameron prepared a second and supplementary post-mortem report which was for the information of the British military authorities only. If that were the case, it could be of course that Professor Cameron's two reports, taken together, omit nothing. Thomas bases his assertion on a private conversation he had with Cameron on the latter's return to Great Britain. The assertion was repeated by Thomas in a letter to Wolf Hess dated January 9, 1988, in which he states that Cameron had confirmed the existence of a second report in an interview with Roy Macardy of Scottish Television.[17]

The personal involvement of Hugh Thomas led to considerable

---

[15]See *Guardian* article, May 20, 1989.

[16]Thomas, Hugh, *Hess: A Tale of Two Murders*, Hodder & Stoughton (1988), 186.

[17]Confirmed to the author also by Hugh Thomas on February 5, 1993, but denied by Cameron in correspondence with the author. Cameron explained that the second report merely supplemented the original report by giving the results of certain laboratory tests.

media interest in connection with the death of Hess, culminating in questions raised in the British House of Commons. Thomas was convinced that Prisoner Number Seven, the sole survivor at Spandau, was murdered on August 17, 1987. But he had a theory that Prisoner Number Seven was not Rudolf Hess.[18] Such was the publicity generated by Thomas's twin assertions during 1988 that eventually the Crown Prosecution Service was instructed to carry out an investigation into the nature and circumstances surrounding the death of Prisoner Number Seven. The work was entrusted to Detective Chief Superintendent Howard Jones of New Scotland Yard's Serious Crime Squad.

Jones's work was apparently restricted to a consideration of the medical evidence only as made available by the two post-mortems, the (confidential) report of the Special Investigations Branch of the British Military Police and the allegations made by Hugh Thomas and Wolf Hess. Jones did *not* interview Professors Cameron, Spann or Eisenmenger or Melaouhi or Jordan, for reasons which are obscure.[19] He also, of course, had no opportunity of seeing Spandau, the summerhouse or its contents.

In November 1989 the Director of Public Prosecutions announced that the Jones report 'provided no cogent evidence' to prompt further investigation into the circumstances of the death at Spandau. That being the case, Mr Rhodri Morgan, MP for Cardiff West, asked that the report be placed in the Commons library. Members could then determine for themselves its cogency of otherwise. Permission was refused by the Prime Minister. Subsequent requests by Hugh Thomas, Wolf Hess and the author for sight of the report have also been refused. Letters addressed direct to Howard Jones by the author have been ignored.

However, some background to the preparation of the Jones report is provided by David Irving, the historian. When presenting a paper on the occasion of the fiftieth anniversary of Hess's flight to Great Britain Irving reported: 'Police officers from Scotland Yard came to me in England. They included Detective Inspector Graham Dennis. I asked him "What is your opinion of the matter?" Dennis's reply was "Scotland Yard are convinced that it was a murder. At the moment, we have the greatest problems with the Foreign Office. After all, it has placed a stumbling block in the way of the investigations. The British authorities under Green (the Director of Public Prosecutions) have

---

[18]Hugh Thomas developed the *Doppelganger* theory extensively in his book, *A Tale of Two Murders*, (Hodder & Stoughton), 1988.
[19]See *Guardian* article, May 20, 1989.

ordered the investigations to be stopped."' If Irving's remarks faithfully record what was said then they point to political interference at the highest level to prevent a historical fact becoming public knowledge. Such a hypothesis sits naturally and easily into the whole pattern of Government reporting relating to Hess the man, his mission and now, his death. History is being determined by political expediency if matters are left as they are.

There is a further difficulty. If the death certificate read 'asphyxia, ligature, throttling' rather than 'asphyxia, ligature, suspension', how is the suicide note explained? Self-throttling, especially by a man in Hess's physical condition, can be ruled out. If Professor Spann's medical evidence is accepted then the only manner in which a suicide note will appear is as a contrived apparatus. This would reinforce Professor Cameron's official findings as to hanging. First impressions are that this could not be the case because the note was written in what is undoubtedly the handwriting of Hess. The note was not dated and an English translation reads: 'Please would the Governors send this home. Written a few minutes before my death. I thank you all my beloved for all the dear things you have done for me. Tell Frieberg I am extremely sorry that since the Nuremberg Trial I had to act as though I didn't know her. I had no choice otherwise all attempts to gain freedom would have been in vain. I had looked forward to seeing her again. I did get pictures of her, as of you all.' The text was signed at the end by the words 'Your Eldest.'

One point may be made straightway. If the note was written 'a few minutes' before Hess's death then it must have been written in the garden summerhouse. So in addition to looping and tying flex around his neck and throwing himself to the floor with sufficient force to hang himself, Hess must also have had time to write his suicide note, all before Jordan reappeared. It is a very improbable, if not impossible, scenario.

Many other points arise in connection with the note. The signature and the laboured reference to Frieburg (a nickname applied to one of his secretaries in 1941) and the Nuremberg Trial take the note back in terms of time to the actual date when it was written. It has nothing to do with Hess's death in 1987. Hess had not used the signature style of 'Your Eldest' since the early 1970s. All Hess's letters written to the family in more recent years, and these included those to his grandchildren, were signed simply 'Yours' or 'Your One' (*der Eure*). This same point as to dating the document is raised by the strange reference to Frieburg and Nuremberg which takes up most of the letter. Frieburg was one of Hess's secretaries and at the time of the Nuremberg trial she was brought in to see Hess when he was pretending to suffer from hysterical amnesia. He was obliged by his pretence not to recognise her and at the time he was very upset. But all that was in 1946. The comment in the note may well have been a sentiment properly expressed some time after its occurrence but certainly not in 1987, forty years after the event. The family had explained the position to Frieburg years previously.

The reference to pictures also reinforces the suggestion as to prior dating. Up to Christmas 1969 Hess had depended upon photographs to keep himself in visual touch with his wife and son, as up to that time he had refused to see them (for reasons which have already been explained).[20] After their first visit at Christmas 1969 they came to see him regularly and photographs became unnecessary. The fact that Hess does not mention his three grandchildren also suggests that the note was written before they were born. It will also be remembered that there was some delay in producing the suicide note. It is of course normal procedure in the case of a death other than from natural causes, to search the body to identify the victim and turn up any clues there may be so as to determine the manner of death. These would include any suicide note. That was not done in this case. The Hess suicide note was found on the body two days after the death. It was apparently found when the body was being undressed for the purposes of the post-mortem. Its findings was witnessed by all four prison directors. There was a further delay in handing over the note to the family. It should have been handed over with the body when it was released on August 20 but was not. It was sent to Wolf Hess a month later, on September 25.

Having regard to all these factors and Hess's medical history while at Spandau it is possible to pinpoint the appropriate date when the note was probably written. It was sometime in late 1969. At that time, Hess was seriously ill with a perforated stomach ulcer and threatened general peritonitis. He had been taken to the British Military Hospital in Berlin. He was not expected to live. The ulcer had been long neglected and general peritonitis was likely to prove fatal in an old man who was also suffering from heart and circulatory problems. At that time, there were no signs of any early release from Spandau and Hess's spirits as well as general health would have been low. In these circumstances, it would be understandable for Hess to address a short farewell note to his family. Such a note was not a suicide note. The statement in the note that it was being written 'a few minutes before my death' gives a premonition of early death, not suicide. A more appropriate phrase

---

[20]See chapter 27.

in the case of suicide would be 'a few minutes before I take my own life', followed by some explanation as to why suicide is being contemplated. Apparently, this is a typical feature of suicide notes. It is conspicuously absent from the Hess note.

If a 1969 date is assumed then all the references and the signature become unexceptional and within the expected content of a farewell note as distinct from a suicide note. It is suggested that the note would have been caught up in the normal prison censoring procedures and retained. It could then have been used as a contrivance to bolster the official suicide verdict based upon Professor Cameron's post-mortem. It is almost as though Professor Cameron and the 'suicide' note were both waiting in the wings to appear immediately the demise of Hess became a fact.

There is an intriguing postscript to Hess's death. Late in 1987, as a result of an article written in South Africa by a lawyer in connection with the Hess death and subsequent correspondence with Wolf Hess, the lawyer, who wished to remain anonymous, attended before a South African judge and swore an affidavit. The content of the affidavit, which is reproduced in full in Appendix IX, is remarkable. The lawyer claims to have had connections with several of the Western intelligence agencies and it is through these connections that his information has been gained. The information and explanation as to the circumstances of Hess's death fit comfortably with the conclusions arrived at in this book. The intriguing question of course is as to why the *Israeli* Secret Service was privy to the murder of Rudolf Hess. It is the author's information that, attached to the Camp David Accords, signed in 1979 by President Jimmy Carter of the USA, Prime Minister Begin of Israel and President Sadat of Egypt, there was a secret protocol and an undertaking that Rudolf Hess would never leave Spandau alive. President Carter has denied that in correspondence with the author, but it is noteworthy that according to the lawyer's affidavit, the Israeli Secret Service was an active partner in seeking Hess's death. What then was the Israeli involvement with Hess? Once again, the question is asked who knew what and when about an impending Holocaust in 1941?

In the early morning of Thursday, March 17, 1988, Rudolf Hess's coffin was lowered gently into the family grave at Wunsiedel, alongside that of his father and brother. Only the immediate family were present, less than a dozen persons in all, including the cemetery staff. Hess's body had laid in a temporary grave until then because an earlier burial at Wunsiedel might have attracted demonstrations. Hess had already written his own epitaph while in Spandau. It referred to the failure of his peace mission and was movingly simple: 'I achieved nothing. I could not end the insanity of this struggle of nations, could not prevent what came, what I saw coming. I could not bring salvation. But I am glad that I tried.'

29

The aftermath

As to Hess, I think the British public should be informed of the substance of Hess's documents to the Government. We are treated too much like children who cannot be trusted with too much of the truth.

LLOYD GEORGE, May 31, 1941

The body of Rudolf Hess may have been laid to rest but the controversy as to his mission to Great Britain in 1941 and his death at Spandau in 1987 lives on. It is one of the great unsolved mysteries of the Second World War.

Of course, the mystery could be resolved tomorrow if the British Government would release into the public domain all the Hess papers currently embargoed. But such an event, judged by past experience, is wishful thinking, even in this age of trumpeted open government. It is this absence of the relevant papers which has led to the building up a number of hypotheses upon which to hang those facts which are available to provide some sort of rational explanation as to Hess's mission and death. These various hypotheses have been presented in a dozen books and countless newspaper articles and TV and radio features. In strange contrast, the personal memoirs of many of the individuals directly involved, including Churchill, Eden, Kirkpatrick, Beaverbrook and Simon, hardly mention the Hess mission.

The subject matter will not go away. To end with the beginning. 'There is more in this than meets the eye.' So there is. But no British Government, from Winston Churchill's to Tony Blair's, has deigned to tell the British public what it is. Worse than that, they have been at best economical with the truth and that fact has whetted the appetites of the truth-seekers. The original official version of the Hess mission of 1941, that it was the act of a deranged madman lacking all backing from his Government, has long since been discarded. The task of the truth-seekers is to build a superstructure in terms of hypothesis upon which all, not some or most but all, the known facts relating to the Hess affair may be hung, so as to sit naturally and comfortably together. The task is not easy.

Some of the facts fit a certain hypothesis but others do not fit the same hypothesis. A good example is the behaviour of Hess during his imprisonment in Great Britain, prior to the Nuremberg trials. It was extraordinary and untypical of the man, having regard to his personal history and character. The facts fit at least three hypotheses. The original, official version was that Hess was deranged. But if the Hess mission was the act of a deranged individual without the backing of his Government, how did this deranged individual fly, single-handed and without permission, an unarmed Me110 aircraft over some of the most heavily defended airspace in Western Europe out over the North Sea, navigate and pilot himself safely to the British coast and then fly in broad daylight across the Borders and Scotland and back again, eluding in their entirety all British air defences by way of fighter aircraft and anti-aircraft gunfire? That may have been the performance of a genius or of a pilot having a lot of German and British help along the way. But it was certainly not the performance of an unbacked, deranged lunatic.

Hugh Thomas, in his intriguing book *A Tale of Two Murders*, suggests a second explanation for the extraordinary behaviour of Hess during his imprisonment: that the man imprisoned was not Hess but an impostor. But if that were so, why did Hess's wife and son not recognise the impostor when they visited him at Spandau? And why did Hess's Nazi colleagues not recognise the impostor when they met at Nuremberg? In this book, a third hypothesis has been suggested: that the extraordinary behaviour was induced by drugs, the fear of drugs and an intellectual game that Hess played with his psychiatric warders which included the feigning of what the psychiatrists diagnosed as hysterical amnesia. But does that hypothesis fit together with all the other known facts? This is the important test.

Very few facts were made available on or immediately after Hess landed by parachute in Scotland on the evening of May 10, 1941. Early releases through the British Ministry of Information mentioned only the fact and manner of his arrival and confirmation as to his identity. There was no mention as to the purpose of the mission. Churchill prepared a draft explanatory statement for submission to the House of Commons. It was never delivered. The British release of information had been preceded by a German release explaining the mission in terms of mental derangement. That was a convenient hook upon which to hang the British explanation of events. Beaverbrook suggested it.

Churchill adopted it. Thereafter, there was a total shutdown of information on the Hess flight from both German and British sources. A policy of 'isolate and forget' was adopted on both sides of the English Channel.

All the remaining facts that are now available have emerged gradually over the years. Foreign governments, Russia in particular, have released relevant papers. The German diplomatic papers are now available (although no doubt weeded by the Allies before publication) and many of the actual participators have given accounts of their personal experiences. These accounts range from those of lead players like the Duke of Hamilton to bit players with nevertheless, important roles, like Cecil Bryant, DFM, the radio operator at Unsworth and Albert James, the Yorkshire Area Secretary of the Transport and General Workers Union. They contrast sharply with the absence of information made available by successive British Governments down to the present day. Churchill's isolate and forget policy of 1941 is still alive and well in 2000.

It is this feature of governmental secrecy which is one of the most baffling and, it is believed, the most important aspect of the continuing mystery. There are documents embargoed at the Public Record Office which have been embargoed for the last 59 years. They are likely to be embargoed for another 59 years. As recently as June 1992 Douglas Hurd, the then Foreign Secretary, when announcing the release of some of the Hess papers (which revealed nothing that was not known previously) stated that 'there was at least one document held back *for reasons of national security*'. How could national security in 1992 be endangered by the release of papers relating to events occurring in 1941? One ponders on the phrase 'national security'. Should it in fact be 'national embarrassment'?

If the facts now known are put together it is not impossible to construct a hypothesis that fits them. That has been the task attempted in the foregoing pages, but there are still one or two areas where the facts fade and the hypothesis becomes conjecture. That is unavoidable under the circumstances. What is now known is that Rudolf Hess flew to this country on May 10, 1941, with the blessing of Adolf Hitler and a small number of the Nazi hierarchy. They were privy to a scheme initiated by Hess to bring the Anglo-German war to an end. Germany had never wanted war with Great Britain. Her preparations for war were aimed exclusively towards the East and in particular the destruction of Russian communism and the opening up of the Russian landmass to satisfy the German need for *Lebensraum.* This major policy objective of Adolf Hitler, chronicled in full in his *Mein Kampf*, may have passed unnoticed by successive British Governments but was certainly discussed openly with British Air Intelligence in the mid 1930s. Even details as to the planned *blitzkrieg* methods which were to be used to open up the Russian hinterland were divulged.

The declaration of war by Great Britain and France in September 1939 had signalled the failure of German foreign policy towards the West, but the military campaigns of 1940 had removed any threat from that direction. Having removed France from the equation, Germany was anxious to formalise a peace with Great Britain before the onset of Operation Barbarossa which would mark out the great ideological battle between fascism and communism. Ever since the Anglo-German war had started, Germany had sought to end it. In May 1941 it was thought that a personalised attempt by the Deputy Führer, held generally in higher regard by the British than his Nazi colleagues, would perhaps have an outside chance of success.

Hess himself was passionately anti-communist and pro-British. He rated his chance of success highly. He and his colleagues in Germany believed in the existence of a British Peace Party headed by people like David Lloyd George, Lord Halifax, Sam Hoare, Rab Butler and the Duke of Windsor and including most of the landed aristocracy (particularly the Scottish) and important members of British business, banking and other financial institutions. There was plenty of evidence available to the Germans of peace seeking activities originated by the British and involving Ministers up to and including Cabinet level, senior diplomats and members of MI6.

It was also known by the Germans that these elements of the British Establishment considered that the biggest danger to the status quo which protected their privileged position came not from Nazi Germany but from communist Russia. Their fear as to communist encroachment into Europe was matched only by that of Nazi Germany. They saw a strong Germany as a shield against that encroachment. Hess expected to meet representatives of the British Peace Party on his arrival in Great Britain, parley with them, make peace and bring down the Churchill Government. His point of contact was the Duke of Hamilton, the senior Scottish duke with strong personal connections with King George VI.

It was agreed between Hitler and Hess that if the mission failed, the 'deranged individual' card would be played. Germany and Hitler, then enjoying unprecedented military and diplomatic success and a complete hegemony over almost the whole of the continent of Europe, would not then be humiliated by the rebuff of a peace initiative and the loss of the Deputy Führer. The flight itself was aided by the co-operation of German air defence over Western Europe and the provision of fighter escorts over the North Sea. There was equivalent co-operation from air defences on the British mainland, not a shot being fired either by aircraft of Fighter Command or anti-aircraft batteries of the army. Hess crossed the coast in broad daylight and then crossed Scotland from east to west and back again entirely unmolested before parachuting to earth, leaving his aircraft to crash.

It is apparent that British Intelligence and in particular, British Air Intelligence must have been involved in arranging this strange acquiescence of the British air defences to the role of non-combatants as Hess's aircraft flew in from the North Sea. It is known that British Air Intelligence had long-standing links with Alfred Rosenberg, friend of Hess and Hitler and the man summoned to Hess's side from Berlin for consultation on the very morning of Hess's departure for Great Britain. This intelligence link had operated since the mid-1930s. It had been used then by no less a personage than King George V and was known to be still in use in early 1941.

It is apparent that something went wrong with Hess's plans after he reached the British coast. His flight plan and landing instructions are unknown and always will be until the embargo on the papers at the Public Record Office is lifted. It appears that he entered British air space in the wrong sector. As a result, he failed to make contact with whatever reception party he had expected to meet. It has of course been suggested that there never was a reception party or for that matter, a British Peace Party. It is said that the involvement of British Intelligence was related to the planning and springing of a trap to lure the Deputy Führer or some other Nazi big fish to Great Britain by holding out the bait of a (non-existent) British Peace Party. If that were so, there is no evidence available to support the conjecture. There is plenty of evidence (from Russian, Czech and French sources) of the involvement of British Intelligence but none of the conspiracy-to-trick theory.

If the Intelligence Services had pulled off such a coup and the Deputy Führer of Germany put in the bag, one would have expected such an achievement to have been trumpeted to the skies and subjected to propaganda use on the grand scale. In fact, the Hess landing was met by a deafening silence and never used for propaganda purposes. Even after the war, when the dust had settled and full rein given to official and unofficial publications, not a single person has ever claimed involvement, let alone claimed credit for their part, in such a remarkable coup. No one has said how the coup was shaped and developed to its fruition. That is extraordinary if in fact there was such a coup. It is suggested that when it became apparent that British Intelligence were involved then they had to be provided with a role. So one was provided.

Another role has been suggested in the foregoing pages of this book. It is a simpler role. It is that British Intelligence, or certain segments of it, were involved as active participants in the Hess peace initiative and were themselves an important part of the British Peace Party. MI6 recruitment, at least up to and including the early years of the war, was almost exclusively from the ranks of the British Establishment. It is likely that the British Establishment was as well represented in the ranks of MI6, as it was in the ranks of the British Peace Party. Stewart Menzies, head of MI6 at the time, was at the very heart of the British Establishment. If parts of the Intelligence Service had in fact acted independently of the (Churchill) Government of the day it was not the first or the last time that the service had acted as a loose cannon. The Zinoviev letter of 1924 and the postwar attempted destabilisation of the Harold Wilson Government provide good evidence of that.

Although Hess met the target of his mission, the Duke of Hamilton, the day after his landing, it was in circumstances far removed from those he had foreseen. The Duke had got off to a rather stuttering start which encompassed some 24 hours of most strange behaviour when it is presumed he was taking advice or instructions or both from persons unknown. Eventually, he decided he was a Churchill man. Hess soon found himself imprisoned and treated as a prisoner of war although he may have fairly claimed, and did at the Nuremberg Trials, that he was a peace plenipotentiary and should have been treated as such.

Churchill too got off to a stuttering start. He had received last-minute intelligence from a private industrial source that Hess was on his way, but at first dealt with the delivered package with uncharacteristic hesitancy and indecision. He then hooked on to the German line of Hess's derangement, which would help to promote the Hess initiative as a non-event. This soon merged into an 'isolate and forget' policy. There was a complete shut-down of news coverage on Hess, his whereabouts, his mission and his motives. Churchill was well aware of the existence of a British Peace Party and the insecurity of his own political position against a background of continuing British military reverses. Hess was an unwelcome additive to this potentially potent mixture and the sooner he was put away and forgotten, the better.

It has been suggested that there may have been another even more important factor which led to the isolate-and-forget policy, which would explain its subsequent implementation in the most extreme and inhuman terms for the rest of Hess's life and may have intervened in the manner of his death 46 years later. It would certainly explain the continuing embargo on the Hess papers at the Public Record Office. It concerns the Jewish question and is linked to Hess's personal motives for his mission. There is no direct evidence that such a factor existed but there is some circumstantial evidence which suggests it.

The Germans in 1941 had a so-called Jewish problem. More accurately, Hitler had a Jewish problem which he had foisted onto the German nation and had used or abused it to explain all Germany's problems. The problem was irrational in nature and potentially vile in its manifestation. Nevertheless, as far as Nazi Germany was concerned, it existed. What was to be done with Europe's Jews? Of all the major Nazi policy objectives it was the only one that was unresolved in May 1941, apart from the destruction of Russian communism.

There were plans afoot to deal with both these remaining problems. Just as Operation Barbarossa was going to deal with the destruction of Russian communism, so the enforced emigration of all European Jews to the French island of Madagascar, where the Jewish homeland was to be established, was to be the answer to the Jewish problem. The Madagascar Plan was the Final Solution to the Jewish question as it stood on May 10, 1941, when Hess flew to Great Britain. So much is not a matter of conjecture but a matter of fact and a matter of record.

One of the most important aspects entered into the record is that the Jewish measures were to form an integral part of any peace treaty to be signed with both France and Great Britain. If Hess was going to talk about peace with Great Britain then he was going to talk about the Madagascar Plan, at least as far as the European Jews were concerned. That is clear from the German official diplomatic documents still on file at Bonn.

It is suggested, however, that Hess talked about more than the Madagascar Plan, that he talked about a possible alternative to it, and that he talked about the possibilities of an impending Holocaust. The Madagascar Plan was the brainchild of the German Foreign Office. It had been approved by Ribbentrop, rubber-stamped by Hitler and agreed by him with Mussolini. But Heydrich, Eichmann and the SS had other ideas, and Hess knew what those ideas were. He knew this through his good friend, Rosenberg, the recently appointed Reich Commissioner for the Eastern Territories. Heydrich's *Einsatzgruppen* (snatch squads) were already under orders to follow the German combat troops into Russia immediately Operation Barbarossa was launched and seek out all Russian Jews and Russian commissars and exterminate them.

Hess himself had long since been alarmed at the literalism with which Hitler's policy objectives had been carried out and the resulting excesses. Operation Barbarossa was going to further fuel that alarm. Hess had helped his hero of early days write a book. It had set out in great detail the main policy objectives of the Nazi Party. But the acting out of the pages of *Mein Kampf* had proved more indigestible to Hess than the writing of them. Hess was a decent and honourable man. He had been much downcast as a young Great War veteran by his country's defeat and much uplifted by the oratory of the young Adolf Hitler, who had promised Hess and millions of young men like him, a resurgence of national pride, honour and dignity.

In those early days Hess had idolised Hitler and would have followed him anywhere. And did. But he was always more of an old-fashioned patriot and hero worshipper than a true Nazi. And the dream had gone sour. Hitler could accommodate the fruits of the literalism with which the policy objectives were pursued. Hess could not. The Night of the Long Knives on June 30, 1934, when Hitler's old friend Ernst Roehm and his followers were liquidated, and the *Kristallnacht* pogrom of November 9, 1938, when full government licence was given to the burning, looting and destruction of Jewish property and lives, proved that.

There is more than one witness to the fact that Hess was appalled by these excesses which were but manifestations of the principles enunciated in *Mein Kampf.* Worse still, as the programme of implementation had unfolded there rose to the forefront of the Nazi hierarchy men endowed with little more than a ruthless ambition for power for its own sake. They were prepared, indeed happy, to embrace the excesses that Hess rejected. If Hess had been apprehensive about earlier excesses, how much more was he desperately afraid of the future with such people at the right hand of Hitler? With people like Heydrich, Eichmann and Bormann pushing to the front, Hess knew what the alternative to the Madagascar Plan would be if his peace initiative failed.

It is no great leap into the dark to suggest that he voiced these fears to his British interrogators. This hypothesis, that the Churchill Government was aware of a possible Holocaust before the event, would help explain the need for Hess's incarceration under the tightest security to the day of his death, 46 years later. Certainly, Churchill's original isolate-and-forget policy seemed to bring the best of all worlds to the British. It effectively prevented Hess from divulging information which Churchill thought was 'not in the national interest'. The initial outcry from the British press, MPs, and the public at large about the lack of information eventually died away. Hess was soon well isolated and in due course of time, almost forgotten.

The imprisonment of Hess at Mytchett Place and Maindiff Court during the four years that led up to Nuremberg was noteworthy not only for the degree of isolation and security which it imposed but also for the fact that he appears to have been treated as a psychiatric guinea pig. No fewer than eight psychiatrists attended upon him during that time. They produced a bewildering battery of obscure and differing symptoms, diagnoses and treatments. It needs hardly be said that none of them found him to be normal. Hess himself joined in the fun. His feigning of hysterical amnesia later warranted particular mention in the medical journals and threw doubts on the true worth of psychiatric diagnosis. In 1941 the practice of psychiatry was not as well developed as it is today. Anyone consigned to the care of a psychiatrist in those days, let alone eight of them, was deemed mad. Perhaps that was the plan as far as Hess was concerned.

Hess's case history during those years was the subject of a book by J.R. Rees, the senior psychiatrist concerned with Hess. It is a strange book. Although it is a medical casebook it includes an uncommon amount of non-medical misinformation as to the flight itself and the background. The flight is described as the act of a deranged individual without backing from his Government. A flight plan is reproduced, reputedly drawn by Hess while at Maindiff Court, showing his Augsburg to Scotland route. This has since been dismissed as a nonsense by Helmut Kaden, the airfield manager at Augsburg, who points out that the early part of the flight is shown as over Western Germany, comprising heavily defended airspace which would certainly have been out of bounds to a lone, unidentified, unauthorised aircraft. The route then locks on to a prime navigational beam in Denmark used by mainstream bombers flying across the North Sea to attack Great Britain. Kaden says that Hess would never have divulged such an operational secret during the war years. He also points out that the plotted route was beyond the range of an Me110 aircraft, even when fitted with extra fuel tanks.

Perhaps more significant are the medical omissions from a book dealing with a medical case history. Nowhere is there any statement as to what drugs were prescribed for the patient. Hess claimed that he was drugged throughout his imprisonment in Great Britain. That may well have been the case. Churchill's isolate-and-forget policy may well have been helped on its way by the administration of drugs. If Hess had not entered into his imprisonment as a psychiatric case it would appear that every effort was made thereafter to make him into one. Thus he could live out the official version of his mental condition.

Hess and his lawyer considered Nuremberg to be a legal farce. Prisoners were indicted by legislation having retrospective effect and individuals were held responsible for offences committed by nation states. Both were principles outlawed by international law until the advent of Nuremberg. Worst of all, representatives of Russia, a nation state which should have been in the dock with Germany in connection with the war of aggression against Poland, sat on the judges' bench. As a result of these perceived absurdities, Hess refused to accept the legal authority of the court and took only an intermittent part in the proceedings. He was found not guilty of war crimes and crimes against humanity but guilty of conspiring with others in the planning of an aggressive war. The fact that he made an attempt to end the war with Great Britain at risk of his own life was not taken into account. He was sentenced to life imprisonment.

The Russian case that led to this sentence was that if the Hess mission had been successful, the loss of Russian lives in the ensuing struggle with Germany would have been even more grievous than was the case. There was a rough logic to the Russian view, but their argument rested on the assumption that Operation Barbarossa would have gone ahead even if Hess's mission had been successful. Hess has since denied this.

Hess's life at Spandau, especially in the later stages, represented a particularly harsh and extreme version of Churchill's original policy. He was incarcerated in Spandau for the remainder of his natural life, a total of 42 years, the last 21 of which were spent in solitary confinement. There was no remission of his life sentence as there had been in the case of Raeder and Funk. The security arrangements remained uncompromising to the end. Even when allowed visits from the family, they were obliged to take place in the presence of all four prison directors. There was to be no physical contact or talk to do with policies, the Nazi Party, the war or his flight to Great Britain. These measures would have been extraordinary in any case, but as applied to an old man of 90, crippled with arthritis and suffering from circulatory trouble and heart failure, it was little short of torture.

The immediate cause of this state of affairs was said to be the intransigence of the Russians. They were unwilling to consider freeing Hess on compassionate grounds, in spite of the most energetic representations made by his son. All that changed however in the spring of 1987, following the advent of Mikhail Gorbachev as President of the USSR and his new policy of *Perestroika.* It soon became apparent that Hess at the age of 93 would be released from Spandau before the end of that year.

It was not to be. On August 17, 1987, Hess died in Spandau. The official verdict was that he committed suicide by hanging himself. It was an extraordinary thing to do in view of his impending release. It was impossible not to link his death with Churchill's original policy of isolate and forget. It seemed that the policy had reached its logical end. There were many unsatisfactory features about the death which indicated not suicide but murder. These included the physical impossibility of a man of 93, crippled with arthritis, carrying out the manoeuvres necessarily associated with hanging, the different versions of the manner of death (all involving an electric extension cord that never existed), the signs of a struggle in the summerhouse, the suspect suicide note, the destruction of the summerhouse and all its contents, the unavailability of the reports of the Special Investigations Branch of the British Military Police and of Chief Superintendent Howard Jones and the political shut-down on the latter's investigation.

By far the most important evidence of a miscarriage of justice lay in the medical evidence apparent from the reports of Professor Wolfgang Spann of the Institute of Forensic Medicine at Munich University, following his post-mortem examination of the body of Rudolf Hess carried out immediately after its release to the family for burial. Spann's findings were fundamentally opposed to those of Professor James Cameron who had carried out the earlier official post-mortem examination. While agreeing with Professor Cameron that death was not due to natural causes but from asphyxia caused by ligature, Spann was of the opinion that the death was more typical of a throttling or strangulation rather than suspension by hanging as reported by Professor Cameron.

If Professor Spann's opinion is correct then the most serious matters of public policy are opened up. If Rudolf Hess was murdered, why was he murdered? If the hypothesis built up in the foregoing pages of this book and summarised above is accepted, then logically Rudolf Hess had to be murdered because of what he might have divulged if set free. He would perhaps have told the world about the constituent members of the British Peace Party of 1941, from royalty downwards. He might have described the true function and involvement of MI6 in his mission. Most important of all, he might have told the world about British (and maybe American) pre-knowledge of an impending Holocaust. It is almost as though the manner of his death explained his mission of 1941.

An attempt is currently being made to re-open the question of Hess's death. Previous attempts to do this have already been made but have failed. Hugh Thomas gained considerable publicity in 1988 following the publication of *A Tale of Two Murders*, in which he suggested that the man who was murdered at Spandau on August 17, 1987, was not Rudolf Hess but an impostor. Thomas's *doppelganger* theory caught the imagination and the headlines. It eventually led to questions being raised in the House of Commons and, ultimately, to the Howard Jones report. There however, the matter rested. The Jones report never saw the light of day. The whole investigation was effectively quashed. It demonstrated in dramatic fashion the failure of the supreme British democratic institution to see through an investigation into a matter of public policy to its logical end. The Government announced that they were satisfied that the man who had died at Spandau was Rudolf Hess. They said precious little else as to the circumstances of his death. It was as though the identity issue had effectively masked the more important issue. It was an important victory for the Thatcher Government. It demonstrated the strength of the political blocking mechanisms.

Present attempts to obtain a review of the position have followed a different tack. The death certificate relating to Hess's death refers to 'asphyxia due to compression of the neck due to suspension'. If Professor Spann's opinion was correct then the certificate should read 'asphyxia due to compression of the neck due to throttling'. Formal application to amend the registration of the death was made to the British Registrar of Births and Deaths Overseas Section on April 24, 1995. The application was supported by personal declarations made by Professor Spann, Professor Eisenmenger, Abdullah Melaouhi, Wolf Hess and the author amounting in total to nearly 400 pages of declarations and exhibits. It was considered that if the Registrar failed to amend the registration then legal remedy might be possible by seeking a judicial review.

Reference has been made in the preface to this book to the difficulties and delays encountered in dealing with Government departments. The Office of Population Censuses and Surveys, to which the application to amend was referred, is no exception. The application was made on April 24, 1995. It was not until August 2 that any substantive reply was received. It was extraordinary. Notification was given that the death certificate had been incorrectly registered under the wrong statute in the first place and was therefore being cancelled. The correction of the error by cancelling the registration had the effect of sidestepping the issue. Prolonged correspondence followed with the Ministry of Defence, to which the matter had been passed, but brought no satisfaction. Their view was that as they had no power to register, they had no power to amend.

Fortunately, the intervention of Rhodri Morgan, MP, has once again proved helpful. In discussion with the new Labour Government Armed Forces Minister, it became apparent that an application could be made to amend the death certificate itself, which had been properly issued, as opposed to its registration which was defective. Such are the issues which feed the frustrations of those seeking only the truth. At the time of writing (January 2000) Wolf Hess is considering the making of a formal request to amend the death certificate. Refusal by the Ministry of Defence to comply will open the door to an application for leave to apply for a judicial review at which would be presented the 400 pages of additional evidence already lodged with the Registrar of Births and Deaths, Overseas Section. Amendment of the death certificate would of course open the door as to the motive for murder.

30

And a postscript

Britain fondly imagined she had won the war. She had not. America and Russia had won the war. Britain had merely, in her finest hour, not lost it.

WINSTON CHURCHILL, 1945

The purpose of Rudolf Hess's mission in May 1941 was to bring to an end a war which Germany had never wanted in the first place. He had said more than once that the only beneficiaries from an Anglo-German conflict would be Russia and America. And so it proved to be. The irony of Great Britain's position was manifest. She went to war in 1939 to prevent one nation, Germany, from dominating Europe and threatening Great Britain's position. She ended up in 1945 with another nation, Russia, dominating Europe and threatening not only the position of Great Britain but that of the whole Western world. There is added irony in the fact that high among the pre-war policy priorities of the first nation (Germany) was the destruction of the second (Russia), a fact apparently ignored by those responsible for British pre-war policy.

After the failure of the Hess mission the then localised war soon broadened into a global conflict, marked by increasing barbarism and excesses on all sides. After 1941, Great Britain played a steadily decreasing role. History will probably adjudge Great Britain's role, honourable though it was, as the last brilliant illumination from the dying fires which marked the decline of British power and influence in the world in the 20th century. American industrial and financial muscle and Russian manpower and military prowess were the dominant factors which led to the defeat of Nazi Germany. But Great Britain, during the years 1939 to 1941, had provided the vital element of time during which the Russian and American preparations for war could be brought to their full potential.

In 1945, after six years of war, Great Britain was exhausted and impoverished. Although her 400,000 casualties were far less than Russia's or Germany's, her economic and financial losses were devastating. From being the world's largest creditor nation in 1939, she became the world's largest debtor nation in 1945. She then owed some £2,879 million in external debt, mostly in convertible sterling balances. The estimates for 1946 were that Great Britain would be spending something like £750 million more abroad than she would be earning. If she was to get anywhere near to balancing her international books she would need to export more goods than she had ever done before, this in spite of the fact that exports for 1945 were 60 per cent down on the pre-war figures.

There were other factors which were to make the difficult task a near impossible one. Her merchant fleet was 30 per cent smaller in 1945 than in 1939 and two of her major exporting industries, textiles and coal mining, had been stripped of essential manpower. But by far the greatest hurdle to surmount in the search for export markets was the loss of the pre-war Imperial Preference status as a result of the lend-lease negotiations of 1941. Nearly all the tariff barriers had come down and world markets were a free for all. In practical terms that meant that they were American-dominated. British manufacturers, so long cosseted by cosy incestual relationships formed behind the walls of Imperial Preference, were slow to react. Worse still, the British populace, exhausted by six years of war and all the privations and aerial bombardment that had gone with it, viewed the early postwar years as their age of entitlement. 'Welfare' was the key word. Imperial greatness and endeavour became matters of history. The British Empire, an institution so admired and envied by Adolf Hitler, soon fragmented and disappeared. Great Britain had not lost the war but she certainly had not won it.

Russia too entered an age of entitlement in the immediate postwar years. Her losses during the war, both in human lives and material, had been the most grievous of all the warring nations. But she demonstrated to the world and perhaps more importantly, to herself, that her military capacity was second to none. She had taken on and eventually destroyed a German military machine which up to the time of launching Operation Barbarossa had proved invincible. Out of 13 million German casualties suffered by their land forces during the whole war, no less than ten million were incurred on the Eastern Front. As a result, they had been bled dry. The Russians brought to bear immense resources in manpower and wedded them to a well equipped military machine. During 1941, the first year of the German invasion, she incurred three million casualties but was still able to deploy an army of four million. Her total casualties were six times those of Germany and 20 times those of the combined British and American forces. For the three year period from 1941 to 1944 the Russians fought the Germans alone. Even after the Normandy invasion in 1944 the Germans were deploying 250 of their best divisions in the East compared with only 90 divisions in the West.

Russia maintained, correctly, that she had always been the main ideological target for Nazi Germany and therefore inevitably, her main adversary on the field of battle. She did not dispute that she had received help from the Anglo-American military contribution but rightly or wrongly, considered it as late in arriving (which she thought was politically motivated) and of comparatively minor importance. On those grounds, Russia considered it her entitlement to stake out her territorial claims in Eastern Europe and to take her place as a major player in the postwar world councils. And she did. In spite of her losses the war established Russia as a front-line world Super Power, to rank with and, in due course, against America.

The real winner of the war was the United States of America. During the 1938 crisis the American President, Franklin Roosevelt, had stated that American productive sources could only be enriched in the event of a European war. The following year, the American neutrality laws were relaxed so as to make legal the supply of arms to the combatants in a European war. This converted Roosevelt's prediction into reality. American production was boosted not only by the domestic requirements of America's own defence programme but also by the supply of arms to Great Britain and France during 1939 and 1940. After the collapse of France, American industry took on board all the British requirements arising under the lend-lease arrangements. She handled them comfortably. There was no inflationary strain on her domestic economy.

By the end of the war, American economic muscle plus Roosevelt's commercial acumen had established America as the most powerful nation on earth. She had suffered little by way of material losses due to enemy action (she had never undergone aerial bombardment) and her casualties were trifling compared with those of the other combatants. Her industrial output was prodigious. In 1939 her aircraft production was 2,100 machines. By 1944 it was 96,300 machines. By that time, two thirds of all the tanks and motor vehicles employed by the British were American made. Great Britain, lacking both manpower and industrial resources, had been reduced to a subsidiary role, almost entirely dependent upon American support. Her power in the councils of war was thus diminished.

Nowhere was this degree of dependency and the humiliations that went with it better illustrated than in the control and use of the first atomic bomb dropped on Hiroshima. By the Quebec Agreement of 1943, British consent was obligatory to the use of an atomic bomb. This right of veto recognised the part-proprietary rights of the British, having regard to their early research work which had led to the development of the bomb. This consenting authority was deputed by the British Cabinet to an inner circle of three, comprising Churchill, Sir John Anderson and Field Marshal Wilson, head of the British Mission in Washington. In fact, the committee was never consulted as to the use of the bomb. Churchill, no doubt under pressure from the Americans, made the decision alone on July 2, 1945. There was no discussion with the British, either as to the moral issue involved or as to how, why, when or where the first bomb was to be dropped. All strategic and operational matters were decided upon by the Americans alone. They seemed unaware that the British had any right to participate and ignorant as to the worth of early research. Such were the humiliations born of economic and financial dependence.

The war established America as the most powerful political as well as economic power in the world, with a truly global perspective. The war also established Russia as a competing Superpower, dominating Eastern Europe and with ambitions far beyond that. It also marked the decline of British power and influence in the world and her economic dependence upon America. Rudolf Hess's prophecies had indeed been fully confirmed by events.

Appendix I

UK organisations in the late 1930s and early 1940s with pro-German/anti-communist/anti-Semitic tendencies

Anglo-German Fellowship
Anglo-German Brotherhood
British Fascists
British People's Party
British Union of Fascists
The Britons
German-English Society
Imperial Fascist League
January Club
Liberty Restoration League
The Link
Militant Christian Patriots
National Citizens Union
National Socialist League
National Workers Party
Nordic League
Pro-British Association
Right Club
United British Advisory Ratepayers' Association
White Knights of England
Windsor Club

Appendix II

Alfred Rosenberg's report to Adolf Hitler on Anglo-German relations, October 1935

'The attempts to find people in England who were eager to comprehend the German movement date back to 1929. Our English agent R. [de Ropp] in Berlin then made possible my first journey to London in 1931. There it was possible to make a number of contacts which worked out well for an Anglo-German understanding. In the forefront here was Squadron Leader W. [Winterbotham], a member of the Air General Staff, who was entirely convinced that Germany and England must move together to ward off the Bolshevik danger. The outcome of the various discussions was the widening of the group amongst the Air General Staff, and the Royal Air Force Club became a centre for fostering Anglo-German understanding.

In the Spring of 1934 Squadron Leader Winterbotham came to Germany and was received by the Führer. The Führer's handling of this matter subsequently resulted in the strengthening of a policy which was already well disposed towards us, and since then permanent contact has never been broken. When there are anti-German activities in London, enquiries always come to us from the Air General Staff as to what reply could be made to favour the German standpoint. The German arguments have then been turned to good account wherever appropriate. Unlike certain English individuals who on the one occasion spoke out enthusiastically for Germany, only to declare the opposite after some months, this firm group in the Air General Staff, led principally by younger officers, showed itself to be firm and keenly aware of its goals in all uncertain situations. Not least of all Baldwin's great speech of the previous year, in which he conceded the right of Germany to air protection, originates from these influences.

The English magazine *The Aeroplane*, appearing under the sponsorship of the Air General Staff, has always strongly opposed

Bolshevism and has declared again and again, when tempers were roused against Germany's alleged militarism, that today it would be entirely to be welcomed if Germany had a strong air force in order to ward off Asiatic barbarism. The English ministers who would not accept this viewpoint were most fiercely attacked. In a reshuffle of the British Foreign Ministry it was not a candidate of the Francophile British Foreign Office who eventually became Foreign Minister, but the one-time Minister of Aviation Samuel Hoare who, still today, maintains his old personal connections with the Ministry of Aviation. At his request a Memorandum inspired by us on the intellectual foundations of National Socialism, has been passed to him, as he wishes to try to understand our Movement more fully.

During MacDonald's term of office direct touch was maintained through MacDonald's private secretary, Mr Badlow, whom I had got to know in 1933 and with whom I had held detailed conversations. Since then he has been kept continuously informed by us and has more than once had heated discussions with MacDonald.

A positive result of the close liaison with the British Air General Staff was that contact between our Air Ministry and the British airmen was established. Yet before it was possible to make known our rearmament, Winterbotham, on the official paper of the English Air Ministry, informed me of a representative of the aero-engine factories which manufacture engines for the British Air Force. Later I received him here in Berlin also. However, as the German industry had already progressed so far, the almost official British furtherance of German air rearmament could not be taken full advantage of. At all events the leader of our English department (Kapitänleutnant A.D. Obermüller) had brought two representatives of the German Air Ministry to London and had undertaken several journeys to London himself. He was the first German to receive an invitation from the Air Vice Marshal to have a thorough look at British air power and equipment. The A.P.A., too, had put a car at the disposal of the Air Marshal when he was in Germany for a sight-seeing tour the previous year. A closer link between our English section and Henry Deterding and his circle has also been taken up. It was possible to straighten out the misunderstanding over the tax situation connected with Deterding's German property. This did prevent changes in the arrangements at Deterding's, or as the case may be, at the Shell works, the result of which would have been the loss to the German State of important commissions.

At the end of last year we were notified that the King of England[1] had pronounced himself dissatisfied with the official press reports. The Duke of Kent's visit to Munich had only worsened the English King's opinion regarding official news reporting, and so one day we received the request from London to make it possible for our English agent to make a trip to London to explain about National Socialism down to the last detail to the Duke of Kent for the purpose of informing the King of England. After careful consultation with me, de Ropp travelled to London where he unobtrusively had a three hour conversation with the Duke of Kent, who then reported it to the King of England. It may be accepted that this meeting contributed very greatly in strengthening the pressure for a reconstruction of the Cabinet and mainly towards beginning of the movement in the direction of Germany.

On Party Day in 1934 a number of Englishmen were invited, some of whom at least were doing work which favourably concerned Germany. First and foremost was Captain MacCaw, the semi-official adviser of the English War Office and liaison officer for other Ministries. Formerly MacCaw had been an adjutant of Lord Kitchener's and, as we ascertained, has for his part worked in a commendable manner in official places for an Anglo-German understanding; and besides him, also, the adjutant of the Duke of Connaught (Uncle of the King of England), a man of sincerity and enthusiasm. Archibald Boyle was actively working towards the same end; he was the official appointment by the Air Ministry to deal with all foreign questions on its behalf. In addition to these most important contacts there are a great number of other acquaintanceships with British politicians, officers and Members of Parliament.

It goes without saying that other people as well in the N.S.D.A.P. had important connections with England and took full advantage of these. All in all, however, I think I can say that, despite many difficulties and opposition, which I will not go into any further, the English section of the A.P.A. has done its utmost to help create the special conditions for an Anglo-German understanding.'

[1]The report is dated October 1935. The King of England at the end of 1934 was King George V.

Appendix III

British Cabinet exchanges and attendant circumstances, May 1940[1]

Friday, May 24
The Cabinet agreed that President Roosevelt be invited to contact the Italians and reassure them that any reasonable territorial and other claims that they may have would receive sympathetic consideration on the conclusion of hostilities with Germany. Both France and Great Britain were concerned that Italy might enter the war at the side of Germany, with consequent danger to the French and British territorial possessions, particularly in the Mediterranean.

Saturday, May 25
During the evening Halifax called on the Italian Ambassador in London, Guiseppe Bastionini. Bastionini was well known to Halifax as a reasonable, personable, middle-of-the-road diplomat. This meeting appears to have been initiated by Halifax, following a suggestion made by Kenneth de Courcy in a letter to Butler openly advocating approaches to both Italy and the USA to act as mediators in the seeking of peace.

The Halifax/Bastionini discussions apparently went well beyond the conditions required to keep Italy out of the war and, in accordance with de Courcy's suggestion to Butler, included the possibility of Italy acting as a mediator for a general peace settlement of all European issues. Halifax said that Great Britain was prepared to consider any such proposals 'provided our liberty and independence were assured'.

From an Italian point of view it appears that Bastionini was attempting to shunt forward Italian claims in return for an offer of mediation.

---

[1]The summary is based upon extracts from those Cabinet records currently available, supplemented by other relevant information and comments.

As far as Halifax was concerned, such a possibility could lead to peace with the preservation of British independence. There is no indication that Halifax had any Cabinet approval for taking the discussions as far as he had.

Sunday, May 26, 9.00 a.m.
Halifax reported to the Cabinet that he had opened up diplomatic channels to Italy 'to assist the French in keeping Mussolini out of the war'. He had of course done rather more than that. Churchill reported on the deteriorating military position and that he expected Reynaud, the French Premier, who was arriving later than morning, to report that French resistance would soon be at an end. Halifax commented that the preservation of the independence of France and Great Britain were now the important matter to consider rather than any question of outright victory over Germany.

Later that morning Churchill met Reynaud and received the latest report as to the deteriorating military position in Flanders. Reynaud was still of the opinion that the Italians should be 'bought off' by (mainly British) concessions in the Mediterranean. At mid-day, Halifax, this time accompanied by Alexander Cadogan, met Bastionini again. No minutes of this meeting have been published.

It is probable that Halifax was confirming his earlier views that Great Britain would be interested in a general peace settlement, providing her independence was guaranteed, and it is possible that he was offering gold from the British treasure chest in the Mediterranean (Malta, Gibraltar, Suez?) to help secure Italian assistance towards that end.

Sunday, May 26, 2.00 p.m.
Churchill reported on his meeting with Reynaud and in particular, Reynaud's request that Italy be 'bought off'. Halifax supported Reynaud's view, but after discussion, it was decided not to approach the Italians direct but rather to wait on the American initiative already taken on May 24. Halifax had of course already made such a direct approach to Bastionini and had widened the discussions with him to a consideration of a general peace settlement, with possible rewards for the Italians.

Before Reynaud returned to Paris, Halifax saw him privately and informed him of the discussion he had already had with Bastionini. In Reynaud's memoirs he reports that he thought 'Halifax was impressed by my arguments but Churchill was hostile to any concessions to Mussolini. The only one who understands is Halifax who is already worried about the future and realises that some overall European solution must be reached. Churchill is always hectoring and Chamberlain is undecided. Halifax had proposed to internationalise the Suez Canal, Gibraltar and Malta in order to be able to negotiate with Italy at once. Churchill would not agree.'

Sunday, May 26, late afternoon

This informal meeting of the Cabinet held at the Admiralty after Reynaud had left for Paris was attended by Churchill, Halifax, Attlee, Greenwood and Chamberlain. This time, the issue of an approach to the Italians to act as mediators in peace talks to effect a general European settlement and what rewards might be offered to the Italians to act in that capacity, was openly discussed. Halifax initiated and seems to have led the discussions. No Secretary was in attendance for the first fifteen minutes of this meeting and no minutes were taken during that initial period.

Halifax formally proposed that a direct approach be made to Mussolini to sound out Hitler as to what terms were on offer for peace, not only for France but also for Great Britain. It was acknowledged that Mussolini would look to Gibraltar, Malta and Suez as a minimum requirement in terms of reward for the mediation services he was being asked to render. Chamberlain was of the opinion that nothing should be done until it was known how much of the army could be lifted from the beaches at Dunkirk. Churchill was against the proposal but his opposition was hardly unequivocal. 'The only thing to do was to show Hitler that he could not conquer this country. We must not get entangled in a position of that kind before we had been involved in any serious fighting.'

Halifax was supported by Chamberlain but Attlee and Greenwood supported Churchill. It was agreed that Halifax should draft his proposed communication to the Italians inviting their participation for further discussion before any actual advance to the Italians was made. It was also agreed that Archibald Sinclair, the leader of the Liberal Party, be invited to attend the next meeting at which the matter would be discussed further and a formal decision reached.

It would appear from a reading of the records relating to this particular meeting that Halifax, rather than Churchill, was in fact 'in the chair'. It was Halifax who took the initiative by proposing that positive steps be taken towards a peace settlement and this had the effect of putting Churchill into a defensive role. At one stage Halifax put to Churchill the specific point that he found compelling to his own mind 'If he (Churchill) was satisfied that matters vital to the independence of this country were unaffected, would he be prepared to discuss terms?'

Churchill's reply is not far removed from Halifax's own view. 'I would be thankful to get out of our present difficulties on such terms, provided we retained the essentials and the elements of our vital strength, even at the cost of some cession of territory.' But, unlike Halifax, Churchill thought that this was all 'pie in the sky' because such terms would not be obtainable from Hitler and even if they were, there was no guarantee that the terms would be kept. This was the crux of Churchill's objection.

The meeting was finally adjourned to the next day, after what was described by Alexander Cadogan as 'a 4-hour wrangle'. (Overnight, according to General Ismay 'The Prime Minister had little appetite for food or drink'. Churchill himself wrote that he felt 'physically sick' at the thought of 'members of my own Cabinet willing to give up without a fight'.)

Monday, May 27, 4.30 p.m.
The War Cabinet comprising Churchill, Halifax, Attlee, Greenwood and Chamberlain was augmented by the attendance of Archibald Sinclair, representing the Liberal Party. There were further reports of the deteriorating position in France. The Dominion Prime Ministers were urging that contact be made with both Mussolini and Roosevelt, with a view to mediation. It was reported that Roosevelt had in fact been in touch with the Italians, as originally suggested on May 24. A reply was awaited.

Chamberlain was instructed to call a meeting of the Dominion High Commissioners and inform them that there was no prospect of giving up the fight even if the French succumbed. Halifax then intervened to say that 'it would not mean that if any terms were offered, they would not be considered on their merits'.

Churchill was in much more dominant mood than the previous day. In his opinion 'the bulk of the people of the country would refuse to accept the possibility of defeat'. He produced a draft of the communication he proposed to send out to all senior officials urging them not to be defeatist and to use confident language in all their communications. He also reminded the Cabinet that he expected them to show good example in this respect. He proposed sending a cable to Reynaud stalling on any decision to make a direct approach to the Italians pending a reply from the American approach.

Halifax again expressed his view that he would not be unfavourable to such an approach 'were Italy willing to collaborate in establishing a peace preserving the independence of Great Britain and France'. He was also prepared to buy off Mussolini with Gibraltar and Malta and grant her some sort of partnership in the Suez Canal if need be. This seems to have precipitated a return to the original fundamental issue as to whether Great Britain should make a direct approach to Mussolini to seek terms of peace from Germany.

Churchill and Halifax were directly opposed on the issue, but this time Churchill gained support from all other members of the Cabinet. Churchill denounced as futile any approach to Italy, making the point that France could not be saved in any case and reiterated his opinion that Great Britain should fight on.

At this point, Halifax came near to resigning. In his diary he wrote 'I thought Winston talked the most frightful rot, also Greenwood and after bearing it for sometime I said exactly what I thought of them, adding that if that really was their view and if it came to the point, our ways would separate'. He made the point that Churchill appeared to have hardened his position since the previous day and was now of the view that 'under no conditions would we contemplate any course except fighting to the finish'. Halifax was not prepared to accept that position if in fact terms could be obtained which preserved the integrity of Great Britain.

Churchill's reply was that Hitler would never make such a offer and there was therefore no alternative to fighting on. He was not prepared to join France in a joint approach to Mussolini. Halifax on the other hand was not prepared to send a flat refusal to France. At the conclusion of the meeting Churchill and Halifax took a walk in the garden together, in an attempt to resolve their differences. They were not successful but it appears that Churchill succeeded in dissuading Halifax from resigning. This was a matter of some importance.

Monday, May 27, 10.00 p.m.
An emergency Cabinet meeting was held to consider the news that the Belgians had capitulated. Halifax remained silent throughout. He was no doubt ruminating on the fundamental differences reflected in the earlier discussions.

Tuesday, May 28, 4.00 p.m.
Halifax reported that there had been 'an entirely negative response' to Roosevelt's approach to Mussolini on the narrow issue of keeping the Italians out of the war but that Mussolini wanted to know if there was any clear indication that he should approach Hitler with a view to agreeing peace terms and an overall European settlement.

During that morning Halifax had seen the French Ambassador to London, Corbin, and confirmed to him that on the previous Saturday (May 25) he had seen Bastionini, the Italian Ambassador in London, and had independently already sounded him out as to the possibility of a direct approach by Great Britain and France to Mussolini through Bastionini for Italy to act as a mediator in terms of a general European settlement. Having received no reply, Halifax had then requested the British Ambassador in Rome, Sir Percy Lorraine, to contact the Italian Foreign Minister, Ciano, and ascertain the position with his enquiry. Ciano had confirmed that he had received the enquiry through Bastionini but had made no reply because there was an embargo on diplomatic traffic because of the imminence of war. Ciano's own diary confirms this position and records on May 28: 'Received British Ambassador who complained about the interruption of the negotiations'.

These independent French and Italian records confirm the extent of Halifax's discussions with Bastionini on the Saturday before the series of Cabinet meetings took place, how far he was prepared to go on acting independently without Cabinet authority and how he was prepared to mislead the Cabinet in his report to them as to the true nature of his discussions with Bastionini. In similar fashion, when he reported to the Cabinet on the failure of the American approach, he made no mention of the stalling of his own personal approach.

During the earlier part of the afternoon Churchill had addressed the Commons in a speech which made it clear that Great Britain would fight on. He was much heartened by the reception to his speech and the support apparent in the Commons. He was therefore of confident mood in Cabinet when Halifax yet again proposed that there should be a joint direct approach to Italy by Great Britain and France.

There was some vacillation by Chamberlain between the Churchill and Halifax views, but in the end he was convinced by Churchill's argument that once Great Britain sat down at the negotiating table they were on a slippery slope and all the resolution to fight on, now present, would disappear. Churchill also repeated his assertion that the Germans would never offer the sort of terms that Halifax had in mind. He thought the odds were 'a thousand to one against'.

At 6.15 p.m. there was an adjournment for Halifax to draft a reply to the French. It was during this adjournment that Churchill addressed Ministers not of Cabinet rank and inspired them with the same message of 'fighting on'. As with the earlier reception in the Commons, Churchill was much heartened by the reaction and support from his Ministers.

Tuesday, May 28, 7.00 p.m.

The Cabinet resumed their adjourned meeting and Churchill reported on the encouraging reception to his remarks from the Ministers he had addressed. 'They had expressed their greatest satisfaction when I told them that there was no chance of our giving up the struggle.'

It was finally agreed (after three days of often volatile debate) that a cable be sent to the French rejecting the suggestion that there should be any direct approach to Mussolini. The cable was sent the next day. This threw up in sharp relief Halifax's personal action in already making such an approach without Cabinet authority.

The Cabinet then rejected a further Halifax suggestion that Great Britain should join with France in making a joint approach to Roosevelt to intercede on their behalf with Hitler. They also rejected a draft cable prepared by Halifax on behalf of the British Government asking the USA to inform Germany that any peace terms offered to Great Britain which affected her independence would thereby affect US vital interests too. This was an attempt by Halifax to ensure that any peace terms offered would in fact conform to the requirement as to British independence with particular reference to the retention of her Fleet. Churchill described it as 'grovelling' and the cable was not sent.

* * *

After May 28 there is no further mention of any contemplated approaches to Italy or the USA in connection with possible peace moves. The above summary of the Cabinet exchanges between May 26 and 28 clearly illustrates that Churchill had more difficulty in carrying his Cabinet with him than the Commons or the nation. Halifax is seen as an implacable protagonist in the cause of peace who was quite prepared to act outside Cabinet authority if need be to further those ends. His efforts in that cause did not finish on May 28.

Appendix IV

British peace initiatives, 1940

(i) *The Prytz affair: 'an unfortunate skeleton'*

The Prytz affair provides one of the best examples of how Halifax and Butler conspired to initiate peace moves in June 1940 without the knowledge and consent of Churchill and in direct contravention with the Cabinet decision of May 28, 1940, to fight on. Unfortunately for those who would have perhaps wished that the details remain unpublished, the Halifax/Butler activities involved the Government of a wartime, neutral country, Sweden and that country and their representatives have from time to time published details of the incident because it forms part of a defence in connection with their own wartime activities.

In June 1940 the Swedes were under intense pressure from Germany to allow the transit of German troops through Swedish territory to reinforce the German garrison at Narvik in northern Norway. They succumbed to this pressure and have always given as their reason for acceding to the German demands the receipt of a cable from their Minister in London, Bjorn Prytz, following a conversation he had with Butler. The cable indicated that the British were about to seek peace and that Halifax would be taking over the premiership from Churchill. If Great Britain was going to give up the fight there was little point in resisting German demands.

At a dinner in Stockholm on October 31, 1944, at the Institute of Foreign Affairs, before an audience of some 200 guests comprising diplomats, journalists and other dignitaries, the guest of honour, the Swedish Foreign Minister, Christian Gunther, told his guests that he had in fact used the Prytz telegram of June 17, 1940, to influence his Cabinet colleagues to bow to German demands. Gunther's remarks received understandable publicity. The official British Foreign Office reaction was that the Butler/Prytz conversations had been misinterpreted by Prytz and the information conveyed by the cable had been used as an excuse and was not the reason why the Swedes had bent to German pressure.

The advice of Sir Victor Mallet, the British Ambassador to Sweden and a guest at the Gunther dinner, was to 'let sleeping dogs lie'. But the sleeping dogs would not lie. In 1945, Prytz was refused permission by the British Foreign Office to include his cable of June 17, 1940, in the official Swedish White Book of diplomatic communications to explain the German transit issue. The White Book was subsequently published in 1947 and in the preface, the refusal of the British Foreign Office to grant permission to publish was noted. Again, the matter received appropriate publicity. A Foreign Office minute at the time is revealing: 'Our stand alone after the fall of France is a matter of outstanding importance which must not be impugned. The personal reputations of Lord Halifax and Mr Butler are at stake'.[1] In 1951, the publication of the Swedish Ministerial Memoirs again included the Prytz cable details, bringing further publicity; and finally, in September 1965, when Prytz was interviewed on Swedish radio in connection with a series concerned with the war years, he repeated his version of the conversations with Butler and was adamant that his cable had faithfully represented the context of those talks. He never retracted this stand to the day he died.

Bjorn Prytz, the Swedish Minister to London since 1938, was a well known, well liked and well respected figure in London's diplomatic and social life, such as it was in the mid-summer of 1940. He was wealthy and drove a 2-seater Rolls-Royce. He was witty, charming and gregarious and for that reason was a much sought after guest of the London social scene. He was in some ways more English than the English, having been educated at Dulwich College and speaking perfect English. He was also a wealthy industrialist, a widely travelled man of the world and an experienced and skilled diplomat. He knew Butler well, both in professional and social terms. According to Butler, Prytz met Butler by chance during lunchtime on Monday, June 17 when Butler was walking in St James's Park. It was the day when France had asked for armistice terms. They started a discussion which was then continued back at the Foreign Office.

In view of subsequent events it is difficult to accept that the meeting was by chance. There are so many factors that suggest otherwise.

---

[1]PRO FO371/24192/243.

It is perhaps of special significance that Halifax had called on the King at Buckingham Palace that very morning. Butler was Halifax's Minister of State and, like his master, was an appeaser and pacifist by nature, training and experience. Prytz was the ambassador of a neutral country admirably placed for handling peace traffic. France had just asked for armistice terms. Halifax was of the opinion that Great Britain could not carry on alone and had said so. There is no British record of the conversations, although Prytz deemed them so important that they warranted his sending of a cable to Sweden that very day.

According to Prytz, Butler said that the British were actively considering the taking up of peace negotiations in view of the downfall of France. 'Britain's official attitude will for the present continue to be that the war must go on', but the reality was that 'no opportunity of reaching a compromise peace would be neglected if the possibility were offered on reasonable conditions'. Also, according to Prytz, Butler confirmed that no 'diehards' would be 'allowed to stand in the way in this connection' because 'Britain had greater possibilities of negotiation today than she might have later on.' At one point when at the Foreign Office, Butler left Prytz but then, according to Prytz, he returned with what he said was a message from Halifax which was that 'common sense and not bravado would dictate the British Government's policy'. The inference must be that the terms 'diehard' and 'bravado' referred to Churchill, and that 'common sense' referred to Halifax.

In addition to his reported conversation with Butler, Prytz also referred in his cable to other conversations with British MPs with whom 'there is an expectation that if and when the prospect of negotiations arises, possibly after June 28,[2] Halifax may succeed Churchill'. All these comments were included in Telegram 723[3] which, after enciphering, was sent off to Stockholm and received there at 10.20 p.m. Swedish local time on that same day, Monday, June 17, 1940.

During the evening of the same day another telegram was sent to Sweden. This was a cable from the Foreign Office to Sir Victor Mallet, the British Ambassador in Stockholm.[4] The contents of this cable have never been published, but the inference is that Mallet was being advised as to the Butler/Prytz conversations and almost certainly formally instructed as to a positive peace initiative. This interpretation is borne out by events in both London and Stockholm the next day, June 18.

---

[2]The significance of this date is not known.
[3]Telegram 723 reposes in the Foreign Ministry Department of the Swedish National Archives.
[4]Ponting, Clive, *1940: Myth and Reality*, Hamish Hamilton (1990), 113.

In London, Chamberlain, not Churchill, presided over the Cabinet meeting held at 12.30. Churchill was absent because he was preparing a speech for delivery in the Commons that afternoon.[5] Item five on the agenda and the relevant minutes are omitted from the public record, but the omission is partly retrieved by a significant entry in the diary of Alexander Cadogan, the Cabinet Secretary, who was present at the meeting. It reads: 'Winston not there. Writing his speech. No reply from Germans.' It is apparent that the missing minutes refer to the Foreign Office and Butler/Prytz twin approaches through Sweden and the expectation of some reaction.

In Sweden on the same day, June 18, the deciphered Prytz cable was in the hands of Foreign Minister, Christian Gunther, by mid-morning. On the same day he was visited by Mallet. Gunther regarded these events as indicating a genuine intent on the part of the British Government to make peace through Halifax/Butler. The contents of the Prytz telegram were distributed widely by diplomatic bag to Swedish diplomats abroad, including those in Russia and the other Scandinavian countries. Gunther also discussed the cable with Arvid Richert, the Swedish Minister in Berlin, who was in Stockholm in connection with the German request for transit rights.

Perhaps more importantly, the contents of the cable and information relating to the call on Gunther by Mallet were sent to Francisco Fransoni, the Italian Ambassador in Sweden, who relayed the details to Count Ciano, the Italian Foreign Minister,[6] on June 19, stating: 'The British representative (Mallet) requested an interview with the Swedish Foreign Minister and notified him that the British Government is inclined to enter into peace negotiations with Germany and Italy. The Secretary General of the Foreign Ministry here immediately informed me and in reply to my enquiry confirmed specifically that this declaration by the British representative is of official character'.[7]

On the next day, June 19, the confusion caused by the deep divides within the British Government became apparent to all and the peace initiative foundered. In Berlin, von Weizsäcker, Secretary of State in Ribbentrop's Foreign Ministry, was confronted with the news of the British approach through Halifax and Butler at the same time as reading transcripts of Churchill's resolute address to the Commons making it clear that Great Britain would fight on and referring to Great Britain's 'finest hour'. As a result, Weizsäcker did not follow up the

---

[5]It was the 'finest hour' speech.

[6]Italy was by this time a belligerent.

[7]Martin, Bernard, *Friedensinitiativen und Machtpolitik im Zweiten Weltkrieg 1939–1942*, Dreste Verlag, Dusseldorf (1974), 272.

Halifax/Butler/Mallet approach.[8] In London, Churchill catching up on Cabinet proceedings during his absence,[9] stepped in immediately and brought matters to an end. Mallet was instructed to refer Gunther to Churchill's speech as the only authorised statement of British policy and Halifax was obliged to send a confirmatory telegram to Mallet. This cable was drafted by Butler, who attempted to explain how Prytz had misunderstood and misquoted his original remarks in conversation.

After the war, Professor Wilhelm Carlgren, a contributor to the official history of Swedish foreign policy during the war years interviewed Prytz and questioned him closely as to the Butler affair. He states: 'Bjorn Prytz was absolutely certain that he had reported accurately'. Not only did Prytz assure Carlgren repeatedly that he had accurately reported his meeting with Butler but he told him that other sources in the Conservative Party had also led him to believe that the Foreign Secretary, Halifax, was considering the possibility of forming a Government that would negotiate with Germany if Churchill continued to refuse to do so.[10]

Churchill's action, or inaction, in dealing with the matter would appear to be significant. First of all there was a week's delay before Churchill admonished Butler, and then he did so in the mildest of terms, set down more in the manner of a letter of enquiry through Halifax than a reprimand. At first sight, this would appear to be extraordinary, uncharacteristic behaviour on the part of Churchill. It does however become understandable in the context of a possible threat from those factions looking for peace and the need to keep them quiescent. Churchill knew all about the Halifax/Butler pacifist enthusiasms but he may not have known the extent to which they represented others. He may therefore well have spent the week prior to June 26, when he finally wrote to Halifax, making his own enquiries as to the existence or otherwise of a functional 'Peace Party' and the seriousness of its intent.[11] His gentle chiding of Butler through Halifax, when it came, is very indicative of a wish not to stir up what could be a

---

[8]It would therefore appear that Churchill's 'finest hour' speech may have had an effect far beyond that which was immediately apparent. There was another reason why there was no immediate German response to the peace initiative of June 17–18. On June 19 British/Swedish diplomatic relations were broken off, following the seizure of some Swedish navy vessels by the Royal Navy in the Azores on June 17, the same day as the Butler/Prytz talks. As a result no diplomatic traffic from Stockholm to London was possible until June 24. Was this by accident or design? Was Churchill more aware as to what was going on than Halifax realised?

[9]He also had the benefit of a deciphering service that 'read' all Swedish cables sent from Great Britain.

[10]Letter Professor Wilhelm Carlgren to J. Costello, March 22 1989.

[11]Churchill had his own intelligence service outside the remit of MI5 or MI6.

hornet's nest or more specifically, precipitate a major political crisis which could have led to the very event which may have been threatened, his own demise and the succession of a peacemaker.

Having only just reported to the Commons and the world that 'the present Government and all of its members are resolved to fight to the death', Churchill must have been furious to learn of the misdemeanours and disloyalty of two of his senior Ministers, but his letter to Halifax of June 26 reflects none of his anger. 'It is quite clear to me from these telegrams and others that Butler used odd language to the Swedish Minister and certainly the Swede derived a strong impression of defeatism... Find out from Butler what he did say.' Halifax showed Churchill's letter to Butler and Butler replied the same day, by a hand-written note to Halifax.[12] It was a half apology, half explanation. Halifax did not send it on to Churchill but penned his own reassurance to Churchill: 'I should be very sorry if you felt any doubt either about Butler's discretion or his complete loyalty to Government policy, of both of which I am completely satisfied.' This tongue-in-cheek remark from a self-styled moralist is truly breathtaking. It was probably accepted by Churchill in the same spirit in which it was given and there matters rested until Churchill felt that his own political position was such that he could at last rid himself of the peacemakers without fear of a political upheaval. Halifax went to America in December 1940 and Butler to Education in June 1941.[13]

(ii) *Kenneth de Courcy: promptings from the Right*

On the evening of Saturday, May 24, 1940, as a prelude to his own personal peace initiatives and running ahead of and outside proper Cabinet authorisation,[14] Halifax called to see the Italian Ambassador in London, Giuseppe Bastionini. The suggestion that he should do so had been made to his Secretary of State, Rab Butler, in a letter of May 15 received from Kenneth de Courcy.

De Courcy was a colourful, even eccentric character, well known in diplomatic circles, independent in political view but with valuable contacts both in America and Europe. He counted among his friends the Duke of Windsor, Bjorn Prytz, Rab Butler and Joseph Kennedy,

---

[12]PRO FP 800/322. Butler to Halifax, June 26, 1940.

[13]There is another possible explanation of Churchill's soft approach to the problem. The continuance in office of two known pacifists always encouraged the German belief that peace overtures were imminent. That may have delayed the onset of military operations against Great Britain and therefore may have been a conscious policy by Churchill.

[14]See Appendix III.

the American Ambassador to Great Britain. Prytz described him 'as a well-known British Conservative publicist with good American contacts who used to be close to Butler'. His politics were extreme right-wing. He was secretary of the Imperial Policy Group and in that capacity was the editor and publisher of a widely read intelligence digest propagating right-wing views. He thought that the war with Germany was a mistake and should be brought to an end as soon as possible. He correctly forecast that France would collapse but even before they did he had bombarded Butler with letters advising him to contact both the Italian and American Ambassadors to enlist their support in the seeking of a negotiated peace.

On June 6, 1940, when acknowledging receipt of a de Courcy letter dealing with another matter, Butler added a hand-written note asking de Courcy to meet him at the residence of his parliamentary private secretary, 'Chips' Channon, the next day, June 7. At the meeting, Butler asked de Courcy if he would act as a go-between with Kennedy in the matter of a draft peace plan which was to be linked with a world conference to settle all outstanding European problems, with US backing and guarantees if deemed necessary. Under the terms of this plan Germany would have to withdraw from most, if not all, of her Western European conquests, under threat of American sanctions and/or involvement. De Courcy was to see Kennedy and sell the idea to him. De Courcy subsequently saw Kennedy at the US Embassy. Kennedy proved to be an enthusiastic recipient of the plan, endorsing it with the words: 'This is a most intelligent idea. I will recommend it to the President'.[15]

A few days later de Courcy met Butler by chance in the diningroom at the Carlton Club. Butler came over to de Courcy's table and congratulated him, saying: 'The [American] Ambassador asked for an interview with my master [Halifax]. He was enormously impressed with the proposal that you made. My master thinks it highly desirable if you saw Kennedy again as soon as possible.'[16] De Courcy agreed and it was arranged that de Courcy and Butler would then meet for breakfast the next morning at Butler's residence in Smith Square in Westminster.

At 4 p.m. the same day de Courcy was telephoned by Victor Raikes, a Conservative MP and a member of the executive committee of the Imperial Group. There was to be no breakfast meeting but de Courcy was requested to take a walk in St James's Park and express surprise when he saw someone he knew as he crossed the bridge. De Courcy

[15]Costello, John, *Ten Days that Saved the West*, Bantam Press (1991), 310.
[16]*Ibid*, 311.

did as he was bid and duly met 'Chips' (Sir Henry) Channon, Butler's parliamentary private secretary, on the bridge. They sat down together on a seat and then Channon warned de Courcy: 'I have a message from my master. You have to go back to Old Queen Street[17] and burn your file with everything that has ever been written between you and Butler'. De Courcy was also told to cancel his further appointment with Kennedy and leave for Scotland. 'If you do not, you will be in very great danger, so will my master, so will Lord Halifax. Churchill has found out everything and is even threatening to lock up Halifax and my master under the 18B regulations'.[18] De Courcy did not flee to Scotland or burn his papers, but he was badly shaken because he had not realised that Halifax or Butler had been acting without the authority of Churchill. He immediately severed his connection with Butler.

After the war, in the summer of 1946, de Courcy met Bjorn Prytz at a dinner party and told him of these circumstances. Prytz was very interested, since de Courcy's story lent weight to the account of his own conversations with Butler on June 17 which had been subsequently described as exaggerated and misunderstood. He accordingly made a note of his conversation with de Courcy and filed the document with the Swedish Foreign Ministry on August 29, 1946. In 1984 de Courcy deposited his personal papers, which would have included his correspondence and notes in connection with his dealings with Butler and Kennedy, with the Hoover Institution in the United States, in a file headed 'World War 1939/1945'. This file has since disappeared from the Stanford Archives.[19,20]

(iii) *David Kelly: of autocratic bent*

David (later Sir David) Kelly was British Minister in Berne, Switzerland, in the summer of 1940. He had been appointed to that position by Halifax in December 1939. Details of his history and background have been given in chapter nine. During the summer of 1940 Kelly met and had a conversation, or conversations (versions differ), with Prince Max von Hohenlohe[21] in Berne.

Hohenlohe was a freelance negotiator with many contacts in diplo-

---

[17]De Courcy's residence.

[18]Costello, John, *Ten Days that Saved the West*, Bantam Press (1991), 311–12.

[19]*Ibid*, 308.

[20]In August 1993 the author had the benefit of a two-hour conversation with de Courcy who confirmed that all the details of the Butler/Kennedy affair were as stated and as recorded by John Costello.

[21]His full title was Prince Max von Hohenlohe-Langenburg of Schloss Rothenhaus.

matic circles throughout Europe. He had acted as an intermediary between the European powers before the war and was known to have been engaged in peace activities since. Although he was a native of the Sudetenland he was thought to be less than enamoured with the Nazi regime. He was well respected by those with whom he dealt. His conversation, or series of conversations, with Kelly were concerned with the possibility of a peace between Great Britain and Germany. Of that there is no doubt, but there are two versions of the event – one from Kelly and the other from Hohenlohe. Hohenlohe's version appears in the official German diplomatic documents as a report from Hohenlohe delivered shortly after the talks occurred. Kelly's version was given some time later, but five years before the German diplomatic papers containing Hohenlohe's version were published after the war.

Kelly states that when he took up his post in Berne in December 1939 he was secretly provided with two names by Robert Vansittart, then Permanent Secretary at the Foreign Office. These names were of agents who might get in touch with the new Minister; if they did, Kelly was to listen and report back. These instructions seem to reinforce the impression that part of the British Government's strategy for waging war in 1939 appears to have been a careful preparation for peace. One of the two names given to Kelly was Hohenlohe. In June 1940, according to Kelly, the former Swiss Minister in London, Paravincini, then in Switzerland, suggested to Kelly that he should meet Hohenlohe. Kelly agreed and, according to Kelly, Hohenlohe met him on three or four occasions during that summer, travelling to Switzerland especially on each occasion. The message conveyed to Kelly, which purported to come from the German Foreign Office, was always the same. Germany would make peace on the basis of a free hand in Europe in return for the guarantee of Great Britain's independence and integrity and that of her Empire.

These terms were of course, the same as those which had been peddled so consistently since before the war. Great Britain had adamantly refused to consider such a 'deal' before the war, but what was the present position in her somewhat more straitened circumstances? On one occasion, according to Kelly, Hohenlohe produced a memorandum, said to have been approved by Hitler, which included a note as to a time limit for the receipt of peace overtures from Great Britain, in the absence of which massed air attacks would commence against the British mainland. This time limit was to expire in early September.[22]

[22]The first mass air attack on London took place on September 7, 1940.

According to Kelly, he responded thus: 'Knowing the vital importance of gaining time, I made a show of interest while in fact, of course, merely reporting to Sir Robert Vansittart what he (Hohenlohe) said without comment. I never received from London any comment or acknowledgement of my unofficial reports, so there was never any question of discussion and still less of negotiations, but it was obvious that every day gained for the production of Spitfires and the training of crews was priceless.'[23]

Hohenlohe's account, written on July 18, 1940, is rather different to Kelly's. Hohenlohe refers to a single meeting rather than a series. On June 30, 1940, Walter Hewel of Hitler's personal staff had sent Hohenlohe a letter saying: 'I would be interested in hearing from you if you again hear of English attempts to approach Germans for the purpose of orientation. While we will certainly make no use of such channels, it is nevertheless interesting to observe exactly the tendency in England.' Hohenlohe then says that he was pressed by Paravincini, the former Swiss Minister in London, and also by Professor Carl Burckhardt, the former League of Nations High Commissioner in Danzig and now like Hohenlohe in the nature of a freelance peace negotiator, to call on Kelly; but he declined to do so until Kelly himself sent him, through the Spanish Minister in Berne and apparently on the instructions of Butler, an express indication of his desire for a meeting. Hohenlohe agreed and the meeting took place. Hohenlohe goes on in his report:

> Immediately after my arrival, Mrs Kelly, a native of Belgium, took me aside and urged me to lose no time and discuss peace possibilities with her husband. Kelly then asked me to go with him to an adjoining room. There he told me, after a few introductory remarks, that he would very much like to talk with me as an old friend of his own friends in England about the situation and the future. He was, to be sure, only the Minister to Switzerland and therefore only available as a messenger. I stated that if he was merely a messenger for Winston Churchill, it was meaningless and the talk could be broken off at once. He (Kelly) replied that he was aware that our common friends in England were Butler, Vansittart[24] and Halifax with followers.[25]

After some (alleged) flowery references by Kelly to Hitler, includ-

[23]Thompson, Laurence, *1940: Year of Legend, Year of History*, Collins Fontana (1968), 156.
[24]The inclusion of this name is a mystery. Vansittart was not a pacifist.
[25]The addition of the word 'followers' is interesting.

ing 'the greatness of his conception',[26] Kelly apparently said that it was difficult to arrive at a lasting settlement of questions since experience had not facilitated reliance on the Führer's word and it was difficult to imagine what sort of definitive guarantees could be given for a general and lasting settlement. Hohenlohe continues:

> We then talked about the forces in English domestic politics and I mentioned that he surely knew, as I did, how untrustworthy a person Winston Churchill was, how he was often under the influence of alcohol and that I could not believe that this man was the embodiment of the English people. Kelly assented to my criticism of Winston Churchill to the extent of saying that Winston Churchill was a bull who was running his head against the wall but that the temperaments of Butler, Halifax and also Vansittart were different. My general impression of the conversation, which was conducted by Kelly with great emotion, ... was that he was engaging in it with frankness and a desire to develop those contacts further. I did not go along with him, however, for the suspicion that conversations are to gain time is an obvious one.[27]

Weizsäcker had been confronted by the Halifax/Butler overtures of June 27 through Bjorn Prytz at the same time as Churchill's bellicose 'fight on' speech in the Commons. In similar fashion Ribbentrop, the ultimate recipient of Hohenlohe's report, was now confronted by the nationwide broadcast by Halifax, put up by Churchill purposely because Berlin knew of Halifax's pacifist learnings, rejecting the overtures made by Hitler in his widely publicised 'peace' speech in Berlin on July 19. As a result, Hewel wrote to Hohenlohe in the following terms:

> As politics are at the moment, there does not appear, in the Minister's (Ribbentrop's) view, to be a (case for the) continuation of such contacts, since thereby wrong impressions might be created on the other side. The Minister therefore requests you to do nothing more at the moment in that direction. The speech of Halifax has definitely destroyed our belief in a conciliation Party over there and the Führer also does not wish that further attempts should be made to build bridges for the English... Nor do I

[26]Kelly's high regard for specified dictators, and Hitler in particular, has already been noted in chapter fifteen.
[27]Thompson, Laurence, *1940: Year of Legend, Year of History*, Collins Fontana (1968), 156–58, and DGFP, Vol 10, 245.

> believe that we can achieve anything over these through unofficial channels at this time, for otherwise the English would at least have restrained themselves a bit in their official utterances.

Hewel's attitude was subsequently confirmed by Ribbentrop himself in a cable to the German consulate at Geneva: 'After Lord Halifax's refusal of the Führer's and Chancellor's appeal to reason, we intend to destroy England.'[28]

According to Hohenlohe, Kelly approached him again in December 1940 and asked him if he had passed on the content of their earlier discussions. Kelly said that he believed an understanding was possible if Germany would guarantee the evacuation of her conquered territories. Hohenlohe replied by asking what Great Britain's attitude would be if Germany gave up claims to all territories other than Poland and Czechoslovakia. Hohenlohe then expressed the opinion, in a further report, that Kelly could see war damaging the internal political and power position of the propertied class to which Kelly belonged.

This last report of Hohenlohe contains some significant passages. The earlier part clearly designates Poland and Czechoslovakia as territories to be retained in possession by Germany. The clear implication is that these territories were required in connection with the proposed drive eastwards. Perhaps even more importantly, Hohenlohe alights upon a possible reason for Kelly's actions in his desire for peace to safeguard the existing social, political and power structures of the landed classes 'of which he was a part'. This agrees precisely with Kelly's own expressed views as mentioned in chapter 15. Having regard to Kelly's history and background, his political beliefs and German sympathies it is not unreasonable to accept Hohenlohe's version of the events occurring in the summer of 1940, illustrating Kelly's anxiety to talk peace.

(iv) *The Lothian intrigues*

If David Kelly in Berne was motivated in his peace efforts by a feeling of kinship for German autocracy, Lord Lothian in Washington was reliant upon more lofty considerations.[29] He was, like Halifax, an out-and-out pacifist emanating from his Christian beliefs. In July 1940 he enlisted the support of an American Quaker friend, Malcolm J. Lovell,

---

[28]DGFP, Vol 10, 295.

[29]Although he had some 28,000 acres of land to worry about in Scotland and England.

to act as a go-between on his behalf with the German *chargé d'affaires* in Washington, Hans Thomson.

On July 19 Hitler had made his much-publicised 'peace' speech in Berlin but had not specified the precise terms that he had in mind to bring the conflict to an end. Lothian determined to find out what those terms were and to indicate to the Germans that, if the terms were reasonable, Great Britain would be interested in negotiation. He accordingly informed his intermediary, Lovell, that there were dissidents in the British Cabinet, namely Halifax and Chamberlain, who were prepared to negotiate a peace. He then asked Lovell to find out from the German Embassy in Washington the kind of peace Hitler had in mind.

Thomson reported on the request to Berlin on July 19, describing the enquiry as 'a British approach'. Churchill became aware of this Lothian initiative[30] and was apparently shocked, although he was of course aware of Lothian's pre-war visits to Hitler and his vigorous pro-German campaign waged through *The Times*. Churchill accordingly advised the Foreign Office that 'Lord Lothian should be told on no account to make any reply to the German Chargé d'Affaires' message'.[31] Halifax in fact did nothing. On July 22 Berlin informed Thomson that Hitler would welcome a fair peace but a query was raised as to Churchill's bellicose speech delivered on July 14. Thomson was instructed to enquire if the speech was intended for 'home and colonial' consumption only, in which case Berlin would not consider it to be an insuperable problem. But if it were otherwise and was a statement of genuine policy and intent, then it would 'change the face of the war'.

During that same day, July 22, a British Cabinet meeting had been held and Halifax had been deputed to broadcast that evening a formal British Government rejection of Hitler's offer of peace. The relevant minutes of this meeting are not available, but there is no doubt that what must have been an act of coercion on the part of Churchill was a masterstroke. Churchill knew that Halifax was the man most associated with possible peace by the Germans. He it was, through Butler and Prytz, who had spoken of 'common sense and reason' and no 'die-hards' getting in the way. He was the man who was now going to formally reject German hopes of peace.

At 7 p.m., shortly before Halifax was to broadcast his speech, Lothian telephoned him from Washington pleading with him 'not to shut the door' as a further approach had been received from Thomson. Halifax actually scribbled down the message that Lothian gave him:

---

[30]Bletchley was 'reading' all German diplomatic traffic.
[31]Winston s. Churchill, *The Second World War*, Vol II, 229.

'Lothian could get the information as to what he (Hitler) means if we want it. Lothian says we ought to find out what Hitler means before condemning the world to one million casualties.'[32] Lothian eventually got his reply from London: 'Tune into Halifax's broadcast this evening.'[33]

The Halifax rejection had a profound effect in Berlin. Rejection of the peace offer was branded as a war crime and Lovell, Lothian's intermediary, was told by Hewel of Hitler's personal staff that 'the Führer does not desire further attempts made to build bridges for the British. If they crave their own destruction they can have it.'[34] Lothian, far from being deterred by the effect of Halifax's broadcast under coercion from Churchill embroiled himself further in peace initiatives which eventually involved the head of British Security Co-ordination in the USA.

On June 6, 1940, Sir William Wiseman lunched with Halifax and was subsequently appointed by Halifax to assist Lothian 'with the work of publicity'. Wiseman was a Cambridge boxing blue who had served with MI6 during the 1914–18 war and had hoped to get his old job back at the outbreak of war in September 1939. His history, background and training were hardly fitting for the post of a publicity agent. According to James D. Mooney, Vice-President of General Motors, Wiseman was instructed by Lothian in a very different capacity. Mooney should know, because together they conspired (in a private room at the Wall Street Bank of Kuhn Loeb) to 'find some method of starting a negotiated peace that would be effective'. Presumably, Halifax was well aware of the true nature of Wiseman's appointment when he engaged him, and no doubt Lothian was pleased to acquire an active baggage man to assist in the pursuit of peace.

The Wiseman/Mooney initiative pursued jointly in London (Wiseman) and Berlin (Mooney) through the good offices of the Vatican during September and October was aborted, apparently because Lothian ordered a slow-down, on the grounds that it was 'not a propitious time for negotiations in London'.[35] At that time, of course, the aerial bombardment of London was in progress. Wiseman quickly found other employment for his talents, however, but still in the same field of activity; this time his cover was not publicity but Secret Service work for Sir William Stephenson, better known as 'A Man called Intrepid'. Stephenson was a Canadian millionaire, ostensibly

---

[32]Sadly, in the event, a serious understatement.

[33]Halifax memo on Lothian's call, PRO FO C7377.

[34]Irving, David, *Churchill's War*, Veritas Publishing (1987), 372.

[35]Mooney papers, Georgetown University Library.

employed as the British passport controllor in New York. In fact, he was the head of British Security Co-ordination in the USA.

Under Stephenson, Wiseman's brief was to establish contact with Fritz Wiedemann, the German consul-general in San Francisco. It was thought that Wiedemann was something less than a safe Nazi and could possibly be used (or abused) by British Intelligence. The intermediary used by Wiseman to establish this connection was a rather flamboyant character, well known to the American FBI, called Princess Stephanie von Hohenlohe-Waldenburg, a distant relative by marriage to Prince Max von Hohenlohe and an associate of Hitler in early days. She had gone to America in December 1939 and was known on the West Coast as the 'Nazi Princess'. She was closely associated with Wiedemann.

On November 27 Wiseman met Stephanie at his suite in the Mark Hopkins Hotel. There was a long conversation and, as a result, Wiseman compiled a 3½ page report upon the proceedings for Stephenson in which he reported that the purpose of the meeting was to brief Stephanie as to the need to 'draw out' Wiedemann and the sort of information that British Intelligence were requiring. Unknown to either Wiseman or Stephanie, the conversation was tape recorded by the FBI, who had 'bugged' Wiseman's suite for that purpose.

Stephanie had been under FBI surveillance for some time, and the conversation had nothing to do with briefing Stephanie in connection with British Intelligence requirements of Wiedemann. It had everything to do with the detailed formulation of British/German peace proposals. The transcripts covered 17 typewritten pages and also referred to two other Wiseman/Stephanie discussions on the same subject on the previous day. Stephanie had promised her personal help in getting the proposals to Hitler and Wiseman made it clear that he 'represented a group of Englishmen who believe that a satisfactory peace arrangement can be brought about between England and Germany'.[36] Terms would be agreed with Wiedemann. Stephanie would alert Ribbentrop as to the fact of the initiative through Thomson at the Washington Embassy.

On the next day, November 20, Wiseman confided his personal status to Wiedemann and told him that Halifax represented 'a certain political party in the House of Lords and in the House of Commons which is very strong'.

As a result of the FBI disclosures the British Establishment washed their hands of Wiseman. The FBI interned Stephanie as an undesirable alien in December 1941, when the USA entered the war. When

---

[36]Costello, John, *Ten Days that Saved the West*, Bantam Press (1991), 401.

Wiseman met Mooney on January 8, 1941, he confirmed that Lothian had been behind all the initiatives. That is not surprising having regard to Wiseman's original appointment by Halifax and what now appears obvious as to the terms of his appointment as Lothian's aide. What is perhaps more interesting is to ponder upon the involvement or otherwise of Stephenson as head of British Intelligence in America. Was he really an innocent abroad? Did he really receive and believe a 'spoof' report from Wiseman as to his discussions with Stephanie, having regard to his original appointment as Lothian's aide, Stephanie's known reputation and FBI involvement? Or was he a main player, together with Halifax, Lothian and Wiseman?

(v) *Livingston and others at Geneva*

According to a report made to the German Foreign Ministry and to German Military Intelligence on July 18, 1940, by Dr Hans Riesser, a German Military Intelligence agent, Henry B. Livingston, the British consul-general in Geneva, had asked to see him, having repeatedly telephoned him during the day. According to Riesser there had then followed a conversation lasting for more than one hour during the course of which Livingston had said that information was reaching him both from Berlin and Italy that there was no great feeling against Great Britain and that there should be a peace. Livingston then apparently informed Riesser that he was 'in a position to inform Riesser that Great Britain also preferred peace to the total destruction of Europe'. According to the Riesser report he then asked three questions of Livingston. Was that Livingston's view or the official view of Great Britain? If the latter, how did that reconcile with recent Churchill speeches? Finally, upon what basis did Great Britain envisage peace?

Livingston answered that a peace objective was the view of the British Government, that Churchill's message was that Great Britain would fight only if attacked and that peace could come from a guarantee of Great Britain's independence and that of its Empire traded against German economic but not political, *Lebensraum* in Europe. There would be no more British guarantees in Europe and Great Britain was prepared to hand back Germany's old colonies. Livingston then queried how negotiations could be started without either side being branded as 'weak' or 'cowards', and asked Riesser to report back to him.[37]

---

[37]Thompson, Laurence, *1940: Year of Legend, Year of History*, Collins Fontana (1968), 153–55, and DGFP, Vol 11, 1048/1049.

In a further report, dated October 7, Riesser reports upon further conversations with Livingston who referred to their earlier discussions. If this second report is to be believed, Livingston's remarks indicate a depressing attitude based upon a 'no win no lose' position reached in October rather than the out-and-out requirement as to peace which was the message of his earlier remarks in July. Since then of course the Battle of Britain had been fought and won, there had been no invasion of Great Britain and the nightly aerial bombing of Great Britain was tending to stiffen British morale rather than destroy it.

According to Riesser, Livingston considered that the time was no longer appropriate for talks of peace, although he referred to a recent attempt having been made through Lisbon. The Italians were making 'wholly unacceptable demands' in connection with African colonies, public morale in Great Britain was 'not bad', and aid from America was increasing, with more to come when Roosevelt was re-elected. The air war would increase in intensity and by the spring of 1941 Great Britain would be able to conduct large-scale air attacks on German cities. 'The madness could go on for years without bringing about a decision. Neither Great Britain or Germany can win. Together, they will destroy Europe.'[38] This apparent 'no win, no lose' deadlock, and the consequent need for a compromise peace to avoid the total destruction of Europe, is further confirmed by a report to the German Foreign Ministry from the German consul general in Geneva dated December 5, 1940. The consul-general reports that a member of the British Conservative Party[39] highly respected in political circles and a boyhood friend of Winston Churchill although not now sharing his political views, had arrived recently from London and had talked 'to one of my most reliable informants' on December 4. Before his departure Churchill had apparently spoken to the informant and said 'I would have only to lift my little finger and I could have peace but I do not want it'.

Churchill was said to lead a faction fanatically committed to carrying on the war but other members of the British Government thought otherwise. They were not allowed to express their opinions in public and even made warlike speeches with which they were not in total agreement. The English people were not shaken (by the bombing) and firmly backed their Government. There were however 'a few big English industrialists inclined towards a compromise peace and they wished to remain in touch with influential circles in Germany'. The

---

[38]DGFP, Vol 11, 1046/1048.

[39]Mentioned in the German report as 'possibly a certain Taylor who was formerly a member of the Finance Sub-committee of the League of Nations or Lord Darventer'.

English informant summarised his views by saying that neither Germany or Great Britain could win the war and it was therefore better for Great Britain to conclude a compromise peace as soon as possible.[40]

(vi) *British Intelligence*

It appears clear both from the German official records and the statements of Dr Fritz Hesse, who had represented the official German News Agency in London before the war and was subsequently adviser on English affairs at the German Foreign Office, that British Intelligence agents were implicated in the active seeking of peace terms from Germany during the summer of 1940. Hesse was close to Ribbentrop and also a confidante of Walther Hewel, a personal aide to the Foreign Minister. In early June, a fortnight before the final French collapse and at about the same time as the de Courcy/Butler intrigues, the German Foreign Office and German Military Intelligence were receiving reports of contacts made by British Intelligence agents which encouraged both Hitler and Ribbentrop to believe that peace talks would be possible.

As an one example, Hesse cites the fact that one British agent instructed by the British consul-general in Geneva, Livingston, had approached the German consul-general in Zurich, Krauel, and also one of Canaris's agents of Military Intelligence, inviting them to open up discussions for peace, Krauel being instructed to approach the British through the Papal Nuncio in Berne. Hesse quite clearly states that it was believed at the time that hundreds of British Intelligence agents had received instructions to establish contact with their German counterparts to find out what Germans had in mind as acceptable peace terms.

Hesse accordingly advised Ribbentrop as to the peace terms which he thought could be acceptable to the British. These included the renunciation by Germany of all conquests in the West, no reparation payments, Germany to give peace guarantees and rejoin the League of Nations, conquests in the East to be defined by the old 1914 frontiers, Germany to guarantee the integrity of Poland and Czechoslovakia (even though not restoring sovereignty) and renunciation of all ties with Russia. Ribbentrop requested a short memorandum for use by German agents when dealing with their British counterparts and Carl

---

[40]DGFP, Vol 11, 791/792.

Burckhardt, the then international head of the Red Cross and previous League of Nations Commissioner at Danzig, was named as a suitable mediator for their use.[41]

If British Intelligence agents were so instructed, who in ultimate terms instructed them? According to the example quoted by Hesse, the British consul-general in Geneva, Livingston, had instructed a British agent who had then presented himself to the German consul-general in Zurich. But who instructed Livingston to instruct the agent? Was it Churchill, intent upon misleading Germany as to British intentions and thus delaying the military onslaught? Was it Halifax and/or Butler as part of their overall peace aims? Or was it the head of MI6, Stewart Menzies, and if so, in what capacity?

(vii) *Mallet in Stockholm*

Sir Victor Mallet was British Ambassador in Stockholm. His implication in the Prytz affair in June 1940 has already been mentioned earlier in this Appendix. Subsequent reports included in the official German diplomatic documents indicate a continuing attitude of defeatism and a willingness to handle further peace traffic. On July 8 only three weeks after the Prytz episode, the German Ambassador to Moscow is reporting to the German Foreign Ministry, following a conversation he had with the Swedish Minister in Moscow after a recent visit to Stockholm by the latter. The Swedish Minister had apparently found Mallet 'extremely depressed'. He had explained that Great Britain was daily expecting a German invasion which might well succeed, in which case the Government would be obliged to operate from Canada where it would become the junior partner to the USA. According to Mallet, the one bar to peace was the assumption that the British Fleet would have to be surrendered and that would never be acceptable to the British people.[42]

A further report in the German archives also refers to Mallet's activities in Stockholm. Dated October 23, 1940, the report is from the Chief of Security Policy and Security Service to the German Foreign Ministry, entered under the reference Berlin VI G/AZ/5766 for the personal attention of Minister Luther. It is headed 'Initiation of unofficial peace negotiations with England' and reports that Mallet had expressed through various Swedish connections that 'his Government might be prepared to ascertain unofficially whether Germany was

---

[41]Hesse, Fritz, *Hitler and the English*, Allan Wingate (1954), 103–05.
[42]DGFP, 126/127.

prepared for peace negotiations'. The report goes on to recall that previous diplomatic initiatives had failed 'but in this case, the Security Services had vetted the authenticity' of the enquiry.

Mallet had stated that he had received instructions from London 'to talk in unofficial terms' to Dr Eckberg, the President of the Swedish Supreme Court, and that the latter had confirmed that he had called on Mallet, at Mallet's invitation. According to Mallet, the British Cabinet was divided and this position had been confirmed by the Finnish Minister in London. Mallet further reported to Eckberg that there had been a secret Cabinet meeting in London at which Churchill had noted that certain internal rights had been granted by Germany to Poland. On that basis Great Britain might be prepared to accept that the granting of 'cultural autonomy' to Poland and to other European conquests could be a way of reconciling British and German requirements and obtaining peace terms without Great Britain losing face. A note on the report indicates that it was submitted to Ribbentrop on November 11, 1940. The contents were apparently reconsidered from time to time and eventually filed on March 25, 1941.[43]

The content of this report, and in particular its references to a 'secret Cabinet meeting' and to 'cultural autonomy', is hardly Churchillian in character. The language and obtuse reasoning employed to arrive at some rather tenuous conclusions is more the stuff of Halifax and Butler. If there was a secret Cabinet meeting was it so secret that Churchill did not attend? Alternatively, was there a large element of wishful thinking included in the German report?

(viii) *The Barlow/Bonde initiative*

Lady Barlow was the niece of Lord Rennell who lived in Scotland and had extensive business interests there. She was an old and dear friend of Baron Knut Bonde, a Swedish diplomat serving in the Swedish legation in Berne, where David Kelly was the British Minister. Bonde had retired before the war but had been brought back into service. He had other English connections, since he had married the daughter of a former colonel of Stewart Menzies's old regiment, the Life Guards. He also had his own Swedish connections and through them, a means of communication to Goering. One of them was Count Eric Rosen, brother of Goering's first (Swedish) wife, Karen. In December 1939 he had worked with Goering on seeking German/British reconcilia-

[43]DGFP, Vol 11, 380.

tion, establishing a reputation with the British Foreign Office as a man of integrity.

Sometime near Christmas 1940 Lady Barlow sent a cable to Bonde in Berne. The cable has not been identified in any official records and its precise contents are therefore unknown. The effect of its receipt was such that Bonde travelled immediately to Sweden and arranged to see Goering. They met on January 14, 1941, and Bonde has since said that if he had been able to present concrete proposals from the British side then peace negotiations could have been started. On returning to Berne, Bonde saw the British Minister, Kelly, who cabled back to London that 'Goering (is) at least sufficiently unsettled as to the future as to welcome any personal message from our side'. Bonde also wrote to Lady Barlow: 'If I could go to London I would try to see Lloyd George and tell him that my conviction is that a peace negotiation undoubtedly could be started through my intermediary... If Lloyd George thinks that he can induce the Government to do something on the lines I suggest, will you send me a telegram? I can see Goering again at any time... A message would reach me through the British legation here.'[44]

It was at this point that Churchill stepped into the picture and closed down the potential negotiations. The Foreign Office had received other confirmation[45] that Goering was prepared to negotiate, but the new Foreign Secretary, Anthony Eden, sent instructions to Kelly in Berne, Mallet in Stockholm and Hoare in Madrid to meet all future soundings from the German side with silence.

---

[44]K. Bonde to Lady Barlow, January 20, 1941. PRO FO371 26542, C610/324/18.
[45]From Sam Hoare in Madrid, citing the Hungarian and Vichy Ministers there (Padfield, Peter, *Hess: Flight for the Führer*, Weidenfeld and Nicolson (1991), 154–55).

Appendix V

The Duke of Windsor in Spain and Portugal, 1940

If the 1940 activities of Halifax and Butler and of some of their senior diplomatic staff and MI6 agents can fairly be described as near-treasonable, then the activities of the Duke of Windsor in Spain and Portugal during June and July of that year were even more questionable. On two occasions during that time the Duke was in direct contact with the King's enemies and on the second occasion he offered help to those enemies. He was never brought to trial for his treason presumably because, as the brother of King George VI, he was a prominent, albeit disgraced, member of the royal family.

On June 17, Marshall Pétain, the new French Premier, announced that 'fighting must cease'. All British forces in France were thereupon ordered to return to the United Kingdom using Mediterranean and Biscayan ports as appropriate. The Duke had been serving on the British Military Mission in Paris, with the rank of Major General, but had left Paris before the end of May, driven south to pick up the Duchess at Biarritz and then journeyed on to Antibes, reaching La Cröe on May 29 where they had by then both taken up residence. This extraordinary opting out of his military responsibilities appears to have had no basis of lawful authority. He had simply walked, or rather motored, out of the fighting and returned to his world of refined domesticity.

By June 10 the Italians had declared war and the Germans were advancing down the Rhone Valley. On June 19 the Duke and Duchess left La Cröe and made not for a Mediterranean port for return to Great Britain, as ordered, but Spain. They arrived the next day and were in Madrid by June 23. A cable from Churchill was awaiting them, instructing them to proceed immediately to Lisbon in Portugal where a flying boat would convey them to England. There then followed a round of correspondence between Churchill and the Duke concerned with the Duke's wish not to return to the United Kingdom for family reasons and in particular the family's non-recognition of the royal status of the Duchess. He looked to Churchill to provide him with a job overseas.

In the meantime, the Germans were beginning to move into the picture. They were very interested in the Duke as a possible figurehead, or even monarch, to preside over a defeated Great Britain – or, perhaps more accurately, a Great Britain which had come to terms with her position and was prepared to accept German dominance over Europe. The Germans knew of the Duke's long-standing sympathy with their cause, his belief in Anglo-German 'friendship', his admiration of the Führer and his fear of the communist threat. All this he had demonstrated in his expressed sentiments while Prince of Wales and during his short kingship, all to the acute embarrassment of Government circles in Great Britain. Not least, the Germans also knew of the Duke's antipathy, even hatred, of his own brother King George VI and his Queen for not 'recognising' Wallis Simpson and of how the Duke would wish to depose them both for that reason. The Duke of Windsor fitted very conveniently into the German picture of Great Britain as she would shortly be if German hopes were realised.

When Ribbentrop was alerted on June 24 by his Ambassador in Madrid, Dr Eberhard Baron von Stohrer, that the Duke and his wife were in Madrid then it seemed to him eminently desirable that the Duke remain in Madrid and that some attempt be made to contact him, with a view to starting some meaningful talks. The original suggestion had already been made to Stohrer by the Spanish Foreign Minister, Colonel Juan Beigbeder Y Atienza, and it is interesting to conjecture whether Beigbeder had been 'tipped off' as to the arrival of the Duke and Duchess in Spain by Sam Hoare, the British Minister in Madrid. Hoare and the Duke were old friends (going back to the time when Hoare was First Lord at the Admiralty in 1936) and perhaps more importantly, had an abiding and common interest in appeasing the Germans and coming to terms with them. Hoare would be as anxious to promote the Duke as the Duke would be to be promoted to the Germans.

Ribbentrop lost no time. His cable arrived in Madrid on June 25, and soon Beigbeder was inviting the Duke and Duchess to remain awhile in Madrid as guests of the Spanish Government. At this stage it is unlikely that the Duke knew what was behind the Foreign Minister's invitation but he was certainly interested in a stay in sunny Spain as a guest rather than an early return to war-stricken Great Britain approaching a national crisis of unprecedented importance and under the threat of impending military action: The Palace of the Caliph at Ronda in Andalucia, which had been suggested as his residence, certainly had attractions.

It was during this 'waiting time' in June and July that, quite ludicrously, the Duke contacted both the Germans and the Italians through a Spanish friend, Don Javier 'Tiger' Bernejillo, and their respective embassies in Madrid, asking if the Duke's two properties together with all their contents at Boulevard Suchet in Paris under German occupation and at La Cröe at Cap d'Antibes under Italian occupation could be protected until after the war was over, when the Duke and Duchess would return to take up residence again. Both Ribbentrop and the Italian authorities ensured that this extraordinary request was honoured. They had a big fish to catch and minor domestic problems were certainly not going to get in the way. At the same time, the compliance with the Duke's wishes placed him to at least some small extent, in their indebtedness. This bizarre incident perhaps demonstrated clearly the Duke's scale of priorities at a time of national emergency and also the fact that he was quite prepared to contact the King's enemies if it so suited his domestic requirements.

A much more serious act of direct dealing with the enemy was to follow. During that same period of 'waiting time' in the Iberian Peninsula, while missives travelled to and fro with Churchill in London, the Duke aired his defeatist views to anyone who cared to listen. He was convinced himself that a British victory was impossible, that the war should not have been started in the first place and that it should be ended with all speed, preferably with American intervention. His views and the manner in which he was expounding them was reported by more than one responsible observer and listener, including Herbert Pell, US Minister in Madrid, Marcus Cheke, junior secretary at the British Embassy in Madrid and direct to Ribbentrop by Hoyningen-Huene, the German Ambassador in Lisbon.

On the morning of Wednesday, July 3 the Duke and Duchess left Spain and entered Portugal. It is not clear why they made this move. Churchill wanted them there as a prelude to their return to Great Britain, but the Duke had not moved from his stated position that he would only return to Great Britain if the 'proper courtesies' were extended to his wife in royal circles. A prolonged stay in Spain was an attractive alternative and at that stage the Duke was almost certainly unaware that German requirements lay behind the Spanish Government's invitation. In Portugal, the Duke and Duchess took up residence with a wealthy Portuguese banker, Ricardo Espirito Santo Silva, at his villa at Cascais, a few miles from Lisbon. Silva was a close friend of Hoyningen-Huene, and was considered by British Intelligence to be pro-German in his views and activities.

The British Embassy viewed this latest indiscretion by the Duke with alarm, but as it was assumed that the Duke would be returning to Great Britain within a matter of days, there was no attempt to take any corrective action. In fact, the Duke and Duchess stayed with Silva throughout July, during which time the Duke succeeded in compromising himself fully and committing an act of treason.

Shortly after taking up residence with Silva the Duke was handed a cable from Churchill in which Churchill reminded the Duke that he was still a serving officer of the British Army and as such was subject 'to obey direct orders of the competent military authority'. In effect, the Duke was being threatened with a court-martial if he did not return to Great Britain. The cable had the desired effect. Arrangements were made for the Duke and Duchess to leave Lisbon by flying boat on Friday, July 5, bound for England. But on the day before he was to leave, the Duke was handed a further cable received from Churchill which offered the Duke an appointment as the Governor and Commander-in-Chief of the Bahamas. The suggestion appears to have originated from either Churchill or King George VI, or both. The motive is perhaps obvious – to remove a potential troublemaker to a backwater where he could do the least harm at a time of national crisis.

The Duke accepted the invitation without delay, typing his own reply to Churchill. He must have thought the governorship of an ex-slave and comparatively unimportant colony was more attractive than having to play second fiddle to his brother in war-torn Britain. The announcement of his appointment was made public on July 9. It was at this point that German interest in the Duke and his future began to be translated into positive action. On July 11 Ribbentrop received a long report from Hoyningen-Huene on the Duke's appointment and his views as reported by some of his Spanish entourage. It is extraordinary in content and it is difficult to distinguish the accurate analysis from the wishful thinking. It states that the purpose of the Bahamas appointment was to keep the Duke out of England since his return would greatly strengthen the position of (the) English friends of peace, whereupon his arrest at the instigation of his enemies could be counted upon. It went on to say that the Duke would be delaying his departure for the Bahamas until August 'in the hope of an early change in his favour'.

According to Hoyningen-Huene, the Duke was of the opinion that the war could have been avoided if he had remained on the British throne and that he was still 'a firm supporter of a peaceful compromise with Germany'. In conclusion, the report states that the Duke was of the opinion that 'continued heavy bombing will make England ready for peace'. Hoyningen-Huene was supplying what Ribbentrop wanted to read. The Duke was suggesting that there was a peace faction or party in England of which he could become a part, or even its head, and that within a few weeks there might be political changes that would favour such a faction. Ribbentrop therefore saw the retention of the Duke and his wife within German control as a matter of prime importance.

A German plan was launched by Ribbentrop's answering cable to Hoyningen-Huene, dispatched immediately, which revealed three requirements. First of all the Duke and Duchess were to be brought back to Spain. It was suggested that this be done through a social invitation by Spanish friends of the Duke. Once the Duke and Duchess came back into Spain they were to be kept there, either voluntarily or by the use of force if necessary, and then approached directly with a message from the Germans that they would like the Duke to hold himself in readiness for the situation after Great Britain's defeat. In particular, the Duke should hold himself in readiness to assume the English throne, together with his wife.

On July 12, the German Ambassador in Madrid called on the Spanish Interior Minister, Ramón Serrano Suñer, General Franco's brother-in-law and a notorious Britain hater (which is why Stohrer had approached him). The Spanish Foreign Minister was considered to be an Anglophile and unfitted to carry Ribbentrop's confidence. Stohrer cabled Ribbentrop that same evening. Suñer had promised full co-operation. The Duke was to be invited back into Spain to discuss certain aspects of Anglo-Spanish relations and to take advantage of a hunting trip. A suitable Spanish emissary had been chosen to deliver the invitation and no hint would be given to indicate the German interest. The Duke would later be 'advised' as to the activities of British Intelligence in Portugal and for that reason invited to stay on in Spain. This would then set the stage for the direct message to the Duke.

In the meantime, the Duke and Duchess, blissfully unaware of the part they were expected to play in a major Nazi intrigue, were making their preparations for the trip to the Bahamas which they had booked for August 1 on the SS *Excalibur*. These preparations illustrate the shallow nature of their characters. The Duke argued long in a series of cables with London which became increasingly acrimonious and which personally involved Churchill at a time when he must have been bowed down with the overall responsibility of conducting the war at a time of national crisis. The cables were concerned with the Duke's requirements as to his personal manservants in the Bahamas, involving the release of men from the Scots Guards and a suggested visit to

New York on the way to the Bahamas, so that the Duchess could see friends and complete her shopping.

At the same time, the Duchess wanted arrangements to be made through the Portuguese and German Embassies in Lisbon for her personal maid, Mademoiselle Moulichon, to travel to Paris (which was in German-occupied France) to pick up, crate and bring to Portugal all the personal silver, furniture, linen, clothing and other chattels which remained in the Duke's residence at Boulevard Suchet in Paris. It was apparent that the war was a very secondary affair as far as the Duke and Duchess were concerned and nothing was to interrupt or interfere with their established mode of living or personal comforts. The Germans for their part were happy to assist Mademoiselle Moulichon. Once she was in occupied France she would be artificially delayed by the bureaucratic machinery, which would also delay the Duke and Duchess's departure from the Iberian Peninsula if Ribbentrop's plan went awry for any reason. As to the Duke's requests to London, permission was refused for a stay-over in New York (no doubt the thought of the Duke's loose mouth in front of American journalists was too much for Churchill to swallow), but his request for the release of Piper Fletcher and Corporal Webster from active service with the Scots Guards, so that he could be correctly dressed at all times, was reluctantly agreed by Churchill.

In the event, the acrimony and rancour that crept into the London/Lisbon cables, arguing these trivia, had an effect out of all proportion to their subject matter. The Duke was not a stable character and when crossed became moody and depressed. As a result of the cables and the opposition which he (rightly) identified in London, he turned wholeheartedly against the proposed appointment in the Bahamas, and was thus laid wide open to the suggestions that were about to be made to him by Stohrer's emissary, Don Miguel Primo de Rivera.

Miguel was well-known to the Duke, who would count him as a personal friend. They had met and become friends when the Duke had visited Spain as the Prince of Wales in 1927. Miguel and his wife dined with the Duke and Duchess at least twice between July 17 and 20 as Stohrer duly reported to Berlin in his despatch of July 23. Miguel had reported that the Duke and Duchess would be happy to return to Spain, but their passports had been surrendered to the British Legation in Lisbon and he would need help from the Spanish Minister for the Interior so that Spanish visas could be obtained. Stohrer also reported that Miguel had said that the Duke and Duchess were thoroughly estranged from King George VI (who the Duke had described as 'stupid') and his wife. According to Miguel the Duke was considering a public disavowal of the current British policy and formally breaking with his brother.

In a further dispatch of July 29 it is apparent that Miguel had, on his own initiative, mentioned the possibility of a return to the English throne as 'the course of the war might produce changes even in the English constitution', at which 'the Duchess in particular became very thoughtful'. At this point, there appears to have been a leak as to the existence of a German plot, and by July 25 David Eccles from the British Embassy in Lisbon was in London giving full details to the Foreign Office and Churchill. The leak had occurred because the Spanish Ambassador in Lisbon, Don Nicolas, brother of General Franco had also been asked to bring pressure to bear upon the Duke and Duchess to return to Spain and had also been informed as to the plot that awaited the Duke upon his return to Spain. What was not known by the Spanish authorities or their German conspirators was that Franco's brother was a less than ardent Fascist and was in fact, in the pay of Eccles.

In the meantime, Ribbentrop in Berlin was unaware of the leak and still of the opinion that the Duke and Duchess could be lured back into Spain, with every hope of them embracing the arrangements the Germans had in mind. He decided, with the approval of Hitler, to send a top German Intelligence agent to the Peninsula to organise the transfer of the Duke and Duchess from Portugal to Spain. The man selected was Walter Schellenberg. Schellenberg although young, held the rank of Major-General in the SS. He had distinguished himself early in the war by organising the capture of Best and Stevens, the two top British Intelligence agents in the notorious Venlo affair. He was one of Heydrich's top men. On July 24 he was briefed by Ribbentrop and the next day flew to Madrid with two aides.

Schellenberg's instructions were simple. He was to bring the Duke and Duchess back into Spain. There was to be both a carrot and a stick. The carrot was the promise of fifty million Swiss francs to be deposited to the Duke's credit in Switzerland, providing 'the atmosphere seemed propitious' and some material offer could be made. The stick was that the Duke and Duchess were to be removed forcibly from Portugal and taken to Spain if that became necessary. In Madrid, Schellenberg talked to Stohrer and the police attaché at the German Embassy, Paul Winzer. He did not wish to use force to effect the necessary move to Spain and he therefore approved the dispatch to the Duke of a second emissary (whose name is not stated in the German official documents or in any of Schellenberg's reports). The emissary was to arrange a few days' holiday for the Duke and Duchess near the Spanish border, to include hunting trips that would carry the hunting party over the border into Spain. The Portuguese frontier guards would be co-operative in the matter of visas and other required documents.

Schellenberg arrived in Lisbon on the evening of Friday, July 26, and immediately began work preparing the ground for the second emissary. He had to ensure full co-operation from those Portuguese officials who could ease the journey of the Duke and Duchess from Portugal to Spain, and nullify the effort of British Intelligence who were determined to keep the couple in Portugal and to ensure their departure to the Bahamas rather than Spain. He was to arrange for further SS and other agent cover to the operation, as necessary.

Obviously, the determining factor which would bring to an end all the intrigues, conspiracies and plans of the interested parties was the attitude of the Duke and Duchess. If they wanted to stay in Spain, co-operate with the Germans and run up the flag of opposition to the Duke's brother, King George VI, and the policies of his Government, then the task of the second emissary and Schellenberg would be considerably eased. But if the Duke wished, or thought he ought, to throw in his lot with Churchill and demonstrate his bottom-line loyalty to his King and country then Schellenberg's task would become almost impossible.

On Sunday, July 28, the second emissary presented himself at the Santos residence and gave the Duke a letter in which were explained full details of the proposed 'hunting' trip and the cross into Spanish territory. Also included in the letter was a blunt warning that the personal safety of the Duke and Duchess was and would be a matter 'of extreme gravity', both in Portugal and the Bahamas, if they were to 'manifest an opinion or act in some way contrary to a decision of the British Government'. Here was the threat intended to help the Duke and Duchess opt out of any allegiance to Churchill and King George VI and take up residence in Spain as a guest of the Spanish Government.

It was not to be. Four days later the Duke and Duchess walked up the gangplank of SS *Excalibur* and set sail for the Bahamas. The immediate occasion for this apparent decision was the visit of Sir Walter Monckton who arrived by flying boat from Great Britain that same Sunday, July 28. Monckton was well known to the Duke. He was a colleague at Oxford before the 1914–18 war, had been the Duke's legal adviser in the early 1930s and had acted as the Duke's intermediary during the Abdication crisis. He had continued to act as an unofficial intermediary between the Duke and the British Government ever since. He was a man the Duke would trust. He brought with him a letter from Churchill to the Duke. After the pleasantries, Churchill warned the Duke against expressing any contrary political views to those held by the British Government when he arrived in the Bahamas.

The precise content of the ensuing Monckton/Duke of Windsor talks are unknown, but presumably Monckton warned the Duke of the British Government's suspicions that some sort of German plot was possibly afoot to take the Duke and Duchess into custody. He may well have said other things to the Duke which had the immediate desired effect. 'Blackmail' is perhaps too strong a word, but there was plenty in the Duke's personal history that would not endear him to the British public in the crisis climate of the summer of 1940 if it was made public. Whether it was the soft persuasion of an old friend or blackmail from the hard men back in London, the effect was the same. The Duke and Duchess would be sailing for the Bahamas on August 1.

On July 29 Schellenberg wrote a final report to Berlin which seemed to acknowledge defeat. It concluded with the prophetic phrase '*Willi will nicht*' ('Willi says no'), 'Willi' being the code name for the Duke. Up to this point, as far as the Germans were concerned, the Duke was unaware of the German plot that lay behind the proposed move to Spain. Schellenberg now proposed a direct approach to the Duke and the disclosure of German plans for the use of the Duke in connection with possible peace arrangements. Stohrer from Madrid advised similarly. Ribbentrop took the cue and on July 31 dispatched an urgent cable to his Ambassador in Lisbon, Hoyningen-Huene. The cable confirmed that the German hand be exposed to the Duke in a last ditch attempt to stop his departure from Lisbon the next day. The cards were to be put on the table by the Duke's host, Ricardo de Espirito Santo Silva, during the morning of August 1.

According to Hoyningen-Huene's cable to Ribbentrop of August 2 – and due consideration has to be given to the Ambassador's integrity and the veracity of the cable's contents – this was done. In his reply, reported Hoyningen-Huene, 'the Duke had paid tribute to the Führer's desire for peace, which was in complete agreement with his own point of view. He was firmly convinced that if he had been King it would never have come to war. To the appeal made to him to co-operate at a suitable time, he gladly consented. However, he requested that it be understood that at the present time he must follow the official orders of his Government. Disobedience would disclose his intentions, prematurely bring about a scandal, and deprive him of prestige in England. He was also convinced that the present moment was too early for him to come forward since there was, as yet, no inclination in England for an approach to Germany. However, as soon as this frame of mind changed, he would be ready to return immediately. To bring this about there were two possibilities. Either England would yet call upon him, which he considered to be entirely possible, or Germany would express the desire to negotiate with him. In both cases, he was prepared for any personal sacrifice and would make himself available without the slightest personal ambition. He would remain in constant communication with his former host and had agreed with him a code word, upon receiving which he would immediately come back over. He insisted that this would be possible at any time since he had foreseen all eventualities and had already initiated all the necessary arrangements. The statements of the Duke were, as the confidant stressed, supported by firmness of will and the deepest sincerity and had included an expression of admiration and sympathy for the Führer.'

If Hoyningen-Huene's report gives an accurate account of the Duke's response to the full disclosure made by Silva then it is difficult to avoid the conclusion that the Duke of Windsor was guilty of treasonable talk on that Sunday morning of August 1, 1940. Later that day he sailed from Lisbon bound for the Bahamas. He did not leave his questionable behaviour behind in Lisbon. He took it with him to the Bahamas.

Appendix VI

Albrecht Haushofer's letter to the Duke of Hamilton, dated September 23, 1940

B Sept 23rd

My dear Douglo

Even if there is only a slight chance that this letter should reach you in good time, there is a chance, and I am determined to make use of it.

First of all, to give you a personal greeting. I am sure that you know that my attachment to you remains unaltered and unalterable, whatever the circumstances may be. I have heard of your father's death. I do hope he did not suffer too much – after so long a life of permanent pain. I heard that your brother-in-law, Northumberland, lost his life near Dunkirk – even modern times must allow us to share grief across all boundaries.

But it is not only the story of death that should find its place in this letter. If you remember some of my last communications in July 1939, you – and your friends in high places – may find some significance in the fact that I am able to ask you whether you could find time to have a talk with me somewhere on the outskirts of Europe, perhaps in Portugal. I could reach Lisbon any time (and without any kind of difficulties) within a few days after receiving news from you. Of course I do not know whether you can make your authorities understand so much, that they give you leave.

But at least you may be able to answer my question. Letters will reach me (fairly quickly, they would take some four or five days from Lisbon at the upmost) in the following way: double closed envelope: inside address: 'DrAH' Nothing more! Outside address:

Minero Silricola Ltd
Rua do Cais de Santarem 32/1
Lisbon, Portugal

My father and mother add their wishes for your personal welfare to my own...

Yours ever

'A'

This is the text of the 'innocuous' letter to be sent by Albrecht to Hamilton, as drafted by Albrecht in English. It was sent without alteration except that the date was changed to September 3. Readers will be able to assess whether in their view it represented a realistic attempt to circumvent censorship and interception and arrive safely in the hands of the Duke with its security intact.

Appendix VII

Prominent members of the Anglo-German Fellowship in 1940

(see *M15*, Nigel West, p168).

Aberdare, Lord (55), Chairman, *Fortnightly Review*.
Airlie, the Earl of (47), Lord Chamberlain.
Arbuthnott, Lord (57), Lord Lieutenant of Kincardineshire.
Arnold, Lord (62), Former Labour MP for Penistone.
Barnby, Lord (56), Former Unionist MP for South Bradford.
Bennett, Sir Ernest, Former Labour MP for Cardiff.
Bertie, Viscount (67), Barrister.
Brittain, Sir Harry (67), Former Unionist MP for Acton.
Brocket, Lord (36), Former Unionist MP for Wavertree.
Ebbisham,, Lord (70), Former Unionist MP for Epsom.
Eltisley, Lord (59), Former Tory MP for Cambridge.
Glasgow, Earl of (66), Vice-Convenor Ayrshire County Council.
Hamilton, Lord Ernest (78), Former MP for North Tyrone.
Hellenden, Lord (68), Former High Sheriff of London.
Hulbert, Sqdn Leader Norman (37), Unionist MP for Stockport.
Knox, Maj. Gen Sir Alfred (70), Tory MP for Wycombe.
Londonderry, Marquess of (59), Former Tory Air Minister.
Lothian, Marquess of (56), Ambassador to Washington.
Lucas, Sir Jocelyn (50), Tory MP for Portsmouth.
Lymington, Viscount (47), Former Unionist MP for Basingstoke.
McGowan, Lord (65), Chairman of I.C.I.
MacNamara, Jack (35), Unionist MP for Chelmsford.

Moore, Sir Thomas (56), Unionist MP for Ayr.
Mottistone, Lord (66), Former Liberal War Minister.
Mount Temple, Lord (62), Former Tory Transport Minister.
Nuffield, Lord (63), Chairman of Morris Motors Ltd.
Nutting, Sir Harold (56), Former ADC to Governor General of Australia.
Pownall, Sir Assheton (61), Unionist MP for Lewisham.
Rennell of Rodd, Lord (81), Former MP and Ambassador to Italy.
Rice, Edward, Former MP.
Sempill, Lord (46), Chairman, Royal Aero Society.
Stamp, Lord (60), Director, Bank of England.
Strang, Sir William (46), Chief Political Adviser, Foreign Office.
Sueter, Adm. Sir Murray (68), Tory MP for Hertford.
Tiarks, Frank C. (66), Governor, Bank of England.
Wellington, the Duke of (66), Boer War veteran.

(Ages in 1940 shown in parentheses.)

Prominent members of The Link

(see *MI5*, Nigel West, p167)

Beazley, Sir Raymond (71), Professor of History, Birmingham University.

Bedford, The Duke of (82), 11th Duke.

Blakeney, Brigadier R.G. (68), Veteran of Khartoum.

Brown, Colonel Sir John, Deputy Director-General of the Territorial Army.

Crawford, Archibald KC (58), Ex-Unionist candidate for Peebles.

Crooke, Sir John, Unionist MP for Deritend, Birmingham.

Domvile, Admiral Sir Barry (62), Director of Naval Intelligence, 1927–30. Retired RN, 1936.

Downe, Viscountess, Former British Union of Fascists candidate for North Norfolk.

Duff, Jasper, Ulster MP.

Fuller, Major-Gen J.F.C., Military tactician.

Jebb, Ralph Gladwyn, Former British Union of Fascists candidate for West Dorset.

Haworth, Sir Lionel (66), Former Indian political officer.

Jerrold, Douglas (47), Historian and publisher.

Laurie, Professor A.P., Fellow of King's College, Cambridge.

Lowke-Bassett, W.J., Labour leader of Northamptonshire County Council.

Mitchell, Edward Rosslyn (61), Former Labour MP for Paisley.

Nuffield, Lord (63), Chairman of Morris Motors Ltd.

Parry, Vice Admiral R.St.P (60), Retired RN, 1931.

Pearson, Lady, Widow of Sir Edward Pearson.

Powell, Vice Admiral G.B.(69), Retired RN, 1926.

Redesdale, Lord (62), Father of the Mitford sisters.

Roe, Lieutenant-Colonel C.D. (50), Indian Army, retired 1931.

Unwin, Captain Edward, VC (76), Hero of Gallipoli.

Ward, Sir Lambert (64), Unionist MP for Kingston-on-Hull.

Westminster, The Duke of (61), 2nd Duke.

White, Major-General H.S. (78), Veteran of the Sudan expedition.

Wilshire, Frederick (72), Recorder of Bridgwater.

Wilson, Sir Arnold (56), Tory MP for Hitchin.

Yeats Brown, Colonel Francis (54), Author of *The Bengal Lancer*.

(Ages in 1940 shown in parentheses.)

Prominent Members of the Right Club

(see *Ten Days that Saved the West*, John Costello, p479)

Agnew, Commander Peter, MP and member of Church Council.

Bennett, Sir Ernest, National Labour MP British delegate to League of Nations.

Carnegie, Lord, Member of Royal Family by marriage to Princess Maud, granddaughter of Queen Victoria. Later Earl of Southesk.

Edmondson, Sir Albert, MP and Government Whip.

Joyce, William, 'Lord Haw Haw'. Hanged for treason, 1946.

Kerr Colonel Charles, MP and Government Whip. Later Lord Teviot.

Montrose, Duke of, Later Minister of Defence in breakaway Rhodesian Government, mid-1960s.

Mitchell, Colonel Harold, Vice-Chairman, Conservative Party.

Redesdale, Lord, Father of the Mitford sisters.

Sempill, Lord, Aviator and Chairman, Royal Aero Society.

Walker, Sir Alexander, Chairman, Johnnie Walker whisky distillery.

Wellington, Duke of, Boer War veteran.

Also included are 'half a dozen larger Scottish landowners' and 'MPs representing Scottish constituencies'.

Appendix VIII

Statutory declaration by Professor Dr Wolfgang Spann, MD, relating to the death of Rudolf Hess

To the Service Registering Officer for North West Europe
In the Matter of the Births, Deaths and Marriages
(Special Provisions) Act
1957
AND in the Matter of the Entry in the Register of Deaths of
RUDOLF WALTER RICHARD HESS

I PROFESSOR DOCTOR. MED., DOCTOR MED.H.C. WOLFGANG SPANN Professor Emeritus of the University of Munich of The Institute of Forensic Medicine, 80337 Munich Frauenlobstrasse 7a, do solemnly and sincerely declare as follows:

1. I am Professor Emeritus at the Institute of Forensic Medicine, 80337 Munich, Frauenlobstrasse 7a. A copy of my curriculum vitae is now produced and shown to me marked 'WS1'.

2. I make this statutory declaration in connection with the death of the former Reich Minister, Rudolf Hess, on 17 August 1987.

3. I have before me the following documents which are now produced and shown to me marked 'WS2'.

    3.1 A copy of the death certificate of Rudolf Hess. Under the heading 'Cause of Death', it states. 'Asphyxia due to compression of the neck due to suspension. Certified by Professor J.M, Cameron MD PhD FRCS FRCPath, Professor of Forensic Pathology, University of London'.

    3.2 The report of the autopsy performed on Hess's body on 19 August in the British Military Hospital by Professor J.

Malcolm Cameron. The autopsy was conducted in the presence of medical representatives of the four Allied powers. The report noted a linear mark on the left side of the neck consistent with a ligature (strangulation device). Professor Cameron stated that, in his opinion, death resulted from asphyxia, caused by compression of the neck due to suspension.

4. Together with my colleague Professor Doctor Eisenmenger, I conducted the post mortem examination of the corpse of Rudolf Hess (hereinafter 'The Deceased') on 21 August 1987 at 9.00 a.m. Present at the autopsy were Dr Seidl and, with his agreement, Police Officer Nefzger with officers of the Munich Criminal Investigations Department. The latter were present solely to observe the proceedings. The report of the examination is now produced and shown to me marked 'HWS3'. There is also produced and shown to me marked 'WS4' a selection of five photographs taken during the post-mortem examination.

5. Our findings are set out fully in the report and I rely on those findings in support of the opinion which I express here.

6. Our findings in the area of the skull and neck indicate that the cause of death was a central paralysis, caused by violence to the neck, accompanied by stoppage of the oxygen supply to the brain. Therefore, the findings ascertained by us agree with Professor Dr Cameron's inasmuch as it is also his opinion that the cause of death was asphyxiation due to compression of the neck. This presupposes that the decisive mechanism causing death lay in a compression of the arterial vessels of the throat, accompanied by stoppage of the oxygen supply to the brain, and not in a compression of the respiratory tract.

7. Dr Cameron's further conclusion that this compression was caused by suspension is not necessarily compatible with our findings. The photographically documented findings in the area of the neck reveal, in the nape of the neck as well as at the front of the throat, an impression mark running roughly horizontally as is generally observed in cases of violence against the neck by means of a ligature (strangulation device). In point 9 of the report, we stated that a distinctly delimited discoloration was evident which ran from the posterior edge of the large sternocleidomastoid muscle 'diagonally downwards in the middle and to the right side'. We had also described, in point 10, a double-track discoloration on the back of the neck running 'almost horizontally'.

This description, however, referred to the condition of the body after an already previously performed autopsy during which conditions on the front of the throat were distorted by the dissection suture proceeding here, so that the diagonal course of the mark described here is of less significance than the almost horizontal course of the impression mark on the nape of the neck, as the skin there was viewed in its original condition. For this reason, the summary of our findings in our report points out specifically that the impression mark proceeding along a circular path around the neck had its highest point in the area behind the left ear, 'as far as still discernible, after the autopsy incision'.

8. This is of especial significance because the findings noted on the neck, combined with the haemorrhagic spots in the conjunctive membranes of the eyelids, indicate that violence against the neck by means of a ligature (strangulation device) did occur. In forensic medicine a distinction has long been drawn between two methods of strangulation with a ligature (strangulation device), namely hanging and throttling. The forensic pathologist's task begins with the differentiation between the two possibilities, based on the anatomical findings, that is, the ligature mark.

9. In forensic science, the course which the ligature mark takes on the neck is considered a classic indicator for the differentiation between the forms of strangulation of hanging and throttling. A horizontally level course of the ligature mark around the neck is considered to be a characteristic sign of throttling. In the case of hanging, on the other hand, the ligature mark ascends in the direction of the fixed attachment point of the strangulation device, in which case the ascension of the marks towards the attachment point can be more or less pronounced.

In the case of so-called typical hanging, which is defined as free suspension of the body with the highest point of ligature impression on the middle of the back of the neck and a single loop of the ligature around the neck, the ascent of the ligature mark as a rule proceeds steeply and symmetrically up both sides of the throat. In the case of atypical hanging, on the other hand – if at least one of the three aforementioned points of definition is not realised – asymmetrical and slight rates of ascent of the ligature mark are possible. Another criterion for assessment is that in the case of throttling, the ligation mark often proceeds at or below the height of the larynx, whereas the mark is as a rule observed above the larynx in the case of hanging.

10. Professor Cameron, in reaching the conclusion that the cause of death was asphyxiation caused by compression of the neck due to hanging, appears to have neglected to consider the other method of strangulation, namely throttling. By definition, throttling entails strangulation by means of a device encircling the throat and the active constriction by another person, or very rarely by the victim himself, whereas in the case of hanging, the compression by the strangulation tool is achieved passively through the weight of the victim's own body or a part of it. Making this distinction would have required an examination of the course of the ligature mark. The precise course of the mark is not reported in Professor Cameron's autopsy report, In the second paragraph of the section of the autopsy report entitled 'External Examination', it is merely remarked that:

'A fine linear mark, approximately 3 in (7.5 cm) in length and 0.75 cm in width was noted running across the left side of the neck, being more apparent when the body was viewed with ultraviolet light... '

Here, neither the course of the strangulation mark on the neck, as we have described it, nor its course on the throat, nor its position relative to the prominence of the larynx has been described and assessed. While every experienced forensic pathologist knows that some skin alterations caused by violence become more easily visible the more time has passed following death, this is practically always a matter of drying-out following injury to the upper continuous layer, whereas in this case the ligature mark – as our photographs verify – was caused by reddening, that is, by displacement of blood, in other words, haemorrhaging. The ligature marks on Rudolf Hess's neck must therefore have been clearly visible during the autopsy carried out by Professor Cameron.

11. This is the reason why we conclude that Professor Dr Cameron's conclusions are not compatible with our findings. Since on the uninjured skin of the neck, where the possibility of distortion through the suture of the dissection incision is ruled out, an almost horizontal course of the strangulation mark could be identified, this finding, as well as the fact that the mark on the throat obviously was not located above the larynx, is more indicative of a case of throttling rather than of hanging. Under no circumstances can the findings be readily explained by so called typical hanging ('suspension'). The burst blood vessels which we

observed in the face, caused by blood congestion, are also not compatible with suspension. As no exact details of the sequence of events and no photographic materials of the discovery scene are available, we cannot rule out special forms of atypical hanging. In German language forensic medicine there is a definition for so called typical hanging, the decisive criteria being that:

1. the highest point of the ligature is located in the middle of the nape of the neck,
2. the body is free hanging,

with some authors giving still another criteria, namely that

3. the ligature encircles the neck with one loop only.

Hanging is described as being atypical if one of the above criteria is not fulfilled. A horizontal course of the strangulation mark and thus of the ligature – as in the case of Rudolf Hess – would in any event presuppose either a throttling or an atypical hanging as no highest point of the ligature was located in the middle of the nape of the neck. An atypical kind of hanging with a horizontal course of the ligature mark is conceivable only if the victim is lying down and the attachment point of the ligature is more or less vertically above the region of the neck.

12. As for the nature of the impression mark, it should be stated that its double-track nature, observed at least on the back of the neck, does not require that a ligature must have been put in place as a double loop. It is perfectly possible that the ligature was an electric cord which was in contact with the skin where the white gap in the area of the neck is especially clear, whereas the double-track reddening came about through tiny haemorrhages into the skin to either side of the ligature mark.

13. Lastly, a short fundamental comment is required with respect to the injuries of the cervical skeleton and the haemorrhages of the soft parts of the throat. In the case of violence against the neck, in whatever manner, it is in keeping with the rules of forensic examination – at least in the German-speaking countries – to perform the dissection of the organs of the throat in a so-called bloodless field and to dissect the musculature off in layers. A bloodless field is achieved in that following the removal of the brain and the opening of the blood vessels leading from the heart to the throat and vice versa, the blood in these vessels is made to drain through tilting movements of the neck. This procedure is

deemed necessary since if these measures are not taken, blood may extra vasate from the still filled vessels during the autopsy, so that the vigour of haemorrhages subsequently observed can no longer be adequately assessed. The proceeding is then noted down in the autopsy report. Such a note is absent from Professor Cameron's protocol. Then, however, Professor Cameron describes an unusual severity of haemorrhages as noted in the soft parts of the neck – namely in the muscle cords on the left side of the neck and on the left edge of the jaw, furthermore in the upper area of the right side of the laryngeal thyroid cartilage, also behind the larynx, especially above the right side, which were said to be as pronounced as the contusions of the muscle cords on the left side of the neck. Over and above that, clearly visible contusions were then said to have been found behind both corniculum laryngis, especially on the right superior cornu. In our experience with post-mortem examinations, such massive haemorrhages at such difference locations are not to be expected in cases of typical hanging (suspension), and unusual, if not to say rare, in cases of atypical hanging as well as of throttling. But as neither the extent of the haemorrhage nor its exact location with respect to the ligature mark on the skin was described and we have no account of the discovery situation, we do not feel we are in a position to conclusively discuss the value of these findings. As is evident from the autopsy report drawn up by Professor Cameron, a video camera was used during the post-mortem. However, no still photos were apparently taken. Hence there is perhaps a film which portrays the autopsy proceedings as well as the individual findings in a more precise manner than does the autopsy report. If such a film exists, as well as the possibility of viewing it, we would be happy to submit a further statement with respect to the findings and their assessment.

14. One can see from the photographs at exhibit 'WS4' that this was clearly not a case of typical hanging. There is a horizontal mark on the nape of the neck without any tendency to peak. Most importantly the line is totally unbroken. This proves that a strangulation device must have been applied and not only fleetingly but long enough to cause these marks. It is the exception that someone strangles himself because when he becomes unconscious his strength goes and he lets go again. An electrical cable with a smooth surface can be expected to slip apart once tension is released.

15. In conclusion, we are of the opinion that the diagnosis of death

> stated in the death certificate is by no means established. Although we agree that the cause of death was asphyxia due to compression of the neck, we do not consider that suspension has been proved to be the cause of death. Our findings indicate rather that death occurred as a consequence of throttling.

Declared at Munich
on 24 January 1995

....

Signed W Spann

Before me, Bernd Hofling Notary Public, Munich

Appendix IX

Affidavid of anonymous South African Attorney claiming involvement of Western Intelligence agencies in the death of Rudolf Hess

AFFIDAVIT

Aware of the penal consequences of a false – even if only a negligibly false – given affidavit, I state herewith,
in lieu of an oath:
Identification:
I am citizen of the Republic of South with the identification number residing in
Republic of South Africa and
in the National Intelligence Service with the civilian profession of attorney.
Facts:
I have been asked about the more detailed circumstances of the death of the German Reich Minister Rudolf Hess.
Reich Minister Rudolf Hess was murdered at the instigation of the British Home Office (Ministry of the Interior). The murder was committed by two members of the British SAS (22nd SAS Regiment, SAS Depot Bradbury Lines, Hereford, England). The SAS ('Special Air Service') is subordinated as military unit to the British Home Office (not to the Defence Ministry). The responsible planning and management of the murder mission was done by MI-5 (usually responsible for the 'domestic' security of Great Britain; secret service, military actions outside Great Britain fall within the competence of MI-6). The secret service action was so hastily planned, that it was not even given a code name, which is absolutely unusual.

Other initiated services were the US American, the French and the Israeli service. KGB and GRU and the German services were <u>not</u> informed.
The murder of Rudolf Hess had become necessary, because the government of the USSR intended to release the prisoner in July 1987 (in connection with the visit of the Federal President v. Weizsäcker in Moscow), but Federal President v. Weizsäcker could negotiate a prolongation of the date until the following Soviet guard period in November 1987.
The two SAS men had been in the Spandau prison since the night of Saturday to Sunday (August 15–16, 1987). The US secret service gave its concurrence for carrying out the murder on Monday (August 17, 1987).
During the afternoon walk of the prisoner in the prison grounds, the two SAS men lay in wait of the prisoner in the summerhouse located in the prison grounds, and attempted to throttle him with an approximately 1.50m long cable, then a suicide through 'hanging' was to be feigned. But since Reich Minister Rudolf Hess resisted and also called for help, and at least one US soldier from the guard squad became aware of the assault, the attempt was broken off and an ambulance of the British military hospital was called. The unconscious Reich Minister Rudolf Hess was brought with the ambulance to the British military hospital; the two assassins left the Spandau prison with the same vehicle and during the trip completed the attempt.
I received the above information on the case orally and personally from an officer of the Israeli service on Tuesday, 18 August 1987 at around 08:00 a.m. South African time. I have known this employee of the Israeli service officially and personally for four years. I am completely convinced that he is sincere and honest and I have no doubt of any nature concerning the truth of what he told me. The purely private character of his conversation with me is equally without doubt.

February 22, 1988

(illegible stamp, presumably a notarisation)
(second illegible stamp, presumably a date of receipt stamp)

BIBLIOGRAPHY

Allen, Peter, *The Crown and the Swastika*, Robert Hale, London, 1983

Block, Michael, *Operation Willi*, Weidenfeld and Nicolson, London, 1984

Bradford, Sarah, *King George VI*, Weidenfeld and Nicolson, London, 1989

Browning, Christopher R., *The Final Solution and the German Foreign Office*, Holmes & Meier Publishers Inc., New York, 1978

Charmley, John, *Churchill: The End of Glory*, Hodder & Stoughton, London, 1993

Cockett, Richard, *Twilight of Truth*, Weidenfeld and Nicolson, London, 1989

Costello, John, *Ten Days that Saved the West*, Bantam Press, London, 1991

Douglas-Hamilton, James, *Motive for a Mission*, Mainstream Publishing, Edinburgh, 1979

Ellis, Major L.F., *The War in France and Flanders 1939–1940*, Her Majesty's Stationery Office, London, 1953

Erickson, John, *The Road to Stalingrad*, Weidenfeld and Nicolson, London, 1975

Fishman, Jack, *The Seven Men of Spandau*, Souvenir Press, London, 1954

Gorbachev, Mikhail, *Perestroika*, Collins, London, 1987

Griffiths, Richard, *Fellow Travellers of the Right*, Constable, London, 1980

Halifax, Earl of, *Fullness of Days*, Collins, London, 1951

Henderson, Sir Nevile, *Failure of a Mission*, Hodder & Stoughton, London, 1940

Hess, Wolf Rüdiger, *My Father, Rudolf Hess*, W.H. Allen, London, 1986

Hess, Wolf Rüdiger, *Who Murdered my Father, Rudolf Hess?*, Reporter Press, Alabama, USA, 1989

Hesse, Fritz, *Hitler and the English*, Allan Wingate, London, 1954
Hitler, Adolf, *Mein Kampf*, Hurst and Blackett, London, 1939
Hitler, Adolf, *Hitler's Secret Book*, Grove Press Inc. New York, 1961
Hoare, Sir Samuel, *Nine Troubled Years*, Collins, London, 1954
Hoare, Sir Samuel, *Ambassador on Special Mission*, Collins, London, 1946
Howard, Anthony, *RAB. The Life of R.A. Butler*, Macmillan, London, 1988
Irving, David, *Hess. The Missing Years 1941–1945*, Grafton Books, 1989
Irving, David, *Churchill's War*, Veritas Publishing, Bullsbrook, Australia, 1987
Kelly, Sir David, *The Ruling Few*, Hollis & Carter, London, 1952
Kippax, Frank, *The Butcher's Bill*, Harper Collins, London, 1991
Knightley, Phillip, *The Second Oldest Profession*, Pan Books, London, 1987
Martin, Bernard, *Friedensinitiativen und Machtpolitik im Zweiten Weltkrieg 1939–1942*, Droste Verlag, Dusseldorf, Germany, 1974
Newton, Scott, *The Anglo-German Connection and the Political Economy of Appeasement*, Frank Cass, London, 1991
Owen, Frank, *Tempestuous Journey. Lloyd George: His Life and Times*, Hutchinson, London, 1954
Padfield, Peter, *Hess: Flight for the Führer*, Weidenfeld and Nicolson, London, 1991
Ponting, Clive, *1940: Myth and Reality*, Hamish Hamilton, London, 1990
Rees, J.R., *The Case of Rudolf Hess*, William Heinemann, 1947
Rhodes James, Robert, *Chips: The Diaries of Sir Henry Channon*, Weidenfeld and Nicolson, London, 1967
Roberts, Andrew, *The Holy Fox: A Biography of Lord Halifax*, Weidenfeld and Nicolson, London, 1989
Rowse, A.L., *All Souls and Appeasement*, Macmillan, London, 1961
Shirer, William L., *The Rise and Fall of the Third Reich*, Pan Books, London, 1964
Simpson, A.W. Brian, *In the Highest Degree Odious*, Clarendon Press, Oxford, 1992
Speer, Albert K., *Spandau: The Secret Diaries*, Macmillan, London, 1976
Taylor, A.J.P., *The Origins of the Second World War*, Hamish Hamilton, London, 1961
Taylor, A.J.P., *English History 1914–1945*, Oxford University Press, Oxford, 1965

Thomas, Hugh, *Hess: A Tale of Two Murders*, Hodder & Stoughton, London, 1988

Thompson, Laurence, *1940: Year of Legend, Year of History*, Collins Fontana Books, London, 1968

West, Nigel, *MI5*, Triad Grafton Books, London, 1983

West, Rebecca, *The Meaning of Treason*, Virago Press, London, 1982

Winterbotham, F.W., *Secret and Personal*, William Kimber, London, 1969

Winterbotham, F.W., *The Nazi Connection*, Weidenfeld and Nicolson, London, 1978

Ziegler, Philip, *King Edward VIII*, Collins, London, 1990

Also:

The Christie papers at Churchill College, Cambridge comprising correspondence and copy reports. Group Captain Malcolm Grahame Christie was born in Edgbaston in 1881. After service with the RFC (later RAF) he was appointed Air Attaché in Washington (1922–26) and subsequently in Berlin (1927–30). In 1930 he retired from active service and took up the position of political consultant on the affairs of Germany and Central Europe for Sir Robert Vansittart of the Foreign Office to whom he made copious notes and reports.

The Stokes papers at the Bodleian Library, Oxford comprising correspondence and interview notes etc. Richard R. ('Dick') Stokes was the right-wing Labour Member of Parliament for Ipswich during the 1939–45 war. He was a confirmed pacifist and critic of Churchill's war policy throughout that period and was constantly in touch with others who were of the same mind including Lloyd George, Liddell-Hart, the Duke of Bedford, Lord Londonderry and Beaverbrook.

German Foreign Office Archives.

Extracts from 'British Foreign Policies during the Second World War' edited by Sir Llewellyn Woodward.

Documents concerning German-Polish relations and the outbreak of hostilities between Great Britain and Germany (HMSO).

Documents on file at the Public Record Office, Kew, London.